Lecture Notes of the Institute for Computer Sciences, Social Informatics and Telecommunications Engineering 229

More information about this series at http://www.springer.com/series/8197

Anthony L. Brooks · Eva Brooks
Nikolas Vidakis (Eds.)

Interactivity, Game Creation, Design, Learning, and Innovation

6th International Conference, ArtsIT 2017
and Second International Conference, DLI 2017
Heraklion, Crete, Greece, October 30–31, 2017
Proceedings

 Springer

Editors
Anthony L. Brooks
Aalborg University
Esbjerg
Denmark

Eva Brooks
Aalborg University
Aalborg
Denmark

Nikolas Vidakis
Technological Educational Institute of Crete
Heraklion
Greece

ISSN 1867-8211   ISSN 1867-822X (electronic)
Lecture Notes of the Institute for Computer Sciences, Social Informatics
and Telecommunications Engineering
ISBN 978-3-319-76907-3   ISBN 978-3-319-76908-0 (eBook)
https://doi.org/10.1007/978-3-319-76908-0

Library of Congress Control Number: 2018934358

Printed on acid-free paper

This Springer imprint is published by the registered company Springer International Publishing AG
part of Springer Nature
The registered company address is: Gewerbestrasse 11, 6330 Cham, Switzerland

Preface

We are delighted to introduce the proceedings of the 6th European Alliance for Innovation (EAI) International Conference on Interactivity and Game Creation (ArtsIT 2017) and the Second International Conference on Design, Learning and Innovation (DLI 2017), held in Heraklion, Crete, Greece, October 30–31, 2017. This conference brought together researchers, developers, and practitioners from around the world who are leveraging and developing modern IT technologies with strong ties to arts interactivity, game creation, design, learning, and innovation in their works.

The ArtsIT series of conferences has been created to provide a platform where researchers and practitioners in the arts and humanities, who have a keen interest in contemporary IT developments, meet with individuals working in the fields of computational technologies and IT who, in turn, have strong ties to the fine arts and the design disciplines in their output. With the extended call for papers including interactivity and game creation, the focus was widened to reflect trends in state-of-the art whereby the art of interactivity and game creation is included to encourage cross-fertilization between these related fields.

Design, learning, and innovation (DLI) frame the world of ICT, play and playfulness opening doors into an increasingly playful world. Whether it is about developing tools, technologies, environments, as well as content and approaches that can spark and nurture a passion for learning and transforming domains such as education, rehabilitation/therapy, work places, and cultural institutions, DLI is a powerful catalyst in empowering individuals to participate, communicate, and create to be able to exceed their own limits in a playful way: Such is the spirit driving the DLI conference. Making this spirit explicit and visible is crucial to identify how specific tools, technologies, methodologies, and solutions shape opportunities for people to learn and engage with the demands of life. Today, challenges in the fields of DLI are often approached by transdisciplinary teams and solutions, such that tools, technologies, methods, and theories developed for other purposes are mobilized to be utilized in unlocking new frameworks for understanding these fields and thereby opening up to partnerships that can enrich learning in formal and informal learning practices. DLI intends to foster such dynamics.

The technical program of the collocated conferences ArtsIT 2017 and DLI 2017 consisted of 52 full papers in oral presentation sessions during the main conferences tracks. Aside from the high-quality technical paper presentations, the technical program also featured three keynote speeches. The three keynote speakers were Prof. Georgios N. Yannakakis from the University of Malta, Dr. Stavroula Zoi and Manthos Santorinaios from Athens School of Fine Arts, Greece, and Prof. Eva Brooks from Aalborg University, Denmark.

We strongly believe that the collocated conferences ArtsIT 2017 and DLI 2017 provided a good forum for all researchers, developers, and practitioners to discuss the science and technology aspects that are relevant to interactivity, game creation, design, learning, and innovation. We also expect that the future ArtsIT and DLI conferences will be as successful and stimulating as indicated by the contributions presented in this volume.

February 2018

Nikolas Vidakis
Anthony L. Brooks
Eva Brooks

Organization

Steering Committee

Steering Committee Chair

Imrich Chlamtac   EAI/Create-Net, Italy

Steering Committee Co-chairs

Anthony Lewis Brooks   Aalborg University, Denmark
Eva Petersson Brooks   Aalborg University, Denmark

General Chair

Nikolas Vidakis   TEI of Crete, Greece

Organizing Committee

Eva Petersson Brooks   Aalborg University, Denmark
Evangelos Pallis   TEI of Crete, Greece
Giorgos Papadourakis   TEI of Crete, Greece

Technical Program Committee Chairs

Ben Challis   Manchester Metropolitan University, UK
Cumhur Erkut   Aalborg University Copenhagen, Denmark
Michael Boelstoft Holte   Aalborg Universitet Esbjerg, Denmark
Fotis Liarokapis   Masaryk University, Brno, Czech Republic
Paul McKevitt   University of Ulster, UK
Dan Overholt   Aalborg University Copenhagen, Denmark

Publicity and Social Media Chairs

Charikleia Chatzaki   TEI of Crete, Greece
Ioannis Kopanakis   TEI of Crete, Greece
Alexandros Roniotis   TEI of Crete, Greece

Workshops Chair

Georgios Triantafyllidis   Aalborg University Copenhagen, Denmark

Panels/Tutorials/Demos Chairs

Tsampikos Kounalakis   Aalborg University Copenhagen, Denmark
Ioannis Pachoulakis   TEI of Crete, Greece
Matthew Pediaditis   Foundation for Research and Technology – Hellas

Antonios Providakis	TEI of Crete, Greece
Panagiotis Zervas	TEI of Crete, Greece

Sponsorship and Exhibits Chairs

Eirini Dhmou	TEI of Crete, Greece
Magda Mpoumakkou	TEI of Crete, Greece
Sofianna Piliaris	TEI of Crete, Greece

Web Chairs

Evangelia Maniadi	TEI of Crete, Greece
Alexandros Roniotis	TEI of Crete, Greece

Publications Chairs

Eirini Christinaki	University of Essex, UK
Anastasia Pampouchidou	University of Burgundy, France
Nikolaos Papadakis	TEI of Crete, Greece

Posters and PhD Track Chairs

Nikolaos Papadakis	TEI of Crete, Greece
Alexandros Roniotis	TEI of Crete, Greece

Local Chair

Evangelia Maniadi	TEI of Crete, Greece

Conference Manager

Lenka Bilska	EAI (European Alliance for Innovation)

Technical Program Committee

Chris Abbott	University of Portsmouth, England, UK
Mark Billinghurst	University of South Australia in Adelaide, Australia
Nanna Borum	Aalborg University, Denmark
Anthony Brooks	Aalborg University, Denmark
Eva Irene Brooks	Aalborg University, Denmark
Ben Challis	Manchester Metropolitan University, UK
Orestis Charalampakos	TEI of Crete, Greece
Line Gad Christiansen	Aalborg University, Denmark
Eirini Christinaki	University of Essex, UK
Jonathan Duckworth	RMIT University
Cumhur Erkut	Aalborg University, Denmark
Pedro Gamito	Universidade Lusofona, Lisbon
Yi Gao	Aalborg University, Denmark
Steven Gelineck	Aalborg University, Denmark

Contents

IGDA Game Accessibility SIG - Research and Development

DLI 2017

ArtsIT 2017

Between Artistic Creativity and Documentation: An Experiment on Interaction with an Installation for Music-Making

Federica Bressan[1]([✉]) [iD], Acatia Finbow[2,3] [iD], Tim Vets[1], Micheline Lesaffre[1], and Marc Leman[1]

[1] IPEM - Department of Art History, Musicology and Theatre Studies, Ghent University, Ghent, Belgium
{federica.bressan,tim.vets,micheline.lesaffre,marc.leman}@ugent.be
[2] English Department, University of Exeter, Exeter, UK
af406@exeter.ac.uk
[3] Research Department at Tate, London, UK

Abstract. This article presents the preliminary results of an exploratory experiment with BilliArT, an interactive installation for music-making. The aim is to extract useful information from the combination of different ways to approach to the art work, namely that of conservation, of the aesthetic experience, and of the artistic creativity. The long-term goal is to achieve a better understanding of how people engage with interactive installations, and ultimately derive an ontology for interactive art.

Keywords: Interactive art · Aesthetic experience · Conservation
Documentation · Digital humanities

1 Introduction

Practices of documentation exists across a number of disciplines, and the definition of documentation can often differ subtly between the various approaches of those doing, using, or observing documentation. Whether written, visual, digital, or even embodied, documents (physical or otherwise) provide 'information' about a central object or phenomenon. Within the arts practice, and particularly within performance studies, documentation practices and products of documentation are problematic, due to the intrinsic impermanence of the phenomenon they try to capture. Beginning with the repeatedly cited claim by Peggy Phelan (Phelan 1993) that performance could not be recorded or saved in any way – the ultimate act of documentation – because of the intrinsic difference between the ephemerality of performance and the endurance of the document. Philip Auslander (Auslander 2008) later countered this by suggesting that it is only through the mediation of performance in another form that we become aware of 'liveness', and he also suggests that disappearance and loss are not exclusive to

© ICST Institute for Computer Sciences, Social Informatics and Telecommunications Engineering 2018
A. L. Brooks et al. (Eds.): ArtsIT 2017/DLI 2017, LNICST 229, pp. 3–12, 2018.
https://doi.org/10.1007/978-3-319-76908-0_1

performance, but are also a part of the material existence of performance documentation. Christopher Bedford (Bedford 2012), considering performance art specifically, has also – like Auslander (Auslander 2006) – advocated for the continuing life of the performance-as-artwork through the performance document, and its journey through time and space. The creation of the documents, and their potential for organisation, retrieval, and use in the future (Briet 1951) constitute complementary problems in building a good body of documentation. The quality of the final *network*, which includes the art work or performance themselves, has to be predicated on a good conceptual model (high level), and has to make sure that the format of each document is easily accessible, interoperable, and implements safety measures against tampering.

In their contribution to this conference in 2013, the authors proposed an abstract model for the preservation of interactive multimedia installations (Bressan and Canazza 2014). In this work, they present the continuation of their work, which aims to explore the nature of *interaction* with an artistic installation. The long-term goal is to achieve a better understanding of how people engage with interactive installations, and ultimately derive an ontology for interactive art. In this article we present the preliminary results of an explorative experiment carried out with an interactive installation for music-making called BilliArT. The aim of the experiment is to extract useful information from the combination of different ways to approach to the art work, namely that of conservation, of the aesthetic experience, and of the artistic creativity.

We move from the assumption that, at this stage of the research, these approaches can inform each other and produce new knowledge. Conservators need to compose a thorough description of the art work, and in order to do so they need a model of the art work. A model for interactive art will have to include interaction, but interaction – especially in aesthetic contexts – is not yet well understood. So a better understanding of interactive processes is functional to the advancement of our preservation models. For their part, artists are interested – among other things – in verifying the "end-user acceptance" (how the audience received the work) and the "overall system usefulness" (effectiveness of the artistic concept), "to get feedback to inform future design" (Abowd and Mynatt 2000) – with a clear parallel with the evaluation of interactive systems (a well developed field in engineering, for example (Bellotti et al. 2013)). Mostly qualitative questions that nonetheless require systematic gathering of quantitative data. Documentation can, in some cases, come to be an artwork in itself, with photographic and film documents often being included in exhibitions, or in data visualisations that hold aesthetic value and can be further manipulated to become part of future works. The participation to the practice of documentation can be seen, in this sense, as part of an expanded artistic practice.

A note on gender: gender mainstreaming (European Commission 2008) is an intrinsic part of this project. One way of implementing gender mainstreaming in gender non-related studies is to monitor gender representation, and to detect eventual differences among gender groups (Balarajan et al. 2011). Within the limits of this article, a reference to gender appears in Subsect. 4.1. The authors are currently developing more sophisticated methods to carry out gender-related tasks across the project activities.

The article is structured as follows: Sect. 2 gives a concise description of the installation; Sect. 3 describes the experimental setup and the types of data; Sect. 4 discusses the preliminary results.

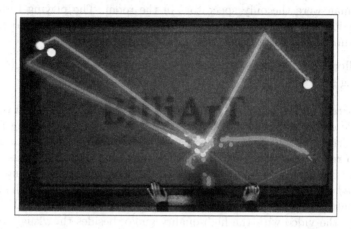

Fig. 1. Balls trajectories graphically reconstructed with the motion capture data log, and superimposed to the real-life video captured from the top of the table.

2 Description of the Installation

BilliArT is a dynamic system in which generative music emerges from the interaction of the participants with a standard carom billiard table. It was developed by Tim Vets at Ghent University, and first presented to the public in 2013 (Saenen et al. 2013). The installation features a jazz-inspired "algomorphic" approach to real-time music composition, combining sampled traditional jazz instruments (guitar, bass, drums) with their electronically manipulated counterparts. BilliArT presents the user with an interface familiar to most people, a standard billiard table: no musical training is required to compose with BilliArT, as the music unfolds as the game evolves. The balls rolling on the table, coated with a reflective material, are tracked by a motion capture system. The balls coordinates are passed to a Pure Data patch (using Open Sound Control) and drive the navigation through various dynamic melodic, harmonic, rhythmic and sonic structures. Standard billiard rules don't need to be respected, both to eliminate the requirement of having to know the rules, and to allow a greater degree of freedom in the exploration of sounds (for example the players can manipulate the balls with their hands, block their free roll or redirect them – but they cannot lift them from the table or remove them from the playing area). There is no standard playing duration and multiple players can interact at the same time. In this study, however, we experimented with a single-user interaction. For a detailed description of the system architecture, see (Vets et al. 2017).

3 Experimental

Setup. For this experiment, BilliArT was set up in a laboratory environment. A short verbal explanation about the installation was given to each participant before the game, then they were encouraged to familiarise themselves with the system by directly interacting with it (1 min training session). A researcher and a cameraman were the only spectators in the room. The playing time of the actual session was free (no time limit: participants were encouraged to follow the structure or the flow of their own musical inspiration).

Data collection. Qualitative as well as quantitative data were collected during the playing sessions:

- **Video recording:** each game was recorded with two fixed cameras: one on the side of the table, in the corner of the room, and one hanging from the ceiling, right on top of the billiard table, to capture the balls movements.
- **Audio recording:** the sonic output (the musical composition) was recorded directly from the line-out of the sound card mixing and redirecting the pre-recorded samples and the synthesised sounds to the speakers; the audio is also contained in the side video recording, providing an additional audio cue to align the video with the high-quality audio, besides the visual cue of the balls movement.
- **Motion capture data log:** the data log from the motion capture system was saved for each game, allowing for quantitative analyses on the games attributes such as exact duration and Quantity of Motion (see Subsect. 4.1);
- **Questionnaire:** a semi-structured anonymous questionnaire requiring the participants to fill in some questions right before and some questions right after the playing session;
- **Interview:** a semi-structured interview was carried out (and audio-recorded) right after the playing session.

There was some intentional redundancy in the data, aimed at integrating eventual missing data (which turned out not to be necessary) and at the verification of the consistency of the data. For example, the balls trajectories were graphically reconstructed starting from the motion capture data log and superimposed to the video recording captured from the top of the table (Fig. 1), to see how much noise was recorded by the motion capture system in the trajectories of the balls[1].

4 Analyses and Discussion

In the next paragraphs, we present the results of two analyses: the Quantity of Motion (Subsect. 4.1) and auto- and cross-correlations for the comparison of different playing sessions (Subsect. 4.2). In (Bressan et al. 2017), we reported

---

[1] A video is available at: http://federicabressan.com/daphnet/billiart/.

the effects of BilliArT on mood, and how previous experiences with installation art may influence the evaluation of BilliArT according to opposite pairs of adjectives (for example, "boring/exciting"). We plan to present the results of the questionnaires and the interviews in a separate article, oriented to qualitative analyses.

4.1 Quantity of Motion (QoM)

As the game develops over time, it's hard to express its characteristics with fixed values. On the other hand, we are not so interested in a real-time reconstruction of the game progression, we don't want to "watch" it again. We want to know "how much" and "how" the players interacted with BilliArT (how long did they play? were they always using all three balls? did they leave a ball still for a long time? how much surface did the balls cover on the table? etc.). So we defined a derived quantity called Quantity of Motion (QoM), that is a useful way of looking into each games characteristics and be able to compare them with other games (see Subsect. 4.2).

For each game, the QoM is calculated first for each ball. The QoM is made of two values: speed and angularity. Speed is the linear distance traveled by the ball during the entire game duration. Angularity is a sudden change in the ball's direction. When it occurs, three cases are possible: the ball hit the rim of the table, or it collided with another ball, or it was redirected by the player's hand(s). Angularity is relevant in the game because – according to the mapping defined by the artist – it triggers a musical event.

Angularity detecting is performed by considering the position of the ball in three consecutive motion capture frames. The angle defined by the ball's position in the current frame (t) and the previous $(t-1)$ is subtracted from the angle defined by the previous frame $(t-1)$ and the one before $(t-2)$. Let $x[t0]$ and $y[t0]$ represent the coordinates of the position of the ball at a given frame, $x[t-1]$ and $y[t-1]$ the coordinates at the previous frame, and $x[t-2]$ and $y[t-2]$ the coordinates in the second-previous frame. Angularity is calculated subtracting $\arctan((y[t0] - y[t-1]) / (x[t0] - x[t-1]))$ from $\arctan((y[t-1] - y[t-2]) / (x[t-1] - x[t-2]))$. When $y[t0] - y[t-1]$ or $y[t-1] - y[t-2]$ (i.e. delta(Y)) is negative, 180° are added to the result in order to obtain that the correct quadrant. However, an accurate calculation of the angularity requires that speed is also taken into account due to the physiological noise of the motion capture system. When a ball is not moving, the motion capture will detect micro-changes in its position, like a slight oscillation of the centre of the ball. And even a micro-change in the position can result in a large angle change. Therefore, by considering speed, we are able to determine whether the ball is in motion or not, and to retain the angularity value or not. This is achieved by multiplying the angle by the speed of the ball (the distance between the positions in the current and the previous frame).

Speed and angularity are then divided by the duration of the game, as each playing session had a different duration. The resulting number is the QoM for each separate ball. The QoM of the entire game is the mean of the sum of each separate QoM value. Figure 2a shows the normalised QoM for male and female participants. The QoM median for female participants is higher, and female also show a greater variance in their game. For both male and female, the QoM of each ball is similar to the mean QoM, confirming that it is a fair representation of the overall game – and not, for example, that participants played with two balls a lot and left one still, yielding the same motion mean value. Defining a quantity to describe motion proves useful in two ways: it helps artists formally abstract some aspects of the playing mode and features, manipulate them intellectually and then decide to introduce (or not) modifications in future re-installations or novel works. In other words it provides a language to talk about one aspect of the interactive process – the definition of which may be adjusted to fit the type of interaction of this specific installation. At the same time, by calling for the formal definition of other aspects of the interaction process, the QoM contributes to the vocabulary that conservator uses to understand, describe and archive the work. In this context, QoM is not intended as the measurement of human gestures – the motion capture system, normally used to track human gestures in studies that involve QoM in this sense (e.g. (Burger et al. 2013; Visi et al. 2014a)), is used in BilliArT to track the balls movement. In human gestures, QoM "is proportional to the translational movement and it is extracted from a global set of features evaluated over time. It gives high values when the body is moving fast and low values when it is more stationary" (Visi et al. 2014b). In BilliArT, QoM combines both the speed and angularity of the balls, and the relation is not necessarily fast movement/high value and stationary/low value.

Finally, QoM was mapped against the participants answers to the question "how much did you feel in control [during the playing session]" (for a description of the questionnaire see Sect. 3). The Likert-scale was grouped in three bins: "not in control", "somewhat in control", "very much in control" (Fig. 2b). Participants who felt less in control have the highest QoM value, while participants who felt 'somewhat in control" or "very much in control" have a similar median, although participants who felt "very much in control" also show a greater variability. The oral interviews reveal that participants who didn't feel in control were more relentless in trying to figure out the relation between balls movement and sound, resulting in a greater activity – as well as in a feeling of frustration, as revealed by the interviews. Conversely, participants who felt in control show a lower QoM because they were not trying so hard to "make" the installation sound, but let the balls roll longer, manipulated them less with their hands, and "listened" more to the co-created composition.

4.2 Comparing Games

We now take a closer look at some features of the playing sessions and compare them. We derive some observations on the participants' perceived sense of control, and on the tension between the concepts of "searching" and "finding" during the game progression. Cross- and autocorrelation matrices were made for the game data recorded by the motion capture system. A set of 12 variables was considered separately, among which the movement of each ball along the x and

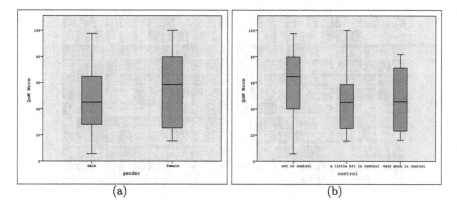

Fig. 2. Left: box plots of the Quantity of Motion (QoM) for two gender groups. Right: box plot of the QoM for groups of participants that evaluated how much they felt "in control" during their interaction with BilliArT.

y axis and the QoM. The raw motion capture data consist of time series that correspond to the three spatial coordinates (x, y, z) for each of the three balls (total of 9 values per sample), with a sampling frequency of 100 Hz. The matrices were generated discarding the value for the z axis (balls roll on the flat table, elevation is not relevant), and calculating the speed and angularity for each ball (totalling a number of 12 variables). Angularity is detected when a ball suddenly changes direction (see Subsect. 4.1).

Each of the 12 values were compared with themselves and the remaining 11, yielding 144 correlation matrices. Figure 3 combines the correlation matrices of two different games, laid out in a 12 by 12 *fingerprint*. The visual impact of the *fingerprints* expresses the overall similarity of the games.

Zooming in on each square gives us more information about the game progress. For example, Fig. 4 shows the auto-correlation of the movements of ball number 2 with respect to the x axis in two different games (a and b) and the correlation of both (c). Time runs on the diagonal line from the bottom left to the top right of the square. As can be readily seen in the auto-correlations, in the first game most activity is concentrated in the middle of the session, whereas in the second it is more spread out over the entire duration. Colour channels in subfigure (c) have been assigned so that green indicates changes taking place predominantly in one of the two games, blue indicates changes taking place in both games simultaneously, and plateaus without change in either game are depicted in pink/purple. Therefore, the green lines in Fig. 4c summarise the difference in activity between the two games where activity refers to every time ball number 2 has crossed the x axis on the billiard table. These data visualisations are a special example of documentation with aesthetic value, in that they were produced by the same artist who authored the installation; they can simply be seen as images, without a reference to their source (data) or meaning (data interpretation); they keep informing the artist's creative process, to feed or inspire future data-driven projects.

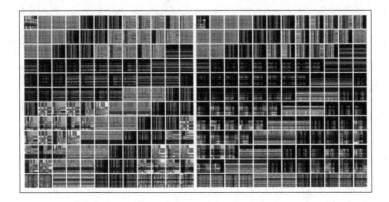

Fig. 3. Fingerprints of games 4 and 9, showing the correlation matrices of 12 parameters.

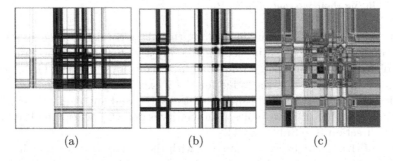

(a)   (b)   (c)

Fig. 4. Auto-correlation matrices (a and b) for the values of the movements of ball number 2 across the x axis in two different games, with angularity transitions emphasised in black; and coloured overlay of both (c). (Color figure online)

Billiard tables have a standard size of $2M \times M$, i.e. their length (x axis) is twice their width (y axis). Moving the balls along the x axis is allows for a greater span than moving them across the y axis. In relation to the musical mapping of BilliArT, it can be said that when the player has the ball cross the y axis, (s)he's trying to "find a new musical idea", while crossing the y axis (s)he's trying to "develop the current musical idea". This allows us to formulate some hypotheses on the musical intention or direction of the player at a given time in the game. Higher activity along the x axis reveal how often the player tried to change the overall musical idea; higher activity along the y axis reveal the desire to explore that idea, to elaborate on it.

5   Conclusions and Future Work

This article presented the preliminary results of an exploratory experiment with BilliArT, an interactive installation for music-making. The aim is to extract useful information from the combination of different ways to approach to the art work, namely that of conservation, of the aesthetic experience, and of the artistic creativity. The long-term goal is to achieve a better understanding of how people engage with interactive installations, and ultimately derive an ontology for interactive art. Future work include the selection of the most suitable indicators about the interactive aesthetic experience, and the design of experiments that refine the emerging concepts and test them on installations other than BilliArT. In a specific example, when we can distinguish the cause of direction change in a ball (hitting an obstacle while rolling, versus manual redirection), we can gain a better understanding on the experience of the player by combining this information with the perceived sense of control reported in the interview, the physical engagement and finding the game "clear" vs. "confusing". Letting the balls freely roll across the table (they only change direction when they hit a rim or another ball) may indicate that the player is more in an "observing" mode of the system, listening to the sounds of the installation without interfering much, trying to understand the mapping behind the movement and the sound; while intense hand manipulation reveals a will to "do", to control, to maximize the amount of sound "extracted" from the system. It may also indicate an inclination to stick to the original game of billiards, where balls are supposed to roll freely, or to engage in the interaction exploiting all the possibilities of the installation, where the rules of the original game don't have to be necessarily respected – actually not respecting them allows for more interesting sounds sequences and combinations.

Of course, regardless of the player's observing or active mode, the questions whether interactive systems such as BilliArT actually allow for *control* are open for debate, just like the question of the *authorship* of the musical output (who is the composer? the artist who designed the installation, the player, or the installation? or all three?). It depends how we define "control" and "authorship", and this is why definitions are not secondary not only in art history and critic for the sake of classification, but in preservation insofar preservation (of interactive art) requires a clear understanding of the phenomenon we're trying to describe, trans-code, and ultimately transmit over space and time.

Acknowledgements. This study was partially supported by the European Union's Horizon 2020 research and innovation programme under the Marie Skłodowska-Curie grant agreement No. 703937.

References

Abowd, G., Mynatt, E.: Charting past, present, and future research in ubiquitous computing. ACM Trans. Comput. Hum. Interact. **7**(1), 29–58 (2000)

Auslander, P.: Liveness: Performance in a Mediatized Culture. Psychology Press, London (1999/2008)

Auslander, P.: The performativity of performance documentation. PAJ: J. Perform. Art **28**(3), 1–10 (2006)

Balarajan, M., Gray, M., Mitchell, M.: Monitoring equality: developing a gender identity question. Research report 75, National Centre for Social Research - Equality and Human Rights Commission, London (2011)

Bedford, C.: The viral ontology of performance. In: Perform, Repeat, Record: Live Art in History, pp. 77–87. Intellect (2012)

Bellotti, F., Lee, B.K.K., Moreno-Ger, P., Berta, R.: Assessment in and of serious games: an overview. Adv. Hum. Comput. Interact. **11**, 1 (2013)

Bressan, F., Canazza, S.: The challenge of preserving interactive sound art: a multi-level approach. Int. J. Arts Technol. **7**(4), 294–315 (2014)

Bressan, F., Vets, T., Leman, M.: A multimodal interactive installation for collaborative music making: from preservation to enhanced user design. In: Proceedings of the European Society for Cognitive Sciences of Music (ESCOM) Conference, pp. 23–26. Ghent University, Ghent (2017)

Briet, S.: What is Documentation? English Translation of the Classic French Text. Scarecrow, Toronto (1951/2006)

Burger, B., Thompson, M.R., Luck, G., Saarikallio, S., Toiviainen, P.: Influences of rhythm- and timbre-related musical features on characteristics of music-induced movement. Front. Psychol. **4**, 183 (2013)

European Commission: Manual for gender mainstreaming: employment, social inclusion and social protection policies. Technical report, European Commission (2008)

Phelan, P.: Unmarked: The Politics of Performance. Routledge, London (1993)

Saenen, I.P., et al.: BilliARt - AR carom billiards - exploration of an AR framework. In: Stephanidis, C. (ed.) HCI 2014. CCIS, vol. 434, pp. 636–641. Springer, Cham (2014). https://doi.org/10.1007/978-3-319-07857-1_112

Vets, T., Nijs, L., Lesaffre, M., Moens, B., Bressan, F., Colpaert, P., Lambert, P., de Walle, R.V., Leman, M.: Gamified music improvisation with billiart: a multimodal installation with balls. J. Multimodal User Interfaces **11**(1), 25–38 (2017)

Visi, F., Coorevits, E., Miranda, E., Leman, M.: Effects of different bow stroke styles on body movements of a viola player: an exploratory study. In: Proceedings ICMC—SMC—2014, Athens, Greece, pp. 1368–1374 (2014a)

Visi, F., Schramm, R., Miranda, E.: Gesture in performance with traditional musical instruments and electronics: use of embodied music cognition and multimodal motion capture to design gestural mapping strategies. In: Proceedings of the 2014 International Workshop on Movement and Computing, pp. 100:100–100:105. IRCAM, ACM, New York (2014b)

Interactive Artist – Affective Painting in Multimedia Sensor Space

Anthony L. Brooks$^{(\boxtimes)}$ (ID)

Aalborg University, Aalborg, Denmark
tb@create.aau.dk

Abstract. Non-arbitrary mapping of computer feedback audio and visuals to affect an artist/painter in performance aligned with human feedback loop closure is reported. Design related 'bouba/kiki' and 'law of effect'. Results suggested higher unconscious than conscious impact to the artist during the process of creative expression. Performance process impact on creative expression by dynamic external stimuli on an artist is inconclusive from this explorative study.

Keywords: Afferent efferent neural feedback loop closure in performance

1 Introduction and Background Narrative

Computer software that empowers creation and manipulation of imaging is positioned from the perspective of two traditional artists (painters) so as to introduce this study.

A positive of digital software is exemplified by the history of an oil painter Jean Detheux[1] who became allergic to natural media and was only able to continue, reawaken and even develop his art via digital empowerment. This first with Painter in 1997 (Fractal Design/MetaCreations – later Corel), and subsequently, around the turn of the century, with Synthetik Studio Artist: Attributes of this twenty-first century product enabling even a 'non-artist' user to automatically paint, draw, and rotoscope, in other words, to create, have fun and experience a satisfying creative expression. However, such inclusive and accessible empowerment was considered negative and threatening by a Danish-based French painter Manu Rich[2] who is subject of herein reported series of studies.

In a meeting in 1999, artist Rich argued negatively against digital software such as Painter and Adobe Photoshop and the threat he considered innate. The author designed to counter by conceptualising how an interactive stimuli environment would affect the artist experience in a painting performance. The concept included with audience experiencing the creative expression activity. The concept related to the author's body of work coined as SoundScapes where empowered gesture-based creative expression is used as a supplement to traditional rehabilitation intervention (e.g. Brooks et al. 1999, 2002, 2011).

Around the time of the meeting the author was invited to feature in the Danish NeWave festival in New York and a linked 'going away' party in Copenhagen. Behind

---

[1] https://news.synthetik.com/tag/jean-detheux/.
[2] http://www.manurich.com.

© ICST Institute for Computer Sciences, Social Informatics and Telecommunications Engineering 2018
A. L. Brooks et al. (Eds.): ArtsIT 2017/DLI 2017, LNICST 229, pp. 13–21, 2018.
https://doi.org/10.1007/978-3-319-76908-0_2

the invitation was that his interactive installation (see in following sections and online video[3]) had toured Museums of Modern Art and culture centres for near two years. Serendipitously, the invitation offered a timely opportunity to create and research the interactive painter concept.

1.1 Concept Foundation

This contribution reports on a three segment explorative study of non-arbitrary mapping of audio and visuals to affect a painter in performance. The concept aligns with the author's related research on human afferent-efferent neural feedback loop closure (Brooks et al. 2002, 2011).

The concept foundation related to audio-visual perceptual 'in-process' linking such as 'bouba/kiki' effect (e.g. Köhler 1929; Ramachandran and Hubbard 2001; Maurer et al. 2006). However, instead of speech sounds linked to visual shapes (i.e. the 'bouba/kiki' effect), this study focused on dynamic stimuli affecting a live painting activity by a professional artist who through his movement dynamics of painting, within a 'prepared' canvas sensor space, triggered and manipulated, thus self-effected, the external stimuli. The self-effective computer feedback interactions were speculated to affect the artist sub-consciously (thus, self-affect) and this was anticipated as being transferred to the creative expression (painting). Also speculated was impact at a conscious level. The author-selected content stimuli to affect, with changes made in real-time, thus the artist had no control of which sound was triggered. A speculation was that 'law of effect' through learning from the stimuli would enhance the artist's experience over time to indicate repeated pleasant consequences in the creative process behaviour and vice-versa (e.g. Thorndike 1932; Goodenough 1950; Kentridge 2005). Three studies were undertaken each resulting in a traditional painting on canvas – see Appendix 1–3 for images of framed pictures.

2   Venues and Overview of Design

2.1   Inaugural Event: Background/Overview

Scandinavian Centre, Aarhus, Denmark
Following the initial meeting with artist Rich, the author's Circle of Interactive Light (COIL) – an interactive large room-size installation that exhibited at leading Museums of Modern Art, City Museums, and main cultural centres throughout 1998 and 1999 – proved a suitable controlled location for the initial event. COIL was at the time hosted at the Scandinavian Centre[4] in Aarhus for approximately six months. It was a mature and tested installation where a live audience could be invited for 'special occasion' evening 'happenings' to experience a centre-stage meta-event and subsequently to experience the interactive spaces. The interactive painter was billed as such a

---

[3] https://www.youtube.com/watch?v=3W4VznlgiU4.

[4] http://www.Scandinavian-Center.Dk.

'happening'. There was also a gratis café set up inside the installation to, as much as possible, ensure a catchment audience.

A large canvas was purchased, mounted and positioned with the artist's paint and tools near to hand. Infrared sensors were mounted around the canvas to enable the sensing of the artist's movements within specific painting spaces (e.g. tracking torso, head, limbs, brush strokes… within a volumetric space). Stereo speakers, MIDI and MIDI/DMX512 translator interfaces mapped sensed motion data to multiple unit auditory and lighting systems via computer feedback software (Cycling74 Max/MSP). Selection of auditory feedback aligned with 'bouba/kiki' effect referring to dynamic 'rounded/jagged' interpretations (e.g. at the extremes a smooth moving synthesizer patch versus a heavy aggressive Hendrix guitar style patch where each effected the painter to smooth and rounded expressions or jagged and aggressive expressions). A video of the event was recorded[5].

See Appendix 1 for resulting painting.

An overview for readers is that COIL was created under the author's 'Ludic Engagement Design for All' (LEDA) umbrella. This aspect of design targeted as wide as possible inclusion and accessibility for diversity across abilities, ages and situation (as aligned within SoundScapes - see Brooks 2011). Hence, the author-contracted agreement with all host venues included opportunities for Monday experience workshops. Monday being typically a museum's 'closed to public day' where staff administration is undertaken. Institutions, communities or groups were promoted to contact the museum of their preferred Monday to book the author-led workshops. In this way wheelchair users or others with disability had freedom to experience without encumbering distraction from traditionally-abled, families, and others. Informing COIL design was a definition of diversity and inclusion from the American Alliance of Museums[6]. This emphasizes diversity as "The quality of being different or unique at the individual or group level" including "the perspectives of each individual shaped by their nation, experiences and culture—and more" and inclusion as the "act of including; a strategy to leverage diversity" whereby "to leverage diversity, an environment must be created where people feel supported, listened to and able to do their personal best." Thus, fitting under this umbrella was considered the negative artist/painter as a unique individual whose difference was through opinion on the potentials of digital in the form of virtual interactive space (Brooks 1999). Through designing and hosting the interactive painter within the COIL installation the author was creating inclusion through the interactive meta-installation as discussed herein. Thus, interpretively, the interactive painter concept aligned with the author hosted Monday workshops at the museums.

Approximately thirty audience members attended the inaugural event. Many gave generally positive reactions following the event when asked open-ended questions. Some attendees even wished to purchase the created painting. This positive response however is lightly taken as attendees can be considered as mostly friends or associates of author and/or artist. It should be noted that the purpose of the 'happening' was not to appease the attending public.

---

[5] https://www.youtube.com/watch?v=KOI16Vih8Xs.

[6] http://www.aam-us.org/about-us/strategic-plan/diversity-and-inclusion-policy.

2.2   Second Event

Life Nightclub, Copenhagen, Denmark
The follow-up event after the initial COIL inauguration of the interactive painter was at a 'going-away' fund raising event towards realizing the Danish NeWave festival to be held in New York City, USA. The event was hosted in Life nightclub in Copenhagen and a similar interactive painter set-up was established, but with the addition of an invited heavy metal guitarist. The role of the guitarist was to offer another level of interaction for the painter who enjoyed heavy metal. The anticipated interaction did not result as predicted so the live musician was discontinued for the final event. A significant audience attended but this was not specific for the interactive painter aspect as a whole evening (and most of the night) was programmed for entertainment. There were insignificant interviews undertaken at this event.

See Appendix 2 for resulting painting.

2.3   Cumulative (Third) Event

Gershwin Hotel and Gallery, New York City. United States of America
Located in the NoMad ("NOrth of MADison Square Park") neighbourhood centred on the Madison Square North Historic District in the borough of Manhattan, New York City, The Gershwin hotel (named after the musician George Gershwin; since 2014 rebuilt as The Evelyn hotel) at 7 East 27th St was frequented by a host of celebrities and was a culture hub with gallery space. The lobby featured original artwork from Andy Warhol and Roy Liechtenstein and each floor had a different artist or art theme. Figure 1, a painting by Andrew Woodward (many thanks for permission to use) illustrates the façade as the author recalls from 1999 and the Danish NeWave event.

The event at the Gershwin included a similar set-up as detailed in previous sections but with the addition of an author-design conductor jacket with strips of retro reflective material sown in the style of feathers over half of the jacket. The body movements of the artist wearing the jacket thus were enhanced through the augmented infrared sensor reflection of the jacket. This augmentation made the computer feedback system, via sensors sourcing the dynamic motion data, highly sensitive to change resulting in a more responsive feedback of stimuli.

An audience of around thirty attended. Immediately following the interaction event there was opportunity for the audience to ask questions. The questions exhibited curiosity, interest and confusion…and hinted at provocation and challenge as targeted under the research design. The performance event was subject to live streaming Online – something of a novelty in 1999 – though the author never saw the footage. Notable was that a group of Greek attendees positively responded by recommending contact to Jonas Mekas, 'the godfather of avant-garde cinema'[7] who was based in New York running the Anthology Film Archives[8] where he is still listed as artistic director. The

---

[7] https://www.theguardian.com/film/2012/dec/01/jonas-mekas-avant-garde-film-interview.

[8] http://anthologyfilmarchives.org/contact/staff.

Fig. 1. Andrew Woodward, "Gershwin hotel," acrylic on panel, $12 \times 18''$ - copyright the artist and used with permission – see http://www.andrewwoodward.com

author followed up by meeting Mekas, however, his interest was solely on film medium and he had no concept of what was being presented as avant-garde interactive digital art. This is a side note of no value for this research publication, thus, not further reported and no disrespect is intended with this comment as the author valued the meeting and the positive recommendation by attendees.

See Appendix 3 for resulting painting.

3   Conclusions

A concept was conceived to affect a live painting event where the artist was challenged through a darkened environment, interactive multimedia stimuli, and live audience. Speculated was that the stimuli would affect the artist's creative painting expression such that, at the extremes from an auditory perspective using physical modelled sounds, a heavy distorted Hendrix style sound would result in an aggressive highly jagged painting motion whilst a synthesizer pad sound would result in a smoother conjoined motion of creative expression.

A triad series of paintings were created upon three 'prepared movement-sensing canvas' performances under the author's SoundScapes concept with different audiences in different venues and situation. The French artist Manu Rich[9] was the painter. A goal

---

[9] http://www.manurich.com.

was to explore afferent-efferent neural feedback loop closure using dynamic stimuli feedback responding to human input i.e. a self-effect/affect loop (see Brooks et al. 1999, 2002, 2011).

Performances (all 1999) consisted of painter Manu Rich plus:-

- (1 @ Scandinavian Congress Center, Aarhus, Denmark – *Circle of Interactive Light [COIL] MoMA exhibition tour*) digital audio-visuals
- (2 @ Life Night Club, Copenhagen, Denmark – *Danish NeWave "Going Away" party*) audio plus live guitarist, and
- (3 @Gershwin Hotel and Gallery, New York City, USA - *Danish NeWave festival*) digital audio via enhanced motion sensor wearable.

A live audience was in attendance at all performances and qualitative assessment was via observations and interviews. In addition, an audience Q & A session took place after the culminating performance in New York City (3). Outcomes from the observations and interviews are inconclusive as to whether 'law of effect' through learning from the stimuli impacted the artist's experience or satisfaction. Likewise, it was also not evident whether behaviour followed by unpleasant consequences or dissatisfaction was not repeated (see Thorndike 1932; Goodenough 1950; Kentridge 2005). Auditory feedback was observed more impactful on the artist's matching dynamics than mixed media, however this needs further investigation to claim with confidence. The 'bouba/kiki' effect was evident, through observations, in how certain of the artist interactions (beyond brushstrokes, as a variety of 'tools' were used) seemed to dynamically match certain feedback changes – especially if they were distinctly at either end of the auditory round-jagged stimuli scale; however, the artist's conscious reflective experience in interview was inconclusive on this. Thus, it is difficult to ascertain the level of impact that the computer feedback (effect/affect) achieved if any. In other words, total closure of the afferent efferent neural feedback loop cannot be claimed. Related to the author's main body of research however, there is alignment with potential unconscious engagement of the subject in responding to the stimuli that augmented the action behaviour. Further studies are needed, with possibly a number of artist/painters and with improved research protocol.

Notable is that even though the artist still gave indifferent responses when interviewed and in the Q & A session after the events, in 2008, almost a decade after the interactive painter series of events, he again 'performed' or 'painted direct' at the RATP (Régie Autonome des Transports Parisiens) Cultural Center – Paris alongside poetry by Paul Sanda and music by Damien Charon (see http://www.manurich.com/biographie). The 1999 events have not been discussed since as the painter returned to Paris following living in Denmark.

4   Coda and Future Work

What inspires an artist (e.g. painter, improvising musician, …) to creatively express? What causes anyone to creatively express? Can such expression be empowering to a person? How does movement relate to creative expression? Can artist movement and creative expression be influenced externally by non-related stimuli? Can afferent efferent neural feedback loop closure be identified and observed in an art-piece? Does it matter? …

Movement related to creative expression is increasingly being investigated since sensor-based interfaces, microcontrollers, and computer advances are readily available commercially and affordable, in part, due to the adoption by games industry. Such interfaces were not as available in 1999 when this study took place. Thus, the bespoke sensors used in the author's movement research within disabled communities were used in this study.

This three segment explorative study of non-arbitrary mapping of audio and visuals (i.e. mixed media) to affect a painter in performance, although inconclusive, offered indications of the potential of interactive stimuli to painter performance. Such potentials are investigated in the author's main body of research titled SoundScapes where performance relates to functional ability. Potentials are also reflected as related to evidence in an independent randomized intervention study where a computer feedback product coined as 'Personics', which resulted from the author's research, was used to effect elderly patients in balance training where reported results were of a "marked improvement that was up to 400% in the training specific performance" (Hagedorn and Holme 2010).

In closing the author deems it necessary to state that, although the research reported was conducted in 1999, the questions asked in, and relating to, this explorative study are to a point still questioned nearly two decades later. But this could be a reflection of the author's naivety or, more recently, his distancing from the field. However, the undertaking and experience of showing his work at the Gershwin gallery as a performance research endeavour was rewarding. From this positioning, and as the text is closing, the author reflects on meetings and communications with the cited Montreal-based artist Jean Detheux who is increasingly acclaimed for his own improvisation concept of interactive painting performance with live musicians: Jean is probably the person who could get closest to answering some of these posited questions.

To end, it is reflected that the opportunity to realize such a study with three diverse venues in different countries, situations, and with a professional artist is rare. Thus, this contribution is shared almost two decades following the actual 'happenings' to promote similar studies where a student-reader researcher can reflect on the weaknesses of this research design to improve and challenge these and related questions on creativity, human expression, and stimuli effect/affect. Maybe a good place for them to start would be to query Mister Jean Detheux!

Appendix 1

Painting result from segment 1 performance: Aarhus, Denmark.

Appendix 2

Painting result from segment 2 performance: Copenhagen, Denmark.

Appendix 3

Painting result from segment 3 performance: New York City, USA.

References

Brooks, A.L.: Virtual interactive space. In: Proceeding of World Confederation for Physical Therapy (WCPT), Yokohama, Japan, p. 66 (1999)

Brooks, A.L.: SoundScapes: the evolution of a concept, apparatus and method where ludic engagement in virtual interactive space is a supplemental tool for therapeutic motivation (2011). http://vbn.aau.dk/files/55871718/PhD.pdf

Brooks, A.L., Camurri, A., Canagarajah, N., Hasselblad, S.: Interaction with shapes and sounds as a therapy for special needs and rehabilitation. In: Proceedings of the 4th International Conference for Disability, Virtual Reality and Associate Technologies (ICDVRAT), Reading University, UK, pp. 205–212 (2002)

Goodenough, F.L.: Edward Lee Thorndike: 1874–1949. Am. J. Psychol. **63**, 291–301 (1950)

Hagedorn, D.K., Holme, E.: Effects of traditional physical training and visual computer feedback training in frail elderly patients. A randomized intervention study. Eur. J. Phys. Rehabil. Med. **46**(2), 159–168 (2010)

Kentridge, R.: Edward Thorndike, puzzle-boxes, and the law of effect. Lecture note, University of Durham (2005)

Köhler, W.: Gestalt Psychology. Liveright, New York (1929)

Maurer, D., Pathman, T., Mondloch, C.J.: The shape of boubas: sound-shape correspondences in toddlers and adults. Dev. Sci. **9**(3), 316–322 (2006)

Ramachandran, V.S., Hubbard, E.M.: Synaesthesia: a window into perception, thought and language. J. Conscious. Stud. **8**(12), 3–34 (2001)

Thorndike, E.: The Fundamentals of Learning. AMS Press Inc. (1932)

Ideal Spaces Exhibition

Michael Johansson[1(✉)] and Ulrich Gehmann[2]

[1] HKR Kristianstad University, Kristianstad, Sweden
Michael.johansson@hkr.se
[2] KIT, Karlsruhe, Germany
ugehm@t-online.de

Abstract. Through the years we have worked with the idea of *gestalt* through artefact creation (including virtual objects and 3D-worlds) as one surface to explore, exploit, test and communicate our ideas and concepts, that are generative rather than produced, where we try to grasp systematic insights through complex generated realities, in which an audience later is invited to interact. In our Ideal spaces exhibition for the 2016 Biennale in Venice, we tried to explore this via a combination of presenting ideal city spaces, active participation of the visitors molding their own spaces, and symbolic representation. Ideal Spaces is also a high-tech project that uses diverse technologies in new ways, also new techniques and programming developed by us.

Keywords: Art · Design · Architecture · Interaction design · Ideal spaces
Animation · Unity3d

1 Introduction

An ideal space is both space imagined, from the Greek idea and eidos; and space "ideal" in the words common use, denoting a space perfected [1]. In that latter meaning, an ideal space is an absolute model of how space should be. In this sense, it is also a utopian space.

Ideal spaces are not only about architecture but about social dreaming and imagination, expressed in 'ideal' spaces with their impacts on architecture, art, and human hopes. We tried to show this via a combination of presenting ideal city spaces, active participation of the visitors molding their own spaces, and symbolic representation. Ideal Spaces is also a high-tech project that uses diverse technologies in new ways, also new techniques and programming developed by us. The exhibition deals with ideal spaces in a double sense: as spaces imagined and as spaces utopian, or perfected. In both its meanings of being 'ideal', an ideal space relates to utopian space, an old theme deeply embedded in our cultural memory which has never lost its actuality and appeal. With a look at recent conditions, we need to re-address it more than ever.

1.1 Our Theme Ideal Spaces

Since it is a mythic theme full of hopes and dreams, and at the same time, very practical. Today, the majority of human beings live in urban agglomerations which are far away from being 'ideal' but chaotic, accompanied by an actual destruction of space

© ICST Institute for Computer Sciences, Social Informatics and Telecommunications Engineering 2018
A. L. Brooks et al. (Eds.): ArtsIT 2017/DLI 2017, LNICST 229, pp. 22–32, 2018.
https://doi.org/10.1007/978-3-319-76908-0_3

unprecedented in history. In parallel, never before so many technical possibilities of imagining spaces existed, allowing for escape into worlds of fantasy, dream, and game. Space is lost, and at the same time multiplied.

But human beings need space, also real ones deserving the name, and they need community. Issues which have to be settled, urgently. One first step in doing so may consist in re-framing them, to look at them anew, from different but nevertheless related perspectives.

We did so by taking the theme's archaic character as a background tale, the myth of a paradise lost and to be regained again [2], and by actively involving the visitors. Today, the question arises of what an ideal space actually is, or could be. We wanted to invite visitors to join this venture, by experiencing spaces conceptualized as ideal ones: shown in a large cave, as worlds of their own, and on an "ideal" cosmic disk presenting them in connection. And by constructing their own spaces, which will allow the visitors to experience their commonly generated spaces together, both as a process and as a result.

The epitomized place for an ideal space is that of the ideal city, also one of the formers' favorized *topoi* in symbolic terms [3]. The ideal city relates to utopia, the *eu*-topia as a place of redemption and liberation in form of a second, and artificial paradise. Exemplary cases of such cities, to be conceived primarily as *space* (and not as cities) were provided on a cave-like screen measuring 3.60×6.0 m, so that the visitors could really "dive" into them, allowing for an experience of the respective space as a world by its own. We also presented the cathedral, a very symbolic space in occidental heritage with regard to the topic of a paradise to be regained. Moreover, at the end of our sequence of worlds, we sketched a favela, both a symbolic and real counterpoint. its symbolic value is not confined to be the epitomized opposite to an "ideal" space, but to offer a new, and different kind of utopia: instead of a pre-planned entity provided by some creators outside [4], the inhabitants of such a space have the possibility to mold it by themselves – an old democratic ideal of participation since the days of the *polis* in a new shape.

What is "ideal" in the spaces presented? The very term *ideal* relates to the Greek words *idea* and *eidos*, to have an 'idea' or an inner image of something; in case of eidos, also one which can become very concrete, and which may serve as a pattern or type [5] – e.g. for constructing an ideal city acc. to a clear and pre-given "inner" image. And as already mentioned in the beginning, *ideal* also stands for something perfected or 'ideal' in the common sense of the term: something which is an end state ('perfect'), in other words [6] (Fig. 1).

Looking at these two meanings of what *ideal* denotes, it is of decisive importance when both these meanings coincide or overlap: when a city shall be constructed as an ideal space, covering both these meanings – even in cases where its constructors have literally 'no idea' what they actually are doing. That is, when they are not decisively and explicitly reaching for utopia but nevertheless built utopian spaces, in fact, by generating a spatiality of the "non-place" addressed by critics as Augé [7] and others (e.g., [8]): a type of placeless spatiality generating real physical but essentially placeless ('*ou*-topian') spaces on the historical remnants of which we all live.

In these cases, the imagery about an ideal space must not always, and not explicitly be utopian. Since in the original meaning of an ideal, an ideal space does not only

Fig. 1. Three of the ideal spaces shown in the exhibition. Babel IId, the Reims Cathedral, and Motopia

denote a space perfected, something that has to be achieved as an optimized final state; but also a space which has been conceptualized at all: an inner image, an idea about a space as it shall look like [9], pouring into plans, concepts, and other concretized imaginations about spatial design; as in city planning, layout of logistic networks, buildings, the construction of spaces for the public, and the like. These are examples which demonstrate that the notion of an ideal space does also include quite practical constructions needed for the purposes of daily life in its concrete terms.

But let's return to the epitome of an ideal space (at least in the occidental realm), the one of an 'ideal' city. Concepts about an ideal city rely upon the idea of an ideal space constructed, to provide both base and frame for a proper unfolding of the human condition, for an ideal *conditio humana*. According to our cultural imagery, the proper and genuine place for humans as "cultural animals" (McLuhan) is the city, from the start of human civilization onwards [10]. Thus, a city has to be erected which is ideal, constructed in such a way that the spatial conditions for that animal shall propagate the advent of the 'positive' traits of a general human nature; or, expressed in mythological terms: after the first, natural paradise being lost, a second one has to be created, a paradise regained by construction. As an environment and a frame of living, these new paradises shall become man's second nature to overcome the shortfalls of existing urban environments.

For the first time in human history, the major part of humanity lives inside the frames and conditions of such environments; and judging from such a background, the topic of an "ideal" city becomes actual more than ever. There exist two major distinctions as regards the notion of an ideal city. In a classical 'old' understanding, an ideal city, as a term, refers to the search of urban theorists and others for a reconstruction of or reaching for the utopian Garden of Eden, for the creation of an ideal place in the metaphysical or religious sense of heaven on earth [11]. The other meaning is an 'ideal' city in the sense of making the best out of the actually available resources, circumstances, and geography, centering on the topics (and goals) of sustainability and of harmony with nature and culture. These distinctions, we have to add, can be understood as directions of meaning as well, to conceive the topic of an ideal space in general.

If we include its secularized variants, the interpretation of an ideal place refers to the utopian direction of meaning; the other, second direction of meaning is more pragmatic: it does not have to be the absolutely perfect end state but 'ideal' only in the sense of making the best out of the existing situation, the conditions which actually prevail. As does any other way of how to handle things in general and how to cope with reality, it presupposes a certain mindset – out of which things are handled in that way and no other, what is conceived as relevant, and so forth. And this finally depends on ideals, on inner images as mental guidelines for how to tackle things in general – in their sum, the 'world' – and for which purposes. So, even the most pragmatic mind cannot avoid ideals. If physics symbolically stands for the barely present, for that what is (also physically) in the moment, then we cannot avoid metaphysics. 'Best' solutions in this sense do not depend on physics, but on ideas, ideals: on inner images.

So, all in all, ideal space and meta- physics seem to belong together; in particular when we speak about the future, and here about a future desired, a state of being which is not present yet, but which shall become present [12]. Moreover, those spaces do not just express some architectural constructions; they are symbolic spaces, spaces which are "standing for" additional meanings behind them [13], meanings which elicited their construction at all. These spaces shall, of course, become real physical spaces then. This addresses once more the aspect of imagination, and the symbolic aspect of these spaces: we, the spectators of their images presented, have to conceive them as real spaces, as parts of an 'as if-world' that can turn into reality. This is, at the same time, a particular mode of experience: we have to look at those spatial images as if experiencing a real world, and we can compare these experiences with those we made in our real spaces we are living in.

The issue of experience and imagination is relevant for all the spaces of our exhibition: those presented as ready-made worlds, those made by the visitors themselves, and those which are symbolized and presented in the world disk. First and foremost, this applies to the worlds we wanted to present as "ready-made" ideal spaces (mostly of utopian character) which appeared in history. What has been called a *concrete utopia* [14]: space where humans shall live in an 'optimized' and planned way; and which has been constructed, or has to be constructed, as a concrete and carefully planned environment.

In other words, these constructions shall enable the 'proper' unfolding of human nature, as an ideal place to live in. And in these regards, it also has to be a space of management and control, a place of actual conduct for such a proper life, which very often has to be supervised to ensure that everything runs according to plan [15].

The basic intention of such conceptions was to create an artificial cosmos, metaphorically speaking, an encompassing *ordo* where everything runs according to plan, serving as a frame for the welfare of its inhabitants. All of our infrastructural networks rely upon such an idea. As an idea going back to Roman times [16], it was to construct an ideal space of functional networks serving as a base for the needs of many individuals [17], up to the actual post-modern state [18].

1.2   The Exhibition and Its Design

So through the years, we have worked with the idea of gestalt through artifact creation (including virtual objects and worlds) as one surface of communicating and testing our ideas and concepts that are generative rather than produced, where we try to grasp systematic insights through complex generated realities.

Our design work which has its roots in the application of artistic discipline to the engineering of technology, in the form of pattern making for mass production, and as styling for product marketing. Later, design, as well as our work, has come into its own as a creative discipline and an origin of innovations rather than only something slapped onto existing ones. The design is one activity of creating the future, not solving old problems as much as inventing new opportunities, still with strong ties to empirical science and engineering but also with the storytelling, of branding and marketing. In parallel, industries and design have evolved from producing products to services, and recently to experiences, expressing basic human tenets to create and tell stories. This, of course, is at the core of rediscovery - learning from the unknown-known and of course fiction, both helping us make sense of what it means to be human, how to plan and live our lives and to find some purpose in our journey.

In this work the friction created by letting ideas and artifacts evolve in specific materials and media (in this project mostly between written conceptual parts [website] and 3d created/generated environments) and in a transdisciplinary team of people set us off for a complex challenge even where to start, how our findings should/could be communicated, how to both ground them in theory and find a way to visually communicate them.

Working with 3d worlds based on a variety of historical documents, interpretations as a source of communication made us explore this area by complex connections through iteration between architectural intentions/typologies, historical forces, digitally generated expressions, physical objects and script/code writing (shaders and camera movements). The key here for us was the ability to work in ambiguity – to explore different possibilities with each ideal space recreated without too early jumping to conclusions nor on how to represent the space nor on how to move through it. Often it means undoing the connections between things, signs, and images which constitutes what we intend as reality. Our design material here, even though being historical also act as generators when they generate new and unforeseen processes, which extend into new and likewise unforeseen contexts. Where all of the ideal space team through our work process can disseminate their knowledge into the 3d worlds at first and then later into the exhibition design, that in itself is a gestalt of its own. This way of working created over its execution the time to add idea upon idea, returning in several steps to the same subject, and allowing each of the ideal spaces to in themselves through our reconstruction to be a space to think within, digest and re-work what has been the object of investigation. Here it is a matter of adding knowledge, linking what we already know, and detect insights in a sequence with other knowledge.

With the idea of Gestalt as a form of inquiry and a process resulting in some knowledge acquired during this process (the 3d worlds 1–7). This process can thus be viewed as a process of knowledge acquisition or learning from the previously unknown-known. The knowledge acquired pertains not only to the particular domain of the 3d worlds but to the gestalt process itself. That is, we acquire knowledge on how to evolve both 3d worlds, possible areas of user interaction and design process.

The exhibition space as a whole, in the final form, consists of three interrelated parts and took about 9 months to realize: The entire exhibition is a system of three related parts: Wall 1 the cave, Wall 2 interactive worlds, and wall 3 the world disk. As a whole, the system is in itself is a gestalt that constantly evolves around the ideal spaces shown on wall one, the user interaction that takes part in wall 2 and the traces of interaction that is revealed on the worlddisc on wall three.

1.3   Wall 1 Cave

The sequence of ideal spaces in history. On the left wing of the cave, the historical sequence of spaces is listed. Historically, the sequence starts with The Cathedral and ends with The Favela (Fig. 2).

Input: Reconstructions of seven ideal spaces (worlds: http://idealspaces.org)
Output: Architectural types, used as building blocks/devices in wall 2

A sequence of worlds the visitor can enter, to experience and to imagine ideal spaces; shown as utopian but inhabitable spaces, built or conceptualized in the course of history. The worlds we show cover the entire span from conceptualized up to realized versions. They are presented in a cave so that the visitor has the opportunity to really stand in the midst of these worlds, having time and the possibility to experience them; and through that, gain an impression of those worlds very aim: to be an ideal space. The sequence starts with the cathedral, a space that is symbolic but points to a final, real space to achieve in a future time, a final paradise to come. It continues with worlds conceptualized, such as da Vinci's ideal city, a first functional city in the Renaissance; as Cité Industrielle, a space of liberation through mechanics; as Motopia or Babel IID, spaces of utopian perfection for a perfect life in the age of modernity. As worlds built but still ideal such as Karlsruhe, a combination of ideal space, domination and civil freedom. It ends with the Favela, a decisive counterpoint to all the constructions shown so far. A favela seems to be the very opposite to any 'ideal' space; but here, in contrary to all the spaces shown before, the inhabitants have the possibility to actively participate in shaping their own environment. It is a one not pre-given any

Fig. 2. Showing wall 1 the cave, Da Vinci Milano sequence and an image from the animated sequence of the Cité Industrielle.

longer as a perfect space made by some God-like demiurges, fixed for all eternity. Instead, it is a space that has the chance to unfold; molded by those who have to live on its terms. Can such a space of co-creation also turn into an ideal space?

1.4   Wall 2 Interactive Worlds

In a possible dialogue with others, you are invited to generate your common space. You mold them with your hands, together with other visitors, on a table. You see your results on the screen above the table. When your world is finished, push the switch to store them. You see a number where you can find your world in our archive, at www. idealspaces.org (Fig. 3).

Fig. 3. Images showing wall 2 interactive worlds

The left side of the table: sand, to mold the terrain of your space imagined. You can directly see the results on the screen above the table.

The right side of the table: Architectural objects to place and move on the table. And flat discs serving as a brush to mold out areas of a certain type (indicated by icons placed on top of them).

Input: Architectural types represented by Architectural objects from the Cave (concepts).

Output: Data of generated worlds (the sequence of how the Architectural objects shaped the world built by the visitor), as input for the World Disc.

Output: Architectural types (as physical representations), used as building blocks/devices in wall two.

The created worlds are composed of different physical elements such as sand and building blocks/devices that generate, in their different combinations, a virtual space projected in front of the visitors. The sand is for forming the terrain, as one element of an ideal space. The building devices, symbolizing certain kinds of architecture, are either mapped directly into the virtual world as landmarks, such as temples, towers, etc.; or represent a local change in the virtual world, such as an area or streets. For the visitors molding the worlds with their own hands, a direct haptic experience becomes possible. By seeing the influence in real time on the spatial gestalt as a visual representation, the space built up appears as a totality. By that, a basic anthropological experience combines with imagination in direct visibility: The ideal space becomes a space immediately experienced, in the making of one's own world. Architectural types derived from the historical sequence of the worlds shown in the cave are serving as input for the building devices offered to the visitors. In this way, the two parts of the exhibition become connected.

1.5   Wall 3 World Disc

As a cosmic symbol of dynamic change, it is a cosmic symbol for the spaces appearing here: of the historical spaces shown and the ones generated by the visitors. Highlighted rings appearing on disc mark the epoch where the respective ideal space is located, in terms of history. In the center, the rings begin with the epoch of the cathedral and ends at the outward rim with the favela Black lines on the disk: evolving and changing constantly, showing the frequency of related objects used in Interactive Worlds The disc is dynamic, changing in appearance over the entire duration of exhibition (Fig. 4).

Fig. 4. Wall 3 world disc. Showing recorded user interaction (left), the world disc image that consists of a hand painted map based on historical references (middle) and to the right the world disc with overlay of user interaction and which world is shown on wall 1

Input: Images from spaces and buildings of the epochs shown; data of the worlds generated by the visitors, from Interactive Worlds
Output: Data for scientific evaluation

Here, the results of those spaces generated by the visitors transform into a real historical process reflected in changes taking place on that cosmic disk during the exhibition's entire duration. It is composed of different rings aligned in a concentric order, each ring representing a century, starting with that of the cathedral in the disc's center, and ending with that of the favela at its outer rim. Each ring is composed of images of typical architecture belonging to the respective century, and those centuries where our worlds in the cave come from appear larger. Thus, the visitor can see where the respective world is located, inside the entire historical context. The disk receives input from the worlds created by the visitors and it translates these inputs into changes taking place on the disk itself. Through that, it reflects what is going on in the process of the visitors' world making, and it does so constantly: each day, the disk will look different, as does a real world formed by human beings. The disk thus connects with the ideal spaces shown in the cave, as well as with the spaces made by the visitors.

In these ways, the three parts of the exhibition align together, to form a coherent system. Since it was our original intention to conceive the topic of ideal spaces as a whole, the single parts of which present a unity, of both experience and of making.

1.6   Lessons Learned

Through this work, we have learned that configuring space through user interaction is not easy. Early in our development, there was a conflict between if a visitor should layout architectural objects, in which the visitor recombines already developed building blocks into city environments- a lego like an approach, based on distributing predefined objects in space. Or if the visitor through a more symbolic system would be able to configure a city space through a set of symbolic rules that could be combined in different ways - a design fiction approach, based on a calculation that generates environments. We ended up with a system in which visitors could create spaces, by connecting different topologies (symbolic objects) extracted from our seven worlds shown on wall 1 and as a series of predefined developed architectural shapes. Even though there was a lot of technological freedom for the user in our designed system (and we could record and store how worlds was created), it, unfortunately, locked the visitors into a very limited process for exploring and expressing spatial ideas - spaces could be laid out but not configured, the user could arrange pre-given architectural objects but was not able to change the ideas and configuration of those objects or the environment - which in the end created spaces that were too similar to each other. Looking back we were not clear on what level of abstraction we wanted to involve the visitors on and what symbolic objects could be used for such explorations.

1.7   Future Work

For our next project, we have chosen to approach the visitor how they can configure and create their own worlds a bit differently. This will be done through navigation and through a series of choices that the visitor constantly has to do navigating the space of our world disc in VR - experience and creating at the same time as they go along and in the choices they make a long that way, when and where they make their transition between different points in time and space - creating their own historical exploration of real and fictitious spaces and that in the end also generate a space based on their choices taking part of this journey. Which is an important part of our future work: to conceive process as gestalt, as an order emerging out from the interaction.

1.8   Conclusion

Through our work, we try to emphasize the importance of a multiperspective view of space and its entities based on the idea to transcend merely scientific or artistic approaches into a more comprehensive and immediate approach and working practice. It is about symbolic objects and entireties (the issue of gestalt), not about mere construction and functions. This can help to re-detect the world and its entities in all the richness and variety they actually have while at the same time transferring new and fruitful knowledge and methodology back to the disciplines. Where we through user interaction try to have them conceiving wholes instead of fragments as a way to re-detect the world could gain new understanding in the domains of science, humanities, and art and therefore increase their explanatory potentials within their already existing domains.

References

1. Eaton, R.: Die ideale Stadt. Von der Antike bis zur Gegenwart, p. 11. Nicoliai, Berlin (2001)
2. Scafi, A.: Mapping Paradise: A History of Heaven on Earth. The British Library, London (2006)
3. Feuerstein, G.: Urban Fiction. Strolling through Ideal Cities from Antiquity to the Present Day. Axel Menges, Stuttgart/London (2008)

4. Seng, E.-M., Saage, R.: Utopie und Architektur. In: Nerdinger, W., et al. (eds.) L'Architecture Engagee. Manifeste zur Veränderung der Gesellschaft, pp. 10–37. Edition Detail, Munich (2012)

5. Knobloch, E.: Das Naturverständnis der Antike. In: Rapp, F. (ed.) Naturverständnis und Naturbeherrschung, pp. 10–35. Wilhelm Fink, Munich (1981)

6. Vercelloni, V.: Europäische Stadtutopien. Ein historischer Atlas, p. 4. Diederichs, Munich (1994)

7. Augé, M.: Non-Places. Introduction to an Anthropology of Supermodernity. Verso, London (1995)

8. Vidler, A.: The Architectural Uncanny. Essays in the Modern Unhomely. MIT Press, Cambridge/London (1992)

9. Summers, D.: Real Spaces: World Art History and the Rise of Western Modernism, p. 320. Phaidon Press, New York (2003)

10. Baumeister, R.: The Cultural Animal. Human Nature, Meaning and Social Life. Oxford University Press, Oxford (2005)

11. Giesecke, A., Jacobs, N.: Nature, Utopia and the Garden. In: Giesecke, A., Jacobs, N. (eds.) Earth Perfect? Nature, Utopia and the Garden, pp. 6–17. Black Dog Publishing, London (2012)

12. Lehmann, G.K.: Macht der Utopie. Ein Jahrhundert der Gewalt, 10ff. Neske, Stuttgart (1996)

13. Böhme, G.: Aisthetik. Vorlesungen über Ästhetik als allgemeine Wahrnehmungslehre, p. 152. Wilhelm Fink, Munich (2001)

14. Mannheim, K.: Ideologie und Utopie, p. 169. Friedrich Cohen, Bonn (1929)

15. Mumford, L.: The Myth of the Machine, vol. 1. Harcourt Brace Jovanovich, New York (1967)

16. Aureli, P.V.: The Possibility of an Absolute Architecture, p. 7. MIT Press, Cambridge (2011)

17. Graham, S., Marvin, S.: Splintering Urbanism: Networked Infrastructure, Technological Mobilies, and the Urban Condition. Routledge, London/New York (2001)

18. Shane, D.G.: Recombinant Urbanism: Conceptual Modeling in Architecture, Urban Design and City Theory. Wiley, West Sussex (2013)

Walking on 2 Legs: 3D-Structured Method Alignment in Project Management

Christian Stary[(✉)]

Department of Business Information Systems – Communications Engineering,
Johannes Kepler University, Altenbergerstraße 69, 4040 Linz, Austria
Christian.stary@jku.at

Abstract. This paper explores the possibility of the use of tangibles in the field of education and project management. We propose an interactive instrumentation based on specific building blocks referred to as W2L (Walking on 2 Legs) that can be used as a (pedagogical) practice to guide and facilitate method structuring and alignment in project design. The need for this instrumentation is motivated by a teaching approach where students are asked to select, assign, and adjust methods pertaining to a specific project design. In order to improve their respective skills, we have designed and implemented W2L for method chaining along project phases or milestones using Lego© bricks and adapting a table-top system. We could test W2L with Knowledge Management students when planning their project to evaluate the effectiveness of the approach. An analysis of feedback and results revealed positive impact on methodologically informed project design.

Keywords: Project planning · Methodological design · Gamification
Lego© · Tangibles · Tabletop interaction · Articulation support

1 Introduction

Project management has become essential in education, as business and management require respective skills increasingly (cf. [12]). Traditional courses explore a systems approach to the selection, design, execution, control, evaluation, and termination of projects to meet project objectives and customer expectations within allocated performance and resources constraints in organizations (cf. [5]). Basic tools and techniques of project management that are explored place emphasis on management and engineering tasks, as the courses have the goal to facilitate the knowledge that will aid project leaders to successfully handle project-specific work structures and achieve a project goal within an certain time and cost frame. Hence, typical course objectives are: Understand essentials of project management and apply the fundamental tools and its methods; Develop knowledge of concepts and methods in the leadership of projects; Perform conceptual design, planning, and scheduling for a project; Develop knowledge for understanding, assessing, and resolving human, technical and administrative issues for deployed projects. The format leading to demonstrate student capability in design, analysis, and evaluation of project management (systems) is traditionally based on (blended learning) class and self-regulated periods. Besides studying (electronic) text and handout material, students take part in class discussions and work on assignments

© ICST Institute for Computer Sciences, Social Informatics and Telecommunications Engineering 2018
A. L. Brooks et al. (Eds.): ArtsIT 2017/DLI 2017, LNICST 229, pp. 33–42, 2018.
https://doi.org/10.1007/978-3-319-76908-0_4

including practical project work. Thereby, lecture material, deliverables, project presentations, and reports are discussed.

Since project management has its focus on organizing, planning, monitoring, and controlling project-specific information and activities, the teacher is used to ask the students to develop a project plan, perform a project, and evaluate the results according to the project's objectives. Testing these skills involves students to get an idea of taking responsibility and to collaborate with other students or project workers according to the project plan while minimizing risks to ensure successful project completion (cf. [7]). Although this approach insists that students become firm in management activities, learning to know how to take responsibility and collaborate needs to be enriched to the dynamics of today's organizations' operations and domain-specific context (cf. [6]). As the study of Lakemond et al. [8] reveals for innovation projects, the flow of knowledge becoming crucial, requiring to put project management in knowledge-management context - the organization's knowledge governance, and thus, core asset matters for the integration of external knowledge into innovation processes.

Becoming aware of opening project management to its application domain and domain-specific objectives motivated us to think about building a tangible interactive support instrument for more informed, enjoyable and lasting experience of selecting and arranging problem-solving methods to meet project objectives. It should focus on increasing the level of involvement using hand gestures and playful elements where achieving a project objective through method alignment even in complex settings is a structured task. In the following, we report on the development of a pedagogical technique to learn method chaining through a structuring mechanism. We performed aspiration and ideation tasks providing a natural user interface and a set of building blocks to students in Knowledge Management. The instrument we have finally implemented enriches conventional project management settings by providing 3D elements and a set of relationships relevant for method application and alignment. It is of use when arranging and completing a chain of methods in a tangible way along project planning and design.

Due to the exploratory nature of research, we followed the design thinking process as proposed by the Stanford D.school (dschool.stanford.edu) when developing the instrument. The process comprises inspiration, ideation, and implementation. After defining the challenge, forming the team and conducting a secondary research it is the inspiration phase where the team conducts the design research that can be considered the core of all the news phases. By the end of this phase, researchers should have a clear understanding about the design challenge to be addressed, aside of a project plan for the timeline, budget, and team. This stage is crucial to ensure the success of the project as it is considered a pivot point where the different stages need to refer to during the measurements and iteration after each of the ideation and implementation phases. In this paper we report on:

- The *inspiration phase* identifying concrete needs and relating project management activities to method structuring and alignment.
- The *ideation phase* driven by students, with design proposals emerging from Lego©-based structuring and aligning methods when planning projects in Knowledge Management.

- The *implementation* of a tangible instrumentation that involves the students to use 3D elements, hand gestures, and visual stimuli to actively participate in the method specification and chaining of a project design process.

The remainder of this paper is organized as follows: In Sect. 2, we describe how the design emerges through revisiting method chaining in the context of project management (inspiration phase), and students dealing with Lego© bricks for method selection, specification, and concatenation (ideation phase). In Sect. 3, we discuss the proposed methodology, and present the setup for interactive manipulation. We also report on feedbacks from first field tests (implementation phase). Section 4 concludes the paper with future directions of research.

2   Emergent Design

In this section we detail the inspiration phase identifying concrete needs and re-considering existing work for a specific application domain, namely Knowledge Management (KM), in Subsect. 2.1, before reporting on the ideation phase driven by stakeholders, with designs emerging from experiments involving KM students in Subsect. 2.2.

2.1   Method Alignment in Knowledge Management Project Design

Project management in Knowledge Management (KM) is similar complex to innovation management, the case mentioned in the introduction. Knowledge managers as project managers need to be aware of techniques and tools handling stakeholder knowledge to become effective for organizations and their development [1]. Project design is driven by several constituents, most important, theories and conceptual frameworks, such as the Knowledge Life Cycle [3], and a set of methods addressing the various KM dimensions, such as Repertory Grids for externalizing implicit knowledge (cf. [4]).

Theories and concepts set up frameworks and lifecycles. They provide the context of methods and their application. The more theoretical underpinnings and conceptual knowledge about methods can be provided, the better KM activities can be set in a coherent way. However, theories or concepts can evolve without being linked explicitly to methods (cf. [14]). For instance, systems thinking [13] is not bound to a certain method. It can be applied in various contexts, and thus implemented by a variety of methods.

When acquiring methodological knowledge KM project managers need also to become aware of specific bundles of KM activities: Acquisition, representation, sharing, processing, and evaluation. They have been introduced to structure knowledge conversion processes, as e.g., proposed by Nonaka and Takeuchi [9]. When planning a KM project, for each of those activity bundles, methods fitting to the inherent KM logic need to be specified and aligned, e.g., knowledge representation follows knowledge acquisition for documenting and storing generated knowledge.

In Fig. 1 some constitutive KM elements are exemplified according to the afore-mentioned categories. Since theories and concepts play a crucial role for putting KM into reflective praxis and affect operational activities, they have been separated (left strand in the figure) from activity bundles (middle strand) and methods (right strand). Figure 1 also shows typical instances of KM theories and concepts (naming some KM proponents), activity bundles, and methods.

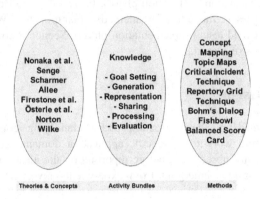

Fig. 1. Sample KM theories and concepts, activity bundles and methods

In addition, project managers have to be aware that methods primarily focus on a certain perspective, such as the Balanced Score Card focusing on financial matters. However, a KM project typically touches several perspectives, including technology, organization of work, social behavior, emotions, and cognition. Whenever a method is applied, the perspective determines the subject of concern, which adds an additional challenge to the selection and alignment process.

A KM project requires to consider each KM strand in an adjusted and mutually aligned way, in order to ensure coherent project settings. An informed setting in this way should prevent reductionist method applications or incomplete project task pro-cedures. Consider an application of Value Network analyses (cf. [15]) without any background on converting implicit to explicit knowledge: It could easily mislead a KM project, e.g., reducing its outcome to codified organizational assets when focusing on tangible elements. Another common example concerns single and double loop learning processes (situated in Theories & Concepts in Fig. 1), as neglecting double loop processes could hinder changing the processing environment (single loop learning). Such lack of scoping restricts organizational value creation through KM projects, and can be prevented by adjusting knowledge generation, representation, and processing in an informed way (cf. [16]).

Finally, it needs to be noted that specific methods may require understanding their respective background and origin, in order to put them to practice effectively. For instance, Repertory Grids [4] open up for the individual exploration of mental models. Albeit gaining individual insights, further (social) interventions are required in the course of subsequent KM activities, such as sharing and consolidating grids, before the acquired knowledge can be processed for organizational change. Hence, the epistemic structure of KM requires informed method selection and mutual alignment in the course of project planning and design.

2.2   Method Alignment Using Lego© Bricks: Starting to Walk on 2 Legs

As indicated above, project management, in particular project planning and design in Knowledge Management (KM) is a non-trivial task. Thereby, project managers need to be aware of KM methods and their context of use to achieve KM project goals. Since we wanted to develop an educational and effective support tool, the students of the postgraduate KM program at the University of Linz were asked to perform a project planning task, including milestone definition and method specification for each project phase. Typically, a KM project starts with the some method application eliciting or acquiring knowledge from domain experts or informed stakeholders, and is followed by documenting acquired knowledge in some repository using a knowledge representation scheme. Each of these tasks needs to be supported by (a federated set of) methods, with interfaces enabling non-disruptive processing and seamless exchange of data. Hence, each method application needs to be checked in how far it fits into the resulting method chain for the project at hand.

In order to identify effective means to support the method specification and alignment process, the KM students were given a set of various Lego© bricks. They were asked to encode and visualize the structuring and alignment of methods according to their project tasks using these bricks in a modular manner. Thereby, they needed to take into account the following constitutional information concerning methods:

1. *Incoming and processed information*: We distinguish the trigger referring to the starting point of a method application from the data to be provided as input, since both are relevant items of project management.
2. *Functional processing or core information*: It specifies not only the name of the method and thus, the function in terms of activities to be set, but also the KM perspective which is taken when a method is performed. In this way, the context can be represented more accurately compared with purely functional specifications.
3. *Outgoing and delivered information*: Again, we distinguish two different elements, once a method application has been completed: The outcome denoting the effect of using a certain method, and the produced data or output for further processing.

For instance, an application of the Repertory Grid technique [4] is triggered by the need to elicit value systems of concerned stakeholders. For successful application as input a theme and the elements related to this theme need to be provided. The grid encodes a human perspective on KM, as it involves interviewing concerned stakeholders. The output is a documented grid with the effect of having externalized a person's value system in terms of construct/contrast elements for a given set of elements.

For each of the project tasks the students generated (several) chains of methods, depending on their understanding of the addressed KM issues and the project. For instance, in case elicited and documented knowledge should lead to business process specifications and prototypical execution for organizational development, methods for modeling and simulating of processes needed to be specified and aligned using the structure mentioned before, according to the students' project objectives.

The students came up with a variety of patterns. In Fig. 2 one of the most common types of structures to encode methods as well as the most common chaining codification for alignment (right part of the figure) are shown. The students used different sizes of bricks and colors to specify methods and their interfaces. In any case a method was encoded as an assembled piece composed of one or two fundamental building blocks extended with the relevant method attributes (trigger, input, outcome, output) serving as interface. The interface elements were positioned in a way to be connected with elements of other method bricks. The left method creation shows a dog-like form, with the tail (left side) being the incoming and the head part delivering information. Other students created two or more legs to encode the 4 interface elements. For incoming and outgoing information not only different colors were used, but also in many cases different types of bricks, e.g., for the incoming part of the left creation big red and small blue bricks, in order to represent the bipartite structure of incoming and outgoing information.

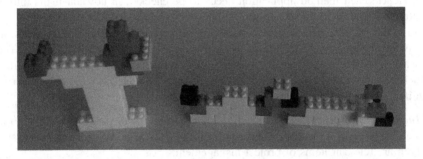

Fig. 2. Sample Lego© brick method structures and a method chain (Color figure online)

The alignment codification of the right creation in Fig. 2 reveals for the outgoing information that in some cases two different method concatenations are possible, as indicated by the two small black input connected to the red output, based on a yellow 'OR'-connector. Some students also marked starting points by shaping the respective method in a unique way (on-top piece in the center of the left method creation in the right part of the figure). Some of them indicated a fit of interfaces, as the right creation shows a fitting connection topped by a green brick. Overall, the students were able to select and utilize bricks not only to encode methods in terms of their structure, but also to link methods through outgoing and incoming information.

3 Walking on 2 Legs

Walking on 2 Legs (W2L) got its name from the objectives of our work as well as the patterns we could identify from the students when codifying the structure and alignment of methods, aiming to meet their project objectives. The name indicates several demands when structuring and aligning methods: (i) Effective method alignment in project management requires an additional source of information, i.e. the context of the problem domain addressed through the project; (ii) It requires two types of constituting interface elements, namely incoming and outgoing information; (iii) Each of them has 2 parts, providing context to input and output, namely the trigger or event initiating the method application, and the effect of applying the method or outcome; (iv) A chain of methods requires at least two method elements to be aligned, in order to complete a project.

In the following we explain the W2L procedure in Subsect. 3.1, before we discuss its digital implementation in Subsect. 3.2 adapting an existing tabletop system supporting tangible structure elaboration.

3.1 Procedure

The proposed procedure distinguishes three groups of project management activities when applying W2L. The first activity contains *required preparation activities (1):*

1.1 Set up a space for method alignment: As a first step, the project manager creates some space for method alignment (e.g., an activity bundle to be discussed when planning) with an appropriate title for the session. Method experts can be invited.

1.2 Provide project or method portfolio: The project manager structures the space with respect to the available method pool and puts in required start information, e.g., method descriptions. It serves as development repository, in order to ensure sharing of documentations and traceability of the planning and design process.

The subsequent set of activities concerns *method refinement/adaptation activities (2).* The following tasks are mainly performed by the participating project team members and method experts, guided by the project manager. Steps 2.1 through 2.4 are running simultaneously and in an iterative manner. They do not have to follow a strict sequence.

2.1 Trigger a group meeting (if required): The project manager invites project team members to a project design meeting. Depending on the project, he/she may ask to acquire additional information and put it into the portfolio.

2.2 Participants scope work packages and project tasks: The manager invites project team members to start specifying the scope of the method chain to be specified, e.g., work packages or project tasks, according to their perception of the current situation, or an already existing project plan.

2.3 Project manager presents current method pool: As soon as the scope has been specified, project team members can propose methods to be used for achieving the objectives of the task or work package. Other team members can ask questions for clarification and issue concerns. The project manager should guide the presentation through time budgeting, re-phrasing, and structuring information.

2.4 Participants acknowledge method pool and selection: Participants provide their acknowledgement in this step for the selected methods. These methods represent the list of candidates to be aligned. This step is considered a milestone for project planning, as the method baseline has been set for a work package or project task.

The third set of activities leads to *method refinement and alignment (3)*, and is performed by the project team:

3.1 Check elements and relations: Team member contributions may vary in providing insights and information. However, each method can be checked for completion ensuring respective interfaces. The project manager keeps track of the progress. A method chain is constructed based on the selected methods.

3.2 Detail required incoming/outgoing information: Project team members provide the attributes for each category of interface information (trigger, input, output, outcome) for all represented methods. The project manager keeps track of the progress.

3.3 Align according to interfaces: Project team members check whether each output/input-pair fits according the previously specified attributes for all represented methods. In case of conflicts proposals for alignment are collected and discussed. It might be required to go back to the pool of methods or/and invite additional experts. The project manager keeps track of the progress.

A method alignment space is creating through representing methods and their interfaces. The fundamental element denotes the method. Each method has a certain structure, as shown in Fig. 3 in diagrammatic form. It consists of the already mentioned name, and incoming and outgoing information.

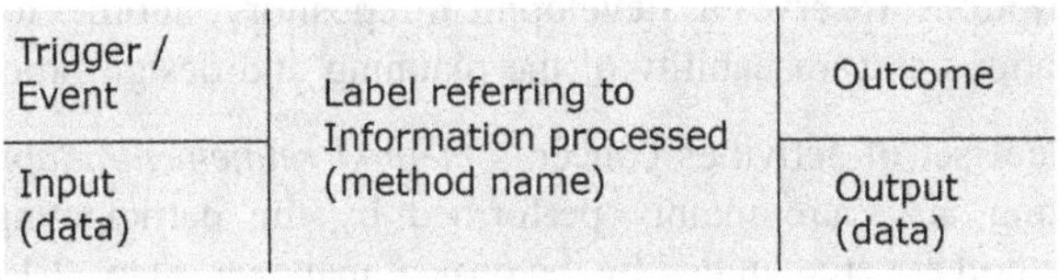

Trigger / Event	Label referring to Information processed (method name)	Outcome
Input (data)		Output (data)

Fig. 3. A diagrammatic representation of a method

3.2 Digital Implementation and Field Test

Interactive digital support can effectively be provided by tangible 3D manipulatives on a tabletop device enabling structure elaboration [10, 11]. Such a platform can be designed to increase digital literacy (cf. [2]) in education and organizational settings, and support domain-specific projects, as already demonstrated in healthcare [15]. For Walking on 2 Legs methods become tangible through their structure. Figure 4 shows a schematic representation of the most condensed and the most elaborated way the system can be used for method structuring and alignment. On one hand, a 3D element can represent a single method, as shown in the upper part of the figure, also indicating the internal parts by mirroring the diagrammatic method representation. Such a use requires information beyond simple naming the manipulative, either to be put into the manipulative through markers, utilizing a container function, or through digital note sticking. The latter allows for each manipulative and displayed relation on the surface to record context information.

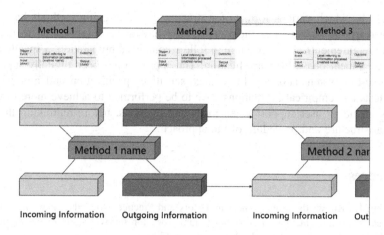

Fig. 4. Structure elaboration support

On the other hand, structuring a method may require up to 5 elements. The latter case encodes the name and each interface in a separate manipulative (see center and lower part of the figure), whereas the single-block representation contains all interface elements under the label of the method. For alignment, the interfaces may be either encoded as relations or manipulatives. As each displayed link on the surface may contain comments, information relevant to alignment may either be stored along a relation or be part of a manipulative. A third variant is using dedicated manipulatives for alignment, either between input and output, or/and between trigger and outcome. When developing method chains, patterns can be analyzed according to the different perspectives as encoded in the relations. Of particular importance are filters when checking correspondence, either between input and output, in order to check their fit, or between trigger and outcome, and for checking the completeness of a method chain.

First field tests of the approach have been performed in the educational setting of Knowledge Management when students needed to plan and design a KM project including method alignment, in order to effectively achieve their project objectives. Thereby, 15 students were asked to report their findings when using W2L. In general, they appreciated the openness to shapes and colors, allowing them to experience methodological design as some kind of game. Although all participants of the field test were able to find a way to structure methods and align them in a coherent way with respect to project objectives, some asked for help on how to evaluate the interface relations, as they were not familiar with handling this type of information. Hence, additional support will have to be provided to that respect.

4 Conclusion

Once projects are also designed from a method perspective, e.g., as required in domain-specific or knowledge-intense settings, methods need to be selected, structured, and aligned to meet project objectives. We followed an exploratory, stakeholder-oriented approach, by which various formats for structuring and aligning methods have been developed by the stakeholders themselves, after having been introduced to minimal structure requirements. The procedure to follow contains a preparation, a specification, and an alignment phase for consolidation. The approach has been digitally supported by a table-top system allowing for context-sensitive specification and arrangement. Future tests and empirical evaluations have to be performed to achieve more practical insights including user support when managing relations, before rethinking the fundamental structure and procedure of the approach.

References

1. Dalkir, K.: Knowledge Management in Theory and Practice. Routledge, New York (2013)
2. Eshet, Y.: Digital literacy: a conceptual framework for survival skills in the digital era. J. Educ. Multimedia Hypermedia 13(1), 93–106 (2004)
3. Firestone, J.M., McElroy, M.W.: Key Issues in the New Knowledge Management. Routledge, New York (2003)
4. Fransella, F., Bannister, D.: A Manual for Repertory Grid Technique. Academic Press, London (1977)
5. Kerzner, H.: Project Management: A Systems Approach to Planning, Scheduling, and Controlling. Wiley, New York (2013)
6. Kraus, J., Boss, S.: Thinking Through Project-Based Learning. Guiding Deeper Inquiry. Corwin, Thousand Oaks (2013)
7. Larson, E., Gray, C.: Project Management: The Managerial Process. McGraw-Hill, New York (2013)
8. Lakemond, N., Bengtsson, L., Laursen, K., Tell, F.: Match and manage: the use of knowledge matching and project management to integrate knowledge in collaborative inbound open innovation. Ind. Corp. Change 25(2), 333–352 (2016)
9. Nonaka, I., Takeuchi, H.: The Knowledge-Creating Company. Oxford University Press, New York (1995)
10. Oppl, S., Stary, C.: Tabletop concept mapping. In: Proceedings of 3rd International Conference on Tangible and Embedded Interaction, pp. 275–282. ACM, New York (2009)
11. Oppl, S., Stary, C.: Facilitating shared understanding of work situations using a tangible tabletop interface. Behav. Inf. Technol. 33(6), 619–635 (2014)
12. Saunders, M.N.K., Lewis, P.: Doing Research in Business and Management: An Essential Guide to Planning Your Project. Pearson, Harlow (2012)
13. Senge, P.M.: The Fifth Discipline: The Art and Practice of the Learning Organization. Broadway Business, New York (2006)
14. Stary, C.: KM curriculum design for reflective practitioner's capacity building. In: Proceedings of 11th International Conference on Knowledge Management, ICKM 2015, pp. 281–290 (2015)
15. Stary, C.: Non-disruptive knowledge and business processing in knowledge life cycles-aligning value network analysis to process management. J. Knowl. Manag. 18(4), 651–686 (2014)
16. Stary, C., Krenn, F., Lerchner, H., Neubauer, M., Oppl, S., Wachholder, D.: Towards stakeholder-centered design of open systems: learning from organizational learning. In: Proceedings European Conference on Cognitive Ergonomics 2015, p. 26. ACM, New York (2015)

Designing a Lighting Installation Through Virtual Reality Technology - The Brighter Brunnshög Case Study

Boa Kim[1], Emmanouil Xylakis[2], Andrei-Ducu Predescu[2],
Georgios Triantafyllidis[2(✉)], Ellen Kathrine Hansen[2],
and Michael Mullins[2]

[1] Department of Sculpture, College of Fine Arts, Seoul National University,
1 Gwanak-ro, Gwanak-gu, Seoul 151-742, South Korea
avo07@snu.ac.kr
[2] Department of Architecture, Design & Media Technology,
Aalborg University Copenhagen, A. C. Meyers Vænge 15,
2450 Copenhagen SV, Denmark
xylakis@gmail.com, {adp,gt,ekh,mullins}@create.aau.dk

Abstract. This paper investigates how VR technology can support the process of designing light installations. Specifically, how visual immersion through digital means can create spatial awareness of an area, without the need of physical presence, thus facilitating the fluency of the design process. The motivation for this study lies in exploring new methods and techniques which can support the process of designing with light. This study attempts to set up an initial design methodology built upon a traditional approach, and expanded based on its three aspects; real-time rendering, flexibility and spatial experience. The project brighter Brunnshög is used as a case study illustrating how a method such as this can be integrated.

Keywords: Virtual Reality · Lighting design · Methodology
Lighting design experiment

1   Introduction

This paper sees the possibility of VR as a product of lighting design and attempts to establish a design model within VR by outlining the immersive condition of designing in VR. With advancements in computing power and the recent release and affordability of Head Mounted Displays (HMD), Virtual Reality (VR) has resurfaced and shown great potential as a tool for industry and education likewise. Specifically, one aspect of VR is of great importance and that is the ability to create spatial experiences via stereoscopy. Being visually immersed in spaces without the requirement of being physically present, can assist the process of design and improve the designer's workflow.

Up until now important steps have already been done in integrating VR tools but mainly in the areas of communication and sharing. The focus of the present study is though how the design process itself can take advantage of VR.

© ICST Institute for Computer Sciences, Social Informatics and Telecommunications Engineering 2018
A. L. Brooks et al. (Eds.): ArtsIT 2017/DLI 2017, LNICST 229, pp. 43–53, 2018.
https://doi.org/10.1007/978-3-319-76908-0_5

The project used as the case has the requirements that relate to interaction and lighting design so the methodology proposed here relates not only to designing a spatial experience but also meaningful ways of interaction with it. The design process model proposed by Hansen and Mullins [1] guides the overall development and is used to explain how a technology such as this can be beneficial.

1.1 Case Project Brighter Brunnshög

It is generally a known fact that people oppose urban development. This effect is known to as the Endowment Effect which refers to the tendency by residents in urban development projects of weighting and emphasizing losses more than gains, i.e. even though residents can get advantages from the urban development, they are critical of losing their routine, heritage and culture due to the construction [2].

Interactive public art installations are suggested to minimize this resistance, and the sense of loss, and which lead to a sense of ownership over development by creating an interactive platform which represents their routines, activities and heritage. This study hypothesizes that by transferring/recreating the experience of a public art piece into a virtual world, it will be possible to recreate its stimulating effect, and as such minimize resistance to development projects in the same way and with the same effect as real works of art.

Brighter Brunnshög, is the first stage of an urban development project in Lund, Sweden, and aims to integrate residents into the development of the area, and spread the word of this new science city and its research centers. This project is conducted under the Lighting Metropolis [3] umbrella, in cooperation with Lund Kommune and Lighting Design in Aalborg University, and funded by Kraftringen.

This VR project is considered as an interactive lighting design product itself, not only as a prototype or testbed for further construction. To enlarge the field of VR into media for lighting design, new design approaches and methodologies are needed based on an understanding of the VR environment, and its comparison with the physical environment.

1.2 Lighting Metropolis Initiative

The case in this investigation, Brighter Brunnshög, is part of the project Lighting Metropolis.

Lighting Metropolis is the first decisive step in realizing a vision for Greater Copenhagen as the world's leading Living Lab for smart urban lighting. The aim is to strengthen the significant role lighting can play in supporting safety, accessibility, identity, health, and education for people in cities.

A second Lighting Metropolis target is to facilitate and support the Greater Copenhagen region by tapping into the significant growth potential of these areas as they expand globally and exponentially [3].

1.3   Motivation

The motivation for this study lies in exploring new methods and techniques for supporting the design development of light in the virtual environment. With the release of "VR editors" [4] (transfer of software environment into the HMD interface), new approaches in design, mainly for the gaming industry, were realized. Using this emerging technology, this study tries to explore its potential and initialize an approach that could potentially change the way that we are designing spaces in VR.

1.4   Related Study

It has been highlighted that VR interfaces with the human perceptual system to a more intense degree, providing a more effective opportunity for computer to human communication. Further, new design interfaces for VR have been suggested which enable designers to work based on their instincts [5]. These attempts, however, focused on developing a tool/system for design, rather than how VR can affect a designer's perception.

To achieve an immersive experience in VR requires gathering various scientific domains to create a robust visual and interactive support for educational setting [6]. This multi-disciplinary framework of VR has been addressed with respects to its pros and cons, and its complexity and flexibility, and requires designers to work in tight collaboration with other experts [7]. Ever since collaboration between multi domains became normal, there have been a lot of theoretical and practical studies of how to integrate the different fields into one. Problem based learning (PBL) [8] and lighting experimental design model highlighted the importance of translating, transforming and testing the data and knowledge from different fields into one project [1].

As such VR offers users spatial experiences with time and lighting, the importance of using VR for presentation in architectural fields has been outlined. Especially for lighting, a multi-dimensional design element which is always connected to time and space [1], its spatial condition can be considered as an ideal design platform in architectural projects.

Aspects of participatory design that constantly get fed into a dynamic system would create the sense "of a living form that is constantly evolving/adapting to the social environment it is embedded in" [9].

Finally, with the decision of using a digital experience as a platform for the above, an extended research on the different types of VR techniques will help in understanding how such technology could host an art installation, that could support its qualities and how it differs from an actual real life installation.

2   Methodology (Design Process Model)

The design process within VR is based on *architectural experiment design model* [1], based on current demands for a transdisciplinary approach with multiple collaborative fields. In this study, the architectural experiment design model is named the *model of lighting design experiment (LDE) as it has been developed for designing with light in architecture* [1]. The design approach is based on one directional procedure where the feedback between creation, adjustment and re-creation is either non-existent, more cumbersome or slower and less dynamic in nature. By contrast, the constant feedback in VR requires the designers within the virtual workplace to have the ability to instantly and simultaneously process results and feed these back into the design itself. The virtual environment which approximates the real world enables the designers to work with their spatial perception. Based on these conditions; fast and constant communication between software, real time workflow, and spatial experience, this study explore how LDE can be optimized in VR.

This VR environment requires designers to take on the responsibility of learning due to the complex relationship between the input and output during the design development. As it provides opportunities for self-directed learning and self-assessment [6], *problem based learning* (PBL) [6] is used as a guideline in VR for optimizing the LDE design process into the multi-dimensional learning and developing design process.

2.1 The Model of Lighting Design Experiment

Since the concept of the project penetrates different domains, the design process is driven by *the model of lighting design experiment (LDE),* the latter of which is a theoretical proposal of how to design with light as a multi-dimensional design element by integrating scientific, technical and creative approaches to light in 5 domains [1]. Drawing from the work briefly outlined in the preceding section, the theoretical framework has been developed on how research traditions can be integrated in trans-disciplinary practice, illustrated in the model for architectural experiments (Fig. 1) [1].

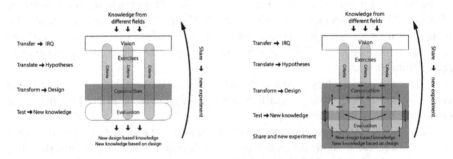

Fig. 1. LDE (left) and LDE in VR (right)

The feedback loops in its structure result in a stepwise process of adjustments and/or improvements. As such each step synthesizes and integrates the data from different fields into the single project. These loops result in an irreversible trend whereby alterations are not undone. The design model structure consists of five steps: (1) Transfer-Image and ask, (2) Translate - Explore and propose, (3) Transform - Link and construct (4) Test and explain - evaluation (5) Share and learn, and run in this sequence in a loop like fashion, where step 5 is followed by step 1 again [1].

The model attempts to resolve the question of how the knowledge of different disciplines can be thoroughly integrated into the design process, create innovative solutions and generate new explicit knowledge [1]. This works not only as a tool for integrating the knowledge from different domains but also as a guideline for the procedure for designers to achieve their goals the most effective way.

2.2 The Model of Lighting Design Experiment in VR

Designing with light in a virtual environment differs from designing in a physical environment in terms of the radically different environments. VR is formulated by the combination of the programming language, data values and graphical assets, and is not a space where tangible objects are created. In other words, designing in VR means basically creating the entire virtual environment including lights, and calculating the relationship of all the graphical components in the scene with high speed processing languages. This critical difference implies the necessity of new design methodologies.

LDE for traditional light installations are developed based on the irreversible factors of the physical world in terms of the scale and the time. If the design can be developed where by time and space can be ultimately controlled, how can the designers operate this flexibility?

The three main factors in VR are defined in terms of real time rendering, flexibility and spatial experience. These factors critically affect the traditional design approach, and can be used to validate the design phases with light in VR and its multi-dimensional elements [1].

2.2.1 Real Time Rendering and Constant Feedback in Design Process of Light

With the latest advancements in virtual environments VR now closely approximates real-world conditions [7]. This highly advanced visual output and the technology of HMD enables designers to use their spatial sense for lighting. The application of LDE in VR, therefore, implies its adaptation, as many aspects within VR fundamentally change the nature of design and workflow.

In VR, the flexibility between VR engaged software and protocols has been the subject of study which has indicated its relevance. The research on VR application has established several VR conditions such as flexible integration and configuration of heterogeneous VR and external software, ease-of-use, lowering the learning curve and empowering end-users [7, 10].

As VR relies on the flexibility and freedom which is easily adjustable depending on the programs engaged, these elements have been developed to be well-compatible with each other, and allow for constant feedback due to instant communication [7]. They can be adjusted and integrated within "a host graphics engine", and as such can be expanded greatly. This system directly influences the way LDE can be applied. More specifically, steps 3 to 5 in LDE; transform - test and explain - share and learn, are engaged more complexly, and the boundary between steps fade somewhat. Further, feedback between the steps is continuous and results in a model where the order of elements is less restricted and more interchangeable.

As indicated by Hadiness [7] "VR is highly controllable and makes procedures repeatable with respect to the design of the environment and the way of interacting with it." Figure 1 (right) outlines the multidimensional communication between the different elements of the model. This model highlights the complex and strong ties of steps 3 to 5. The design, test and evaluation keep repeating during the design progress.

Imported models interact much faster in the game engines as these enable rendering of the visual asset and allow interactions with virtual environments in real time and in a highly realistic manner. In addition, body position, pointing direction, and exploration movements can be measured with high precision in real time [7] (Fig. 2).

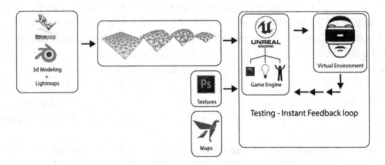

Fig. 2. Continuous feedback between the steps in VR development.

2.2.2   Spatial Experience in the Design Process of Light

The spatial aspects of VR have been highlighted and considered the strongest point of the vision of VR in different industries and as such the human experience is based on spatial environment. Regarding the spatial factor of VR, Hardness outlined that firstly "manipulations of the environment, of viewpoints or metrics of the virtual space (e.g., physical inconsistencies or non-Euclidean metrics), and of interactions with the virtual reality are possible in real time." Secondly, "different sensory modalities related to spatial perception can be tested selectively and can be brought into competition with one another in order to estimate their relative contributions for a given task." Lastly, "virtual reality enables the measurement of spatial behavior in large-scale environments also under real walking conditions (e.g., treadmill or walking sphere)." For these reasons VR has been proposed as a more cost effective and safer replacement of physical projects which might be inappropriate or impossible to be realized due to inaccessibility, cost, security issues [7].

Besides the aforementioned impact on user experience, the spatial conditions in VR equally affect the method of the design process itself. More specifically, it enables designers to experience the light while they are simulating the light and creating the scene. In this process, the field of perception moves constantly between 2D flat screens and the virtual workplace.

This temporal and spatial approximation of the real world is relatively precise, and enables designers to propose lighting scenarios based on real situations, and find the best solutions. However, VR requires the designers to react almost instantaneously to its constant feedback during the design, and at the same time the designers are expected to exploit this flexibility and freedom with absolute control through blueprints and scripts etc. In addition, this real-time and fast feedback requires the lighting designers to either obtain more broad and precise knowledge about other fields integrated in the project or, as Haan [11] commented, need to collaborate closely with domain experts. In other words, when creating a scene in VR, each element has to be introduced and adjusted simultaneously, the latter of which implies knowledge of e.g. botany, architecture, construction, besides understanding such aspects as reflectance of materials and trees when dealing with the lighting. Moreover, these different methodologies enable lighting designers to join the project from its early stage of development.

3   Development

3.1   Setup and Tools

Choice of tools relied on factors such as ease of integrating external interfaces, availability of tutorials and size of community around them, ability to fulfill requirements connected to real world. As the main platform for development, the engine Unreal Engine 4(UE4) was chosen and the HMD interface, HTC VIVE.

Data from user interactions is being collected dynamically and in real time with the use of arduino and sensors within the engine.

3.2   Analysis and Initial Designs

The project initially seeks to answer the question: "How can public art reduce the sense of loss during urban development projects?". The three design criteria of awareness, mutuality and flexibility were formulated according to client needs, focus interviews etc. aimed at answering the question from different perspectives. These three criteria are transferred into lighting (awareness), structure (flexibility), and interaction (mutuality) in VR, as the initial criteria were originally formulated without considering the distinction of the virtual environment.

Lighting (awareness): Lighting in this case study is the main media which enables users to recognize themselves as a part of the development project, and become aware of their area and environment by lighting up the virtual area. Lighting scenarios aiming to solve the problem from different perspectives were designed and simulated in the engine for testing. Figures 3, 4 and 5 illustrate the more distinct cases. The idea behind the design is to put the participant in the position of the designer/artist and light would represent his palette. Virtual "LED screens" placed at the inner side of the tunnel allows for content to be displayed and manipulated according to user's input (Fig. 5). Characteristics such as hue, intensity, motion and patterns are being altered thus resulting by the end of each session a finished installation according to his/her decisions.

Structure (flexibility): The modular structure of the tunnel initially aimed to transform its physical structure to be able to adapt different spaces during the development. The physical body of the installation can correspond to VR itself as the media delivering the

Fig. 3. Initial lighting design and experiment with linear led light

Fig. 4. Tunnel lighting simulation and setting

design. VR as a media is chosen for its ultimate flexibility which can simulate any time and place. In addition, VR is a platform which connects different graphical, and programing languages, i.e. it allows the designers to work with ultimate freedom.

To create the desired environment in Brighter Brunnshög the designers had to go through different combination of these values, test them, return to the basic model and constantly optimize the results. This process is conducted using multidimensional

Fig. 5. Lighting pattern and LED screen simulation

feedback during the development as the settings are continuously affected by small changes. The strength of VR is that these can be tested immediately, as they are developed and proposed.

Interaction (mutuality): Interaction in the virtual environment aims to provide the setting for a mutual relationship between the users and the area. More specifically, it enables not only the users to learn about the area and its vision, but also the Kommune, companies, and public/private organizations can learn from the users. Further interaction between the installation and the users is that in which the users can design the light in the tunnel. VR realizes this idea by transferring that control to the user via different types of sensors. For the more direct interactive elements motion controllers and infrared sensors are being used parallel with ambient interaction sound and radar sensors, which were tested inside the engine.

3.3 Transform and Prototyping

Physical mockups in the step above helped establishing the physicality of the installation and enabled idea generation and details around its form. Taking that further into a VR Environment would help gain an understanding of the installation within its space and experiment with features such as lighting, tunnel motions material shaders and interactions.

With the room-scale VR technique, a physical space (room) was chosen according to the physical dimensions of an active area of the tunnel. This step is important in simulating the experience of walking inside the tunnel and create a sense of scale.

Sensors' input is mapped to actor's parameters such as light intensities, tunnel motions, etc. This helped in understanding an area of interest across gathered data from each type of sensor. Diagram below illustrates the process (Fig. 6).

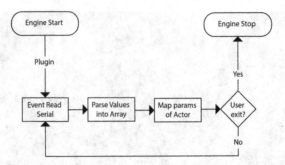

Fig. 6. Process of data collecting from sensors

3.4   Test and Share

Lastly, other than integrating sensor functionality for prototyping/experiments, UE4 is being used as the communication platform for the Installation. By generating the environment around the installation with the use of height maps and procedurally create the foliage, we were able to recreate a big part of the area of Brunnshög and with the use of the HMD visually immerse users into the area. That serves the purpose of communicating the installation's presence in the area.

Secondly a qualitative approach in evaluating the experience would yield valuable results as to how well the virtual experience communicated the design idea of the installation.

4   Discussion

This study aims to initialize an approach to lighting design with the use of virtual reality technology as part of the design process. An approach to design by utilizing digital design tools such as VR, comes with the responsibility of understanding their roles and limits [12]. A stronger interdisciplinary approach in media technology, lighting phenomenology, physics and architecture is required by designers that make use of these tools. While this methodology comes with advantages in communication, evaluation/testing and cost efficiency, meanwhile demands dedicated hardware and special interfaces (HMDs, powerful workstations).

5   Conclusion and Future Work

It is clear that VR offers users the immersive experience based on its spatial aspects which is very close to the experience in the physical environment. This is the one of the strong reasons of VR for designing with light, a multidimensional element in space. Despite this similarity between VR and the physical world, these two worlds rely on different systemic environments, i.e., VR is created by graphic programs and programming which are very flexible and give the designer ultimate control. These three aspects of VR means designing with light in VR can be different from designing in the physical environment. The Brighter Brunnshög case study explored how the design model can be adjusted in VR, and its potential as a media for lighting design. Evaluating this approach is seen as our next step by a qualitatively answering questions like: how did the design process improve by integrating it, which phases during the process could get the most out of these tools and how embodiment was achieved. A successful evaluation of this methodology would assist in optimizing this embodiment as well as the development of dedicated software to accompany it. We are still at the dawn of understanding how to best make use of these tools and truly realize their potential in order to help us design our lighting, our buildings, our living.

Acknowledgements. This work was held in the context of the project Lighting Metropolis, a collaboration between Kraftringen, Aalborg University Copenhagen and Lund Municipality. The authors would like to especially thank Sara Kralmark and Eva Erdös from Kraftringen for their great feedback and support.

Video: https://www.kraftringen.se/Om-Kraftringen/Projekt/Brunnshog/brighter-brunnshog/virtuella-brunnshog/.

References

1. Hansen, E., Mullins, M.: Lighting design: toward a synthesis of science, media technology and architecture. In: eCAADe, vol. 2, no. 1, pp. 613–620 (2014)
2. Kahneman, D., Tversky, A.: Choices, values, and frames. Am. Psychol. **39**(4), 341–350 (1984)
3. Lighting Metropolis (2017). http://lightingmetropolis.com/. Accessed 26 June 2017
4. http://www.cgchannel.com/2017/03/epic-games-unveils-new-vr-editing-tools-in-unreal-engine
5. Alger, M.: Visual design methods for virtual reality (2015)
6. Aiello, P., et al.: A constructivist approach to virtual reality for experiential learning. E-Learn. Digit. Med. **9**(3), 317–324 (2012)
7. Hardiess, G., Mallot, H., Meilinger, T.: Virtual reality and spatial cognition. In: International Encyclopedia of the Social Behavioral Sciences, pp. 133–137 (2015)
8. Mullins, M.: Evaluation of learning in architectural education. In: Kolomos, A., Fink, F., Krogh, L. (eds.) The Aalborg PBL Model – Progress, Diversity and Challenges, pp. 209–218. Aalborg University Press, Aalborg (2004)
9. Hu, J., Wang, F., Funk, M., Frens, J., Zhang, Y., Boheemen, T., Zhang, C., Yuan, Q., Qu, H., Rauterberg, M.: Participatory public media arts for social creativity. In: 2013 International Conference on Culture and Computing (2013)
10. Mullins, M.: Interpretation of simulations in interactive VR environments: depth perception in CAVE and Panorama. J. Arch. Plan. Res. **23**, 328–340 (2006)
11. de Haan, G., Koutek, M., Post, F.: Flexible abstraction layers for VR application development. In: 2007 IEEE Virtual Reality Conference (2007)
12. Reffat, R.: Revitalizing architectural design studio teaching using ICT: reflections on practical implementations (2007)

Improving User Experience for Lost Heritage Sites with a User-Centered Indirect Augmented Reality Application

Christian L. Jakobsen, Jon B. Larsen[✉], Mads Luther Nørlem, and Martin Kraus

Aalborg University, Aalborg, Denmark
{clja13,jbla13,mnarle13}@student.aau.dk, martin@create.aau.dk

Abstract. Using digital media technology, e.g. augmented reality, to convey information about cultural heritage, is becoming increasingly more common. While augmented reality is considered useful and innovative for this purpose, systems based on this technology do at times fail to meet the end users' needs. This paper describes the continued user-centered development and evaluation of an indirect augmented reality application, used to convey information and to visualize the lost Viking ring fortress of Aggersborg, with the larger goal of improving the user experience currently available at the Aggersborg site.

The app was evaluated on users representing the visitors of Aggersborg. The participants were evaluating their user experience of the Aggersborg information board with and without the app as well as the usability of the app by answering user experience and usability questionnaires. It was found that the app did significantly increase user experience for children, while not doing so for seniors.

Keywords: Augmented reality · Indirect augmented reality
User experience · Virtual cultural heritage · Narrative

1 Introduction

Mediating cultural heritage to the public using digital technologies is a field that keeps evolving. Cultural heritage sites, which have been eroded away by time, often suffer from poorly representative visualizations of what the sites looked like in their prime. Use of digital technologies is therefore considered useful in this context [1]. Augmented Reality (AR) has in particular been claimed to be a useful means of conveying information about cultural heritage [2]. AR is currently being integrated into cultural heritage exhibits to provide the user with an interactive experience [3]. However, it has been claimed that there is a gap between the end users and the designers of such applications, indicating a lack of understanding of the users' needs [4,5].

This project is the continuation of previous work done by Jakobsen et al. in collaboration with Vesthimmerlands Museum [6]. The overall aim of this project

© ICST Institute for Computer Sciences, Social Informatics and Telecommunications Engineering 2018
A. L. Brooks et al. (Eds.): ArtsIT 2017/DLI 2017, LNICST 229, pp. 54–63, 2018.
https://doi.org/10.1007/978-3-319-76908-0_6

is to develop a smartphone application that visualizes and conveys information about the Viking ring fortress of Aggersborg through Indirect Augmented Reality (IAR). An interactive base system, which allows users to explore Aggersborg in IAR from three preset locations has previously been developed [6]. An iterative, user-centered design process has been employed in the development, with Vesthimmerlands Museum as primary sparring partner.

The main contribution of this project is a summative evaluation of a user-centered designed and implemented IAR application in terms of usability and user experience compared to experiencing the existing signage at the Aggersborg site.

2 Previous Work

This section provides an overview of the field of cultural heritage, presence in relation to Virtual (VR)- and Augmented Reality (AR), Indirect Augmented Reality (IAR) and digital storytelling.

2.1 Cultural Heritage

Over the past years, efforts have been put into preserving cultural heritage in digital forms [7]. Systems need to be adapted to make use of what current technologies offer, they have to meet the requirements of potential visitors [4,7]. By doing so, the digitized cultural heritage becomes more accessible, available and usable to the public [7]. According to Bachi et al., cultural heritage belongs to the public through the use of digitalization, which encourages more participation from the public. Here mixed reality can be used to virtually transport the user through time and space to a cultural heritage site as it would appear during its prime. Slater described telepresence and place illusion as the concepts of a user feeling located at another place or time and adapting to different bodies of the self [8].

2.2 Indirect Augmented Reality

The proposed system is based on the concepts of conventional AR, meaning superimposing imagery on top of a live camera feed on a handheld device [9]. However, as the terrain of the Aggersborg site is barren of features easily trackable by a computer vision system, alternative methods had to be investigated. Here Indirect Augmented Reality (IAR) can be a substitute for conventional AR without the same problems.

Wither et al. have found that the prominent issues related to conventional AR in outdoor use include either the requirement of computer vision to track features in the real environment, or that it relies on the use of integrated sensors which can result in imprecise alignment [10]. These factors make the alignment of a virtual visual element on top of a live camera feed a challenge. IAR addresses the alignment issue by compositing a 3D-rendered layer on top of a panoramic image of the real-world location; thereby eliminating the need for calculating the alignment between the virtual and real elements in real time. Similar projects have been published by Liestøl et al. who employed a completely pre-rendered environment and GPS locations of the user to use AR systems as a window into the past. Liestøl et al. named this method "situated simulations" [11–14].

3   Materials

The application that was made in this project builds on a foundation which was developed in a previous project [6]. The previous application used IAR to display a 3D-rendered model of Aggersborg on top of 360° photos taken at three locations at the Aggersborg site: at a platform, at the north gate and in the center of the structure. An interface allowed the user to switch between viewing the three preset locations, each showing the ring fortress from a different perspective. In order to align the virtually rendered scenes with the real world, a calibration interface was implemented. The user has to physically stand at the platform and align the app by framing the nearby church in a live camera view and pressing a button. This produces a reference direction, from which an offset can be calculated. This offset is then used to produce a virtual scene, correctly aligned with the real world.

The contribution of the present work is a collaborative design and development process with Vesthimmerlands Museum who acted as the user experts. This collaboration was carried out through multiple meetings with both museum staff, exhibition creators and archaeologists. At these meetings it was decided that to improve the user experience of Aggersborg the system should contain an added narrative and auditory as well as visual elements that help support the users' immersion, when using the app as well as convey factual knowledge. The interface should be intuitive and easy to use, with high affordance, since users span a wide range of age and experience with using apps.

One of the important aspects of the application is its user-centered development. For example, it was considered important to account for both totally absent gyroscopes as well as gyroscopes with poor accuracy in the design. This was achieved by allowing users to disable gyroscope orientation completely, if the accuracy was too poor to produce a satisfying result, and instead use touch to look around in the scenes. In case that no gyroscope was available, the touch navigation would be the default and only option.

Furthermore, an eight-screen tutorial was added at the start of the application, which provides especially new users with a means of understanding the interface and functionality. While it contains a lot of text, it ensures that a thorough description is available for inexperienced users. By adding a skip button, the users can also opt to skip past the tutorial.

The Graphical User Interface (GUI) also exemplifies the user-centered focus. The GUI, including the visual representation of the guide, went through several iterations. Its foundation in terms of design was initially conceived with the collaborators at the museum, using storyboards to consider possible use cases that might be encountered when situated in the context. Various heuristic evaluations and quick and dirty tests helped inform further iterations of the GUI. To make it as user friendly as possible, its buttons were kept simplistic and clear. Because of their non-trivial functions, descriptive text was preferred over icons to illustrate the buttons' functionality. Rather than nesting all buttons in a menu, most buttons were placed in corners of the screen, providing easy access to currently available and relevant functionalities.

3.1 Description of System for Testing

The prototype of the application that was used for testing, see Fig. 1, functioned as follows. When entering the app, the users encounter an introduction, followed by the tutorial. After this, the interface guides the users through aligning the app. After the alignment process, the users are presented with a skybox showing the 360° platform scene, which they can rotate and explore using either the gyroscope of their phone or by dragging on the screen. As a big focus was on the narrative and immersive elements, Svend, a fictive local Viking would act as a virtual guide for the site. When pressing his portrait, he tells a distinct story for each of the three locations, thereby providing factual historical information that is not mediated through the visuals of the app. A treasure hunt mechanic acts as an incentive for users to explore the site; a hidden object is present in each of the three locations for users to find, and once found, users are able to inspect the object more thoroughly in 3D by rotating it and zooming in on it. Textual background information about the object is included as well. For the case of misalignment, a recalibration guide instructs the users how to go through the calibration process again.

Fig. 1. Example of the final iteration of the developed application.

4   Evaluation

The aim of the evaluation was to assess the current prototype iteration in terms of user experience and usability, when using it in its intended context. The purpose of this was primarily to evaluate the application as a supplement to the existing possible activities at Aggersborg, as well as to inform the future design processes by identifying potential usability issues and issues detracting from the user experience.

Based on this, the following research question of the project was formulated:

How does an IAR application, which was developed using user-centered design affect the user experience of visiting the Aggersborg exhibit when compared to the existing information board?

In order to evaluate if the application was a positive addition to the site, as originally intended by the museum, the evaluation was approached as a comparison between the existing outdoor activity at Aggersborg, the information board, and the app. If the app yields a more positive user experience in terms of being a more interesting and fun activity than reading the existing information board, then the app is considered a positive addition to the site. Also, an evaluation of the usability of the app was conducted.

4.1   Test Design

It was chosen to conduct the tests at the Aggersborg site, thereby mimicking the intended context that the app should support. Also, this location allowed for evaluating the user experience of the app in comparison with the information boards. The study relied on questionnaires for gathering anonymous responses from the participants, in the hope that this and their anonymity would decrease the chance of reactivity and experimenter effects as well as demand characteristics, which are important factors to consider when relying on self-reporting [15].

The questionnaire for evaluating the user experience was based on a mix of intrinsic motivation index (IMI) questions for evaluating users' interest [16], as well as relevant questions of our own design. Standard Usability Scale (SUS) questions were used for evaluating the usability and interface of the app [17]. In order to obtain interval data, 7-point Likert scales were used on all questions. After having evaluated both the information board and the app, a short, comparative questionnaire was administered at the end. This questionnaire asked for preferences between the two experiences, and also allowed for the participants to provide more elaborate feedback. Vesthimmerlands Museum estimated that the primary visitors of the site were people aged 60+ as well as families with children. Based on this, people aged 60+ and children were selected for the test. Since the two target groups were vastly different, the questionnaires were kept short and concise. In order to obtain representative samples of these two demographics, the museum was helpful in providing access to 70 school children for testing as well as eight people aged 50+.

4.2 The Field Tests

Two field tests were conducted over the course of two spring days at the Aggersborg site in order to evaluate. This was primarily done in order to evaluate the user experience on the two main target groups and to identify usability issues. The first study encompassed the school children and the second study, conducted two weeks later, encompassed the 60+ participants (hereafter denoted test A and B, respectively). In order to maintain validity, both tests were conducted in identical settings; only participants would differ. One Samsung Galaxy S7 and two Galaxy S6 Android phones were used for testing. In order to be comparable in terms of validity and reliability, the field tests were kept as identical as possible.

Test A Description. On arrival, the 70 children were split into three groups of equal size by their teacher. During the first test, it quickly became obvious that the school children spent far longer time filling out the questionnaires than expected. Also, since some children took longer than others to fill out the forms, and others not complying with the instruction of filling them out, it became difficult to determine which child needed to fill out remaining forms. This lead to inconsistencies in the resulting questionnaires. In total 18 questionnaires for the information board, 22 for the app and 36 comparative questionnaires were answered.

Test B Description. The test session with the 60+ participants was conducted with exactly the same setup as for the children. The participants were all locals from the civic association and were gathered by the museum. The test yielded data from eight senior participants aging from 50 to 68.

5 Results

The data of the two groups of children and seniors was kept separate as the data showed that there were some differences between the groups. A two sample t-test was conducted on the questionnaire, which showed that there was a significant difference in many of them, such as "Was this activity boring?" ($p < 0.05$). Here, the seniors were much less likely to deem the information board boring than the children were.

For the evaluation between the participants experiencing Aggersborg with and without the app, a dependent paired t-test was conducted and the results with a distribution plot of the answers can be seen in Fig. 2. The results show that the difference in user experience for the seniors ultimately does not vary greatly between the information board and the app. The results show that there is no significant difference, as questions such as "Did you enjoy the experience?" ($p > 0.05$) showed that there is only minor variance in the distribution. The method of using a dependent paired t-test was also used for investigating the children's answers. Contrary to the seniors, the results show that there is a significant difference between the information board and the app when it comes to the enjoyment of the experiences. Especially questions such as "This activity was fun" (p < 0.05) show that the children found the app to be more fun to use and that they found it better to hold their attention.

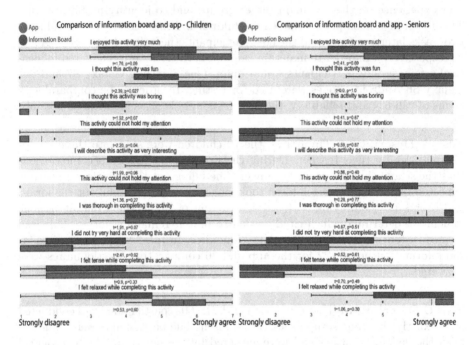

Fig. 2. Boxplots showing the distribution of the answers given on the questionnaire when the seniors and children were asked to assess the information board (blue) and the app (green). The x axis shows the answers given on a Likert scale from 1 to 7. 1 is strong disagreement with the question, while 7 is strong agreement with it. (Color figure online)

5.1 Test A & B Observations

The app was generally received positively by participants in both groups. A number of similar usability issues were observed in both test A and B; specifically in the tutorial section, which at times led participants to either not complete tasks correctly or at all. The following sections summarize the observations from both tests.

Test A Observations. The children generally seemed engaged with using the app, although some of the errors they made might suggest that they did not read the tutorial text. An example of this was seen in the alignment procedure, where several of the children seemed confused by the tutorial. Another example was that a group of children went into the terrain looking for physical artifacts rather than searching for the artifacts within the app. Another group of children thought that the live camera feed for alignment was the actual experience the app had to offer, and needed guidance for entering the IAR scene. Several children seemed impatient when listening to the virtual guide, and promptly shut him off when told that they did not have to listen to it all.

In spite of the initial difficulties with the tutorial, 70% went physically to all of the three locations, and seemed able to follow the instructions of the app.

Test B Observations. The seniors similarly had difficulties with the tutorial. From their behaviour, it was clear that most read all the available text, but rather than just exploring the app, as the children did, many were hesitant to move forward through the interface, and had several follow-up questions. This indicated that the tutorial, which contained only brief texts, was not sufficient to be self-explanatory for this user segment.

6   Discussion

As shown in the results, the app did not statistically improve the user experience of Aggersborg for the seniors, but did so for the children. While the user experience for the seniors was not necessarily improved by the app, they did prefer the app when directly asked to evaluate their preferences. The children did find the application to be more engaging and exciting compared to the information board. As it was better at keeping their attention, it might be more successful in conveying the information of the site; especially the visual appearance of the no longer existing fortress.

The results for the participants' self-perceived competence showed that for both the seniors and the children found the app both intuitive and easy to learn and use. The seniors assessed that most visitors would be able to learn to use the app by themselves, despite that half of the senior participants reported that they did not have a lot of experience with mobile apps in general. Most felt that they did not need long to learn to interact with the app. This is considered important, as the app needs to be easy to use and engage with for visitors of Aggersborg. However, a large part of the children felt more insecure in using the app by themselves, which might be less important as most children visit Aggersborg in some sort of group. Lastly, when asked about intrinsic motivation questions, both groups showed statistically no difference between the two experiences. This indicates that the app was not more intimidating than the information board, despite having more features. However these self evaluations are somewhat contradicting the observed behavior of the participants. Some participants were not able to execute the commands in the tutorial, and some did not indicate to fully understand parts of the interface.

All of this indicates a positive impact on the user experience as a whole, suggesting that both the mediation of information as well as the user experience were satisfactory to the participants. The results point towards that the user experience of visiting Aggersborg was improved for the children, while for the seniors it was on par with that of the information board. The fact that the app appears to provide the users with a positive experience when visiting the site, gives the indication that the approach and its content is able to meet the needs of the users of Aggersborg.

The tests first and foremost posed concerns in terms of the small sample size for the 60+ segment, which threatens external validity and generality. Also, since these participants are connected with the civic association, they are likely biased towards favoring any new action taken to improve upon the site, as also reported by the museum. However, this bias may also be affected by the participants' experience with technology, as the information board is simpler than the app. This, as well as the fact that they volunteered for the test may also be of concern in terms of both internal and external validity [15].

In general, efforts were made to reduce group threats by randomizing all participants as well as counterbalancing the order of events, but because of the small sample of 60+ participants, as well as the chaotic nature of the session with the children, it was not possible to counterbalance all results. Also, allowing the participants to team up with whom they chose within their designated, randomized group, has likely reduced randomization. However, was assessed to be a more accurate representation of the likely behaviour of users when using the app on the site.

7 Conclusion

In conclusion, the IAR application improved the user experience for children by giving them a more overall complete experience compared to that of solely the information board. The user experience of the seniors was not improved in the same way, as they already had a positive experience from the information board in the first place. Despite this, the collaboration with the museum made it possible to develop an IAR application that could be enjoyed and utilized by both children and seniors, which would allow for historical correct information to be conveyed in a more interesting way than the information board. The application allows the users to explore and experience the site in their own way and pace, as it offers various functionalities to experience if desired. From the evaluation, it was found that while the various age groups have different opinions on the information board, they do in general find the application both engaging, easy to use and interesting.

Acknowledgment. We would like to thank Vesterhimmerlands Museum, especially museum cultural heritage supervisor Maria Clement Hagstrup. The collaboration throughout the semester resulted in invaluable knowledge and feedback on the topic of Aggersborg, what content was important to focus on developing as well as crucial assistance during the evaluation of the project.

References

1. Simon, N.: The participatory museum. In: Museum 2.0 (2010)
2. Dunleavy, M., et al.: Affordances and limitations of immersive participatory augmented reality simulations for teaching and learning. J. Sci. Educ. Technol. **18**(1), 7–22 (2009)
3. Kounavis, C.D., et al.: Enhancing the tourism experience through mobile augmented reality: challenges and prospects. Int. J. Eng. Bus. Manag. **4**, 10 (2012)
4. Cipolla Ficarra, F.V., Nicol, E., Cipolla-Ficarra, M.: Usability, communicability and cultural tourism in interactive systems: trends, economic effects and social impact. In: Cipolla Ficarra, F.V., de Castro Lozano, C., Nicol, E., Kratky, A., Cipolla-Ficarra, M. (eds.) HCITOCH 2010. LNCS, vol. 6529, pp. 100–114. Springer, Heidelberg (2011). https://doi.org/10.1007/978-3-642-18348-5_10
5. Schiavottiello, N., Brigola, J.: ArkTeller: a new 3D real-time storytelling platform for cultural heritage interpretation. In: 2015 Digital Heritage, pp. 753–754 (2015)
6. Jakobsen, C.L., et al.: Reviving Aggersborg - conveying lost heritage sites through indirect augmented reality. In: VRIC 2017, Laval, France (n.d.)
7. Bachi, V., Fresa, A., Pierotti, C., Prandoni, C.: The digitization age: mass culture is quality culture. Challenges for cultural heritage and society. In: Ioannides, M., Magnenat-Thalmann, N., Fink, E., Žarnić, R., Yen, A.-Y., Quak, E. (eds.) EuroMed 2014. LNCS, vol. 8740, pp. 786–801. Springer, Cham (2014). https://doi.org/10.1007/978-3-319-13695-0_81
8. Slater, M.: Place illusion and plausibility can lead to realistic behaviour in immersive virtual environments. Philos. Trans. R. Soc. Lond. B Biol. Sci. **364**(1535), 3549–3557 (2009)
9. Bimber, O., Raskar, R.: Modern approaches to augmented reality. In: ACM SIGGRAPH 2006 Courses. ACM, New York (2006)
10. Wither, J., et al.: Mobile augmented reality: indirect augmented reality. Comput. Graph. **35**(4), 810–822 (2011)
11. Liestøl, G.: Augmented reality and digital genre design; situated simulations on the iPhone. In: 2009 IEEE International Symposium on Mixed and Augmented Reality - Arts, Media and Humanities, pp. 29–34 (2009)
12. Liestøl, G., et al.: Exploring situated knowledge building using mobile augmented reality. Qwerty - Open Interdiscipl. J. Technol. Cult. Educ. **11**, 26–43 (2016)
13. Liestøl, G., Morrison, A.: The power of place and perspective: sensory media and situated simulations in urban design. In: Sheller, M., de Souza e Silva, A. (eds.) Mobility and Locative Media, pp. 207–223. Routledge/Taylor and Francis Group, New York (2014)
14. Liestøl, G., Rasmussen, T.: In the presence of the past: a field trial evaluation of a situated simulation design reconstructing a Viking burial scene. In: Szücs, A., Tait, A.W. (eds.) Proceedings of EDEN 2010. European Distance and E-Learning Network Budapest (2010)
15. Field, A., Hole, D.G.J.: How to Design and Report Experiments. Sage Publications Ltd, Thousand Oaks (2003)
16. Self-Determination Theory: Intrinsic Motivation Inventory (IMI). http://selfdeterminationtheory.org/intrinsic-motivation-inventory/
17. usability.gov: System Usability Scale (SUS). https://www.usability.gov/how-to-and-tools/methods/system-usability-scale.html

Facilitating Asymmetric Collaborative Navigation in Room-Scale Virtual Reality for Public Spaces

Sule Serubugo[✉], Denisa Skantarova, Nicolaj Evers, and Martin Kraus[iD]

Aalborg University, Rendsburggade 14, 9000 Aalborg, Denmark
serubugo-sule@outlook.com, dskantarova@gmail.com,
nevers12@student.aau.dk, martin@create.aau.dk

Abstract. This study investigates asymmetric collaboration in public room-scale Virtual Reality (VR) setups to address the isolating experience provided by single-user Head-Mounted Displays (HMDs). In our field study, participants wearing an HMD had to find their way in a virtual maze with the help of co-located participants without an HMD. The non-HMD participants could either see a mirrored HMD view, a map of the maze, or a combination of the two. We evaluated which of these three conditions facilitates more collaboration and engagement for the non-HMD participants and spectators, as well as the HMD participants. Our findings can be used when facilitating engaging asymmetric experiences for public VR setups.

Keywords: Virtual reality · Asymmetric collaboration
Room-scale virtual reality · Visualization · Public spaces
Computer graphics

1 Introduction

Virtual Reality (VR) is of growing interest for public cultural centers such as museums and libraries that are increasingly often setting it up for the public to present cultural information. It has become a new way of providing information and entertaining their visitors [1,2]. The technology has brought new advances such as room-scale virtual reality that is capable of allowing people to freely move around in the play area as they walk and explore a virtual environment. One of the limitations of this technology is that single Head-Mounted Displays (HMDs) can be worn only by one person at a time, which often means that the other people standing by the setup cannot engage in the experience [2,3].

The single-person experience is an important limitation specifically for public cultural centers that are devoted to large groups of visitors [2]. There have been attempts to bring a social experience into VR, such as using multiple HMDs to bring several users into the same virtual environment. However, this is currently a costly setup for public centers who have to manage large groups of visitors.

A. L. Brooks et al. (Eds.): ArtsIT 2017/DLI 2017, LNICST 229, pp. 64–73, 2018.
https://doi.org/10.1007/978-3-319-76908-0_7

In commercial products like VR The Diner Duo [4] and Keep Talking and Nobody Explodes [5], a different approach has emerged that allows for an asymmetric collaboration between one HMD participant and the non-HMD participants. However, there is a lack of research that explores this asymmetric phenomenon for the public setting.

To address this problem, we investigated asymmetric collaboration between the HMD participant in room-scale VR and the non-HMD participants following along on a side display near the VR setup in the scenario of a public cultural center. We compared the views on the side display in three different conditions: a mirrored view of what the HMD participant sees, a map of the virtual environment, and a combination of the two. The comparison investigated their influence on collaboration and engagement of the participants and spectators in the public setting.

2 Related Work

The limitation of a single-person experience in VR can be addressed by creating an asymmetric collaboration, which is rarely considered for public VR setups. Several studies [3, 6–9] that support collaboration and multiplayer experiences made use of similar building blocks. These include unification of participants' experiences through story and theme, use of multiple media, assigning different roles, and emphasizing communication.

Schmitz et al. [8] explored role-based asymmetric collaboration using a media combination of Oculus Rift and CAVE. They gave participants a collaborative task to maneuver a ship around a sea, which was split into two roles – the captain and the crew. In Liszio and Masuch's [3] game Lunar Escape, participants used an Oculus Rift DK2 and two tablet PCs to fulfil a collaborative task. Similarly, in the game Keep Talking and Nobody Explodes [5], users collaborate to defuse a virtual bomb, where one wears an HMD and the other uses a paper manual.

Sajjadi et al. [6] studied the influence of the medium on the participants' game experience and collaboration in serious collaborative games. In their maze-game, participants were given two media – one Oculus Rift and one set of Stifteo cubes. The participant wearing the Oculus Rift was presented with an overview of the maze and obstacles in VR and was able to direct the other participant with the Stifteo cubes to safely find a way out of the maze. Results from their study showed no significant difference between the two media, implying that both participants found their experience equally positive.

These studies show the importance of roles and media, as these mean that participants have to depend on each other's abilities and communicate in order to accomplish the objectives. However, related work has not evaluated the effect of using a side display as means of asymmetrically involving the non-HMD participants for public VR setups. A typical public VR setup could have one HMD and a side display placed close by, showing the virtual environment. In this setup, we compared the different views on the side display to investigate their influence on collaboration and engagement of non-HMD participants, spectators, as well as HMD participants.

3   Materials and Method

3.1   The VR Experience

To explore how the view presented on the side display influences the asymmetric collaboration, a VR experience with two roles was set up for a public library. The non-HMD participants were assigned a navigator role and used a map of a maze on the side display to assist the HMD user, who took the role of an explorer and had to find the way to a diamond in the maze.

The VR setup consisted of the HTC Vive HMD and its Lighthouse bases to provide room-scale tracking in a 2.5 m × 2.5 m area, and a regular monitor close by. In this setup, the HMD role had an ability to freely walk in a large virtual maze, which was designed to fit in the 2.5 m × 2.5 m physical space using self-overlapping architectures [10]. In two conditions, the non-HMD role had information about the overview of the maze and location of the diamond on a map, and had therefore an ability to direct the HMD participant towards the goal. Figure 1 shows the design of the VR experience with the maze and the map.

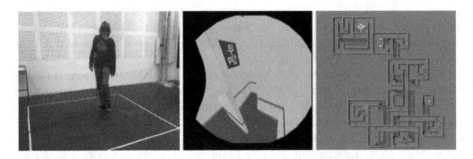

Fig. 1. The 2.5 m × 2.5 m physical space (left), the self-overlapping maze as seen in the HMD (middle), and the map of the maze with the diamond (right)

3.2   Experiment Design

The experiment was set up as an observational study, where three conditions were tested with different views for the non-HMD participants: the mirror display condition (MIR), where only the HMD user's view was mirrored on the side display, the map condition (MAP), where only the map was shown on the side display, and a third combination condition (COMB), where the side display was split to show both the mirror display and the map. The three conditions for the side display can be seen in Fig. 2.

To compare the three conditions, hypotheses were made to find out which of the conditions facilitates more collaboration and engagement for participants and spectators in a public setup. As discussed in related work, roles are an important element of facilitating asymmetric collaboration; thus one hypothesis was

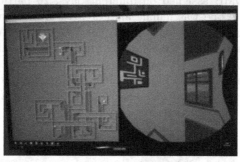

Fig. 2. The side display in MIR (top left), MAP (top right), and COMB (bottom) conditions

that conditions with the map would encourage more collaboration because participants have different roles with different information and abilities. This would not be the case in the MIR condition because the non-HMD participant does not have unique abilities and information compared to the HMD role. Furthermore when the two map conditions are compared, we hypothesized that the collaboration in the COMB condition would be more effective than in the MAP because in the COMB condition, the virtual world is more unified for both participants. It would therefore be easier for the non-HMD participants to give directions to the HMD participant. Based on these assumptions, the following two hypotheses were formulated about collaboration.

H1: The map in conditions MAP and COMB facilitates more collaboration than only the mirror display in condition MIR.

H2: The combination of the map and mirror display in the COMB condition facilitates a more effective collaboration than only the map in MAP condition.

Besides collaboration, observations were also made for participant engagement in the three conditions. Due to the fact that roles brought about by the map conditions allow both participants to contribute towards a common goal, one hypothesis was that the MAP and COMB conditions would be more engaging than the MIR condition. Furthermore, the mirror display in the COMB condition would make it more engaging than the MAP condition. The following two hypotheses were formulated for engagement of both participants and spectators.

H3: The map in MAP and COMB conditions facilitates more engagement than only the mirror display in MIR.

H4: The combination of the map and the mirror display in COMB facilitates more engagement than only the map in MAP condition.

3.3 Participants

At a public library, the experiment was run for three days, with the conditions MIR, MAP, and COMB assigned on different days. 20 participants tried the MIR condition, where one was female and 19 were male with their ages estimated between 10 and 28 years ($M = 16.35$, $SD = 4.6$). The MAP condition was tried by 23 participants, three female and 20 male, whose estimated ages were between 4 and 40 years ($M = 16.09$, $SD = 11.07$). Lastly, 28 participants tried the COMB condition, of which 13 were female and 15 male, and their estimated ages were between 7 and 34 years ($M = 15.07$, $SD = 7.44$). Figure 3 shows images of participants during the experiment.

Fig. 3. HMD participant walking in the VR maze (left) and non-HMD participants using the side display (right)

3.4 Procedure

Participants were instructed at the start that their task is to collaborate to find a diamond in the maze, and the HMD participant was helped to put on the HMD. Their playthrough was observed by two observers nearby. One playthrough was considered to be the period from when participants started to move in the maze until they either found the diamond or stopped the experience due to giving up, changing roles, or the system breaking. As is summarized in Table 1, for each playthrough, the observers noted which roles participants had and how they used them, communication, engagement, spectators, and participants' comments. Communication was counted as utterances for the HMD and non-HMD participants, where one utterance was considered as a piece of speech when a person starts talking until holding a clear pause or until another person starts talking. Two-way communication was also observed, where each utterance of the HMD participant that is replied to by the non-HMD participants or vice versa was counted as one instance.

Observations for engagement included how many times participants tried the HMD and non-HMD role. Spectators were also counted based on their involvement in the experience as passive, moderate, or active. Passive spectators would be considered as people standing nearby and watching, while moderate were people who approached to watch the side display. Lastly, the active spectators would be the ones who approached the side display and helped to guide the HMD participant at some point during the playthrough.

Table 1. Observations noted in the experiment

Topic	Observations
Collaboration	How they use their roles
	Amount of communication: HMD and non-HMD utterances, two-way communication
Engagement	Playthroughs per participant
	How many try one role more than once
	Do they complete the maze
	Number and involvement of spectators: passive, moderate, and active

4 Results and Discussion

The observations from the experiment were analyzed using statistical tests with a significance value of $\alpha = 0.05$. During the experiment, participants in the MIR condition made a total of 18 playthroughs, in the MAP condition 29 playthroughs, and in the COMB, 40 playthroughs were made.

4.1 Collaboration

The system's ability to facilitate collaboration in the different conditions was evaluated by observing whether the participants used their roles, thus contributed to the goal, how much they communicated, and what directions they used. Pearson's chi-squared test showed that there was a significant difference for use of roles (MIR 83%, MAP 97%, COMB 100% used roles), however this was not significant in post-hoc pair-wise comparison tests.

For communication shown in Fig. 4, Tukey HSD test showed that the MIR condition ($M = 4.04$), $p = 0.049$, and COMB condition ($M = 3.84$), $p = 0.03$, had significantly more HMD participant utterances per minute compared to the MAP condition ($M = 2.50$). Similarly, MIR ($M = 13.50$) had significantly more two-way communication than MAP ($M = 6.48$), $p = 0.0002$, and COMB ($M = 9.48$), $p = 0.046$. Further, the COMB condition encouraged significantly more two-way communication, $p = 0.006$ than the MAP condition. Although the MIR condition had most two-way communication, observations indicated that this communication consisted mainly of participants discussing at junctions about where to go next and whether they have been at the same place before: "don't go back here, I think it's a dead end" or "wasn't that the way you came from?".

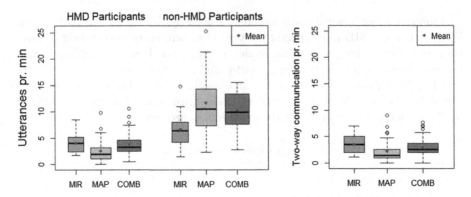

Fig. 4. HMD and non-HMD participant utterances per minute (left) and two-way communication per minute (right)

In contrast to the HMD participant making more utterances in the MIR condition, the non-HMD participants had significantly more utterances per minute in the MAP condition ($M = 11.69$), $p = 0.0003$, and the COMB condition ($M = 10.28$), $p = 0.01$, than in the MIR condition ($M = 6.64$). From observations, this difference in non-HMD utterances in the MAP and COMB conditions was due to the non-HMD participants giving directions, and guiding the HMD participants towards the goal. The communication in the COMB condition was however similar to the MIR condition with regards to HMD utterances and two-way communication, but with many more non-HMD utterances. With the use of roles not having significant differences, the data from communication alone has not shown enough evidence for accepting the hypothesis *H1* that the map conditions MAP and COMB would facilitate more collaboration than the MIR condition. It could therefore be reasoned that merely observing utterances might not be sufficient for accurately evaluating collaboration. Also the fact that the participants in all conditions were instructed to collaborate on completing the goal may have made them feel as if they were required to talk. On the other hand, the communication results showed that the two map conditions encouraged the non-HMD participants more to collaborate than the MIR condition. The hypothesis *H2* that compares the MAP and COMB conditions can be accepted as the COMB condition, where the participants' world was more unified, facilitated more effective collaboration than the MAP condition.

4.2 Engagement

The three conditions' ability to facilitate engagement in the participants has also been analyzed. This was measured through number of playthroughs, spectators and completion rate to evaluate hypotheses *H3* and *H4*. Observations showed that participants had an engaging experience with both roles in all conditions and nine people said that it was "cool", one said that "it was not bad to walk around" and that he "never tried to control virtual reality before – it was fun".

For the playthroughs shown in Fig. 5, Dunn's multiple comparison test showed that there were significantly more playthroughs per participant in COMB ($M = 3.11$) than in MIR ($M = 1.90$), $p = 0.02$, and MAP ($M = 2.78$), $p = 0.03$. A participant would also try the non-HMD role significantly more times in COMB ($M = 1.89$) than in MIR ($M = 1$), $p = 0.008$. There was no significant difference when the COMB condition was compared to the MAP condition ($M = 1.74$), $p = 0.08$. Furthermore, trying the HMD role was not significantly different across conditions, $H(2) = 3.12$, $p = 0.21$. Significantly more participants retried one role several times in MAP (52%), $p = 0.03$, and COMB (89%), $p < 0.0001$, compared to MIR (17%) and in COMB compared to MAP, $p = 0.007$.

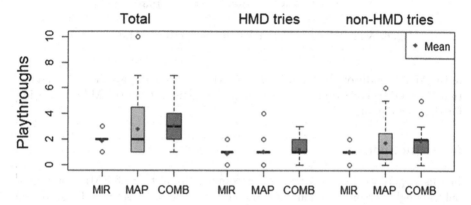

Fig. 5. Number of playthroughs, and tries of the HMD and non-HMD role per participant

The MAP condition ($M = 6.31$) had the most amount of total spectators, as shown in Fig. 6, compared to MIR ($M = 2.17$), $p < 0.0001$, and COMB ($M = 2.88$), $p < 0.0001$. Out of all spectators, the percentage of those who actively directed the HMD participant was significantly higher in MAP (21%), $p = 0.007$, and in COMB (26%), $p = 0.003$, than in MIR (3%). This suggests that MAP provided the most engaging viewing experience. Regarding completion rate, we observed that in more than half (56%) of the MIR playthroughs, participants stopped playing due to frustration, while nobody did in both the MAP and COMB conditions. This also suggests that the MIR condition was overall less engaging. In five out of the 18 playthroughs in the MIR condition, non-HMD participants were observed disengaged and were for instance checking messages on the phone. Six were also observed saying that "I think we are stuck", "we have been all the ways" and one saying "I'd like a minimap". This shows that participants were stuck and disengaged without the map.

Overall, the hypothesis *H3* that the map in conditions MAP and COMB facilitates more engagement than MIR for participants and spectators, can be accepted due to the low completion rate of the MIR condition, the number of retries of one role in the two map conditions, and the high spectator engagement

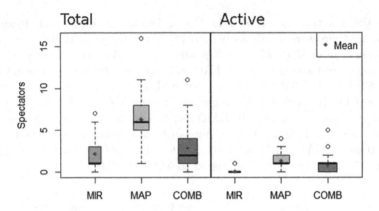

Fig. 6. Number of all spectators (left) and active spectators (right)

of the MAP condition. For hypothesis $H4$, the experiment also showed evidence that the COMB condition facilitates more engagement than the MAP condition for the participants.

5   Conclusion

In this paper, we have addressed the common limitation of HMDs providing only a single-person experience for public room-scale VR setups. To overcome this limitation, the study has proposed and investigated asymmetric collaboration based on different views displayed on the side display for the non-HMD participants. Three conditions, the mirror display, the map, and the combination of the mirror display and the map, were compared in order to find out which condition facilitates more collaboration and engagement for both participants as well as spectators. Based on the statistical analysis of communication between participants, it was not possible to conclude that the two conditions with the map facilitate significantly more collaboration than the mirror display condition. However, the two conditions with the map involved non-HMD participants in the collaboration more than the mirror display condition. In terms of engagement, observations showed that there were significantly more retries and successful completions of the maze in the conditions with the map than in the mirror display condition. There was also a significantly higher number of spectators in the map conditions than in the mirror display condition.

This study has demonstrated how a side display can be used to encourage asymmetric collaboration for a public VR setup. Our findings can be generalized and applied in different areas working with VR setups that aim to include bystanders. This could also be explored in further studies, where inspiration could be drawn from games and interaction theories to create content that can engage the non-HMD viewers even more. Other media such as smartphones that are typically used by people in public places could also be explored for how they can be used as controllers, thus giving the non-HMD role new abilities.

References

1. Massis, B.: Using virtual and augmented reality in the library. New Libr. World **116**(11/12), 796–799 (2015)
2. Carrozzino, M., Bergamasco, M.: Beyond virtual museums: experiencing immersive virtual reality in real museums. J. Cult. Heritage **11**(4), 452–458 (2010)
3. Liszio, S., Masuch, M.: Designing shared virtual reality gaming experiences in local multi-platform games. In: Wallner, G., Kriglstein, S., Hlavacs, H., Malaka, R., Lugmayr, A., Yang, H.-S. (eds.) ICEC 2016. LNCS, vol. 9926, pp. 235–240. Springer, Cham (2016). https://doi.org/10.1007/978-3-319-46100-7_23
4. Whirlybird Games. VR The Diner Duo. [Steam] (2016). http://store.steampowered.com/app/530120/VR_The_Diner_Duo/
5. Steel Crate Games. Keep Talking and Nobody Explodes. [Steam] (2015). http://store.steampowered.com/app/341800/Keep_Talking_and_Nobody_Explodes/
6. Sajjadi, P., Cebolledo Gutierrez, E.O., Trullemans, S., De Troyer, O.: Maze commander: a collaborative asynchronous game using the oculus rift & the sifteo cubes. In: Proceedings of the First ACM SIGCHI Annual Symposium on Computer-Human Interaction in Play, CHI PLAY 2014, pp. 227–236 (2014)
7. Wendel, V., Gutjahr, M., Gobel, S., Steinmetz, R.: Designing collaborative multiplayer serious games for collaborative learning. In: CSEDU, vol. 2, pp. 199–210. SciTePress (2012)
8. Schmitz, M., Akbal, M., Zehle, S.: SpielRaum: perspectives for collaborative play. In: Proceedings of the 2015 Annual Symposium on Computer-Human Interaction in Play, CHI PLAY 2015, pp. 427–432 (2015)
9. Azadegan, A., Harteveld, C.: Work for or against players: on the use of collaboration engineering for collaborative games. In: Foundation of Digital Games, 3–7 April 2014, Lauderdale, FL, USA (2014)
10. Suma, E.A., Lipps, Z., Finkelstein, S., Krum, D.M., Bolas, M.: Impossible spaces: maximizing natural walking in virtual environments with self-overlapping architecture. IEEE Trans. Vis. Comput. Graph. **18**(4), 555–564 (2012)

Authoring a Serious Pervasive Game for Reflecting upon Urban Spaces

Vanessa Santos[✉] and Roc Parés Burguès

Department of Communication, Pompeu Fabra University,
Roc Boronat 138, 08018 Barcelona, Spain
santosvaness@gmail.com, roc.pares@upf.edu

Abstract. This paper investigates how pervasive games, which explore the potential of storytelling on mobile and locative media, can transfer knowledge about serious topics regarding public space. The discussion anchors on *Chronica Mobilis* (Barcelona 2014), a situated playing experience devoted to supporting critical thinking about contemporary cities' issues. The authors expose the inception, interaction design, implementation and public presentation process of the mentioned artwork, as well as a qualitative analysis of the participants' experience. They evaluate the manner in which this serious pervasive game manifests as a ludic mechanism to inform the reflection on the immigration and gentrification phenomenon.

Keywords: Serious games · Storytelling · Urban space · Locative media
Situated learning

1 Introduction

The exponential rise of digital gaming in popular culture has been an opportunity to expand the use of these cultural forms to support teaching processes. This increasing interest in adopting computer games for educational purposes relies on the belief that they positively facilitate learning by evoking high levels of engagement [1–3]. The growing field of "serious games" embraces such playing applications, whose goals transcend the purpose of mere entertainment [4]. The difference, when the 'serious' adjective qualifies these ludic activities, refers to the prior objective of supporting critical thinking and the learning and training process in a variety of areas.

The game industry concentrates mainly on producing fun and enjoyment experiences [5], though relevant content can also appear as a topic to let players learn about a particular universe in this manner. Even such games devoted solely to leisure have learning as one of their fundamental motivations, because the formal structure of goals, rules, and challenges can entertain as well as instruct. The learning process can be latent and involve the skills needed to overcome the challenges established by the gameplay [6]. The formal characteristics of a game, the competitive and collaborative strategies it demands, the choices it requires, the fantasy it creates can also influence and incentivize the discussion of serious topics.

Digital gaming can transfer knowledge across diverse contexts, even though it happens in quite a different manner when compared to traditional teaching methods [7].

© ICST Institute for Computer Sciences, Social Informatics and Telecommunications Engineering 2018
A. L. Brooks et al. (Eds.): ArtsIT 2017/DLI 2017, LNICST 229, pp. 74–84, 2018.
https://doi.org/10.1007/978-3-319-76908-0_8

This paper investigates how to facilitate learning experiences in alternative ways, by making players reflect on and learn about determined topics by situating them within the discussed context. The focus is on the potentialities of pervasive games, or on "the construction and enacting of augmented and/or embedded game worlds that reside on the threshold between tangible and immaterial space" [8]. These playing activities, which include a range of formats and technologies, adopt computational procedures of a post-desktop paradigm, including wearable and mobile media to facilitate the physical environment for gameplay.

This paper considers this particular genre and a specific subset that figures among the broad spectrum of serious game-based applications: those devoted to supporting reflection upon urban spaces[1]. It discusses the potential that a situated and collaborative game experience has in generating debate and promoting interest in community issues. It investigates how to enhance critical thinking by fostering situated, embodied and collaborative activities supported by mobile and locative media[2].

The authors analyze such a possibility through a case study approach based on *Chronica Mobilis*[3], a pervasive game that uses the computational and communication infrastructure of cities, working to integrate virtual and physical elements into the game world. The piece turns portable technology into a delivery channel, recording and incorporating player position meaningfully in the rules that govern the play activity, and considers the mobility features of the supporting medium in the game mechanisms. The resulting playful experience brings attention to a local reality, inviting a discussion about the serious topic of gentrification in the urban planning field.

2   A Situated Game Experience About Gentrification

Chronica Mobilis does not have the explicit intention of creating an experience that could serve to define itself as a learning game. Rather, it proposes a narrative with game dynamics that aims to bring attention to the current situation taking place in Poblenou, a neighborhood in the city of Barcelona. In the late nineteenth century, it was an industrial district largely inhabited by low-income people. The area, characterized by abandoned factories, is currently experiencing an urban renewal. The 22@Barcelona technological district project[4]. has triggered profound changes in the lifestyle of the residents as well as in the profile of the community. The gentrification process, akin to

---

[1] In this particular domain, designers have been adopting the gameplay dynamics for creating playful public participation in urban planning. For example, see: [9].

[2] This paper defines locative media according to Lemos and Josgrilberg [10], as the technological interfaces, such as mobile phones with Global Positioning System receivers, 3G and Bluetooth technologies, which allow interaction between the physical, social and digital networks, by generating data that identifies the location of people and objects in physical space.

[3] http://chronicamobilis.net.

[4] The project 22@Barcelona claims that it will transform "two hundred hectares of industrial land of Poblenou into an innovative district offering modern spaces for the strategic concentration of intensive knowledge-based activities. This initiative is also a project of urban refurbishment and a new model of city". See: http://www.22barcelona.com/.

that in Poblenou, is a global phenomenon and a serious topic within the research agenda of contemporary cities [11].

The narrative embedded in *Chronica Mobilis* has gentrification as the central conflict responsible for triggering a series of story events represented and split into three subplots. Each stands for a moment in the life of a character: childhood, adolescence and adulthood. The childhood plot brings us to a neighborhood deteriorated, abandoned and neglected by government policies. Adolescence frames the time in which the area becomes gentrified, affecting long-term residents like the protagonist, who must leave his home. Adulthood marks the return of the character to the place where he grew up, a moment surrounded by the memories of the past and the newly gentrified reality of the present. Chronological, the whole narrative with its three subplots shows how the protagonist and the urban space changes significantly over the time. While the story is very linear, the discourse formation is interactive and gains its motive with a structured game dynamic.

Chronica Mobilis investigates the rhetoric potential of mobile and locative media by stressing the connections between the content and the space in which participants experience it. Following the tendency of projects enabled by location-aware technologies, it integrates some historical, ethnographic and architectural information provided by the cityscape as a layer of meaning [12]. Narratives that geolocate their content normally operate by reinforcing the relation between site, story, and participants, creating an embodied experience rooted in particular places and moments, lived and shared. Immersive and compelling experiences can result from such dialogue, making participants engage with the space mapped out for the diegesis that can even be the original location of the represented events.

Chronica Mobilis geolocates its embedded story in Poblenou area. Real sites in the neighbourhood function as locative nodes containing a virtual layer of added content. The story, organized in a network architecture, appears fragmented into twelve audiovisual scenes. Only an explorative journey through the area can discover and trigger the geolocated content. Three groups of players take part in this rewarding and collaborative experience. Stimulated by a positive spirit of inquiry, they reveal the invisible fictional story which inhabits the places they visit. They see the geographical space of Poblenou turning into both: an extension of the embedded narrative and a game board for a site-specific experience.

Such integration between place and content involved studying the neighborhood through exploratory journeys. These practices followed the premises of the Situationist technique of dérive [13]. The process allowed the perception and integration of some resonance of the area, found on a denotative and immediate level, as well as on a connotative deeper and inferred dimension. The reality of the district and the fictional story establish a productive dialogue, as the narrative contains much of the current situation experienced by the residents of Poblenou. In the fictional narrative, for instance, the house of the protagonist is demolished when local gentrification starts. The site in the neighborhood chosen to geolocate this scene is an empty lot containing the remains of a demolished building protected by a construction fence. In front of it, a large sign announces the sale of a new and modern enterprise. Should players look through the metal plates, they see written on the walls: "speculation: the neighborhood virus". The video geolocated there depicts story events recorded in the same place, which are the protagonist returning to the gentrified district, looking for his former house, discovering that it was demolished. Such parallels and connections enrich the situated experience and blur a possible line built in participants' mind separating fiction from non-fiction Fig. 1.

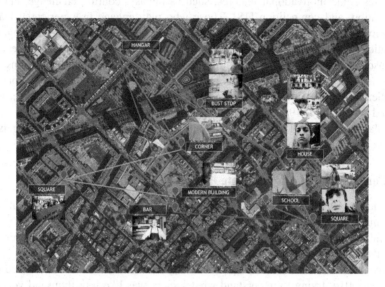

Fig. 1. Locations in Poblenou, where players can find the video fragments.

Players in *Chronica Mobilis* engage with a geohistorical and sociopolitical tension, whose conflict relates to demographic shifts, gentrification issues, and preservation concerns. They become immersed and participate in that particular context transpiring in Poblenou. The environment they are placed in serves as a source of information to support critical thinking about these topics through observation. Players have the opportunity to experience, acquire and learn information and skills in the physical and social environment. Such situated learning is one of the educational values of serious pervasive games [14]. It represents a valuable opportunity, considering that meaningful learning experiences encourage understanding by calling on the reflection and connection between gaming and life situations [15]. While situated learning facilitates the development of critical thinking and skills, it also increases the potential for players to later transfer the learned knowledge to other similar situations in new contexts [16]. In the case of *Chronica Mobilis*, though it became a site-specific work, the narrative also translates some of the issues, shifts and consequences gentrification can cause in other places. Though the narrative experience points to the particular process in Poblenou, on a broader level the fictional story emphasizes a multifaceted and global phenomenon of contemporary cities.

3 Engagement with Experiential Learning

A logical structure governs the situated experience proposed by *Chronica Mobilis*. The schema foregrounds the player's participation in the game and with other players [17]. It explores some motivational features, such as fantasy, control, challenge, curiosity, collaboration, and competition [18]. Those who play engage in experiential learning with active participation in tasks based on problem-solving, decision-making, communication and team-playing. Rather than giving didactic instructions about the serious topic discussed, the acquisition of knowledge comes from the players' actions. They need to analyze the context they are engaged with, gather the necessary information and articulate it to solve the challenges posed by the gameplay. In such cases, as observed by Rooney [19], critical thinking is one of the cognitive skills they acquire while playing, but the knowledge resulting from such experiential learning is also cognitive, physical and emotional.

3.1 Formal Structure to Motivate Playing

As previously stated, the narrative embedded in *Chronica Mobilis* involves immigration, gentrification and preservation issues. When discussing a serious topic in a game, the definition of a pleasurable metaphor able to create fantasy and to raise curiosity is one of the core aspects in achieving and sustaining the motivation of players [18]. In *Chronica Mobilis*, a futuristic metaphor makes players enact the role of archaeologists in the year 6014, trying to understand what society was like four thousand years ago. There are no digital or analog registers from the past. By collecting geolocated memories embedded in the game, they can retrieve some objects that a determined person kept hidden. These are the last analog recordings remaining from the past. The metaphor justifies and enhances the interest in the game activity. It also determines a clear task to players, letting them identify their roles and responsibilities within that playing context, which is an important feature to generate motivation [19].

While goals are responsible for shaping the player's experience and keeping their desire to move forward [14], maintaining the player's relationship to the goal is a challenge [20]. *Chronica Mobilis* achieves this by establishing short-term tasks to bring instant gratification, while players wait for the delayed long-term outcome. These step missions nurture the core mechanics and maintain engagement until the end. The goal creates pleasure, while a set of fixed, binding and repeatable rules sustains motivation [20]. The first rule: each of the three teams playing the game has to define who will play online and who will go to the streets. These two sub-teams will be in different spaces and with a particular set of equipment and technology. Those online must stay inside the exhibition space playing from computers connected to the Internet. Those in the city carry mobile phones enabled with GPS and connected to a 3G network.

The essential rules of the game stem from the predefined manner in which these two categories of player have to communicate and interact. Presented with the goal, they identify their roles: players on computers guide their partners through the city, whereas those in the city find and visit determined locations. According to the rules, street players must send audiovisual streaming showing their experience in the city, receive instant text messages with guidance, and send location data to inform their team of their spatial location. On the other side, online players watch the auto-report streaming and observe the location and displacement in the map, to send text messages with guidance Fig. 2.

Fig. 2. Layers of content generated as a result of the playing.

The rules of *Chronica Mobilis* pose difficulty by preventing teams from directly and freely communicating, as well as setting a limited time for the game activity. The intention is to increase difficulty but preserve equilibrium between challenge and frustration. They do not let play be so easy as to result in apathy and do not make the task too difficult to master, which could generate tension. Avoiding anxiety or boredom, the degree of difficulty and the restrictions in the gameplay try to create a flow between the skills and the challenge to overcome, between anxiety and pleasure [21].

The dynamics of reward and punishment also integrate a psychological operant conditioning into the core mechanics of the game, which encourages or discourages certain players' behaviors and influences their actions, motivation and overall experience [17]. Player activity in *Chronica Mobilis* is intrinsically rewarding, in an attempt to involve them in the desire to achieve more and more. They receive a reward every time they visit a place that geolocates a story fragment: a video featuring a memory of events that took place in a determined narrative temporality at that precise location. The final bonus is gaining access to the whole story of the protagonist and his analog belongings from the past.

3.2 Player Positioning in the Interaction Model

Chronica Mobilis integrates different levels of engagement that correspond to two reception conditions: contemplative and interactive. The contemplative audience does not interact but follows the game activity. Some audience members are in the exhibition space, while others watch streamed footage on the project website. They have a secondary and mediated experience of Poblenou, which comes in part from the data that street players generate as a result of their playing activity, and in part from the audiovisual fragments exhibited every time they manage to find a location. The videos of the embedded story are meant to be memories of a character, so they simulate a subjective view of situations he has lived through as they occurred in the past. It shows, from a first person perspective, the same physical locations in Poblenou in which the audience sees the players Fig. 3.

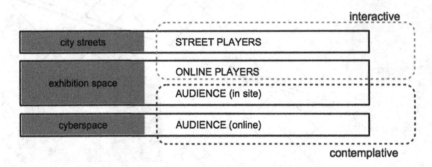

Fig. 3. Modes of engagement in *Chronica Mobilis*.

In contrast to the audience, players assume an interactive position and can either play inside or outside the exhibition space. The game's demand for collaborative strategies integrates the online and situated positioning of players. Both categories have to act as a coordinated team; communicating, sharing information and formulating their strategies using the technologies available to them. Collaboration is also relevant among the three teams of players, as the narrative embedded in the game works like a jigsaw puzzle with its parts assembled collaboratively by the work done by each group.

Those playing outside have a direct experience of Poblenou. On the other hand, online players experience a simulation of being in the streets, because they contribute to decisions regarding the destiny of their partners' exploration of the neighbourhood. They act to control street players' navigation as if they were directing an avatar. The mediated experience they have from the computer screen simulates a third person perspective of Poblenou.

4   Agency in the Construction of the Meaning

One of the major discussions in the game studies field regards the Ludology versus Narratology question, or whether these cultural forms possess a narrating instance [22–24]. *Chronica Mobilis* has a design devoted to exploiting the controversial interrelation of both traits. Working as a narrative of discovery [19], it combines two layers of meaning: a predefined and embedded story about gentrification and an emergent story based on the ludic exploration of the urban space.

The embedded story is a predefined narrative, whose plot follows the classic linear structure and the discourse organizes according to an interactive scheme. As a reward-based storytelling, it comes fragmented in the format of cut-scenes presented every time players complete a step-mission. Its fragments linked to sites in the city serves as a kind of treasure hunt that those engaged in the game will have to encounter. The game turns players into storytellers, giving form to the narrative discourse exhibited to the contemplative audience following their progress. Nevertheless, the playing activity does not restrict itself to the recounting of the events in this embedded narrative. The meaning does not come only from the scenes players collect through the city. The interaction model of *Chronica Mobilis* enhances the sense of personal control, allowing players to build a parallel story based on their performative playing activity. The range of strategic options given in the gameplay open space to rule-governed actions carried out by them [23]. They have the possibility of creating an emergent story that also possesses narrativity, as it contains some basic elements - actions, events, characters, and a setting - organized into a story-like order [24]. This narrative is not told but performed by players. Their actions within the game world are what depict the representational level [22].

They enact the story of archeologists of the future searching for invisible memories living under the visibility of Poblenou. This emergent storytelling, concurrent and complementary to the embedded one, is relatively unstructured, with unexpected and unscripted events and actions. It is dependent on the interaction with the built environment, thusly representing the neighborhood experienced and seen from the players' perspective. They control the storytelling by exploring the space, unlocking its secrets, and producing diversified layers of content: a psychogeographic map, messages and audiovisual content reporting the exploratory experience of the neighborhood. Players become authors and characters, agents and spectators, which live through and watch the gentrification phenomenon. They are expected to conclude their experience motivated by the retelling of the embedded narrative and that which they experienced in the streets. In both cases, the retelling includes critical thinking motivated by situated experiential learning.

5   Evaluation of Participants' Experience

Immediately after the presentation of *Chronica Mobilis*, participants completed a questionnaire with open-ended questions that served as an essential mechanism to the understanding of their experience. It allowed self-reporting in order to gather qualitative data about the different participation modes. The responses given by five street players, nine online players, and twenty-one audience members correspond to three levels: cognitive (feeling and satisfaction), system (technical, interaction and usability aspects), and content (story and discursive strategy).

Streets players qualified their experience employing adjectives, such as exciting, interesting and original. The sense of adventure in discovering the sites within the real city appeared as one of the recurrently referred aspects. Some mentioned how they felt responsible for the mission; others pointed to the amusing ludic dimension of running through the streets. They also commented how the atmosphere set for the game motivated and created a futuristic feeling for them. Nevertheless, some of the street players also complained of exhaustion caused by the physical effort required by their situated play activity. Concerning the narrative, the majority of the comments mentioned the emergent rather than the embedded story. They evaluated positively the feeling of agency, which was seen as an opportunity to freely create their own story based on the exploration of Poblenou. Wrote one participant: "It felt like being a documentary, reporter creator [sic]".

Online players reported the originality and the novelty as positive aspects influencing their experience. "Motivating", "exciting", "intriguing" were some of the adjectives employed by them. They evaluated the game activity as enjoyable, though they spent their time sitting in an enclosed space attached to a computer screen. Many of them justified the enjoyment, mentioning the game dynamics and its demand for collaborative strategies. Rather than commenting on the narrative content, online players referred more to the system level. They described positively the infrastructure, the presentation based on the combination of multiple sources, and the use of geolocation data. They also mentioned the accessible nature of the media employed, or the "easy technology" as one described. As a negative aspect, the main complaint also concerned the system level, especially the delay and inconsistency of the tracking system, which occurred due to the low bandwidth connection of the 3G network.

The audience members also considered the experience original and exciting. They emphasized the fun and ludic dimensions, even though they did not play any role in the game. "As the public, I did not expect to have so much fun. I believed that the players would enjoy more, but the public too [sic]", wrote an audience member. Another made associations with the memories of his childhood: "It was like being a child again in a game of discovering". Regarding the narrative, the most frequently mentioned aspect was the discursive strategy, or the manner in which they discovered the story. They referenced the interesting and important role of the gameplay for the storytelling act, or "the idea posed as a game", as one described it. Some of the audience members also praised the narrative content of the embedded story, by saying that it contained "very powerful memories", or mentioning "the poetry of the fiction". Regarding the emergent story, they emphasized how the enthusiasm of street players in their exploration of Poblenou had spread a vibrant energy through those following them, which was associated with the futuristic metaphor of the game. The negative aspects listed by the audience members referred mainly to the difficulty in following the different layers of content. They reported that sometimes the complex combination of different data sources resulted in confusion.

6 Conclusion

This paper focused on the field of pervasive games, investigating the potential for combining learning and playing activities to support reflection on serious issues in contemporary cities. The discussion anchored on *Chronica Mobilis*, a situated experience about gentrification, a controversial topic in urban planning. The authors detailed how this serious pervasive game draws attention to the Poblenou neighborhood and its sociopolitical and historical issues, by situating players in the center of a conflict.

The description included design decisions taken in the creative process; from the definition of the content and the manner chosen to geolocate it, to the game strategies created to generate motivation and engagement.

By unveiling the authoring process of *Chronica Mobilis*, the authors also explained how the game overcomes the Narratology vs. Ludology dilemma. They showed a scripting, design and implementation method, which integrates production and dissemination as roles to be actively and critically played in a location-aware process of co-creation. The paper presented experimental results based on the feedback given by players to support a better comprehension of their experience. Despite the importance of such findings, further investigation could be done to obtain a deeper evaluation of whether the playing experience did result in participants' critical thinking and willingness to engage in local issues. Future works based on such data could enrich the analysis of the potential of serious pervasive games in directing people to learn and reflect upon the urban space.

References

1. Shaffer, D.W., Squire, K.R., Halverson, R., Gee, J.P.: Video games and the future of learning. Phi Delta Kappan **87**(2), 105–111 (2005)
2. Gee, J.P.: Getting over the slump: innovation strategies to promote children's learning. The Joan Ganz Cooney Center at Sesame Workshop, New York (2008)
3. Smith, R.: Game impact theory: the five forces that are driving the adoption of game technologies within multiple established industries. Games Soc. Yearb. **1**, 1–32 (2007)
4. Susi, T., Johannesson, M., Backlund, P.: Serious Games – An overview School of Humanities and Informatics. University of Skövde, Sweden (2007)
5. Blythe, M.A., Wright, P.C.: Introduction: from usability to enjoyment. In: Blythe, M.A., Overbeeke, K., Monk, A.F., Wright, P.C. (eds.) Funology: From Usability to Enjoyment. Human-Computer Interaction Series, vol. 3, pp. 13–19. Klumer Academic Publishers, Dordrecht (2005)
6. Crawford, C.: The Art of Computer Game Design. McGraw-Hill/Osborne Media, Berkeley (1984)
7. Egenfeldt-Nielsen, S.: Beyond Edutainment: Exploring the Educational Potential of Computer Games. Lulu.com, Morrisville (2011)
8. Walther, B.K.: Pervasive game-play: theoretical reflection and classifications. In: Magerkurth, C., Röcker, C. (eds.) Concepts and Technologies for Pervasive Games – A Reader for Pervasive Gaming Research, vol. 1, pp. 67–90. Shaker Verlag, Leipzig (2007)
9. Poplin, A.: Playful public participation in urban planning: a case study for online serious games. Comput. Environ. Urban Syst. **36**(3), 195–206 (2012)
10. Lemos, A., Josgrilberg, F.: Comunicação e mobilidade. EDUFBA, Salvador (2009)
11. Wyly, E.: Gentrification. In: Short, J.R. (ed.) A Research Agenda for Cities, pp. 113–124. Edward Elgar Publishing, Massachusetts (2017)
12. Hight, J.: Narrative Archaeology: reading the landscape. In: 4th International Conference on Media in Transition, Massachussetts Institute of Technology. http://www.academia.edu/203311/narrative_archaeology
13. Debord, G.: Theory of the Dérive. In: Internationale Situationniste, vol. 2, pp. 50–54 (1958)

14. George, S., Serna, A.: Introducing mobility in serious games: enhancing situated and collaborative learning. In: Jacko, J.A. (ed.) HCI 2011. LNCS, vol. 6764, pp. 12–20. Springer, Heidelberg (2011). https://doi.org/10.1007/978-3-642-21619-0_2

15. Rooney, P.: A theoretical framework for serious game design: exploring pedagogy, play and fidelity and their implications for the design process. Int. J. Game-based Learn. 2(4), 41–60 (2012)

16. Pivec, M.: Editorial: Play and learn: potentials of game-based learning. Br. J. Educ. Tech. 38 (3), 387–393 (2007)

17. Salen, K., Zimmerman, E.: Rules of Play: Game Design Fundamentals. MIT Press, Cambridge (2004)

18. Malone, T.W., Lepper, M.R.: Making learning fun: a taxonomy of intrinsic motivations for learning. In: Snow, R.E., Farr, M.J. (eds.) Aptitude, Learning and Instruction, vol. 3, pp. 223–253. Lawrence Erlbaum, Mahwah (1987)

19. Prensky, M.: Digital Game-Based Learning. McGraw-Hill, New York (2001)

20. Jenkins, H.: Game design as narrative architecture. In: Harrington, P., Frup-Waldrop, N. (eds.) First Person, pp. 118–130. MIT Press, Cambridge (2002)

21. Csikszentmihalyi, M.: Flow: The Psychology of Optimal Performance. Cambridge University Press, Cambridge (1990)

22. Neitzel, B.: Narrativity in computer games. In: Raessens, J., Goldstein, J. (eds.) Handbook of Computer Game Studies, pp. 227–245. MIT Press, Cambridge (2005)

23. Aarseth, E.: Genre trouble: narrativism and the art of simulation. In: Wardrip-Fruin, N., Harrigan, P. (eds.) First Person: New Media as Story, Performance, and Game, pp. 45–55. MIT Press, Cambridge (2004)

24. Ryan, M.L.: Avatars of Story. University of Minnesota Press, Minneapolis (2006)

Deep Convolutional Generative Adversarial Network for Procedural 3D Landscape Generation Based on DEM

Andreas Wulff-Jensen, Niclas Nerup Rant,
Tobias Nordvig Møller(✉), and Jonas Aksel Billeskov

Department of Architecture, Design and Media Technology,
Aalborg University Copenhagen, AC Meyers Vænge 15,
2450 Copenhagen, SV, Denmark
awj@create.aau.dk, {nrant14, tnma14,
jbille14}@student.aau.dk

Abstract. This paper proposes a novel framework for improving procedural generation of 3D landscapes using machine learning. We utilized a Deep Convolutional Generative Adversarial Network (DC-GAN) to generate heightmaps. The network was trained on a dataset consisting of Digital Elevation Maps (DEM) of the alps. During map generation, the batch size and learning rate were optimized for the most efficient and satisfying map production. The diversity of the final output was tested against Perlin noise using Mean Square Error [1] and Structure Similarity Index [2]. Perlin noise is especially interesting as it has been used to generate game maps in previous productions [3, 4]. The diversity test showed the generated maps had a significantly greater diversity than the Perlin noise maps. Afterwards the heightmaps was converted to 3D maps in Unity3D. The 3D maps' perceived realism and videogame usability was pilot tested, showing a promising future for DC-GAN generated 3D landscapes.

Keywords: GAN · Deep Convolutional Generative Adversarial Network
PCG · Procedural generated landscapes · Digital Elevation Maps (DEM)
Heightmaps · Games · 3D landscapes

1 Introduction

A major part of videogames is the worlds the player can explore. These worlds establish the foundation of the games and set the mood for the gameplay. Over the years many different worlds have been created for games; from the small worlds of Age of Empires 3 [5] to the billions of planets created in No Man's Sky [3].

Each world has been created to suit the needs of the gameplay and constructed with techniques, which allow for such worlds to be made. Whether the game is set in space, the forest or in a medieval village, different techniques may prove useful for different situations. Some techniques may require a lot of man-hours for modeling and hand-crafting each hill and lake while others may require time to develop an algorithm to generate the maps for them (for examples see [6–9]).

© ICST Institute for Computer Sciences, Social Informatics and Telecommunications Engineering 2018
A. L. Brooks et al. (Eds.): ArtsIT 2017/DLI 2017, LNICST 229, pp. 85–94, 2018.
https://doi.org/10.1007/978-3-319-76908-0_9

With respect to the latter, this study aims to expand on the algorithms used by proposing the usage of a deep machine learning algorithm called Deep Convolutional Generative Adversarial Network (DC-GAN) [10] as the main framework for the map generation. An advantage of this framework compared to other procedural map generation algorithms is the wide and general applicability not commonly found in others [3, 7], as it can be trained to generate multiple different kinds of outputs with distinct features such as tundras, ravines and mountains not limited to one category. Potentially this could become a tool for game developers to generate landscapes faster and more customizable than unassisted procedural content generation. This method should be considered a combination between an unassisted and assisted method [11], where the developer can influence the output while still maintaining diversity and randomness, as it creates multiple landscape entities at ones, not obtainable by other experience-agnostic procedurally generated landscape solutions [12]. Furthermore, it goes beyond the popular idea of using Perlin noise [13, 14] or Digital Elevation Maps (DEMs) [15] as the basis for creating game maps (see for example Minecraft [4], No Man's Sky [3] and Cities: Skyline [16]), due to Perlin noise's popularity the diversity of the generated maps lacks variety, thus increasing the chance of a dull gaming experience. With respect to the DEM for some simulation games like Cities: Skyline it can be engrossing to work with a familiar environment, while in other games such as first person or third person games it can counteract the experience as the environments are not deviating as much.

2   DC-GAN and Its Previous Applications

In 2014 Ian Goodfellow et al. introduced the Generative Adversarial Networks (GANs). They were used to generate images that look photographically authentic compared to the training image dataset [17]. GANs are based on adversarial training, where two players learn from each other by pursuing conflicting goals. GAN consist of two neural networks, one called the generator and another called the discriminator. The discriminator's goal is to distinguish between the training data and the generated data, which is learned through traditional supervised learning. The goal for the generator's is to generate images, which are similar to real images such that the discriminator network cannot tell them apart from the real data. Thus, enabling the generator to learn through reinforcement learning. This method makes the two networks compete against each other thus constantly improving the other's abilities. The overall goal of the GAN is to generate images that look like the images from the training dataset to a point where the discriminator is not able to tell whether the image is real or fake. In theory, this process of continuously producing more realistic images will continue until the goal is reached. This competition is also called a min-max game or zero-sum game [18], where each adversary is trying to minimize its own loss in worst case scenario.

With respect to the functions and architectures of the networks. The discriminator is a four-layer deep convolutional network with ReLu activation functions. It is represented by a differentiable function D and training data x. x is convoluted from start input of 64X64X3 through the network to 4X4X512 feature maps, which is fully connected to a single output neuron [10]. This neuron determines if the input is a generated image $D(x) = 0$ or an image from the dataset $D(x) = 1$. Therefore, will the discriminator try to do the following for the input data: maximize D(x) for every image from the training data distribution, and minimize D(x) for every image generated by the generator.

The generator, on the other hand, is a deconvolution network embedded with ReLu activation functions. It starts with a random vector z of 100 values. This vector is sent through a four-layered deep deconvolutional network ending with a 64X64X3 image. The generator is represented by a differentiable function G. G(x) has the reverse goals of D(x), meaning it tries to minimize D(x) for every image from the training data distribution, and maximize D(x) for every image generated by the generator [18].

The presented GAN network has been trained on a multitude of generation problems with different degrees of success. Lotter et al. [19], used GAN to predict the next frame in a simple head rotation animation. However, multiple models were used to create sharp output images, as a single GAN tended to blur eyes and ears. Ledig et al. [20] later demonstrates that a modified GAN can recover a low-resolution image to its high-resolution stage, due to its ability to generate multiple right answers compared to other tested algorithms. Zhu et al. [21] created an interactive GAN application in which the user can draw. Afterwards the machine converts the drawing to a detailed realistic photo. A similar application was created by Brock et al. [22]. In this application GAN was used to interpret rough sketch modifications edited unto a realistic image, and convert it to the realistic counterpart. The interpretation and conversion between sketch and realism have been used by Isola et al. [23] as well. They have trained GAN to convert satellite images to sketches and sketches of, for example bags, to realistic looking bags. Lastly, Zhang et al. and Reed et al.

[22–24] have achieved to create multiple images based on text description. However, the usual GAN did not create as diverse output as wished, but a modified version called StackGAN corrected this problem.

The investigated studies all showcases perfect examples of how a well-trained and adjusted GAN can work. Some of the problems being harder than others, for instance the interactive GANs seems to be harder, as they may require a big database within their core to be able to guess rather accurately what the user tries to draw. While on the opposite side of the spectrum there is the GAN, which presumably only has been trained with a limited number of images to be able to create for instance a high-resolution image based on the low-resolution input.

Furthermore, a challenging problem faced by [18] is the task of creating animals based on classes from ImageNet [27]. Through this training the GAN created distorted abominations with wrong amounts of different limbs and even concatenations of different creatures. Thus, showcasing one of the limits of GAN.

3 Data Collection for Map Generation

Through the review of how the GAN works and with what it has been utilized, it is certain that to create diverse, but still realistic game maps we need a dataset with the same, yet diversely utilized set of features. Such dataset can for instance be found in heightmaps like DEMs, which is contained within a database called viewfinder-panoramas [15]. In this database the Alps and Norway was chosen, as they have different slopes, attitudes and mountain types. The Norway dataset set was later discarded, because it contains coastlines, which initiated oddly placed lakes in the generated maps, thus reducing the realism of the generated maps. The database from the Alps was sampled into 360,000 images using a program called Auto Hotkey, which was employed to automatically take screenshots of different areas of the Alps. Every 3 s an image of a random location of the Alps was taken, then sliced into 9 smaller pieces to fit the 64X64 entry space of the Discriminator. The process lasted 30 h (an example of the DEM screenshots can be found in Fig. 1).

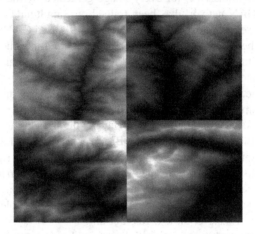

Fig. 1. Example of images scraped from DEMs

4   Evaluations

To evaluate and optimize the system three different methodologies have been employed. The focus of the first is to optimize the network, while the second and third concentrates on objective and subjective parameters of the generated maps.

4.1   Optimizing the Network

The network has different hyper parameters which can be adjusted to make the network perform better or worse with different advantages and disadvantages. The two parameters we will look at are batch size (BS) and learning rate (LR). BS being how many data samples the network is fed with before updating the weights inside the system. LR is how big of a step the gradient decent moves at each learning epoch. Too big BS can result in having too little data to train with, thus the network will never learn correctly. While too little BS could lead to overfitting. The LR can be adjusted to make the system learn faster with a big LR, but at the cost of missing the global minimum. With a small LR, the network will take long time to learn and to even reach a minimum, which unfortunately is likely to be the local minimum.

The evaluation will evaluate three different BSs (16, 64 and 256) and Three different LRs (0.002, 0.0002 and 0.00002). The most optimized network will be the one reaching a satisfying result with the fewest number of epochs, showcasing an output least influenced by repetitive noise patterns.

4.2 Diversity Evaluation

For the objective measuring method, diversity tests between the generated maps and Perlin Noise will be conducted. The diversity is accessible through two image processing algorithms, Mean Square Error (MSE) and Structured Similarity Index (SSIM). MSE has previously been used to estimate the similarity of the pixel intensity between an original image and a distorted image [1]. Therefore, it can be valid to use to measure the difference, thus diversity between two images within a dataset. SSIM goes beyond intensity and investigates the difference in luminance, contrast and structure, by running a kernel through the images we want to compare. Thus, comparing smaller subsets at a time instead of the whole image [2]. The SSIM will allow for a closer inspection of the diversity.

From both tests the diversity within the images datasets will be established. The greater the MSE value the more difference does exist between the images in the sample sets. The smaller SSIM value the greater are the differences between the images.

4.3 Preliminary Usability Test

While the other evaluations focus on how to improve the system and to access the diversity of generated images, a small usability test is needed to test for the aesthetics, traversability and realism of the game maps. Seeing the maps are still heightmaps, thereby not usable to explore in game settings. We will use Unity3D to convert the heightmaps to 3D landscapes with preliminary texturing using Unity's built-in terrain tool. For the test, we will recruit a small sample of participants. Each will spend five minutes walking around three of the generated maps. Afterwards, they will be asked eight questions:

1. Does the map look realistic to you?
2. How does this landscape compare to other video games you have played?
3. How was the landscapes' traversability?
4. How did you feel about the diversity of the landscapes?
5. Does the map look like something you would see in the real world?
6. What kind of game do you see these maps being in?
7. What landscape from the real world does the maps remind you off?
8. Do you have any general comments or suggestions for further implementations?

With question 1, 4, 5, and 7 we wish to evaluate the realism of the generated landscapes, as they are derived from a dataset based on the real world.

Question 2, 6, and 8 examines the usability and in which situation the user could see these maps be used in, and at the same time understand if they have any comments or suggestions for improvements.

At last question 3 is about how well the user could traverse in the landscape without getting frustrated or felt like they exploited the physics.

5 Results

5.1 Optimizing the Network

For all the batch sizes, a progressive improvement of the output based on the steadily increasing number of epochs can be seen (see Fig. 2).

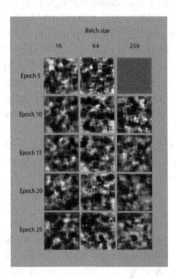 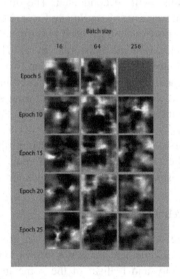

Fig. 2. Output from 3 different batch sizes, through 5 different epochs and 2 different sized images from the Alps dataset

The batch size 16 learned quicker, as the noise is non-visible already in the early epochs. The images look sharper compared to those with batch size of respectively 64 and 256 as they look blurred. Furthermore, the noise is still a bit visible even in the last epoch for batch size 64 and 256. This observation could indicate that the networks need more epochs or more training data to train properly, as some of the noise from the z vector is still persistence. From the 10th epoch the 16-batch size network seems to generate noise free inputs, which compared to the other network witnesses that increasing the batch size seems to only worsen the output. Additionally, at the 5th epoch the batch size of 256 showed no learning at all, as it only shows noise, while the other two have already learned the initial steps towards creating a heightmap. Given the current dataset this evaluation indicates, that a batch size of 16 gives the best possible output.

To further optimize the output the next step is to change the learning rate to see if the previous results can be improved. The results for changing the learning rate, from the default value of 0.0002 to respectively 0.002 and 0.00002, showed no improvements. The results got significantly worse when it was set to 0.002, where the network did not learn at all and continued to generate noise. When the learning rate was set to 0.00002 the network learned, but the final output was worse than the original. Thereby, it was chosen to work with the following hyper parameters: Learning rate: 0.0002. Batch size: 16.

5.2 Diversity Evaluation

The diversity tests' results found in Table 1 are derived from 10000 comparisons between either 500 generated images or 500 Perlin noise images, in which it was ensured that the same two images were not compared twice.

Table 1. Shows the descriptive results of both diversity tests. PN = Perlin Noise, GAN = Generated heightmaps from the GAN network.

	PN - SSIM	GAN - SSIM	PN - MSE	GAN - MSE
Mean	0,7247	0,3109	2829,2957	6021,6372
Median	0,7260	0,3106	2739,2960	6002,5174
SD	0,0241	0,00306	788,5848	706,6115
SE	0,0007617	0,00066779	7,8858	7,0661

Descriptively it is evident that there is a higher degree of diversity within the generated image dataset compared to the Perlin noise dataset. MSE mean GAN > PN and SSIM mean GAN < PN. Statistically this observation is well supported through the Wilcoxon Ranked Sum test which showed p = 0 thus $p < 0.05$, and a H-value = 1. A parametric test could not be utilized as an Anderson Darling test showed that neither of the result datasets were normally distributed.

5.3 Preliminary Usability Test

For this test three students, 1 female and 2 males, were recruited. The feedback from those were positive in terms of realism. Generally, the participants could relate the landscape to real world settings, and thought in general that the landscapes looked like something from the real world (an example of the landscape can be found in Fig. 3). The diversity in the heightmaps, was noticed, but not apparent. Another positive thing was the traversability of the landscape, as all the participants found it easy to traverse.

Fig. 3. One of the final landscapes implemented in Unity, which was shown to the participants in the third test.

The textures in the landscape were roughly implemented, and even though the participants were told to focus on the height of the landscape, the participants had difficulties with excluding the textures in their judgement - both in terms of realism and diversity. This indicates that both parameters cannot be fully satisfied without proper texturing as it goes hand in hand with the landscapes.

6 Discussion

The results from the three tests showed both the possibility to create diverse height-maps and make them usable within the context of games. However, the diversity measures could be questionable, as they are based on pixel value comparisons. This could unintentionally have inflated the test results to show more diversity, than what is real. Another measure to go beyond the per pixel or group of pixels comparison could be through considering the frequency domain and compare the frequency distribution between the images. This will in turn showcase where on the spectrum, and thus which level of detail there are mostly diverse within the group of images. Nevertheless, it is subject for another study. For this paper and the chosen algorithms, it can be justified that on the pixel level the datasets are significantly different from each other.

With respect to the third test the diversity between the landscapes and the texturing were questionable. Even though, there was only 3 subjects in the test these factors were clear drawbacks. The observation nicely illustrates, that isolating the heightmaps of a terrain from textures and other aesthetic elements is hard for the user, thus showing that all of it is intertwined. By further developing the textures of the terrain and add a procedural content generator to create trees, grass and rocks would highly enhance the aesthetic appreciation of the landscapes, and thus heightening their perceived usability. The texture of a future development could be developed by the GAN as well. Seeing that the heightmaps are based on real world photos, the same locations can be found on Google Earth. By training the GAN with the Google Earth images, the output images can be used as basis for the textures. This improvement will make the texture creation more automatic and possibly with greater diversity compared to the textures used by the terrain editor in Unity. Furthermore, a test with just 3 participants are proven to be biased, as it can rarely be replicated, but such small preliminary test can give valuable guidelines without giving the full solid picture. A last remark we want to discuss is the network it-self and its hyperparameters. Through the test we saw that a batch size of 16 was most efficient in producing the best results. However, it is still questionable if a lower batch size with our dataset could have improved the network even further, or if the batch size of 16 is the most optimal. Another thing is the learning rate, which performed best at 0.0002. With respect to this and the conducted tests a more efficient network could possibly be found if the learning rate was only slightly adjusted either up or down compared to the big steps to 0.002 or 0.00002.

7   Conclusion

The focus of this study was to investigate the usability of a deep convolutional generative adversarial network to generate 3D landscapes for video games, which could challenge conventional methods of game map generation. We attempted solving this problem by proposing a novel pipeline, using DEMs gathered from the Alps as a dataset for a Torch implementation of a DC-GAN. Afterwards the generated heightmaps were used in Unity to create 3D landscapes. Through the study three different evaluation of the product was conducted. One testing the optimization of the networks, one testing the diversity of the output, and one qualitative test for general feedback and realism of the landscapes. The first test showed good results when lowering the batch size to 16 with a learning rate of 0.0002. The second test showed greater diversity within the generated heightmaps compared to Perlin noise maps. The third test gave mixed results as the test participants had a hard time excluding the textures from their perception of the landscapes, but overall thought the landscapes were easy to traverse and looked like landscapes from areas in the real world. Combined, all the tests showed an ability to create functional landscapes based on real world areas. We believe that our attempt to use machine learning to generate maps for video games was overall successful, and can in fact challenge the use of Perlin noise for map generation. Furthermore, there is basis for continued research and experimentation in this area of machine learning and procedural generation.

Exploring the use of DCGAN's applications with procedurally generated landscapes could lead to more interesting possibilities including but not limited to combining landscapes, generating buildings and fauna, adding lakes or oceans and generating textures, which in the future could be done interactively e.g. [21–23] and be implemented to create game maps on the fly or endless terrains wherever a user moves.

References

1. Wang, Z., Bovik, A.C.: Mean squared error: love it or leave it? IEEE Sig. Process. Mag. **26**, 98–117 (2009). https://doi.org/10.1109/MSP.2008.930649
2. Wang, Z., Bovik, A.C., Sheikh, H.R., Simoncelli, E.P.: Image quality assessment: from error visibility to structural similarity. IEEE Trans. Image Process. **13**, 600–612 (2004). https://doi.org/10.1109/TIP.2003.819861
3. Cook, M.: We've Run Out of Planets - Procedural Generation After No Man's Sky. Cut Garnet Games (2016)
4. Mojang, A.B.: Minecraft. Stockholm, Sweden (2013)
5. Microsoft: Age Of Empires III. Microsoft, Redmond (2013)
6. Yannakakis, G.N., Togelius, J.: Experience-driven procedural content generation. IEEE Trans. Affect. Comput. **2**, 147–161 (2011)
7. Togelius, J., Preuss, M.: Towards multiobjective procedural map generation
8. Shaker, N., Asteriadis, S., Yannakakis, G.N., Karpouzis, K.: Fusing visual and behavioral cues for modeling user experience in games. IEEE Trans. Cybern. **43**, 1519–1531 (2013). https://doi.org/10.1109/TCYB.2013.2271738

9. Shaker, N., Togelius, J., Nelson, M.J.: Procedural Content Generation in Games: A Textbook and an Overview of Current Research. Springer, Berlin (2014). https://doi.org/10.1007/978-3-319-42716-4
10. Brandon, A.: Image completion with deep learning in TensorFlow. GitHub (2016)
11. De Carli, D.M., Bevilacqua, F., Pozzer, C.T., Cordeiro D'Ornellas, M.: A survey of procedural content generation techniques suitable to game development. In: Brazilian Symposium on Games and Digital Entertainment, SBGAMES, pp. 26–35 (2011). https://doi.org/10.1109/sbgames.2011.15
12. Yannakakis, G.N., Togeliu, J.: Artificial Intelligence and Games (First Public Draft) (2017)
13. Perlin, K.: Improving noise. In: Proceedings of the 29th Annual Conference on Computer Graphics and Interactive Techniques, SIGGRAPH 2002, p. 681 (2002). https://doi.org/10.1145/566570.566636
14. Rose, T.J., Bakaoukas, A.G.: Algorithms and approaches for procedural terrain generation. In: 2016 8th International Conference on Games and Virtual Worlds for Serious Applications, VS-Games 2016, pp. 4–5 (2016). https://doi.org/10.1109/vs-games.2016.7590336
15. De Ferranti, J.: Viewfinder Panoramas (2012)
16. Paradox Interactive: Cities: Skyline. Paradox Interactive. Stockholm, Sweden (2015)
17. Goodfellow, I., Pouget-Abadie, J., Mirza, M., Xu, B., Warde-Farley, D., Ozair, S., Courville, A., Bengio, Y.: Generative Adversarial Networks, pp. 1–9. (2014). https://doi.org/10.1001/jamainternmed.2016.8245
18. Goodfellow, I.: NIPS 2016 Tutorial: Generative Adversarial Networks (2016). https://doi.org/10.1001/jamainternmed.2016.8245
19. Lotter, W., Kreiman, G., Cox, D.: Unsupervised learning of visual structure using predictive generative networks, pp. 1–12 (2016). https://doi.org/10.1109/iccv.2015.465
20. Ledig, C., Theis, L., Huszar, F., Caballero, J., Cunningham, A., Acosta, A., Aitken, A., et al.: Photo-realistic single image super-resolution using a generative adversarial network (2016)
21. Zhu, J.-Y., Krähenbühl, P., Shechtman, E., Efros, A.A.: Generative visual manipulation on the natural image manifold. In: Leibe, B., Matas, J., Sebe, N., Welling, M. (eds.) ECCV 2016. LNCS, vol. 9909, pp. 597–613. Springer, Cham (2016). https://doi.org/10.1007/978-3-319-46454-1_36
22. Brock, A., Lim, T., Ritchie, J.M., Weston, N.: Neural photo editing with introspective adversarial networks (2016). https://doi.org/10.1177/1470320311410924
23. Isola, P., Zhu, J.-Y., Zhou, T., Efros, A.A.: Image-to-image translation with conditional adversarial networks (2016)
24. Zhang, H., Xu, T., Li, H., Zhang, S., Huang, X., Wang, X., Metaxas, D.: StackGAN: text to photo-realistic image synthesis with stacked generative adversarial networks (2016)
25. Reed, S., Akata, Z., Yan, X., Logeswaran, L., Schiele, B., Lee, H.: Generative adversarial text to image synthesis (2016)
26. Reed, S., van den Oord, A., Kalchbrenner, N., Bapst, V., Botvinick, M., deFreitas, N.: Generating interpretable images with controllable structure. In: ICLR 2017, pp. 1–12 (2016)
27. Krizhevsky, A.: Learning Multiple Layers of Features from Tiny Images. Technical report, Science Department, University of Toronto, pp. 1–60 (2009). 10.1.1.222.9220

Real Time Evaluation of Education Methods via Smart Mobile Technology

George Tsamis[1(✉)], Nikos Papadakis[1], Evangelos Tzirakis[1],
Evi Katsaraki[2], Maria Rousaki[1], John Nikolopoulos[3],
and Kostas Vassilakis[1]

[1] Technological Educational Institute of Crete, 71410 Heraklion, Greece
{gtsamis,npapadak,kostas}@cs.teicrete.gr,
vagelis.tzirakis@gmail.com, mrousaki@windowslive.com
[2] University of Crete, 70013 Heraklion, Greece
evi_katsaraki@hotmail.com
[3] Pointnet, 71409 Heraklion, Greece
jnikolop@pointnet.gr

Abstract. We design, implement and evaluate performance of Exantas application which is compatible with Android Operating Systems Smartphone devices. As Exantas tool was able to show ancients travelers the correct route to follow we show that our application can help educational staff to improve their skills and evaluate on the fly how efficient is the educational style that they follow. Results can help teachers measure while teaching how much of the lessons content has been successfully absorbed by students and what are the topics that need further analysis or even a completely new explanation approach. As experiments show, Exantas is able to reduce teaching efforts and to reveal real lessons comprehension status since Teachers can make multiple Questions to all students and receive answers in seconds. Moreover, all answers are processed anonymously ensuring anonymity and integrity since students are not afraid to provide their actual answer.

Keywords: Android · Application · Real time · Education methods
Evaluation

1 Introduction

In the student-centered environment, emphasis is placed on the student's previous knowledge and skills rather than on the teacher's. According to diagnostic teaching, students try to discover their beliefs and their misunderstandings about a problem [1] rather than teachers try to improve their teaching methods or techniques. As Vygotsky (1978) claimed, the active role of students is very important during teaching. An issue supported by his bigger idea, that children grow into the intellectual life of those around them (teachers included).

Nowadays, it is very important every teacher to know the background of students during teaching. This fact could reduce teaching effort, because he is able to adapt his education method depending on the needs of his students. Furthermore, teacher can

© ICST Institute for Computer Sciences, Social Informatics and Telecommunications Engineering 2018
A. L. Brooks et al. (Eds.): ArtsIT 2017/DLI 2017, LNICST 229, pp. 95–104, 2018.
https://doi.org/10.1007/978-3-319-76908-0_10

locate possible misconceptions of students and explain again topics that students didn't fully and clearly understand. Using this approach, instructor can help the procedure of correctly modifying the students' perspective, based on the fact that knowledge can be considered as a building in which each store is supported by its previous one.

More specifically, knowledge transfer is based on the cognitive background of each student and on the collaborative learning. Each transfer either simple or complex can lead to a negative or positive outcome. This means that teachers should ensure that knowledge transfer has a positive impact on students [2] and is successive. An issue that is pointed out in this work [3].

Nowadays, the educational science provides a variety of educational methods and mechanisms for more effective teaching procedures. This is why, all teachers should evaluate and apply the suitable education method for them.

Every method's evaluation takes place through appropriate research tools or applications. For this reason, the paper presents a useful, adaptive application through which the educational method will be evaluated in real time. According to principles of learning and understanding, evaluation should take place continuously during teaching and inform teacher, pupils and parents about students' cognitive level [1].

There are many different methods that can be used for learning [4]. They measure the effectiveness and satisfaction on the student's side and ignore Teachers skill. Moreover, as previous research has shown, students found the use of an electronic device to be more satisfying and attractive for teaching purposes that conventional means [5, 6]. Last but not least, research [7–10] has verified that concerning university students, more than 96% of them makes use of real time communication, 89% uses internet to search for information and 86% of them owns at least one smartphone device which they always carry. In addition, research found that there was no statistical difference between males and females or among student age. Therefore, we introduce Exantas, an education assisting application for Android smartphone devices.

The rest of this paper is structured as follows: In Sect. 2, we present the implemented user interface of the application. In Sect. 3, we briefly describe the entity – relationship model of the database. In Sect. 4, we describe the experimental results. Finally, in Sect. 5, concludes this paper and presents directions for future work.

2 Application Design and Implementation

Application core functionality is a mix of different but necessary technologies such as PHP, MySQL, SQLite, MPAndroidChart (A powerful Android chart view/graph view library), Volley (used to make HTTP calls library). Notice that in order to operate successfully Exantas application is demanding a Wi-Fi or 3G connection which means that user must provide device hardware access and Internet permissions.

In order to establish communication with the server side applications (which hold registering data and all results from all available researches) and complete a correct and safe interaction with MySQL database we need to implement some functionalities

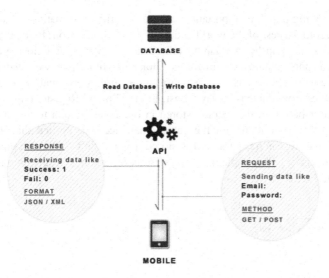

Fig. 1. Database communication mechanism

which are necessary. This mechanism will be able to respond into requests initiated by users, make SQL transactions with existing dedicated database to our application and finally forward results back to the specific user.

As Fig. 1 shows our server accepts requests using GET, POST methods. On server php files are able to communicate with database and make insertion or retrieve data which are forwarded back to the user in JSON format.

2.1 Researcher Identification and Registration

In details, previously mentioned database communication mechanism involves the following when an already registered teacher is asking for identification or a new one is asking for a new account creation (notice that teachers are considered to be Researchers by the application since they are conducting a survey). On the server 5 files are waiting for a request to arrive (Table 1).

Table 1. Server side content.

File name	Internal operation
Config.php	Contains necessary data to connect to MySQL database
DB_Connet.php	Able to successfully establish a database connection
DB_Functions.php	All functions that are necessary to manage MySQL database content
Login.php	Able to identify a registered user
Register.php	Responsible for a new user registration

On the Config.php file important database security information is stored which must be secret to the rest of the world and can be called only from Exantas application. On the DB_Connet.php file we handle safe database opening and closing connection. DB_Functions.php contains all functions implementations that we need in order to communicate with the database e.g. new user insert, user's information receive, update or delete entries from database arrays. Last, Login.php and Register.php files are used to identify user based on the records stored in our database and to add a new one if there is no other user matching the same email account. Notice that all sensitive information like Researcher password is stored using 128bit AES encryption ensuring safety and integrity. The implemented interface for login or registration activity is shown in the Fig. 2.

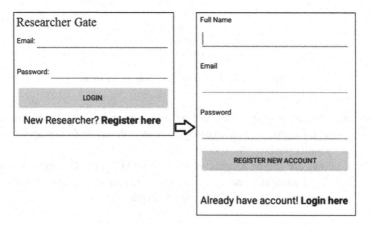

Fig. 2. Login and register activity interface

2.2   Selecting a Specific Research from Database

Each research is described by a unique ResearchID or a QR code which contains the ResearchID in a computer accessible form. Application users (considered as Voters by the database) can either insert the ResearchID by typing it, using device keyboard, or by scanning a figure of QR code which is generated by our application. This approach makes specific Research choosing process easier for users and reduces human error possibility since all procedures are made as automatic as possible. Android compatible zxing library is used to generate and parse two dimensional barcode and its core functionality is included inside app package and there is no need for external software installation. If a correct ResearchID has been provided then VotingActivity is called and a request is raised for a specific research content. Otherwise, user is informed that given research ID does not corresponds to an existing research and is asked to retry to select a specific ID (Fig. 3).

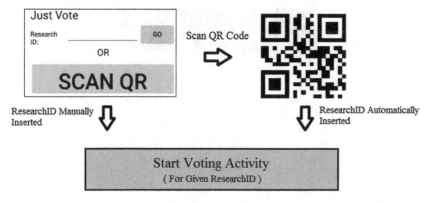

Fig. 3. ResearchID selection procedure

QR code (Quick Response Code) [11], is the trademark for a type of matrix barcode (two-dimensional barcode) first designed for the automotive industry in Japan. The QR code consists of black squares arranged in a square grid on a white background and can be easily scanned by smartphones camera or other image input hardware. Encoded data can be extracted from patterns that are present in both horizontal and vertical components of the image. Internal information translating mechanism provides even error correction features ensuring data transfer correctness. Its main benefit is that it offers an easy machine readable barcode reading mechanism which can efficiently store content using four standardized encoding modes (numeric, alphanumeric, byte/binary, and kanji). QR representation has become very popular nowadays even outside of the automotive industry which was initially designed for, since it offers an easy way to transport data between different platforms which might otherwise be incompatible.

2.3 Creating or Improving a Research

Every Researcher is able to create one or more Researches, or different instances of the same Research. On the other hand Researcher should be able to make important editions if necessary. For each one of them, as shown in the Fig. 4, the system is requiring a Research Title which will be the same for all included Queries that Researcher will provided in next steps. After that Researcher is asked to insert for each Query the Question that will be asked to users, all possible Answers that will be shown and finally mark the correct answer so that system can automatically and correctly cross-check between the correct answer and all answers provided by users. Notice that application is able to consider more than one of the answers as correct if Researcher is demanding it, achieving higher rates of flexibility. Navigation between Queries is supported through Previous and Next buttons. Finally, research is saved in database when Finalize button is pressed.

Fig. 4. Create or edit research interface

2.4   Monitoring Research Results

Making use of MPAndroidChart library users answers that are stored in database can be retrieved, processed and visualized in a human friendly interface. In this way, Researcher reduces effort and saves important time which can be better consumed in data mining and information extraction. Collected data can be extracted and stored locally for further examination.

Except the fact that Researcher can monitor the amount of correct and wrong answers for each Query three main visualization approaches are provided by Exantas application in its current version. First one, provides information about the amount of Correct and Wrong Answers per Question and the ability to measure how many users have selected each Answer making use of Pie and Bar charts as Fig. 5 shows in case (a) and (b). In second one, Researchers can observe how many correct Answers have been counted in each Query. Based on this feature, which is presented in case (c), important and critical information can be quickly extracted about where there are spots of misunderstanding or need of further explanation since e.g. presentation audience has failed to answer in many Questions that are related to each other. In third and last visualization technique, as shown in case (d), Researcher can monitor the average time duration of users spent during voting activity, realizing in this way the difficulty of Queries.

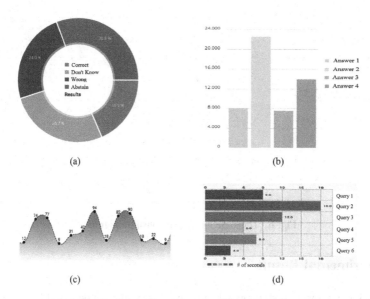

Fig. 5. Research results visualization interface

2.5 Voting Activity

Implemented voting interface looks a lot like Research Creation Activity in a more minimalistic version. In this case we have tried to make Voting Activity as simple as possible since as we all know users get tired or confused very easily. Users are free to choose one or multiple number of Answers and are informed only at the last step that they answered correctly in e.g. 5/8 (five correct Answers out of eight Queries). Using asynchronous communication Exantas database is informed for each selected Answer of any user. Notice that if Internet access is not present or connection is temporally interrupted application will not allow user to answer any Query ensuring information integrity.

3 Database Implementation

The Entity Relationship model shown in Fig. 6 describes basic Entities, Relationships and Cardinality. Implementation is using a MySQL database on a Linux operating system server platform. In details, our implantation of Exantas database has as primary object the Researcher which means that all stored information belong to at least one Researcher and without him database can't retrieve information from users. One Researcher can create one or more Researches. Each research has a Title which helps a lot distinguishing different database entries and can contain multiple numbers of Queries, and each Query is referencing a variable number of Answers. Last, Results Entity contains information selected from all users that have participated in our Research.

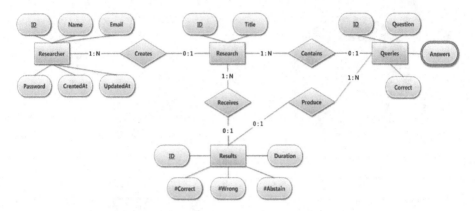

Fig. 6. Database entity relationship diagram

4   Experimental Results

As we all know almost all students when asked if they have understand lecture content they answer positively or ignore question. Measuring the results of this experiment when Exantas application is used we saw that reality differs from students' previous answer. As Fig. 7 shows when this scenario is used in a classroom of 20 random students $\sim$70% to $\sim$85% believed that they have correctly understood topics stated in the presentation when asked from teacher. Results extracted from Exantas app revealed that actually only $\sim$40% to $\sim$60% have in fact understood presentation content and making use of this information teacher had to repeat certain sections and explain again questions that student failed to answer.

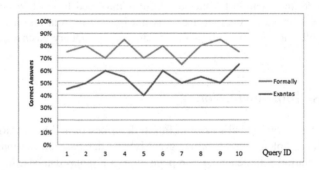

Fig. 7. Queries results asked from teacher versus Exantas

Continuing and extending the previous scenario, as Fig. 8 shows, we measured the amount of correct answers after each time that teacher was using Exantas app on the same package of Queries. Results show that student answers are getting better each time achieving a maximum rate of almost 90% correct answers starting from $\sim$45%. Doubling the amount of correct answers is not something easy but Exantas application can help significantly.

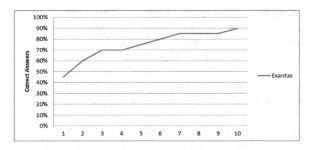

Fig. 8. Amount of correct answers when teacher consults Exantas app

5 Conclusions and Future Work

We designed and implement Exantas application, a fully functional education assisting algorithm, compatible with Android OS, which is able in real time to provide important anonymous information to Queries stated by Teachers or Professors in order to test their teaching methods, measure students' misconceptions and reveal their perspectives. As experiments show, Teachers can significantly improve their skills and avoid time or effort spending procedures.

As a future work we are planning to redesign application in a more functional and user friendly interface providing the necessary internal mechanism to self-adapt Queries content based on previous answers provided by users.

Moreover, we plan to perform performance evaluation and test the limits of the complete chain of dataflow using many simultaneous users answering on the same or not Research ensuring at the end the so cold quality of service.

We are also working on a more simplistic mechanism which implements all basics core functionalities but can be used not only for academic purposes but also for industrial or marketing purposes. Last but not least, porting the algorithm in other platforms such us iOS is considered to be a critical and essential step as well as releasing new and stable version in Google Play Platform and making it available to anyone.

References

1. National Research Council: How People Learn: Brain, Mind, Experience, and School, Expanded edn. National Academies Press, Washington (2000)
2. Abachi, H.R., Muhammad, G.: The impact of m-learning technology on students and educators. Comput. Hum. Behav. **30**, 491–496 (2014)
3. Taspinar Sener, Z., Una, H., Aydin, H.: Using metaphors to investigate pre-service secondary mathematics teachers' perceptions of mathematics and mathematics teacher concepts. Anthropologist **23**(1–2), 291–302 (2016)
4. Furió, D., Juan, M.C., Seguí, I., Vivó, R.: Mobile learning vs. traditional classroom lessons: a comparative study. J. Comput. Assist. Learn. **31**(3), 189–201 (2015)

5. Luckin, R., Clark, W., Avramides, K., Hunter, J., Oliver, M.: Using teacher inquiry to support technology-enhanced formative assessment: a review of the literature to inform a new method. Interact. Learn. Env. **25**(1), 85–97 (2017)
6. Nam, S.Z.: Evaluation of university students' utilization of smartphone. Int. J. Smart Home **7** (4), 175–182 (2013)
7. Paige, K., Bentley, B., Dobson, S.: Slowmation: an innovative twenty-first century teaching and learning tool for science and mathematics pre-service teachers. Aust. J. Teacher Educ. **41**(2), 1–15 (2016)
8. Shi, Y., Qin, W., Suo, Y., Xiao, X.: Smart classroom: bringing pervasive computing into distance learning. In: Nakashima, H., Aghajan, H., Augusto, J.C. (eds.) Handbook of ambient intelligence and smart environments, pp. 881–910. Springer, Boston (2010). https://doi.org/10.1007/978-0-387-93808-0_33
9. Sun, J.C.Y.: Influence of polling technologies on student engagement: an analysis of student motivation, academic performance, and brainwave data. Comput. Educ. **72**, 80–89 (2014)
10. Zheng, B., Warschauer, M., Lin, C.H., Chang, C.: Learning in one-to-one laptop environments: a meta-analysis and research synthesis. Rev. Educ. Res. **20**(10), 1–33 (2016)
11. Soon, T.J.: QR code. Synth. J. **2008**, 59–78 (2008)

In-Store Shopping Experience Enhancement: Designing a Physical Object-Recognition Interactive Renderer

Jianze Li[1,2], Jun Liu[3], and Stephen Jia Wang[1,4(✉)]

[1] School of Design, Royal College of Art, Kensington Gore, Kensington,
London SW7 2EU, UK
stephen.wang@rca.ac.uk
[2] Department of Design, Faculty of Art Design & Architecture,
Monash University, Melbourne, VIC 3145, Australia
[3] Academy of Arts and Media, China University of Geosciences, Wuhan, China
[4] International Tangible Interaction Design Lab, Monash University,
Melbourne, Caulfield, VIC 3145, Australia

Abstract. Following the rapid spread of online-shopping services on both internet and smart devices, the traditional way of promoting and trading in physical retail stores has been challenged. To increase sales, retailers have spent an enormous amount of resources to maintain the attractions of 'traditional' physical store in a digital shopping behaviour dominated world. Unfortunately, the outcome leaves much to be desired.

This study discusses the need of such hybrid-shopping style through an integrated process of customer investigation, observation and user testing. This paper using footwear shopping as a case study. The authors proposed an inventive installation to re-strengthen the inter-connections among customers, products and retailers using physical object recognition and 3D projection mapping technologies. This interactive installation allows customers to personalize their preferences through manipulating the physical products with Augmented Reality (AR) rendering effects. Furthermore, this system also provides an alternative solution to reform the product-promotion and production progress. This design can be applied to the promotion of many other kind of products.

Keywords: Innovative design · Interaction design · Experience design
Shopping behaviour · Physical component recognition · Projection mapping
Tangible interactivity

1 Introduction

Due to the rapid development of on-line shopping for nearly two decades, the consumers' shopping behaviour has been fundamentally changed. When thinking of shopping, the first action most people would take is to browse the shopping item(s) online, browse the reviews, compare the prices, and often may even purchase the item(s) through the internet. Certainly, such online shopping behaviour is the direct consequence

© ICST Institute for Computer Sciences, Social Informatics and Telecommunications Engineering 2018
A. L. Brooks et al. (Eds.): ArtsIT 2017/DLI 2017, LNICST 229, pp. 105–115, 2018.
https://doi.org/10.1007/978-3-319-76908-0_11

of the fast-spreading high-speed internet services; there are certain benefits to consumers by implementing such shopping behaviour. However, a huge negative impact has occurred on the retailer stores. According to The Fiscal Times (TFT) news, there is an incredibly rapid decline in American retail stores [1]. Some data illustrated that this situation has occurred since 2010 but is now getting faster [2, 3].

Following this trend, some valuable relationships during the traditional shopping process have already been lost, for instance, the traditional connection in product manufacturing has been pushed to the limit [4]. Losing the direct interaction with the real products and physical store atmosphere is the key factor which has significant influence on customer's behaviour, satisfaction and expenditures [5]. Furthermore, regarding the 2015 Time-Trade State of Retail Report, most consumers prefer to shop in stores rather than online or digital shopping because they like being able to actually touch and feel the products during shopping [6]. From the producers' perspective, thousands of manufacturers have to shift their strategies to answer such changes in customer thinking, shopping behaviour patterns, crowd feed & evaluations, and expectations in various sections.

Globally, there is also much effort to attract consumers back to the physical retailer stores. Even the online shopping giants are opening physical stores and have been implementing the latest technologies to enhance in-store shopping experience, such as Alibaba's supermarket stores in Beijing and Shanghai, and the Amazon's physical stores in New York, Washington and several US major cities.

In this paper, the authors have studied the factors which affect or potentially affect the customer shopping behaviour. These factors help in formulating design principles and in generating new concepts to achieve a richer shopping experience. Specifically, the main focus is on:

- User research on purchasing behaviour (use 'footwear purchasing behaviour' as a case study)
- Physical (touchable and wearable) components based recognition and communication system development
- Real-time spatial augmented realty
- Future development possibilities.

The paper proceeds as follows: Sect. 2 investigates the current market and consumer requirements. Section 3 presents the rationale of this design. Section 4 describes the technology and features of the design. Finally, Sect. 5 discusses the findings and also potential future development.

2 Research and Investigation

From a general viewpoint, a good design must engage consumers and create behaviour changes with a full understanding of users and their context [7]. Likewise, the way the user interacts with devices is strongly affected by the way the devices are designed [8]. Thus, it is crucial for designers to create and solidify the concept based on a deep understanding of shoe buyer behaviour patterns. In this study, the authors present design to support in-store footwear shopping behaviour as a case study. Compared with online shopping, what is the motivation for consumers to come to retail stores? Which inherent characteristics of current physical retailers still benefit consumers, and which are expected to change?

2.1 Market Research

As the first step, a US market review was implemented with a focus on both market and user-related statistical data to obtain a clearer grasp of the trends of consumers' shopping behaviour and then to identify the gap between consumers' expectations and existing services in the conventional footwear stores. Looking at the US market, the growth of e-commerce is still outpacing the overall growth of retail sales; retailers are continuing to close brick-and-mortar outlets. While total US retail sales grew 3.7% in the fourth quarter of 2014 compared with the same quarter in 2013, e-commerce sales jumped 14.6% in the fourth quarter. One year earlier, total sales grew 3.8% year-over-year, while e-commerce sales increased 16.0%. In fact, all kinds of traditional stores are urgently facing the need to adapt to new technology, including the Internet of Things [9]. However, according to the Omni Channel Shopping Preferences Study, most people are willing to combine online shopping and physical store together to complete their purchase. Also, interestingly, the 2015 Time Trade State of Retail Report found that eighty-five percent of customers say they prefer to shop in physical stores [6]. Furthermore, most of them suggested that they would even prefer to shop at an Amazon store over Amazon.com if possible [6]. Essentially, people shift their shopping method but physical stores still play an irreplaceable role in our life. Meanwhile, customers have higher expectations for the in-store shopping environment than ever before [10]. The Internet enables e-retailers to better understand each customer's needs, which facilitates provision of specially tailored offers and preference promotions [3]. If the retailers cannot entice customers in their stores and keep them interested, they will choose to stay home and shop online [1].

2.2 Consumer Survey Findings

Secondly, a survey study on the shoe purchasing behaviour was implemented. A total of 62 subjects participated, including 30 males and 32 females. Of these, 56 respondents are from age 18–27, four from 28–37, two from 38–54. The key findings are:

(A) 54.8% (34) of the respondents were willing to pay $100–$199 for purchasing a pair of customized shoes. Interestingly, a group with four people (with three females and one male) expected to spend less than $49; in contrast three people (all males) were willing to spend more than $250.

(B) When a customer intends to purchase a pair of shoes, 85.5% of the total participants (53 subjects) suggested that they prefer to use a physical retail store to be able to physically hold and check the real shoe products, and 13 of these subjects suggested that they need further assistance to purchase shoes even using the physical stores. Only 9 subjects suggested that they are happy with online-shopping environment mainly due to time-consumption reasons.

(C) Regarding the most important factors affecting their decision-making for shoe purchasing, 69.3% of the respondents (43 subjects) considered *Comfort*; which compared to 38.9% (21 subjects) selected *Brand*, 30.6% (19 subjects) chose *Price*; and 25.8% (16 subjects) chose *Colour Scheme and Shape* respectively.

Other findings were based on a series questions related to *Customization (pre-designed order)*. The authors found out that 56.5% (35 subjects) of the total respondents were willing to complete their shoe design through an online website or smart device and then be able to try them on in the physical store; 25.8% (16 subjects) prefer to design their shoes in an in-store environment with assistance from the shop staff, and only 19.4% (12 subjects) were willing to complete their design with the online shopping tools only. Interestingly, 45.2% (28 subjects) of the respondents were willing to pay a part of the price as a deposit before they get the actual product and 38.7% (24 subjects) were willing to pay the full payment before they get the actual product. Only 9.7% (6 subjects) consider the question of 'if I cannot get the actual shoes at the first time in the store why should I have to come into the physical store?' as a serious issue.

Considering the time consumption in the design and production process of a customized order, the survey found that 85.5% (53 subjects) of the respondents were more than satisfied if the time span could be limited to less than a week from ordering to receiving the actual products. Further details are shown in Table 1.

Table 1. Satisfaction for delivery time after your design

	Disappointed	Normal	Satisfied	Very satisfied
Less than a week	0	7	19	**34**
One to two weeks	5	14	**25**	13
Two to three weeks	**19**	17	17	3
Three to four weeks	24	**25**	9	1
Four to five weeks	**38**	18	1	0
Five to six weeks	**56**	5	1	0

Furthermore, respondents were mostly interested in modifying and redesigning 'sneakers', which occupied 67.8% (42 subjects) of the respondents, including 25 male subjects. The secondary type was 'boots' with a percentage of 38.7% (24 subjects), including 14 female subjects in this group. It is worth noting that over 60% of the respondents were interested in adding personalized patterns and viewing it both digitally and physically.

Through this survey study, it has become clear that:

1. Tangibility drives customers to visit a physical retailer store, as they want to try on the actual footwear;
2. Customization answers customers' passion to create their own shoes, responds to their unique expectations. Even in the situation they cannot take their customized request away immediately, they still prefer to view it both digitally and physically;
3. Waiting period is an inevitable issue for delivery, but, in general, customers prefer to receive the ordered goods as soon as possible, preferably 'now';

4. Information exchange, especially for the youth generation, smart device access has been considered as one of the most crucial items in their daily activities. Using smart devices as a linkage to connect people with products might be an attractive approach to engage people in the customization process.

The shopping experience typically aims to maximize either efficiency or entertainment according to retail management theory [11]. The online market maximizes the advantage of convenience that motivates consumers to shop online through the internet [12]. People collect information and compare goods in a much faster way compared with the current way of in-store shopping. Thus, based the above investigations, we could see that the physical stores have not been improved in an adequate manner to satisfy the changes of customers' expectations.

3 Design Rationale

Based on our market research and user studies, it is clear that in-store retailers have a significant potential to maximize benefit by enhancing the physical environment and customizing services. With this design concept, it is possible to enhance in-store shopping experience with higher product browsing efficiency, richer interactivity and visualization. The target product is shoe manufacture, the target end-users are young people from sixteen to thirty-years old who intend to purchase a pair of shoes. The features of interactive renderer developing based on consumer research allows customer to participate in a design process, to preview shoes in real-time mode. Choosing real shoes as rendering object meets the needs that were identified from the user research. Use tangible physical manipulation tool as rendering controlling input device rather than merely virtual digital buttons on screen is aiming to increase the usability and able to customer to preview materials physically [13, 14].

3.1 Design of Tangible Components

Generally, the design contains two main parts. One is wearable pure white shoes. The customer is able to touch and put them on as with normal shoes. Before rendering, they are able to put them on and check the conformability. The second part consists of tangible controllers. To recognize the rendering effects that will apply to the shoe, all controllers' materials are made with real materials, the same as the shoes (Fig. 1).

Fig. 1. Tangible controllers

Moreover, using tangible controllers as an input method rather than a multi-touch screen not only avoids misunderstanding of interface design but also provides the possibility for several people to play with it and exchange their markers to share their design template. To communicate with the physical components recognition system, all tangible components including shoes and controllers are attached with a unique fiducial marker at the bottom which are used for physical components recognition.

3.2 Physical Components Recognition

Physical components recognition is a key feature leading innovation to close the gap. Once customers put controllers on a table, the markers will be detected by the camera underneath. Every fiducial stands for a different instruction used for sending messages to physical components recognition system. The markers were designed as two main types (Fig. 2). One is for shoe models. Another is for controllers, which stand for different types of shoe deign template. Theoretically, only two kinds of markers put on the table together will enable shoe objects will be rendered. In addition, all controller's fiducial design is also working for smart device MYSHOE App. Users can use an iPad, tablet or smart phone through the application to discover possible shoe designs, modify them and preview them digitally.

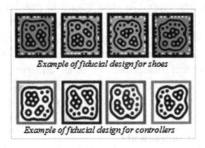

Example of fiducial design for shoes

Example of fiducial design for controllers

Fig. 2. Example of fiducial designs

3.3 3D Projection Mapping

Also known as video mapping or Spatial Augmented Reality (SAR) [15] the projection mapping technique is used for adding a variety of layers to a physical object in order to augment the object with digital content [16]. In this case, 3D projection mapping effects applied to the shoes model (Fig. 3) and it can be modified by replacing tangible controllers. To maximize the physical feature, 3D projection mapping techniques are the optimal choice for this project. First, it retains a touchable physical product, which is essential to physical shopping. Compared with augmented reality (AR) and virtual reality (VR), SAR allows the customer to put on the actual product and touch real materials and goods rather than in a virtual world play with a well-designed digital image. Second, it offers a chance for the customer to participate in design process, to create personalized products and to render them in real-time mode. It also saves plenty of inventory space, thus reducing the operating cost. However, it does have a

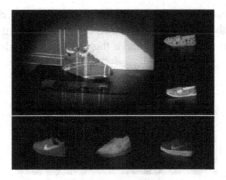

Fig. 3. 3D projection mapping calibration

drawback, which is lighting interference. According to the final prototype user testing, this technique pretty much relies on the environment. If strong light surrounds it, it will seriously affect the rendering results. To ensure getting an optimized rendering in a public place, it is necessary to create a light-block space for demonstration.

3.4   Intangible Components

The design also includes a smart device application, which allows the customer to discover shoe information in or out of a store through an App called MYSHOE. Essentially, it includes two modes, the in-store and the online modes. System structure is shown in Fig. 4.

The in-store mode allows customers to preview and modify the 3D rendering effect virtually through the smart device. Once the customer is satisfied with their selected favourite colour, pattern and shoe model, it will show all the details about purchasing,

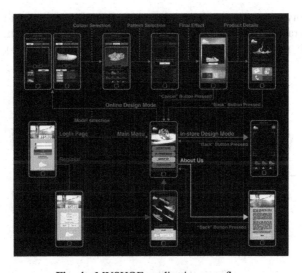

Fig. 4. MYSHOE application user flow

such as introduction, recommendation, price and payment option etc. Most importantly, the purchaser can find the marker ID that stands for corresponding controllers and shoe. Then users are able to real-timely observe their design through interactive rendered results (Fig. 5).

Fig. 5. Online mode discovery

The online mode provides an interface as the crucial part that brings together the online retailer and consumers [3] and also a chance to encourage them back to the store to physically make their shoes. Through that mode, the customer is able to browse and select shoes, then modify the colour, add patterns, and finally preview it digitally with 2D and 3D rendering effect, and make the payment as with e-retailers.

4 Technology

The latest prototype contains an interactive rendering table and a smart device application. The interactive rendering table (Fig. 6) is based on Adobe Flash, enabling it to receive a UDP message from the detecting software (reacTIVision), then send a

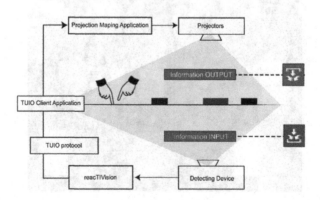

Fig. 6. Overall system structure

message to projection mapping software (TouchDesigner). Finally, it can present the designed shoe model through projected images which are overlapped on a blank (white) shoe model. The App named MYSHOE is based on Unity3D and Vuforia SDK, and uses the physical recognition system to find the corresponding digital images or models, then show the 2D and 3D digital effect to the users.

5 Discussion and Potential Development

With the global popularity of online shopping proceeding at an incredible speed, many business institutions and services have noticed the significant impact of online-retail sales by adjusting their business processes [4]. The traditional physical retailer business model may be replaced by a hybrid one due to the trend of integration of internet and physical store shopping. Through enhancing the tangible interactivity between customers and products, retailers could have the ability to provide consumers with a more enjoyable in-store shopping experience.

In this study, a 3D projection-mapping technique has been implemented to provide an alternative in-store shopping solution which enables multiple users to participate. A higher level of service customization leads to higher customer satisfaction [17], and the aims of customization are to satisfy as many needs as possible for each individual customer [18]. Thus, this tangible SAR-enabled product display and ordering system was designed for the customer to further explore the features of the products and intuitively customize their orders.

One of the most direct benefit of this technology is that users can experience an Augmented Reality product presentation, which can be more readily shared compared with a Head-Mounted VR technology [19]. For instance, people's position can be more flexible, and users can view the displayed products from various angles simultaneously. In responding to a 360° display need, multiple projectors also could work together (with additional projection edge-blending technologies) to achieve an omnidirectional vision. Furthermore, seeking peer opinions and having discussions are common behaviour needs during purchasing shoes, which requires the installation with multi-user participation capacity. Responding to this need, the authors have integrated the functions of *feelings sharing*, *opinions of similar idea* and *specific design requirements* before place orders.

Regarding the prototype user testing, the authors have found the following three main drawbacks.

Firstly, tangible components design must follow the design principle of 'less is more' to keep it simple and support intuitive operations. However, using 'tangible controllers' as the only input method could make the users feel that it 'lacks interactivity'. Users nowadays expect much richer interactive experience to enhance their explorations and customization (design) possibilities.

Secondly, the visual feedbacks (rendered AR effects) which based on SAR technology is sensitive to the environmental lighting. Any kind of strong light source will have a significant impact on the rendering effect.

Finally, the software selected (Adobe Flash in this study) as a tool receiving and sending messages was not a stable solution, which has randomly caused entire system crashes. It's necessary to explore a better alternative solution to process the input data. A video demo is available at YouTube; the link is shown below.

- Interactive Renderer 1.0: https://www.youtube.com/watch?v=T9dcOa08Jfk
- Interactive Renderer 2.0: https://www.youtube.com/watch?v=oFt1dc5SkI4&t=49s.

Acknowledgments. This project is supported by the International Tangible Interaction Design Lab (ITID Lab) at Monash University. The authors are also grateful for all effective feedback, and technical support received from lecturer Warwick Molloy supported on Unity 3D & Vuforia SDK; proofreading support from Adjunct Prof Patrick Moriarty; and TouchDesigner support from Matthew Ragan and Baoruo Si. The authors also thank seminar participants at Monash university and all respondents involved in project research survey and user testing.

References

1. PWC: making a difference global annual review 2016. PWC (2016)
2. Gustafson, K.: The Incredible Shrinking American Retail Store. The Fiscal Times, 23 January 2014. http://www.thefiscaltimes.com/Articles/2014/01/23/Incredible-Shrinking-American-Retail-Store
3. Tsai, H.-T., Huang, H.-C.: Determinants of e-repurchase intentions: an integrative model of quadruple retention drivers. J. Inf. Manag. **44**(3), 231–239 (2007). Department of International Business, Yuan Ze University, Chung-Li, Taoyuan, Taiwan, ROC
4. Chiagouris, L., Ray, I.: Customers on the web are not all created equal: the moderating role of internet shopping experience. Int. Rev. Retail Distrib. Consum. Res. **20**(2), 251–271 (2010)
5. Mobach, M.P.: The impact of physical changes on customer behavior. Manag. Res. Rev. **36**, 278–295 (2010)
6. Wallace, S.: The State of Retail. TimeTrade Systems, Inc., Tewksbury (2015)
7. Daae, J., Boks, C.: A classification of user research methods for design for sustainable. J. Clean. Prod. **106**, 680–689 (2015)
8. Norman, A.D.: The Design of Everyday Things. MIT Press, London (1988)
9. Watch, M.: 10 retailers closing the most stores. Accessed 25 Mar 2015
10. Pavitt, D.: Retailing and the super high street: the future of the electronic home shopping industry. Int. J. Retail Distrib. Manag. **25**, 38–43 (1997)
11. Reimers, V., Clulow, V.: Retail centres: it's time to make them convenient. Int. J. Retail Distrib. Manag. **37**, 541–562 (2009). Emerald Group Publishing Limited
12. Chen, S.-J., Chang, T.-Z.: A descriptive model of online shopping process: some empirical results. Int. J. Serv. Ind. Manag. **14**(5), 556–569 (2003). MCB UP Ltd
13. Wang, S.J.: Fields Interaction Design (FID): The Answer to Ubiquitous Computing Supported Environments in the Post-information Age. Homa & Sekey Books, Paramus (2013)
14. Wang, S.J., Moriarty, P., Wu, S.Z.: Tangible interaction design: preparing future designers for the needs of industrial innovation. Procedia Technol. **20**, 162–169 (2015)
15. Bimber, O., Raskar, R.: Spatial Augmented Reality: Merging Real and Virtual Worlds. A K Peters, Wellesley (2005)

16. Rowe, A.: Designing for engagement in mixed reality experiences that combine projection mapping and camera-based interaction. J. Digit. Creat. **25**, 1–14 (2014). Routledge
17. Coelho, P.S., Henseler, J.: Creating customer loyalty through service customization. Eur. J. Mark. **46**(3/4), 331–356 (2012)
18. Itamar, S.: Determinants of customers' responses to customized offers: conceptual framework and research propositions. J. Mark. **69**(1), 32–45 (2005)
19. Siegl, C., et al.: Real-time pixel luminance optimization for dynamic multi-projection mapping. J. ACM Trans. Graph. (TOG) **34**(6), 1–11 (2015)

Interact with Show-Window at Stores: Exploratory Study and Design Solution for Physical Retailers' Product Demonstration

Jianze Li[1,2], Andreas Hamacher[3], Daniel Waghorn[3], David Barnes[3,4], and Stephen Jia Wang[1,5(✉)]

[1] School of Design, Royal College of Art,
Kensington Gore, Kensington, London SW7 2EU, UK
stephen.wang@rca.ac.uk
[2] Department of Design, Faculty of Art Design & Architecture,
Monash University, Melbourne, Caulfield, VIC 3145, Australia
[3] Monash Immersive Visualisation Platform, Monash University,
Clayton, VIC 3800, Australia
[4] Faculty of Information Technology, Monash University,
Clayton, VIC 3800, Australia
[5] International Tangible Interaction Design Lab, Monash University,
Melbourne, Caulfield, VIC 3145, Australia

Abstract. Facing the rapidly shrinking trend of in-store shopping, this study aims at developing an interactive environmental prototype that provides the in-store customer with a more intuitive and enjoyable experience. Based on an intensive market research and evaluation process, we suggest that it is necessary to establish a new type of connection among customers, products, and retailers. Therefore, it is vital to provide stores with a better solution which could integrate an advanced product displaying method with object tracking and recognition and user behaviour interaction approaches. The designed solution proposes an interactive show-window, which emphasizes customized product visualization and direct interactivity to reinforce the connection, during physical shopping, between goods and consumers. We explore the possible feedback when people interact with the interactive show-window using a qualitative study, which has also been facilitated through an interactive show-window installation. The results demonstrated a meaningful outcome for this designed solution.

Keywords: Interactivity · Tangible interaction design · User experience
Shopping behaviour · Physical shopping experience
Physical product demonstration · Transparent screen · Object recognition
Object tracking

1   Introduction

With the booming trend of online shopping in the recent two decades, there is a significantly negative impact on the physical retail stores which can be seen as a miniature of the many domains of human interaction already affected dramatically in

© ICST Institute for Computer Sciences, Social Informatics and Telecommunications Engineering 2018
A. L. Brooks et al. (Eds.): ArtsIT 2017/DLI 2017, LNICST 229, pp. 116–126, 2018.
https://doi.org/10.1007/978-3-319-76908-0_12

the twenty-first century. Such trends have also already established new conventions in how people share information, and it creates an entirely new business model and consumer behaviour. As the number of Internet users continues to increase, the opportunities for online shopping will unavoidably continue to expand as well [1]. However, consumers also seem willing to go further to a mall with more comfortable shopping environment and with more diversified and cheaper products [2].

The tangible (physical) shopping experience is one of the primary attributes that drives most consumers to physical stores. Compared with the rapid development of online shopping, physical shopping urgently requires integration with innovative technologies to enhance shopping experiences in the physical store context. Keeping technology up-to-date is an important way to satisfy the ever-changing shopping habits [3]. However, there is a gap between customers' in-store shopping expectations with current retailer stores' environment and available services.

There is an enormous opportunity when implementing potential technologies in physical retail stores. The success heavily relies on a good understanding of (a) what are the key factors affecting customer shopping behaviours; (b) what is the established way for physical retailers to catch consumers' curiosity; (c) how to demonstrate their product; and (d) what they focus on to improve the physical shopping experience.

The following issues are the main focus:

1. Curiosity in shopping - Market research and analysis on the advantages and dis-advantages of how physical retailers currently integrate new technologies to showcase product and arouse consumer's curiosity
2. Factors for satisfaction - What are the most important aspects being focused on to increase customer shopping satisfaction
3. Intuitive interactions - Design and evaluate possibilities for altered shopping process and product presentation by using object recognition and tracking technology
4. Overlapping/combined displays - Further develop the potentials for an 'interactive front store window' concept using transparent-screen technology

2   Market Research and Analysis

In a world flooded with visual stimulation, visual aspects of branding have become the central factor affecting shopping behaviours [4], even as branding itself has become ever more crucial to bringing significant market value to a business [5]. Thus, shopping malls and individual physical retailers are aiming to establish their unique brand image and maximize their features on either efficiency or entertainment [6]. Moreover, recreational shopping behaviour, which focuses on the shopping activity and the experience itself [7] is also a good way to keep potential customers engaged. Retailers should focus on customer satisfaction, trust and commitment through the implementation of customer-oriented selling, thus leading to a long-term relationship [8]. There are many examples of retailers re-building their shopping environment to satisfy the customer's expectation for in-store shopping, but the results are still limited. Here market research was used to evaluate several ways of product presentation in the current market. Based on usability, flexibility, price, and functionality enabled a deeper understanding the in-store consumers' expectations, and the core factors affecting in-store (physical) purchase satisfaction.

The physical static decoration is the most common method for re-building the in-store shopping environment, but the shortcomings are also evident (Table 1). Dynamic decoration as an upgraded version of physical decoration which increases the effect attract people's attention, but still, neglects the information connection and connection between the customer and actual products. In most cases, customers expect to give their feedback in their own words on evaluating items [9], which is a great potential connection that can be established between consumers and products. Moreover, considering shopping as a *process*, composed of a set of distinct components linked together in a particular sequence [10], an effective way implant technology to shopping processes might alter the shopping process, making it more efficient and joyful. For instance, *Interactive WayFinder* and the *Interactive Mirror* both offer shopping-related information to the customer, such as location, opening hours, inventory availability and digital fit-on effect. Those designs are focusing on data interactivity using gestures as the main input method. Bettman in 1979 highlighted that situational variables affect in store decision making in various ways [11]. With the advanced technology available, people should not be restricted to gesture, hands or fingers as the input method. Human interactivity has a tremendous potential for any kind of tangible objects rather than screen-based display or a smart phone. Physical and digital space penetrate one another, to achieve an enhanced shopping experience [12]. All those possible input methods can be considered as situational variables affecting in-store decision-making during shopping (Fig. 1).

Table 1. Evaluation on wayfinding solutions in the current market

Current solutions	Advantage	Disadvantage
Static physical decoration	1. Most common way to improve the shopping atmosphere in a physical shop	1. Long construction time 2. High cost 3. Environmental impact by waste material
Interactive WayFinder	1. Save labour 2. Low cost 3. Interactive communication	1. Limited information support 2. Limited interaction
Dynamic showcase	1. Better visual effect 2. Build luxurious & distinctive brand images	1. High cost of maintenance and construction
Interactive mirror	1. Modifiable user interface 2. Convenient to customer browse items and check inventory 3. Enrich customer shopping experience through virtually fit-on	1. Unnatural fit effect 2. Relatively low usability
Interactive gaming machine (claw gaming machine)	1. Increase amusement interactivity	1. As an accessorial machine cannot directly facilitate final purchase

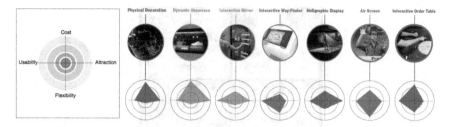

Fig. 1. Products marketing usability evaluation

3 Exploratory Technology Practicability

Concerning the study and evaluation of the current approach that physical retailers demonstrate their products, *interactivity, customization,* and *visualization* are three key factors affecting customer's shopping satisfaction and shopping behaviour. In this section, based on shopper's needs and latest technology, the design will first come up with the innovative concept, then test, evaluate, redesign it to get closer to the core of consumer needs.

3.1 Concept One: Trackable Overlay Augmented Reality

In this concept (Fig. 2), the physical product is situated behind the transparent screen, using overlay effect through transparent display rendering the actual product. The overlay effects appear on display which can be modified by the user; meanwhile, it will follow the user's position to ensure the overlay effects align with the actual product.

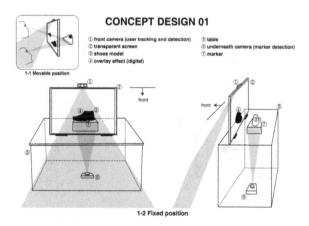

Fig. 2. Explorative concept design 1

However, as Fig. 3 shows, the outcome cannot satisfy the design goals, even though the layer can be matched with eyes perfectly, it still cannot achieve the ideal

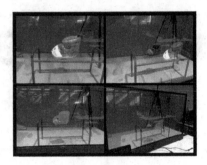

Fig. 3. Explorative concept design test 1

composite rendering effect. The transparent screen is also affected by the lighting, overlaying effect on the actual product, the colour aberration should be considered.

3.2 Concept Two: Trackable Overlay Augmented Reality Rendered by a Mirror Reflection

To achieve a better rendering effect by using transparency, we present the secondary concept as shown in Fig. 4, which put the transparent screen toward to a mirror. The user was able to modify the rendering effect appear on the screen through smart devices. The final rendered effects can be seen from the reflection on the mirror (Fig. 4). The advantage of this concept is that it allows the customer to actually wear the actual product, and to track the position of user's feet through front camera detection. Most interestingly, it is also possible to apply it to a several users with multi-object moving setting and render the augmented images at the same time.

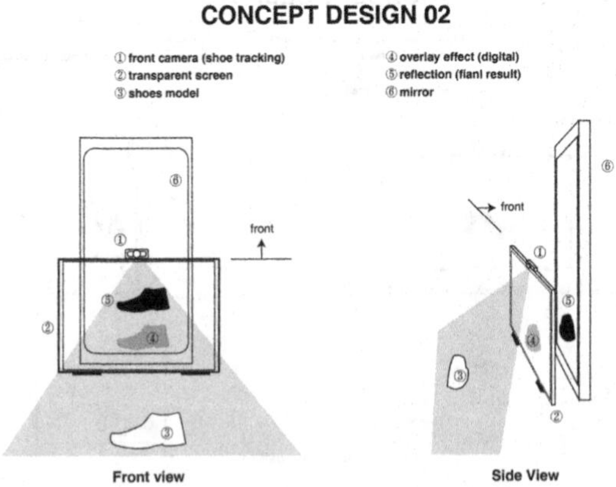

CONCEPT DESIGN 02

① front camera (shoe tracking)   ④ overlay effect (digital)
② transparent screen   ⑤ reflection (fianl result)
③ shoes model   ⑥ mirror

Front view   Side View

Fig. 4. Explorative concept design 02

After the test, the outcome is a rendering effect as natural as the design expectations (Fig. 5). Several people tested this prototype; they said that when they look at the

Fig. 5. Explorative concept design test 2

reflection in the mirror, they feel uncomfortable, because they will automatically look at their shoes rather than only observe the reflection in a mirror. Some of the testers also suggested that the augmented imaging effects were not natural enough, it looks like they are wearing a digital shoe, even though they can modify the colour or pattern and view it in a mirror. Mostly they will not go to complete their purchase if they cannot see the actual customized shoes.

3.3   Concept Three: Interactive Showcase

Whereas a forward overlay effect will not match with the real object, a reversed overlay effect through a mirror fails to offer a natural result. To overcome these issues, we imagined concept design three (Fig. 6), an interactive showcase which puts several products on a moving track behind the transparent screen, depending on the timing when certain products come to the centre position to load different items or products information on the screen. The transparent screen is simply and only used to add annotation explaining key information or specifications of the items.

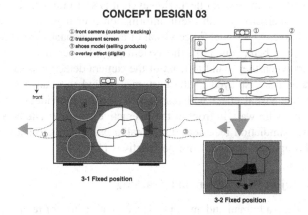

Fig. 6. Explorative concept design 3

In this concept, the physical product remains the focus of the consumer, and the technology is simply being used to engage the consumer via a 'Want to know more?' paradigm. The test result is reasonably positive; most of the testers suggested that the effect is natural and if the item is close enough to the transparent screen, the position of the annotation is not a big issue. However, it needs to be built with useful interactivity which can create the linkage between customer, product, and retailer. Significantly, the designer needs to figure out a way to attract customers' attention and deliver useful/valuable information to them. Examples could include, asking for product evaluation or feedback, and keeping the customer engaged with product demonstrations.

4 Executable Concept and Design Rationale

After various potential concept designs and tests, the most feasible solution was the interactive store-front window. The possibility of implementing transparent display and object tracking technology to enhance physical interaction between the shopper, and visualization of, the product, has been emphasized through all the tests. To rationalize functionality of this design, the designer went through market research and evaluation of the current methods that physical retailers use to present their products. With the feature of visual interactivity, the interactive window was able to stimulate potential customers' curiosity and dynamically schedule selectable advertisements. The feature of transparent display integrated with infrared multi-touch input, satisfied those people who were: willing to make a quick purchase; queuing outside a store; or anyone interested in new arrival products. Finally, physical object recognition and tracking technology enrich the method of input instruction.

4.1 Visual Interactivity

The visual effect is one of the most critical factors to be considered when building a physical in-store shopping environment. There are some cases in the current market or shopping mall with strong visual effect. However, it is still rare to integrate the visual effect and human interactivity with useful information exchange, which could provide interesting interactive experience. Since visual or audio feedback is crucial for guiding the user's interactive behaviour [13], the system provides sensitive visual and audio feedback to users when they stand in front of the camera detection area. Visible target product information is displayed to the customer behind the transparent screen. An interactive dynamic visual effect will respond to passing individuals' positions, and entice those people who walk in front of the interactive window. The benefits of using the virtual reality simulation technique may enable participants to show their preferences simply through different viewing perspectives [14].

4.2 Physical Object Recognition and Tracking

Interactivity between a human and an object is a crucial factor for retailers to focus on. With a variety of advanced technology released, customer behaviour should not be merely restricted to static physical objects and/or smart phones. Physical object recognition and tracking technology is the key to opening a new linkage between customers and products which enables users to interact with a machine with the real-time positions of their head/face rather than limited gesture such as swap, click, scale etc.

In this concept, the transparency and the infrared multi-touch input are the two main features used to facilitate interactive shopping behaviours. Traditionally, the store-front window emphasises its own attribute as a physical barrier that demarcates the shopping area from the street/mall. This concept unleashes the potential of transparent show-window including overlay effects and product annotations, associated directly with the actual product. Importantly, it could monitor the user's interactive behaviours (including both touch and gestural) which enables the retailer to obtain first-hand information leading to a better understanding of individual customer's needs [15]. Moreover, it could potentially provide a fast shopping solution. The customers could have a chance to review an item and complete their purchase even outside the store.

Regarding to the above-mentioned visual effects, a big potential advantage for physical retailers in implementing such technology is the ability to build linkages through user's eyes, arms, legs even entire body movements as an information input. Furthermore, designers can build up visual effects corresponding to the position of a human face. It provides an active feedback to draw potential customers' interest and give a focus and real-time response to keep customers engaged. Such experiences could provide better support to facilitate the completion of trade (Fig. 7).

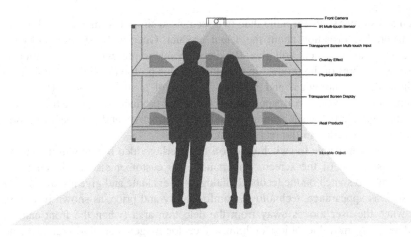

Fig. 7. Explorative concept design 4

5 Technology

Using the well-known tools Unity3D and OpenCV, we developed a functional prototype based on our interactive store-front window concept (Fig. 8). This prototype includes three main modes: (a) screen protection mode (default mode), (b) attracting mode, and (c) discovery mode.

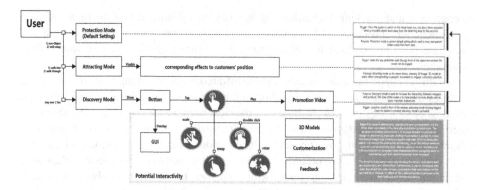

Fig. 8. Interactive store-front-window system structure diagram

The screen protection mode is the system default mode, which is used for energy-saving and to prevent burn-in on the transparent screen. This mode is activated once the customer moves away from the front camera detection area for longer than five seconds. When anyone walks into or goes through the front camera detection area it will automatically switch to attracting mode.

Attracting mode is designed to attract people's attention and arouse their curiosity. In this prototype, the application of Adobe After Effect was used to build a multi-group video effect which can play on the screen in a position corresponding to the location of the person's face.

When a customer stays for more than two seconds, a simplified menu will show up containing brief information about the actual product. Once the customer clicks the button, a video advertisement will play. Retailers are able to present key information to showcase the features of the product in the video. In this prototype, we created a video to highlight the technological and material features of a shoe product. The video advertisement as an overlay corresponding to the actual product behind the transparent screen. This augmented visualization provides an attractive and unique visualised information layer overlay to the real product.

The customer was able to switch on or off the overlay video by tapping the button on the right-side top of the screen. Importantly, the customer also could click the feedback button to switch on the feedback dialog, then evaluate and give a score on that product such as appearance, technology, comfortability and price, as shown in Fig. 9. Finally, when the user moves away from the detection area (when the front camera cannot detect any movable object or human face for longer than five seconds), the system goes back to the default screen protection mode.

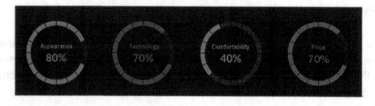

Fig. 9. System feedback menu

6 Discussion and Future Work

This study provides an overview of using transparent display technology, object recognition and tracking technology, to augment the physical product presentation in a physical in-store shopping context. We started with market research concerning current modes of physical product presentation in a shopping mall and an analysis of their limitations, then went through design concept development, discussion and rebuilding to come up with the final executable solution - interactive shop-front window. During this overall development process, we have taken a user-centred approach, with a specific focus on creating innovative solutions to satisfy the consumer's needs during in-store shopping, utilising the above mentioned technical features [9].

After building a low-fidelity prototype for the interactive window concept, we tested it with 5 university lecturers, 5 potential shoe buyers, and 5 researchers. Through the observation and conversation with them, useful feedback was obtained. *For example:*

- *"the visual effect is indeed impressive and draw a significant attention from them";*
- *"it achieves the goal to give a focus to customer allowing them to look at specific item in front of them";*
- *"people are trying to move their body, hand or head even rotate their body to check out what will happen next".*

Those comments inspired the designer to increase the use of various facets of human behaviour as input, instead of monotonic position of face or body detection.

Furthermore, to solve the lightless area around the actual product, LED lights can be attached on the top of the showcase to light up the products behind the transparent screen. However, the 'customization' function takes the primary consideration during the testing. The main functionality of this design is to arouse potential customer's interests, attract them to go into the store to discover more on what they could be potentially interested in exploring further. On the other hand, responders proposed that the customization possibility through the outside interactive window could be an advantage for customers who want to make a quick purchase, and also enable them to purchase products out of opening hours. To further develop this concept, more user research is required, such as consumer psychology and behaviour to optimize the shopping experience.

Our prototype is different from other existing tools in the current market. The functionality of an interactive window not only focuses on human's multi-touch as an input method but also captures human behaviours, extending the possibility of inter-activity between human and machine, such as eye tracking, body movement, facial recognition and so on. A responsive visual effect which matches with the pedestrian's movement can be an effective way to attract people attention, and emphasize or promote a specific product.

The next step for polishing up the concept will focus on enhancing visual attraction including a graphic user interface and a refined visual effect. For example, providing a pull-down menu will enable customers to modify the user interface to achieve a flexible user experience. For a more energy-saving solution, the visual effect could be triggered by people passing nearby through a body movement detection system.

Acknowledgment. This project was greatly supported by the International Tangible Interaction Design Lab (ITID Lab). We thank the Faculty of Engineering at Monash University for providing access to the transparent screen used in this research. As part of the activity in the Master of Interaction Design program, the authors also want to thank all effective feedback and technical support from lecturer Warwick Molloy.

References

1. Overby, J.W., Lee, E.J.: The effects of utilitarian and hedonic online shopping value on consumer preference and intentions. J. Bus. Res. **59**, 1160–1166 (2006)
2. Gould, J., Golob, T.F.: Shopping without travel or travel without shopping? An investigation of electronic home shopping. J. Transp. Rev. **17**, 355–376 (1997)
3. Eroglu, E.: The changing shopping culture: internet consumer behavior. Rev. Bus. Inf. Syst. **18**, 35 (2014)
4. Da Silveira, C., Lages, C., Simões, C.: Reconceptualizing brand identity in a dynamic environment. J. Bus. Res. **66**, 28 (2013)
5. Phillips, B.J., Mcquarrie, E.F., Griffin, G.W.: How visual brand identity shapes consumer response. Psychol. Mark. **31**, 225–236 (2014)
6. Lewison, D.M.: Retailing. Prentice Hall, Upper Saddle River (1996)
7. Jack, E.P., Powers, T.L.: Shopping behaviour and satisfaction outcomes. J. Mark. Manag. **29**, 1609–1630 (2013)
8. Williams, M.R.: The influence of salespersons' customer orientation on buyer-seller relationship development. J. Bus. Ind. Mark. **13**, 271–287 (1998)
9. Burke, R.R.: Technology and the customer interface: what consumers want in the physical and virtual store. J. Acad. Mark. Sci. **30**, 411–432 (2002)
10. Peterson, R.A., Balasubramanian, S., Bronnenberg, B.J.: Exploring the implications of the internet for consumer marketing. J. Acad. Mark. Sci. **25**, 329–346 (1997)
11. Bettman, J.R.: Memory factors in consumer choice: a review. J. Mark. **43**, 37 (1979)
12. Valentina, C., Mark, G.: Futuristic retail spaces. Archit. Des. 138–141 (2009)
13. Wang, J.S.: Fields Interaction Design (FID): The Answer to Ubiquitous Computing Supported Environments in the Post-information Age. Homa & Sekey Books, Paramus (2013)
14. Berneburg, A.: Interactive 3D simulations in measuring consumer preferences: friend or foe to test results? J. Interact. Advert. **8**, 1–13 (2007)
15. Dewan, R., Jing, B., Seidmann, A.: Product customization and price competition on the internet. Manag. Sci. **49**, 1055–1070 (2003)

The Impact of Virtual Reality Training on Patient-Therapist Interaction

Daniel J. R. Christensen and Michael B. Holte[(✉)]

Department of Architecture, Design and Media Technology,
Aalborg University Esbjerg, Niels Bohrs Vej 8, 6700 Esbjerg, Denmark
djrcl2@student.aau.dk, mbh@create.aau.dk

Abstract. This paper presents the development and evaluation of a Virtual Reality Kitchen to study the impact of VR rehabilitation on patient-therapist interaction in comparison to conventional rehabilitation. The study was conducted on 10 patients; 5 in an experimental group and 5 in a control group continuing with their conventional rehabilitation at NeuroRehab Centre Sydvestjysk Sygehus in Grindsted, Denmark. The therapists at NeuroRehab were supervising the test sessions for physical and verbal guidance over a period of four weeks requiring the patients and therapists to use the system three times per week for 30 min. A semi-structured interview was conducted with each participant from both groups. Additionally, each test session was video recorded to observe the physical and verbal interaction between the patient and the therapist and possible conversations. The outcome of this study indicated a clear difference between the therapists and their way of interacting with the patients. The therapists with experience in VR rehabilitation approached the patients, as in a conventional training session, utilising verbal and physical guidance, including hand gestures and commands, whereas the therapists with no VR rehabilitation experience did not.

Keywords: Interaction · Motivation · Patient-therapist interaction
Stroke · Virtual reality rehabilitation

1 Introduction

According to Hjerneskadeforeningen [1], approximately 12.000 people are suffering a stroke every year in Denmark with a surviving rate of 70%. To this end, over 75.000 people are living with consequences of a stroke, who need regular medical supervision, which is a significant expense for the government. In 2013, the Danish government spent 73 billion Danish kroners on disability and rehabilitation, and the costs are increasing year by year. Conventionally, a stroke survivor will be placed in a rehabilitation centre, facilitating both physical and cognitive rehabilitation in close collaboration with different therapists. A regular rehabilitation process in these centres can last up to 6 weeks. Afterwards, some of the patients return to their homes while others remain institutionalised. Within the last few years and with the release of diverse commercial Head-Mounted Displays (HMDs) researchers have been shifting their focus towards Virtual Reality Rehabilitation, due to its opportunities.

© ICST Institute for Computer Sciences, Social Informatics and Telecommunications Engineering 2018
A. L. Brooks et al. (Eds.): ArtsIT 2017/DLI 2017, LNICST 229, pp. 127–138, 2018.
https://doi.org/10.1007/978-3-319-76908-0_13

This study aims to investigate how a virtual reality training system (VRTS) influence the patient-therapist interaction compared to conventional training within a stroke rehabilitation program. The VRTS consists of a HMD (Oculus Rift DK2), a motion sensor for hand tracking (Leap Motion) and a personal computer to run a Virtual Environment (VE). This was developed specifically for stroke patients with a team of therapists from Sydvestjysk Sygehus Neurological Rehabilitation Grindsted, Denmark, and contains both physical and cognitive tasks. The tasks were created around Activities of Daily Living tasks (ADL). To do so, a conventional training program was studied, consisting of ADL training in a kitchen.

2 Related Work

Patient-therapist interaction has been a focus of research for many years, and can be divided into three different interaction models [2]. All three models focus on the needs of the patient, and that each patient is an individual with personal values and background:

1. *Client-centred practice* focuses on patient autonomy; the responsibility is shared between patient and therapist. The goal is to create a caring and empowering environment where the patient is in control of the direction of their rehabilitation.
2. *Patient-centred care* focuses on the patients' perspective on rehabilitation. The therapist informs the patient regarding their condition and discusses the rehabilitation options, in order for the patient to understand their condition and the value of rehabilitation.
3. *Patient-focused care* focuses on the philosophy of care, including the physical, emotional, social, and spiritual needs of the patient. Here the patient-therapist relationship is equal, and striving to give information and a simplification of choices for the patient.

The following section provides details on patient-therapist interaction and their relationship in conventional rehabilitation.

2.1 Patient-Therapist Interaction in Conventional Rehabilitation

A systematic observation was conducted by Talvitie [3] to study the communication between patients and therapists, which indicated the therapist to be more verbally active than the patient. The therapist spoke the most of the time under the study to communicate instructions and corrections, whereas the patient only made short comments and asked few questions regarding their performance. This can be related to the therapist's need to communicate a specific task under training. This is usually done with a mix of verbal instructions and explanations, combined with physically demonstrating the specific task and physically aiding the patient under movement. Therapists with experience in the field of motivation tend to use verbal encouragement and tactile cues combined with constant hand communication and physical aid more often than therapists with less experience [4].

Lettinga et al. [5] discovered that physical aid and verbal guidance prevent the patients from making mistakes, hence, they are not able to evaluate their own performance or learn from it. This can be argued to be applicable for all stroke patients; however, cognitive impairments, as neglect, can affect the patients' self-awareness, and therefore, they need to rely on the therapists' aid and guidance [5].

There exists an inconsistence in how patients are informed about their diagnosis, due to the patients' own knowledge and experience of the rehabilitation. Usually, the therapists do not consider these factors; therefore, they do not convey the information [6]. The Therapists tend to focus on a symptom oriented approach instead of considering the individuals' background and knowledge, leading to a disconnection in the new established relationship between patient and therapist in the early stage of conventional rehabilitation [7]. However, Slingsby [8] describes a new approach to the rehabilitation, a relationship-centred model, developed in three parts:

1. *Patient motivation:* considered to be related to the rehabilitation outcome and can be increased by effective patient-therapist interaction.
2. *Personal relationships:* determined to be the primary factor in the rehabilitation process, as the relationship between the therapist and patient "it is the key to successful stroke rehabilitation", as stated by Slingsby [9].
3. *Professional behaviour:* can be defined as the therapists' ability to adapt their behaviour and way of communicating according to the patients. This is described as a tool to foster personal relationships with the patient and the patient's family [9].

2.2 Advantages and Disadvantages of VR Rehabilitation

Recently, Virtual Reality has undergone a significant development. As a result, custom created displays and commercial HMDs are currently becoming more available. Moreover, due to the advance of technology, both hardware and software, VEs are becoming more immersive and interactive. Rizzo and Kim [10] developed a SWOT analysis on VR rehabilitation, analysing the potential future of VR rehabilitation. The SWOT analysis consists of Strengths, Weaknesses, Opportunities and Threats related to VR rehabilitation. Their findings can be seen in Table 1.

The strengths of VR rehabilitation include real-time feedback for the patients while interacting with the VE; Enhancement of motivation through gaming factors and self-guiding exploration; along with adaptability through interface modifications. For a commercial level, the strengths are its low-cost duplication and distribution, error-free learning and safe test and training environment.

The weaknesses of VR rehabilitation include the interface. 3D user interfaces need further development to design a more efficient and easy to understand way of interacting with the VE. Another weakness is the possibility of motion sickness; this can be induced when the VE runs in low frame rate both in static and dynamic environments, combined with low resolution on the display. Furthermore, the wires influence in a negative way the user experience, as they become a distraction when used in dynamic environments.

The opportunities of VR rehabilitation is highly related to the increased focus on VR. The commercial HMDs: Oculus Rift, HTC Vive and PlayStationVR were released

Table 1. SWOT analysis on VR rehabilitation [10].

Strengths	Weaknesses
• Enhanced ecological validity • Stimulus control and consistency • Real-time performance feedback • Cuing stimuli to support "error-free learning" • Self-guided exploration and independent practice • Interface modification contingent on user's impairments • Complete naturalistic performance record • Safe testing and training environment • Gaming factors to enhance motivation • Low-cost environment that can be duplicated and distributed	• The interface challenge 1: interaction methods • The interface challenge 2: wires and displays • Immature engineering process • Platform compatibility • Front-end flexibility • Back-end data extraction, management, analysis, visualisation • Side effects
Opportunities	**Threats**
• Emerging tech 1: processing power and graphics/video integration • Emerging tech 2: devices and wires • Emerging tech 3: real-time data analysis and intelligence • Gaming-industry drivers • VR rehabilitation with widespread intuitive • appeal to the public • Academic and professional acceptance • Close-knit VR rehabilitation scientific and clinical community • Integration of VR with physiological monitoring and brain imaging • Telerehabilitation	• Too few cost/benefit proofs could impact VR rehabilitation adoption • Aftereffects lawsuit potential • Ethical challenges • The perception that VR will eliminate the need for the clinician • Limited awareness/unrealistic expectations

to the public in 2016, and innovators around the world are currently developing and investigating ways to make HMDs wireless and improve the resolution. Furthermore, the companies behind the HMDs are developing commercial drivers and hardware in order to achieve higher realism and accessibility. The most important opportunity is to minimise the cost of rehabilitation processes. This technology is appealing to the public and is brining excitement and enjoyment among patients. There is a universal academic and professional acceptance that this is the future of rehabilitation, and that it can strengthen the relationship between the clinicians and patients.

The main threats that VR Rehabilitation is facing are that there is no tangible low cost/benefit proof due to its novelty. People may have unrealistic expectations of VR since the awareness is still limited, and some clinicians have the perception that the system will replace them.

2.3   Patient-Therapist Interaction in VR Rehabilitation

There are no studies at present time on patient-therapist interaction within the field of Virtual Reality due to the novelty of VR. Many works focus on the physical or cognitive improvement or physiological measurements in order to validate the clinical efficiency of VR Rehabilitation rather than the effect of VR on the patient-therapist interaction. Hence, the contribution of this study is to investigate the patient-therapist Interaction in VR rehabilitation.

3   Methods

This section introduces the system development and its functionality. Next, the target group and ethical considerations will be introduced. Finally, the test procedure and data treatment are presented.

3.1   System Development and Functionality

The virtual reality system consists of:

- *Hardware:* Leap Motion – a tracking device which is motion sensitive to different gestures and movements, Oculus Rift Development Kit 2 – a head mounted display headset displaying the VE, and a desktop computer (PC).
- *Software:* a custom-built task simulator – Virtual Reality Kitchen (VRK).

The Leap Motion is mounted on the Oculus Rift to give higher accuracy and realism. The tracking camera from Oculus Rift was positioned 70 cm in front of the patient and at 130 cm height. Artificial lighting supported good functionality of the devices.

VRK simulates training exercise from ADL that are usually part of the stroke rehabilitation at NeuroRehab Centre at Sydvestjysk Sygehus, Grindsted, Denmark. The task simulator game is a PC-based game displayed on both Oculus Rift and a monitor display, and controlled with Leap Motion. The in-game tasks involve physical exercises for recovery of motor functions in the upper extremities and the trunk. The movements include: *reaching, grabbing, leaning, pinching* and *grasping.*

There are two tasks in the VRK: *coffee making* and *grocery sorting.* Additionally, a *calibration scene* was developed. In the *coffee making* scene the patients are required to complete eight actions in order to get a score of 60 points. These actions are: *opening tab, lifting coffee machine lid, filling the glass with water, pouring the water then the coffee in the machine, placing the jug in the machine, closing the lid* and *pressing the on/off button.* The scoring is divided so 10 points is given for the five actions and an additional 10 points if the tasks were completed in less than 3 min. In the *grocery sorting* task, the participants are required to sort and place 17 items in one of the three possible locations: *freezer* (left side), *fridge* (right side) or on *fours shelves* (frontal). 10 points are given for every correct placement with a total possible score of 170 points. The maximum achievable total score was 180 points. The aim of the calibration scene is to define a training space based on individual capabilities and limitations. The interactive objects are only placed in the training space to achieve an appropriate individual level of difficulty per task. To calibrate the game, the participants were required to reach as far as possible in three directions: left, right and top.

To develop the VE, a free source 3D modelling software, Blender was utilised. The objects were designed to resemble an entirely furnished kitchen. For actions and interaction, the system was developed in Unreal Engine 4 – a suite of tools for design and system development purpose. Unreal Engine 4 provides an important feature (the Blue Print) which is a visual scripting system enhancing simple design and development. The programming language used for the scripts is C++.

3.2   Target Group

A sample of 10 participants and 5 physiotherapists involved in a rehabilitation program at NeuroRehab Centre, Sydvestjysk Sygehus, Grindsted, Denmark were included in the experiment. The patients consist of 3 women and 7 men who suffered a stroke no longer than two months before the experiment. The therapists were 3 women and 2 men. Patients were divided in two groups: a control group, where conventional rehabilitation treatment was applied; and an experimental group, where subjects utilised the VRK system instead of their conventional rehabilitation. All the patients were pre-tested using a Box and Blocks scale, which determined their physical motor condition. Randomisation of the participants was effectuated based on different factors such as: Box and Blocks score, stroke location, paraplegic side, gender and age, see Table 2.

Table 2. Patient information (BB: Box and Blocks, R: Right arm, L: Left arm).

Nr.	Name	Age	Gender (M/F)	Stroke location	Paraplegic side	BB score (R/L max: 150)	Group (E/C)
1	P	58	M	Left side	Right	R20:L22	C
2	PV	77	M	Right side	Left	R19:L6	E
3	L	74	M	Left side	Right	R15:L49	C
4	J	74	M	Cerebellum	Right	R15:L23	E
5	S	70	F	Left side	Right	R45:L63	C
6	M	61	M	Both sides	Right	R46:L50	E
7	PO	80	M	Right side	Left	R44:L39	C
8	F	85	M	Right side	Left	R50:L18	E
9	R	62	F	Frontal lobe	Both	R46:L46	C
10	B	60	F	Left side	Right	R40:L45	E

3.3   Ethical Considerations

Ethical considerations were discussed and applied regarding informed consent, deception, debriefing, confidentiality and protection from physical and psychological harm. Considering that the nature of the study was rather sensitive, the therapists and the patients were completely instructed in all the aspects of the experiment and asked to sign a consent form. The aim of the form was to acknowledge their understanding of the study and to allow the researchers to video record the sessions. The sessions were entirely conducted with physiotherapists to avoid any harm. Furthermore, a researcher was partially observant of the experiment to ensure a good functionality of the system. All the parties involved had the right to stop the experiment at any time. Their names and personal data were utilised only for the purpose of research.

3.4   Test Procedure, Data Gathering and Treatment

To test how a virtual reality training system (VRTS) influences the patient-therapist interaction compared to conventional training within a stroke rehabilitation program, a qualitative research method was applied. The experiment was conducted at NeuroRehab, Grindsted, Denmark. The duration of the experiment was four weeks, where the experimental group had 3 weekly interactions with the system of 30 min duration in accordance with National Clinical Guidelines for Rehabilitation [11], while the control group followed their conventional rehabilitation treatment. A semi-structured interview was conducted with each participant from both groups. Additionally, each test session was video recorded to observe the physical and verbal interaction between the patient and the therapist and possible conversations.

The qualitative data was extracted through semi-structured interviews and video recordings of interviews and test sessions. The semi-structured interview consists of five questions as follows:

1. How important is the role of the therapist in your rehabilitation process?
2. If the system was plug-and-play, how would you feel if you would have to use it by yourself without your therapist?
3. Do you trust your therapist with providing you the right guidance for your rehabilitation process?
4. Is your therapist motivating you through the process of rehabilitation?
5. Is the VR system changing the interaction between you and your therapist?

The questions were adapted for each group and the therapists; however, the meaning of the questions was identical for each participant. The questions were translated into Danish (the participants' native language), and the interviews were also conducted in Danish. All of the interviews were video recorded and transcribed and the transcriptions were translated into English, read and categorised in different themes such as: physical aid, verbal guidance and patient confusion, and the themes were compared between groups. The video recordings were utilised to support the results from the semi-structured interviews, hence, each session was transcribed and translated into English, and patterns were established and compared between groups.

4   Results

This section will present the results obtained from the test following the procedure presented in Sect. 3.4.

4.1 Semi-structured Interviews

The primary findings from the semi-structured interviews of the therapist and patients are presented in Table 3.

Table 3. The primary findings of the semi-structured interviews.

Question	Therapists' answers
1	*Therapist without VR experience:* the therapist role is paramount, it is us who have the knowledge and works with it every day, so I think it is important to guide and give good advices
2	*Therapist with VR experience:* For the patients who it fits and where there is motivation, I can see VR as a great tool. You can train specific goals as a patient to which is motivating
3	*Therapist without VR experience:* Yes, the patients trust me. I know it is not always realistic but then you have to find a middle ground
4	*Therapist with VR experience:* I think motivation is an important part, and to give the right feedback to the patient. It is very motivating when they use the HMD
5	*Therapist with VR experience:* Yes, it is changing the interaction with the patient, a bit; he is disappearing into another world. However, this is also the challenge; how much should you aid and guide the patient and how little *Therapist without VR experience:* Yes, it does, it has done that in this case. We have come to know him better and he has come to know us, and we know how much we can push him
Question	Patients' answers
1	*PV:* It cannot be described, the therapists are crucial; if I did not have them, then I would be lost. They came to me with the solution of moving to another rehabilitation center, but I said no way! I want to stay here until I am at the level where I can go home. Not before. And they accepted that
2	*F:* In the morning after the coffee, I sat down with one of the occupational therapist balls and practiced a bit, and then I went over and did knee flexion. So, I could absolutely use it without my therapist; I do not just sit and watch TV
3	*PV:* I Completely trust my therapist 100% *JB:* I have to trust my therapist; I do not know better. So, for me it is simple
4	*JB:* I assume that. It requires motivation to deal with some cases. It is often her last push that keeps me going, when we think it is a waste of time
5	*PV:* Not at all. Now it is this thing we concentrate on and then we go on to something else. It is like any other training tool

4.2 Patterns in Patient-Therapist Interaction

Patterns were discovered and labelled according to the themes mentioned above:
Therapist with Prior Knowledge of VR Rehabilitation

- The therapist physically aids the patients while interacting with the system.
- Aids the placement of the patient's left hand (support hand) to the table in order to use the right hand to control the system.

- Asks the patient to move back in order to get a better sitting position.
- Compliments the patient for his performance.
- Tries to verbally guide and motivate the patients.
- Motivates the patients by explaining he is doing a good job and physically showing with his hands which areas are active under the movements.
- Uses physical aid in order for the patient to understand the in-game grabbing.
- Motivates the patient as he fails to place objects and gets confused.

Therapist without Prior Knowledge of VR Rehabilitation

- Therapist's body interferes with the infrared light from the Leap Motion and moves out of the area of video recording.
- Standing aside and does not provide guidance when patients are confused.
- Uses no physical aid and only observes the patient.
- Stands far away from the patient.
- Following the patient but not commenting on the patient's performance.
- Sits down next to the patient and motivates the patient while the system is restarting and the HMD is taken off the patient.

5   Discussion

This section discusses the presented results in order to draw a conclusion of the study.

Interference with Hardware. There is a clear difference in the way the therapists interact with their patient while they have the HMD on. The therapists with experience in VR rehabilitation sit next to their patient in order to aid the patient, e.g., as it was observed under the test of PV, while the less experienced have a tendency to stand or sit with some distance to the patient. This can be due to their limited knowledge of the VRTS, as they do not know how much they can aid the patient without interfering with the system. E.g., this was observed under the second test of B, where the therapist interferes with the Leap Motion, and as a result, moves further away from the patient, where she stands for most of the testing period. In contrast, the therapist with more experience shows no fear of interfering and aids the patient and moves his hand out of frame when it starts to be tracked instead of the patients. All the therapists answered under the semi-structured interview that they did not feel any influence of the VRTS on the interaction with the patients, even though contrary facts have been observed. It can be argued that the therapists are not aware of their changed behaviour with patients utilising the VRTS compared to conventional rehabilitation.

Patient Confusion. Patient confusion can be seen under all preliminary tests as the patients are new to the system. B uses the first test session to learn how to manipulate the in-game objects with the Leap Motion, as the grabbing need to be controlled and precise. E.g., when the therapist asks her to grab an object the answer is that the patient is too afraid to grab it. This fear and confusion diminished over the following weeks while B is interacting with the system. One of the patients, JB, a 74 years old with a stroke in his cerebellum, had difficulties in understanding how to interact with the system and grabbing using the Leap Motion. JB decided to quit the experiment after the first week of training, as he felt "defeated". He could not understand why the in-game objects could fall out of his hand when the Leap Motion stopped tracking or when he did not look at the hand. Furthermore, he could not understand cognitively where different objects had to be placed, even with verbal guidance and physical aid from the therapist. A male patient, PV, who had the lowest score in the pre-test, also experience intensive struggling while using the system. He pushed objects without grasping the hand, as he did not have any tactile feedback and therefore could not understand when to grasp. An experienced therapist, who was supervising his testing sessions, verbally guided and physically aided the patient without any response. Therefore, the therapist used a physical box in order to simulate the grasping of the in-game object which aided the patient in completing the task.

Physical Aid. Again, the therapists can be divided into two groups: with and without VR rehabilitation experience. The therapists with VR rehabilitation experience aided the patients while testing, they manipulated with the patients' paraplegic arm in order for the patients to either use it as support or to manipulate the in-game objects. The therapist who was supervising the first test of patient B used his own hand as a weight to hold the patients left hand on the table. The reason of the therapist actions was to support a good sitting position of the patient, when he was using right hand to manipulate the VE. The same therapist was accompanying PV in his test session, where he again used physical aid to assist the patient. PV was using his left hand for playing while the therapist was supporting the patients back, as PV had the tendency to push his body to the left side, due to neglect. The less experienced therapists did not utilise physical aid, as they were not in range of the patient and did not react when the patient needed aid. It was observed that the patients assisted by less experienced therapists learned the mechanics of the game faster than the patients with more experienced therapists. This is in correlation with the discovery made by Lettinga et al. physical aid can minimise the patients' ability to learn from their mistakes.

Physical Guidance. Physical guidance is hard to achieve as the patient is using a HMD, and therefore cannot see the therapist's body and hands. This results in a higher degree of verbal guidance from the experienced therapist and acts as a barrier for the therapist with less experience. The therapist who assisted PV in his test sessions used physical guidance after the HMD were taken off. Therefore, the patient received physical guidance regarding his position and the way of grabbing for the following session.

Verbal Guidance. All the therapists with VR rehabilitation experience intensively utilised verbal guidance, and assisted the patients under the entire testing sessions, whereas the therapists with less experience used no form of or little verbal guidance. This could be a result of their lack of knowledge of the in-game tasks or their fear of interfering with the system. The patients who received verbal guidance performed more proper movements compared to the one who did not. Consequently, those without verbal guidance performed improper movements while trying to reach the objects faster in any way possible, as no therapist prevented it. This can be especially seen in the test of PV and first test of B, where the therapist guides the patient in every move to readjust their sitting position when it is incorrect. Under the semi-structured interviews, all the patients expressed gratitude and trust towards the therapists and their guidance, and the therapists expressed trust in the patients to follow their guidance.

Motivation. Therapists with no VR experience did not motivate the patients while using the VRTS. However, they sustained in the interview that they used motivation in the rehabilitation and training of each patient. Again, this can be a result of their lack of experience with VR rehabilitation and fear of interfering, or insufficient introduction to the VRK. The more experienced therapists (e.g., JB's therapist) used motivation to convince the patient to participate in more sessions. Furthermore, the therapist supervising PV asked the patient to place a few more objects and complimented his performance in order to encourage him to continuing playing.

6 Conclusion

The purpose of this paper was to evaluate the difference in the interaction methods between patients and therapists when utilising a VRK compared to conventional rehabilitation. The testing sessions indicated a clear difference between the therapists and their way of interacting with the patients. The therapists with experience in VR rehabilitation approached the patients as in a conventional training session utilising verbal and physical guidance, including hand gestures and commands. Furthermore, they physically aided the patients throughout the test by supporting the paraplegic hand and arm [3], and motivated the patients by giving compliments, establishing a closer therapist-patient bond. Whereas, the therapists with less VR rehabilitation experience demonstrated a lack of therapist-patient interaction, as they did not use any of their regular methods to interact with the patients. Consequently, the system could be a barrier between patient and therapist, because of the fear of interfering with the system or a lack of training in VR rehabilitation. Therefore, it can be concluded that a VRK affects the interaction between patient and therapist. However, proper training in VR rehabilitation can eliminate many of the barriers so the VRK can be used as any other tool in rehabilitation without any influence on the interaction.

Acknowledgments. The authors would like to thank Erling Pedersen from CoLab Vest, Jonas Drefeld from Syddansk Sundhedsinnovation, Tobias Theodorus Perquin from Teknologisk Institute, and the therapists at NeuroRehab, Sydvestjysk Sygehus, Grindsted, Denmark.

References

1. Hjerneskadeforeningen: Tal og Fakta om Hjerneskader. https://hjerneskadet.dk/om-hjernes kader/tal-og-fakta-om-hjerneskader
2. Weston, W.W., Brown, J.B.: Overview of the patient-centred clinical method. In: Patient-Centred Medicine: Transforming the Clinical Method, pp. 21–113. Sage Publication, London (1995)
3. Talvitie, U.: Guidance strategies and motor modelling in physiotherapy. Physiother. Theor. Pract. **12**(1), 49–60 (1996)

4. Jensen, G.M., Shepard, K.F., Hack, L.M.: The novice versus the experienced clinician: insights into the work of the physical therapist. Phys. Ther. **70**(5), 314–323 (1990)
5. Lettinga, A.T., Siemonsma, P.C., Van Veen, M.: Entwinement of theory and practice in physiotherapy: a comparative analysis of two approaches to hemiplegia in physiotherapy. Physiotherapy **85**(9), 476–490 (1999)
6. Heath, C.: The delivery and reception of diagnosis in the general-practice consultation. In: Drew, P., Heritage, J. (eds.) Talk at Work: Interaction in Institutional Settings, pp. 235–267. Cambridge University Press (1992)
7. Thornquist, E.: Profession and life: separate worlds. Soc. Sci. Med. **39**(5), 701–713 (1994)
8. Slingsby, B.T.: The nature of relative subjectivity: a reflexive mode of ethical thought. J. Med. Philos. **30**(1), 11–39 (2005)
9. Slingsby, B.T.: Professional approaches to stroke treatment in japan: a relationship-centred model. J. Eval. Clin. Pract. **12**(2), 218–226 (2006)
10. Rizzo, A., Kim, G.J.: A SWOT analysis of the field of virtual reality rehabilitation and therapy. Presence: Teleoperators Virtual Environ. **14**(2), 119–146 (2005)
11. Sundhedsstyrelsen: National Klinisk Retningslinje for Fysioterapi og Ergoterapi til Voksne med Nedsat Funktionsevne som følge af Erhvervet Hjerneskade, Herunder Apopleksi – 8 Udvalgte Indsatser (2014). https://www.sst.dk/da/udgivelser/2014/ ∼ /media/F3A5AAE7 542049FE8854C25109E40D1C.ashx

The Influence of Biofeedback on Exercise Correctness and Muscle Activity

Laurentiu Toader, Nicolai B. K. Jensen, and Michael B. Holte(✉)

Department of Architecture, Design and Media Technology,
Aalborg University Esbjerg, Niels Bohrs Vej 8, 6700 Esbjerg, Denmark
{ltoade12,nbkjl2}@student.aau.dk, mbh@create.aau.dk

Abstract. This paper examines the effect of an electromyography (EMG) biofeed back fitness application, and its potential to improve resistance training and exercise execution using the measure of muscle activity. To examine this, an application was built and tested using biceps curl as the reference exercise. The participants were divided into three conditions: the first condition did not receive any feedback, the second condition received feedback from a personal trainer, and the last used the feedback presented by the application. The focus is to investigate the participant's ability to activate muscle fibres in the biceps, and improve the execution in regards to minimising the shoulder involvement over three sets. The results of the study do not provide any statistically significant improvements using biofeedback versus no feedback. However, the participants with the applicational support, as well as the participants within the personal trainer condition, show a slight improvement on the visual correctness of the exercise execution. The lack of statistically significance, important observations and indications are discussed.

Keywords: Biofeedback · EMG · Exercise correctness · Fitness
Muscle activity

1 Introduction

The Danish board of health recommends that the average person should perform approximately 30 min of moderate physical activity a day, reason being that physical activity is essential to maintain an adequate personal health [1]. However, encouraging people to perform physical activity, such as strength training, is difficult, since it requires general knowledge on how to perform a certain exercise and what exercise to choose in order to improve a personal weak area [2–4]. It is therefore important to find new effective ways to provide people with the right information on fitness and health.

The technological advancement regarding health information and fitness technology, such as heart rate monitors, step counter, exercise trackers, fitness and health apps, etc., have become more accessible to the public. Studies have shown that fitness and health technology have the potential to improve physical health, and increase health-care awareness with the use of fewer resources [5–8]. However, many of these applications and technologies have deficiencies and limits, because they are not based on behavioural theories and guidelines from the medical and health industry [5, 6]. In

© ICST Institute for Computer Sciences, Social Informatics and Telecommunications Engineering 2018
A. L. Brooks et al. (Eds.): ArtsIT 2017/DLI 2017, LNICST 229, pp. 139–150, 2018.
https://doi.org/10.1007/978-3-319-76908-0_14

the field of rehabilitation and strength training, studies have shown that the use of biofeedback technology can significantly improve the health and mobility of people suffering from brain injury, cerebral palsy and stroke [9–11]. To this end, in the field of sport science, fitness and health technology, more specifically electromyography (EMG), is used to determine the effectiveness of a certain movement or exercise in muscle activity science [12–15].

This paper hypothesise: *an EMG-based biofeedback fitness application can improve exercise execution correctness and muscle activity during strength training in comparison to conventional training.* This research will verify this hypothesis by developing and evaluating an EMG-based fitness application. The evaluation will be conducted by comparing the effectiveness of the EMG application versus conventional instructions on a specific strength training exercise.

2 Theoretical Background

This section presents general theory of physical strength training and an explanation of EMG and its means of use.

2.1 Strength Training

When developing an application, which uses EMG feedback to evaluate muscle activity and exercise correctness, it is critical to understand the physiology during strength training, in order to understand the feedback provided by EMG.

Strength training is defined as the process of breaking and rebuilding muscle tissue. When an athlete is actively performing strength training, they are inflicting a form of stress on themselves both physically and mentally. The body's reaction to this stress is to adapt by reshaping and rebuilding muscle, which can withstand this impact [16, 17]. During heavy strength training, the chemical environment of the muscle changes through the process of energy stores depletion and lactic acid accumulation, which gives the feeling of fatigue. This, alongside the breakdown of muscle tissue, is what provides the body with the signal to improve from its current state [17].

A human consists of a frame (the skeleton) which becomes mobile through the functions of the muscles. All human movement is usually triggered by a contraction of one or several muscles. When a muscle, or muscles, contract, it creates a force which affects the relevant bones and creates movement in that specific part of the body [17]. This contraction happens due to the internal structure of the muscles and the function of the neuromuscular system.

The muscle is a highly complex tissue, consisting of muscle fibres, which can contract and expand depending on the signal received from the brain. The muscle fibres are connected by connective tissue, such as tendons and ligaments, which makes up the elastic components of the muscle [16, 17]. After a long period of strength training one would see an increase in the amount of fibres and cross-sectional area and volume, which is referred to as hypertrophy.

A muscle needs a signal from the brain to active a contraction, this process is handled by the neuromuscular system. The neuromuscular system is built from the muscles themselves and the central nervous system. When a simple movement has to be made, the brain sends an impulse through the nerves to a giving motor neuron, which then activated the contraction of the muscle fibres. The speed, in which the motor neuron can activate the synchronisation of the muscle fibres, is what determines the force developed [16]. When doing a specific strength training exercise, the correct muscle activation and force developed is essential in order to perform the exercise properly. The muscle contractile force depends on the intensity and frequency of nerve impulses to be sent to the muscle. Thus, the ability to develop muscle power depends on both neural, muscle structural and biomechanical properties [16]. The intensity of a nerve impulse from the motor neurons, and the contractile force, is what can be measured by EMG.

2.2   Electromyography

Electromyography (EMG) is the study and evaluation of the electrical potential of the muscles and nerves, and is the foundation behind electro diagnostic medical consultation [12–15]. Through EMG it is possible to obtain information about the activities within the muscles and nerves, and it is mostly used in the medical field to determine nerve or muscle damage, and in sports medicine to investigate muscle activity during movement [12, 13]. EMG provides easy access to the physiological processes, which generates force within the muscles and produce movement.

The electrical signal conducted by the muscle tissue is called Muscle Unit Action Potential (MUAP) and can be detected by the electrodes in the muscles or on the surface of the skin. The MUAP is a depolarisation of the motor neuron, which occur when the central nervous system sends a signal to contract a given muscle. This depolarisation passages along the muscle fibres and produces an electrical wave which can be detected by the recording electrodes [13, 15]. When using a two-electrode EMG system, the MUAP is represented by a triphasic signal, which is the potential difference between pole A and B (see Fig. 1).

There are several factors that can influence the quality of the signal detected by the electrodes, of which some can be controlled by the user, i.a., the placement of the electrodes, the distance between the recording electrodes, orientation in regards to muscle fibres and the type of used electrodes [13, 14]. Furthermore, one of the electrical factors that can influence the fidelity and signal is the noise-to-signal ratio. This factor is the ratio between the amplitude of the EMG signal and the amplitude of the noise signal. The noise signal is defined as the signal which is not a part of the EMG signal, such as electrical interference [13, 14]. The EMG signal is relatively low, which means that amplification is needed; here, usually a differential amplifier is used (see Fig. 1). The next step is then to filter the noise from the EMG signal; here, it has been proven effective to use low pass and high pass filters to eliminate the low- and high frequencies [13, 14]. In most cases the signal is rectified and averaged to indicate the EMG amplitude, which indicates the MUAP.

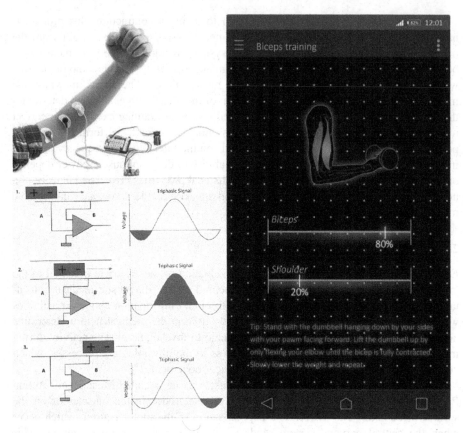

Fig. 1. On the top-left: a Grove EMG Detector sensor connected on a forearm, bottom-left: a differential amplifier generating a triphasic signal, and on the right: the application interface. (Color figure online)

3 Related Work

This section presents related work on the use of EMG feedback in rehabilitation and strength training, similar applications and important findings from related studies.

EMG has a wide range of utility and its use has been proven effectively on biofeedback applications. EMG is often used in sports and exercise studies, where it is a valuable tool to analyse movements, or compare the effect of different exercises on muscle activity, coordination and hypertrophy [18–20]. Bird et al. [19] used EMG to determine what abdominal exercise was most effective when activating the muscle fibres. In the study the EMG activity of the external oblique, upper rectus abdominis and lower rectus abdominis was collected. The data collected from the EMG allowed the investigators to analyse in what phases, concentric and eccentric, the different muscles were active, and conclude that the crunch exercise was overall better than the ab-slide [19]. Similar usages of EMG have been presented in several studies, and prove the overall effectiveness of the EMG for exercise evaluation [18–21].

Also in the field of rehabilitation the EMG has proven an indispensable tool; here, the data being received from the EMG, along with the guidance of a physiotherapist, has proven most effective on the early rehabilitation stages [9–11]. Studies on biofeedback applications and rehabilitation have showed that the use of EMG, as direct biofeedback to the user, has proven highly effective on muscle strength development and range of motion, in post-stroke- and cerebral palsy patients [9–11]. Furthermore, the use of EMG biofeedback and gamification has indicated a higher level of adherence and motivation in comparison to traditional rehabilitation exercises [9, 11]. Common for these studies is the use of EMG presents the user, physiotherapist and investigator with valuable information on the muscle activity during exercises, and the information on how to correctly guide or adjust the exercise to insure the highest amount of MUAP.

Conventional methods for measuring and improving exercise execution involve physiotherapists or personal trainers, who observe and correct the person performing the exercise. This method has proven highly effective and motivating for the user [3, 4]. However, this method has significant deficiencies in cost, accuracy, opportunity, coverage and adherence. A physiotherapist or a personal trainer typically splits their attention among several patients at different locations, which means that the patients or clients have to be self-sufficient at some level. Self-reporting is often used to ensure that the patients or clients execute the exercises themselves. However, this is often inaccurate due to forgetfulness or un- and intentional misreporting, or lack of knowledge on how to perform the exercises correctly [2]. Researches have investigated how to improve this by using wearable sensors to recognise, classify and report activities, and most studies have proved the effectiveness of wearable sensors on activity recognition [22–25]. However, the majority of this research has been conducted in controlled environments with the focus on rehabilitation, and in most cases solely GPS and accelerometers have been used [5, 22–25, 27].

In regards to the realisation outside the scientific field and towards the commercial market, there are many applications created for the purpose of improving fitness and health. Since mobile devices are both highly available and have several sensors that can be used, many application developers have created a vast number fitness and health applications with the purpose of information distribution, exercise libraries, training logging and tracking tools [5, 26, 27]. The state-of-the-art applications mostly use accelerometer and GPS; however, in some cases heart rate monitors and calorie counters are also used [5, 26, 27].

4   Design and Development

In this section decisions behind the application is presented, and the design choices for the interface justified.

The Application. Since the purpose of this application is to provide straightforward and effective biofeedback, and the nature of this study is to observe the effect of such an application, a non-intrusive method of EMG was chosen, also known as surface EMGs.

Since this study aims to prove that biofeedback can improve exercise execution, it is decided that a simplistic exercise should be used. The biceps curl is chosen due to is accessibility to measure, and because it is a simple exercise for conducting movement analysis [16]. The formal description of the biceps curl is [28]:

1. Stand up straight with a dumbbell in each hand at arm's length. Keep your elbows close to your torso and rotate the palms of your hands until they are facing forward. This will be your starting position.
2. Now, keeping the upper arms stationary, exhale and curl the weights while contracting your biceps. Continue to raise the weights until your biceps are fully contracted and the dumbbells are at shoulder level. Hold the contracted position for a brief pause as you squeeze your biceps.
3. Then, inhale and slowly begin to lower the dumbbells back to the starting position.
4. Repeat for the recommended amount of repetitions.

The Interface. Data sliders are used to display the feedback to the user. It is presented by a percentage scale, which is additionally supported by a colour gradient from red to green. The right value of how much the specific muscle should be included, within the executed exercise, is shaded in a green area (see Fig. 1). Furthermore, the application delivers an animated gif, which shows the execution of the exercise. The visualisation is reduced to solely display a human torso and the active muscles in this exercise for simplification, give a good overview, and to prevent information overload [29, 30].

EMG Recording. The physical part of the prototype consists of an Arduino Uno to which an Arduino shield is connected in order to provide direct connectivity to the four pin harness jump wires that are specific to the EMG sensors. Two Grove EMG Detector sensors are applied; one being reserved for the biceps, and the other for the deltoid. The sensors are connected to the muscle through 3.5 mm connector cables, which present three data collection caps. Each cable is connected to three disposable surface electrodes, which are placed on the muscle, so one is situated at the base of the muscle, another at the middle of the muscle, and the last one on a prominent bone, thus grounding the electrical circuit (see Fig. 1).

In this study the software reads the amplitude received from the EMG sensors at 50 Hz, and records the data using PLX-DAQ software. However, an EMG sensor measures noise along with the essential signal. Hence, an exponential moving average (EMA) band pass filter with a low cut-off alpha value of $\alpha_L = 0.3$ and a high cut-off alpha value of $\alpha_H = 0.5$ is implemented:

$$L_{co}(t) = \alpha_L \times x(t) + (1 - \alpha_L) \times L_{co}(t - 1)$$
$$H_{co}(t) = \alpha_H \times x(t) + (1 - \alpha_H) \times H_{co}(t - 1)$$

$$(1)$$

Where $x(t)$ is the sensor value at time t, and L_{co} and H_{co} are the low cut-off and high cut-off values, respectively.

5   Methods

For the evaluation of the prototype, each participant underwent two stages: a Max Voluntary Isometric Contraction (MVIC) pre-test and a proof-of-concept test. The tests were conducted in the campus fitness at Aalborg University Esbjerg.

Test Participants and Procedure. For the proof-of-concept test 15 participants volunteered for the test, 12 healthy males and 3 healthy females (age: 23 ± 3 years), all with little to no previous strength training experience. The exercise chosen for this test is the biceps curl, based on its availability for measuring and since this exercise is often miss executed [16, 31]. The electrodes were placed on the biceps brachii short head and the deltoideus posterior, since these are the muscles involved in the exercise. All the participants were assigned to one of three conditions: baseline, Personal Training (PT) and application. The baseline condition group tested the control condition, which means that they had no feedback before or during the exercise execution. The Personal Training condition group had the aid of a personal trainer both before and during the exercise execution, and the application condition had the assistance of the application. To ensure balance between groups, the test participants were artificially allocated into the three condition groups based on the MVIC pre-test, which determined the weight they could execute a single repetition of the given exercise. The MVIC pre-test was conducted by measuring the EMG amplitude generated when lifting a max weight in an isometric contraction.

Assessment. Three sets of eight repetitions had to be completed with a weight equivalent to 40% of their MVIC. The groups underwent a between-groups independent measures design, meaning that none of the participants in a given group A could be part of group B, and each participant tested the exercise individually. Both an inter-group and an intra-group comparison analysis were conducted to investigate if one condition performed better than the others, and to acknowledge any improvement between sets. The recorded data was given in MUAP from the sensors predestined for the bicep and the deltoid, respectively. Each set per individual was recorded in a separate Excel file, and afterwards all three sets were added to a file labelled for the participant.

To analyse and compare the EMG data, the data had to be normalised. Root mean square (RMS) normalisation was used to compare the intra-group and inter-group relations [18]. Since biceps curl is an exercise intended to isolate the biceps and to limit the activation of the front shoulder, the ratio between the two muscles was used, in order to compare.

Expected Results. Based on the literature review, it is expected that the application condition is equal or more effective than the PT condition, and significantly more effective than the baseline condition. Meaning that, the participants testing the application condition would show higher increase in muscle activity through the EMG values, and better exercise execution, than the PT and baseline condition.

6   Results

In this section, the results from the proof-of-concept test are presented (See Fig. 2). The data is checked for normality using Shapiro-Wilks normality test and homogeneity of variance using the Levene's variance analysis test. Next, the data is analysed using the parametric one-way independent analysis of variance (ANOVA).

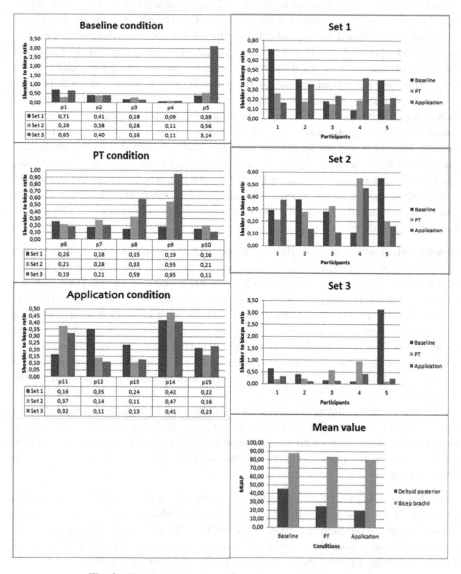

Fig. 2. The experimental results represented by histograms.

Intra EMG Ratio Result. In this subsection, the results of the intra-group analysis are presented. The data is segmented accordingly to the three conditions: baseline, personal training (PT) and application, to show if any improvements between sets are found within the groups.

For all three conditions, a one-way independent ANOVA is performed to investigate the difference between the three sets. The result of the ANOVA shows that the variances for all the sets are equal for the baseline, PT and application conditions ($f = 1.06$, $p > 0.05$; $f = 0.92$, $p > 0.05$; $f = 0.23$, $p > 0.05$, respectively).

Inter EMG Ratio Result. In this subsection, the results of the inter-group analysis are presented. Here the difference between each group is investigated, looking for a significant difference within set. In other words, if baseline condition performed better than PT- or application condition, within each set.

The data for each set underwent a one-way independent ANOVA, in order to investigate the difference between the three conditions. The result of the ANOVA shows that the variances for all the conditions for set 1, 2 and 3 are equal ($f = 1.55$, $p > 0.05$; $f = 0.31$, $p > 0.05$; $f = 0.97$, $p > 0.05$, respectively).

Inter EMG Biceps Average Result. To discover whether one condition achieved better bicep activation than the others, the Biceps and the Deltoid MUAPs are analyses between the three conditions. However, again, the ANOVA does not show a statistically significant difference between the conditions.

7 Discussion

The results of this study showed that there were no statistically significant differences between the three conditions, in both the MUAP ratio between biceps and deltoid, and the bicep and deltoid alone. Even though no statistically significant results were obtained during this study, observations showed that the application had some potential in assisting the user, similar to the personal trainer.

As mentioned in Sect. 4, the biceps curl is categorised as an isolation exercise, since only a few muscles are required in the execution of the exercise [31]. In other words, the biceps curl is an exercise which focuses on isolating the biceps muscle by avoiding the incorporation of other muscles, such as the deltoid. This could justify the lack of significant results, since the exercise might be too simplistic, which makes it hard to determine whether an individual performs better than another solely based on EMG data. Despite this, visual improvements of the execution were observed between the groups and sets during the sessions.

Based on observation, a frequent event occurred in the baseline condition, which involved a tendency of increasing the involvement of the deltoid when executing the exercise, in contrast to the PT and application conditions. This observation was strengthened when analysing the MUAP values of the deltoid activity, where the baseline condition shows a higher value than the other conditions, as seen in Fig. 2. Particularly, test participant 5 in the baseline condition group has a very high shoulder to bicep ratio during set 3, which was verified by the visual observation showing signs of fatigue and poor exercise execution. However, the baseline condition also has a higher MUAP value of the bicep, resulting in similar ratio between bicep and deltoid as the other conditions. Additionally, it was noticed that the participants in the baseline condition executed the repetitions faster than the other conditions, specifically from 1–2 s in comparison to 2.5–4 s for the PT condition and the application condition. This observation may be a contributing factor to that no difference between the three conditions was found, due to the fact that when performing strength training several factors affect the MUAP of the muscle: load, repetitions, sets, pause and time under tension [16]. In this study, all factors were normalised for all conditions, except the time under tension (TUT). All conditions performed three sets of 8 repetitions with a weight corresponding to the 40% MVIC, and with a pause of 60 s between sets. However, the TUT was determined by the individual alone, or given by the personal trainer or application. This may have resulted in the larger rate of force development in the baseline condition than the other conditions. Furthermore, this means that the baseline condition activated their muscle fibre more synchronised, making it a more explosive movement with a higher MUAP, but over a shorter period of time. This can result in being able to lift more weight, but not with better execution.

As mentioned in Sect. 3, the use of EMG biofeedback has proven highly effective in behavioural change, muscle strength development and range of motion, in post-stroke- and cerebral palsy patients [9–11]. The same kind of behaviour change and exercise improvements was observed during the testing sessions. The baseline condition did not change their execution between sets, whereas the two other conditions did. The participants in the PT condition all tried to improve their execution and performance based on the feedback given by the personal trainer. Likewise, the application condition changed their execution based on the feedback provided by the application. However, some of the participants, within this condition expressed confusion towards the feedback. Hence, the limited information might have been too inferior for the participants to fully understand the corrections needed to improve execution. Nevertheless, all participants concluded that the meaning of the feedback was to increase bicep activation and lower shoulder activation, as intended. Additionally, the participants in the application condition visually improved the execution of their repetitions by better isolating the bicep. The results in Fig. 2 also hint this tendency.

In spite of the circumstances and factors discussed above, in this study a small sample group was recruited for the testing sessions. Hence, significant results might be found in a larger sample group based on the tendencies highlighted in this study.

8 Conclusion

The main goal in this paper was to investigate the effectiveness of a developed electromyography (EMG) biofeedback fitness application and its potential improvement of strength training exercise execution using the measure of muscle activity. The results obtained from this study hinted that participant without any feedback did not alter their execution between sets. The PT- and application condition indicated a better execution visually; however, no statistically significant results were found to support this observation. Furthermore, the application condition suggests that even though the feedback presented was not perfect, the participants did in fact improve between sets, which are supported by the literature [9–11]. The lack statistical significant results, leads to the conclusion that more extensive and thorough testing of these conditions is needed in order to obtain more definitive results.

Acknowledgments. The authors would like to thank the participants for volunteering for this study, the Department of Electronic Engineering at AAU Esbjerg for the collaboration on creating the software, and a special thanks to Jennifer Matthiesen for the cross-semester collaboration.

References

1. Andersen, L.B.: Fysisk Aktivitet: En Håndbog om Forebyggelse og Behandling, 3rd edn. Sundhedsstyrelsen, København (2011)
2. Chandra, H., Oakley, I., Silva, H.: Designing to support prescribed home exercises: understanding the needs of physiotherapy patients. In: ACM 7th Nordic Conference on Human-Computer Interaction: Making Sense Through Design, pp. 607–616 (2012)
3. Jeffery, R.W., Wing, R.R., Thorson, C., Burton, L.R.: Use of personal trainers and financial incentives to increase exercise in a behavioral weight-loss program. J. Consult. Clin. Psychol. **66**(5), 777–783 (1998)
4. Richard, M., Christina, M.F., Deborah, L.S., Rubio, N., Kennon, M.S.: Intrinsic motivation and exercise adherence. Int. J. Sport Psychol. **28**(4), 335–354 (1997)
5. Boulos, M.N.K., Brewer, A.C., Karimkhani, C., Buller, D.B., Dellavalle, R.P.: Mobile medical and health apps: state of the art, concerns, regulatory control and certification. Online J. Public Health Inform. **5**(3), 229 (2014)
6. Cowan, L.T., Van Wagenen, S.A., Brown, B.A., Hedin, R.J., Seino-Stephan, Y., Hall, P.C., West, J.H.: Apps of steel: are exercise apps providing consumers with realistic expectations? A content analysis of exercise apps for presence of behavior change theory. Health Educ. Behav. **40**(2), 133–139 (2013)
7. Liu, C., Zhu, Q., Holroyd, K.A., Seng, E.K.: Status and trends of mobile-health applications for iOS devices: a developer's perspective. J. Syst. Softw. **84**(11), 2022–2033 (2011)
8. Kranz, M., Möller, A., Hammerla, N., Diewald, S., Plötz, T., Olivier, P., Roalter, L.: The mobile fitness coach: towards individualized skill assessment using personalized mobile devices. Pervasive Mob. Comput. **9**(2), 203–215 (2013)
9. Yoo, J.W., Lee, D.R., Sim, Y.J., You, J.H., Kim, C.J.: Effects of innovative virtual reality game and EMG biofeedback on neuromotor control in cerebral palsy. Bio-Med. Mater. Eng. **24**(6), 3613–3618 (2014)
10. Coleman, K.: Electromyography based human-computer-interface to induce movement in elderly persons with movement impairments. In: EC/NSF Workshop on Universal Accessibility of Ubiquitous Computing: Providing for the Elderly, pp. 75–79 (2001)
11. Shusong, X., Xia, Z.: EMG-driven computer game for post-stroke rehabilitation. In: IEEE Conference on Robotics, Automation and Mechatronics, pp. 32–36 (2010)
12. Türker, H., Sözen, H.: Surface electromyography in sports and exercise. In: Electrodiagnosis in New Frontiers of Clinical Research, p. 181 (2013)
13. Lamontagne, M.: Application of electromyography in sport medicine. In: Puddu, G., Giombini, A., Selvanetti, A. (eds.) Rehabilitation of Sports Injuries, pp. 31–42. Springer, Heidelberg (2001). https://doi.org/10.1007/978-3-662-04369-1_4
14. Reaz, M.B.I., Hussain, M.S., Mohd-Yasin, F.: Techniques of EMG signal analysis: detection, processing. Classif. Appl. Biol. Proced. Online **8**(1), 11–35 (2006)

15. Zwarts, M.J., Stegeman, D.F.: Multichannel surface EMG: basic aspects and clinical utility. Muscle Nerve **28**(1), 1–17 (2003)

16. Bojsen-Møller, J., Løvind-Andersen, J., Olsen, S., Trolle, M., Zacho, M., Aagaard, P.: Styrketræning Brøndby, 2nd edn, vol. 2. Danmarks Idræts-Forbund (2006)

17. Borch, C.M., Milandt, J., Bundgaard, N., Meiborn, J., Bundgaard, T., Egstrup, G., Tybjerg-Pedersen, E.: Fysisk Træning, Brøndby, 5th edn. Danmarks Idræts-Forbsund (2006)

18. Fukuda, T.Y., Echeimberg, J.O., Pompeu, J.E., Lucareli, P.R.G., Garbelotti, S., Gimenes, R. O., Apolinário, A.: Root mean square value of the electromyographic signal in the isometric torque of the quadriceps, hamstrings and brachial biceps muscles in female subjects. J. Appl. Res. **10**(1), 32–39 (2010)

19. Bird, M., Fletcher, K.M., Koch, A.J.: Electromyographic comparison of the ab-slide and crunch exercises. J. Strength Cond. Res. **20**(2), 436–440 (2006)

20. Son, J., Kim, S., Ahn, S., Ryu, J., Hwang, S., Kim, Y.: Determination of the dynamic knee joint range of motion during leg extension exercise using an EMG-driven model. Int. J. Precis. Eng. Manuf. **13**(1), 117–123 (2012)

21. Saeterbakken, A.H., Fimland, M.S.: Muscle activity of the core during bilateral, unilateral, seated and standing resistance exercise. Eur. J. Appl. Physiol. **112**(5), 1671–1678 (2012)

22. Buttussi, F., Chittaro, L., Nadalutti, D.: Bringing mobile guides and fitness activities together: a solution based on an embodied virtual trainer. In: ACM 8th Conference on Human-Computer Interaction with Mobile Devices and Services, pp. 29–36 (2006)

23. Lester, J., Choudhury, T., Borriello, G.: A practical approach to recognizing physical activities. In: Fishkin, K.P., Schiele, B., Nixon, P., Quigley, A. (eds.) Pervasive 2006. LNCS, vol. 3968, pp. 1–16. Springer, Heidelberg (2006). https://doi.org/10.1007/11748625_1

24. Chang, K.-H., Chen, M.Y., Canny, J.: Tracking free-weight exercises. In: Krumm, J., Abowd, G.D., Seneviratne, A., Strang, T. (eds.) UbiComp 2007. LNCS, vol. 4717, pp. 19–37. Springer, Heidelberg (2007). https://doi.org/10.1007/978-3-540-74853-3_2

25. Ermes, M., Pärkkä, J., Mäntyjärvi, J., Korhonen, I.: Detection of daily activities and sports with wearable sensors in controlled and uncontrolled conditions. IEEE Trans. Inf. Technol. Biomed. **12**(1), 20–26 (2008)

26. Liu, C., Zhu, Q., Holroyd, K.A., Seng, E.K.: Status and trends of mobile-health applications for iOS devices: a developer's perspective. J. Syst. Softw. **84**(11), 2022–2033 (2011)

27. Chen, Y., Pu, P.: HealthyTogether: exploring social incentives for mobile fitness applications. In: ACM Second International Symposium of Chinese CHI, pp. 25–34 (2014)

28. Digital Træningsværktøj. http://exorlive.com/dk

29. Müller, J., Wilmsmann, D., Exeler, J., Buzeck, M., Schmidt, A., Jay, T., Krüger, A.: Display blindness: the effect of expectations on attention towards digital signage. In: Tokuda, H., Beigl, M., Friday, A., Brush, A.J.B., Tobe, Y. (eds.) Pervasive 2009. LNCS, vol. 5538, pp. 1–8. Springer, Heidelberg (2009). https://doi.org/10.1007/978-3-642-01516-8_1

30. Seto, M.A., Scott, S.D., Hancock, M.: Investigating menu discoverability on a digital tabletop in a public setting. In: ACM International Conference on Interactive Tabletops and Surfaces, pp. 71–80 (2012)

31. Delavier, F.: Strength Training Anatomy, 3rd edn. Human Kinetics, Champaign (2010). Chapter 1

BubbleFeed: Visualizing RSS Information in Public Spaces

Effie Karuzaki[1(✉)], Nikolaos Partarakis[1], Margherita Antona[1], and Constantine Stefanidis[1,2]

[1] Institute of Computer Science,
Foundation for Research and Technology – Hellas (FORTH), N. Plastira 100,
Vassilika Vouton, 700 13 Heraklion, Crete, Greece
{karuzaki, partarak, antona, cs}@ics.forth.gr
[2] Department of Computer Science, University of Crete, Heraklion, Greece

Abstract. Public interaction displays contribute to upgrading the quality of public spaces since they attract many users and stimulate social interaction. In this paper, BubbleFeed is presented, a system for visualizing RSS news from multiple sources in public spaces. RSS news headlines are displayed inside virtual interactive bubbles ascending from the bottom of a vertical screen to the top, resembling the bubbles formed in a glass of soft drink. Besides touching the bubbles to expand and read the respective news stories, playful user interaction is supported to promote better engagement and motivate multiple users to participate. To support custom news feeds and Facebook posts in addition to RSS feeds, we have built a tool and a library that produce RSS files from the respective sources. BubbleFeed also supports displaying weather information, hosting media galleries and providing useful information such as Wi-Fi hotspot maps.

Keywords: Information visualization · RSS feed · Public spaces

1 Introduction

Public spaces are social spaces that are generally open and accessible to people. They have a social impact on people present by involving necessary, optional and social activities [1] and by hosting exhibits that provide public information. The latter include for example advertising stands and bus-routes as well as tourist information such as weather forecast data, shop and sightseeing open hours, shop offers, and city news and events. To improve the quality of the information provided, researchers propose to encourage user-interaction with the data in an aesthetic manner, instead of statically displaying them on stands or screens. In this sense, information visualization techniques can help towards conveying information without overwhelming the users and playful interaction can help towards arousing user interest and attracting the public.

This paper presents BubbleFeed, a system for visualizing RSS information in public spaces. To support custom news content provided from stakeholders, a tool and a library have been built which produce RSS files from user-provided data and public Facebook pages respectively. The title of each news item, along with a key thumbnail, are displayed within a graphical color-coded bubble, called NewsBubble, which animates from the bottom of a large vertical touch screen to the top, resembling the bubbles formed in a glass of soft drink. Users who are interested in reading more about a topic can expand the related bubble into a bigger square-shaped one by touching it. The full news article also contains all the multimedia received from the RSS feed; however, they are displayed at the end of the news article instead of inside the text flow, so that users who are only interested in seeing the multimedia can find them more easily. Users can also interact with the bubbles in a playful manner, i.e., by dragging them around, colliding them together and bursting them. Additionally, the BubbleFeed system can display weather forecast information and can host image and video galleries as well as a WiFi hotspot map. A screenshot of the BubbleFeed display is shown in Fig. 1, while a video of the system is available on youtube[1].

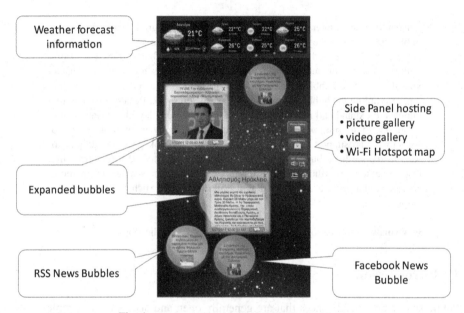

Fig. 1. A screenshot of the BubbleFeed system.

2 Related Work

2.1 Information Visualization

Visual representations of data, i.e., information visualization, is generally agreed to reinforce human cognition. Today, researchers and users of Information Visualization are convinced that it has great potential [2]. Information such as news are often visualized to achieve better organization and understanding, allowing users to infer additional data. For example, TweetViz [3] offers visualizations that represent topic

---

[1] https://www.youtube.com/watch?v=pjW2V7I4U6M.

distribution in a set of tweets, while TwitInfo [4] uses visualization to highlight peaks of tweet activity regarding a given topic. Many systems have also been built to help users browse large amounts of news articles. For example, sentiment maps [5] help users determine distinction in sentiments among multiple web sites concerning a given keyword, while Galaxy of News [6] is an old tool that allows users to quickly understand a news base using abstract presentations that cover the entire information base and interactions that progressively refine the information details. Other Information visualization systems can integrate information in some kind of art displayed on digital screens. For instance, Spark [7] uses informative art to visualize physical activity, while Redstrom et al. use a composition similar to the style of an abstract painter to show weather information in six cities, and a piece of "landscape art" to give a view of recent earthquake activity [8]. Ferscha in [9] display information as specific parts of an existing painting e.g., the number of birds in the sky represent the number of unread emails. In the same context, Partarakis et al. use informative art to represent mailbox information encoded within a painting through the appearance and disappearance of items representing specific email categories (e.g. urgent, email from colleagues, etc.) [10].

BubbleFeed visualizes RSS items from various sources as bubbles ascending in a large vertical display. To provide extra information and facilitate users in locating news articles they are interested in, bubble colors are used to indicate the type (limited time offer, ferry route delay update, etc.) or the origin of information presented (RSS, Facebook, custom content provided by the stakeholders). In cases where the news article contains images, a key thumbnail is displayed on the bubble so that users can perceive at a glance what the contained news is about.

2.2 Visualization in Public Spaces

Visualizing news information on digital screens and multi-touch displays can encourage content sharing and user interaction [11]. More specifically, authors in [11] present the CityWall, a large multi-touch display installed in a public space, and show that it acted like a stage, where users at the display attract other users. To encourage content sharing, Churchill et al. [12] developed a network of digital, interactive, bulletin boards, called 'Plasma Posters', that can replace the traditional cork boards in a building. Another work in this direction is the Notification Collage [13], a groupware system where distributed and co-located colleagues can post media elements onto a surface that all members can see. To resemble physical public bulletin boards, NC randomly places incoming elements like desktop snapshots and vacation photos on its surface. Apart from collaboration screens and bulletin boards, visualization systems can also be used in public spaces to display information of common interest. For example, authors in [14] designed a real-time visualization of bus departure times and deployed it in a public space with very positive results. MAGICBoard [15] is another public display deployed in a university setting that solicits electronic votes and opinions of bystanders on trivial topics, while EMDialog [16] is an interactive information presentation that was part of a museum exhibition and visualized the diverse and multi-faceted discourse about an artist, aiming to inform and provoke discussion.

BubbleFeed installations in public spaces allow people to read news, see the weather forecast, browse through media galleries and find interesting information such as the location of the Wi-Fi hotspots. Visualizing such information in public spaces can stimulate interaction among the users accessing it, thus more users can be attracted.

2.3   Playful Interaction with Information

Playful interactive interfaces (instead of merely interactive interfaces) are often proposed especially for exhibits installed in public places. Play and playfulness encourage exploration and creativity and stimulate social interaction [17], while in the context of public displays it is found that a large portion of the people interacting with them seem to be more concerned about playing 'with' the display rather than exploring its content [18]. In this vein, more and more work featuring public interaction displays make use of playful characteristics. For example, FizzyVis [19] is a playful multi-touch interface for information browsing, which visualizes information as animated interlinked bubbles reacting to touches. Other examples include Ubinion [20], a service that allows young people to interact with large interactive displays in urban spaces in order to provide feedback on municipal issues to local youth workers, and the playful installation presented in [21] which features a spherical display at the center of a circle made of interactive light-boxes that encourages users to "enter the circle" to explore it.

BubbleFeed enables user interaction with the bubbles in a playful manner, allowing users to expand them, drag them freely around the display, collide them together to "push" them away and burst the small ones. The colors used for indicating the type and/or the origin of news in the NewsBubbles are also carefully chosen so as to give an extra playful note to the overall installation.

3   Iterative Design

An iterative User Centered Design process using high-fidelity prototyping was followed in the development of the BubbleFeed system. Firstly, a high-fidelity prototype was built that was initially evaluated in-lab and after reaching a mature state installed in three different locations. The reason for choosing the high-fidelity prototype methodology was to enable both end-user and stakeholders' evaluation and to get actual usage statistics within different contexts of use, as well as collecting useful comments from the client stakeholders. The evaluation results along with the comments received were carefully analyzed, and a final system was built to replace the prototype.

3.1   BubbleFeed Prototype

The BubbleFeed prototype was designed to facilitate large interactive displays both for tabletop usage and as a wall mounted information point. To this end, tangible interaction with real objects in the context of a multi-touch surface device was initially considered. The initial design iteration was conducted by exploiting the Microsoft Surface 2.0 SDK and a Microsoft Surface 2.0 device. The first prototype was build using the Windows Presentation Foundation (WPF) and specific controls of the

Microsoft Surface 2.0 SDK. The in-lab evaluation of this initial design with usability experts and users concluded that the object manipulation paradigm (object that integrate fiducial markers that can be detected by the surface design) was not usable in terms of public space deployment as they could be lost or stolen. Furthermore, the interaction with objects in a completely free environment was not well perceived by all user groups (e.g., elder users). A simplification of this design was done by selecting a vertically oriented large size touch screen display in a kiosk style of operation that could support both multiple users at the same time (through multi-touch) and a solid containment for the equipment in terms of public spaces with security considerations (public buildings, airports, city squares, etc.). In such usage context, this set-up could be safeguarded through specialized equipment such as industrial grade touch screens for 24/7 operation, anti-vandalism structures for outside use etc. An initial prototype was implemented, evaluated in lab and deployed for public usage in the context of FORTH-ICS collaboration with Heraklion and Hersonissos municipalities and the port authority of Heraklion to address the needs of providing information to public library visitors, tourists of Hersonissos and cruise visitors of Heraklion respectively.

These exhibitions, which also represent different contexts of use, are permanent in the context of a larger effort to promote tourism and culture in Crete. As presented in Table 1, the content of each information display at the installation sites was adjusted to meet the requirements of the respective stakeholder. More specifically, in the library the content is aligned more towards informing visitors regarding events hosted by the municipality and the library itself than providing tourism information, while in a public information point such as the one of Hersonissos, the information presented is related to events such as concerts, exhibitions, bazaars, alterations of bus routes and attraction opening hours, as well as weather forecast information. Moreover, information such as "you are here" maps and Wi-Fi Hotspots is integrated together with photo and video libraries that are usually sought by tourists who want to remember the beauties of the locations they visit. Regarding the port installation in the case of cruises, the presented information is similar but tailored to the specific day covered by the cruise hop. The system design was also adapted to the concept of each space hosting it as shown in Fig. 2. For example, the Hersonissos info-point (Fig. 3.) followed a monochrome design approach to map the info-points interior. The prototype installed at the port authority was designed to match the sea colors, while for the one at the library a more sophisticated book-case like design was used.

Table 1. Features included in each prototype installation

	Multiple RSS feeds	World news feeds	Multi-language info	Weather forecast	Practical info	360° tourism info	Tourism promo videos	Send news by email
Vikelaia municipality library	X	-	X	X	-	-	-	X
Heraklion port authority	X	X	X	X	X	-	X	X
Info-point at the Hersonissos Municipality	X	X	X	X	X	X	X	X

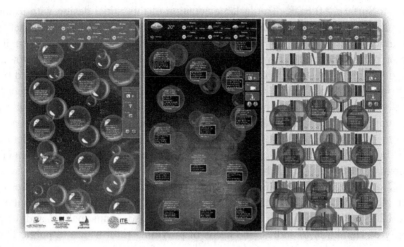

Fig. 2. Design approaches followed in each of the installations: Heraklion port authority (left), Info-point at the municipality of Hersonissos (middle) and Vikelaia municipality library (right)

Fig. 3. The BubbleFeed prototype installation at the Hersonissos info-point

3.2   Prototype Evaluation

During the pilot period of the permanent installation of the prototype, several modifications have been made to the system to automatically record usage statistics, while at the same time informal interviews with the stakeholders have been organized so as to gather their feedback and suggestions for improvement.

Usage Statistics Analysis

Usage statistics essentially measure user engagement, and include user interaction time and number of users attracted. More specifically, the statistics tracked include: (a) usage of the main sections of BubbleFeed (photos, videos, news, bubble items),

(b) time spent in each section, (c) amount of information browsed per sessions (heuristically indicated by pauses larger than five minutes between subsequent usages), (d) number of emails send per day and per session (e) number of POIs of the Wi-Fi hot spots and location map accessed, number of user simultaneously accessing the prototype (through detection of multiple touch inputs). As expected, in all the installations user engagement was quite high. In the case of the library, users were more relaxed and read more news than in the other two setups, mainly due to the fact that the library attracts mainly local citizens who have more time to spare during a library visit than a passing by visitor of a cruise stop or at an info point. However, tourism information users spent an average of 2.3 min in front of the installation as they read a few news bubbles and navigated through the map to find the Wi-Fi hotspots. The security and emergency information available in the BubbleFeed versions that were installed at the port were not as commonly used as expected by the port authority (only an average of 2 times per day for the emergency and 5 times per day for the security).

Stakeholder Feedback

Although BubbleFeed generally received positive comments from stakeholders, there were a few short-comings reported that resulted in the reengineering of the design and enhancement of several features in the final version of the system.

- *News from Facebook pages.* The BubbleFeed prototype supported showing news items extracted from posts on public Facebook pages using the Facebook Public Feed API[2]. However, this API stopped working and is not available anymore (since API V 2.0). Maintaining this functionality is extremely important for stakeholders that have active engagement in the social media.
- *Custom news content.* The prototype system only supported publicly available RSS feeds; however, all three stakeholders requested a way to also display custom news items as well. For example, the library asked to display current book offers and discounts of the library's bookstore, the municipality asked to announce emergent traffic reroutes and the port authority asked to display ferry delays, ticket availability, and offers at the port shopping center.
- *Playfulness.* After analyzing the statistics kept during the evaluation period, it was clear that the users had just the expected interaction with the BubbleFeed prototype for accessing information. Each user stayed in front of the screen for about 2 min accessing maximum three news and there was no interaction among users that were simultaneously accessing the prototype. Although this was expected, it was decided that the updated version should be more playful to incite users to spend more time with the system.
- *Limited weather information.* BubbleFeed screens received many clicks onto the weather icons, meaning that end-users wanted to get more weather information than the displayed ones. This also indicated misinterpretation of the design, as users conceived parts of the weather display as interactive controls.

---

[2] https://developers.facebook.com/docs/public_feed.

4 BubbleFeed Implementation

After consolidating the evaluation results of the pilot installations and taking into account the comments received from the stakeholders, a new enhanced version of the BubbleFeed system was built. This final version is based on Unity3D, a well-known cross-platform game engine that allow supporting a playful interface in order to achieve better user engagement and promote user-to-user interactions. The new version of BubbleFeed features all the functionality of the prototype, plus:

A playful interface: The NewsBubbles do not ascend in a straight line but follow a sinusoidal one. Also, extra decorative bubbles have been added with transparency values to enhance the feeling of screen depth.

Playful user interaction: NewsBubbles can interact with each other; more specifically, they can collide with each other like billiard balls. Moreover, users can freely drag them around the screen or force them to hit other bubbles. Users can also break the decorative bubbles on touch.

Displaying news from a public Facebook page. The Facebook Graph API was used to build a library that accesses public Facebook pages and produces RSS feeds from their posts. These RSSs are then loaded and displayed normally in BubbleFeed.

Displaying custom news content. A common request among the stakeholders was to display extra news that do not exist in any publicly available RSS feed, nor have been posted on a Facebook page, such as limited time offers or updates for short ferry delays. To this end, we developed a tool called MaRSS (Make RSS) that essentially enables stakeholders to produce tailor-made RSS feeds. Figure 4 shows a screenshot of the tool: users can add news items by pressing the "Add" button and by filling in the news details on the form shown at the right hand side. MaRSS produces a valid RSS feed that can be read by all RSS readers, thus the fields "title", "link" and "description" are mandatory. Images can include both image links and local images, while videos support local videos, video links and YouTube video links. Local resources are copied in a specific folder on the computer where the system is installed, along with the RSS xml file and BubbleFeed reads it periodically in the same way it reads a publically available RSS to get the fresh news.

Color-coded information visualization. The newer version of BubbleFeed supports assigning colors to bubbles containing certain type of information, such as emergency information, limited time offers, ferry delays etc. Different colors can also be applied to NewsBubbles that origin from different sources, e.g., facebook or RSS. Color-coded bubbles actually play a dual-fold role: they serve more information to the users without overwhelming the display, and also they make the interface more interesting and playful, arousing the curiosity of people passing by and thus attracting more users.

Displaying more weather information for the 7-day forecast. More specifically, additional to the weather description, wind speed and temperature displayed in the prototype version of BubbleFeed, wind direction, humidity levels as well as

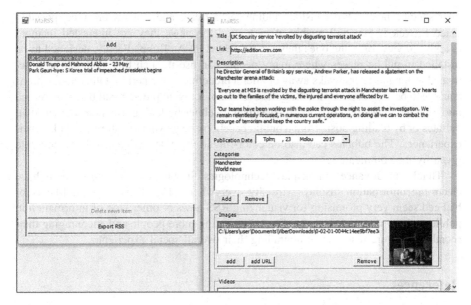

Fig. 4. A screenshot of the MaRSS tool. On the left, the news library is displayed. On the right, the news item editor is shown.

minimum and maximum day temperature are displayed. To display weather data, we u small icons instead of text, essentially achieving both displaying more information in the same screen space while keeping the interface clean for users to read and understand.

5 Conclusions and Future Work

This paper has presented the BubbleFeed system for visualizing RSS information in public spaces. In order to build BubbleFeed, an iterative process was followed based on a high-fidelity prototype that was installed in three public spaces: a public library, a public square and a port. Depending on the installation site, the information content and the overall system appearance were adapted to meet the needs of the respective stakeholders. Although all three installations attracted many users and received positive comments, a careful analysis of the usage statistics data collected along with the feedback provided by the stakeholders led us to some redesign of the BubbleFeed system in its final version. The latter enables the display of more information while adding playful notes that help engaging more users and lead to better information visualization.

The next step is to replace the prototypes with the renewed version of the BubbleFeed system after a new evaluation cycle is conducted to assess the impact of the new features and especially of the playful interaction. We will also contact other stakeholders such as the airport, hotels and local stores and adapt BubbleFeed to target their specific needs. We consider adding news filters and a news browser (possibly voice activated) that will enable users to find the news they are interested in more quickly, or view only the ones they are interested in. As BubbleFeed is designed to be installed in public places where many people can use it, such filters should be deactivated as long as users walks away or after a predefined time period. Other applications could also be supported by the BubbleFeed setup; for example, it could be easily turned into a public guestbook of a tourist-destination, either by letting users create their own bubbles or by reading posts from a public Facebook page where visitors would lay their experiences. The bubbles can also be color- highlighted depending on the review rate given by the commenters.

Thanks to advances in display technologies, it will soon be possible to have electronic information displays virtually everywhere [14]. Thus, systems like BubbleFeed seem very promising for visualizing RSS news or other kind of information in public spaces to upgrade their quality via attracting more people and encouraging their social interaction, resulting in upgrading their overall social experience.

References

1. Brignull, H., Rogers, Y.: Enticing people to interact with large public displays in public spaces. In: INTERACT 2003, pp. 17–24 (2003)
2. Fekete, J.-D., van Wijk, J.J., Stasko, J.T., North, C.: The value of information visualization. In: Kerren, A., Stasko, J.T., Fekete, J.-D., North, C. (eds.) Information Visualization. LNCS, vol. 4950, pp. 1–18. Springer, Heidelberg (2008). https://doi.org/10.1007/978-3-540-70956-5_1
3. Stojanovski, D., Dimitrovski, I., Madjarov, G.: TWEETVIZ: Twitter data visualization. In: Data Mining and Data Warehouses (SiKDD) (2014)
4. Marcus, A., Bernstein, M.S., Badar, O., Karger, D.R., Madden, S., Miller, R.C.: TwitInfo: aggregating and visualizing microblogs for event exploration. In: CHI 2011, p. 227 (2011)
5. Kawai, Y., Fujita, Y., Kumamoto, T., Tanaka, K.: Using a sentiment map for visualizing credibility of news sites on the web. In: WICOW 2008, pp. 53–58 (2008)
6. Rennison, E.: Galaxy of news: an approach to visualizing and understanding expansive news landscapes. In: UIST 1994, pp. 3–12 (1994)
7. Fan, C., Forlizzi, J., Dey, A.: A spark of activity: exploring informative art as visualization for physical activity. In: 14th UbiComp 2012, pp. 81–84 (2012)
8. Redstrom, J., Skog, T., Hallnas, L.: Informative art: using amplified artworks as information displays. In: DARE 2000, pp. 103–114 (2000)
9. Ferscha, A.: Informative art display metaphors. In: Stephanidis, C. (ed.) UAHCI 2007. LNCS, vol. 4555, pp. 82–92. Springer, Heidelberg (2007). https://doi.org/10.1007/978-3-540-73281-5_9
10. Partarakis, N., Kartakis, S., Antona, M., Paparoulis, G., Stephanidis, C.: Classic art for modern people. In: Stephanidis, C. (ed.) HCI 2011. CCIS, vol. 174, pp. 529–533. Springer, Heidelberg (2011). https://doi.org/10.1007/978-3-642-22095-1_106
11. Peltonen, P., Kurvinen, E., Salovaara, A., Jacucci, G., Ilmonen, T., Evans, J., Oulasvirta, A., Saarikko, P.: It's mine, don't touch! In: CHI 2008, p. 1285 (2008)
12. Churchill, E.F., Nelson, L., Denoue, L., Girgensohn, A.: The plasma poster network: posting multimedia content in public places. In: INTERACT, pp. 599–606 (2003)
13. Greenberg, S., Rounding, M.: The notification collage. In: CHI 2001, pp. 514–521 (2001)

14. Skog, T., Ljungblad, S., Holmquist, L.E.: Between aesthetics and utility: designing ambient information visualizations. In: INFOVIS 2003, pp. 233–240 (2003)
15. Tang, A., Finke, M., Blackstock, M., Leung, R., Deutscher, M., Lea, R.: Designing for bystanders. In: CHI 2008, p. 879 (2008)
16. Hinrichs, U., Schmidt, H., Carpendale, S.: EMDialog: bringing information visualization into the museum. IEEE Trans. Vis. Comput. Graph. **14**, 1181–1188 (2008)
17. Tsekleves, E., Darby, A.: The role of playfulness and sensory experiences in design for public health and for ageing well. In: Sensory Arts and Design, pp. 49–66 (2017)
18. Tomitsch, M., Ackad, C., Dawson, O., Hespanhol, L., Kay, J.: Who cares about the content? An analysis of playful behaviour at a public display. In: PerDis 2014, pp. 160–165 (2014)
19. Coutrix, C., Kuikkaniemi, K., Kurvinen, E., Jacucci, G., Avdouevski, I., Mäkelä, R.: FizzyVis: designing for playful information browsing on a multitouch public display. In: DPPI 2011, pp. 27:1–27:8 (2011)
20. Hosio, S., Kostakos, V., Kukka, H., Jurmu, M., Riekki, J., Ojala, T.: From school food to skate parks in a few clicks: using public displays to bootstrap civic engagement of the young. In: Kay, J., Lukowicz, P., Tokuda, H., Olivier, P., Krüger, A. (eds.) Pervasive 2012. LNCS, vol. 7319, pp. 425–442. Springer, Heidelberg (2012). https://doi.org/10.1007/978-3-642-31205-2_26
21. Williamson, J.R., Sundén, D.: Enter the circle. In: PerDis 2015, pp. 195–200 (2015)

Expressive Human Pose Deformation Based on the Rules of Attractive Poses

Masaki Oshita[(✉)], Kei Yamamura, and Aoi Honda

Kyushu Institute of Technology, 680-4 Kawazu, Iizuka, Fukuoka 820-8502, Japan
{oshita,aoi}@ces.kyutech.ac.jp, yamamura@cg.ces.kyutech.ac.jp

Abstract. We propose a method of deforming a human pose based on the rules of attractive poses. In our previous research, we proposed an approach for obtaining the rules of attractive poses from a set of attractive poses with a specific style and another set of unattractive poses by creating a decision tree based on the low-level pose features. In this paper, we propose a heuristic kinematics-based pose deformation method based on the discovered rules of attractive poses. The rules can be applied to any input pose with any specified scale. We evaluated our method through a user experiment. The results show that our method can deform a pose to realize a specified style, although not all rules are applicable to all kinds of poses and an appropriate style and deformation scale must be selected by the user.

Keywords: Human pose · Attractive poses · Pose deformation

1 Introduction

Attractive poses of human characters often appear in various types of media content such as movies, animations, computer games, illustrations, comics, and action figures. The creators must design attractive poses that fall within a certain style and are novel and eye-catching. Because there are no specific definitions or rules of attractive poses, the creators must design them based on their experience and through trial and error. This is a difficult and time-consuming task.

In our previous research [1], we proposed an approach to obtain the rules of attractive poses from a set of attractive poses with a specific style and another set of unattractive poses by creating a decision tree based on the low-level pose features that are computed from the example poses. We implemented our approach for two kinds of attractive poses, Hero and JoJo standing poses, and successfully discovered the rules of these styles. We also developed a heuristic pose deformation method specialized for the discovered rules.

In this paper, we propose a method of deforming a human pose. We developed a heuristic kinematics-based pose deformation method based on the discovered rules of attractive poses. This method is generalized and can work with any rules based on our low-level pose features. The rules can be applied to any input pose with any specified scale. Using our system, a creator can interactively design

© ICST Institute for Computer Sciences, Social Informatics and Telecommunications Engineering 2018
A. L. Brooks et al. (Eds.): ArtsIT 2017/DLI 2017, LNICST 229, pp. 162–171, 2018.
https://doi.org/10.1007/978-3-319-76908-0_16

novel poses. We evaluated our method in a user experiment. The results show that our method can deform a pose to realize a specified style, although not all rules are applicable to all kinds of poses and an appropriate style and deformation scale must be selected by the user.

Attractiveness is an important factor in content creation. However, it is a difficult factor to evaluate. Although there are subjective evaluations for human motions [2], the specific rules of attractiveness are still unclear. In this research, we developed a pose deformation method based on the rules of attractive poses that we discovered in our previous work [1]. For pose deformation, we implemented a kinematics-based method. Although similar approaches have been used before [3,4], our method focuses on the pose features that appear in the discovered rules of attractive poses. High-level pose features have been introduced in previous studies [5]. However, such high-level features are only applicable to a specific range of poses. To handle a wide range of poses, many pose features would be required.

2   System Overview

We have developed a pose deformation method and system. Figure 1 shows screen shots of our system. The user can specify an input pose, a class of attractive poses, and a deformation ratio. The system deforms the input pose interactively. An input pose can be specified in several ways. The system has a user experiment mode that we implemented for our experiments. This mode is explained in Sect. 5.1.

(a) pose deformation mode   (b) user experiment mode

Fig. 1. Developed pose deformation system. (a) The pose deformation mode allows the user to apply the rules of attractive poses to an input pose. The input pose is shown on the left side. The deformed (output) pose is shown on the right side. The class (style and category) of attractive poses is selected via the menu at the bottom. Whether the input pose satisfies the rules of the class is shown on the top left by a circle (yes) or a cross (no). The deformation scale is controlled by the slider on the top right. (b) The user experiment mode shows a randomly selected example pose and a deformed pose. The user is asked which pose has the indicated style.

Given a human skeleton model, a pose is represented by the position and rotation of the pelvis and the rotations of all joints. We used a skeleton model with 16 joints and 15 segments. A skinned human model is used to display poses, as shown in Fig. 1. Our system provides several ways to input a pose such as the use of a mouse-based pose editing interface [1].

3   Rules of Attractive Poses

In this section, we briefly explain the rules of attractive poses for two kinds of example poses. For the details, the reader can refer to our previous work [1].

We define each type of attractive pose using examples. Given a set of attractive poses with a specific style and another set of unattractive poses, we determined rules with which to separate the two sets of poses by creating a decision tree. Our research focuses on the static standing poses of a male character with an average physique who does not hold any props. We also assume that the attractiveness of a pose is view independent and it does not change when the pose is mirrored (i.e., flipped horizontally).

3.1   Pose Features

We compute a large number of low-level pose features for each example pose (381 in total). Of them, a decision tree automatically chooses a few important features that are effective for separating attractive and unattractive poses.

We use simple pose features such as the positions and orientations of the body segments and joints that can be computed from the pose representation using forward kinematics. All pose features are represented by a (signed or unsigned) one-dimensional scalar value. Three-dimensional positions and rotations are divided into a combination of single variables.

As mentioned above, the attractiveness of a pose should not change when the pose is mirrored (i.e., flipped horizontally). Therefore, instead of using pose features from the right and left sides (limbs) of the pose, we use the average and absolute difference between values from the two sides. Additionally, as the horizontal position and direction of the pose do not affect the attractiveness of the pose, horizontal positions and angles are discarded. The pose features are categorized as follows.

1. Rotational angles of the center joints.
2. Rotational angles of the limb joints (the average and difference angles of the right and left side joints).
3. Relative orientation angles between the center body segments.
4. Orientation of the center body segments with respect to the ground.
5. Body segment heights.
6. Body segment distances.
7. Height of the center of mass.

3.2   Example Pose Sets

We implemented our approach for two styles of attractive poses: Hero and JoJo styles. We chose these two styles because they are well-known popular styles in Japanese culture and materials such as picture and illustration books about these styles are available.

We created 30 example attractive poses for each style based on example poses that are taken from the picture and illustration books. In addition, we created 30 examples of unattractive poses.

Hero poses (Fig. 2) are the first type of attractive pose used in this study. Suited action heroes in Japanese movies often appear in Hero poses. When a hero or heroine faces the villain during a fight scene, they often adopt strong and defiant poses. The example poses are chosen from a picture book [6] that is meant to provide examples for creators.

JoJo poses (Fig. 3) are the other type of attractive pose considered in this study. The JoJo standing poses appear in the comic series *JoJo's Bizarre Adventure* by Araki [7], which is famous and popular in Japanese culture. The JoJo standing poses have a unique style. They are often imitated in many other media as well. The example poses were chosen from an illustration book [8].

Unattractive poses (Fig. 4) are ordinary standing poses. They were chosen from various books [9,10]. Of the many possible example poses, we selected ordinary poses that are dissimilar to the Hero and JoJo poses.

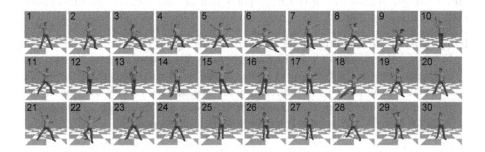

Fig. 2. Examples of attractive Hero poses

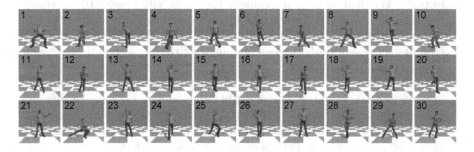

Fig. 3. Examples of attractive JoJo poses

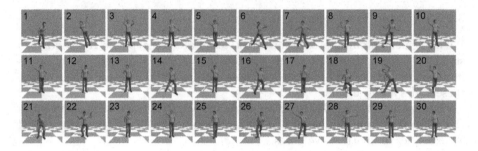

Fig. 4. Examples of unattractive poses

3.3 Discovered Rules of Attractive Poses

Decision trees are a non-parametric supervised learning method used for classification [11,12]. The results are represented as simple trees, which are visible and easy interpreted. By changing a parameter that determines the processing condition, different trees with similar accuracies can be generated. We chose a decision tree that contains fewer pose features and conditions and provides intuitive rules. Some styles have more than one category of poses. The rules for five classes (style and category) were obtained as follows.

Hero Poses. Almost all of the Hero poses can be categorized into one cluster with conditions as follows.

Hero pose: The bending angle of head with respect to the neck should be between −0.045 and 0.15. If the bending angle is between 0.15 and 0.045, the absolute value of the horizontal angles of the head with respect to the trunk and waist should be less than 0.11 and 0.77, respectively. In short, when both the bending and orientation angles of the head are small (i.e., the head is facing forward), the pose is considered to be a good pose.

JoJo Poses. JoJo poses are categorized into four clusters as follows.

JoJo pose A: When the bending angle of the trunk with respect to the ground is less than −0.063 (i.e., bent backward), the bending angle of the head with respect to the pelvis should be should be less than 0.22. In short, when the trunk is bent backward, the bending angle of the head should be straight. Typical poses in this category are poses 1 and 24 in Fig. 3.

JoJo pose B: When the bending angle of the trunk with respect to the ground is between −0.063 and 0.46 (i.e., straight), the absolute value of the difference between the bending angles of the left and right knees should be larger than 0.59. In short, when the trunk is straight, the bending angles of the knees should be asymmetrical. Typical poses are poses 9 and 16 in Fig. 3.

JoJo pose C: When the bending angle of the trunk with respect to the ground is between −0.063 and 0.46 (i.e., straight) and the absolute value of the difference between the bending angles of the left and right knees is smaller than 0.59, the absolute value of the horizontal orientation of the neck with respect to the trunk should be between 0.0078 and 0.01. In short, when the trunk is straight, the head should be facing forward. Typical poses are poses 11 and 26 in Fig. 3.

JoJo pose D: When the bending angle of the trunk with respect to the ground is larger than 0.46 (i.e., bent forward), the absolute value of the difference between the bending angles of the left and right elbows should be larger than 0.15. In short, when the trunk is bent backward, the bending angles of the elbows should be asymmetrical. Typical poses are poses 12 and 29 in Fig. 3.

4   Pose Deformation

We developed a pose deformation method based on the discovered rules of attractive poses. The rules can be applied to any input pose with any specified scale. We defined pose deformation parameters based on the pose features that are used in the rules. Using these parameters, an input pose can be deformed using a heuristic kinematics-based method.

4.1   Adjusting Pose Features

The target values of the pose features are determined according to the selected style and category and the specified scale of attractiveness. As the scale increases, each target pose value approaches to the desirable range and value in the discovered rules. When the scale is between 0.0 and 0.5, it is linearly interpolated from the initial value, which is computed from the initial pose to the threshold using the discovered rules. When the scale is between 0.5 and 1.0, it is linearly interpolated from the threshold to an extreme value that is manually specified in advance. If the rules define a feature range, the center of the range is used as the extreme value.

4.2   Pose Deformation

Given an input pose and desired pose features, the input pose is deformed through the following three steps.

Step 1. Deformation of the upper-body pose. Joint rotations of the upper-body joints and the pelvis are computed. Joint rotations, segment orientations, and segment positions can be controlled by one or a few joint rotations. When the pose feature is mapped to a single joint rotation, the joint rotation is determined according to the desired pose feature value. When the pose feature is mapped to multiple joint rotations, the rotations of these joints are computed according to the desired pose feature value and the weights of joints that are manually defined in a way similar to [13]. The head orientation, for example, can be controlled by rotations of the neck, trunk, and pelvis. When there are multiple conditions that control the same joint, the order of conditions must be determined manually.

Step 2. Balance correction control. Deformation of the upper-body pose may result in an unbalanced pose. The lower body pose is controlled through the position of the pelvis. All joint rotations on both legs are computed using inverse kinematics [14] so that the positions of both feet are kept. The horizontal (two-dimensional) position of the pelvis is computed to keep the balance so that the horizontal position of the center of mass remains in the same place after deformation of the upper-body pose.

Step 3. Deformation of the lower-body pose. The lower body pose is controlled via the lateral (one-dimensional) position of the pelvis under the constraints of balance and foot position. The lateral axis is determined according to the positions of the two feet. Balance can be maintained as long as the pelvis moves along the lateral axis. The target lateral position is linearly interpolated between the initial value and foot position.

The pose features contain the rotations of the lower-body joints. However, it is not possible to simply change them, because such pose deformation breaks the constraints of contact between the feet and ground. We therefore control them by moving the pelvis along the lateral axis; e.g., the difference between the bending angles of the two knees is controlled. When the pelvis is moved over the right foot, the right knee is bent and the left knee is extended. Note that the required pose feature may not be satisfied depending on the input pose. When the two feet are close to each other, for example, there is little room in which to control the lateral pelvis position without moving the foot positions. This is a limitation of our method.

5   Experimental Results and Discussion

5.1   User Experiment

We conducted a short user experiment to evaluate the effectiveness of our pose deformation method and the discovered rules of attractive Hero and JoJo poses. We evaluated whether the subjects could recognize that the poses deformed using our method have the intended styles compared with the original poses. Nine university students participated in the experiment. The participants were moderately familiar with Japanese subcultures including Hero and JoJo, although they were not content creators. Before the user experiment, images of example poses of Hero and JoJo (Figs. 2 and 3) were presented to each participant so that they could grasp the features of these styles. During the experiment, our system randomly chose an example pose from the set of 30 ordinary poses, a class of attractive poses from five classes (style and category), and a deformation scale from 0.5 or 1.0. There were thus 300 combinations (patterns). The system showed the original example pose and the deformed pose for a random placement as shown in Fig. 1(b). The participant was then asked to choose which pose has the indicated style compared with the other pose. The participant could change the viewing orientation of the pose using a mouse. Each participant went through 300 trials, which took about 30 min.

5.2 Results and Discussion

We measured whether the participants chose the deformed pose correctly for each pattern of example pose, class and deformation scale. Because this is a two-choice question, the ratio of correct answers should be around 50%, if our pose deformation method is ineffective. The results are shown in Fig. 5. High accuracy ratios exceeding 70% were obtained for 24.66% of patterns. This demonstrates that our method can realize the intended style successfully on many patterns. Meanwhile, a low accuracy ratio less than 30% was obtained for 14.0% of patterns. This shows that the combination of an input pose and a class is important, in that some combinations could have negative effects. However, this is not a problem in practice for our system. As the user can choose the class and deformation scale interactively, they can avoid such ineffective combinations.

Examples of successful and unsuccessful patterns are shown in Figs. 6 and 7, respectively. We analyzed some unsuccessful examples to see why our deformation method had negative effects. One reason that we found was the problem of incomplete rules of attractive poses. For example, in Fig. 7(g), the head faces down in the deformed pose, whereas Hero poses are expected to have the head facing forward. This is because our rules of Hero poses happened to be based on the local neck rotations and keep it straight. When the body faces down, the head faces down too. This kind of problem should be avoided by refining the decision trees.

Another reason that we found was the problem of local pose deformation. As our deformation method only deals with a small part of the pose without considering the full body, infeasible poses may be produced. In Fig. 7(h), for

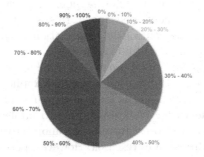

Fig. 5. Results of our user experiment. A histogram of all 300 patterns based on the ratios of answers that correctly chose the deformed pose matches the indicated style over the original pose.

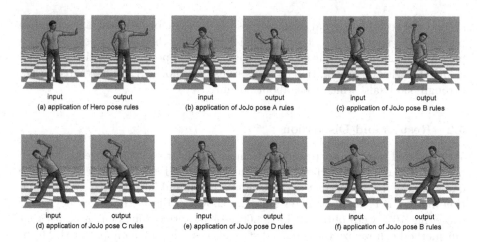

Fig. 6. Examples of successful pose deformation. Rules of the selected type and category are applied to the input.

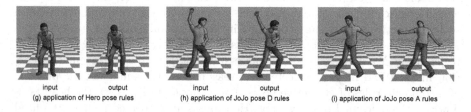

Fig. 7. Examples of unsuccessful pose deformation.

example, the deformation method extends the right arm and bends the left arm without considering shoulder rotations and collisions. As a result, the right arm pose looks infeasible and the left arm penetrates into the body. In Fig. 7(i), the upper body is too bent and the resulting pose looks infeasible. As explained in Sect. 4.1, we set extreme motion feature values manually. By setting smaller extreme values, such a problem does not happen. However, some poses may need higher extreme values. As mentioned above, this is not a problem in practice, as the user can interactively control the deformation scale to avoid deformation parameters that are too large and infeasible poses.

We successfully applied our approach to small numbers of example Hero and JoJo poses. Our pose deformation should be applicable to other rules for different kinds of attractive poses as long as the rules are described according to the low-level pose features. We are planning to implement our approach to a wider range of attractive poses. Introducing more advanced pose features is also a possible future direction of research. However, pose deformation becomes a difficult problem, because human poses have more degrees of freedom and it is hard to make a reasonable pose on the basis of a small number of pose features.

6   Conclusion

We developed a heuristic kinematics-based pose deformation method based on the discovered rules of attractive poses. We evaluated our method through a user experiment. The results show that our method can deform a pose to realize a specified style. Although we still need to experiment on different types of attractive poses, we believe that our approach is promising and can be an effective way to create novel attractive poses.

Acknowledgment. This work was supported in part by Grant-in-Aid for Scientific Research (No. 15H02704 and No. 15K05003) from the Japan Society for the Promotion of Science (JSPS).

References

1. Oshita, M., Yamamura, K., Honda, A.: Finding rules of attractive human poses using decision tree and generating novel attractive poses. In: Computer Graphics International, Article No. 33 (2017)
2. Hoyet, L., Ryall, K., Zibrek, K., Park, H., Lee, J., Hodgins, J., O'sullivan, C.: Evaluating the distinctiveness and attractiveness of human motions on realistic virtual bodies. ACM Trans. Graph. **32**(6), 204 (2013). (SIGGRAPH Asia 2013)
3. Neff, M., Kim, Y.: Interactive editing of motion style using drives and correlations. In: Eurographics/ACM SIGGRAPH Symposium on Computer Animation, pp. 103–112 (2009)
4. Phillips, C.B., Badler, N.I.: Interactive behaviors for bipedal articulated figures. In: SIGGRAPH 1991, pp. 359–362 (2001)
5. Guay, M., Cani, M.P., Ronfard, R.: The line of action: an intuitive interface for expressive character posing. ACM Trans. Graph. **32**(6), 205 (2013). (SIGGRAPH Asia 2013)
6. BOS Action Unity: Action Pose Pictures - Be a Hero! Pie International (2012). (in Japanese)
7. Araki, H.: JoJo's Bizarre Adventure Comic Series. Shueisha (1987–2017). (in Japanese)
8. Araki, H.: JOJO6251 - The World of Hirohiko Araki. Shueisha (1993). (in Japanese)
9. Yamaguchi, K.: Action Pose 500: Basic Poses. Graphics (2001). (in Japanese)
10. Maar: Dynamic Stop Motion Poses 2: Basic Actoins. Maar (2002). (in Japanese)
11. Kass, G.V.: An exploratory technique for investigating large quantities of categorical data. Appl. Stat. **29**(2), 119–127 (1980)
12. IBM: SPSS statistics ver. 24 (2016)
13. Monheit, G., Badler, N.I.: A kinematic model of the human spine and torso. IEEE Comput. Graph. Appl. **11**(2), 29–38 (1991)
14. Tolani, D., Goswami, A., Badler, N.I.: Real-time inverse kinematics techniques for anthropomorphic limbs. Graph. Models **62**(5), 53–388 (2000)

Reconsidering Registration: New Perspectives on Augmented Reality

Hanna Schraffenberger[1,2(✉)] and Edwin van der Heide[1]

[1] Media Technology, LIACS, Leiden University, Leiden, The Netherlands
h.schraffenberger@ru.nl, e.f.van.der.heide@liacs.leidenuniv.nl
[2] TiCC, Tilburg University, Tilburg, The Netherlands

Abstract. Augmented reality (AR) projects typically involve interactive systems that align virtual objects with the real world. This process is called registration and can make it seem as if virtual objects existed in the otherwise real environment. Registration is widely accepted as a defining and necessary characteristic of augmented reality. In this paper, we reconsider the need for registration on two levels. First of all, we argue that the intended presence of virtual objects in real space can be achieved without registration by an interactive AR system. Secondly, we suggest that the perceived spatial presence of virtual content in real space is not necessary for AR in the first place. We illustrate both points with examples and propose a more encompassing view of AR that focuses on relationships between the virtual and the real rather than on registration.

Keywords: Augmented reality · Registration
Virtual-real relationships · Theory · Information · Illusion · Presence
Mobile games · Sound art

1 Introduction

With the advent of augmented reality (AR), the presence of virtual content in real space has gained a new dimension. Virtual objects no longer simply appear on the screen of computers, tablets, mobile phones, smart watches, digital information boards, advertisement screens or other digital displays. Rather, they appear to exist right here, in our physical space, just like real objects do: Wearing a Head-mounted display (HMD), virtual, three-dimensional game characters appear to walk on real streets [1]. Looking at the environment through a mobile phone's screen, site-specific information, such as where to find nearby restaurants, metro stops and ATMs appears to be floating through the space in front of us [2]. More recently, Microsoft's HoloLens headset promises the possibility of building landscapes and filling our living rooms with virtual building blocks rather than physical lego bricks [3].

The presence of virtual content in real space that characterizes so many AR scenarios is typically simulated by an interactive system that aligns the virtual and the real and gives virtual objects a position in the real world. This process

© ICST Institute for Computer Sciences, Social Informatics and Telecommunications Engineering 2018
A. L. Brooks et al. (Eds.): ArtsIT 2017/DLI 2017, LNICST 229, pp. 172–183, 2018.
https://doi.org/10.1007/978-3-319-76908-0_17

is called registration. A look at AR research reveals that registration is widely seen as a defining and necessary characteristic of AR (see, e.g., [4,5]). Most prominently, Azuma's [6] wide-spread survey describes AR in terms of interactive systems that not only combine the virtual and the real but also register (align) virtual and real objects with each other in 3D and in real-time. By now, this view of AR—and with it, the need for 3D registration by an interactive system—has been widely accepted (cf. [7]).

However, not everyone shares the view that registration is necessary. For instance, the call for papers of the 14th edition of the International Symposium on Mixed and Augmented Reality (ISMAR 2015)—the leading conference on AR—explicitly lists "augmented reality without 3D registration" as one of the two emerging areas of particular interest [8]. Furthermore, some researchers provide broader descriptions and definitions of AR. For instance, Manovich [9] suggests that "a typical AR system adds information that is directly related to the user's immediate physical space" (p. 225). Similarly, Klopfer and Squire [10] define AR in terms of "situation[s] in which a real world context is dynamically overlaid with coherent location or context sensitive virtual information" (p. 205). We, too, have argued that relationships between the virtual and the real characterize AR [11]. While these views suggest that the virtual has to relate to the real, they do not state that the information has to be *registered* with the real world in 3D.

In the light of these different views, we wonder what role registration plays in AR. Is it actually a prerequisite for AR—and if so, why? Could it be that we unnecessarily limit AR, if we only consider scenarios where an AR system registers virtual content with the real world in 3D? Is there a chance that other links between the virtual and the real, too, result in augmentation? In this paper, we address these questions and challenge the common understanding of AR in terms of interactive systems that align virtual and real objects in 3D.

The paper consists of five sections. In Sect. 2, we investigate the purpose of registration. This investigation reveals that registration is used to make it seem as if virtual objects were part of the otherwise real environment. It furthermore becomes clear that this effect is typically achieved by means of an interactive system that aligns the virtual and the real in 3D and in real-time. Subsequently, in Sect. 3, we show that this type of registration by an interactive AR system is not always necessary for virtual content to appear as part of real space. We illustrate this point with three examples. Following this (Sect. 4), we challenge the need for registration more fundamentally. We suggest that the (simulated) presence of virtual content in real space is not necessary for AR in the first place. We argue that virtual content can augment the real world in other ways and in particular, by informing us about the real world. Two examples demonstrate this point. Finally, in Sect. 5, we discuss our findings and propose a broader understanding of AR that focuses on relationships between the virtual and the real that participants experience rather than on the registration of the virtual and the real by an AR system.

We limit our discussion to visually and auditory augmented reality because the need for registration primarily surfaces in this area. Whereas registration is commonly approached from an engineering perspective, we approach the topic from a conceptual and experience-focused perspective. Technological questions, such as how to best implement or improve registration fall out of the scope of this paper. The paper reflects on existing projects from the domains of art, gaming and augmented reality. It aims to advance AR theory and practice through a better understanding of what AR is and potentially can be. As such, it does not present new empirical results.

2   The Apparent Presence of Virtual Objects in Real Space

There are many ways to present virtual content in the real world. For instance, virtual content can be displayed on a computer screen, projected onto a wall, broadcasted on loudspeakers or played back on head-phones. However, according to the prevailing opinion, merely displaying or presenting virtual content in the real environment does not suffice in order to create AR. Instead, researchers argue that virtual content has to be registered with the real world or aligned with real objects in 3D. So what is registration, why is it regarded necessary—what purpose does it serve?

Strictly speaking, opinions on what registration entails vary slightly. However, registration generally refers to the process of giving virtual objects a position in real space. For instance, Azuma et al. [4] uses the term to refer to the alignment of virtual and real objects with respect to each other and Drascic and Milgram [12] use registration to refer to the alignment of "the coordinate system of the virtual world with that of the real world" (p. 129).

The challenge of properly aligning the virtual and the real is commonly referred to as "the registration problem" and regarded one of the key issues in AR research (e.g., [5,6]). How this problem is addressed differs from project to project. However, registration is generally realized by an interactive computer system that aligns the virtual additions with the real world in real-time and in three dimensions (e.g., [6]). In the following, we refer to this form of real-time 3D registration by an interactive system as *registration in the traditional sense*.

Judging from AR literature, registration is such a prominent issue in AR, because it can create the illusion of virtual objects being part of and existing in the real environment. This is one of the primary goals in existing AR research [6,13]. According to existing research, registration not only serves the illusion of virtual objects existing in real space but is *necessary* for it. For instance, Azuma [6] writes: "[t]he objects in the real and virtual worlds must be properly aligned with respect to each other, or the illusion that the two worlds coexist will be compromised" (p. 367). Similarly, Vallino and Brown [14] point out "[t]o maintain the illusion that the virtual objects are indeed part of the real world requires a consistent registration of these two images–the major challenge for augmented reality systems" (p. 195). Likewise, Bajura and Neumann [15] write:

"Accurate visual registration between real and computer-generated objects in combined images is critically important for conveying the perception that both types of object occupy the same 3-dimensional (3D) space" (p. 52).

To some degree, practical AR projects seem to back up these concerns. A popular example of a mobile game, which does not properly register virtual content in real space is Pokémon Go. This game takes place in the real world, where players can use their phone to chase and capture so-called Pokémon (animal-like creatures). In the AR view of this game, virtual Pokémons are displayed on the mobile's screen, superimposed on a player's live view of the environment.

The application makes use of GPS coordinates and the phone's compass and gyroscope in order to include the Pokémon and other game-related content in the otherwise real environment [16,17]. This approach of placing virtual content in the real world suffers from several weaknesses: First of all, it has poor accuracy [18]. Furthermore, because the camera image is not analyzed, the application has no knowledge about spatial structure of the physical environment. In the case of Pokémon Go, these drawbacks can cause Pokémons to appear in unrealistic positions in the environment or can make them look like an independent overlay that floats on top of the camera feed, rather than as part of the environment. This can be seen in the first two images in Fig. 1. As these images show, inaccurate alignment of the virtual and the real indeed can hurt the perceptual illusion of virtual Pokémon existing at a position in the real environment.

Fig. 1. At times, Pokémon appear at unrealistic positions and on top of the real world (images on the left). At other times, the virtual creatures appear to be part of the real environment (images on the right).

However, such issues are usually temporary. Despite the rather low accuracy, the virtual creatures regularly appear to be present in our real environment. We can see screenshots of such cases where virtual Pokémon seem to be a part of the real world in the two images on the right in Fig. 1.[1]

On first sight, the Pokémon Go example seems to support the reviewed claims that accurate registration is necessary for virtual objects to appear in real space.[2] However, poor registration has not prevented Pokémon Go from becoming one of the most popular mobile games so far [19]. The success of the game suggests that players seem to enjoy the game despite improper registration. This gives us reasons to believe that worthwhile AR experiences can be created without accurate registration.[3] Judging from the personal experience of the authors, we accept the virtual Pokémon as a believable part of real space even if they do not appear properly aligned. In fact, it even can be a fun aspect of the game, to actively move the phone around in order to manually align the displayed Pokémon with the environment and make them blend in with the real world. In any case, the example of Pokémon Go suggests that accurate and stable registration in 3D space is not always necessary. It raises the question whether AR applications have to 'fool' us perceptually in order to create the experience of virtual objects being part of the real environment. It furthermore suggests that the participant can play a more active role in aligning the virtual and the real, e.g., by moving the phone until the creatures seem to fit with the environment. We will explore this possibility further in the next section.

3 Alternative Approaches to Placing Virtual Content in Real Space

There is no doubt that interactive AR systems that align virtual and real content in 3D can make it seem as if virtual objects were part of real space. However, we wonder whether there are other ways of placing virtual content in the real world. In the following, we discuss three examples that suggest that this is possible. Next to visually augmented reality we will also consider sound-based forms of AR. After all, the concept of registration is closely tied to the idea of visual augmentations. Additional possibilities for integrating virtual content into the real world might exist when dealing with non-visual virtual content.

Forest walk. Early examples of AR experiences that are created without registration by an interactive system include Cardiff's audio walks [20], such as *Forest walk*. The artist provides participants with prerecorded soundscapes that are played back on traditional CD players or iPods while on a predetermined walk

---

[1] The author has positioned the phone manually to make the Pokémon appear at realistic locations. However, similar situations regularly arise without such efforts.

[2] Of course, one example does not allow us to draw general conclusions.

[3] Players can also turn off the AR mode entirely. If players approach a Pokémon with AR mode switched off, the creature appears in a virtual environment, rather than overlaid onto the camera feed. However, Pokémon are still positioned on a virtual map of the actual surroundings and in this sense, placed in the real environment.

[20]. Listening to the recordings on headphones while navigating the otherwise real environment, the recorded sounds often appear to originate in the physical environment[4] and mix in with our real surroundings. How is this possible?

One crucial aspect that contributes to the spatial quality of Cardiff's recordings is the used recording technique. Cardiff's audio walks have been recorded with binaural audio. Binaural audio is a recording technique that captures the complete auditive experience—including the three-dimensional spatial information of the sounds. Another important aspect is that the audio mimics the environment in which it is played back to the listener. The artist explains that "[t]he virtual recorded soundscape has to mimic the real physical one in order to create a new world as a seamless combination of the two" [20]. In line with this, Cardiff has recorded the audio material in the same environment that the listener navigates during the walk. "Forest Walk", for instance, includes natural sounds of the forest, such as the sound of crows [21]. Because Cardiff makes use of binaural soundscapes that were recorded in the listener's actual environment, the virtual sounds appear to be a spatial part of the real environment, even though there is no interactive system that aligns them with the real world.

Does this mean we are dealing with AR without registration? Not necessarily. One could argue that Cardiff's walks make use of a *different* (and much looser) form of registration: the participant is told where to start the walk and press play, and the audio mix includes instructions that tell the participant where to go and where to look. Indirectly, the instructions determine the participant's position in and movement through the space, and consequently, also roughly determine where the virtual sound sources appear in space.

One potential reason why this loose alignment suffices is that the recorded sounds not necessarily have to appear at a specific position in the surrounding space. For instance, no exact 3D registration is necessary when dealing with flying elements such as crows, as it does not matter where exactly they appear in the environment.

Mozzies. Another application that makes virtual objects appear in real space without 3D registration is the early mobile game *Mozzies*. This game was installed on the Siemens SX1 cell phone that launched in 2003 [22]. The mobile application used to show flying mosquitoes, overlaid on the live image of the environment captured by the phone's camera. Players could shoot the virtual mosquitoes by moving the phone and pressing a button when aiming correctly [23]. In contrast to Cardiff's work, the game makes use of an interactive system. However, the application does not make use of registration in the traditional sense, but instead, 'only' uses the camera as a motion sensor [23] and applies 2D motion detection [24]. Yet, judging from the images that can be found of this (and similar) games online, it appears as if mosquitoes were flying through the space in front of the phone's lens.

---

[4] This claim was confirmed by Zev Tiefenbach, the studio manager of Cardiff/Miller, who in turn confirmed this with Janet Cardiff (personal communication).

Presumably, this works because mosquitoes (like the crows mentioned above) 'only' have to appear to be flying *somewhere* in the surrounding space rather than at an exact position. To achieve this, exact registration seems not to be necessary. However, because the creatures are not registered in 3D, is not possible to walk around the virtual insects and look at them from all directions and angles. Furthermore, the virtual mosquitoes can not disappear behind real objects. (The same constraints currently hold for Pokémon Go.)

NS KidsApp. A third example of AR without registration in the traditional sense is the NS KidsApp. This mobile application by the Dutch railway operator *Nederlandse Spoorwegen* (NS) is primarily aimed at children (and their parents), and it introduces a short story with the two characters *Oei* and *Knoei*.

There are several playful assignments for the player that allow them to make videos with Knoei appearing in the otherwise real environment. For instance, the player is asked to put the camera against the window and film the outside. As a result, one can see Knoei flying next to the train in a superman kind of fashion. Likewise, when filming another player, one can see Knoei hovering over a train chair, showing off his muscles to his neighbor (see Fig. 2).

Fig. 2. The NS Kids app shows Knoei flying next to the train (left) as well as next to a player showing off his muscles (right) on the camera feed. Screenshots by Hanna Schraffenberger and Jurriaan Rot.

This application, too, creates the illusion of virtual content seemingly existing in real space, without the use of registration in the traditional sense. Like in Cardiff's case, instructions are part of the game. Here, they make sure that what the participant sees will serve as a fitting background for the virtual overlay.

4   Alternative Approaches to Augmented Reality

The previous section has revealed that the apparent presence of virtual content in real space does not always require registration by an interactive AR system. In this section, we challenge the need for registration more fundamentally and question whether virtual content has to appear as if it were spatially present in the real surroundings. Our idea is simple: Aside from registration, other links between the virtual and the real are possible. These potentially lead to other forms of AR. For instance, the virtual can inform us about our real surroundings. In our opinion, this can also augment the environment. We support this idea with two examples.

Audio Guides. The idea of virtual additions that inform us about the real world is common in the cultural sector. For instance, many museums provide additional information in the form of audio tours that guide the visitor through a museum, and which supplement the real world and ideally, enhance our experience of the exhibition. In our opinion, such audio tour guides can accompany a user and augment a user's experience of their real surroundings, even if they do not appear to be spatially present.

We are not alone with the opinion that audio tours and audio guides can be considered AR. For instance, Bederson [25] argues "[o]ne place a low-tech version of augmented reality has long been in the marketplace is museums. It is quite common for museums to rent audio-tape tour guides that viewers carry around with them as they tour the exhibits" (p. 210). Furthermore, Rozier [26], refers to audio tours as "perhaps the earliest form of 'augmented reality'" (p. 20).

Whereas audio guides typically provide factual information about the real surroundings, other possibilities exist. For instance, the artist Willem de Ridder has realized an audio tour in the "Stedelijk Museum" in Amsterdam in 1997 that told visitors about the meaning of 'invisible' elements in the museum [27]. This shows that the virtual information can relate the surroundings more freely.

Google Glass. The concept of using a virtual layer of information to enhance our everyday lives is also at the basis of the Google Glass project. Google Glass is essentially a head-mounted display in the shape of eyeglasses. A small display in one corner presents additional information (such as text and/or images) as an overlay on top of a user's view of the world.

The information displayed by Google Glass can be completely unrelated to a user's context (e.g., a random text message from a friend) but it can also relate to the user's real surroundings. For instance, the device can be used to translate advertisements and overlay driving instructions onto a user's view.

The role of Google Glass in AR is controversial. As we know, 3D registration is commonly considered necessary. This view excludes all Google Glass applications from the realm of AR. However, the 2015 call for papers of the leading AR conference ISMAR suggests Google Glass as an example of "augmented reality without 3D registration" and argues that "[l]ightweight eyewear such as Google Glass can be used for augmenting and supporting our daily lives even without 3D registration of virtual objects" [8]. In line with this, some researchers consider head-mounted displays like Google Glass in the context of augmented reality. For instance, Liberati and Nagataki [28] consider Google Glass an AR device, and distinguish among two types of current and future AR glasses: (1) AR glasses that inform the user about their surroundings and provide "informational text" to the user and (2) AR glasses that present additional objects, that are embedded in the real world and that potentially can interact with the real world as if they existed physically.

We, too, believe that virtual information can modify (our perception of) real objects. Arguably, it can add to and affect our experience of the real world and in this sense become part of and augment the environment. However, we believe such augmentations are possible independently of how the virtual information is presented. In other words, information can augment our surroundings no matter whether it is, e.g., overlaid with AR glasses, displayed on a phone's screen or delivered by a recorded voice on headphones.[5]

5 Discussion and Conclusion

Is registration necessary for AR? This question remains (to some degree) a choice. Definitions are not set in stone. It is up to us—the AR research community—to define AR and draw the lines on the emerging AR landscape.

There is no doubt that registration in the traditional sense plays a crucial role in AR. It is at the heart of almost all AR applications. Registration can make it seem as if virtual objects were present in the real space. In many contexts, such as in the medical domain or in a manufacturing setting, the need to accurately align virtual information with the real world is self-evident. Yet, we believe that by defining AR in terms of interactive systems that register the virtual and the real interactively, in real time and in 3D [6], we unnecessarily limit AR.

We have identified two main reasons to adopt a broader understanding of AR: First, the apparent presence of virtual content in real space, which seems to motivate the need for registration, also can be achieved *without* 3D registration by an AR system in the traditional sense. For instance, the participant can align the virtual and the real by moving in space until the right perspective is obtained. Also, many settings require less strict forms of registration. E.g., an exact alignment might not be necessary when dealing with flying objects. Second and more fundamentally, not all forms of AR require the spatial presence of virtual objects in real space in the first place. In particular, virtual content can inform us about the real world, and by doing so supplement and augment (our experience of) the real world. For instance, virtual museum guides do not have to look or sound as if they were spatially present in order to accompany our visit and affect our experience with their words. We see such scenarios as a form of AR that is based on the content-based relationship between the virtual and the real. We thus conclude that registration in the traditional sense plays a key role in AR, but is not necessary for AR per se. This raises one final question: If real-time registration by an interactive system in 3D is no defining factor, what then does define AR?

Strikingly, all encountered AR scenarios have one characteristic in common: *virtual content is experienced in relation to the real world.* In some cases, the link

---

[5] In many ways, information defies the terms virtual and real. Arguably, information can have the same effects, no matter whether it is presented virtually or physically.

between the virtual and the real is primarily spatial. For instance, the mosquitoes in *Mozzies*, the character Knoei in the *NS KidsApp* as well as the sounds in Cardiff's *Forest walk* all seem spatially present in the real surroundings. In other cases, the participant experiences a relationship between the virtual and the real on the content-level. For instance, the information provided by an audio guide typically relates to a physical artifact content-wise and consequently, is also experienced in relation to this artifact. Similarly, navigation instructions, such as provided by Google Glass and other mobile devices, relate to a participant's environment and are normally interpreted in relation to the real surrounding space. In line with these examples, we see AR environments as spaces in which the participant experiences a relationship between the virtual content and their real surroundings.

In contrast to common notions, our view focuses on the relationships between the virtual and the real rather than on registration and on the experience of the participant rather than on enabling technologies. Taking the participants' experiences into account is important because AR systems typically aim at providing the participant with an augmented experience of their environment. Instead of defining the field in terms of technologies that create such scenarios, we suggest defining the field in terms of the environments and experience we actually want to create. This will allow us to study the actual area of interest, even if enabling technologies change or take unforeseen form (such as in the case of Cardiff's audio walks).

Our view of AR is much broader than the common understanding of AR in terms of interactive systems that align the virtual and the real interactively, in real-time and in 3D [6]. Yet, it allows us to distinguish AR from other environments that include both virtual and real content. In particular, it sets AR apart from scenarios where the virtual and the real merely coexist in the same space and where both are experienced as *independent* from each other. For instance, our definition does not include scenarios where participants are immersed in virtual worlds and where they experience virtual elements as independent from their actual, real environment. Likewise, it does not comprise situations where a participant listens to an audio book and experiences this story as independent from and unrelated to their actual environment.

Our understanding of AR is not new—we have proposed the same view in previous publications (e.g., [11]). Furthermore, the above-reviewed definitions by Manovich [9] and Klopfer and Squire [10] also focus on the relationship between the virtual and the real. However, our paper sets itself apart from such earlier publications because it provides a detailed rationale for deviating from commonly accepted views of AR. Furthermore, our proposed definition differs from views such as put forward by Manovich [9] and Klopfer and Squire [10] with its focus on the participant's *experience*.

Our investigation reveals two main forms of AR: First, cases where a participant experiences the presence of virtual content in the real environment. We propose calling this "presence-based AR". Second, cases where the virtual augments the real on a content-level. We suggest calling this "content-based AR".

In future research, it would be desirable to explore if yet different forms of AR exist. For instance, can the virtual become part of the real world similarly to how a soundtrack becomes (a non-spatial) part of a movie? More generally, we would like to systematically explore what factors contribute to the experience of virtual content being part of the real space. We can imagine that next to registration, aspects such as the participants' imagination and an underlying narrative can play a major role in AR.

Our view of AR suggests that when it comes to creating AR scenarios, we have to consider and give form to the relationships between the virtual and the real. However, we have to keep in mind that establishing a relationship between the virtual and the real not automatically ensures that a participant also experiences this relationship. What is more, a participant might experience relationships that have never been created or intended. For instance, a museum visitor might listen to a virtual museum guide, but associate the information with the wrong artwork. Similarly, the same scenario might be experienced as AR by one person but not by another. In our opinion, the question whether a scenario should be considered AR can not be answered based on what a system does or displays. Instead, it remains a question of personal experience.

The main contribution of this paper is that it provides a better understanding of what AR is and potentially can be. It shows that aside from using traditional AR systems, alternative approaches to placing virtual content in real space exist. Furthermore, it shows that aside from making virtual objects appear in real space, alternative approaches to creating AR experiences exist. In addition, our paper complements technology-focused AR research with its focus on the participant's experience.

Our investigation has revealed various examples of interactive applications that defy existing definitions of AR but yet, augment our experience of our physical surroundings. This shows that narrow definitions not necessarily prevent practitioners to think outside of the box and to come up with different forms of (arguably) augmented reality. Yet, we expect that a better and broader understanding of AR will highlight those possibilities and hopefully, inspire even more and new forms of AR.

References

1. Piekarski, W., Thomas, B.H.: ARQuake: the outdoor augmented reality gaming system. Commun. ACM **45**(1), 36–38 (2002). ACM
2. Layar [mobile application software]. http://www.layar.com
3. Microsoft HoloLens (2015). http://www.microsoft.com/microsoft-hololens/
4. Azuma, R., Baillot, Y., Behringer, R., Feiner, S., Julier, S., MacIntyre, B.: Recent advances in augmented reality. IEEE CG&A **21**(6), 34–47 (2001)
5. Bimber, O., Raskar, R.: Spatial Augmented Reality: Merging Real and Virtual Worlds. A. K. Peters Ltd., Natick (2005)
6. Azuma, R.: A survey of augmented reality. Presence **6**(4), 355–385 (1997)
7. Zhou, F., Duh, H.B.L., Billinghurst, M.: Trends in augmented reality tracking, interaction and display: a review of ten years of ISMAR. In: ISMAR 2008, pp. 193–202. IEEE Computer Society, Washington, D.C., USA (2008)

8. International Symposium on Mixed and Augmented Reality: Call for papers (2015). http://ismar2015.vgtc.org/ismar/2015/info/call-participation/call-fullshort-papers/

9. Manovich, L.: The poetics of augmented space. Vis. Commun. **5**(2), 219–240 (2006)

10. Klopfer, E., Squire, K.: Environmental Detectives—the development of an augmented reality platform for environmental simulations. Educ. Tech. Res. Dev. **56**(2), 203–228 (2008)

11. Schraffenberger, H., van der Heide, E.: Towards novel relationships between the virtual and the real in augmented reality. In: De Michelis, G., Tisato, F., Bene, A., Bernini, D. (eds.) ArtsIT 2013. LNICST, vol. 116, pp. 73–80. Springer, Heidelberg (2013). https://doi.org/10.1007/978-3-642-37982-6_10

12. Drascic, D., Milgram, P.: Perceptual issues in augmented reality. In: Electronic Imaging: Science and Technology, pp. 123–134. International Society for Optics and Photonics (1996)

13. Regenbrecht, H.T., Wagner, M.T.: Interaction in a collaborative augmented reality environment. In: CHI 2002 Extended Abstracts, pp. 504–505. ACM (2002)

14. Vallino, J., Brown, C.: Haptics in augmented reality. In: ICMCS 1999, vol. 1, pp. 195–200. IEEE (1999)

15. Bajura, M., Neumann, U.: Dynamic registration correction in video-based augmented reality systems. IEEE CG&A **15**(5), 52–60 (1995)

16. Pope, T.: Which phones work with Pokémon GO? (2016). http://www.gottabemobile.com/2016/08/12/which-phones-work-with-pokemon-go/

17. Koll-Schretzenmayr, M., Casaulta-Meyer, S.: Augmented reality. disP - Plan. Rev. **52**(3), 2–5 (2016)

18. Blum, J.R., Greencorn, D.G., Cooperstock, J.R.: Smartphone sensor reliability for augmented reality applications. In: Zheng, K., Li, M., Jiang, H. (eds.) MobiQuitous 2012. LNICST, vol. 120, pp. 127–138. Springer, Heidelberg (2013). https://doi.org/10.1007/978-3-642-40238-8_11

19. Allan, R.: Pokémon GO usage statistics: the most popular U.S. mobile game ever (2016). https://www.surveymonkey.com/business/intelligence/pokemon-go-usage-statistics/

20. Cardiff, J.: Introduction to the audio walks. http://www.cardiffmiller.com/artworks/walks/audio_walk.html

21. Cardiff, J.: Forest Walk [audio walk] (1991). http://www.cardiffmiller.com/artworks/walks/forest.html

22. López, M.B., Hannuksela, J., Silvén, O., Vehviläinen, M.: Interactive multi-frame reconstruction for mobile devices. Multimed. Tools Appl. **69**(1), 31–51 (2014)

23. Wikipedia: The Free Encyclopedia: Siemens SX1 (2016). https://en.wikipedia.org/w/index.php?title=Siemens_SX1

24. Reimann, C., Paelke, V.: Computer vision based interaction techniques for mobile augmented reality. In: Proceedings of the 5th Paderborn Workshop Augmented and Virtual Reality in der Produktentstehung, pp. 355–362 (2006)

25. Bederson, B.B.: Audio augmented reality: a prototype automated tour guide. In: CHI 1995, pp. 210–211. ACM (1995)

26. Rozier, J.M.: Hear&there: an augmented reality system of linked audio. Ph.D. thesis, Massachusetts Institute of Technology (2000)

27. Stedelijk Museum, history and archive. http://www.stedelijk.nl/en/artours/history-and-archive

28. Liberati, N., Nagataki, S.: The AR glasses' "non-neutrality": their knock-on effects on the subject and on the giveness of the object. Ethics Inf. Technol. **17**(2), 125–137 (2015)

The Engagement Effect of Players' Agency over their Characters' Motivation

Daniel S. Christensen[✉], Mette Jakobsen, and Martin Kraus

Department of Architecture, Design and Media Technology, Section of Medialogy,
Aalborg University, Aalborg, Denmark
{daniel,mette}@galdrastudios.com, martin@create.aau.dk

Abstract. Story-rich games are increasingly popular, and with this popularity comes the demand for more engaging narratives in games. This paper investigates how the players' engagement is affected by providing them with agency over the player character's motivation through a game mechanic, which we call Hover-text. An experiment was conducted in which a test- and control group played through a visual novel with or without the Hover-text. Using questionnaires to measure their engagement in the three categories of agency, empathy and roleplay, it was found that players who were exposed to the Hover-text reported that they felt more involved with the player character's feelings. These findings suggest an alternative to the way games can encourage empathic engagement. More research is necessary to clarify the role of the player character's personality, and whether using the Hover-text on a blank-slate character differs from using it on a fully-fleshed character.

Keywords: Video games · Narrative · Agency · Engagement
Player character · Character motivation

1 Introduction

Video games are a digital medium which surpasses other digital media, such as audiovisuals and music, when it comes to interactivity and agency. With the introduction of player agency come the challenges of the Narrative Paradox: the trade-off between providing the player with more agency and providing the author with more power to create immersive narratives [1]. The player character (PC) reflects this paradox by either being a pre-described character, aiming to induce readerly pleasure, or a blank-slate character for the player to apply their own traits, which instead gives the player agency. Games have a tendency to compromise back and forth between these two extremes when it comes to designing the PC. Lankoski [2] proposed that engagement within a game can be derived from goal-related and empathic engagement. Goal-related engagement is an "I" experience, where the player acts to reach their goals. Empathic engagement happens when the player reacts to a character's actions: recognition, alignment and alliance.

© ICST Institute for Computer Sciences, Social Informatics and Telecommunications Engineering 2018
A. L. Brooks et al. (Eds.): ArtsIT 2017/DLI 2017, LNICST 229, pp. 184–193, 2018.
https://doi.org/10.1007/978-3-319-76908-0_18

We propose that by providing the player with agency over the PC's motivation and personality, it is possible to shift a player's engagement from goal-related to empathic. We also propose this as a way to give the author some power to tell an immersive story, while still providing the player with some feel of agency. We developed a prototype, in order to test this hypothesis. The prototype is of the visual novel genre, in which players choose their actions from a menu of options in order to progress. The test group was given extra text in the form of an inner monologue describing the character's feelings about that particular choice. The inner monologue text, referred to as the Hover-text, was written to fit within three different tones: sneaky, no-nonsense and social-butterfly, allowing the player to base their choice not only on the action itself, but on what kind of character they wanted to be. The control group could only choose based on the action they wanted to perform. We evaluated the prototype in an online experiment with 184 participants playing the game and evaluating it with a questionnaire. We measured the players' engagement on three main categories: agency, empathy and roleplay, where roleplay items are items asking whether the players felt they were acting "in-character" or on their own accord. The questionnaire consisted of ten 5-point Likert scale items.

The results from our test showed a significant difference in players' feel of being involved with the feelings of the PC, when exposed to the Hover-text.

2   Related Work

The relationship between player and PC has been well investigated. Besseire et al. [3] found that players in the online game World of Warcraft sculpted their avatars to reflect their ideal selves, and they would act in this role when playing. Blake et al. [4] took another approach and investigated the tendency for the player to shift their self perception to fit the character they were playing. These are instances where players are either given a character with defined motivations, or a blank-slate character to fill out themselves. Our research expands on this and investigates players' reaction to a PC, when they have agency over their character's motivation. We want to see how a mechanic that gives the player the ability to pick from different motivations affects their experience within the parameters of agency, empathy, and roleplay.

The illusion of agency was tested by Fendt et al. [5] in a scenario where players interacted with different story structures, namely the branching tree against the flowchart. It was found that by giving specific feedback it was possible to give an illusion of agency, a conclusion they based upon feedback in the form of questionnaires. Another test, which used questionnaires to measure agency, was conducted by Thue et al. [6]. They tested their prototype PaSSAGE, and found that arranging the way in which available interactions are presented (based on what the player was most likely to choose) was sufficient to create an illusion of agency. Our motivation for looking into agency stems from our design, in which we add more context to a player's choice. The additional weight to the choice does not give them more agency over the story, but it is interesting to see if it creates an increase in perceived agency.

When talking about the emotional affection of games, research is quick to focus on the effect of violence on players, however, Belman et al. [7] argue in their paper, that games can also be used to foster more positive reactions, such as empathy towards marginalized groups. For measuring empathy, Davis' [8] questionnaire is often used. He divides empathy into four categories, one of which is fantasy, i.e., a person's ability to empathise with fictional characters, which makes it relevant to our research.

Games often provoke feelings towards the self: excitement, frustration, relief, and curiosity. Even if the game story does involve emotions such as love or jealousy, those are not the emotions motivating the player to rescue the princess [9]. Combining emotional immersion with interactivity is problematic, because it requires players to feel empathy towards a computer-controlled character, which also serves a purpose in the interaction, either as a messenger, helper or hinderer of the player's objective [9]. If, however, the player's lucid interest in the character, as a means to an end, can be combined with the narrative interest of the character as a person, then it elevates the character from being a game object, into a human being [10, 11].

The PC's motivation and players' ability to recognize it is part of the emphatic engagement defined by Lankoski [2]. He also defines goal-related engagement as the player's goal being the same as the goal of the game. Empathic engagement and goal-related engagement does not have to cancel each other out, but it is quite clear that a lot of games rely on the goal-related engagement. With our research, we want to explore whether providing the player with knowledge and agency over their PC's motivation could provoke empathic engagement.

Summary. We propose that providing the player with knowledge and agency over their character's motivation influences the player's feel of agency, empathy, and roleplay.

3   Experimental Design

In order to test our hypothesis, an experiment was conducted. A game was developed with a specific mechanic designed to give the player access to, and agency over, the PC's inner thoughts. This mechanic was named Hover-text and was mainly inspired by the game Dreamfall Chapters [12]. The new game was put online for testing, and evaluated using a questionnaire.

3.1   The Game

The game was designed as a visual novel, in which players had to solve a murder mystery by interacting with different characters. It features purposeful-selective interaction [9], where the player picks from menus with options to decide how they wish to respond. An example can be found in Fig. 1. The crime theme was picked due to it being what-suspense [9], which in itself does not encourage empathy, but rather indulge the player with the intellectual satisfaction of solving a puzzle. A setup was needed which allowed for the possibility of a difference between the PC's motivation and their actions. This setup was inspired by Cluedo [13], because this interaction is inherent to the game. The characters all wear masks to symbolize that the game world is one of deception. The structure of the narrative is a flowchart [9], in order to ensure that every player gets approximately the same content, and to avoid combinatorial explosion by having a true branching tree.

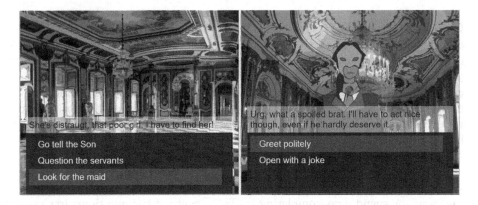

Fig. 1. Screens from the game Court of Madness, showcasing the Hover-text.

The Hover-Text. The player interacts with the game through menus. Each option has an action-text describing the action the PC will perform, if that option is selected. The Hover-text refers to a text that appears when the player hovers over an action. The text is an inner monologue, written as if spoken by the PC, and gives context to the action. For some options, the Hover-text will reflect the action of the PC, but other times they can be contradicting. For example, a player could pick the action "Greet politely" to act nicely toward a person, while the Hover-text would reveal that the PC in fact does not like the other character. The Hover-text is written so that the player may choose between three distinctive personalities: sneaky, no-nonsense and social-butterfly. The player will be able to then base their choice on not only the action they wished to take, but which of the three personalities they might wish to roleplay. A control group was also tested, which were given the action-text but not the Hover-text.

3.2 Online Test

The online model was chosen due to a number of reasons. The game needed to be a certain length, in order to get a proper dramatic arc, and give the player enough time to get familiar with the characters. Having the test online would make it possible to run multiple tests, unsupervised, at the same time, making testing more time efficient on our part. This was necessary due to the length of a play session and because the expected required sample size is too large to realistically achieve in a supervised setting. The test environment was also more representable for how the participants would usually play such a game, since they were allowed to play it however they felt comfortable. Finally, by reaching out online, it was possible to get a more diverse test group, although the participants fall into the demographic of being users of the social media used to recruit them.

Quality of Data. Several measures were taken to ensure the quality of the collected data. The user's IP was logged to make sure they did not appear in the data several times. A player's choices during play was also logged, making it possible to trace how they navigated the game world. The entries were sorted to ensure a balanced sample, first by gender, then by current sample size, and lastly gaming experience. Gaming experience was chosen above other features, due to the experiment by Thue et al. [6], where they found that player experience had an influence on their data. When asked about gender, the players were able to fill out "other", in addition to male and female because participants who do not identify as male or female, might not be proper representatives for either. All actions were logged with time stamps, making it possible to check if players rushed through the game, or spend days completing it. The layouts of the questionnaires were made to look the same as the game, in order to create continuity, and make the ending of the game less of an exit point. We wanted to mitigate the number of participants who left the test before completing the post-test questionnaire. Players were recruited through social media: Facebook, Twitter, and in various game- and narrative oriented groups on Reddit.

3.3   Questionnaire

The player experience was measured using a questionnaire with items in three categories: agency, empathy, and roleplay. The three categories were chosen based on previous research, summarized in the related work section, and from the results of a pilot test, where participants played an early version of the game followed up by an interview. The two first items were taken from Fend et al.'s questionnaire [5] for the illusion of agency. For empathy, items 3–6 were taken from Davis' questionnaire [8]; however, the original items were meant for literature, and therefore had to be reformulated to fit a game. Finally, the remaining four items were formulated to measure the player's self-perceived role when playing:

1. When playing the game, I was able to see the results of my actions.
2. I felt that the story would have been different if I had made different choices.
3. While playing the game, I could relate to how the player character was feeling.
4. I did not get involved with the feelings of the main character in the game.

5. When playing the game, it was difficult for me to view things from the player character's perspective.
6. I tried to imagine myself in the player character's shoes when making a choice.
7. I made choices based on what I felt the player character would do.
8. I made choices based on what I felt I would do.
9. I made choices based on what I felt would yield the best result.
10. I felt, I was not part of the story, but rather someone off screen, guiding the player character to the right path.

4 Results

The test was online for two weeks and at the end of the test, 263 IPs had been logged, while there was a total of 184 completed entries by unique IPs, meaning 70% of participants played the entire game and filled out the post-questionnaire. Out of the 184 participants, 4 participants were excluded because they admitted in the comment field of the post-test questionnaire that they did not read the text. The 7 participants who chose "other" as gender were also removed. Participants who were major outliers in terms of finishing the game too fast were removed, due to the likelihood of them not having taken proper time to read the text. It was decided to look at the 12 participants from the pilot test as a reference for finding outliers, as these entries were recorded without breaks. In the results from the final test, players were able to take long breaks, effectively increasing the median of the data set, and thus making a bad representation for what the minimal time would be for someone who did not take any breaks. The threshold was found by using John Tukey's outlier filter, with IQR times three and this gave a threshold of 10 min and 57 s. 32 outliers were found by players who finished the game in a time below the threshold, leaving a total of 143 samples. Out of all the entries removed, 27 were found in the control group and 9 in the test group, which ended up skewing the sample sizes a bit, leaving the test group larger than the control group. A summary of the demographics of each group can be found in Table 1.

Table 1. Summery of demographics.

	Test group	Control group
Gender	59M/21F	46M/17F
Mean age $\pm$ SD	25.20 $\pm$ 6.77	23.70 $\pm$ 4.15
Mean game experience $\pm$ SD	2.62 $\pm$ 1.76	2.59 $\pm$ 1.47
English as first language/other	33/47	21/42
Total participants	80	63

4.1   Questionnaire Data

The questionnaire data was tested using the Mann-Whitney U test and significant differences were found in item 4 and 8. A graphical visualisation, using diverging stacked bar charts, can be found for each of these items in Figs. 2 and 3. Red is used for those who strongly disagree, orange for disagree, grey for neutral, light blue for agree, and dark blue for strongly agree. In addition to looking at the test- and control group, we also investigated the differences when looking at each specific gender and when looking at whether the players spoke English as their first language or not.

The differences in the answers to the remaining 8 items were not found to be significant. There were other items which showed a trend towards being significant, and all of the p-values can be found in the Table 2.

Table 2. All p-values across the ten items, calculated using the Mann-Whitney U test. Bold numbers in the table indicated a significant result. For gender and first language, the Bonferroni correction was considered for the results, meaning the significance level was divided by the number of tests, in this case 3.

	Item	1	2	3	4	5	6	7	8	9	10
	All	0.565	0.593	0.398	**0.035**	0.105	0.457	0.837	0.732	0.386	0.662
Gender	Male	0.249	0.494	0.452	**0.015**	0.356	0.325	0.947	0.600	0.602	0.805
	Female	0.383	0.925	0.730	0.990	0.068	0.765	0.500	0.745	0.483	0.184
First language	English	0.097	0.870	0.823	**0.017**	0.158	0.639	0.442	**0.005**	0.222	0.808
	Other	0.718	0.673	0.298	0.287	0.471	0.671	0.922	0.120	0.613	0.912

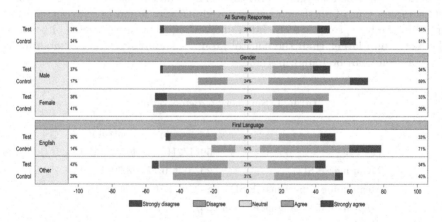

Fig. 2. The p-value for the difference between the answers to item 4 of the test- and control group is 0.035. If only looking at male participants, the p-value is 0.015, and if only looking at participants who have English as their first language, the p-value is 0.017. (Color figure online)

8.   I made choices based on what I felt I would do.

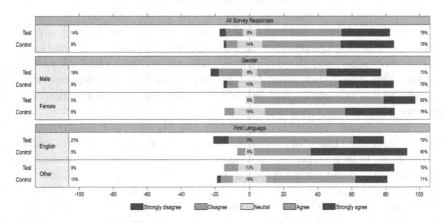

Fig. 3. *p*-value for the difference between the answers to item 8 of the test- and control group is 0.732. When only looking at participants who had English as their first language, the *p*-value becomes 0.005. (Color figure online)

5   Discussion

From the data gathered in the experiment, we can conclude that in this particular game, players who were exposed to the Hover-text expressed that they were more involved with the feelings of the PC, and native English speakers expressed that they made choices based on what they themselves would do, to a lesser degree. We observed no significant differences in the two groups' expressed feel of agency, which suggests players felt neither more or less in control of the game, by having the Hover-text.

The fact that players expressed that they were more involved with the feelings of the PC suggests that by allowing players to make decisions based on the inner thoughts of their character, they will be more aware of the fact that the PC has inner thoughts, and perhaps that leads to the feeling of involvement. This would reflect the proposal by Lankoski [2], that empathic engagement is linked to the knowledge of a character's alignment. We did not observe any difference in the other empathy questions, which prompted us to look more into the formulation of these items. Item 3 asks the player if they could relate to the PC's feelings. If the player was not roleplaying a character, is it then possible for them to relate to it? Item 5 asks about the player's ability to view things from the PC's perspective, which also requires that the player perceives the PC as a character. This can also be argued for the case of item 6, which asks players if they were imagining themselves in the PC's shoes, when making a choice. It can therefore be argued that giving the player agency over the PC's motivation, does not provoke empathy, if the player does not perceive the PC as a character. By having the 3 different personas to chose from, it is possible for the player to change the motivation of their character quite drastically, and participant No.

154, from the test group, wrote the following in the comment field: "That the player character starts quite malicious but can change his mind and become sympathetic so easily makes him hard to identify with, a bit wishy washy."

It is possible that the results would be different, had the PC only had one distinctive personality, and the different motivations written to fit that particular persona. This would then mean that players would have to roleplay a character they do not necessarily find likeable, but that does not necessarily have to influence whether the player can empathise with the character or not.

From the data it would also appear that the player's spoken language has a stronger influence than other features, such as gender. With the data gathered there appears to be no difference correlated to the player's gender, but the sample size between male and female is too far apart to make a proper conclusion. When only looking at native English speakers, item 8 becomes significant. Here the sample size is 54, which is 38% of the data set. Item 8 is in the roleplay category, suggesting native speakers are either more likely to not base choices on what they themselves would do, or they are better at self-asserting when they are doing it. It is possible that non-native speakers would have rated roleplay the same way native speakers did, were it not for potential language barriers.

6   Future Work

There appeared to be a correlation between players being native speakers, roleplay, and the use of the Hover-text. For further studies it might be interesting to look into how native speakers perceive a narrative differently from non-natives speakers, and this might be useful for reducing noise related to language barriers.

It is also interesting to dig further into the role of the PC, either as a blank-slate character or as a more fleshed out character. By writing all Hover-text to match the most popular persona in our experiment, one could diminish the number of players who did not perceive the PC as a character, due to irregular motivation. Then the player will have to play as a set, but fully-fleshed, character, while still being able to base their choices on this character's motivations. In this way, significant differences might be found in more of the empathy items, between the test- and control group.

References

1. Aylett, R.: Narrative in virtual environments - towards emergent narrative. In: Working Notes of the Narrative Intelligence Symposium, 1, November 1999
2. Lankoski, P.: Player character engagement in computer games. Games and Cult. **6**(4), 291–311 (2011)
3. Besseire, K., Seay, A.F., Kiesler, S.: The ideal elf: identity exploration in world of warcraft. Cyberpsychol. Behav. **10**(4), 530–535 (2007)
4. Blake, C., Hefner, D., Roth, C., Klimmt, C., Vorderer, P.: Cognitive processes involved in video game identification. In: Herrlich, M., Malaka, R., Masuch, M. (eds.) ICEC 2012. LNCS, vol. 7522, pp. 75–84. Springer, Heidelberg (2012). https://doi.org/10.1007/978-3-642-33542-6_7

5. Fendt, M.W., Harrison, B., Ware, S.G., Cardona-Rivera, R.E., Roberts, D.L.: Achieving the illusion of agency. In: Oyarzun, D., Peinado, F., Young, R.M., Elizalde, A., Méndez, G. (eds.) ICIDS 2012. LNCS, vol. 7648, pp. 114–125. Springer, Heidelberg (2012). https://doi.org/10.1007/978-3-642-34851-8_11
6. Thue, D., Bulitko, V., Spetch, M., Romanuik, T.: A computational model of perceived agency in video games. In: Proceedings of the Seventh AAAI Conference on Artificial Intelligence and Interactive Digital Entertainment (2011)
7. Belman, J., Flanagan, M.: Designing games to foster empathy. Int. J. Cogn. Technol. **15**(1), 11 (2010)
8. Davis, M.H.: A multidimensional approach to individual differences in empathy. JSAS **10**(85) (1980)
9. Ryan, M.L.: Narrative as Virtual Reality 2: Revisiting Immersion and Interactivity in Literature and Electronic Media. Johns Hopkins University Press, Baltimore (2015)
10. Nitsche, M.: Video Game Space. MIT Press, Cambridge (2008)
11. Ryan, M.-L.: Interactive narrative, plot types, and interpersonal relations. In: Spierling, U., Szilas, N. (eds.) ICIDS 2008. LNCS, vol. 5334, pp. 6–13. Springer, Heidelberg (2008). https://doi.org/10.1007/978-3-540-89454-4_2
12. Red Thread Games. Dreamfall chapters (2014)
13. Pratt, A.E.: Cluedo. Waddingtons, Parker Brothers, Hasbro and Winning Moves, Leeds (1949)

Self-overlapping Maze and Map Design for Asymmetric Collaboration in Room-Scale Virtual Reality for Public Spaces

Sule Serubugo[✉], Denisa Skantarova, Nicolaj Evers, and Martin Kraus[ID]

Aalborg University, Rendsburggade 14, 9000 Aalborg, Denmark
serubugo-sule@outlook.com, dskantarova@gmail.com,
nevers12@student.aau.dk, martin@create.aau.dk

Abstract. This paper addresses two problems of public room-scale Virtual Reality (VR) setups. These are the lack of walkable space due to the restricted room-scale tracking area, and the isolating experience provided by a single Head-Mounted Display (HMD). We propose and demonstrate a design for constructing a naturally walkable self-overlapping maze and a corresponding unfolded map to facilitate asymmetric collaboration between the participant wearing an HMD and the co-located participants without HMDs. Two experiments were conducted to evaluate the usability of the design and participants' experience. Our work can be useful when designing self-overlapping architectures for limited physical spaces and when supporting asymmetric experiences in public VR setups.

Keywords: Self-overlapping space · Virtual reality
Asymmetric collaboration · Room-scale virtual reality
Impossible spaces · Visualization · Public spaces · Computer graphics

1 Introduction

Virtual Reality (VR) is a rapidly developing technology that is increasingly often used by public cultural centers such as libraries and museums to entertain and immerse their visitors [1,2]. Recent advances such as room-scale virtual reality that is capable of tracking users' motions within physical room-sized areas allow for natural interaction as well as locomotion in virtual environments. However, this technology has two limitations when set up in public spaces. Walking in virtual environments requires a significant play area [3], which is often hard to find in a public space. Additionally, head-mounted displays (HMDs) tend to isolate users in single-person experiences [2].

We propose a design that addresses these limitations, where we develop a system that is capable of allowing people to walk in a large virtual environment, but also facilitates more engagement through asymmetric collaboration with the bystanders (non-HMD participants). The proposed design consists of a walkable self-overlapping VR maze as it represents a simple navigation-based task,

© ICST Institute for Computer Sciences, Social Informatics and Telecommunications Engineering 2018
A. L. Brooks et al. (Eds.): ArtsIT 2017/DLI 2017, LNICST 229, pp. 194–203, 2018.
https://doi.org/10.1007/978-3-319-76908-0_19

and a map visualizing it on a side display near the VR setup for the non-HMD participants. The design is evaluated through two usability experiments to find out whether HMD users can walk in the expansive maze without interruptions. Furthermore, the design of the map is evaluated for whether it can be understood and used by the non-HMD participants. In summary, this paper makes the following novel contributions:

- A formal design and demonstration of how a self-overlapping maze-like architecture can be constructed for public VR setups
- Demonstration of how to visualize self-overlapping architectures on a map
- Evaluation of the system with the self-overlapping architecture with a large audience in a public cultural center

2 Related Work

Navigation in the real world is a universal task based on sensory information from several cognitive processes such as vision, proprioception, and vestibular information [4]. In VR, navigation is often achieved by using traditional navigation tools (controllers, keyboard, mouse, etc.), however these usually only facilitate visual information, and have a tendency to induce motion sickness [3,4]. Ruddle and Lessels [4] found that this can be overcome by free walking in VR.

A limitation with free walking in large virtual environments is that it requires a large tracking space. Several researchers [3,5,6] have attempted to overcome this in two ways. The first manipulates users' motion such as in the technique "redirected walking" [5], where the users' perceived motion is slowly amplified or diminished as they walk in the virtual environment [3]. The second manipulates the virtual environment with techniques such as the perceptual phenomenon "change blindness", where instantaneous architectural shifts are made to the virtual environment without users noticing [7]. Another technique is "self-overlapping architectures", where a large virtual environment is compressed into a smaller physical area by overlapping parts of the environment [3,6]. The advantage of self-overlapping architectures over the other techniques is that it is less affected by the spatial requirement and does not require a directed experience. However, it has not been studied how this technique can be applied to the limited space in public VR setups and visualized unfolded on a map, which is what is investigated in this study.

To overcome the single-user experience limitation, bystanders can be involved in the experience through an asymmetric collaboration with the HMD user, an approach rarely used for VR in public. In studies [8–10], asymmetric collaboration is facilitated by unifying participants' experiences through a common story and theme, using multiple media, different roles, and communication.

An example of a role-based asymmetric collaboration in room-scale VR is the local multiplayer game VR The Diner Duo [11], where two participants are assigned roles of a cook and a waiter that have to collaborate to serve the guests. However, the game makes little use of natural navigation in the room.

In our study, we want to extend this using self-overlapping architectures to allow natural navigation and also support asymmetric collaboration via a side display in a public VR setup.

3 Design

Room-scale VR is a design paradigm that uses 360° tracking equipment to monitor the user's physical movement in all directions inside a tracked play area. There are essentially two high-end room-scale solutions – the HTC Vive setup with a play area of approximately 3.5 m × 3.5 m, and Oculus Rift for a play area of 2.5 m × 2.5 m. Our design and the experiments conducted use the HTC Vive setup, however findings can also be used for the Oculus Rift. Based on the equipment and related work, the design aims to fulfil the following criteria:

- The maze has to be walkable in VR in a limited physical space that is approximately 2.5 m × 2.5 m
- Using the technique of self-overlapping architectures, changes for updating the maze should not be noticeable to the HMD participant
- The overall area of the walkable maze should be perceived larger than the actual physical space
- To support asymmetric collaboration, the maze should be visualized on a map allowing non-HMD participants to engage in the experience

3.1 Constructing a Self-overlapping Maze

We define one part of the virtual environment that fills the 2.5 m × 2.5 m physical space as a "cell". Each cell of the self-overlapping maze can consist of informational rooms and transitional corridors. Rooms provide natural open area for placing objects, which is more constrained in corridors. Decorative and thematic content can be added that can be game-related, such as treasure and puzzles, or culture-related, such as architecture and historical structures like cathedral interiors. Transitional corridors are passageways whose primary purpose is to connect different rooms. When positioned right, corridors can help change the direction the user is walking in, thus breaking the pattern of for instance walking in a circle. Despite being transitional, they can also include game or cultural content such as scenery that can be seen through windows.

A cell can be split into a grid layout to define the placement of corridors and rooms in the virtual environment. With the average width of a person being approximately 0.456 m [12], different grid layouts were considered as shown in Fig. 1.

Without use of doors, the smallest grid that would allow for having corridors split in branching paths in the maze, is a 3 × 3 grid. This grid would consist of nine tiles, each with a size of 0.75 m × 0.75 m. On the other hand, taking into account the minimum corridor, which the users would need to walk in, the largest grid is a 5 × 5 grid. It would consist of 25 tiles, each with a size of 0.5 m × 0.5 m.

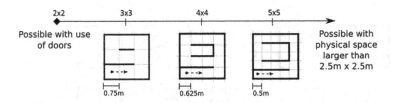

Fig. 1. Possible grid layouts for the 2.5 m × 2.5 m self-overlapping maze

Choosing the right grid layout would be based on the size of the physical tracking area and the amount of variation needed for a single cell, while still considering the minimum width for a person. For this study with a 2.5 m × 2.5 m tracking space, a 4 × 4 grid layout is used, which consists of 16 tiles, each with a size of 0.625 m × 0.625 m. Findings from our design can however also be applied for the other grid layouts. Grid layouts can also be combined to add variation to the width of corridors and rooms.

In order to create a self-overlapping maze, several cells are made and placed on top of each other. These are then swapped one after the other, allowing the user to move forward. The result is an architecture whose perceived area is larger than the physical space of 2.5 m × 2.5 m. When swapping one cell out with another, the tile where the user is positioned and the content seen on its neighbouring tiles have to be maintained and duplicated on following cells until they are out of the user's field of view. Figure 2 demonstrates a walkable VR maze designed with 26 cells. Windows are also added at places marked by double lines. The transitional tiles, where one cell is swapped for the other, are marked by numbers.

3.2   Visualizing a Self-overlapping Maze on a Map

In order to encourage asymmetric collaboration with the non-HMD participants and engage them in the experience of the HMD participant, a map is designed to represent the self-overlapping maze in a top-down orthographic view. To accurately visualize the maze on the map, the overlapping cells in Fig. 2 are reused. They are unfolded in such a way that they do not overlap. This is achieved by laying each cell next to the side of its previous cell depending on the direction that the user would be heading to when swapping to the new cell. Unfolding cells leaves gaps between the transitional tiles (marked by numbers in Fig. 3) that have to be connected. This is achieved by adding tiles in the gaps to prolong some of the corridors so that they connect with the following cells, as is demonstrated in Fig. 3 for instance between transitional tiles 2 and 3.

In some cases, it is not possible to place the connected cells right next to each other, and therefore in order to continue the unfolding, the next cell is placed further away, resulting in some prolongations crossing over each other. These crossings form prolonged bridges and tunnels, which is also demonstrated in Fig. 3 in the orange transition for example between transitional tiles 3 and 4.

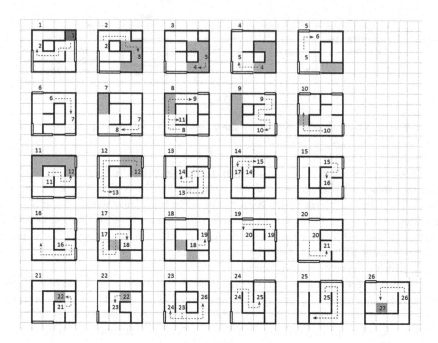

Fig. 2. A self-overlapping maze with 26 cells. Double lines mark the windows and orange tiles mark the tunnels corresponding to the map (see Sect. 3.2) (Color figure online)

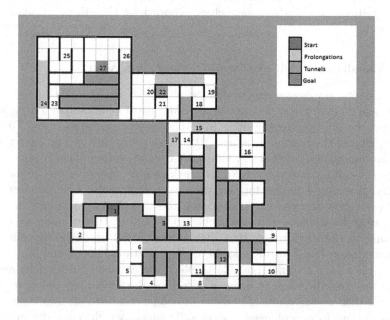

Fig. 3. A map visualization with an unfolded version of the self-overlapping maze

The bridges and tunnels that emerge on the map have to also be replicated in the overlapping cells in Fig. 2. In this case, they can be represented in form of small tunnels – areas with lower ceiling in the maze (marked as orange tiles in Fig. 2). Besides the self-overlapping architecture, the map has to also represent the movement of the HMD users and the direction they are facing for the non-HMD participants to be able to guide them. This can be achieved using a mimicking object, an avatar, with clear indication of the front side, such as a circle with a pointy edge. This avatar can mimic the HMD user's movement, and when it reaches the prolonged areas, the movements can be scaled to cover the prolonged distance in the map.

3.3   Implementing the Design

The proposed design was implemented in the Unity 3D game engine with the SteamVR plugin for VR development, and 3D models were created in Blender. As shown in Fig. 4, a 3D cell consisted mainly of wall and floor tiles and was set up in a Unity scene to fit in the 2.5 m × 2.5 m tracking area. In each cell, Unity's colliders were added on the transitional tiles to detect the user and when to swap to the next cell. Finally, the 3D cells were unfolded to form the map.

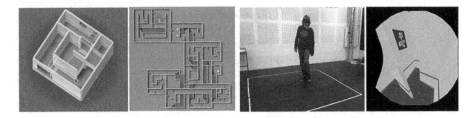

Fig. 4. From left: a 3D cell with colliders marked by yellow rectangles; the map; the 2.5 m × 2.5 m physical space; and the view in the HMD (Color figure online)

The map from Fig. 4 is presented on the side display for the purpose of facilitating asymmetric collaboration between the HMD and non-HMD participants. Here, two roles emerge based on the medium, which can be combined with a theme. We set the theme of exploration in a castle, with the role of a navigator for the non-HMD participants and the role of an explorer for the HMD participant. After implementing, the design was evaluated in two experiments described in the following sections.

4   Experiment 1: Testing the Design in a Lab

To evaluate the experience and usability of the proposed design, a usability test was conducted in a VR lab. In total, 18 participants between the age of 20 and 34 were tested in pairs. One participant was equipped with an HMD and acted as an explorer, while the other with the role of the navigator was instructed to guide the HMD participant to the end of the maze. After completing the maze, each participant was given a separate questionnaire based on their role to rate the five-point Likert items shown in Table 1. Furthermore, open questions were added to the HMD questionnaire to get responses on whether the HMD users noticed updates to the maze and their estimation of the size of the whole maze. Lastly, a short semi-structured interview was conducted with every participant.

Table 1. Likert items for the HMD and non-HMD role on a five-point scale (1: Not at all, 5: Very much)

Role	Items
HMD	**HQ1:** To what extent did the maze allow you to freely walk in the VR environment?
	HQ2: I got motion sick during the experience
	HQ3: To what extent did the help from the person without the HMD help you progress in the maze?
	HQ4: To what extent did you use the guidance of the other participant without the HMD?
Non-HMD	NQ1: How representative was the movement of the HMD participant on the map?
	NQ2: To what degree did the sudden speeding up of the HMD participant's movements on the map affect your guidance and communication?
	NQ3: To what extent did the map involve you in the VR experience?
	NQ4: To what extent did the map facilitate collaboration between you and the HMD participant?

4.1   Results and Discussion

Responses from the Likert items are summarized in Fig. 5. They show that HMD participants could freely walk in the self-overlapping maze (HQ1: $M = 3.44$) and generally did not notice the updates in the maze. When asked about the size of the whole maze, most HMD participants gave larger measurement than the actual physical size of $2.5\,\mathrm{m} \times 2.5\,\mathrm{m}$. Responses from the experiment also show that natural walking in the self-overlapping maze did not elicit motion sickness (HQ2: $M = 1.89$).

For the map, most responses show that the non-HMD participants rated the avatar's movement to correspond well with that of the HMD participant (NQ1: $M = 3.89$, NQ2: $M = 2.56$). The directions from the non-HMD participants were also rated as mostly helpful (HQ3: $M = 3.67$). Observations showed that some non-HMD participants struggled to find the exit of tunnels that were placed too close to each other, as was also mentioned by seven participants.

In terms of asymmetric collaboration, observations showed that participants used their roles, and the HMD participants used the guidance from the non-HMD participants (HQ4: $M = 3.89$). In the interviews, two HMD participants

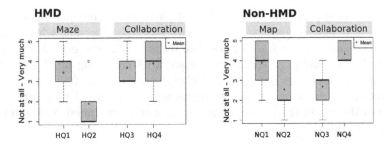

Fig. 5. Box plots of ratings on HMD and non-HMD experience from Table 1

mentioned that they "couldn't have continued without help from the non-HMD participant". Non-HMD participants also stated that the map facilitated their collaboration with the HMD participants (NQ4: $M = 4.33$), and a few mentioned in the interview that the fact that their directions were followed made them more part of the experience. Two participants said: "I felt part of the experience because she was reacting to what I was saying, we worked on it connected". Further improvements are however needed since the ratings showed that the map facilitated only average involvement of the non-HMD participants in the VR experience (NQ3: $M = 2.67$). Non-HMD participants could for instance be given more tasks for their role or be presented with more information and a mirrored view of the virtual world.

5 Experiment 2: Testing the Design in a Public Library

After testing in the lab, the second experiment was conducted as an observational study to evaluate the proposed design in a public library. Before testing, the system was improved to include more spacing around tunnels. The proposed system was tried by a total of 20 participants, of which two were female and 18 male with an estimated age of 9 to 40 years. Figure 6 shows pictures taken from the experiment, where the participants were instructed to collaborate and find a diamond in the maze.

Fig. 6. The setup of the experiment and participants interacting with the system

During the experiment, the number of participants and playthroughs was counted. One playthrough was considered the whole session where participants maintained their roles. Besides this, intuitiveness and usability were also observed by how far participants progressed without giving up. Furthermore, to evaluate collaboration, we observed whether participants fulfilled their roles and were communicating. Lastly, engagement was evaluated by whether they completed the maze, tried the system again, and by the number of spectators standing by and watching.

5.1 Results and Discussion

The system was played through 21 times. Based on the observations, as can be seen in Table 2, results on the intuitiveness and usability from the field study are similar to those from Experiment 1. 16 (78%) playthroughs completed the maze and found the diamond. The remaining five either accidentally pulled out the HMD wire or got confused at a more complex tunnel junction. All participants were observed to be engaged in the experience. 17 (81%) out of the 20 participants tried both the HMD and non-HMD role. There were only four participants observed to have retried their roles, which could be attributed to the fact that there only was one maze for them to solve. Lastly, a total of 30 spectators were observed in 13 (62%) out of 21 playthroughs, which shows that the system is able to asymmetrically involve the co-located people outside VR.

Table 2. Observations from the test. See Fig. 3 for transitional tiles 3 and 13

Observation	Count
Number of playthroughs	21
How many reach transitional tile 3 - understand the prolongations	21 (100%)
How many reach transitional tile 13 - understand the complex tunnels	17 (81%)
Do they collaborate - helping and using each other's contribution	21 (100%)
How many completed the maze	16 (78%)
Number of participants	20
How many participants tried both roles	17 (85%)
How many participants tried one role more than once	4 (20%)

6   Conclusion

This paper has proposed a self-overlapping maze that the HMD participant can naturally walk through, and a corresponding unfolded map to asymmetrically involve the non-HMD participants in a public VR setup. We have demonstrated a design for how to construct such a self-overlapping maze by creating cells that overlap to fit in a limited physical space of 2.5 m × 2.5 m. Furthermore, we presented how to create a map that can show the whole maze at once, where prolongations, tunnels, and bridges are added to create transitions from one cell to the next. Two experiments were conducted, one in a lab and one in a public library, to evaluate the proposed design. Results show that the self-overlapping maze is experienced as freely walkable while the map is mostly understandable with only visualization of tunnels requiring improvements.

Our work can be generalized and applied in other areas working with VR setups that can be walkable in small physical spaces or include non-HMD participants. Such areas could include architectural installations, where the designed buildings could be experienced through natural walking. Future work should investigate how to improve the visualization of the tunnels and bridges on the map, so that the non-HMD participants can clearly see where the tunnels start and where they lead. Lastly, the possibility of creating the self-overlapping maze and map procedurally, and the influence of sound could be further investigated.

References

1. Massis, B.: Using virtual and augmented reality in the library. New Libr. World **116**(11/12), 796–799 (2015)
2. Carrozzino, M., Bergamasco, M.: Beyond virtual museums: experiencing immersive virtual reality in real museums. J. Cult. Herit. **11**(4), 452–458 (2010)
3. Suma, E.A., Lipps, Z., Finkelstein, S., Krum, D.M., Bolas, M.: Impossible spaces: maximizing natural walking in virtual environments with self-overlapping architecture. IEEE Trans. Vis. Comput. Graph. **18**(4), 555–564 (2012)
4. Ruddle, R.A., Lessels, S.: The benefits of using a walking interface to navigate virtual environments. ACM Trans. Comput.-Hum. Interact. **16**(1), 5:1–5:18 (2009)
5. Razzaque, S., Kohn, Z., Whitton, M.C.: Redirected walking. In: Proceedings of EUROGRAPHICS, vol. 9, pp. 105–106 (2001)
6. Vasylevska, K., Kaufmann, H., Bolas, M., Suma, E.A.: Flexible spaces: dynamic layout generation for infinite walking in virtual environments. In: 2013 IEEE Symposium on 3D User Interfaces (3DUI), pp. 39–42 (2013)
7. Suma, E.A., Clark, S., Krum, D., Finkelstein, S., Bolas, M., Warte, Z.: Leveraging change blindness for redirection in virtual environments. In: 2011 IEEE Virtual Reality Conference (VR), pp. 159–166. IEEE (2011)
8. Liszio, S., Masuch, M.: Designing shared virtual reality gaming experiences in local multi-platform games. In: Wallner, G., Kriglstein, S., Hlavacs, H., Malaka, R., Lugmayr, A., Yang, H.-S. (eds.) ICEC 2016. LNCS, vol. 9926, pp. 235–240. Springer, Cham (2016). https://doi.org/10.1007/978-3-319-46100-7_23
9. Sajjadi, P., Cebolledo Gutierrez, E.O., Trullemans, S., De Troyer, O.: Maze commander: a collaborative asynchronous game using the oculus rift & the sifteo cubes. In: CHI PLAY 2014, pp. 227–236 (2014)
10. Schmitz, M., Akbal, M., Zehle, S.: SpielRaum: perspectives for collaborative play. In: CHI PLAY 2015, pp. 427–432 (2015)
11. Whirlybird Games. VR The Diner Duo. [Steam] (2016). http://store.steampowered.com/app/530120/VR_The_Diner_Duo/
12. First In Architecture. Average Male and Female Dimensions/Heights (2017). http://www.firstinarchitecture.co.uk/average-male-and-female-dimensions/. Accessed 12 Apr 2017

The Post-virtual Reality: From the Interactive Experience to the Connective Experience

Eli Borges Jr.(✉) and Massimo Di Felice

University of Sao Paulo, Atopos USP International Center for Studies in Digital Networks, Av. Lucio Martins Rodrigues, 443, Sao Paulo, SP 05508-020, Brazil
{eli.borges,massimo}@usp.br

Abstract. This paper aims to problematize the concept of "virtual reality" in light of the hypothesis that there is a contemporary transformation of the nature of the interaction between the spectator and the artwork. New technologies such as Google Tilt Brush, seem to require a new reading of this relationship, whose complexity suggests surpassing the limits of the notion of interactivity. In this sense, we present an alternative concept of "connectivity", which seeks to cover the three effects that we point on this transformation: the destabilization of conventional notions of time and space; the shuffling of notions of subject and object; the advent of a new form of fruition, which we propose to call "post-virtual reality".

Keywords: Virtual reality · Augmented reality · Interactivity · Fruition
Google Tilt Brush

1 Presentation of the Problem

Despite all the debate around the concept of "virtual reality"[1], which unfolds in the two sharp edges of the "virtual" and the notion of "reality", it seems increasingly complicated the task of characterizing certain technological devices from that expression. At the same time, the advancement of these technologies and their new potential[2] suggests a significant differentiation between them and the first resources, giving rise to a series of totally unpredictable ways, which tend to change the contours of the contemporary relationship between the human and technique.

From an experience of interactivity, further characterized by a fundamental distinction between human element and the machine, and, therefore, by the description of an action that suggests the first always as the irradiator pole or action receiver[3], what

---

[1] Expression that will appear in this text also by the abbreviated version "VR".

[2] Potentialities that resonate in the most varied spheres of life: in the arts, in the elaboration of games, in our practical life – our displacements in space, our work –, in education, in the medical area; there are several examples in which devices applications of the so-called "virtual reality" have emerged today. In this sense, large technology conglomerates, such as Google and Facebook, have shown considerable interest in the area, channeling specific efforts to promote it within their productive processes. An example of this was the creation in early 2016 of Google's VR project division.

[3] On the subject of action, described in the context of contemporary experiments between art and technology, see [1].

© ICST Institute for Computer Sciences, Social Informatics and Telecommunications Engineering 2018
A. L. Brooks et al. (Eds.): ArtsIT 2017/DLI 2017, LNICST 229, pp. 204–212, 2018.
https://doi.org/10.1007/978-3-319-76908-0_20

we seek to discuss here, even briefly, is the hypothesis that this relationship might be described from various contours: no longer as an experience of interactivity, but as an experience of "connectivity". What would this distinction mean, in turn, and why this distinction is necessary to rethink, in theory, all about this extremely diverse constellation that today we insist on calling "virtual reality"?

We start here from the notion that new so-called resources would be enabling a diverse experience of fruition, never before experienced: something that seems to transform our familiar notions of time, the relationship with our surroundings, and, more than that, our own exercise of perception. Unlike perspectives that seek to escape from the thematizations between the concepts of real and virtual, as in the works of Lévy [2], online and offline, addressed by Beiguelman [3], these devices seem to go beyond as they invite us to think of even more acute transformations. In this sense we could even read them, without exaggeration, as the emergence of a new dwelling condition, that is marked by the dissolution of the boundaries between subject and object, spectator/user and environment. These relations would ground no longer in the exchange between one and another – and, therefore, in recognition of their separate dimensions – but in a dynamic capability of reinventing their concepts and the relationship between them: in place of this scenario of "interactivity", we propose the concept of "connectivity" [4].

Before exposing, however, the reasons why we present this proposition, let us make a very brief overview of some notions that exploit the concept of "interactivity" and then introduce our hypothesis itself. As a way to delineate it, albeit in embryonic way, we will present the representative case of Google Tilt Brush, a resource recently launched by Google and that seems to offer new frontiers for thinking the interaction and the creation in the contemporary relationship between arts and technology. Once this is done, then we will pass to the theme of "connectivity" as an important operative concept in order to reread the peculiarities of a new dwelling condition brought about by such devices.

2 The Experience of Interactivity

It is true that Benjamin [5], reflecting on the effects of the cinema on the sensory body of the viewers, already announces there, to some extent, the ability to think, for example, the movie theatre as an ambience capable to establish a dwelling condition that is diverse from the one experienced by modern life. Benjamin calls our attention to a type of fruition of the image that is different from the one experienced until then: the technical reproducibility in the arts, mainly represented by the photography and film, destabilizes the traditional model of the contemplation – which is based on a mainly rational association – and transforms it to an immediately sensory perception model. This notion is founded by Benjamin to point out what he calls "disruptive effect" of cinema, able to "target" the viewers in its most immediate layer, in a primarily aesthetic effect, not rational.

Likewise, it must also recognize that Benjamin's interpretation of the relationship between spectator and film technology reflects a certain idea of communication as mechanical transmission of messages, an idea that delimits quite clearly the boundaries between the subject that perceives and the perceived thing. This relation, to some extent, is described as almost without possibilities of intervention by the spectator itself, that, when is "targeted" for such images would not be able to do anything more than to react in a certain way to its effects. Not much beyond a relation between stimulus and response.

Direct symptom of that seems to be the very importance that Benjamin attributes to the film and its ability to release the public of their lethargy simply because of a shock effect of its moving images on the sensory apparatus of the spectators[4]. Saved all the great importance of Benjamin's reflection, what seems to announce here is therefore a fundamentally dual interaction model – spectator and screen, human and machine – that will be reproduced by several researchers of the image, evidently with interesting variations, but that, in most of the cases, ends up culminating in a still dualistic reasoning. The terms may vary: "interaction" is, at times, replaced by "interactivity"; in others, it appears to be equivalent; however, it would not be an exaggeration to say that, in general, there is a certain tendency to draw clear boundaries between a human element and a technological element and, from a more accurate perspective, on converging them to a supremacy of the first one. The action tends to be bound fundamentally to this human dimension.

In a slightly different context, characterized by the advance of the electricity and the consequent advent of the electronics, Ascott [7] explores the topic of human-machine inspired by the fundamental view of the Norbert Wiener's cybernetics [8], noting, instead, the possible changes that the computer could bring to artistic experimentations. Although spectator and machine appear here under a perspective still quite definitive, with clearly defined roles, it is certain that an important space of unpredictability in the relationship between them is opened, something that the prospect of Benjamin's disruptive effect does not seem to admit. This would allow us to say that, for Ascott, there is a more open concept of interaction, a perspective that gives us some gaps within which we may trace the high level of participation of current technologies as performers or even action producers [1].

The experimental efforts in the second half of the twentieth century, particularly after the 60's, will thus be strongly marked by the presence of new technologies, exploring, in good part, the interaction potentialities offered by them: interaction that could have effect among the spectators themselves or even between the spectator and the artwork. Admittedly, the Bauhaus, decades earlier, would be an important inspiration for this, but the proliferation of computer and video, and the ease of access to them would lead the experimentations to consequences never before imagined. The presence of these new technologies in performance, happenings and even in conventional arts, would lead to an absolutely multifaceted scenario, disfiguring the classic separation between "fine arts": the new genres of video art, art installation, dance theatre, and cyberart are other important examples, creating many possibilities for reconfiguring the very idea of interaction or interactivity with such devices.

---

[4] More on this model of the fruition of the technological image, also called "distracted attention", in Benjamin [6].

In order to organize this panorama, Julio Plaza undertakes a specific reflection on the notion of interactivity and what he calls the "degrees of openness of the artwork" to the reception. Plaza attributes "a plurality of meanings" to the first of the three degrees, a plurality that would allow a certain freedom of interpretation by the spectator. These degrees grow according to the opening of the artworks to participation: in the second degree, the artwork can be manipulated or even modified by the spectator, although this happens in accordance with certain restrictions. To the third degree of openness, however, it is reserved a particular way of interactivity, with a more active participation, which Plaza exemplifies with artworks constructed in interaction with the computer. As asserted by him in these last cases, "the interactivity is not only a technical and functional convenience; it implies physically, psychologically and sensitively the spectator into a practice of transformation" [9]. As we see with this analytic perspective, Julio Plaza seems to cover the various modes of interaction "author-artwork-reception"[5], although ultimately, he still seems to situate the action on the human element: no wonder his model is based on the degree of "activity" of the spectator.

In a similar effort, Edmond Couchot calls into question the relationship between author, artwork and spectator. He says that the exercise of the latter, in the digital interactive art, no longer would be reduced to the role of contemplating, but to the role of expanding the artwork, of "enlarging it" and, ultimately, of providing the very existence of it, insofar as, without interaction, the artwork would remain as a "not perceptible computational potentiality". The production of the artwork would thus take shape in a real verbal, visual, gestural or tactile dialogue between author and enjoyer [10], an idea that later would be developed by Couchot in his concept of "second interactivity" [11].

These examples of reflections on the concept of interaction and interactivity seem to constitute a way of thinking that reinforces one aspect of frontality between the subject that watches and the artwork watched, although there is a major effort to point out the attempts of "openness" of contemporary artworks. The direct consequence of that – which justifies our discussion – is that newly presented technologies tend to explode this logical interaction: they no longer seem to function according to these models, not even within the concept of "interaction" or "interactivity". But how particular would these technologies be to require new models of interpretation? That is what we intend to discuss in the next section of this paper.

3   The Post-virtual Reality: The Experience of Connectivity

The discussion about "art forms" – if we can precisely use this mode of expression – or even about "categories" in the arts, tends to become considerably more explosive when it counts as a special ingredient: the participation of new technologies of image, in particular, digital devices that in many cases seek to reposition or, in the limit, reread certain traditional practices. It was and still is the case, for instance, of the use of

---

[5] Expression that gives the title to his paper [9].

software or electronic interfaces in the production of new sound styles[6] or the example of insertion of video technologies in the creation of new scenic forms, seeking to bring together traditional elements within the known formats of theatre, film or performance[7].

But it is about the painting that we would like to present an interesting case suggesting the disruption of the frontality boundaries, which seems to mark the relations between art and technology as they are experienced nowadays. We bring here the example of Google Tilt Brush[8], a device released by Google in April 2016 which has fostered a number of experimentations in the visual arts, design, and even in the diverse and dynamic world of games. Armed with virtual reality glasses and a number of resources that are available by the device software, the user has at his or hers disposal a wide range of work tools with which he can draw on the immersion space offered by the glasses, with the possibility of adding diverse 3D visual effects to this new ambience: brightness, movements and colors in the most different shades[9].

The repercussion of the device and its potentialities has generated a number of initiatives, both inside and outside Google. Among the most important of them, it is the creation of an artist residency program, the Tilt Brush Artist in Residence (AiR), which assembled more than 60 artists, according to the company, "from a variety of disciplines", including "graffiti artists, painters, illustrators, graphic designers, dancers, conceptual artists, creative technologists and cartoonists"[10].

Another interesting result of this movement is the emergence of what could point to as a new kind of artistic practice, which has brought together traditional operating modes, and the dynamics and infinities of features offered by the device. An emblematic case about this is the meeting of graffiti conducted by Opposable VR in Bristol[11], United Kingdom, or, above all, the works of the artist Anna Zhilyaeva, which bring together Google Tilt Brush effects to the paper, the canvas, the brush or the crayon[12].

---

[6] This is the case of free improvisation experiments, which seek to break the limits of the idea of musical note, exploring, much more, its dimensions as "sonorities". More in [12, 13].

[7] On the participation of digital technologies in the contemporary performing arts, see [1].

[8] It is worth checking the homepage of the device, with information and videos on the modes of operation and some potentialities of the resource. Available at: <https://www.tiltbrush.com/>. Accessed on: 09 May 2017.

[9] The Google Tilt Brush homepage highlights: "Painting from a new perspective. Tilt Brush lets you paint in 3D space with virtual reality. Your room is your canvas. Your palette is your imagination. The possibilities are endless". Available at: <https://www.tiltbrush.com/>. Accessed on: 09 May 2017.

[10] As Google describes in the Youtube page dedicated to AiR. Available at: <https://www.youtube.com/watch?v=LBJPIgNXUDI>. Accessed on: 09 May 2017.

[11] Meeting held in December 2015, even before the official launch of Google Tilt Brush, in April of the following year. A brief video of the meeting can be viewed on the Opposable VR channel on Youtube. Available at: <https://www.youtube.com/watch?v=jtoLmZwbyG0>. Accessed on: 09 May 2017.

[12] About Zhilyaeva's artworks, access her Youtube channel, available at: <http://www.youtube.com/channel/UCKEfXMw7538wvuulXy_RNcQ>. Accessed on: 09 May 2017.

The advent of Google Tilt Brush can lead us to many issues, but the most evident one, and the central point of our paper, is to investigate the nature of the experience of the device user, as an artist, a "builder" of the artwork or an enjoyer of it.

On the one hand, in relation to the artist's work, we can glimpse a certain recovery of the gestures of drawing and traditional painting[13], something that the computer, from its keyboard or its mouse, had reduced to the mere touch of buttons. The "new painting" seems to be emancipated from the fingertips, arms, and a static body of the painter, to remake the most daring gestures, able to describe themselves, the very strength of the created images. We could perceive, in this case, a certain reconfiguration of the painting as a body performance, brought to the limits by the intensity of the contemporary works of Ushio Shinohara or Franck Bouroullec, for example.

On the other side, but very close, there is the point that interests us and that could be described as a transformation of the relationship between artwork/spectator, also taken to its extreme by the device: this transformation would be characterized especially by a dissolution of frontality between these instances, a dissolution that would even confuse them in the end. Thus, as a result of this dissolution, we would point three other effects: the destabilization of conventional notions of time and space; the shuffling of concepts of subject and object; the advent of a new form of fruition, which challenges the expression "virtual reality". Each of them is briefly discussed below:

1. The destabilization of conventional notions of time and space: when we experience artworks like the ones of Steve Teeple (known as Teeps) or Tamiko Thiel, artists of Google AiR Program, we are immersed in a condition in which the cardinal points seem to get completely overwhelmed, bringing what Massimo Di Felice characterizes as a "loss of sense of place" [15].
   This spatial disorientation, accompanied by the result of a time confusion, is related to what Di Felice characterizes as an "atopic form of dwelling"[14], an expression that here is very timely. In environments built by these artists, we are immersed in "atopic" spatiality and temporality in the sense of "a-topos", or "out of place", "paradoxical", even "strange". The loss of these references would lead us, ultimately, to a certain physical discomfort, a common reaction among those who first experience the 3D glasses.
2. The shuffling of concepts of subject and object: the separation that traditionally outlines the relationship between the spectator and the oil on canvas that he contemplates, in the constructed experiences, seems to migrate to another condition in which the action provoked by the artwork merges with the action of the spectator-subject himself. Therefore, the operation dynamics of it with the various

---

[13] As Borges Junior briefly pointed out in [14].

[14] According to Di Felice, the digital technologies provide new ways of inhabiting the contemporary world, completely influencing our perceptions of time and space. These devices would not only be an "extension" of our bodies, as McLuhan asserts [16], but rather elements endowed with "action", in constant relation with humans and other organic and inorganic entities. As Di Felice adds: "The atopic form of dwelling is thus characterized as a 'transorganic' form of the being that begins to experience its own essence and existence itself through a hybrid and *protean* form capable of changing the spatiality and its perception by the dress of an interface or software" [17]. Italic by the author.

elements of the artwork is the founder and characterizer aspect of this experience. In this sense, placed next to that ambience and, at the same time, literally "inside" it, the boundaries between spectator and artwork, subject and object, which mark the notions of "interactivity" – especially those that we have just briefly discussed –, fog in favor of a relationship that seems to describe otherwise something that is also able to express the action of non-human elements: those that, in some way, leave some kind of "trail" [18].

There arises another kind of interaction, a "connectivity" [4]. Distinctly from "interactivity", which presupposes a relation *between* elements of different natures (organic and inorganic, e.g., human and computer; artist and work), the concept of "connectivity", referring precisely to the universe of digital networks, refers to a condition in which the original nature of such elements is converted into a third and only format: information, capable of bringing together organic elements to inorganic elements and convert them into a nature not exclusively organic or inorganic, but hybrid, which we call "transorganic" [4]. In so far as everything is transformed into "connected information", the notion of interactivity seems to make no further sense, for it denotes an idea of "distinction" *between* two entities, presupposed separated. In this new condition, space and time are converted in that format, in which physical spaces and bodies merge to the informative nature of the ambiances offered, for instance, by Tilt Brush. The result is a symbiotic relationship between the various elements, clearly distinct from each other (humans, technological devices and territorialities), but whose relationship suggests the overcome of the duality subject/object, and thus the mere logic of stimulus/response. The relation of "connectivity" becomes more complex and, therefore, leads to a problematization of the own roles of the artist, artwork and spectator.

3. The advent of a new form of fruition: these artworks signal thus for the emergence of a new feeling, which destabilizes the very traditional notion of fruition, without limits between "inside" and "outside", referring, in turn, to Edgar Morin's "*principe hologrammatique*": the whole and the parts are not defined by clear boundaries, they amalgamate themselves and belong to each other, without losing, however, its specificities [19]. Thus, we propose in this paper, the passage of a dimension of "interactivity" to a perspective of "connectivity": these artworks, from the way they articulate the spectator and the technological devices as well as the way they operate the notions of space and time, suggest us no longer an interaction of elements of a diverse nature, artwork/spectator or artwork/artist, but another relation, "connective", that transforms the "ecology of interactions" [4].

In this new context, older dilemmas between online and offline, real and virtual, do not fit since the connectivity condition seems to break such extremes: it emerges there another form of reality, a "post-virtual[15] reality" that no longer distinguishes material and immaterial and therefore orders us an intensification of feeling, able to activate in us much more than just the vision. The vision is constituted in the primal sense of what can be called "Virtual Reality" or, ultimately, of "Augmented

---

[15] "Post-virtual" which here is re-signified and is not related to other examples of employment of the term, as in [20].

Reality". In the post-virtual reality, the feeling is kinesthetic; in it, the art no longer pursues the obligation to mimic the reality, but it is operationalized by the creation of a new reality.

4 Conclusions

What we propose here is much more an attempt to question the concept of "virtual reality", in the face of the advent of a different dwelling condition that has been brought by new technological devices, than a detailed presentation of representative cases of the potential of these technologies.

As a track to this, we chose to question the concept of interactivity and its theoretical suitability as a way of thinking the nature of relations that are made possible by these new devices. We hold, therefore, that such concept – in the way it suggests to guard a distinct separation between artwork and spectator, subject and object, and thus still maintaining a frontality among them – ultimately clash with the numerous possibilities offered by technologies like Google Tilt Brush, and its artistic works, which seems to break through the boundaries of the frontality of the painting. As a result, we point out a destabilization of conventional notions of time and space, and, ultimately, an advent of a new form of fruition, which we describe as an experience of "connectivity", and we relate to the emergence, in these artworks, of another condition that we call "post-virtual reality".

Our effort integrates, in a wider perspective, an attempt to reread the technological phenomena of our time mainly when they seem to exercise a direct action on various fields of modern life. As a scientific work, it is an evolving process that is therefore open and subject to the productive contributions of other reflections.

Acknowledgments. This paper is a result of a PhD fellowship: grant #2016/03588-7, São Paulo Research Foundation (FAPESP).

References

1. Borges Junior, E.: Tecnodionysos: Digital Technologies and Networked Action in the Contemporary Scene. ECA/USP, Sao Paulo (2014)
2. Lévy, P.: Qu'est ce que le virtuel? La Découverte, Paris (1998)
3. Beiguelman, G.: Admirável mundo cíbrido. In: Brasil, A., et al. (eds.) Cultura em Fluxo: novas mediações em rede. PUC Minas, Belo Horizonte (2004)
4. Di Felice, M.: Net-attivismo: dall'azione sociale all'atto connettivo. Edizioni Estemporanee, Roma (2017)
5. Benjamin, W.: Illuminations: Essays and Reflections. Edited by Hannah Arendt and translated by Harry Zohn. Schocken Books, New York (1969)
6. Arantes, O.B.F.: Os novos Museus. Novos Estudos CEBRAP, no. 31, Sao Paulo (1991)
7. Ascott, R.: Behaviourist art and the cybernetic vision. In: Packer, R., Jordan, K. (eds.) Multimedia: From Wagner to Virtual Reality. W. W. Norton & Company, New York/London (2002)

8. Wiener, N.: Cybernetics, or Control and Communication in the Animal and the Machine. MIT Press, Cambridge (1961)
9. Plaza, J.: Arte e interatividade: autor-obra-recepção. ARS, Sao Paulo, vol. 1, no. 2, pp. 9–29, p. 15 (2003)
10. Couchot, E.: A arte pode ainda ser um relógio que adianta? O autor, a obra e o espectador na hora do tempo real. In: Domingues, D. (ed.) A arte no século XXI. UNESP, São Paulo (1997)
11. Couchot, E.: Des images, du temps et des machines dans les arts et la communication. Actes Sud, Paris (2007)
12. Costa, R.: Música errante: o jogo da improvisação livre. Perspectiva, Sao Paulo (2016)
13. Solomos, M.: De la musique au son: l'émergence du son dans la musique des XXe - XXIe siècles. Presses Universitaires de Rennes, Rennes (2013)
14. Borges Junior, E.: Forma espetacular e imagem bipolar: reflexões sobre abstração e concretude na fruição da imagem midiática contemporânea. In: XXXIX Congresso Brasileiro de Ciências da Comunicação, pp. 1–16, p. 13. Intercom, Sao Paulo (2016)
15. Di Felice, M.: Paysages post-urbains: la fin de l'expérience urbaine et les formes de l'habiter. CNRS Éditions, Paris (2016)
16. McLuhan, M.: Understanding Media: The Extensions of Man. Routledge & K. Paul, London (1964)
17. Di Felice, M.: Paysages post-urbains: la fin de l'expérience urbaine et les formes de l'habiter, pp. 268–269. CNRS Éditions, Paris (2016)
18. Latour, B.: Reassembling the Social: An Introduction to Actor-Network-Theory. Oxford University Press, New York (2007)
19. Morin, E.: La Méthode, vol. 5. Séuil, Paris (2003)
20. Beiguelman, G.: Arte pós-virtual: criação e agenciamento no tempo da Internet das Coisas e da próxima natureza. In: Cyber-arte-cultura: a trama das redes. Seminários Internacionais Museu Vale, Vila Velha, pp. 147–171 (2013)

Sensory Augmentation: Toward a Dialogue Between the Arts and Sciences

Alwin de Rooij[1]([✉]), Michel van Dartel[2], Antal Ruhl[2],
Hanna Schraffenberger[1], Bente van Melick[1], Mathijs Bontje[1],
Mischa Daams[2], and Michel Witter[2]

[1] Tilburg University, Warandelaan 2, 5037 Tilburg, AB, The Netherlands
alwinderooij@tilburguniversity.edu
[2] Avans University of Applied Sciences,
Parallelweg 21–24, 5223 Den Bosch, AL, The Netherlands
mf.vandartel@avans.nl

Abstract. People sense the world by exploiting correlations between their physical actions and the changing sensory input that results from those actions. Interfaces that translate non-human sensor data to signals that are compatible with the human senses can therefore augment our abilities to make sense of the world. This insight has recently sparked an increase in projects that explore sensemaking and the creation of novel human experiences across scientific and artistic disciplines. However, there currently exists no constructive dialogue between artists and scientists that conduct research on this topic. In this position paper, we identify the theory and practice of *sensory augmentation* as a domain that could benefit from such a dialogue. We argue that artistic and scientific methods can complement each other within research on sensory augmentation and identify six thematic starting points for a dialogue between the arts and sciences. We conducted a case study to explore these conjectures, in which we instigated such a dialogue on a small scale. The case study revealed that the six themes we identified as relevant for a dialogue on sensory augmentation emerge rather spontaneously in such a dialogue and that such an exchange may facilitate progress on questions that are central to the theory and practice of sensory augmentation. Overall, this position paper contributes preliminary evidence for the potential of, and a starting point for, a dialogue between the arts and sciences that advances our understanding of sensory augmentation and the development of applications that involve it.

Keywords: Art-science collaboration · Cognitive science · Interfaces
New media art · Sensory augmentation · Sensory substitution

1 Introduction

"Art being a thing of the mind, it follows that any scientific study of art will be psychology", states Friedlander in Gombrich's book *Art and illusion* [1] (p. 3). In the dialogue between the arts and psychology that Gombrich advocates however, art plays a mere instrumental role in the development of theory on perception. For instance, pictorial artworks are discussed as support for a representational theory of perception,

© ICST Institute for Computer Sciences, Social Informatics and Telecommunications Engineering 2018
A. L. Brooks et al. (Eds.): ArtsIT 2017/DLI 2017, LNICST 229, pp. 213–223, 2018.
https://doi.org/10.1007/978-3-319-76908-0_21

yet such theory is not explicitly considered to hold any value for the creation of art. It has been shown that theory of perception can however also advance the field of art. In turn, artistic work that is grounded in such theory can be relevant to the study of perception [2]. In this position paper, we argue that this especially goes for research that considers perception as action (i.e., the sensorimotor coordination approach [3]), rather than a passive processing of symbols (e.g., computational approaches to perception [4]).

Theory that considers perception as an activity suggests that people make sense of the world by exploiting the correlations between their physical actions and the changing sensory input that results from those actions, i.e. sensorimotor contingencies [5]. Parallel to the emergence of such scientific theory, recent art theory suggests that art is no longer something to look at or listen to from a distance, but a call to action that challenges us to understand or make sense of something [6], and that art practices can be considered modes of thought based on acts of creation [7]. As perception research shifts to studying the correlations between sensory input and physical actions, art is shifting focus to intervening and subverting such active relationships between humans and their surroundings [8]. This suggests that a dialogue on perception research between artists and scientists is possible now more than ever. Besides novel scientific insight inspiring new artistic experiences, such a dialogue could also be mutually constructive because "in the sciences […] the subjectivity that accompanies experience is usually seen as an undesired variable that is to be controlled rather than enhanced" whereas "creative research practices emphasise the role of personal or subjective experiences" [9] (p. 90). Thus, where science aims to understand subjective phenomena, such as perception, attempts to rule out rather than enhance the 'undesired variable' of subjectivity can be in the way of progress. Therefore, the arts and sciences can complement each other, yet need to be desegregated. In what follows, we identify the art and science of *sensory augmentation,* identify six themes as point of departure for a dialogue between the arts and sciences, and present a small case study on what this dialogue could bring about.

2   Sensory Augmentation in the Arts and Sciences

Interfaces that translate non-human sensor data to signals that are compatible with the human senses can augment our abilities to make sense of the world, and are used across the sciences and the arts [2, 10]. One fundamental experiment to the field of sensory augmentation has resulted in both acclaimed artistic and much-debated scientific outcomes; a class of experiments often referred to as 'inverted vision'. In these experiments, goggles with mirrors that alter the visual consequences of moving one's eyes, e.g. reversing up and down, are typically used. While experiments by scientists Stratton [11] and Kohler [12] are often taken as empirical proof for active approaches to perception [3], and continue to inspire research on the topic (e.g., [13]), these experiments also had their impact on the arts. Artist Carsten Höller, for instance, has extensively researched the application of 'inverted vision' in aesthetic experiences, pioneering a novel type of active relationship between an artwork and its audience [8].

Sensory substitution goes one step further in intervening and subverting correlations between the sensory changes that result from the movement of our sensors. It takes the sensory changes of one (artificial) modality and correlates these to sensory changes in another. By doing this consistently, the sensory correlations that we are accustomed to within one modality transfer to another and augment the original sensory experience. A classic example is a series of experiments by Bach-y-Rita [14] for which he developed an interface that substituted visual information into tactile stimulation by mapping a low-res camera image onto a grid of solenoids worn on the stomach or back. After training, subjects reported the experience of 'seeing with the skin'. This work demonstrates the possibility of developing interfaces to establish novel sensorimotor relationships, through which new contingencies can be mastered to make sense of and experience the world; experiences otherwise non-existent. Although sensory augmentation has since been widely explored scientifically (see, e.g., [10, 15]), the potential initially projected on Bach-y-Rita's breakthrough findings has yet to be fully realized in both art and science. First, laboratory studies have shown that learning sensorimotor contingencies follows generalisable lawful patterns [16], but reports of participant's having novel subjective sensory experiences during such studies, such as "seeing with the skin", are mostly anecdotal [17]. Second, laboratory studies into sensory augmentation have been argued to neglect testing users for "novel kinds of stimuli [...] for which they lack pre-existing knowledge" [18], which omission draws into question whether sensory augmentation interfaces can elicit truly *novel* sensory experiences. We argue that investigation of such novel experiences (i) calls for a broad imagination on what such *"novel kinds of stimuli"* [18] could entail, and (ii) requires the creation of personal subjective experiences and modes of research that allow for unavoidable *subjective and personal experiences* (see also [19]). Such imagination, as well as the creation of personal subjective experiences, are key to the domain of art [2, 6, 8, 9]. This suggests that the generalisability that comes with the scientific method can help develop new theory, on the basis of which new subjective experiences can be designed. Reversely, artistic exploration of subjective experiences can form a basis to advance theory. Therefore, we propose an integrated approach to advance the theory and practice of sensory augmentation based on the instigation of a dialogue between art and science on the topic.

3   Themes for a Dialogue Between the Arts and Sciences

To facilitate the envisioned dialogue between art and science we develop six *themes* that emerged consistently in discussions between the authors of this paper and that can be used to structure the envisioned dialogue in a manner that advances both domains.

3.1   Understanding Sensory Augmentation

Three themes for the envisioned dialogue emerged that may advance our theoretical understanding of sensory augmentation: (i) *apparatuses*, (ii) *mapping*, and (iii) *contingency learning*.

First, the *apparatuses* that artistic and scientific projects use to effectively achieve sensory augmentation should be a theme in the envisioned dialogue on sensory augmentation. Where scientists typically develop apparatuses to map sensor data to human senses, e.g. Bach-y-Rita's TVSS interface [16], artists may conceive completely new types of senses or enable the body's senses in unlikely places [2]. An example of the latter is the *Blind Smell Stick* by artist Peter De Cupere, which extends the olfactory sense via a long rigid tube that hovers just above the ground, sucks in air, and blows it into the user's nose, providing a novel way of navigating and experiencing cities [21]. Scientific apparatuses for sensory augmentation, such as Bach-y-Rita's TVSS interface, as well as artistic apparatuses, such as De Cupere's *Smell Stick*, help us to understand human experience better and inspire new research. While hitherto such pieces of equipment predominantly inspired new research within the domain within which they were conceived, it seems plausible that scientific analysis of the aesthetic experience of sensing at a distance, as brought about by the *Smell Stick,* may advance theory of perception, while artistic analysis of TVSS interfaces may just as well advance theory of aesthetics.

Second, effective and meaningful sensory augmentation also depends on how the *mapping* from an (artificial) sensor to a human sense is designed [20]. For instance, [19] showed that speech-to-touch mapping leads to signal loss because speech is sensed at a dimensionality that exceeds the actuation capabilities of a haptic interface. However, mapping speech signals to movement patterns, rather than to static touch points on the skin, increased the ability of people to accurately classify the content of the speech signals. Artistic work has a long history of evoking experiences associated with one sense by using another [22–25]. In doing so, it provides worthwhile leads for developing new mappings, which can enable effective sensory augmentation.

Third, the meaning and richness of the experiences that sensory augmentation elicits also depends on the context in which *contingency learning* is achieved. Where scientists typically use operant conditioning in a lab context with limited success [16, 20], artists pioneered contingency learning through narratives [2] and "in the wild" [7]. In one of Carsten Höller's artworks, for instance, participants wore inverted-vision goggles on a rooftop terrace with a spectacular view over London. After a brief period of adaptation, some relatively easily managed to walk to the edge of the terrace, to be rewarded with a reversed view over London. Interestingly, the period of adaptation to the inversion was characterized by social play and 'having fun' [8]; signaling their importance in learning sensory contingencies. Thus, a dialogue about contingency learning may help to understand how sensory augmentation can achieve rich and meaningful experiences.

3.2 Applying Sensory Augmentation

Three other themes for the envisioned dialogue emerged that may advance the practical application of sensory augmentation: (i) *test environments,* (ii) *new application domains,* and (iii) *commercial potential.*

First, developing effective sensory augmentations can benefit from a dialogue about *test environments.* Ideally, these enable user-testing to optimise the way sensory augmentation is achieved. Virtual reality (VR) may be particularly suitable as a starting point due to VR's psychological realism [26, 27], ability to simulate interfaces and environments [28], and shared history in art and science [27]. For example, simulated variations on distance-to-audio mappings have been tested in a virtual maze to study what mappings lead people to navigate through the maze the quickest [28]. The same flexibility may help adapt scenarios and narratives to pre-test how to achieve rich and meaningful immersive sensory experiences effectively.

Second, utilising the questions that artists and scientists tend to ask can help to explore *new application domains*. Art is often driven by 'What if?' questions, while science explores 'How?' questions [2, 18]. Conveying the experience of a sensory augmentation and asking 'What if?' can reveal its utility, complementing the need to understand 'How' it works. This way, new applications can be probed to see whether (further) research and development is justifiable. Illustrative of such new domains is augmented navigation. For example, [29] studied how a tactile-vision navigational aid could support the visually impaired. A similar interface was used by [30] to suggest spatial dimensions to an audience by exploring their ability to use such augmentations and how this impacted their experiences. These findings suggest that combining art and science can support the exploration of new application domains.

Third, artists have set up 'spoof' companies to probe the *commercial potential* of innovative products, including sensory augmentation interfaces. For instance, 'Eye Candy', a lollipop–like device inspired by Bach-y-Rita's BrainPort tongue interface, was marketed online as an off-the-shelf product by Eye Candy Can Ltd. [31]. The product was 'released' in six different flavours; the 'FOCUS' flavor, for instance, promised a tactile sense of "Direction giving arrows that help to improve focus and attention". Approximately 68.000 people attempted to purchase 100.000 lollipops [2], yielding the online venture a commercial success. Such artistic work can gauge what kinds of sensory augmentation are commercially viable and may help guide the development of sensory augmentation interfaces in the direction of their commercial potential.

4   Case Study: A Sensory Augmentation Masterclass

We conducted a small case study to confirm whether or not the selected themes could form a constructive starting point for the envisioned dialogue and to gather preliminary evidence for its potential. To instigated a dialogue between artists and scientists we organised a masterclass on sensory augmentation in which they explored sensory augmentation interfaces that are commonly used in scientific and artistic research practices.

Participants. Besides two session leaders, 13 early to mid-career professionals participated in the study; an architect, writer, curator, material scientist, stylist, two cognitive psychologists and two media artists and three media designers. The masterclass was held during the STRP Biennale in Eindhoven (NL) on March 28, 2017.

Masterclass. The masterclass was structured on the basis of Wallas' four stage model [31]. First, participants engaged in two *preparatory activities*: (i) an introduction by the session leaders to the art and science of sensory augmentation, which included a discussion of the six themes introduced above, and (ii) a demonstration session in which four participating researchers demonstrated four sensory augmentation interfaces (Fig. 1): (i) *Inverted-vision goggles*. Five goggles with prisms that alter the visual consequences of moving one's eyes, reversing up and down (from [33]); (ii) *Pupil size-auditory feedback interface*. An eye tracker with software that maps pupil size to sound; (iii) *Haptic vision interface*. An interface that maps camera images to the tactile sense via a grid of solenoids; and (iv) *Magnetic north interface*. A vibrating belt that indicates the direction of the magnetic north (from [16]). These demonstrations were followed by the formation of breakout groups that each explored one or two of the interfaces. Each demonstrator chaired a breakout group and the remainder of the participants were distributed over the groups, on the basis of their individual prefer-ence. The two smallest groups, with those who selected the inversion goggles or haptic vision interface, were merged together to create groups of similar sizes. Using the interfaces as discussion starters enabled participants to first-hand explore how such interfaces can augment our experience of the world. After being given ample time to explore the sensory interfaces and share initial thoughts amongst the group, participants took a lunch break of approximately 45 min. This enabled them to replenish and *incubate*, benefitting subsequent *idea generation* [32, 33]. Third, the groups purpose-fully explored the interfaces to elicit ideas on (i) new research questions and (ii) new concepts and prototypes that could lead to insight into these questions. Fourth, the questions, concepts, and prototypes were presented, demonstrated, and discussed in a plenary session. This allowed for *verification and reflection* of the research questions, concepts, and prototypes developed.

Fig. 1. The sensory augmentation interfaces used in the study: (a) Inverted vision goggles, (b) pupil size-auditory feedback interface, (c) haptic vision interface, (d) magnetic north interface. (Photos by Stanley Obobogo Badoana)

Documentation. The masterclass was documented photographically throughout the day. The plenary closing session was also filmed. On the basis of this documentation we were able to cite several key observations about the research questions and concepts developed in the masterclass, which we will discuss in the section below.

5 What Did the Case Study Reveal?

The masterclass resulted in three new research questions and concepts that fitted the previously selected *themes*, and touched upon the creation of novel *subjective experiences* and the development of *novel kinds of stimuli* (Sect. 5.1). It also led to general observations regarding the dialogue it instigated, which may prove useful leads for future work toward the envisioned dialogue between the arts and sciences (Sect. 5.2).

5.1 New Research Questions and Concepts

Three new research questions and concepts resulted from the masterclass:

(i) *Haptic Vision: Using haptic augmentation to support inverted vision.* The group that explored the *inversion goggles* and *haptic vision interface* conceived and developed the research question: "Can one measure the effects of sensory substitution using an inverted vision task?", investigating the themes *contingency learning* and *test environments*. The participants created a game in which two participants compete to trace a zigzagged line as fast as possible, from top to bottom with one hand. Both contesters wear inverted vision goggles, yet one of them also wears the haptic vision interface on the hand with which the line is traced. The contester that first reaches the bottom of the line wins. Playing the game led to several interesting observations: (i) Re-learning hand-eye coordination under inverted vision can benefit from haptic-vision substitution support when it is used strategically, e.g. as error feedback (i.e., "..checking if I am still on the line.", as one contestant called it); (ii) Strong reliance on the haptic interface can also interfere with attempts to overcome disorientation (e.g. "The haptics provide too much input", one contestant yelled out to his competitor); (iii) even within the limited time of the closing session, repeated performance seemed to suggest a learning curve for contestants wearing the haptic device, which might indicate that participants improved their ability to interpret the distorted visual sense and haptic information simultaneously; and (iv) a hybrid interface, which combines sensory substitution with other forms of augmentation, points in interesting directions for future research. The range of fundamental questions that were elicited during the short plenary presentation of this outcome, attests to the usefulness of allowing and enhancing *personal and subjective experiences* in sensory augmentation research.

(ii) *The pupil DJ: Emotion regulation by sensing pupil size.* The group that explored the *pupil size-auditory feedback interface* conceived and developed the research question: "Can sensing pupil size be used to regulate emotion?" To this end, the group touched upon the *apparatuses* theme. The interface was originally designed to map pupil size to sound, but after some exploration of the interface the group decided to focus on the link between pupil size and emotion instead. Based on the assumption that pupil size correlates with emotion, the group investigated the link between music and emotion, for which the interface was slightly adapted. Initial testing showed that pupil size indeed varies between songs, and that some changes roughly correspond to the emotional reaction to a song. The group subsequently discussed the potential of selecting and playing songs on the basis of pupil size, as a means to regulate emotion, and speculated on a novel apparatus to explore whether meaningful relationships could emerge from a sensorimotor loop between pupil size and music selection. With this, they alluded to pupil behaviours made perceptible as *novel stimuli* that enable an added sense of one's own emotions; and suggest a *new application domain* for sensory augmentation based on pupil size.

(iii) *Spouse detector: A novel sense for the (un)faithful.* The group that explored the *magnetic north interface* conceived and developed the research question: "Can a belt that vibrates in the direction of your spouse support a relationship?". The interface was conceptualised as providing location awareness of one's partner, rather than the magnetic north. In this concept, a set of *mappings*, i.e. vibration patterns, provide a sense of objective support that "augments the ability to connect and stay faithful to a romantic partner, even in his or her absence", as the group described it. Vibration patterns were elaborated to establish a sense of the other's presence and potentially tangibly convey their emotional states. The concept led to constructive discussions on (i) the usefulness of augmenting such directional awareness with a tactile representation of the other's inner rhythms, e.g. breathing or heartbeats, and (ii) whether people could learn to interpret such patterns as meaningful information about the other or should rely on algorithms to classify such information for them. By exploring *novel stimuli,* tuned to the consequences of one's actions for romantic relationships, this concept illustrates how the dialogue we envision may break open unexpected *new application domains* for sensory augmentation interfaces.

5.2 General Observations

Although each group followed its own unique trajectory towards the outcomes described above, four general observations can be made regarding their dialogues.

The *preparatory activities* gave rise to highly divergent discussions in each breakout group. Although the interfaces and demonstrator's practices were provided as a starting point for a dialogue, these almost instantly diverged in very different directions. Two general observations can be made regarding the dialogues overheard during this phase of the masterclass: First, discussions commonly veered towards the practices of the participants; and second, each group displayed a tendency towards thought experiments in which the interface is applied to everyday situations, such as to listening to music or to maintaining romantic relationships. This may indicate that 'the everyday' makes fruitful common ground for researchers to explore when individual backgrounds vary.

After the replenishment and *incubation* during the break, it took each group relatively long to transition towards *idea generation*. In fact, most of the two hours reserved after the break to converge towards a research question and concept, was consumed by exploring multiple ideas in parallel or by diverging even more by formulating yet more new ideas. Only when the session leaders announced that each group had 5 min left to finalise their presentations, each group rapidly converged by abandoning secondary ideas or combining several ideas into one presentable outcome. The importance of time pressure for convergence [34], can therefore be added as a third general observation.

The *verification and reflection* that followed during the closing plenary session revealed that the research questions, concepts, and prototypes (i) matched several of the *themes* identified in Sect. 3, and (ii) supports the arguments developed in Sects. 1 and 2. That is, the range of observations made during the case study attest to the potential of allowing and even enhancing otherwise confounding variables, such as those that associate with *personal and subjective experience*, and at least two outcomes alluded to the creation of *novel kinds of stimuli*; relative location to a spouse or audio-feedback based on pupil size. Thus, a fourth observation can be added; the study's results attest to the potential of a dialogue between the arts and sciences about sensory augmentation.

6 Conclusion

In this position paper, we argued that a dialogue between the arts and sciences may advance our understanding of *sensory augmentation* and can be useful for developing novel sensory augmentation applications. As a starting point we introduced six themes, around which this dialogue could be structured, and presented a small case study in which a dialogue between artists and scientists was initiated. The study yielded several new research questions and concepts that (i) indicate how informative *personal and subjective experiences* can be, strengthening our claim that a dialogue between art and science may help overcome the scientific limitation that the subjective is generally considered an 'undesired variable' (Sects. 1 and 2); (ii) alluded to *novel kinds of stimuli*, suggesting that a dialogue between art and science can indeed benefit the broad imagination needed to conceive the "novel kinds of stimuli" for which we lack "pre-existing knowledge" [18] that is required to advance the field (Sect. 2); and (iii) the majority of the described *themes* emerged during the dialogue, supporting the use of the selected themes as a starting point for the envisioned dialogue (Sect. 3). Thus, this paper contributes preliminary evidence for the potential of, and a starting point for, a dialogue between the arts and sciences that advances our understanding of sensory augmentation and the development of applications that involve it.

References

1. Gombrich, E.H.: Art and Illusion. Phaidon, London (1977)
2. Schwartzman, M.: See Yourself Sensing: Redefining Human Perception. Black Dog Publishing, London (2011)
3. Noë, A.: Action in Perception. MIT Press, Cambridge (2004)
4. Marr, D.: Vision. W.H. Freeman, San Francisco (1982)
5. O'Regan, J.K., Noë, A.: A sensorimotor account of vision and visual consciousness. Behav. Brain Sci. **24**(5), 883–917 (2001)
6. Noë, A.: Strange Tools: Art and Human Nature. Hill and Wang, New York (2015)
7. Manning, E., Massumi, B.: Thought in the Act. University of Minnesota Press, Minneapolis (2014)
8. Van Dartel, M.F.: Aesthetics in the Wild: Art and Design Practices and Pedagogies after the Situated Turn. Avans, Breda (2016)
9. Biggs, M., Karlsson, H.: Research in the Arts. Routledge, New York (2012)
10. Froese, T., McGann, M., Bigge, W., Spiers, A., Seth, A.K.: The enactive torch: a new tool for the science of perception. IEEE Trans. Haptics **5**(4), 365–375 (2012)
11. Stratton, G.M.: Vision without inversion of the retinal image. Psychol. Rev. **4**, 463–481 (1897)
12. Kohler, I.: The Formation and Transformation of the Perceptual World. Psychological Issues, vol. 3. International University Press (1964). Monograph 12
13. Miyauchi, S., et al.: Adaptation to left-right reversed vision rapidly activates ipsilateral visual cortex in humans. J. Physiol. Paris **98**, 207–219 (2004)
14. Bach-y-Rita, P., Collins, C.C., Saunders, S.A., White, B., Scadden, L.: Vision substitution by tactile image projection. Nature **221**, 963–964 (1969)
15. Kercel, S.W., Bach-y-Rita, P.: Noninvasive coupling of electronically generated data into the human nervous system. In: Akay, M. (ed.) Wiley Encyclopedia of Biomedical Engineering, pp. 1960–1974. Wiley (2006)
16. Kaspar, K., König, S., Schwandt, J., König, P.: The experience of new sensorimotor contingencies by sensory augmentation. Conscious. Cogn. **28**, 47–63 (2014)
17. Ward, J., Meijer, P.: Visual experiences in the blind induced by an auditory sensory substitution device. Conscious. Cogn. **19**, 492–500 (2010)
18. Deroy, O., Auvray, M.: Reading the world through the skin and ears: a new perspective on sensory substitution. Front. Psychol. **3**, 457 (2012)
19. Sha, X.W.: Poiesis and Enchantment in Topological Matter. MIT Press, Cambridge (2013)
20. Novich, N.: Sound-to-touch sensory substitution and beyond. Ph.D. thesis. Rice University (2015)
21. De Cupere, P.: Blind smell stick (2012). http://www.blindsmellstick.com/index.php/about. Accessed 2 Nov 2016
22. De Rooij, A., Broekens, J., Lamers, M.H.: Abstract expressions of affect. Int. J. Synth. Emot. **4**(1), 1–31 (2013)
23. Evers, F.: The Academy of the Senses: Synesthetics in Science, Art and Education. ArtScience Interfaculty Press, The Hague (2012)
24. Kandinsky, W.: Composition VIII (1924). https://www.guggenheim.org/artwork/1924. Accessed 2 Nov 2016
25. Ramachandran, V.S., Hubbard, E.M.: Synaesthesia: a window into perception, thought and language. J. Conscious. Stud. **8**(12), 3–34 (2001)

26. Maidenbaum, S.: Practical sensory substitution in real and virtual worlds: development, accessibility and neuroscience. In: Proceedings of the 33rd Annual ACM Conference Extended Abstracts on Human Factors in Computing Systems, pp. 211–214 (2015)
27. Van Dartel, M., Misker, J., Nigten, A., Van der Ster, J.: Virtual reality and augmented reality art explained in terms of sensory-motor coordination. In: Proceedings of 4th International Conference on Enactive Interfaces (2007)
28. Maidenbaum, S., Chebat, D.R., Levy-Tzedek, S., Namer-Furstenberg, R., Amedi, A.: The effect of expanded sensory range via the EyeCane sensory substitution device on the characteristics of visionless virtual navigation. Multi Sens. Res. 27(5–6), 379–397 (2014)
29. Froese, T., Spiers, A.: Toward a Phenomenological Pragmatics of Enactive Perception. Cognitive Science Research Papers, 593 (2004)
30. O'Rourke, K.: Walking and Mapping. MIT Press, Cambridge (2013)
31. Studio Eyal Burstein: Eye Candy Can Ltd. (2007). http://www.eyalburstein.com/eye-candy/1n5r92f24hltmysrkuxtiuepd6nokx. Accessed 2 Nov 2016
32. Wallas, G.: The Art of Thought. Harcourt Brace, New York (1926)
33. Grand Illusions. Reversing goggles. http://www.grand-illusions.com/acatalog/Reversing_Goggles.html. Accessed 19 Apr 2017
34. de Rooij, A., Jones, S.: Mood and creativity: an appraisal tendency perspective. In: Proceedings of the 9th ACM Conference on Creativity and Cognition, pp. 362–365 (2013)

IGDA Game Accessibility SIG - Research and Development

User Interfaces and 3D Environment Scanning for Game-Based Training in Mixed-Reality Spaces

Artur Krukowski[1(✉)] and Emmanouela Vogiatzaki[2]

[1] Intracom S.A. Telecom Solutions,
19.7 km Markopoulou Av., 19002 Athens, Greece
krukowa@intracom-telecom.com
[2] Research for Science, Art and Technology (RFSAT) Ltd.,
311 Shoreham Street, Sheffield, UK
emmanouela@rfsat.com

Abstract. Game-based rehabilitation systems gain much interest recently due to fast advancement of natural human-machine interfaces including Augmented and Virtual Reality headsets, near-real time 3D body motion understanding and 3D environmental scanners. Game-based training and rehabilitation has quickly recognized the advantage of improving personal physical capabilities using games and competition as incentives for boosting patient's compliance. Such systems call for new types of user interfaces, which seamlessly engage natural human senses and allow interaction as if one was in his/her natural environment. Furthermore, a possibility to exercise within a familiar home environment further improves the effectiveness of the rehabilitation. The core of the work presented here originates from the FP7-ICT-StrokeBack project and includes more recent advances in 3D scanning of large scale environments and introduces high precision 3D object modelling for realistic gaming environments from Horizon'2020-Reflective-SCAN4RECO project, both co-funded by the European Commission from FP7 and Horizon'2020 programs.

Keywords: Rehabilitation · Mixed reality · Human-machine interfaces
Body motion capture · 3D photogrammetry · MS Kinect

1 Introduction

Vast number of people suffering from both physical and mental disorders have been proven to benefit from rehabilitation training. Until recently this has been done primarily in specialized centers with assistance of trained staff. However, recent advances in ICT technologies including gaming engines, realistic Virtual Environment and intuitive Human Machine Interfaces (HMI) paves a way to possibilities of performing such exercised in a comfort of their own home, at their leisure, while still supervised remotely by their physicians. Such an approach offers much greater advantage in patient compliance with doctor instructions, less stress associated with change of environments and the element of fun and competition.

© ICST Institute for Computer Sciences, Social Informatics and Telecommunications Engineering 2018
A. L. Brooks et al. (Eds.): ArtsIT 2017/DLI 2017, LNICST 229, pp. 227–237, 2018.
https://doi.org/10.1007/978-3-319-76908-0_22

The system originally developed through collaborative effort of the StrokeBack consortium [20] comprises a telemedicine system to support ambulant rehabilitation at home settings for the stroke patients with minimal human intervention. It is complemented by a Patient Health Record (PHR) system in which training measurements and vital physiological and personal patient data are stored. Thus, PHR provides all the necessary medical and personal information for the patient that rehabilitation experts might need to evaluate the effectiveness and success of the rehabilitation, e.g. to deduce relations between selected exercises and rehabilitation speed of different patients as well as to assess the overall healthiness of the patient. In addition, the PHR can be used to provide the patient with mid-term feedback e.g. her/his, rehabilitation speed compared to average as well as improvements over last day/weeks, to keep patient motivation high. Furthermore, the focus is on increasing patients' motivation when exercising with tools like a gaming console. It aims at exploiting the fact the patients feel better at home, that it has been shown that patients train more if the training is combined with attractive training environments [4, 13]. First, the patients learn physical rehabilitation exercises from a therapist at the care center or in a therapists' practice. Then the patients can exercise at home with the StrokeBack system monitoring their execution and providing a real-time feedback on whether the execution was correct or not. In addition, it records the training results and vital parameters of the patient. This data can be subsequently analyzed by the medical experts for assessment of the patient recovery. Furthermore, the patient may also receive midterm feedback on her/his personal recovery process. To ensure proper guidance of the patient, the therapist also gets information from the PHR to assess the recovery process enabling him to decide whether other training sequences should be used, which are then introduced to the patient in the practice again.

2 Game-Based Rehabilitation

The use of virtual, augmented or mixed reality environments for training and rehabilitation of post-stroke patients opens an attractive avenue in improving various negative effects occurring because of brain traumas. Those include helping in the recovery of the motor skills, limb-eye coordination, orientation in space, everyday tasks etc. Training may range from simple goal-directed limb movements aimed at achieving a given goal (e.g. putting a coffee cup on a table), improving lost motor skills (e.g. virtual driving), and others. To increase the efficiency of the exercises advanced haptic interfaces are developed, allowing direct body stimulation and use of physical objects within virtual settings, supplementing the visual stimulation.

Immersive environments have quickly been found attractive for remote home-based rehabilitation giving raise to both individual and monitored by therapists remotely. Depending on the type of a physical interface, diverse types of exercises are possible. Interfaces like Cyber Glove [2] or Rutgers RMII Master [3] allow the transfer of patient's limb movement into the virtual gaming environment. They employ a set of pressure-sensing servos, one per finger, combined with motion sensing. This allows therapists to perform e.g. range of motion, speed, fractionation (e.g. moving individual fingers) and strength (via pressure sensing) tasks. Games include two categories:

physical exercises (e.g. DigiKey, Power Putty) and functional rehabilitation (e.g. Peg Board or Ball Game) ones. They use computer monitors for visual feedback. Cyber Glove has been used by Rehabilitation Institute of Chicago [4] also for assessing the pattern of finger movements during grasp and movement space determination for diverse stroke conditions. Virtual environments are increasingly used for functional training and simulation of natural environments, e.g. home, work, outdoor. Exercises may range from simple goal-directed movements [5] to learn/train for execution of everyday tasks.

Current generation of post-stroke rehabilitation systems, although exploiting latest immersive technologies tend to proprietary approaches concentrating on a closed range of exercise types, lacking thoroughly addressing the complete set of disabilities and offering a comprehensive set of rehabilitation scenarios. The use of technologies is also very selective and varies from one system to another. Although there are cases of using avatars for more intuitive feedback to the patient, the use of complicated wearable devices makes it tiresome and decreases the effectiveness of the exercise [1]. In our approach, we have been exploring novel technologies for body tracing that exploit the rich information gathered by combining wearable sensors with visual feedback systems that are already commercially available such as Microsoft Kinect [6] or Leap Motion [7] user interfaces and 3D mixed reality visualization.

The environment aims to provide a full 3D physical and visual feedback through Mixed-Reality interaction and visualization technologies placing the user inside of the training environment. Considering that detecting muscle activity cannot be done without wearable device support, our partner in the project, IHP GmbH, has been developing a customizable lightweight embedded sensor device allowing short-range wireless transmission of most common parameters including apart from EMG, also other critical medical signs like ECG, Blood Pressure, heart rate etc. This way the training exercises become much more intuitive in their approach by using exercise templates with feedback showing correctness of performed exercises. Therapists are then able to prescribe a set of the rehabilitation exercises as treatment through the EHR/PHR platform(s) thus offering means of correlating them with changes of patient's condition, thus improving effectiveness of patients' recovery.

3   Concept Architecture

A concept system architecture is presented in Fig. 1. The Patient System is deployed at home and provides physiological remote patient monitoring, executes rehabilitation games and offers full integration with online Personal Health Record (PHR) used for sharing information between patients and their physicians.

Such a system offers full support to immersive user interfaces like Kinect [6], Leap Motion [7], Emotiv EEG [8] and other ones, combined with a range of virtual and augmentation systems to enable fully immersive gaming experience. As shown in Fig. 2 we support a range of client devices, such as 3D Smart TVs, AR/VR headsets, user interfaces, 3D scanners and 3D screens/projectors. The system offers full support for mobile devices like smartphones, tablets etc. An affordable integrated gaming solution for both near field and full-body exercises, called "Smart Table", was also developed, which supporting use of physical objects along with virtual ones, while providing access

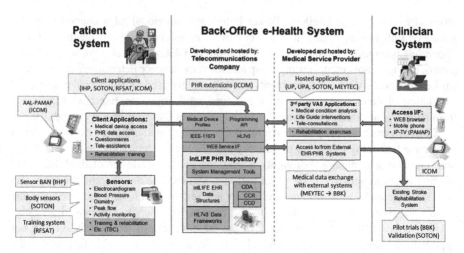

Fig. 1. The architecture of the complete rehabilitation training system from StrokeBack project

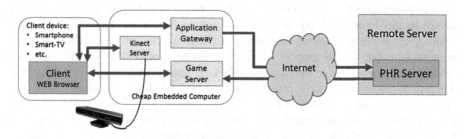

Fig. 2. Kinect Server for game management with game server running locally

to back-office PHR data repository for constant monitoring of patients' condition through the clinician part of the system. The progress of their rehabilitation and other relevant physiological data including audio-visual connection are also provided, if needed. The back-office services are currently based on open-source solutions like Open EMR [9] platforms.

The gaming system has been designed using client-server approach allowing us to store the game repository and game provision of the PHR server, thus maximally lowering the load on the client devices. This allowed us from one side to run games on such devices as Smart TVs or Smartphones, while offering us flexibility of maintaining the latest versions of the games without the need of updating the clients.

4 Body Sensing and User Interfaces

To track the correctness of performed exercises automatically without the constant assistance of the physicians, an automated means of tracking and comparing patient's body movement against correct ones (templates) has to be developed. This is an ongoing part of the work due to the changing requirements from our physicians. Although many methods are in existence, most of them employ elaborate sets of wearable sensors and/or costly visual observations. When better accuracy is required that offered by 3D scanners then additional micro embedded sensor nodes are employed, e.g. gyros (tilt and position calibration) and inertial/accelerometers. Such are readily available from e.g. Shimmer EMG sensor platform that we use for detecting muscle activity during the exercises.

Muscle activity poses problems for measurement since it has been well known for many years [10] that the EMG reflects effort rather than output and so becomes an unreliable indicator of muscle force as the muscle becomes fatigued. Consequently, measurement of force, in addition to the EMG activity, would be a considerable step forward in assessing the effectiveness of rehabilitation strategies and could not only indicate that fatigue is occurring, but also whether the mechanism is central or peripheral in origin [11]. Similarly, conventional surface EMG measurement requires accurate placement of the sensor over the target muscle, which would be inappropriate for a sensor system integrated within a garment for home use. Electrode arrays are, however, now being developed for EMG measurement and signal processing is used to optimize the signal obtained. Several different solutions have been investigated to offer sufficiently reliable, but economic muscle activity monitoring. We used EMG sensors on 2R Shimmer platform for system development, moving towards a dedicated sensor node by IHP GmbH towards end of the project.

However, EMG is not the only sensor that is needed for home hospitalization of patients suffering from chronic diseases like stroke. This requires novel approaches to combining building blocks in a body sensor network. Existing commercial systems provide basic information about activity such as speed and direction of movement and postures. Providing precise information about performance, for example relating movement to muscle activity in a given task and detecting deviations from normal, expected patterns or subtle changes associated with recovery, requires a much higher level of sophistication of data acquisition and processing and interpretation. The challenge is therefore to design and develop an integrated multimodal system along with high-level signal processing techniques and optimization of the data extracted.

The existing techniques for taking measurements on the human body are generally considered to be adequate for the purpose but are often bulky in nature and cumbersome to mount, e.g., electro-goniometers, and they can also be expensive to implement, e.g. VICON cameras [12] or Xsens MoCap sensors [13]. Their ability to be used in a home environment is therefore very limited. In this context, we have decided to address those deficiencies by extending the state-of-the-art in the areas of:

- Extending the application of existing sensor technologies: For example, we tend to use commercially available MEMS accelerometers with integrated wireless modules to measure joint angles on the upper and lower limbs for wireless, low-cost sensor nodes optimized for information content and spatial location.
- Novel sensing methodologies to reduce the number of sensors worn on the human body, while maintaining information quality. With the advent of the Xbox Kinect system, the position and movement of a human will be possible to be monitored using a low-cost camera mounted on or below the TV set.

- Easy system installation and calibration by non-experts for use in a non-clinical environment, thus making this solution suitable for use at home for the first timer and with support or untrained caretakers and family.
- Transparent verification of correct execution of exercises by patients may be based on data recorded by Body Area Networks (BAN), correlation of prescribed therapies with medical condition thus allows to determine their effectiveness on patient's condition, either it is positive or negative.

4.1   Kinect Based User Interaction

The principal user interface used to control our games has been Microsoft Kinect. Its combination of distance sensing with the RGB camera proved perfectly suitable for both full body exercises (exploring its embedded skeleton recognition) as well as for near-field exercises of upper limbs. Since Kinect has not been designed for short range scanning of partial bodies, the skeleton tracking could not be used and hence we had to develop our own algorithms that would be able to recognize arms, palms and fingers and distinguish them from the background objects. This has led to the development of the "Kinect server" based on open source algorithms. The software was built for both MS Windows and Linux platforms.

The gaming system has been built using client-server approach allowing us to store the game repository and game provision of the PHR server, thus maximally lowering the load on the client devices (Fig. 2). This allowed us from one side to run games on such devices as Smart TVs or Smartphones, while offering us flexibility of maintaining the latest versions of the games without the need of updating the clients. However, since any networked based system needs to anticipate that connectivity may not be always maintained, we have built into our system two scenarios: when network is constantly available and when it is not (Fig. 3). In the former case, game server is executed remotely, while in the latter one it can be executed locally and use games downloaded earlier. Similarly, physiological data and game progress info can be either uploaded on the fly or pre-stored and uploaded when network link is re-established. The main can restrict the depth of visibility, filtering the background beyond a given distance, to distinguish among individual objects etc. Following the requirements from physiotherapists we replaced the standard keyboard arrows with gestures of the palm

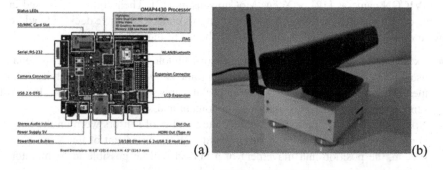

Fig. 3. Embedded Kinect Server (a) deployed on a Panda board (b)

(up, down, left, right and open/close to make a click). Such an interface allowed for the first game-based rehabilitation of stroke patients suffering from limited hand control. The tests were first made with Mario Bros game where all controls were achieved purely with movements of a single palm. The algorithm for analyzing wrist position and generating respective keyboard clicks has been developed initially in Matlab and then ported to PERL for deployment along with the Kinect server on an embedded hardware.

Kinect sensors are known for the need for high-performance computers to use them and compatibility with certain Operating systems only. Availability of drivers for other systems has been also limited, making us to investigate alternative approaches.

This has led to the development of the "Embedded Kinect Server" or EKS, implemented on a Panda board as shown in Fig. 3. Using micro embedded computers allowed the client device to run the game by accessing data from the EKS over local network. Such an approach allows also to remove the physical connectivity restriction of the Kinect and allow 3D scanning capability from any device if it was connected to a network. Various embedded platforms were investigated: from Raspberry PI [14] to Panda board [15] (Fig. 5) and many other ones. The tests have revealed the inherent problem with the Kinect physical design that is shared between the Xbox and the subsequent Windows version that is the need to draw high current from USB ports to power sensors despite separate power supply still required.

5 Rehabilitation Games

The principal user interface used to control our games has been Microsoft Kinect. Its combination of distance sensing with the RGB camera proved perfectly suitable for both full body exercises (exploring its embedded skeleton recognition) as well as for near-field exercises of upper limbs. Since Kinect has not been designed for short range scanning of partial bodies, the skeleton tracking could not be used and hence we had to develop our own algorithms that would be able to recognize arms, palms and fingers and distinguish them from the background objects. The attractive game type supported by Kinect Server mixed virtual and real objects was a game where patients were requested to through a paper ball at the virtual circles displayed on the screen as shown in Fig. 4.

The Kinect sensor synchronized with location of projected object detects physical ball reaching the distance of the wall. Combined with its XY coordinated, this allows to detect the collision. Such a game allowed patients to exercise the whole arm, not just the wrist. Hitting the circle that represented a virtual balloon was rewarded with an animated explosion of the balloon and a respective sound. Such games proved to be very enjoyable for the patients letting them concentrate on perfecting their movements while forgetting about their motor disabilities, increasing effectiveness of their training.

Full immersion games were also implemented that used either synthetic virtual environments or 3D scanned environments (Fig. 7). While the former one could be designed from 3D objects from a library, the latter one required 3D scanning of the space for creating its virtual representation for both visualization and real-time detection of collisions between the virtual and real objects.

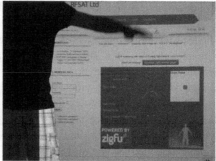

Fig. 4. Mixed-reality game of throwing paper balls at virtual balloons (left) and fully-immersive body exercise (avateering) within Virtual Environment replicating movement of the user (right)

6   Photogrammetric 3D Scanning of Real Spaces and Objects

For the virtual space to resemble the real one, it is important to be able to scan the real environment with high accuracy, especially their geometry. Currently available solutions using high accuracy laser scanning are both expensive and often unsuitable for scanning e.g. small indoor spaces and objects, most attractive elements to be used for immersive gaming. Various technologies have appeared recently, from ranging sensors like Structure [16] to depth detecting visors like MS HoloLens [17].

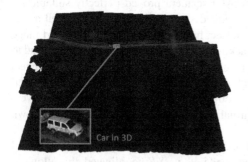

Fig. 5. Photogrammetric 3D scanning of large areas from UAV (left) and indoor spaces (right)

However, being able to immerse the used into the mixed-reality space, they lack the ability to accurately represent the real objects. The photogrammetric 3D scanning is a way to produce accurate representations of objects and spaces from multiple images taken from different viewpoints, allowing precision of object modelling down to micro levels as it has been proven already in the SCAN4RECO [8] project, subject to following certain rules when capturing images. In this project, objects of Arts have been successfully scanned to 50 μm accuracies with 50MPixel Canon camera and such software like Pix4D [18] or Autodesk ReMake [19], while environments to the levels of single centimeters (Fig. 7). Such spaces can be used to create highly realistic virtual gaming or training environments, like the one in Fig. 5 (right).

7 Evaluations and Conclusions

Both technical system validation tests and subsequent evaluations with real patients have been performed. We tested both assisted (under supervision of a physician) and individual training. In both cases, the PHR monitored and analysed the execution of tasks and exercises and generates respective feedback. Finally, training results and acquired scores are uploaded to PHR. Patients could see the final evaluation and score of an exercise after finishing it. The validation tests have proven the viability of the design approach adopted. The suitability of selected user interfaces and game development under Unity3D has been confirmed. The focus was on the motion capture and recording of the real person (therapist) for subsequent use for demonstration of correct exercises by animating his/her avatar within a virtual space (Fig. 6).

Fig. 6. Virtual Table for limb training (left) and "Endless Runner" game executed on it (right)

Various types of games have been tried, from "Endless Runner" where specific body motion/gestures were translated to control the game, to mind games and full-body training in synthetic environments built from 3D scanned spaces [1, 21]. Alternative exercises used also physical objects (e.g. cubes) transferred into virtual environment, some of those using embedded sensors to detect accurately their movement and orientation, embedding a GHOST micro-sensor developed by IHP. Results of such exercised were compared against classical approaches aimed to manipulate everyday objects while observed by therapists [1].

In the real evaluations, all aspects of therapeutic interventions have been evaluated, from simple limb movements to complicated body motions. Although in rehabilitation we still rely on the common occupational therapy, automatic clinical assessment of patient's motor skills/recovery progress according to the WMFT is clearly beneficial both for patients and therapists, feasible for occupational training with real objects. Use of such tools in home environments with remove supervision, without a need for

Fig. 7. Playing with standard objects (left), "Smart Cube" (center) in a virtual game (right)

appointment and going to the medical center was outlined as an important benefit by all involved stakeholders. Even that in many cases, physical intervention of the physician is needed for rehabilitation, the use of IT-enabled tools brings benefits especially for patients requiring repetitive exercises that may require less supervision. Having results taken automatically and stored in the PHR, gives an added benefit of providing continuous objective metrics of patient progress in their recovery. Embedding elements of fun and competition was also indicated by patients as providing additional stimulation to performing training exercises with less strain.

Acknowledgments. Research leading to these results has been partially funded by the European Union 7th Framework Program (FP7/2007-2013) under grant agreement n° 288692 "Stroke-Back" and Reflective Societies program of the Horizon'2020 Research Framework under Grant Agreement N° 665091 "SCAN4RECO".

References

1. Vogiatzaki, E., Krukowski, A. (eds.): Modern Stroke Rehabilitation through e-Health-based Entertainment. Springer, Cham (2016). https://doi.org/10.1007/978-3-319-21293-7
2. Virtual Technologies Inc., 17 June 2017. http://www.cyberglovesystems.com/all-products
3. Bouzit, M., Burdea, G., Popescu, G., Boian, R.: The Rutgers Master II—new design force-feedback glove. IEEE/ASME Trans. Mechatron. **7**(2), 256–263 (2002)
4. Rehabilitation Institute of Chicago, 17 June 2017. http://www.ric.org/conditions/stroke/
5. McNeill, M., et al.: Immersive virtual reality for upper limb rehabilitation following stroke. In: IEEE International Conference on Systems, Man and Cybernetics (2004). ISBN 0-7803-8566-7
6. Microsoft Kinect, 17 June 2017. http://kinectforwindows.org
7. Leap Motion, 17 June 2017. https://www.leapmotion.com
8. H2020-SCAN4RECO project WEB site, 17 June 2017. http://www.scan4reco.eu
9. Open EMR, 17 June 2017. http://www.open-emr.org
10. Edwards, R., Lippold, O.: The relation between force and integrated electrical activity in fatigued muscle. J. Physiol. **28**, 677–681 (1956)
11. Enkona, R., Stuart, D.: The contribution of neuroscience to exercise studies. Fed. Proc. **44**, 2279–2285 (1985)
12. VICON Reality, 17 June 2017. https://www.vicon.com/products/camera-systems
13. XSense, 17 June 2017. https://www.xsens.com
14. Raspberry PI, 17 June 2017. http://www.raspberrypi.org

15. Panda Board, 17 June 2017. http://www.pandaboard.org
16. Structure sensor, 17 June 2017. https://structure.io
17. MS HoloLens, 17 June 2017. https://www.microsoft.com/en-us/hololens
18. Pix4D Mapper Pro, 17 June 2017. https://pix4d.com/product/pix4dmapper-pro
19. Autodesk ReMake, 17 June 2017. https://remake.autodesk.com
20. FP7-STROKEBACK project WEB site, 17 June 2017. http://www.strokeback.eu
21. Vogiatzaki, E., Krukowski, A., Gravezas, Y.: Rehabilitation system for stroke patients using mixed-reality and immersive user interfaces. In: European Conference on Networks and Communications (EuCNC 2014), Bologna, Italy, 23–26 June 2014

Design of a Game Community Based Support System for Cognitive Game Accessibility

Sammy Yildiz, Anton Carlsson, Henrik Järnbrand, Tomas Sandberg,
and Thomas Westin[✉]

Department of Computer and Systems Sciences, Stockholm University,
Kista, Sweden
thomasw@dsv.su.se

Abstract. Cognitive game accessibility concerns removing unnecessary barriers for people with cognitive disabilities to participate in game play. Cognitive accessibility may involve the content of the game that requires work by game designers with limited time but also perhaps limited awareness of the issues and opportunities. The focus here is on people in the game community without cognitive disabilities to contribute with content for cognitive accessibility. The problem is that there is no support system for game community-based contributions of simplified texts and other modalities in games. This paper presents three iterations of a support system, within a design science framework with prototypes, interviews and observations, to answer: Which requirements need to be met for a game community-based system for making quest descriptions more accessible for people with cognitive disabilities affecting language? How can a system for contributions of simplified text be designed from the perspectives of experienced gamers? The conclusions were: (1) a set of requirements and a digital prototype available online; (2) experienced gamers understood how the interface of the prototype worked; and (3) further support functionality would benefit the users of the system. Future work is to evaluate community contributions by involving people with mild cognitive disabilities in game play studies.

Keywords: Cognition · Game · Accessibility · Community · Simplified text

1 Background

Game accessibility is to remove barriers unnecessary for playing a game. Cognitive game accessibility is a field that requires more attention and relatively few games have been developed for people with cognitive disabilities [1]. Previous related work is e.g. Grammenos, Savidis [2] who developed a structured method to design universally accessible games with design alternatives and user attributes (including cognitive impairment) to create user profiles. Another method is to simulate personas with impairments [3]. These methods are especially useful to identify issues early with less effort. Barriers for cognitive accessibility need to be addressed manually [4, 5], but dynamic adaptation can be made of settings, interaction and difficulty [6]. E.g. creating an easy to read text need manual work, but text selection can be done dynamically or

© ICST Institute for Computer Sciences, Social Informatics and Telecommunications Engineering 2018
A. L. Brooks et al. (Eds.): ArtsIT 2017/DLI 2017, LNICST 229, pp. 238–247, 2018.
https://doi.org/10.1007/978-3-319-76908-0_23

automatically. Furthermore, designs for people with cognitive disabilities should consider three individual configurations, found by Torrente, Blanco [7]: (1) identity, for instance having a character resembling themselves; (2) goals, e.g. a task-list in the game; and (3) the user interface. One example could be if the player accepts a quest (or mission) in a game, specific actions to complete the quest could be inserted into a task-list.

Text based quest descriptions are common in role-playing games, one of the most popular genres. Text is one of the modalities that can be a challenge as language is affected by e.g. autism, learning disabilities, Alzheimer and acquired brain injury [8]. Simplified text is an easier to understand version of the same text [9]. While simplified text is not the only solution, it may be a first step. In addition, audio, video and images of quests may be a multimodal approach but takes more resources to store and create. As cognitive game accessibility involves the content of the game such as quest descriptions, it requires work by game designers who may lack budget, awareness or both to address the issue. Thus, there is a need to define requirements for developing and evaluating a support system where people in the game community (including game designers) can contribute with simplified quest descriptions.

The system design may be inspired by wikis with considerations taken for games, as well as usability, accessibility and motivation mechanisms for contributing. The latter may be achieved with social rewarding systems with author rankings [10]. Ling, Beenen [11] says that uniqueness of contributions is important for motivation, which may be achieved by limiting the number of highest ranked contributions and also showing which quests are currently being simplified by others. Requirements may include non-text, linear formats for information and guidance; minimize the need for decisions and memory; and have adaptable contrasts as well as size of buttons and texts, based upon the review by LoPresti, Bodine [8]. This paper presents results based on two bachelor theses (study 1 and 2 below), supervised by the last author.

1.1 Problem and Research Questions

People with cognitive disabilities affecting language may be excluded from playing games where language is central, such as role-playing games. The problem is that there is, to the best of the authors' knowledge, no system for game community-based contributions of simplified texts and other modalities in games. The research questions were: (1) Which requirements need to be met for a game community-based system for making quest descriptions more accessible for people with cognitive disabilities affecting language? (2) How can a system for contributions of simplified text be designed from the perspectives of experienced gamers?

2 Methods

Two studies were conducted within the framework of design science, where different approaches and methods can be iterated to explicate problems, define requirements, and develop, demonstrate and evaluate an artefact [12]. Here the artefact is a support system developed in three main iterations with the target group of contributors.

2.1   Methods in Study 1 and Iteration 1

In iteration 1 an example interface was prototyped as a slideshow with hyperlinks and used during data collection. A list of requirements for iteration 1 was based upon basic design principles by Norman [13] such as established conceptual interaction models in game menu interfaces and guidelines for defining requirements [12]. Four participants were selected with purposive sampling, i.e. selected on basis of being part of the gaming community as gamers, representing the target group of contributors to the system. The aim in study 1 was to define requirements for a support system to contribute with simplified texts. Thus, focus was on usability rather than accessibility, and none of the participants identified as disabled.

Each participant first tried the interactive slideshow prototype, and were asked to think-aloud concurrently while being observed. Following the observation, the participants were interviewed on what requirements they would have on the interface, what they thought about the functionality of the prototype, how they could be motivated to contribute with simplified texts and what they would like to add. Finally, they were shown the list of requirements and were asked what they thought about the requirements, and if some should be edited, removed or added. A semi-structured interview guide was used with main and follow-up questions. Observation notes and transcriptions were analysed thematically. After each interview, the requirement list was updated before the next interview. Interviews were about fifteen minutes each.

2.2   Methods in Study 2 and Iterations 2 and 3

In iteration 2 a paper prototype was created and tested, with the different interface layouts presented on sheets of paper. Interactive elements were cut out and placed based on user interactions, which is more flexible than an interactive slideshow used in iteration 1. In iteration 3 a digital game prototype was developed with approximately one minute of game play. It contained a simple, linear game level to focus on quest descriptions rather than game play in general, where two quests appeared with many words relative to the content. It was developed in HTML5 and JavaScript to be easily available online. Requirements for iterations 2 and 3 were based upon the results in the first study.

Semi-structured interviews of approx. twenty minutes each was the main method for data collection in both iterations, while a minor observation was made while the participants interacted with the interface before the interviews. Similar to study 1, participants were here also experienced gamers (who played at least seven hours per week, or approx. one hour per day) to enable a deeper understanding of games related to the second research question. There were three and six participants in iteration 2 and 3, respectively (nine in total). They were asked also to add e.g. a new text or vote on someone else's text. A web camera was used to record the audio of the interviews and transcribed after. Questions were about the interface design and their interaction with it including why they acted as they did. Thematic analysis was made using comments in Microsoft Word with both in-vivo and descriptive coding, resulting in categories that were grouped in themes that affected the design of the system based upon the second research question.

3   Results and Analysis of Study 1

Study 1 comprised iteration 1 (a set of requirements).

3.1   Initial Requirements and Development of the First Prototype

The initial interfaces (Figs. 1, 2, 3) in iteration 1 were based upon basic design principles by Norman [13]. Standard controls like scrollbars were used for recognition from
other applications, and high contrasts were used to ease finding interface elements. This
first prototype was developed as a slideshow with hyperlinks to demonstrate the basic
idea of the artefact to the participants, to ease grasping the concept and be able to
provide data for requirements.

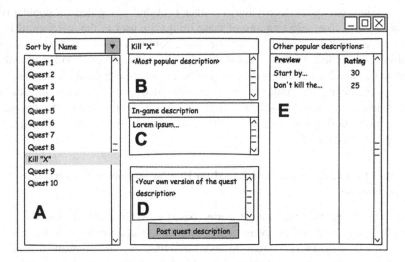

Fig. 1. Quests with existing descriptions and an input field.

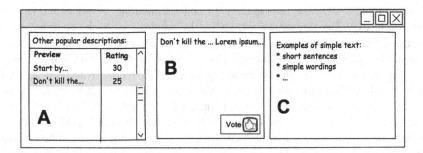

Fig. 2. Quests with other popular descriptions and guidance for evaluation and voting

Fig. 3. An option to evaluate the quest description and contribute upon finishing a quest.

In Fig. 1, the different areas of the interface can be described as follows: A: the quests were listed top down, where a selected option could be highlighted; B: the most popular description, i.e. the one with most likes; C: the original description; D: an input field to write your quest description; E: other contributions sorted by popularity for inspiration or to like; selecting any of these brings the user to the interface in Fig. 2, where the interface areas were: A: list of existing contributions where the selected item could be highlighted; B: the selected description, with a "Vote" with a thumbs-up button to like the description, modified to not be mixed up with similar buttons in social media applications; C: guidance to write simplified texts. Figure 3 illustrates an example interface when a player has completed a quest and is asked if s/he was pleased with the quest description. If not s/he may choose to provide a better description by opening the interface in Fig. 1.

3.2   Iteration 1: Requirements Based on Demonstration of the First Prototype

The following requirements are categories based upon think-aloud observations followed by semi-structured interviews: (1) A ranking system to promote the best contributions; (2) A moderating group to avoid cheating and other unwanted behaviour; (3) Search and sort functions of all content; (4) A list with highest ranked authors and contributions to reward authors and aid readers; (5) Support of multiple languages but also other modalities than text; (6) A function to mark favourite authors and contributions to more easily find them again; (7) Control formatting, grammar and length of contributions; (8) The size of rewards should be proportional to the contribution and ranking, but not in a form that is central to game play. As one participant expressed it: "It would be unfair if you could use this [the support system] to get a lot of advantages or xp [in the game]"; (9) Support creativity by enabling more advanced descriptions and guides, including other modalities such as arrows, pictures and waypoints as well as dynamic bullet-lists that is automatically updated when something is done; this could be a meaningful reward in itself for gamers who like to create guides; (10) Peer feedback and feedback on use of contributions to each author, to further increase motivation to participate; (11) A standards-based, accessible interface that can be individually adapted on demand; (12) Mark quests with complex descriptions to ask for help; (13) Report improper or low quality descriptions, which also must have consequences; and (14) The ranking system must be easy to find and use in the game, also accessible for people with other disabilities or limitations.

4   Results and Analysis of Study 2

Study 2 comprised iteration 2 (a paper prototype) and iteration 3 (a digital prototype).

4.1   Iteration 2: Demonstration of the Second Prototype

The second prototype was based upon the requirements in iteration 1 with an additional requirement: (15) Recent: New descriptions should be shown separately to have a chance of discovery. Figure 4 shows one example of the paper-based prototype with the interface for viewing, selecting or creating a simplified text.

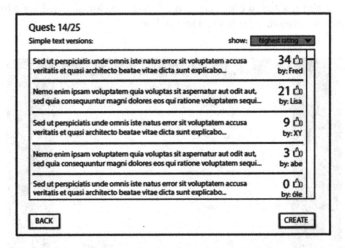

Fig. 4. Paper prototype example in study 2

Themes (in *italics*) and categories (underlined) from the prototype demonstrations:

- *Symbols and buttons.* Unclear: While the symbol for voting for a text was a thumbs-up (Fig. 4), the symbol for marking a favourite author was a star. The participants mixed up these two symbols. Wishes: Descriptions of the functions of buttons, and quick navigation to go directly between Create text, Return to quest text, and Switch original/simplified text.
- *Texts.* Unclear: An issue with the paper prototype (Fig. 4) was the non-semantic text examples, which caused some confusion. As this text had no meaning, the participants could not guess what would happen before selecting it and had to learn by trial and error.
- *Design.* Unclear: Have uniform positioning of buttons across interfaces to avoid confusion. Clear: Use well-known standards. Wishes: Use a position that is more associated with the simplified text contribution for the button group used to like, flag and comment. Requirements: The system should be simple and easy to use.

- *Functions*. Unnecessary: Having both voting of texts and favourite authors as well as four ways of sorting texts could be too complex. Editing: Support for synonyms and alternative sentence structures could aid while editing. Read-out loud: Support for text-to-speech could help people with reading disability. Incentive: Response in the form of likes was seen as valuable incentives to contribute with more texts. Moderation: This was viewed as crucial for sustainability of the system. Flaws: Too much work (clicking) to find and select a simplified text.

4.2   Iteration 3: Development, Demonstration and Evaluation of the Third Prototype

In the third iteration, a digital prototype (Fig. 5) was developed based upon the findings from the second iteration, and is available online[1].

Fig. 5. Selecting simple text versions of a quest

Themes (in *italics*) and categories (underlined) from prototype demonstrations:

- *Use*. Clear: The interface was perceived as familiar and easy to use. Incentive: Interaction with others through visible response on contributions and having followers was motivating. Attitude: Participants expressed a positive view of the system and its purpose.
- *Design*. Clear: The design was logically structured. Bad: The design could be more aesthetically appealing. Suggestion: Two participants missed the Guidelines button in the interface for creating new texts (Fig. 6); a participant suggested that the Browse buttons could be moved down and the most important guidelines could be viewed in the top right position.
- *Buttons*. Clear: The buttons seemed easy to understand, perhaps due to extra information when hovering over buttons, and/or following conventions from

---

[1] Digital prototype. https://github.com/Jaernbrand/Thesis_Prototype [Accessed 2017-06-09]

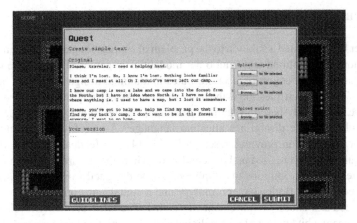

Fig. 6. Create simplified text

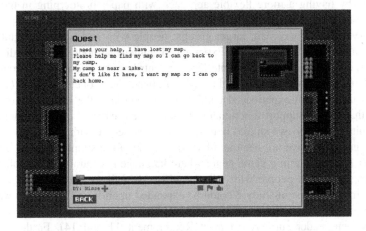

Fig. 7. Quest interface with simplified text and audio descriptions

Youtube and Facebook as one participant expressed it. Unclear: The purpose of the plus sign (Fig. 7) was unclear (although all selected correctly), and the Browse buttons (Fig. 6) could need better descriptions. Suggestion: Replace the plus sign with something more clearly related to favourites. The flag (Fig. 7) was red if someone requested a simplified text; this symbol was perceived a bit too severe; perhaps a different colour could be enough.

- *Functionality.* Wishes: Voting and flagging of comments was wished for as a self-sanitizing feature, as well as having a mean score of each writer to sort on. Restrictions: Participants viewed moderation of texts and comments as crucial to make the system popular and useful. Also, instead of uploading local images the Browse buttons could show a list of screenshots from the within the game only.

5 Discussion and Conclusions

This paper has suggested a solution to the problem of support for game community-based contributions of simplified texts and other modalities in games. This may be used as a design alternative for cognition user attributes in a unified design method of accessible games [2]. The research question in the first study was: Which requirements need to be met for a game community-based system for making quest descriptions more accessible for people with cognitive disabilities affecting language? A set of 14 requirements were argued for, based upon previous research [8–11, 14] and feedback from participants. These requirements were used in the second study where the research question was: How can a system for contributions of simplified text be designed from the perspectives of experienced gamers? Both a paper prototype and a digital game prototype was designed and evaluated and another requirement was added. The order of fidelity levels of prototypes may seem a bit backward with a digital slideshow first and then a paper prototype. This partly reflects the fact that this paper is based upon two studies, with two groups of students who made their choices of methods independent of each other. However, it was motivated by having a more flexible approach with paper prototyping in the second iteration, when interacting with participants and discussing the design.

The system has two main target groups; people with and without cognitive disabilities in the game community. Experienced gamers without cognitive disabilities have been involved to evaluate the interface for contributing with simplified texts, which was the aim of the system for input of texts in this paper. The conclusions are: (1) a set of requirements; (2) that experienced gamers understood how the interface worked, but also (3) that further support functionality would benefit users of the text input system.

A limitation of the two studies in this paper is that people with cognitive disabilities affecting language have not been involved in the use of the simplified texts. This may be further studied within a game genre where language is central such as role-playing games, together with people with mild cognitive disabilities affecting language. The digital game prototype in study 2 could be expanded upon for such a study, where the interface for selecting a simplified text may need further work for accessibility, such as adding screen reader support (to meet Requirement 11 and 14). Furthermore, the selection of participants was not randomized and it is also a small sample. With the existing prototype, a larger study could be done including all game students at a department or several departments through surveys to more easily be able to generalise about the game community, and interviews of people with cognitive disabilities affecting language regarding the simplified texts produced by people without cognitive disabilities.

References

1. Yuan, B., Folmer, E., Harris, F.: Game accessibility: a survey. Univ. Access Inf. Soc. **10**(1), 81–100 (2011)
2. Grammenos, D., Savidis, A., Stephanidis, C.: Unified design of universally accessible games. In: Stephanidis, C. (ed.) UAHCI 2007. LNCS, vol. 4556, pp. 607–616. Springer, Heidelberg (2007). https://doi.org/10.1007/978-3-540-73283-9_67

3. Scott, M.J., Spyridonis, F., Ghinea, G.: Designing accessible games with the VERITAS framework: lessons learned from game designers. In: Antona, M., Stephanidis, C. (eds.) UAHCI 2015. LNCS, vol. 9177, pp. 547–554. Springer, Cham (2015). https://doi.org/10. 1007/978-3-319-20684-4_53

4. Torrente, J., del Blanco, Á., Serrano-Laguna, Á., Vallejo-Pinto, J.Á., Moreno-Ger, P., Fernández-Manjón, B.: Towards universal game development in education. In: Popescu, E., Li, Q., Klamma, R., Leung, H., Specht, M. (eds.) ICWL 2012. LNCS, vol. 7558, pp. 160–169. Springer, Heidelberg (2012). https://doi.org/10.1007/978-3-642-33642-3_17

5. Torrente, J., et al.: Towards a low cost adaptation of educational games for people with disabilities. Comput. Sci. Inf. Syst. 11(1), 369–391 (2014)

6. Jones, R.: Adaptive play: a prototype of a responsive children's videogame for greater inclusivity. In: Proceedings of the 9th Nordic Conference on Human-Computer Interaction, pp. 1–6. ACM, Gothenburg (2016)

7. Torrente, J., del Blanco, Á., Moreno-Ger, P., Fernández-Manjón, B.: Designing serious games for adult students with cognitive disabilities. In: Huang, T., Zeng, Z., Li, C., Leung, C.S. (eds.) ICONIP 2012. LNCS, vol. 7666, pp. 603–610. Springer, Heidelberg (2012). https://doi.org/10.1007/978-3-642-34478-7_73

8. Lopresti, E.F., Bodine, C., Lewis, C.: Assistive technology for cognition: understanding the needs of persons with disabilities. In: IEEE Engineering in Medicine and Biology Magazine, pp. 29–39. IEEE (2008)

9. Saggion, H., et al.: Text simplification in simplext. Making text more accessible. Procesamiento del Lenguaje Natural 47, 341–342 (2011)

10. Hoisl, B., Aigner, W., Miksch, S.: Social rewarding in Wiki systems – motivating the community. In: Schuler, D. (ed.) OCSC 2007. LNCS, vol. 4564, pp. 362–371. Springer, Heidelberg (2007). https://doi.org/10.1007/978-3-540-73257-0_40

11. Ling, K., et al.: Using social psychology to motivate contributions to online communities. J. Comput. Mediated Commun. 10(4) (2005). http://onlinelibrary.wiley.com/doi/10.1111/j. 1083-6101.2005.tb00273.x/full

12. Johannesson, P., Perjons, E.: An Introduction to Design Science. Springer, Cham (2014). https://doi.org/10.1007/978-3-319-10632-8

13. Norman, D.A.: The Design of Everyday Things. Basic books, New York (2002)

14. Rello, L., et al.: Simplify or help?: text simplification strategies for people with dyslexia. In: Proceedings of the 10th International Cross-Disciplinary Conference on Web Accessibility, pp. 1–10. ACM, Rio de Janeiro (2013)

DLI 2017

Designing Inclusive Reflective Learning with Digital Democratic Dialogue Across Boundaries and Diversities

Elsebeth Korsgaard Sorensen(✉) and Eva Brooks

Department of Learning and Philosophy, Aalborg University,
Kroghstraede 3, 9220 Aalborg Ø, Denmark
{elsebeth, eb}@learning.aau.dk

Abstract. This paper deals with the challenge of designing online learning architectures for master students. From different theoretical concepts and with a netnographic methodological research approach, the paper discusses theoretical concepts, challenges and mechanisms significant to designing and structuring the "walls" of a digital learning architecture conducive to the establishment of a social, inclusive, empowering and interactive learning climate online. It makes a plea for using an approach of dialogic design with meta-structures in the communicative fora in order to promote inclusiveness, reflection, empowerment and ownership amongst learners.

Keywords: Meta learning · Inclusive · Learner empowerment
Dialogic · Democratic citizenship · Collaborative knowledge building
Reflection · Diversity · Digital affordances · Quality of dialogue

1 Introduction

Within the last couple of decades teaching and learning with digital technology have grown rapidly all over the Globe. This has happened hand in hand with the increasing development and succeeding availability of digital environments [1–3], but for different reasons and with different motivations. Some of these reasons are of a rational and economic nature, others are based on different, but equally rational and pragmatic ground. Only a small part of the resulting digital learning architectures is designed with a prim goal of enhancing the "internal" quality of the learning process and design, such as the incorporation of quality criteria such as "inclusion" and "space for diversity" in the learning design.

Parallel to this development, teaching and learning in digital and blended environments offer integrated access to Open digital Educational Resources (OERs). Amongst these, inclusive digital tools and technologies [3]. Among other things, this is happening in order to meet the educational needs of society and to prepare diverse groups of learners for a growing global learning arena. The educational world needs inclusive approaches when building bridges across diversity - e.g. disciplines, physical distances, and other differences - social, academic and psychological [4].

© ICST Institute for Computer Sciences, Social Informatics and Telecommunications Engineering 2018
A. L. Brooks et al. (Eds.): ArtsIT 2017/DLI 2017, LNICST 229, pp. 251–261, 2018.
https://doi.org/10.1007/978-3-319-76908-0_24

There is a need for novel learning designs to be incorporating and understanding and will to promote space for diversity [5, 6], (meta-) dialogue, democratic dialogic principles, and make use of inclusive pedagogic strategies in digital or blended learning context and environment.

There is also a need for understanding more deeply the affordances of the digital environments, so this digital potential can be married more fundamentally with innovative pedagogies in order to establish insights in what constitutes a fruitful sustainable digital online learning architecture and process that can work for learner empowerment and inclusion [6].

The aim of this paper is - through the glasses of relevant theoretical concepts and on the basis of an evaluation of the design and delivery of a Master's module – to assert to what extent the learning environment and the learning design prove to be supportive of an establishment of an inclusive and empowering collaborative learning process based on a dialogic approach to design [7]. Does the particular way the module is pedagogically designed, support inclusive collaborative learning and dialogue? Are there specific significant features, of both the virtual environment and the learning design, that seem essential with respect to ensuring inclusiveness, interaction, collaboration and inclusiveness in the online learning process.

2 Theoretical Perspective

Several concepts are relevant for the approach and gaze of this paper. They are presented in the section below.

2.1 Values and Attitudes

Innovative initiatives in terms of designing good quality pedagogic online learning architectures that promote an atmosphere of inclusion, often appear the result of individual teachers' personal bottom-up processes (their own practices) [8].

In the view of the authors, in particular educators, carry a principled responsibility for creating awareness and self-awareness about these issues. It is through education – and what is learned through educational processes – that we cultivate values and attitudes of *good quality,* such as e.g. a *democratic attitude*, an *inclusive attitude* towards our global fellow citizen, learner empowerment and a view of diversity and sharing as a common resource [4].

But, more precisely, what are the goals, challenges and possibilities that we, as designers and educators, face in a context of digital tools and digital environment? To what extent is the dialogic design inclusive in generating important and good quality teaching and learning that work for learner empowerment [9] and democratic global citizenship? How may a conceptual framework, which supports the envisioned goal, look?

2.2 Digital Affordances for Dialogic Inclusion

Digital learning environments are often noted as having a non-hierarchical infrastructure in the communication process [3, 8, 10]. One clear and concrete design potential of digital technology is to provide structure. However, as confirmed by Dalsgaard [10, 11], the formal educational potential of digital technologies and environments cannot be easily overlooked, especially as they empower the learner's in terms of *agency*. The learner's possible initiatives are strengthened in two ways: *Dialogic participation* and *democratic negotiation*, and *creation and sharing* of knowledge and digital resources.

2.3   Collaborative Dialogic Democratic Meta-Learning

In a dialogic perspective, "dialogue" is understood *as a way of knowing*; in other words, as a kind of epistemology [12]. This implies that there are no fixed meanings that can be obtained or learned, as meaning is situated in a dialogic context. A dialogic context always appears open to potentially new re-assessing views and comments. With reference to the insight of Bakhtin (1986), Wegerif [12] concludes that there is neither a first nor a last word. And there is no limit at all to the dialogic context, as it extends retrospectively into the "boundless past" and ahead into the "boundless future" [13].

Wegerif [12, 13] adds a final affordance to the pedagogic vision about digital technology relevant to this study. Pointing to digital networks, Wegerif emphasizes their potential for building digital learning contexts that promote fundamental democratic, dialogic skills and empowering educational attitudes, such as e.g. an urge to listen to other "voices" in other dialogues than ones own. The ability to relate dialogically becomes a needed competence in an intercultural, globally oriented world.

The hypothesis of the authors is that there exists an un-explored and not yet utilized space for higher-level-learning, especially concerned with learner attitudes (Fig. 1) in virtual learning environments. In the voice of Bateson [14] and assuming the different communicative "walls" of the digital learning space, it clearly follows that we are facing a virtual potential for inclusive-learning-for-collaborative-awareness (meta-reflection). Thus, we need a learning architecture (a model) promoting valuable inclusive meta (reflective) space, like e.g. the model of Sorensen and Takle [21], refined further by Sorensen and Murchú [22]:

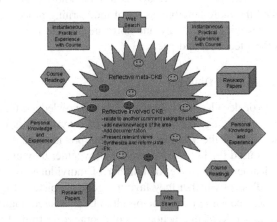

Fig. 1. Learning and collaborative knowledge building through online digital dialogue. Involved interaction (learners-learners and teachers-learners), and reflective meta-interaction (teacher-learners and learners-learners) [16].

The framework assumes that participatory resources enter dynamically from outside the formal learning space (i.e. knowledge and references from the participants as well as through the teacher). The framework denotes a digital dialogic inclusive collaborative knowledge building process, constructed by participants.

3 The Online Master Module

The entire Master's program is a part-time master study for professionals, with a value of 60 ECTS extended over two years. The module in question weighs 5 ECTS, and it is the initial module of the entire program. The topic of the module is concerned with learning how to utilize digital technology in design of digital teaching and learning. The module (as it is the case with the entire program) uses a VLE as the main learning environment. The asynchronous online study process was interrupted twice by a two-day f2f-seminar.

The 29 students attended the explored module have different backgrounds. A part comes from all levels of education, a few come with a background in business. The students come from all over Denmark, a few from Norway, and a few from Faroe Islands and Greenland.

3.1 Participants

The goal of the design of the specific first module was to establish an including dialogic continuous collaborative learning process, in which the students were exposed to a digital dialogic democratic blended learning architecture [7] as a laboratory and method for collaboratively generating new knowledge about designing teaching and learning with digital technology.

The learning process was intended to unfold, partly asynchronously through Moodle as the virtual learning environment (VLE), and partly interrupted by four physical f2f-seminars (2 seminars per semester). While the asynchronous online environment was used as a collaborative discussion and knowledge building space, the f2f-seminars handled the more tangible issues of the learning process (e.g. workshops, and practical exercises with technology and software), where the students engaged in f2f-dialogue with their teachers and peers.

3.2 Roles as Catalyst for Dialogue

Over the last couple of decades it has been widely acknowledged that in a process of dialogic collaborative learning, the *establishment of interaction* is essential. This is regardless of which one of the various types of interpretation of the concept of collaborative learning is used [9, 17–22]. Regardless of whether they use the parameter in their definition of learner perspective, of number of individuals, or of organizational methods - and regardless of whether they favour a general epistemological approach to learning that is socio-constructivist, socio-cultural, or shared-cognitive - they all emphasise the essential role of interaction in collaborative learning [9, 15, 22].

The framework above on D-Roles (Table 1) was implemented to stimulate both kick-start, the "knitting together" and the "raising of dialogic awareness" (meta-learning).

Table 1. D-Roles: Dialogic roles in small online groups, to be used for the plenum debate.

Dialogue roles	Description
Presenter	The task linked to the role of the presenter is to write a contribution (in the advised plenum forum of the small group) presenting a, potentially controversial, topic/problem statement for discussion. The statement should have a rationale with references to the course/theme literature, to the presenter's experiences, and to learning theoretical positions. The contribution should be approximately 20–30 lines
Opponent	The task linked to the role of the opponent is to challenge - qualified and with serious arguments and references to literature - the views in the statement of the presenter. In other words, the opponent should pose a contrasting view rhetorically in a way that fosters further dialogue and discussion. **Note:** When the debate has been kick-started and evolves continuously, the opponent should stop opposing as a principle - and, instead, participate genuinely according to his/her own views and convictions (i.e. take the role of commentator)
Moderator	The task of the moderator is to support and weave the discussion started by his/her small group. The moderator encourages comments and reactions in relation to the statement made by the small group presenter, and challenges "lurkers" to comment. The moderator also keeps the discussion on a fruitful track and weaves to create communicative cohesion between the comments of the evolving dialogue. **Note**: The moderator has the final responsibility for summarizing the debate elicited and posting this summary
Commentator (all participants)	The task of a commentator is to comment generally on the ideas emerging from and presented by other participants, and to contribute in a qualified way to the collaborative knowledge building discussions. This role should be applied by each participant at all times in the plenum forum, so that each one contributes also to also the discussions lead by other groups

3.3   Assessment Framework

In order to ensure not only dialogicity and the establishment of interaction amongst participants in the period of debate, but also to in retrospect be able to assess the level of dialogicity and the individual participants' dialogic behavior, the process-oriented assessment framework (PAA) was implemented first by Sorensen and Takle [21], later modified by Sorensen and Murchú [22] (Table 2):

The framework was used, both *prescriptively* for scaffolding the dialogic process and later, as a set of criteria, *for the purpose of assessment* of *dialogicity* and *inclusiveness*.

Table 2. Dialogue roles in small online groups, to be implemented in the plenum debate.

Dialogic requirements (per participant)	
Quantitative	Submit **at least** 5 contributions, out of which 2 should be your own identifications, and 3 should be responses to your peers
Qualitative	Contributions that ask for clarity; contributions that oppose; contributions adding new knowledge to the discussion; contributions of relevance; contributions that build on logical argumentation in relation to others; contributions that sum up and synthesize and take a new point of direction; etc. (open-ended list)

4 Research Design and Methodology

The overall research approach in the current study is inspired by Netnography[1], a research approach applied to understanding dialogue and interaction in digital communication contexts. In this approach the data are produced through online interactions [23, 24].

In addition, the authors are attracted to the idea of Appreciative Enquiry (AI), which we see as a way of moving our thinking forward a positive premise, while focusing at generating NEW knowledge and insights and discover other inclusive strategies and techniques. Also elements from Content Analysis have been applied with this intention. Ultimately, we wished to remain focused on a sustainable meta-learning process of Learning2Learn. As emphasized by Wegerif [12]:

It implies that we must not be content with teaching the facts or knowledge as we see them, these will soon be out of date, instead we need to teach students how to engage in the dialogues through which knowledge is constantly being constructed, deconstructed and reconstructed [12:60]

The social-constructivist point of departure acknowledges that reality is created in social relations through communication and assignment of meaning [25:43–47]. The underlying suspicion is that we might have exhausted traditional problem solving, and that "appreciative enquiry" is a more effective way of a transforming investigations, which are able to inspire, mobilize and induce change in creative and innovative ways [26–28]. As stated by Cooperrider [25] the future may ask for methods, which confirms, convinces and accelerates predicted learning based on a higher degree of community [25:31] – and a higher degree of including attitude, we may add.

The attitude of an AI approach appears attractive in a perspective of *inclusion* – and *dialogicity*. Thus, the authors of this study attempt to identify signs of inclusiveness and dialogic behavior in digital student dialogue. We look for a tendency for students to become more inclusive in their collaborative process and to build on and invite participation and the meanings/views of other learners into the collaborative knowledge building process in their shared endeavor of seeking NEW knowledge in an inclusive

---

[1] Netnography uses these conversations as data. It is an interpretive research method that adapts the traditional, in-person participant observation techniques of anthropology to the study of interactions and experiences manifesting through digital communications [24].

collaborative atmosphere. Thus, such analysis is positively concerned with *signs of inclusive and democratic attitudes* (i.e. listening to and incorporating the opinions of fellow students, and it asks perspectives/questions, such as (1) can we identify an attitude of dialogicity, and, if so, (2) how is an inclusive attitude expressed?

After the delivery of the module, it was evaluated orally at a f2f seminar with the students. The students were asked about their experience in three categories: (1) pros, (2) cons and (3) constructive comment for future iterations of the module.

The participants were asked, when they signed up for the program, to accept that the data generated in their study would potentially be used for research purposes - of course, with the usual respect, rules and requirements in terms of anonymity of the scientific society.

5 Findings and Discussion

The digital technology acted, not only as a medium for the module delivery process, but also, it constructed a practical collaborative learning experience for the participants. Essentially, the module unfolded in the intersection between dialogic interaction between peers on both theory and practice – and, in addition, also unfolded at a meta-level, as meta-reflections on module interactions (meta-learning). Small groups (4 participants) distributed communicative roles (Fig. 2) and presented an identified problem/question/wondering.

The various small groups presented in three **plenum fora**, and the groups themselves moderated the succeeding discussions on three topics: *(1) Theory and ict-supported practice; (2) The reflective learning potential of Ict; (3) Quality, Inclusion and Digital Education.* Two **meta-fora** were offered: *(a) About the module; (b) "Online dialogue as method in collaboration and learning".* Participants were asked to prepare in the small online groups, on the basis of recommended readings and distributed group roles, involving also an initial 1–2 weeks of in depth individual reading, raising questions/wonderings for a process of *plenum debate with peers* and teachers. The group roles were applied to the discussion, and the dialogic endeavor had started.

The *teachers* were present in the two meta-fora with the function of (1) supporting the meta-learning around the method (online dialogue as a method for collaboration and learning), and (2) being present for Q's about the module. The teacher was only allowed to comment in the three topical fora with an attitude of "equal participant" (to avoid "authority-style" and to not disturb the process and feeling of empowerment and ownership amongst the individual participants).

The **META-forum "Dialogue ABOUT the module"** produced **109 contributions** The nature of them were e.g. questions, answers, information-passing, etc. The **META-forum "Online dialogue as method ..."** produced **98 contributions** that illustrate the motivating and including attitude and effect of relations and the motivations hidden in a dialogic learning process[2]:

---

[2] Text in bold in the contributions from participants indicates a selection of the authors, and it is also the authors who are responsible for the translation of the contributions from Danish to English.

Topic: Half-way reflections in module 1
It has been hard to related to Moodle, there are so many threads. I have lost the overview. When you want to go back to something in a thread, it is difficult to remember where it is. Unfortunately, I have had a tendency to lurk to much and then when I did want to write a contribution, I was overtaken by someone else. E., at a point in time, urged us to write, saying that everybody's opinion counted, but I lost my breath with all the long contributions. It seems so pointless to write that I agree with A and B…But, in contrast, **it has been extremely motivating to read all the exiting contributions and it has caused me to reflect a lot**. It is exiting to read all the different perceptions and I feel that I have come to know quite a few peers. It is a good replacement for not often meeting f2f in the module…..I have had to re-think my way of participating. My Moodle is now on my mobile….learning and participating as I go along.

Topic: Overwhelmed….information overload
"So much has happened within the last week. From using many hours considering how one best express one-self, and how one should navigate in the enormous amount of contributions/views….to becoming so occupied with them that I (almost) forgot that it was a part of a study program… To be asked to use theories to argue for positions and attitudes in practice in daily life has been enormously productive/giving, because you exactly need to relate yourself to something – and not just learn it by heart. What a pity it is, that there is not more time and space for this type of thing in the common daily life of a teacher…The more I know, the more I realize what I do not yet know, and this module has given me courage and appetite to explore and to wonder about what I have not yet learned….

The **FIRST plenum forum, "Theory and ict supported practice",** hosted 3 small groups and generated 56 contributions. The contribution below is an example that mirror an (embracing) including, inviting comment from a participant, asking with an interested attitude, if others have similar thoughts on the matter:

Topic: Digital Natives….
"Digital natives" and "Digital immigrants" ("On The Horizon", Prensky m. (2001 a). This will in my view result in big challenges for everyone in the near future. (…) I was so lucky in my previous work place to obtain permission to participate in a pilot project concerned with the recording of teaching….**Is there someone amongst you, who feel a resistance towards recording of teaching with the students? (I believe it is a question of accepting the conditions of the surroundings, where everyone records random things ….**We – the group of educators – must go through the same kind of continuous educations as our students, as it-tools continue to provide with new possibilities, which we at the current point in time are not able to relate to.

The **SECOND plenum forum "The reflective learning potential in digital network"** hosted 3 small groups and generated 42 contributions. A contribution that mirrors an including dialogic attitude asking peers to share knowledge and insights:

Topic: Which pedagogical criteria should be fulfilled in order for children to become motivated to participate in learning in digital networks?
In another thread it is discussed which pedagogic criteria it takes to motivate adults to participate in digital teaching/learning processes. In my view, it cannot be the same as those relevant to kids. **Therefore, I would like to hear your opinions on what it takes to motivate kids?** … There are six points (Knowles),which look at the motivation of adults…..The question is, how do we make learning motivating to kids, if there is no immediate need for learning. The Danish Institute of Evaluation (EVA) has investigated   (http://www.eva.dk/projekter/2013/undervisning-pa-mellemtrinnet/notat-det-siger-forskningen-om-god-undervisning-i-skolen/notat-det-siger-forskningen-om-god-undervisning-i-skolen) this. They concluded with the following points: 1) the teacher creates a positive climate in the class, which then is positively focused on learning, 2) the teacher constructs the goal for the kids, 3) the teacher works with evaluation and feedback in teaching, 4) the teacher includes the kids, 5) the teacher teaches with variation….**Now, how do YOU think that these points can be implemented in a digital teaching environment?**

The **THIRD plenum forum "Quality, inclusion and digital education"** hosted 4 small groups and generated 91 contributions. Below is an example of a contribution that mirrors an including attitude in terms of collecting a mandate for the overall view.

Topic: Digital education ("Bildung") and sociale media
This week Politiken has publiced two articles "Robotics guides your news" about young peoples' use of social media as their most important news channels... (...) **When I point to this article, it is because I think an interesting discussion should be taken around the responsibility of the educational institutions,** when it comes to digital education and social media...and the imprint on young peoples' learning? Is there reason for being worried?....In "Digital Dannelse" Lotte Nyboe writes that (...) young people in this culture are not only "audience", but also "users" and "consumers" ...(Nyboe, 2009, p. 51). To move around reflectively and critically in this media culture must require a high degree of "digital literacy", or what Nyboe names "media literacy" (Nyboe, 2009, p.93)... Does the articles critic also imply a critic of the users' relationship to social media? And **how should we as educators act in relation to the socialization of young people that takes place through social media?**....What do you think??
Borre, M. & Vuorela, M. (24. September 2014). Robotter styrer din
nyhedsstrøm. Politiken: http://politiken.dk/kultur/medier/ECE2405754/robotter-styrer-din-nyhedsstroem/
Vuorela, M (25. September 2014). Denne artikel vil ryste dig for altid.
Politiken: http://politiken.dk/magasinet/feature/ECE2406191/denne-artikel-vil-ryste-dig-for-altid/
Nyboe, L. (2009). Digital Dannelse. København: Frydenlund.

The evaluating comments from the participants illustrated the initial frustration. Nevertheless, in general, the course had been perceived as a positive experience. Some participants initially found it to be a stressing experience due to the large amount of comments and difficulties in maintaining an overview, but others expressed the contrasting view that it had been an exiting and stimulating experience to be engaged in and sharing an explosion of dynamic CKB. A smaller part of the participants expressed some frustration that the course did not have the more traditional roles of a teacher and a student.

Inclusive and *democratic attitudes* were looked for in the knowledge building tapestries that were generated during the module. From the netnographic point of view of the authors, the tapestries mirrored high interaction between participants. Peers made use of (i.e. listened to) each other's views and took further departure from the new insight. This process seems to have created ownership in participants. In the dialogic tapestries the signs and indicators of *inclusive* and *democratic attitudes* were quite clear in most comments. On the basis of the contributions of participants, it was as if the social "intentionality" (dialogicity) was practiced and created stronger relations amongst participants and illustrated a dialogic urge, an social attitude in the string of dialogues, and a wish to engage in knowledge building with peers for NEW knowledge building [29]. We may say that most participants contributed to what we call "the glue" in the dialog. Many of the comments mirror how the author reaches out to peers in order to learn more. They provided new view, relating to those of peers, and they themselves found relevant references to add to the conversation. In other words, learner ownership and empowerment flourished.

6   Conclusion

This study has explored the dialogic design and character of a professional online Master's module on the overall question of how to implement digital technology in learning processes. The overall research approach in the current study was inspired by

Netnography in an attempt to capture the motivating and inspiring potential of social dialogic interaction in a dialogic approach to design learning and meta-learning in a digital communication contexts. The exploration was carried out in a flavor of Appreciative Enquiry and incorporate elements of content analysis.

Spawning an inclusive learning process of good dialogic quality and a flat social learning endeavour amongst participants, it seems fair to conclude that the learning design had identified and implemented important elements in the learning design. The design produced a process of good dialogic learning quality and a socially including learning endeavour that made room for learner empowerment and ownership to develop. While the experience was blessed with a lot of dialogic "glue", it also carried a subtle promise and perhaps tentative suggestion that the path of inclusiveness and meta-learning, as conceptualized in this paper, is a fruitful direction for further studies in the cultivation of inclusive democratic skills and attitudes in digital teaching and learning programs for adults.

References

1. Bates, A.W.: Teaching in a digital age. Guidelines for designing teaching and learning. Tony Bates Associates Ltd, Vancouver (2015). Ebook ISBN 978-0-9952692-0-0; Print ISBN 978-0-9952692-1-7
2. Tait, A.: Distance and e-learning, social justice and development: the relevance of capability approaches—the mission of open universities. Int. Rev. Res. Open Distance Learn. (IRRODL) **14**, 1–18 (2013)
3. Conole, G.: Designing for Learning in an Open World. Springer, New York (2013). https://doi.org/10.1007/978-1-4419-8517-0
4. Sorensen, E.K. Andersen, H.V.: Solitude or co-existence – or learning-together-apart with digital dialogic technologies for kids with developmental and attention difficulties. EAI-J. Int. J. Arts Technol. (2017). Special Issue – Brooks, E. (ed.)
5. Hoskins, B., Jesinghaus, J., Massimiliano, M., Munda, G, Nardo, M., Saisana, M., Van Nijlen, D., Vidoni, D., Villalba, E.: Measuring Active Citizenship in Europe. CRELL Research Paper 4. EUR 22530 EN. Office for Official Publications of the European Communities, 1 January 2006
6. Bruce, A.: Inclusion's Final Frontiere. ICT and Innovation in Transformative Education. ULS, Dublin (2016)
7. Sorensen, E.K.: Dialogic e-learning2learn: creating global digital networks and educational knowledge building architectures across diversity. Multicult. Educ. Technol. J. **1**(3), 162–177 (2007)
8. Andersen, H.V., Sorensen, E.K.: Technology as a vehicle for inclusion of learners with attention deficits in mainstream schools. In: EURODL, Vol II, 2016. First published as an DOUBLE AWARD PAPER in Proceedings of the European Distance and E-Learning Network 2015 Annual Conference: Expanding Learning Scenarios Opening Out the Educational Landscape, pp. 720–730. EDEN, Barcelona (2016)
9. Sorensen, E.K.: Promoting Awareness and Ownership in Digital Processes of Teaching and Learning. In: Proceedings of the European Distance and E-Learning Network 2014 Research Workshop (RW8), Challenges for Research into Open & Distance Learning: Doing Things Better – Doing Better Things, Oxford, 27–28 October 2014. ISBN 978-615-5511-00-4

10. Dalsgaard, C.N.: Internettet som personaliseret og social medie. Læring & Medier (LOM), no. 5 (2010). ISSN 1903-248X
11. Dalsgaard, C., Sorensen, E.K.: A typology for Web 2.0. In: ECEL, pp. 272–279 (2008)
12. Wegerif, R.: Dialogic education: what is it and why do we need it? Educ. Rev. **19**(2), 58–67 (2006)
13. Wegerif, R.: Applying dialogic theory to illuminate the relationship between literacy education and teaching thinking in the context of the Internet Age. In: Brindley, S., Juzwik, M., Whitehurst, A. (eds.) Contribution to a Special Issue on International Perspectives on Dialogic Theory and Practice, L1-Educational Studies in Language and Literature, vol 16, pp. 1–21 (2016). http://dx.doi.org/10.17239/L1ESLL-2016.16.02.07
14. Bateson, G.: Steps to an Ecology of Mind. The University of Chicago Press, Chicago (1976)
15. Dillenbourg, P., et al.: The evolution of research on collaborative learning. In: Reimann, P., Spada, H. (eds.) Learning in Humans and Machines. Towards an Interdisciplinary Learning Science, pp. 189–211. Pergamon, Oxford (1995)
16. Kaye, T.: Learning together apart. In: Kaye, A.W. (ed.) Collaborative Learning Through Computer Conferencing. NATO ASI Series, vol. 90, pp. 1–24. Springer, Heidelberg (1992). https://doi.org/10.1007/978-3-642-77684-7_1
17. Scardamalia, M., Bereiter, C.: Knowledge building. In: Guthrie, J.W. (ed.) Encyclopedia of Education, 2nd edn. Macmillan, New York (2003)
18. Koschmann, T.: Conversation analysis and learning in interaction. In: Chapelle, C.A. (ed.) The Encyclopedia of Applied Linguistics, pp. 1038–1043. Wiley-Blackwell, Oxford (2013)
19. Harasim, L.: Learning Theory and Online Technologies. Routledge, New York (2011). ISBN 9780415999762
20. Sorensen, E.K.: Learning online through linguistic interaction. Int. J. Crit. Pract. **2**(2), 12–17 (1997)
21. Sorensen, E.K., Takle, E.S.: Collaborative knowledge building in web-based learning: assessing the quality of dialogue. Int. J. E-Learn. **1**(1), 28–32 (2002)
22. Sorensen, E.K., Murchú, D.Ó.: Identifying an appropriate, pedagogical, networked architecture for online learning communities within higher and continuing education. In: Sorensen, E.K., Murchú, D.Ó. (eds.) Enhancing Learning Through Technology, pp. 226–251. Idea Group Inc., Hershey (2006)
23. Kozinets, R.V.: Netnography: Doing Ethnographic Research Online. Sage Publications, Thousand Oaks (2010)
24. Kozinets, R.V.: Handbook of Qualitative Research Methods. Sage Publications, Thousand Oaks (1998)
25. Cooperrider, D., Whitney, D., Stavros, J.: Håndbog i anerkendende udforskning, 1st edn. Dansk Psykologisk Forlag, Copenhagen (2011). Chaps. 1 and 2
26. Darsoe, L.: Innovationspædagogik. Samfundslitteratur, Frederiksberg (2011)
27. Petersson, E. Brown, D.: Perspectives on games for rehabilitation. In: Games and Rehabilitation. Springer (2017)
28. Brooks, E.P., Brooks, A.L.: Digital creativity: children's playful mastery of technology. In: Brooks, A.L., Ayiter, E., Yazicigil, O. (eds.) ArtsIT 2014. LNICST, vol. 145, pp. 116–127. Springer, Cham (2015). https://doi.org/10.1007/978-3-319-18836-2_14
29. Nowotny, H.: Cultures of technology and the quest for innovation. Berghahn Books, New York (2006). Conference Details: Cultures of Technology and the Quest for Innovation. Kulturwissenschaftliches Institut (KWI), Essen, April 2003. ISBN 9781845451172

Promoting Inclusion and Global Democratic Citizenship Through Digital Dialogic Collaborative Learning: Diversity Matters!

Elsebeth Korsgaard Sorensen[(✉)] [iD]

Department of Learning and Philosophy, Aalborg University,
Kroghstraede 3, 9220 Aalborg Ø, Denmark
elsebeth@learning.aau.dk

Abstract. This paper addresses the problem of inclusive, creative and innovative learning quality of digital collaborative learning designs and their
potential for amplifying digital democratic citizenship in learners - digital
democratic citizenship with inclusive, empowering and teaching/learning processes at both a macro and micro level. The use of digital technologies for
inclusion in processes of teaching and learning is illustrated through the findings
from a Danish research project funded by the Ministry of Education. On the
basis of these insights and the continuous development of new technologies,
such as e.g. humanoid robotics, the paper concludes with a hypothetical theoretical exploration of a not-yet-utilized social-emotional meta-learning space and
the tentative identification of its educational potential for inclusive learning and
development, positioned in the interactive, communicative space between the
learner and the robot. The paper finalizes with a possible conceptual, principled
recommendation for digital learning designs that may be a step in the right
direction towards sustaining global educational use of digital technologies for
the purpose of digital democratic citizenship and social inclusion.

Keywords: Inclusion · Social robots · Digital technologies · Ict-based learning
Digital learning architecture · Democratic dialogue · Meta-learning
Computer Supported Collaborative Learning (CSCL)

1 Introduction

Our global society is marked by imbalance in a variety of ways [1–3]. By political
differences, by inequality, by exclusion, by illiteracy, by exploitation of some for the
benefit of others, and by cultural intolerance - just to mention a few. The leaders of the
globe faces serious political and educational challenges in the striving for democracy
and for cultivating the vision of "education for all" (EFA)[1] through our educational
systems, through our political attitudes to inclusion, through the efforts made (or not

---

[1] The Education for All (EFA) movement is a global commitment to provide quality basic education
for all children, youth and adults. At the World Education Forum (Dakar 2000), 164 governments
pledged to achieve EFA and identified six goals to be met by 2015. Governments, development
agencies, civil society and the private sector are working together to reach the EFA goals. http://
www.unesco.org/new/en/education/themes/leading-the-international-agenda/education-for-all/.

© ICST Institute for Computer Sciences, Social Informatics and Telecommunications Engineering 2018
A. L. Brooks et al. (Eds.): ArtsIT 2017/DLI 2017, LNICST 229, pp. 262–272, 2018.
https://doi.org/10.1007/978-3-319-76908-0_25

made) towards supporting global citizenship, and the cultivating of learner empowerment in the educational system, etc. [4–9]. Nonetheless, while politics and politicians play their games, it is inevitable that a major responsibility for societal development and the direction it takes, is put on the field of education.

2 A Vision of Educational Change

The world society has taken up the challenge of equality in education. In the 1980's, the United Nations standard rules about *equal possibilities for people with handicaps* were agreed upon.

In 1994, the Salamanca Declaration[2] was agreed upon, - a dynamic new statement on the education of all disabled children that called for *inclusion to be the norm*. The Salamanca declaration was launched, stating that every child has a fundamental right to education and should be given the possibility to achieve and maintain an acceptable learning level; every child has unique characteristics, interests, abilities and needs of learning. Finally, the educational systems and processes should be tailored and initiated in a way that respects diversity in abilities and needs.

In 2006/2009, the United Nations Convention on the rights of persons with Disabilities[3] stated that persons with disabilities should be guaranteed the right to *inclusive education at all levels*, regardless of age, without discrimination and on the basis of equal opportunity. Children with disabilities should not be excluded from free and compulsory primary education, or from secondary education. Adults with disabilities should have access to general tertiary education, vocational training, adult education and lifelong learning. And, finally, persons with disabilities should receive the necessary support, within the general education system, to facilitate their effective education; and effective individualized support measures are put in place to maximize academic and social development.

The vision from 2015 is the Incheon Declaration: Education 2030[4], towards an inclusive and equitable quality education and lifelong learning for all. Its visions and principles for education 2030 that there should be equal opportunity and benefit for all, student's views are listened to and taken seriously, and diversity should be viewed as a resource instead of a problem.

> [Inclusion and equity in and through education is the cornerstone of a transformative education agenda, and we therefore commit to addressing all forms of exclusion and marginalization, disparities and inequalities in access, participation and learning outcomes. No education target should be considered met unless met by all. We therefore commit to making the necessary changes in education policies and focusing our efforts on the most disadvantaged, especially those with disabilities, to ensure that no one is left behind] (The Incheon Declaration: http://unesdoc.unesco.org/images/0012/001275/127583e.pdf).

---

[2] The Salamanca Declaration (1994): http://www.unesco.org/education/pdf/SALAMA_E.PDF.

[3] United Nations Convention on the rights of persons with Disabilities (2006/2009): http://www.un.org/disabilities/documents/convention/convention_accessible_pdf.pdf.

[4] The Incheon Declaration (2015): http://en.unesco.org/world-education-forum-2015/incheon-declaration.

In other words, the situation envisioned is that of inclusive and equitable quality education and lifelong learning for all.

2.1 The Role of Digital Technologies?

In this unbalanced global context, educators and educational designers are offered the learning potential of the rapidly and continuously developing digital technologies, tools and their unique potential [1, 3, 10]. These technologies may help us to innovate and to create learning designs through playful experiments [11, 12] and *collaboratively*, through *dialogue and peer interactions* [13], while building *"educational bridges"* over a variety of gaps in the course of enabling people to connect in dialogue across power structures and hierarchies [14]. To build bridges over the vast variety of social gaps in our global society.

3 How to Design for Digital Inclusive Education?

As we have seen, inclusive education builds on societal learning and insights in the shape of declarations of intentions from the United Nations and Unesco. They form a beautiful political vision of a global society, in which everyone has the same access and possibilities of participating in the democratic processes of society, as well as equal access to the resources of society [2, 9]. In addition, its beauty also encompasses for all learners the right, individually and collaboratively, to engage and participate. The work for democracy and inclusive educational approaches is not a challenge only left for digital technology visions and insights of politicians [1]. Political decisions may have serious impact on how digital technologies are implemented in society. And as such these decisions may in many ways be "defining for the conceptual space" they leave for the "how" digital technology gets implemented broadly and, thus, for *the methodological freedom* and *liberating power* [9, 15], in terms of supporting the advancement of democratic education, of how digital technologies are put to work at the various levels of a society.

The pedagogical making of an aware *democratically oriented global citizen* takes its point of departure in the implementation in the digital space of the educational methodology. This plays a significant role in the education and self-understanding of the global citizen. As a result, part of the responsibility for the *"Bildung" of a democratic citizen* becomes a ball thrown in the turban of educators as well as educational designers [7, 15]. Desirable characteristics of educated, ethically aware, democratically oriented global citizens [6, 16]:

- Demonstrates tolerance and support towards fellow human beings
- Demonstrates will and ability to continuously learn anew
- Demonstrates the essential competency of modern life, the ability to continuously learn anew
- Demonstrates openness and responsiveness to ideas and alternative solutions of others, as well as a will and ability to listen to others and incorporate their views

- Demonstrates will and ability to dialogue, collaborate and share knowledge for the course of shared goals
- Demonstrates no wish to take initiatives to control others
- Demonstrates no will to succumb to authoritarian methodology/pedagogy in any area, but instead induce and promote a respect for the quality of the argument.

In essence, we need inclusive education of this kind in order to become decent responsible citizens that can advance our education ("Bildung") for the purpose of peaceful co-existence [16]. While working for democracy, we have an ethical obligation to take every player onboard and include the socially disadvantaged and the disabled, physically and psychologically, in our creative thinking about the challenge of using digital technologies for design of creative playful teaching and learning [9, 11].

To a large extent the key to unlocking these learning qualities lies in the hands of educators. Future inclusive designs of teaching and learning with digital technologies should evolve as a continuing process of practice – strengthening and sustaining the participation of all students, teachers, parents and community members in the work of the school. Restructuring the cultures, policies and practices in schools to respond to the diversity of learners within their localities, providing support for staff as well as learners.

4 The iDIDAKT Project

iDIDAKT was a 3-year research project funded by the Danish Ministry of Education [17]. The ambition of the project was to develop and test a toolbox of didactics, digital tools and learning methods, which can contribute to increased inclusion of students with developmental and attention problems in school. Assuming a potential in the technology as a tool for inclusion, we wanted to identify how this potential could be brought into play in the classroom by trying different technologies, and in collaboration with participating schools and teachers develop digital learning methods and interventions associated with them. This section describes and reports on the findings from the iDIDAKT project.

4.1 Research Problem and Project

The overall research question of iDIDAKT was: How is it possible to use technology to support inclusion of children with developmental and attention deficits in mainstream schools? The project worked with general inclusive approaches on the one hand, targeting individual student needs, and, on the other, a special focus was given to challenged *children* with ADHD and ASD-like traits that had difficulties with (1) hyperactivity and frustrations, (2) attention and focus, (3) listening to and following oral instructions, (4) managing, organizing and completing tasks and activities, and (5) lacing social competencies.

Also the *teachers* had difficulties with the task of inclusion. They were struggling with (1) lacking competencies and tools, (2) resources structure and management of the school, (3) behavioral problems of focus learners, (4) other learners' perspectives, and (5) lack of understanding from parents etc.

It was a very complex field of research. The project was developed within an Educational Design Research Approach where we in collaboration with the teachers developed new practices and – through Action Research – changed their practices. Many stakeholders were involved: 3 municipalities, 11 schools, 15 classes (grade 1–10), 46 teachers, and 500 learners (56 of which were focus learners[5]). Data were collected through (1) teacher statements at seminars, (2) teachers' written reflections in research blog, (3) interviews, (4) surveys and (5) observations.

4.2   Findings

Our analysis shows that focus learners gain a lot of help, support and opportunity from teachers' interventions with digital tools [18].

The findings demonstrate how digital technologies and interventions to a certain extent seem to provide focus learners with "handy" methods and tools for managing and participating in learning processes. It seems vital in *the process of becoming aware* to employ digital tools to *facilitate reifications* (visualization, organizations, etc.) in such a way that the focus learners get to see/realize what they themselves KNOW. Our investigation employed digital tools and interventions in learning situations with the aim of supporting, in particular (a) the facilitation of PROCESS, (b) the creation of PRODUCTS and, finally, (c) the ASSISTANCE with aspects of production and dissemination [21]. The author assert that important strategies are: (1) to *invite and support participation and dialogue* – also in the *planning of the learning process of the individual focus learner*; (2) *to* incorporate tools and *structures for construction* and *dissemination* of learners' knowledge (to demonstrate "I am able to" and "I know"); (3) to offer multimodal and assistive digital modes for communicating, collaborating and contributing – and *opportunities for reflection*.

It also became clear, that teachers not always perceive technologies as simple pedagogic tools [18]. In between we met with disillusioned statements from teachers who felt powerless in their use (or non-use) of digital tools: "I have downloaded the software, but it does not work, neither on my own iPad, nor on the iPad of the school" (teacher, School A). "I cannot come back again after an attempt to mail my text out of iVoice, and I cannot find an overview of the texts that I have recorded" (teacher, School C). "There is not enough time to teach learners how to use these technologies" (teacher, School B).

But technologies also caused disruptions: "A student by accident erases everything, it is difficult on iPads, on which there is no undo-bottom in apps" (teacher, School I, 2nd grade). It appeared very important that the teachers "master" the technology in a way that they are able to both help the learner with such unintended actions, and that they are able to exploit the affordances of the technologies in their pedagogical practice.

By far, *the most significant/worrying discovery* from the project was an identified clear tendency among teachers to latently accept digital technology to "take over" and

---

[5] "Focus learners" is the term used to denote children with developmental and attention deficits.

"park" the learner – done! This perception was very general amongst the teachers - mostly not accompanying this with elements from the pedagogical competencies of the teacher.

To be included is, in itself, a life value for the unique individual/learner. *To feel included*, a learner must feel safe and secure in the learning endeavor. The reversibility of learning actions in a digital learning environment makes it much safer for focus learners to navigate in a "safe" environment. Reducing risks in the processes of creating learning products and reifying processes of learning is important in order to ensure that focus learners will have a voice in the choir of change and the democratic advancement of society. More concretely, learning interventions with digital technologies: make focus learners thrive *with access to a more multimodal way* of expressing themselves through a repertoire of modalities in their academic tasks. *Images can support lacking memory*, and videos can expand written assignments and compensate for writing disabilities. While it invites and enables the learners to act in a new way, the digital technologies also empower them to take *collaborative and multimodal communicative initiatives* and, thus, express themselves more and better. Using digital technologies enables learners to observe, inspect and reflect upon their own learning (their level of knowledge and process of learning). Using digital technologies enables learners to *disseminate, demonstrate and make visible* – through reifications – their own learning.

Thus, Ict-based interventions seem to *act as a vehicle for enabling inclusion* of focus learners through (1) making visible what focus learners are actually able to do and what they know; this transparency can, positively, impact, their self-esteem ("see what I – as a learner – can do"); (2) provide teachers with precious insight for evaluating the special educational support ("what else must we – as teachers – do"?).

5   The Emerging Potential of Robots for Socio-Emotional Difficulties?

An emerging recent special trend of technological development, which appears to hold great promises for groups of socially disadvantaged learners, is the initiatives happening within socially interactive robotics (SIR) [19]. Robots applied in teaching and learning situations are becoming increasingly more recognized. Bertel [19] emphasizes the assistive including aspects of the robot technology. Especially, since social-emotional and interactive skills in many cases are considered prerequisites for the establishment of interaction between humans, and between humans and technologies.

In addition, to many learners digital technologies in general, but perhaps robots in particular, possess an inherent fascination and invitation to play. The added value of the digital humanoid robotics is that they offer the social emphatic role of a friend to do things with – to learn with.

This section take a look at two examples of humanoid robots, used for children with developmental and attention deficits. In addition, the nature of the potential of the social space between learners with attention deficits (or special education learners) is elucidated.

5.1 NAO

The NAO robot[6] is a humanoid robot (i.e. a humanoid technological interface) that has been used for challenges in special education, in particular in contexts of autistic children. NAO has an attractive effect on children. Among other things he raises the quality of communication and interaction through creating communication bridges between an autistic child (children with ASF) and the people around him/her. For the course of education, NAO contributes to reducing the anxiety of the children. For education, and for teaching and learning, NAO offers a lot of help. He is engaging, predictable, tireless, and patient.

NAO contributes to creating trust and reducing fears. He offers patient encouragement, and he never gets tired of repeating instructions. Whether through Via touch, voice or vision, NAO offers interactions in a variety of ways.

5.2 Buddy

The BUDDY robot[7], another humanoid robot (i.e. a humanoid technological interface), is created for companionship, like in the case of NAO, for children with ASD. It has been used for a variety of situations in special education - again, in particular in contexts of autistic children. Children with autism spectrum disorder (ASD) are often disturbed by anxiety. They often have no interest and ability to interact, no interest to communicate, and they often show repetitive behaviors and distress – especially in situations of change. It is difficult to imagine not to be able to understand paralinguistic communication (facial expressions, gestures, body language, etc.). It has been demonstrated that the learning of interaction skills and reading of feelings are enhanced and improved, when robots have been implemented in the role-playing game. Again, the "patience" and "tolerance" of the Buddy robot get emphasized, and it is noted that the results observed in the context of autistic children have been strikingly positive.

6   Unexplored Socio-Emotional Space – Learner(s) and Robot

It is the hypothesis of the author that there exists an unexplored socio-emotional and socio-pedagogic space – a reflective meta learning space for the consolidation of learner identities - that opens itself up for exploration, a potential pedagogic action in the interactive process between learner(s) and robot. This reflective and interactive meta-space, potentially knitted together with emotions (as e.g. in case of a feeling of friendship with the robot) may, as an element of the interaction itself, be acting as a kind of reflective identity-stimulating mirror[8] and make room for the self-development

---

[6] The NAO robot: http://www.robotlab.com/store/ask-nao-autism-solution-for-kids.

[7] The Buddy robot: http://www.roboticstrends.com/article/how_buddy_is_helping_autistic_children/persona.

[8] "Self-phychology", Heinz Kohut (1913–1981) https://da.wikipedia.org/wiki/Heinz_Kohut.

of learners with socio-emotional difficulties [20, 21]. The mirror gets established by the interacting robot in the unexplored communicative/interactive meta-learning space, and the learner's (predicted/programmed) interaction within the unexplored space between the learner and the robot. But perhaps this insight and benefit of using humanoid robots could be transferred to more general areas of school education. Many children outside special education could benefit from the sustained aspects of his "character" (engaging, predictable, tireless, patient, etc.) (Fig. 1).

Fig. 1. The unexplored socio-emotional dialogic space between learners/peers and a humanoid robot

Empathy is essential for human development and change [20, 22]. It is developed throughout early childhood. The idea is that the emphatic attitude of a therapist will promote a learner's self-perception and ability to perform (i.e. a healthy kind of narcissism, which strengthens the effort of an individual to realize personal abilities and possibilities).

Attempts to generally apply social robots to the educational arenas are relatively scares, but experiments are happening within the field of special education, such as e.g. therapeutic-educational initiatives in relation to autistic children.

From the recent research reported on (the iDIDAKT project), addressing the general potential of digital technologies within contexts of children with developmental and attention deficits [17], the project confirmed the problematic areas related to social skills, such as communication and interaction. Bertel [19] presents a taxonomy for socially interactive robots (Table 1):

This framework may form a fruitful optic for further research directed towards exploration of the identified socio-emotional interactive space in an attempt to, pedagogically in learning design situations, make use of the socio-emotional and socio-pedagogic space that opens itself up in the intersection of learner and robot.

Table 1. Bertel [19] presents a taxonomy for socially interactive robots

Socially interactive robots		
Properties	Description	Example
Morphology	Establishes social expectations of the interaction and provides information about the intended use of the robot	Anthropomorphic Zoomorphic Caricatured Functional
Emotions	Facilitate credibility in HRI and serve as feedback to the user about the robot's internal state	Anger, fear, sadness, joy, surprise, neutral and combinations
Dialogue	Exchange and interpretation of symbols and information about the context of the interaction	Synthetic language Natural language Non-verbal cues
Personality	A set of qualities particularly significant for a specific robot	Tool (reliable), Pet (lovable), Character, Supernatural, Human-like
Perception	Perceptual abilities for engaging in social interaction with humans	Face/gaze tracking Speech/gesture recognition Tone of voice
User modeling	The ability to adapt to and shape the interaction in relation to specific user characteristics	Technological literacy Experience Cognitive abilities
Situated learning	Transferring information, skills and tasks between robots and humans	Imitation Machine learning
Intentionality	For people to be able to assess and predict a robot's behavior, expressions of intention are necessary	Targeted movement and behavior Theory of mind Joint attention

7 Conclusion and Future Perspectives

The general primary goal of educational inclusion is that a learner - through a life-long process of developing identity through reflection and meta learning processes in the meeting with in the educational system - obtains digitized learning-to-learn competences (L2L) on his/her learning trajectory and, hopefully, becomes an active, empowered, independent, participating citizen in societal, democratic processes of life.

In essence, the lifelong learning arena coupled with digital technologies offers an overwhelming potential for the advancement of inclusion, both at micro-level in terms of including the disadvantaged learner or the learner "at risk", but also in a global perspective concerned with the further advancement of an inclusive global society. A society which in principle offers possibilities for educators - using digital technologies - for remaining focused on creating and designing fruitful lifelong learning processes that advance the collaborative, innovative, creative, inclusive, dialogic and democratic learning aspects of life and learning. Processes, which are the ones that preserve the meta-qualities of democratic dialogic negotiation – processes, which are likely to advance the inter-human ethical qualities of global intercultural co-existence.

A last important sustainable insight and priority for future designs of inclusive learning – for design challenges at both the macro and micro level - should be put forward: The importance of designing digital democratic learning architectures that incorporate diversity and that allow for the cultivation of digital democratic dialogue for the purpose of negotiating and advancing inclusion for all.

References

1. Bates, A.W.: Teaching in a Digital Age. Guidelines for Designing Teaching and Learning. Tony Bates Associates Ltd., Vancouver (2015). Ebook ISBN 978-0-9952692-0-0, Print ISBN 978-0-9952692-1-7
2. Tait, A.: Distance and e-learning, social justice and development: the relevance of capability approaches—the mission of open universities. Int. Rev. Res. Open Distance Learn. (IRRODL) 14(4), 1–18 (2013)
3. Conole, G.: Designing for Learning in an Open World. Springer, New York (2013). https://doi.org/10.1007/978-1-4419-8517-0
4. Sorensen, E.K., Takle, E.S.: Collaborative knowledge building in web-based learning: assessing the quality of dialogue. Int. J. E-Learn. (IJEL) 1(1), 28–32 (2002). First published as the AWARD for best research paper among 1100 papers in the Proceedings of the 13th World Conference on Educational Multimedia, Hypermedia & Telecommunications (ED-MEDIA 2001), held 25–30 June 2001 in Tampere, Finland
5. Sorensen, E.K., Murchú, D.Ó.: Designing online learning communities of practice: a democratic perspective. J. Educ. Multimed. (CJEM) 29(3), 189–200 (2004)
6. Sorensen, E.K.: Dialogic e-learning2learn: creating global digital networks and educational knowledge building architectures across diversity. Multicult. Educ. Technol. J. 1(3), 162–177 (2007)
7. Hoskins, B., Jesinghaus, J., Massimiliano, M., Munda, G., Nardo, M., Saisana, M., Van Nijlen, D., Vidoni, D., Villalba, E.: Measuring Active Citizenship in Europe. CRELL Research Paper 4. EUR 22530 EN. Office for Official Publications of the European Communities, 1 January 2006
8. Meyer, B., Haas, C., Rørbech, H., Dahl Madsen, K.: Demokratisk dannelse til aktivt interkulturelt medborgerskab. Sprogforum 13(41), 14–20 (2007)
9. Bruce, A.: Inclusion's Final Frontiere. ICT and Innovation in Transformative Education. ULS, Dublin (2016)
10. Dalsgaard, C.N.: Internettet som personaliseret og social medie. Læring & Medier (LOM) – no. 5 (2010). ISSN 1903-248X
11. Brooks, E.P., Brooks, A.L.: Digital creativity: children's playful mastery of technology. In: Brooks, A., Ayiter, E., Yazicigil, O. (eds.) Arts and Technology. ArtsIT 2014. LNICST, vol. 145, pp. 116–127. Springer, Cham (2015). https://doi.org/10.1007/978-3-319-18836-2_14
12. Petersson, E., Brown, D.: Perspectives on games for rehabilitation. In: Games and Rehabilitation. Springer (2017)
13. Sorensen, E.K., Murchu, D.Ó.: Enhancing Learning Through Technology, pp. 226–251. Idea Group Publishing, Hershey (2006)
14. Nowotny, H.: Cultures of technology and the quest for innovation. Berghahn Books, New York (2006). ISBN 9781845451172. Cultures of Technology and the Quest for Innovation, Kulturwissenschaftliches Institut (KWI) in Essen, Germany, April 2003

15. Boelt, A., Sorensen, E.K.: Digital "Bildung" in the Danish Higher Technical Examination Programme. Accepted for presentation at the European Conference on E-Learning (ECEL), to be held 26–27 October in Porto (2017)
16. Sorensen, E.K.: Promoting awareness and ownership in digital processes of teaching and learning. In: Proceedings of the European Distance and E-Learning Network 2014 Research Workshop (RW8), Challenges for Research into Open & Distance Learning: Doing Things Better – Doing Better Things, Oxford, 27–28 October 2014. ISBN 978-615-5511-00-4
17. Andersen, H.V., Sorensen, E.K., de López, K.J., Jensen, R.H.S.: It-baseret inklusion af elever med udviklings- og opmærksomhedsproblemer i folkeskolen. Rapport for Undervisningsministeriet. Aalborg Universitetsforlag (2016)
18. Andersen, H.V., Sorensen, E.K.: Technology as a vehicle for inclusion of learners with attention deficits in mainstream schools. In: EURODL, vol. 2. First published as an DOUBLE AWARD PAPER in Proceedings of the European Distance and E-Learning Network 2015 Annual Conference: Expanding Learning Scenarios Opening Out the Educational Landscape, pp. 720–730. EDEN, Barcelona (2016)
19. Bertel, L.B.: PEERs: persuasive educational and entertainment robotics: a design-based research approach to social robots in teaching and learning. Aalborg Universitetsforlag. (Ph. d.-serien for Det Humanistiske Fakultet, Aalborg Universitet) (2016). https://doi.org/10. 5278/vbn.phd.hum.00039
20. Kohut, H.: Selvets psykologi. Hans Reitzel, Kbh. (1990)
21. Sorensen, E.K., Andersen, H.V.: Solitude or co-existence – or learning-together-apart with digital dialogic technologies for kids with developmental and attention difficulties. EAI-J. Int. J. Arts Technol. (2017). Special Issue - eds. Eva Brooks)
22. Bateson, G.: Steps to an Ecology of Mind. The University of Chicago Press, Chicago (1976)

GLOBE – Learn and Innovate Digitization by a Virtual Collaboration Exercise and Living Lab

Markus Bresinsky and Florian von Reusner[(✉)]

Department of General Science and Microsystems Engineering,
Ostbayerische Technische Hochschule Regensburg (OTH-R),
University of Applied Sciences,
Galgenbergstraße 30, 93053 Regensburg, Germany
markus.bresinsky@oth-regensburg.de,
reusnerf@gmail.com

Abstract. This paper presents an advanced interactive learning platform .dot that implements the GLOBE exercise, using innovative information and communication technologies to enhance learning and development of management and leadership skills in a complex organizational setting. GLOBE on the one hand focuses on competences around ICT and virtual collaboration, and on the other hand on digital transformation, technologies and tools at higher education institutions. By this applied science, learning and developing on the real-world platform, analysis and drive of digital innovation and transformation can be fostered. The main goal is to co-create knowledge and solutions in the following focused subjects: Management and leadership of multidisciplinary, multinational and multicultural virtual and real collaboration in a complex organizational environment. GLOBE uses real world scenarios (e.g. United Nations mission) and involves real world actors.

This comprehensive educational approach should enhance learning techniques and leverage learning progress with hands-on experiences and applied science in the context of ICT and virtual collaboration, and the embodied dynamics of behavior to support innovation and development.

Keywords: Human factors · ICT · Virtual collaboration · Experiential learning
Problem-based learning · Interactive and collaborative learning
Open innovation · Living Lab · Digitization

1 Introduction

Digital transformation is shaping organizations as well as societies in a rapid and comprehensive manner. Until today scope and extent of the upcoming changes are not fully understood or even known. In recent years, researchers, authors and decision-makers have shown an increased interest in the causes and consequences of digitization for economies, states and societies [1]. One common denominator in the discussion about the possible consequences is the urgent need of skill and competence development, e.g. digital literacy, data analytics or virtual collaboration, for future employees

© ICST Institute for Computer Sciences, Social Informatics and Telecommunications Engineering 2018
A. L. Brooks et al. (Eds.): ArtsIT 2017/DLI 2017, LNICST 229, pp. 273–281, 2018.
https://doi.org/10.1007/978-3-319-76908-0_26

and decision-makers. In this context two different but interdependent developments can be identified: on the one hand innovations in digital technologies drive the need for transformation and adaption in organizations, but on the other hand digital innovation is also shaped by the changing demands and requirements of users implementing these innovations. Thus, to understand the impact it is necessary to address both sides of digital transformation, new technologies and tools as well as changing user requirements through digital innovations. Higher education institutions as universities of applied sciences play a crucial role in this context. Not only they are specifically oriented to practical science based problem-solving in a digital world but also provide a platform for teaching and learning skills for the digital world.

Therefore, the aim of this paper is to outline and discuss a concept that incorporates the idea of digital innovation and competence oriented learning in one single platform. OTH Regensburg together with the partner universities Federal University of Applied Science Mannheim and TEI Heraklion has developed a unique exercise platform called .dot (digital organizational training). Within this .dot-platform one training instance is the GLOBE exercise, which provides a real world scenario based learning and training environment. Powered by the platform, GLOBE can be used for analyzing and driving digital innovations and transformation of organizations.

Digital Innovation and Transformation of Organizations

Digitization will comprehensively change the way how organization will be managed and led [2]. Especially, for highly digitized organization it is crucial to understand and manage digital innovations. Domains in which these organizations are rapidly and comprehensively innovating are virtual collaboration and data analytics. This implies for management and leadership not only to scout, assess and plan the implementation of new technologies but also to take into account the impact of these innovations on members of the organization. Hence, digitized organizations need to focus on both technology domain and social domain for a successful transformation.

A lot of research has been carried out on innovation management [3, 4]. Up to now, there exists an elaborated concept for digital innovation called Living Lab (LL) [5]. The LL concept incorporates Cooperative or Scandinavian Design processes [6], the European Social Experiments with IT [7] and the Digital or Smart City Initiatives [8]. The LL approach is combined with the underlying methodologies of Soft System Thinking, Appreciate Inquiry, Action Research, Open and User Innovation, Co-Creation, NeedFinding, or User Centered Design among others. This concept of LL cooperates all stages of a development process – ideation, conceptualization, testing, prototyping, validating, developing, exploiting and commercialization – in a participatory real-world context network approach, bridging the gap between exploration & exploitation and knowledge & solutions. LL is an evolvement indicating an in-situ nature of Research & Development & Innovation, combining multi-stakeholder, multi-method, multi-context and real-life approach with clear user focus on co-creation. One main idea of Living Lab calls for involving all stakeholders of an innovation, private and public actors and as well as people in a real world setting, which is called the Quadruple Helix Model [9]. By this, Living Lab tries to exploit the opportunity of co-creation; i.e. innovations are not only driven by companies and organizations behind closed doors of laboratories, but also by involving users in a real world setting and utilizing their feedback for improving innovations. This concept can be seen as a testbed or experimentation platform, to experiment and validate innovations for, with and by all participants of a Quadruple Helix. Therefore, Living Lab can be seen as a concept to support both innovations and social learning for a sustainable transformation.

Whilst some research has been carried out on digital innovation, best practice by which required skills and competencies for the digital transformation can be identified and trained have not been fully established. The LL concept offers opportunities to connect innovation management and organizational transformation. GLOBE can be seen as one use case how this connection can be implemented successfully.

Connection of Learning and Innovation in a Real World Scenario
GLOBE focuses on the management and leadership of a multinational operation headquarter implementing (1) a forward response team acting in a complex crisis scenario and (2) a supporting headquarter component which cooperates also with (3) associated headquarters. All three elements use virtual collaboration and data analytics to conduct, control and support time sensitive operations in a complex mission environment. By this organizational scenario different digitized processes and technological tools are used and scrutinized under real world conditions.

For example, GLOBE uses the scenario of a United Nations Mission in crisis countries, depicting the organizational structure of a country team managing projects in the area supported by the United Nations Headquarter and associated partner organizations. Time sensitive crisis developments triggered by the scripted scenario, multinational actors shaped by organizational roles with different intentions and digital technologies challenged by users result in a stress test for the comprehensive organizational setting. By modular architecture and adaptive steering GLOBE is flexible and dynamic to address both specific training and analysis needs. GLOBE can easily and quickly be adapted to other scenarios, e.g. entrepreneurial and societal transformation.

In the past, main objective of GLOBE was to offer advanced training for students in virtual collaboration and data analytics. However, GLOBE advanced and offers now the opportunity to implement digital innovations and to analyze the impact of those innovations on different organizational settings in several modularized scenarios. Interestingly, by the combination of learning and innovation it tackles the above mentioned interdependent feedback between digital innovation and skill development and provides a framework to investigate the mutual impacts.

In sum, GLOBE is used twofold: (1) to provide a learning environment for students not only to familiarize with real world scenarios like multinational crisis management but also to advance their skills in project management, leadership, and digital competencies (2) to investigate the interplay of human factors [10], under psychological and management aspects. Both use cases together can be implemented in the Living Lab concept. By that, innovation by co-creation and experiential learning go hand in hand for the purpose of organizational transformation.

2 Implementation of the GLOBE Project

From Teaching to Testing

The GLOBE exercise was developed by a cooperation of the Federal University of Applied Administration Mannheim (FUM) and Prof. Dr. Bresinsky at the OTH-R in the year 2013. Since then, the exercise was conducted twice a year in total nine runs. Firstly, the idea and goal was to train and teach virtual collaboration, management and leadership of a multinational Humanitarian Aid Mission. Therefore, GLOBE uses real world scenarios like the United Nation Assistance Mission Afghanistan.

In the first runs of GLOBE 40 to 60 students at the partner university in Mannheim and 20 student in OTH-R participated.

Through the years, a development to a comprehensive exercise through the semester with project management, real-world networking and simulation exercise has been established. With a total number of 45 students formed of the OTH-R, the stable partner TEI Crete, and the new partners University of Dubrovnik, Charles University Prague and the University of Glasgow additional to the 40–60 students of the FUM, the GLOBE exercise changed its character from a pure training to a test and experimentation platform. Not only the scenario was enriched by incorporating subject matter experts like data analysts, security advisers, psychologist, and real word non-governmental as well as governmental organizations.

The following list shows the specific implementations of GLOBE (Table 1):

Table 1. Specifications of GLOBE

Year and name of GLOBE exercise	Scenario	Partners and participants	Character
2013 ADRESS/BYWAYS	United Nations Mission with headquarter (HQ) and deployed country team (CT); 6 h time shift between HQ and CT; comprehensive approach with GO, NGO and other actors; scripted real life role play, incidents and injects; time pressure, crisis development and complex problem-solving tasks;	Federal University of Applied Science Mannheim (FUM) Total: 60	Training virtual collaboration (VC) in multinational missions
2014 COMPREHENSIVE/DEPLOYED		FUM Total: 80	and application of digital analysis tools
2015 ENGAGED/FACILITATE		TEI Heraklion (TEI), FUM Total: 90	Test of different HQ structures, IT platforms
2016 GO/HORIZON		University of Dubrovnik (DIU), TEI, Subject Matter Experts (SME) Total: 120	Test of different HQ processes, IT tools
2017 IMPACT/JOINT		University of Glasgow, FUM, TEI, DIU, SME Total: 160	Controlled quasi experiment of different HQ processes

Training Objectives for Digital Competencies

So far, a systematic investigation what digital literacy implies and how it is achieved is missing in the scientific literature. Therefore, it is rather understudied which specific skills and competencies are needed for highly digitized organization [11]. From a more general perspective and based on analysis of the GLOBE exercise it can be said, that there are at least four important skill and competence domains relevant: (1) the domain of communication, (2) the domain of situational awareness, (3) the domain of information and knowledge management, and (4) the domain of data analytics. Under these domains we can identify several specific and shared skills and competencies. It is important to note, that in each domain digital hard- and software is the common factor and various digital systems, tools, and application are used for the management of the organization at all.

The following skills and competencies are of upmost relevance, regarding their specific domains:

(1) In the domain of communication:

- Synchron and asynchrony digital communication methods;
- Prioritize, sustain, and moderate communication channels;
- Affective and emotional communication management in restricted and poor communication channels; Utilization of language and text codes;
- Target and client oriented communication;

(2) The domain of situational awareness based on the domain of communication:

- Perception management and perceptual bias avoidance;
- Maintenance of individual and team situational awareness; Prediction of developments; Implementing and administrating alert and warning system

(3) In the domain of information and knowledge management:

- Platform management; Data storage management;
- Version control and management; Deconflicting and synchronizing;

(4) In the domain of data analytics:

- Management of search algorithms; Assessment of references and research results; Critical thinking and analysis
- Management and application of tool based data analysis;

The above list of skills and competencies is not comprehensive. Nevertheless, based on this list the GLOBE exercise can be adapted in a flexible manner to address special objectives. The following sample provides some specific examples to illustrate the possible features in design and scenario of the GLOBE exercise:

(1) Communication domain:

- Time shifts, availability of actors; Task overload and urgency response;
- Mixing, denying or scramble communication channels;
- Intercultural incidents, foreign languages, stress and time pressure;
- Restricting vocabulary, volume or bandwidth;

- Multiple stakeholder and social networks;

(2) Situational awareness:

- Intercultural incidents, fake news, white noise;
- Organizational changes and task management; crisis development;

(3) Information and knowledge management:

- Multiple platform requirements;
- Data corruption and loss; System downtime;

(4) Domain of data analytics:

- Big data, statistics and scenario technique;
- Heterogeneous, unreliable and missing sources;

From Experiential Learning to Testing and Experimentation in a Living Lab
From the beginning, the main trigger for the implementation and development of GLOBE was providing a learning and training platform. GLOBE uses the experiential learning approach developed by KOLB [12]. Through experiential learning as a multidisciplinary approach, comprehensive learning and understanding can be implemented. The learning process is an iterative cycle of active experimentation, concrete experience, reflective observation and abstract conceptualization [12]. The combination of different dimensions and levels of learning is increasing the effective learning outcomes of all participants. The participatory, problem-based learning puts the learner in the focus, and combines existing knowledge with their application to (co-) create solutions [13]. One important finding is, that the concept of experiential learning seems similar to the Living Lab approach. LL is a user-centered, open innovation and social learning process in real-life context to mediate and transfer knowledge and technology by engaging all participants in a process of learning, development and co-creation of pre-commercial demand [14, 15]. GLOBE utilizes both approaches experiential learning and LL in a combined concept.

The concept GLOBE offers the possibility to analyse non standardized management and leadership processes in multinational operations in a real world scenario. Furthermore, it aims to test tools and technology utilized in virtual collaboration and digitization. The LL concept serves as a test and experimentation platform, enabling all participants to be actively involved and empowered in the development and learning process for creating products and innovations, with the essential elements [16]:

(1) Infrastructure and technology
(2) Organization and legal entity
(3) Lifespan, involvement of public authorities, companies, academia and people
(4) Context (real-life)
(5) Concept of experimentation and testing
(6) Method and Activities: Co-creation, exploration, experimentation, evaluation, retention, exploitation and commercialization
(7) Principles: Continuity. openness, realism, empowerment, spontaneity.

The iterative cycles of experimentation and learning in GLOBE can be seen as suiting both the process of experiential action learning [12] and the different phases of the LL concept, integrating real-world partners and context in the academic curriculum.

The LL implies a Quadruple Helix, as multiple participants co-creating innovations and knowledge. As Public Authorities, Companies, Academia and People, which are present in the GLOBE concept as external experts from companies and organizations, the students both as Academia and People, and the FUM and experts as Public Authorities. This network provides opportunities for profound research and real-life experiences for students to prepare them for future employability.

The GLOBE concept embodies the essential elements of the Living Lab concept to offer comprehensive learning and development opportunities:

Context: As the environment and testbed infrastructure to test and experiment in real-world context with multiple stakeholders. The multinational approach scenario with the real-world partners FUM and external experts embody crisis management, leadership and management processes and product development around digitization.

Concept: Studies on innovation activities in real-life context with versatile structures, actors and roles to organize innovation, development and learning with the testbed environment. GLOBE offers a diverse set of roles within the scenario to serve as platform to experiment and test. The participants are grouped into the (1) project-management team, with Exercise Management, stakeholder analysis, scripting, documentation and Exercise Evaluation; and the (2) Training Audience as Wide Cell, Exercise Control, and participants.

Method: Within the experiential active learning and co-creation process, users and people are central to generate innovations and knowledge within the whole process. The iterative cycle of ideation, contextualization, conceptualization, development, experimentation, retention, observation, feedback and exploitation creates innovations through hands-on experiences. The GLOBE scenario combines multiple tools, as Role Play, applied project management, simulation game, inverted classroom, data analytics, observation and feedback as a mixture of traditional and innovative experimentation and learning tools in real-life context.

The GLOBE concept as a Living Lab offers the opportunity to create a real-life learning, experimentation and development environment with real-world partners to enhance learning beyond the traditional curriculum. The established concept of innovation hubs, used in technical fields can be applied to social sciences and adapted to various fields of interest to observe, test and validate technology and behaviour. The GLOBE scenario allows to examine and experiment in the urgent fields of digitization and virtual collaboration.

3 Conclusion

The set of needs and tools, as analytics, soft skills, situational awareness, intercultural competences, problem-solving and decision-making [11, 17] are not yet fully integrated in the broad curriculum of German higher education. The OTH-R is one of the first institution of higher education to implement such an integrated exercise platform.

However, trends [18] suggest that concepts like inverted classroom, blended learning and action learning concepts transform and bring benefit to learning results in education. Combination to digitization is with these concepts both necessary and possible, to teach skills towards an interactive, intensive and collaborative collaboration with ICT and personal development [18]. The Globe scenario as proposed concept to integrate these learning approaches could enhance applied learning towards future work and leadership skills. This innovative concept integrates traditional theoretical learning, with activating and collaborating approaches towards a comprehensive concept, stimulating maximum learning results.

Participatory approaches shift the learner from passive recipient of knowledge towards active co-creators and applicants of knowledge. Virtual collaboration and digitization as main part of the scenario are both vehicle to learn and experiment these new skills and tools, and object for further study to develop academic curriculum and academic research of dynamic behaviour within virtual collaboration. Globe focuses on the need of developing a set of skills for the digitization, namely confident dealing with information and privacy issues, complex problem solving, analytical thinking, collaborative and self-organized working in heterogeneous teams, agility, interpersonal, social and intercultural skills [18]. The scenario combines concepts to integration & collaboration, gaming & simulation and blended learning [18] to combine all innovative with traditional approaches for digitization and traditional education. This adaptive and agile concept will suit the complex requirements of modern education.

This combined innovative education project defines a comprehensive learning platform, bridging theory and practice in the fields of virtual collaboration, use of ICT, dynamic social behaviour and basic theories of 'Management and leadership of a multidisciplinary project under guidance of a UN mission'. The virtual and real interaction is addressing the concept of active and experiential learning theories and introduces innovative features for a comprehensive learning environment at Universities of applied sciences throughout Germany.

References

1. Brynjolffson, E., McAfee, A.: The Second Machine Age: Work, Progress, and Prosperity in a Time of Brilliant Technologies. W.W. Norton & Company, NY (2014)
2. Geschwill, R., Nieswandt, M.: Laterales Management. Das Erfolgsprinzip für Unternehmen im digitalen Zeitalter, Springer, Wiesbaden (2016)
3. Bogers, M., West, J.: Managing distributed innovation: strategic utilization of open and user innovation. Creativity Innov. Manag. **21**(1), 61–75 (2012)
4. European Communities: Empowering people, driving change. Social innovation in the European Union. https://doi.org/10.2796/13155, https://publications.europa.eu/en/publication-detail/-/publication/4e23d6b8-5c0c-4d38-bd9d-3a202e6f1e81
5. Eriksson, M., Niitamo, V.P., Kulkki, S.: State-of-the-art in utilizing Living Labs approach to user-centric ICT innovation - a European approach. Center for Distance-spanning Technology, Lulea. Lulea University of Technology, Sweden, Lulea (2005)
6. Ehn, P.: Work-Oriented Design of Computer Artifacts. Lawrence Erlbaum Associates, Hillsdale (1989)

7. Qvortrup, L. (ed.): Social Experiments with Information Technology and the Challenges of Innovation, vol. 114. Springer, Heidelberg (1987)
8. Paskaleva, K.: The smart city: a nexus for open innovation? In: Proceedings of the SIGCHI Conference on Intelligent Buildings International, University of Maribor, Maribor, vol. 3, No. 3, pp. 153–171 (2011)
9. Etzkowitz, H., Leydesdorff, L.: The dynamics of innovation: from National Systems and "Mode 2" to a Triple Helix of university–industry–government relations. Res. Policy **29**(2), 109–123 (2000)
10. Badke-Schaub, P., Hofinger, G., Lauche, K. (eds.): Human Factors - Psychologie sicheren Handelns in Risikobranchen, 2nd edn. Springer, Berlin (2012)
11. OECD: OECD Skills Outlook 2015: Youth, Skills and Employability, OECD Publishing (2015). http://dx.doi.org/10.1787/9789264234178-en
12. Kolb, D.: Experiential Learning: Experience as the Source of Learning and Development. Prentice-Hall, Englewood Cliffs (1984)
13. Savery, J.R.: Overview of problem-based learning: definitions and distinctions. Interdiscip. J. Problem-Based Learn. **1**(1) (2006). https://doi.org/10.7771/1541-5015.1002
14. European Commission (EC) (2017). http://s3platform.jrc.ec.europa.eu/living-labs?inheritRedirect=true
15. Almirall, E., Wareham, J.: Living Labs: arbiters of mid- and ground-level innovation. Technol. Anal. Strateg. Manag. **23**(1), 87–102 (2011)
16. Bergvall-Kåreborn, B., et al.: A milieu for innovation - defining Living Labs. In: The 2nd ISPIM Innovation Symposium - Stimulating Recovery - The Role of Innovation Management, New York City, USA (2009)
17. Stifterverband für die Deutsche Wissenschaft e.V. & McKinsey & Company Inc.: Hochschul-Bildungsreport 2020. Hochschulbildung für die Arbeitswelt 4.0. Jahresbericht 2016. Essen (2016)
18. Hochschulforum Digitalisierung (HFD): The Digital Turn - Hochschulbildung im digitalen Zeitalter. Arbeitspapier Nr. 27. Berlin (2016)

Analysis of Motivation in Virtual Reality Stroke Rehabilitation

Paula Epure and Michael B. Holte[(⊠)]

Department of Architecture, Design and Media Technology,
Aalborg University Esbjerg, Niels Bohrs Vej 8, 6700 Esbjerg, Denmark
pepure12@student.aau.dk, mbh@create.aau.dk

Abstract. This paper investigates the post-stroke adult population and their motivation to use virtual reality rehabilitation in the rehabilitation process. The study was conducted on 10 patients, part of a rehabilitation program at NeuroRehab, Sydvestjysk Sygehus, Grindsted, Denmark. The sample of patients was divided into a control group and an experimental group, where the experimental group practiced additionally 30 min of training using a virtual reality rehabilitation system. The system consists of: a head mounted display – Oculus Rift, a motion sensor controller – Leap Motion, a desktop computer and a custom built task simulator game. To study the patients' motivation, a questionnaire based on the Intrinsic Motivation Inventory, play performance measurements, and video recordings were utilised. It is concluded that the patients who utilised the virtual rehabilitation system indicated slightly increased motivation compared to the control group.

Keywords: Motivation · Stroke · Virtual reality rehabilitation

1 Introduction

Stroke has been declared the leading cause of disability and death around the world. The majority of the surviving population experience chronic motor deficits and reduced quality of life [1]. To generate neuro-plastic change and functional motor recovery of patients' impairments, extensive amounts of practice are required, as neurophysiological data shows [2]. However, previous data indicates that patients generally perform a rather limited number of repetitive movements in conventional therapy, which is problematic for the recovery process [3]. Moreover, the efficiency of conventional rehabilitation is limited by a considerable amount of factors such as: logistical, financial, environmental and individual barriers [4]. Consequently, extensive research is focused on improving the conventional rehabilitation. A novel direction towards optimisation is the use of Virtual Reality (VR). VR can be described as a human-computer interface which invokes real-time simulations of a certain activity or environment, enabling user interaction through multiple sensory modalities [5]. VR therapy can offer a range of advantages: complete control over the stimuli (including consistency and variation of complexity), reliable records of patients' performance, a safe learning environment, individualised treatment, and increased motivation by introducing "gaming" in the rehabilitation process [6].

© ICST Institute for Computer Sciences, Social Informatics and Telecommunications Engineering 2018
A. L. Brooks et al. (Eds.): ArtsIT 2017/DLI 2017, LNICST 229, pp. 282–293, 2018.
https://doi.org/10.1007/978-3-319-76908-0_27

The aim of this study is to explore the patients' motivation in utilising VR as part of their rehabilitation process, and thereby verify the hypothesis: *the post-stroke adult population indicates superior motivation when utilising VR therapies as part of their rehabilitation program.* To verify the hypothesis an explanatory sequential design method is utilised, in which game scores, questionnaire results and video recordings are gathered for an experimental group and a control group. The experimental group utilised a VR system consisting of: a motion sensor, a head mounted display (HMD), a computer desktop and a custom built VR task simulator game.

2 Background

This section presents a summary of conventional rehabilitation describing the consequences of stroke and the common treatment applied. Subsequently, VR therapy is introduced and its possible improvements for conventional rehabilitation. Lastly, the notion of motivation is described from therapists' perspective, as well as the gaming perspective.

2.1 Conventional Rehabilitation

Generally, the post-stroke population experiences deficits which may lead to persistent or permanent functional limitations, involving paralysis, abnormal control of movements, loss of coordination, loss of range of motion, abnormal posture, spasticity, memory deficits, spatial neglect, aphasia, dyspraxia and more. These impairments are an impediment towards performing activities of daily living (ADLs: eating, dressing, waling, etc.) and Instrumental ADLs (IADLs: cooking, laundering, shopping, etc.). Hence, the post-stroke population has no capacity for living independently and being self-sufficient. On a physical level, the motor impairment following stroke starts with complete paralysis in one side of the body, usually the opposite side of the brain where the stroke occurred (hemiplegia). Subsequently, severe physical weakness is experienced in the same side as hemiplegia (hemiparesis) [1]. Motor impairment is experienced by 55% to 75% of stroke sufferers and is usually associated with reduced quality of life [2]. These patients need to re-learn basic movements in order to regain their independence. While recovery is possible, most patients will remain with permanent limitations and impairments [3].

Conventional clinical practice for stroke rehabilitation depends on clinical studies and evidence from basic science of the high potential for brain remodelling as a result of neuroplasticity after neurological injury [2, 4]. Neuroplasticity or neural plasticity represents the mechanism utilised by the brain to encode experiences and learn new behaviours. Moreover, it is also the mechanism utilised for re-learning lost behaviour in the case of a damaged brain. For neuroplasticity to occur the training has to be challenging, repetitive, task-specific, motivating, salient and intensive [4]. Currently, the resources available through conventional rehabilitation are not able to fulfil the requirements for enhancing post-injury neuroplasticity. The limitations of standard rehabilitation are: time-consuming, labour and resource intensive, dependent on patient compliance, limited geographical availability, modest and delayed effects in some patients, initially underappreciated benefits by stroke survivors, and it requires cost/insurance coverage after the initial phase of treatment. Although, through conventional rehabilitation patients can benefit of partial recovery, neuroplasticity should be more stimulated. Therefore, research is conducted to indicate the possibility of introducing Virtual Reality in conventional therapy [5].

2.2   Virtual Reality Therapy

Virtual Reality can be defined as a computer-based technology which enhance user interaction with a multisensory stimulated environment and provides real-time feedback on user performance. Currently, most of the VR systems are primarily audio-visual experiences utilising either a computer screen or a HMD to immerse the user in a virtual environment. Additional sound information is provided through speakers or headphones. Furthermore, advanced VR systems are using haptic feedback technology, which has the advantage of stimulating the sense of touch by applying forces, vibrations or motions as tactile information. VR has been introduced in various fields (military training, architecture, sports, art, medicine, etc.). For stroke rehabilitation, VR has the possibility of applying relevant concepts such as: high repetition, high intensity, and task-oriented training of the paretic side [5]. The benefits that VR can offer for stroke rehabilitation are extensive: specificity and adaptability to each patient and disease, ability to provide patient engagement, tele-rehabilitation and remote date-access, precise assessment and safety [6]. However, for this study the focus is on repetition and motivation.

As previously stated, repetition is crucial for neuroplasticity to occur, therefore patient compliance and motivation has a highly important role in the rehabilitation process. A functional outcome of the therapy depends primordially on active cooperation of the patient. Motivation can be increased by applying a serious game format to the training sessions [6]. The benefits of increased motivation are not only towards a more active participation but also towards longer and more lasting training sessions. Therefore, greater physically and cognitively recovery can be achieved if specialists will acknowledge and implement more motivational factors in the rehabilitation process [7]. However, currently, only a few prototype systems for this population exist, and the games are rather simplistic and often neglected in terms of effectiveness and suitability for the rehabilitation process.

2.3   Motivation

There is a common belief, among specialists in rehabilitation, that motivation of patients has a determinant role in the outcome of rehabilitation. However, the understanding of the term *motivation* varies from one physiotherapist to another [8]. Rehabilitation literature indicates no consensus regarding the nature and determinants of motivation, as specialists often disagree over the meaning of "motivation". There is a common belief that motivated patients have higher performances in rehabilitation exercises, and are expected to recover faster and more successfully compared to unmotivated patients. Specialists in rehabilitation are constantly aware of patients' motivation and try to improve it based on personal beliefs [9]. Maclean et al. [9]

conducted a study in which they interviewed 32 professionals regarding patients' motivation. When listing the determinants factors of the rehabilitation outcome, all the professionals mentioned the term motivation, even though the interviewer never introduced the topic. The results of the experiment indicated different factors that affect motivation: personality traits, clinical factors (age, stroke severity, cognitive function and depression), family, culture, rehabilitation environment, and therapists' behaviour. The results exposed that there are three major techniques to improve patients' motivation: setting relevant rehabilitation goals, providing information about rehabilitation, and accessing and using the patient's cultural norm [9].

Ryan et al. [10] investigated motivation for computer game-play and its effects on well-being by applying the Self-Determination Theory (SDT) developed by Lanyi et al. [11]. They hypothesised that the reason behind increased motivation in gaming is that players experience autonomy, competence and relatedness while playing. Consequently, a satisfactory experience causes motivation to play, while a frustrating experience results in a deficit in persistence. SDT focuses on factors that are facilitating or undermining motivation, both extrinsic and intrinsic. According to SDT, the core type of motivation for play and sports is the intrinsic motivation. This is applicable for when playing games also, as, like sport, players do not acquire extra-game rewards or approval – most players play to be involved in gaming activities and sometimes they face disapproval. Therefore, the motivation to play games is intrinsically satisfying because players are seeking "fun". Hence, this paper focuses on intrinsic motivation.

There are several factors that can support or undermine motivation such as: autonomy, competence, presence and intuitive controls [10]. Autonomy relates to willingness or a sense of volition when performing a task. Autonomy in games can be enhanced by: provision for choice, use of rewards as informational feedback and non-controlling instructions. Competence refers to a need for challenge and experiencing efficiency. Factors that enhance competence are: opportunities to acquire new skills, optimal level of challenge, and receiving positive feedback. Perceived competence is one of the most important satisfactory factors in games, as it enhances the players' experience of feeling accomplished and in control [12]. Another factor to be considered in game motivation is presence, which refers to the experience that one is within the game world. Presence is widely associated with the concept of flow [13] which is an intrinsic motivation theory. To enhance presence, game designers attempt (s) to create a realistic and authentic VE with a focus on compelling storylines and graphic environments. Lastly, another variable of interest is intuitive controls which can determine the level of players' satisfaction. Intuitive controls are defined as game controls that are easily understandable and do not interfere with the sense of presence [12]. Based on this theory, there is a need to apply the same motivational factor for rehabilitation game as they are in entertaining games.

Although motivation has been discussed in several studies in the field of virtual reality for rehabilitation, there is a need to measure it and acknowledge its importance within the field.

3   Methods

This section presents the target group and ethical consideration involved in the experiment conducted. Next, the system development and functionality is explained. Lastly, the data gathering and treatment methods are introduced.

3.1   Target Group and Ethical Considerations

The experiment was conducted at NeuroRehab Centre, Sydvestjysk Sygehus, Grindsted, Denmark on a sample of 10 test subjects. The sample was formed by three women and seven men with a recently stroke occurrence (no longer than 2 months). The test subjects were split in two groups: a control group where no extra treatment was applied, and an experimental group utilising a VR system for 30 min.

For a balanced randomisation of the two groups, a pre-test was applied. Each test subject performed a Box and Block [14] test for motor skills evaluation purpose. To gain validity and replicability of the experiment, different factors were considered when allocating the patients, such as: pre-test score of the Box and Block test, stroke location, gender and age. The patient information can be seen in Table 1.

Table 1.   Patient information (BB: Box and Blocks, R: Right arm, L: Left arm).

Nr.	Name	Age	Gender (M/F)	Stroke location	Paraplegic side	BB score (R/L max: 150)	Group (E/C)
1	P	58	M	Left side	Right	R20:L22	C
2	PV	77	M	Right side	Left	R19:L6	E
3	L	74	M	Left side	Right	R15:L49	C
4	J	74	M	Cerebellum	Right	R15:L23	E
5	S	70	F	Left side	Right	R45:L63	C
6	M	61	M	Both sides	Right	R46:L50	E
7	PO	80	M	Right side	Left	R44:L39	C
8	F	85	M	Right side	Left	R50:L18	E
9	R	62	F	Frontal lobe	Both	R46:L46	C
10	B	60	F	Left side	Right	R40:L45	E

Due to the medical sensitivity of the study, vigorous ethical considerations were discussed and applied regarding: informed consent, deception, debriefing, confidentiality and protection from physical and psychological harm. The therapists and the patients were fully informed about the experiment and asked to sign a consent form. The test subjects agreed to be video recorded, accepting that the recordings will only be used for research purpose. All the patients were supervised by their therapist during the experiment to avoid any physical and/or psychological harm. The patients had the right to quit the experiment at any time, and their names and personal data remained confidential (only their initials are used as reference).

3.2   System Development and Functionality

The proposed system constitutes: a hand-tracking device (Leap Motion) motion sensitive to different movements and gestures, a HMD (Oculus Rift) simulating the Virtual Environment (VE), a desktop computer (PC) and a custom build task simulator game – Virtual Reality Kitchen (VRK). The tracking device is placed on the headset for higher accuracy and realism. The positional tracking camera for the headset is placed approximately 70 cm in front of the patient at a height of 130 cm. The room used for the experiment contained solely artificial light for a more accurate functionality of the tracking device and camera.

VRK is a task simulator game that replicates training exercises from Activity of Daily Living (ADL), which are conventionally applied in rehabilitating stroke patients. VRK is a PC-game, controlled with Leap Motion using the headset as a display. The game has been designed to replicate tasks for upper extremities and trunk rehabilitation with a focus on: reaching, grabbing, leaning, pinching and grasping.

The VRK contains two tasks: *coffee making* and *grocery sorting*, and a *calibration scene*. The coffee making scene implies eight actions such as: *opening tab, lifting coffee machine lid, filling the glass with water, pouring the water then the coffee in the machine, placing the jug in the machine, closing the lid* and *pressing the on/off button.* A maximum amount of 60 points is rewarded for completion, in which 10 points are given as time bonus if completed in less than 3 min. The grocery sorting scene implies sorting and placing of 17 items in one of three possible locations: freezer in the left side, fridge in the right side and four shelves on the wall in front of the patient. Each correctly placed item is awarded with 10 points, consequently a maximum amount of 170 points. The maximum achievable total score including the 10 point bonus is 180 points. The calibration scene is specifically designed to define an individual's playing space based on the patients' abilities. To ensure an appropriate level of difficulty for the tasks, all the possible interactions are occurring in the calibrated space. The requirements for calibration are reaching as far as possible to the left side, right side, and top.

The VE is replicating a fully furnished kitchen with custom created objects designed in Blender (a free source 3D modelling software). The system was developed in Unreal Engine 4 (a suite of tools utilised for design and game development). This software was chosen for its important feature – the Blue Print – a visual scripting system utilised for quick design and development. The language used for the scripts is C++.

3.3   Test Procedure and Data Gathering

For this study an explanatory sequential design method is utilised. The experiment was conducted at NeuroRehab, Sydvestjysk Sygehus, Grindsted, Denmark, over period of four weeks. The experimental group had 3 weekly interactions with the system of 30 min duration in addition to their conventional rehabilitation in accordance with National Clinical Guidelines for Rehabilitation [7]. For each test session, in-game scores were registered and video were recorded for each patient in the experimental group, while the control group followed their conventional rehabilitation treatment. To measure the patients' motivation, a questionnaire was applied at the end of the last test session for both the control and the experimental group. Consequently, the data gathered consisted of quantitative data: in-game scores and questionnaire answers (Likets scale), and qualitative data: video recordings.

The analysis of the in-game scores and the motivational indicators of the questionnaire will indicate if there is a correlation between motivation and performance. The applied 7-point Likert scale questionnaire consists of 16 items adopted from the Intrinsic Motivation Inventory – a multidimensional measurement tool for assessing participants' subjective experience regarding a certain activity in laboratory experiments [15]. The questionnaire's scale is used to assess participants' *interest/enjoyment, perceived competence, effort/importance, pressure/tension* and *value/usefulness*. These five sub-scale represented different factors influencing motivation. The items were selected, adapted and translated to Danish (the native language of the participants). The wording of the items is identical except the activity. However, there is a difference between questionnaires based on which group it was applied to. The experimental group has phrases such as "playing" and "using system", while the control group has phrases such as "physical training" and "exercising". For grading the items a colour scheme was designed with seven circles coloured from red to green, where red signifies 1 point, yellow: 4 points, and green: 7 points. The points signify: 1: not true at all, 4:

Table 2. Results of the motivation questionnaire.

IMI	Control group patients					Experimental group patients				
Item	P	L	S	PO	R	PV	J	M	F	B
Q1	6	6	–	6	–	3	–	7	6	6
Q2	7	2	–	6	–	7	–	6	7	7
Q3	6	7	–	7	–	7	–	6	7	7
Q4	6	5	–	6	–	5	–	7	6	7
Q5	7	7	–	7	–	5	–	6	7	7
Q6	6	6	–	3	–	6	–	7	5	7
Q7	4	7	–	6	–	4	–	6	6	7
Q8	7	6	–	7	–	6	–	6	7	7
Q9	5	2	–	6	–	4	–	6	5	7
Q10	6	4	–	6	–	4	–	7	7	7
Q11	7	6	–	7	–	5	–	6	7	7
Q12	2	6	–	6	–	7	–	6	6	7
Q13	7	7	–	7	–	4	–	6	6	7
Q14	7	7	–	7	–	6	–	4	7	7
Q15	5	7	–	7	–	7	–	6	5	7
Q16	5	5	–	6	–	4	–	7	7	7
Total	93	90	–	100	–	84	–	99	101	111
Mean	5.8	5.6	–	6.2	–	5.2	–	6.1	6.3	6.9
Mean	5.8					6.1				

somewhat true, and 7: very true. The purpose of the colour scheme is to simplify the grading by offering additional visual cues, as the participants suffer of cognitive impairment. Finally, video recordings were analysed and partially transcribed with focus on actions and speech that are relevant for the concept of motivation. To this end, the patients' reactions and attitude towards the system were analysed based on motivational factors used in questionnaire.

4 Results

This section presents the results from the Intrinsic Motivation Inventory questionnaire applied to both groups (Table 2), the results from the in-game scores showing the patients performance in the experimental group (Table 3), and extracted themes from the video analysis (Table 4).

Table 3. In-game scores for the experimental group.

Patient	Week	Day	Score 1st scene	Score 2nd scene	Total score	Mean SD
PV	1	1	10	10	20	
PV	2	1	10	20	30	45
PV	2	2	10	50	60	23.8
PV	3	1	10	60	70	
M	1	1	60	170	230	
M	1	2	60	160	220	
M	2	1	60	150	210	223,3
M	2	2	60	160	220	8.16
M	2	3	60	170	230	
M	3	1	60	170	230	
F	1	1	50	140	190	
F	1	2	50	140	190	
F	2	1	50	160	210	205
F	2	2	60	160	220	12.24
F	2	3	50	160	210	
F	3	1	60	150	210	
B	1	1	50	170	230	
B	1	2	60	120	180	
B	2	1	60	170	230	220
B	2	2	60	170	230	22.36
B	2	3	60	170	230	

Table 4. Observations from video recordings.

Patient	Overall reactions - motivational factors				
	Enjoyment	Competence	Effort	Tension	Importance
PV	Negative, frustrated	Not perceived, defeated	Very high	Very high	Useless, very low
M	Positive, joy, fun	Not mentioned	Very high	High	High
F	Positive, joy, fun	Average perceived	High	Medium	Medium
B	Positive, excitement, happiness	Highly perceived	High	Medium	Very high

5 Discussion

This section discusses the results by comparing questionnaire results and in-game scores in-between patients.

The highest obtainable average score for the questionnaire is 7, as it is based on a 7-point Likert scale. The highest average score registered is 6.9 by B in the experimental group. However, the lowest average obtained by PV 5.2 is also in the experimental group. A total average score was calculated and it indicates that the experimental group score (6.1) is slightly superior to the control group score (5.8). Hence, it can be assumed that the motivation of patients from the experimental group was slightly higher compared to the control group. However, during the experiment three patients decided to stop participating in the experiment: two from the control group were discharged faster than expected, and one from the experimental group quitted because his condition was too poor to exercise with the VRK.

Maclean et al. [9] suggest that relevant rehabilitation goals, providing information regarding rehabilitation and using the patient's cultural norm were primordial factors for increasing motivation. The VRK succeeded to deliver relevant rehabilitation, as the tasks were following ADL training exercises. However, the VRK did not provide information regarding rehabilitation which might have led to decreased motivation. The patient's cultural norm is a factor included in VRK, as all the objects and the environment were designed to appeal the elderly Danish population. Patient B reacted positively to the environment, sustaining that she could easily identify all the objects, which were familiar to her. This might have influenced her attitude towards the VRK, as she truly believed the game was suitable for her. On contrary, the video recordings show that one of the patients, PV, could not identify any of the objects present in the VE, due to his cognitive impairments. This might have influence his decision to quit the experiment.

Ryan et al. [10] sustain that to increase motivation in gaming players should experience autonomy, competence and relatedness while playing. In the VRK competence was achieved by implementing the calibration scene which allowed the players to establish an appropriate level of difficulty for their tasks. Therefore, each time they calibrated the game they could observe the improvement by comparing the dimension of the playing space. Because the differences were sometimes low and hard to observe, some of the therapist were always discussing and comparing their movement range. Autonomy was also implemented in the system through the usage of the HMD Oculus Rift, which allows the user to visually separate from the real world. Even though the therapists were supervising the test sessions and the patients were not alone, wearing the HMD gave the patients a sense of independence. E.g., after patient F finished playing the game in one of the test session, he reported that he "came back from the virtual world". This indicates a sense of presence that he experienced and it correlated with the flow theory [12]. The relatedness of the tasks for the patients is debatable. Although the tasks were extracted from the ADL model utilised for conventional rehabilitation, some of the patients felt more related than others. During the experiment some of the men stated that they were not particular interested in kitchen activities. PV who chose to quit the experiment, sustained that he could not recognise nor relate to the environment at all. Moreover, he could not see the purpose of the VR training, as he was not familiar with the tasks or objects in the VE. However, the only woman from the experimental group, B, felt highly related to the environment. It can be assumed that the tasks and the VE were genre related. However, they were adapted based on ADL, and are conventionally part of a rehabilitation program.

According to Ryan et al. [10], a satisfactory experience increases motivation to play, while frustration results in decreased persistence. This can be seen in Table 3, as PV obtained a very low in-game score, which led to lowering his persistence from one test session to another, thus quitting the experiment. As a result, he had the lowest score registered for the questionnaire with an average of 5.2. Although considering that the highest possible achievable score is 7, and that his experience was rather negative, the obtained score is relatively high. On contrary, the patients who obtained the highest scores were motivated to continue playing as many times as possible. Both M and F tested the system six times (Table 3). M achieved the highest in-game scores and the lowest SD, although he scored average (6.1) in the questionnaire on motivation. This might be due to the fact that M was not able to communicate enough during the testing sessions. Besides the feedback received from in-game scores, the patients received verbal and sometimes physical feedback from their therapists. For M the lack of responsiveness caused by his condition might have influenced his overall perception of the system.

Based on the video recordings it was discovered that the patients had an overall positive reaction to the VRK and experienced excitement during the test sessions. However, B had an outstanding reaction by being constantly highly immersed in the game. She was laughing continuously and cursing when the system was not reacting as she wanted to. On contrary, M was very quiet during his interactions with the system. It was observed that M was highly immersed in the game and aspired to gain the maximum score every time. F verbalised his reactions, however, his immersion and motivation were perceived to be lower compared to B and M. Contrary, PV experienced negative reactions towards the game. In general, the encountered differences in how the patients perceived the system correlate well with the findings of Maclean et al. [9]: personality traits, clinical factors (age, stroke severity, cognitive function and depression), family, culture, rehabilitation environment, and therapists' behaviour.

6 Conclusion

The hypothesis of this study: *the post-stroke adult population indicates superior motivation when utilising VR therapies as part of their rehabilitation program*, proved to be true. Based on the discussion above it can be concluded that the patients in the experimental group presented slightly higher motivation when utilising VRK, as part of their rehabilitation process in comparison to the control group. Furthermore, the three factors from the STD: autonomy, competence and relatedness were important in determining the level of motivation of patients. However, other factors, such as: personality traits, clinical factors, family, culture, rehabilitation environment and therapists' behaviour seem to be factors of influence.

Acknowledgments. The authors would like to thank Erling Pedersen from CoLab Vest, Jonas Drefeld from Syddansk Sundhedsinnovation, Tobias Theodorus Perquin from Teknologisk Institute, and the therapists at NeuroRehab, Sydvestjysk Sygehus, Grindsted, Denmark.

References

1. Perry, J., Andureu, J., Cavallaro, F., Veneman, J., Carmien, S., Keller, T.: Effective game use in neurorehabilitation: user-centered perspectives. In: Felicia, P. (ed.): Handbook of Research on Improving Learning and Motivation through Educational Games: Multidisciplinary Approaches, 1st edn., pp. 683–725. IGI Global (2011)
2. Duncan, P., Zorowitz, R., Bates, B., Choi, J., Glasberg, J., Graham, G., Katz, R., Lamberty, K., Reker, D.: Management of adult stroke rehabilitation care: a clinical practice guideline. Stroke **36**(9), 100–143 (2005)
3. Krakauer, J.: Motor learning: its relevance to stroke recovery and neurorehabilitation. Current Opin. Neurol. **19**(1), 84–90 (2006)
4. Kleim, J., Jones, T.: Principles of experience-dependent neural plasticity: implications for rehabilitation after brain damage. J. Speech Lang. Hear. Res. **51**(1), 225 (2008)
5. Saposnik, G., Levin, M.: Virtual reality in stroke rehabilitation: a meta-analysis and implications for clinicians. Stroke **42**(5), 1380–1386 (2011)
6. De Mauro, A.: Virtual Reality based Rehabilitation and Game Technology. In: EICS4Med, p. 48 (2011)
7. Flores, E., Tobon, G., Cavallaro, E., Cavallaro, F., Perry, J., Keller, T.: Improving patient motivation in game development for motor deficit rehabilitation. In: ACE International Conference on Advances in Computer Entertainment Technology, Yokohama, Japan, pp. 381–384 (2008)
8. Maclean, N., Pound, P., Wolfe, C., Rudd, A.: Qualitative analysis of stroke patients' motivation for rehabilitation. BMJ **321**(7268), 1051–1054 (2000)
9. Maclean, N., Pound, P., Wolfe, C., Rudd, A.: The concept of patient motivation: a qualitative analysis of stroke professionals' attitudes. Stroke **33**(2), 444–448 (2002)
10. Ryan, R., Rigby, C., Przybylski, A.: The motivational pull of video games: a self-determination theory approach. Motiv. Emotion **30**(4), 344–360 (2006)
11. Lanyi, C., Szucs, V.: Motivating rehabilitation through competitive gaming. In: Vogiatzaki, E., Krukowski, A. (eds.) Modern Stroke Rehabilitation Through e-Health-Based Entertainment, pp. 137–167. Springer, Cham (2015). https://doi.org/10.1007/978-3-319-21293-7_5

12. Ryan, R., Deci, E.: Self-determination theory and the facilitation of intrinsic motivation, social development, and well-being. Am. Psychol. **55**(1), 68–78 (2000)
13. Nakamura, J., Csikszentmihalyi, M.: The concept of flow theory. In: Snyder, C., Lopez, S. (eds.) The Oxford Handbook of Positive Psychology, 2nd edn., pp. 89—105. Oxford University, New York (2002)
14. Mathiowetz, V., Volland, G., Kashman, N., Weber, K.: Adult norms for the box and block test of manual dexterity. Am. J. Occup. Ther. **39**(6), 386–391 (1985)
15. Deci, E., Ryan, R.: Intrinsic Motivation Inventory (IMI). http://selfdeterminationtheory.org/intrinsic-motivation-inventory

A Review on Individual Assessment of Strength Training Using Smartphone Applications

Nicolai B. K. Jensen and Michael B. Holte$^{(\boxtimes)}$

Department of Architecture, Design and Media Technology,
Aalborg University Esbjerg, Niels Bohrs Vej 8, 6700 Esbjerg, Denmark
nbkj12@student.aau.dk, mbh@create.aau.dk

Abstract. This paper presents a state of the art review of popular strength training applications. The literature review and heuristic evaluation presented in this paper show that there is a large selection of strength training applications on the Android Market, which is not build on behavioural change theories. Furthermore, these provide very limited variety and use of sensory feedback. Additionally, only few applications deliver extended and detailed instructional information, meaning that the user needs prior strength training knowledge to achieve full usage. Nevertheless, it is believed that these applications could have great potential to fill a hole in the fitness and health market, and provide users with more affordable and available strength training support.

Keywords: Fitness · Health · Human-computer interaction
Mobile applications · Skill assessment · Strength training

1 Introduction

Exercising regularly is a key factor for maintaining personal health and physical well-being. The Danish board of health recommends that the average person should perform approximately 30 min of moderate physical activity per day to insure personal health [1]. However, to maintain motivation and encourage people to perform physical activity, such as strength training, is difficult, since it requires a general knowledge on exercise selection and execution, in order to improve personal weak areas and avoid injuries [2–4]. Therefore, it is important to find new effective ways of providing people with the right information regarding fitness and health.

Maintaining an exercise regime and getting effective over an extended period, requires a significant level of discipline and motivation. Here, it has been proven highly effective having access to a personal trainer, both on adherence and motivation [3, 5]. The continuous monitoring of exercise execution, individualized advice and corrections, and motivational feedback, are just some of the roles undertaken by a personal trainer, which can lead to successful results [3, 5]. However, having a personal trainer can be costly and intrusive, depending on the extent of the inquired service [3]. Studies have shown that fitness and health technology have the potential to improve physical health, and increase healthcare awareness with the use of fewer resources [5–8].

Mobile phone or smartphones are rapidly becoming more essential and widespread part of modern life. These smartphones are embedded with powerful sensors, such as

© ICST Institute for Computer Sciences, Social Informatics and Telecommunications Engineering 2018
A. L. Brooks et al. (Eds.): ArtsIT 2017/DLI 2017, LNICST 229, pp. 294–303, 2018.
https://doi.org/10.1007/978-3-319-76908-0_28

accelerometer, digital compass, gyroscope, GPS, microphone and cameras, all of which allows for great utility and possibilities [9]. These technological advancements have allowed health applications to utilise these sensor information for health and fitness feedback, such as heart rate monitors, step counter, exercise trackers, etc. [5]. However, many of these applications and technologies have deficiencies and limits, because they are not based on behavioural theories and guidelines from the medical and health industry [6, 7].

In the field of rehabilitation and strength training, studies have shown that the use of biofeedback technology can significantly improve the health and mobility of people suffering from brain injury, cerebral palsy and stroke [10–12]. However, very few commercial applications have directly been made for the purpose of strength training.

This paper performs a state of the art review of current commercial applications and scientific studies on strength training support, inspired by a previous study [5], and provide recommendation for future applications. This is done by firstly investigating what criteria is needed for a strength training application to be considered successful, then reviewing how similar applications are used within the scientific field to improve fitness and health (Sect. 2). Next, we review the current top 10 strength training applications on the android market, and make a heuristic evaluation of the current applications on the market (Sect. 3), along with future design recommendations for the development of a successful strength training application (Sect. 4). Finally concluding remarks are given (Sect. 5).

2 Literature Review

As stated in the organisation of this paper, the literature review first investigate what criteria is needed for a strength training application to be considered successful (Sect. 2.1), then reviewing how similar applications are used within the scientific field to improve fitness and health (Sect. 2.2).

2.1 Criteria of Success for Strength Training

In order to define the criteria of success for a strength training application, it is needed to have an understanding of what makes a successful strength training regime. However, since strength training is a large area of sports medicine and biology, which spans over both biomechanical and physiological areas, and is larger than can be addressed in this review, this paper will solely provide a basis for understanding the general aspects of strength training, which can provide a basis for the criteria of success.

What is Strength Training? The human body consists of a frame (the skeleton) and expanding and contracting tissue called muscles. It is through the function and positioning of these muscles that the human body becomes mobile. During strength training the muscles becomes stronger and more effective. Strength training is defined as the process of breaking and rebuilding muscle tissue. This process implies inflicting a form of stress on the body, both physically and mentally. The body's reaction to this form of stress is to adapt by reshaping and rebuilding muscle tissue, which can withstand this impact [13, 14]. The chemical environment of the muscle changes during strength training, by the process of energy stores depletion and lactic acid accumulation, which gives the feeling of fatigue. This, alongside the breakdown of muscle tissue, is what signals the body to improve from its current state [14]. Unexpectedly, the process of self-repair and improvement happens, not during the execution of strength training, but in the resting period that follows [13].

What Make a Successful Training Regime? A successful strength training regime is dependent on many variables, such as *intensity, volume, frequency, periodization* and *exercise selection*.

When designing a strength training program, *intensity* is one of the crucial variables to maximize strength. It refers to the load or poundage used during an exercise. *Intensity* is described as the percentage of the one rep maximum load (1RM) lifted [15]. The body's reaction to a high training intensity is to adapt by increasing neural activation; increased peak in electromyographic activity in the muscle, which relates to an increased rate of force development [13–15].

Training *volume* is defined as the total volume performed over a given exercise, and is calculated by the repetitions × sets × weight used. As well as *intensity*, *volume* is an important factor when trying to gain strength, since one has to increase volume over time in order to increase muscle fibre activation and size [13, 15]. Also related to *volume* is the *frequency*, since the total volume over a week is determined by the number of times one hit certain muscle parts during a week. The *frequency* is therefore defined as the number of time one workout a particular muscle. Here it is recommended that one workout each muscle part at least twice a week [13, 15].

The concepts of *periodization* builds on the principle that the training year is often divided into different periods of training, with different focus for each period, to achieve improvement. Within each sport, there are large individual differences, as some athletes are planning a relatively short duration (days/weeks) to achieve a peak once or twice a year, while other athletes in a long season are expected to peak every weekend. Strength training athletes often use the principle of training with high volume and low intensity in the individual exercises, when there is a long time to form the peak, and gradually increase the intensity and maintain or gradually reduce the amount as the peak approaches. Strength training is heavily dependent on other training activities (technique, endurance, etc.) during the week [13, 15].

Lastly, in an effective strength training program several exercises for each muscle/muscle group are used, such that the benefit of small differences in the activation, affect the muscle slightly differently. The order of the exercises within a training program can be varied. However, it is recommended that firstly one train the large muscle groups, so that they are not fatigue by the peripheral muscle groups, thereby determining whether one can lift heavy loads [13, 15].

Taking this information into consideration, it can be assumed that any successful strength training application allows for individual control of these factors. It must provide the user with the ability to, firstly, select exercises based on the needs, and track one's intensity, volume and frequency. To this end, it must provide a means of periodization for the user, since this is a fairly complex task, which requires extensive knowledge. Lastly, it must provide a basis for tracking one's performance over time.

2.2   Related Work

With the intention of providing future application developers with recommendations based on the review of other studies and applications, it is necessary to look into what have currently been done within the community and what do the current applications utilise. In this section, related work, studies and similar application are reviewed.

Automatic Assessment of Physical Activity. Conventional methods for measuring and improving exercise execution involve physiotherapists or personal trainers, who observe and correct the person performing the exercise. This method has proven highly effective and motivating for the user [3, 4]. However, this method has significant deficiencies in cost, accuracy, opportunity, coverage, and adherence. A physiotherapist or a personal trainer typically splits their attention among several patients at different locations, which means that the patients or clients have to be self-sufficient at some level. Self-reporting is often used in order to ensure that the patients or clients execute the exercises themselves; however, this is often inaccurate due to forgetfulness or un- and intentional misreporting, or lack of knowledge on how to correctly perform the exercises [16].

Researches have investigated how to improve self-reporting, by using wearable sensors to recognise, classify and report activities done. Most studies have proven the effectiveness of wearable sensors on activity recognition [2, 17–19]. However, the majority of this research has been done in controlled environments and with the focus on rehabilitation, and in most cases solely GPS and/or accelerometers have been used [6, 8, 16–18, 20].

In regards to the realisation outside the scientific field and towards the commercial market, there are many applications created for the purpose of improving training and health. Since smartphones are both highly available and have several sensors that can be used, many application developers have created a vast number of fitness and health applications with functionality, such as information distribution, exercise library, training logging and tracking tool [5–7, 20]. The state of the art applications mostly use accelerometer and GPS, and in some cases heart rate monitors and calorie counters are also used [5–7, 20]. However, reviews of these applications have shown that they are not based on behavioural change theories or guidelines, and lack biofeedback [6, 21].

Several studies have looked into creating embodied virtual trainer applications, which use all of the above mentioned features to improve health, execution and adherence [5, 16]. These studies found that the use of mobile devices and virtual trainers has big potential; however, the applications should integrate behavioural change theories into the design, and sensors should be implemented to improve the effectiveness. There are several different behavioural change theories which could be implemented [22]. The common factor for all, are that they are focusing on using response-efficacy. However, in several studies it is noted that the use of self-efficacy can provide a stronger base for change in human health behaviour [22, 23]. The notion of behavioural change theories in the design should encourage change within the user towards health behaviour and facilitate a long-term success [22, 23]. Additionally, the feedback shown on the mobile device needs to be presented in a useful manner to ensure correct usage [16, 24, 25].

3 Comparison of Smartphone Applications for Strength Training

In this section, the design space of current popular strength training smartphone applications is evaluated in a comparative review. For this purpose, applications from the Health and Fitness category on the Android Market are reviewed. In order to review most satisfying and the highest quality applications available at the time, the 10 most popular applications based on the user rating (stars) from the most popular list on the Android Market were considered (see Table 1).

Table 1. Overview of the 10 most popular smartphone applications for strength training based on the user rating (stars) from the most popular list on the Android Market.

Category	Name	Developer	Downloads	Stars
Workout planner	5 × 5	Stronglifts	500.000–1.000.000	4.9
Workout planner	30 days fitness challenge	Leap fitness group	5.000.000–10.000.000	4.8
Training journal	Fitnotes	James Gay	1.000.000–5.000.000	4.5
Workout planner	Gym workout tracker & trainer	Fitness 22	500.000–1.000.000	4.5
Training journal	Fit journals	Sultan Seidalin	50.000–100.000	4.5
Exercise archive	My fitness – strength training	Andrey Tsaregorodtsev	10.000–50.000	4.5
Exercise archive	Female fitness – bikini body	VGFIT LLC	500.000–1.000.000	4.4
Training journal	WorkIt Gym log workout tracker	WorkIt	50.000–100.000	4.4
Training journal	Strength training planner	Szabolcs Erdelyi	100–500	4.1
Workout planner	Wodster			

3.1 Heuristic Evaluation

A two-step analysis of the selected applications is carried out using a heuristic evaluation, in order to assess the functionality and features of the applications (inspired by [5]). To discover and structure the different types of applications on the market, the first step is a classification of each individual application based on the core functionality into a number of descriptive categories. In the second step, each application is used during several strength training sessions over the course of three weeks, in order to assess the features and usability.

Four heuristics were used to assess the most important aspects of strength training applications, which are explained below, based on the literature reviewed.

The application *usability* and *effectiveness* for strength training are evaluated based on interaction features (control, appropriate output and ease of use) and customizability, i.e., if the users can modify the application to their specific needs. Additionally, it is assessed whether the application allows for proper tracking of strength training features mentioned in the literature review, such as intensity, volume, frequency, periodization and exercise selection.

The *Instructional features* of the application are examined, i.e., how well the instructions of the exercises are presented on the smartphone. This included the clarity and level of instructions, sufficient level of detail, etc., providing the user with sufficient knowledge about the given exercise.

Next, the *sensor data usage* is evaluated. In other words, to what extent the application utilises the smartphone sensor capabilities, acquired information (e.g., GPS, accelerometer data, etc.) and external sensor output.

Lastly, the applications ability to *motivate* is examined. Hereunder, how well the application is suited for generating adherence and long-term motivation based on variety in the training experience and proper statistical feedback on training progress to maintain extrinsic motivation.

3.2   Results and Discussion

The classifications process identified three categories of strength training applications: *training journal*, *workout planner* and *exercise archive*.

Training journals are classified as applications, whose core feature is to work as a diary and calendar for the exercises done. Here the users can plot in their training program, exercises, set, repetitions and weight, and the application keeps track of the progress through the use of statistics. However, the applications do not propose a program regime or have in depth descriptions of each exercise.

Workout planners are applications which have pre-programmed workout regime that the users can choose between based on their needs and desire. The applications include pre-programmed weight, repetitions, sets and progress based on the 1RM value of the user.

Exercise archives are applications which provide the user with a large, detailed, browsable library of exercises that can be selected for one's training program. The applications have either a visual/written or video explanation of each exercise with key points on executions and performance.

The results of the second step of the heuristic evaluation deliver key insights into the strengths and limitations of the most popular strength training applications.

Firstly, even though the Android Market has a large selection of strength training applications, these provide very limited variety. As shown by the former classification, there are only three primary classes within the Health and Fitness category on the Android Market. To this end, when examining the different applications and categories many deficits are revealed.

The *training journal* applications lack the motivational aspect, since they provide limited progress feedback. Most of these applications present feedback in a statistical format, which requires detailed knowledge on how to use this information. As a result, they are not well suited for beginners; however, they offer great usability through the use of customisation of exercises and the information presented to an intermediate user with sufficient strength training knowledge.

The *workout planners* are very rigid and only allow for small individualization. Furthermore, even though these applications offer a large collection of workouts, they provide only limited advice and information on which workouts are best suited to one's level of experience.

The main deficit of the *exercise archive* applications is that the exercise collections are very limited in comparison to what can be found on the web. Furthermore, they lack details on how to execute the exercises correctly, and to what extent the exercises are useful.

Overall the applications provide limited to no suggestions and corrections, in order to maintain adherence and motivation. Additionally, the applications require physical interaction, meaning that the users have to divert their attention from training to log their performance, in order to get precise tracking of exercises. Additionally, even though most smartphones have a large variety of sensors available [9], the majority of applications use very limited sensory feedback.

4 Guidelines and Recommendations

When taking into account the information that has been presented in the literature review and the findings of the heuristic evaluation, this review deduce some general guidelines and recommendations for future strength training applications. These guidelines and recommendations are summarised in four core points: *foundation, usability, instructional information,* and *adherence and motivation.*

As stated in the criteria of success, a strength training application should build its *foundation* on providing the user with sufficient knowledge on how to structure the *intensity, volume, frequency, periodization* and *exercise selection* [13–15]. This can be done by providing examples based on different needs, which again can be tailored to each individual.

Furthermore, to improve the current *usability* of the applications, the way the information is presented to the user should be simplistic and easy to understand to avoid confusion and frustration [5, 16, 24–27]. Furthermore, current applications use very limited sensory feedback; despite several studies indicating that the use of the advanced sensor possibilities of modern day smartphones can be used for activity recognition and thereby limiting unnecessary interaction during workouts [5, 6, 8, 9, 16, 20, 24].

Regarding *instructional information*, the current applications have many deficits, which could easily be corrected by using existing exercise libraries such as Exorlive [28]. To this end, the possibility to expand these libraries through user customization, based on user experience and training level, could provide a larger and more detailed exercise register.

As mentioned, the conventional methods for improving *adherence and motivation,* and improving exercise execution involve physiotherapists or personal trainers who observe and correct the person performing the exercise [3, 4]. Similar studies have shown that most health and fitness applications are not based on behavioural change theories, meaning that they lack the ability to insure lifestyle changes, which is a key part of a successful strength training regime [3, 4, 13–15, 21]. Some important behavioural change theories are: goal setting, reward system, social support, and behavioural feedback [21].

Lastly, behavioural change theories are well grounded medical and scientific foundations; hence, implementing these into the design could potentially improve the overall effectiveness of the applications. Here it is advised to ensure the of use self-efficacy, through providing goals, structure and confidence in the user's progression [22]. Additionally, it should be considered whether future strength training applications should implement assessment theories from the field of sports science, where the use of external sensors such as electromyography is vital for the analysis of movement and rehabilitation [29–32].

5 Conclusion

The main goal of this paper was to perform a state of the art review with the purpose of providing the next generation of strength training applications with design recommendations and guidelines based on literature and a heuristic evaluation of the current top ranked strength training applications. The results of this review show that there is a large selection of strength training applications, which to some degree are built upon theories behind strength training. However, these applications provide very limited variety and use of sensory feedback. Additionally, only few delivers extended and detailed instructional information, meaning that the user needs prior strength training knowledge to achieve full usage. Nevertheless, based on the literature reviewed, it is believed that with the implementation of behavioural change theories [21] and assessment theories from the fields of sports science [29–32], these applications have great potential for the fitness and health market, and can provide the users with more affordable and available strength training support.

References

1. Andersen, L.B.: Fysisk Aktivitet: En Håndbog om Forebyggelse og Behandling, 3rd edn. Sundhedsstyrelsen, København (2011)
2. Chandra, H., Oakley, I., Silva, H.: Designing to support prescribed home exercises: understanding the needs of physiotherapy patients. In: ACM 7th Nordic Conference on Human-Computer Interaction: Making Sense Through Design, pp. 607–616 (2012)
3. Jeffery, R.W., Wing, R.R., Thorson, C., Burton, L.R.: Use of personal trainers and financial incentives to increase exercise in a behavioral weight-loss program. J. Consult. Clin. Psychol. 66(5), 777–783 (1998)
4. Richard, M., Christina, M.F., Deborah, L.S., Rubio, N., Kennon, M.S.: Intrinsic motivation and exercise adherence. Inter. J. Sport Psychol. 28(4), 335–354 (1997)

5. Kranz, M., Möller, A., Hammerla, N., Diewald, S., Plötz, T., Olivier, P., Roalter, L.: The mobile fitness coach: towards individualized skill assessment using personalized mobile devices. Pervasive Mob. Comput. **9**(2), 203–215 (2013)
6. Boulos, M.N.K., Brewer, A.C., Karimkhani, C., Buller, D.B., Dellavalle, R.P.: Mobile medical and health apps: state of the art, concerns, regulatory control and certification. Online J. Pub. Health Inf. **5**(3), 229 (2014)
7. Cowan, L.T., Van Wagenen, S.A., Brown, B.A., Hedin, R.J., Seino-Stephan, Y., Hall, P.C., West, J.H.: Apps of steel: are exercise apps providing consumers with realistic expectations? a content analysis of exercise apps for presence of behavior change theory. Health Educ. Behav. **40**(2), 133–139 (2013)
8. Liu, C., Zhu, Q., Holroyd, K.A., Seng, E.K.: Status and trends of mobile-health applications for IOS devices: a developer's perspective. J. Syst. Softw. **84**(11), 2022–2033 (2011)
9. Lane, N.D., Miluzzo, E., Lu, H., Peebles, D., Choudhury, T., Campbell, A.T.: A survey of mobile phone sensing. IEEE Commun. Mag. **48**(9), 140–150 (2010)
10. Yoo, J.W., Lee, D.R., Sim, Y.J., You, J.H., Kim, C.J.: Effects of innovative virtual reality game and emg biofeedback on neuromotor control in cerebral palsy. Bio-Med. Mater. Eng. **24**(6), 3613–3618 (2014)
11. Coleman, K.: Electromyography based human-computer-interface to induce movement in elderly persons with movement impairments. In: ACM EC/NSF Workshop on Universal Accessibility of Ubiquitous Computing: Providing for the Elderly, pp. 75–79 (2001)
12. Shusong, X., Xia, Z.: EMG-driven computer game for post-stroke rehabilitation. In: IEEE Conference on Robotics, Automation and Mechatronics, pp. 32–36 (2010)
13. Bojsen-Møller, J., Løvind-Andersen, J., Olsen, S., Trolle, M., Zacho, M., Aagaard, P.: Styrketræning, 2nd ed., vol. 2. Danmarks Idræts-Forbund. Brøndby (2006)
14. Borch, C.M., Milandt, J., Bundgaard, N., Meiborn, J., Bundgaard, T., Egstrup, G., Tybjerg-Pedersen, E.: Fysisk Træning, 5th ed., Danmarks Idræts-Forbund, Brøndby (2006)
15. Tan, B.: Manipulating resistance training program variables to optimize maximum strength in men: a review. J. Strength Cond. Res. **13**(3), 289–304 (1999)
16. Buttussi, F., Chittaro, L., Nadalutti, D.: Bringing mobile guides and fitness activities together: a solution based on an embodied virtual trainer. In: ACM 8th Conference on Human-Computer Interaction with Mobile Devices and Services, pp. 29–36 (2006)
17. Lester, J., Choudhury, T., Borriello, G.: A practical approach to recognizing physical activities. In: Fishkin, K.P., Schiele, B., Nixon, P., Quigley, A. (eds.) Pervasive 2006. LNCS, vol. 3968, pp. 1–16. Springer, Heidelberg (2006). https://doi.org/10.1007/11748625_1
18. Chang, K.-H., Chen, M.Y., Canny, J.: Tracking free-weight exercises. In: Krumm, J., Abowd, G.D., Seneviratne, A., Strang, T. (eds.) UbiComp 2007. LNCS, vol. 4717, pp. 19–37. Springer, Heidelberg (2007). https://doi.org/10.1007/978-3-540-74853-3_2
19. Ermes, M., Pärkkä, J., Mäntyjärvi, J., Korhonen, I.: Detection of daily activities and sports with wearable sensors in controlled and uncontrolled conditions. IEEE Trans. Inf. Technol. Biomed. **12**(1), 20–26 (2008)
20. Chen, Y., Pu, P.: HealthyTogether: exploring social incentives for mobile fitness applications. In: ACM Second International Symposium of Chinese CHI, pp. 25–34 (2014)
21. Yang, C.H., Maher, J.P., Conroy, D.E.: Implementation of behavior change techniques in mobile applications for physical activity. Am. J. Prev. Med. **48**(4), 452–455 (2015)
22. Kritsonis, A.: Comparison of change theories. Int. J. Sch. Acad. Intellect. Divers. **8**(1), 1–7 (2005)
23. Strecher, V.J., McEvoy DeVellis, B., Becker, M.H., Rosenstock, I.M.: The role of self-efficacy in achieving health behavior change. Health Educ. Q. **13**(1), 73–92 (1986)

24. Fox, S., Duggan, M.: Mobile Health 2012: Half of Smartphone Owners use Their Devices to get Health Information and One-Fifth of Smartphone Owners have Health Apps. Pew Internet and American Life Project, California Healthcare Foundation (2012)

25. Handel, M.J.: mHealth (Mobile Health) – using apps for health and wellness. EXPLORE: J. Sci. Heal. **7**(4), 256–261 (2011)

26. Galitz, W.O.: The Essential Guide to User Interface Design: An Introduction to GUI Design Principles and Techniques, 3rd edn. Wiley Publishing Inc., Indianapolis (2007)

27. Borchers, J., Deussen, O., Klingert, A., Knörzer, C.: Layout rules for graphical web documents. Comput. Graph. **20**(3), 415–426 (1996)

28. Digital Træningsværktøj. http://exorlive.com/dk

29. Fukuda, T.Y., Echeimberg, J.O., Pompeu, J.E., Lucareli, P.R.G., Garbelotti, S., Gimenes, R.O., Apolinário, A.: Root mean square value of the electromyographic signal in the isometric torque of the quadriceps, hamstrings and brachial biceps muscles in female subjects. J. Appl. Res. **10**(1), 32–39 (2010)

30. Bird, M., Fletcher, K.M., Koch, A.J.: Electromyographic comparison of the Ab-slide and crunch exercises. J. Strength Cond. Res. **20**(2), 436–440 (2006)

31. Son, J., Kim, S., Ahn, S., Ryu, J., Hwang, S., Kim, Y.: Determination of the dynamic knee joint range of motion during leg extension exercise using an EMG-driven model. Int. J. Precis. Eng. Manufac. **13**(1), 117–123 (2012)

32. Saeterbakken, A.H., Fimland, M.S.: Muscle activity of the core during bilateral, unilateral, seated and standing resistance exercise. Eur. J. Appl. Physiol. **112**(5), 1671–1678 (2012)

Playing a City

Annika Olofsdotter Bergström(✉) 🆔 and Pirjo Elovaara

Technoscience Studies, Blekinge Institute of Technology,
Pirgatan, 374 35 Karlshamn, Sweden
{aob,pirjo.elovaara}@bth.se

Abstract. This paper is based on exploratory interventions in a small city in the south-eastern part of Sweden. The interventions were inspired both by the art movement of Situationists and site-specific games. The activities were also supported by a diversity of theoretical perspectives. During winter 2016 eight women explored by developing playful methods what a city, understood both as a social and material space, could mean for a group of women recently moved to the city. Through the playful approach the project opened up room for participatory design and abled the group to formulate eight rules, also available for other city explorers in other cities.

Keywords: Site-specific games · Rules · Playful · Explorative method
Participatory design · City

1 Background

This paper is based on a series of exploratory interventions in a small city in the south-eastern part of Sweden. The project described in this paper is part of a bigger research project about how site-specific games and play in cities can create engaging citizenship.

During one year (2016–2017) we (the authors) met a group of 6–8 Syrian women every second week, and together we experimented with our joined playfulness, different locations in the city. The aim was to study and develop participatory methods of playful design for citizenship with help of urban places.

The focus of this paper is to present and discuss specific methods of experimenting and intervening with site-specific playfulness in public spaces. This method development project is a pre-study of how big data that cities produce (like population, income, education, political affiliations traffic, and air quality) could be used for making playful cities [1].

The structure of this paper is as follows:

In the *Research frame* chapter, the paper explains within what fields this transdisciplinary project is situated. *The introduction* describes how cities often are represented as a future artifact and, wants to give the reader a picture of how the project got its spark.

A relational city tells how the project started and what important questions were raised. *Walkers and walking women* is a short description of why walking was an important method for the project. *Let's move on - Let's play* is about the experimental approach while playing together. *The rules* is the chapter where the rules made out of the explorative interventions are listed. *Threads* section is a playful rulemaking how to encounter with the references for the paper. The *Final concluding thoughts* chapter closing the paper with a discussion about the role of site-specific play in cities.

2 Research Frame

This work is transdisciplinary [10] and thus finds inspiration and methods both from academic fields, in our case from Participatory Design and site-specific games. But we also looked for inspiration from the Situationists, the art and activist movement. These approaches together created a rich combination that gave the project the character of an exploration with an open ending and sometimes also a messy excursion.

As our first point of departure, we turned to site-specific games as a field for research and practice [1, 8, 15] to playfully handling signs and systems in the urbanity.

This genre of games is played on a specific physical site, usually, in an urban space; using the player's' full bodies and the material in a surrounding to create a game experience. Site-specific games embrace physical environments and the everyday life while playing [15]. By locating and integrating the game with the urban space playing no longer occurs in solitude but becomes rather a performance and manifestation in public.

To consider the specific site with its history, social networks, culture and fauna, even languages is to situate and impute meaning to the game in creating urban engagement [6]. The play transforms the consciousness of our everyday life meanwhile exploring the participatory possibilities of city spaces.

Our goal was also to connect our study and interventions to the field of Participatory Design (PD) [19]. PD has its roots in the Scandinavian labor market in the 1970s, aiming to develop inclusive means and methods to involve employees in the design of computer-based processes. The core ideas for PD was and still is, the democratization of the society as a whole. In design processes, the implementation of democratic participation demands inclusive arenas open for experiences of people, whose lives, design results are going to affect. Since the early days of PD tools and means of participation have expanded widely and found their way to areas outside working life. In our specific case; projects connected to urban development and planning [7, 20] have inspired and encouraged us to develop further the ways citizens and urban environments can be connected. Being inspired of PD we especially wanted to carry on the work already initiated in PD and further develop the topic of how citizens experience their lived environment and focus on how playful means and tools can be designed as a collaborative exercise in participatory ways for urban participation. Inspired by the many years of designing the very participation within diverse and numerous design processes, we were able to phrase questions guiding our own participatory intervention, and in that way bringing PD based ideas with us to the field of game/play. We entered the study with an open-ended question: Can we create a process where the methods and goals are not decided in beforehand by us, the researchers? This indicated that we needed to challenge our own expertise and be open and responsive to the participants' ideas, suggestions and comments in the planning, decision-making of the interventions and also during the interventions conducted during the study.

Our desire to play in the city took us to the fifties, when the artistic and activist movement of Situationists (1957–1972), took the dandy strolling further by making walking to a practice of political action of the everyday consciousness. They played with rulemaking for specific city routes to get new perspectives and to move away from the representation of lives into a more experimental behaviour. Under the representation of the city, the true city was hidden, away from the spectacle [17]. To move rapidly in different atmospheres that the city offered to experience that specific situation was the main idea [17]. The Situationists perceived space both as a political and as a philosophical action of everyday situations, which have inspired artists and game developers to explore urban spaces for playfulness [17].

3 Introduction

Frozen cities
If you open up a Swedish local paper and see a visual presentation of a future suburb, you might be surprised. Everything is clean, quiet, the few (white) people present in the picture sit neatly. Not too near each other. There is no noise. No disturbances. No friction. No contradictions. The city in this picture is a substantive, a stable assemblage [9] not shakable. There is no invitation to join or even enter. The city is a presentation. A pre-defined object [2] which is already in place without troubles and so clean. An illusion of harmony and stability. The city is done as a readymade package. The slice of the city presented in the picture '*is*' - a perfect object we can talk about and like because it is impossible to dislike its seductive perfection.

There is, of course, an alternative story of the city, the back side. With dirt, discomfort, and noise. Crowded places, traffic. Worn down houses. Dark tunnels.

Echoing parking lots. But this contradictory presentation of the city would as well be a frozen story. As a result, we would only get an either-or story, a binary story based on dichotomies but still a substantive. The city still '*is*' something, still an object we can talk about, dislike because it is impossible to like.

These two frozen presentations of a city, disturbed us, the authors. How could these two city pictures be unfrozen and translated into complex zigzags, and uncover other stories? Could we break the frozen images as they were imposed on us, and from the shards make new images, stories and understandings? What is a city we asked ourselves?

We wanted to experiment and in non-fixed ways play in public places. Compose actions that could be transformed into engagements with and in the spaces. We did not want to be the only explorers, but to find other curious co-explorers to join our team. This is what we had in our mind. But where could we find bold people ready to step in our endeavor willing to challenge frozen images, to become brave but modest explorers in a city? To be ready to be affected and to affect?

3.1   A Relational City

To find the brave ones, we also needed to find a context interesting, inspiring and challenging enough to locate and situate our experiments and interventions.

People are on the move. Not as nomadic border transgressing subjects [4] but as involuntary refugees. During the last couple of years, approximately 850 persons ended up in a small city in the south-eastern Sweden looking for a peaceful asylum and waiting for a permit required for a permanent stay in Sweden. This small city underwent a transformation, not made by representations but rather through resistance, desires and wishes.

Our experiments and methods presented and discussed in this paper took off when refugees from Syria started to arrive in the city with the hope of a non-violent future.

The governor and her allies decided that the county of Blekinge, where the city is located, would be the county in Sweden that would manage best to integrate immigrants. A lot of so-called integration projects and activities in order to welcome the newcomers to the city were set into motion. Everything from formal Swedish courses to singing in choirs, football and bandy training, sewing circles, and dinner parties. Authorities, schools, voluntary organizations, charity organizations, sports clubs, and individuals started to act and contribute in a variety of ways. All under the umbrella term of integration.

Taking a closer look at all these positive initiatives some aspects need to be reflected upon. Who are the initiators? Who are the ones who exercise power to organize and 'open their hearts' (a slightly modified phrase of the Swedish prime minister from 2014)? Who is integrated to what? And what is integration all about?

In critical reflections upon the 'what is' and 'who is' and the trajectory of the notion and practices of integration, we (the authors) were keen to see if there could be other ways and also reasons to create a more messy and mobile socio-material assembly consisting of the city and its diversity of inhabitants.

We started to think what the small Swedish city might mean for the newcomers. If and how they could be part of shaping the city. Maybe their eyes, ears, and feet could tell us new stories about the city? What would the city mean for us already staying there? Could our eyes, ears, and feet together make new versions of the city? What if the city could tell stories of its own, seldom heard or already forgotten?

What would become if we brought our bodies, memories, and questions into the city with its own body and started to walk, disturb and claim space? Our very first question when moving further on from thinking and discussing was: how can our interventions change our perceptions and feelings of this seemingly boring and a bit tired small city? How can our joint interventions start to change the place? Without any pre-defined goals and boundaries of what and who as static entities [2] we started to imagine to challenge the city as an assemblage of humans and non-humans [9] through walking, playing and talking.

However, a city as an open arena for everyone is not always reality. All functions that exist in a city side by side; spatially, juridical, economically, culturally, and socially are related to gender and class relations [13]. The possible interactions a city can offer, occasionally meetings of different kinds are restricted by the difference of what social relations citizens are included in and in what spaces they belong to [13]. Women's mobility has been restricted historically and culturally [14] and women's lives and experiences are defined as private and men's as public, and even though women have changed their position in the public over the last century, men still take a bigger part of the public life [13].

But we wanted to carry on, taking both the possibilities and constraints with us, and via the training course, 'Swedish for immigrants', we got in touch with six Syrian women in the age of twenty-three to fifty-five.

We asked them: "Do you want to play with us?" and they all said "Yes."

3.2   Walkers and Walking Women – Methods for Exploration

To walk can be an inspirational movement [13] if you spontaneously follow up what you see or meet on your path.

Influences from the Situationists inspired us as a group of women with restricted movement patterns, to explore how we can take action over places instead of letting the places rule over us [17]. As a group, we wanted to be part of the city and well as observing, being observed, to make a statement of our participation in the city.

To go from looking at the map of the city to start walking into the city and its places was an exploration of the existential moments [16]. By walking and traversing the streets, the conversation about how we perceived the city tied us together and created narratives of what places have been in the past and how places and objects could become something else. Together with the city, we started to reformulate places by using our bodily senses expanding the spatiality.

With the experiments of mapping spaces outside ourselves but as well as within our bodies [16], we were teased to create our own site-specific games, momentarily designed by us and by the places while encountered them. For us the site-specific game as an inspiration and frame is to connect to power, gender and ethnicity and as questions how alienated patterns are transformed to everyday life matters. By walking we stitched together parts of the city to become our playground to turn space into place.

4   Let's Move on - Let's Play

We, the group of eight women, took walking as a rhythm to explore the city chosen by us, stopping to re-name a statue of a naked woman. Imagined the creek full of cro-codiles and waggled the icy downhill like penguins. We played with each other, made new paths and expanded our movements. Collectively we co-created situations by picking up on each other's inventions and ideas. The playing emerged for a while and dissolved into an embodied touch when stopped taking part of the play. Slowly a relationship between us and the city developed. Our re-engagement with the city also became a reclamation of a space as a collective manifestation. The reclamation grew bigger for each time we pushed our spatial expansion [16] further, tried our 'do not' to 'why not'. Who could we become in these places trying out new belongings?

All the playful explorations we did during several months made us wondering. To stand in the dark forest screaming out a wish to the stars made a connection to the future. We (the authors) analyzed and reflected on our expeditions with the group, read notes, listened to the recordings, watched the photos and drawings. Made open frames for next occasion. Sometimes we sighed over the mess in our planning or the rush we always felt before meeting the women. Do we have the pens and the paper? Where is the recorder? But every time when playing together, our bodies told us that we were heading towards something in the becoming, something unexpected.

For several months we played crossed boundaries, challenges ourselves and the city. Asked four young men on a park bench if they knew where the other benches, usually standing there, where? Getting the answer from one of them knowing that the benches needed to be renovated.

From the map, we chose spots to visit and brought some props to play with.

With open minds, we explored and did not expect much. Is it possible to invite citizens to come to the city square to claim their space by drawing a chalk circle around their feet?

When we finally zoomed out there it was: eight co-designed rules which defined a set of different activities to play with [18].

Rules are what make a game's fundamental [18] and in this game, the rules were not made from moral, not from regulations or norms, but aimless and unpredictable. They dictated how the game behaved [18]. If you follow them you can make friendships, get to know your city in a new way, challenge your everyday life or just have a moment of fun. The set of rules that were developed are explicit rules, do this and do that. But in between these commands, the space for implicit rules is embedded and welcoming negotiations and renegotiations of the rules [18].

The ambiguity of the rules opens up possibilities for a leap of joy from an everyday activity into a playful moment which simultaneously initiates a situation of participation.

Our rulemaking became a pattern of accepting and giving in a motion towards the unknown. The city turned into a companion and together we revealed the secrets of entanglements instead of splits.

5 The Rules Designed

We **mapped** places that we visited often, or never visited or wanted to visit. Places we avoided.

We **walked** to a place chosen on the map, explored it, talked about it. We left a mark and we took something from the place to bring with us.

We **lighted** a dark forest playfully. In the darkest spot, we shouted out a wish.

We **transgressed** boundaries, stopped in front of people's houses and asked ourselves which place felt welcoming and which do not.

We **reformulated** by randomly cutting out sentences from books and made new stories.

We **asked** strangers questions that we had made up from nowhere.

We **measured** the town square carefully with a yardstick and counted every object in the square.

We **claimed** the square by inviting citizens to come and draw a colorful circle around their feet.

6 Threads as a Possibility for New Rules

The project we have lived with and loved for one year and a half has been an act of crossing of many vibrant threads. Like Donna Haraway's [9] figuration, or game as Haraway also calls it, of *cat's cradle* we have taken a combination of doing/thinking/making together. Creating occasional patterns by receiving and proposing threads coming together and apart. Sometimes threads form patterns and co-operate kindly, though momentarily. Sometimes threads misbehave and just end up in an endless tangling so you have to make a violent cut. A cut which opens up for something unexpected, a new entanglement.

Playing the cat's cradle is a never ending play, there is no final goal to strive for. It is more a resistance to fixity and dominant visions. Something ever changing is hard to catch but gives the rhythm of playfulness.

By inviting interesting people and their texts and experiences to think together with us, we can highlight some of the threads in our cat's cradle and invite texts and thoughts to continuously play with us. We want to challenge the understanding of how we can read and intervene with theories while making playfulness.

The Rule-Make a cat's cradle

Read Donna Haraway's article about the cat's cradle from 1994.
Find someone to play with. Choose the threads. Create a pattern. Play until it is not playful and fun anymore. Start again. Stop. Keep on going. There is no end.

Thread number 1 Cross boundaries

Re-read Donna Haraway's text about cat's cradle.
Cross boundaries, both visible, physical and imaginary in your city. Do not stop there. Ask instead what kind of work boundaries do. What kind of city do they produce for you? Can you survive? Do boundaries of the city hurt you?

Thread number 2 Let the city fluid

Read John Law's and Vicky Singleton's article about object lessons from 2005.
Find a park bench. Sit down. Ask yourself: Am I sure everything I see is fixed? Things, people, animals? Imagine a city as a fluid space. Does the city keep its shape? Does a city have to keep its shape? Can a city come in many shapes?

Thread number 3 Forget objects and subjects

Read Karen Barad's book about agential realism, intra-actions, apparatuses and cuts from 2007. Read once more. And one more time.
Choose a place in a city. Look around. Gather everything you see. Do not categorize. What's going on? Surprise yourself and tell a new story you have never told before. What and who acts? What did you include in your story? What did you exclude? What are the consequences of your choices?

Thread number 4 Know & care

Read Maria Puig de la Bellacasa's article about knowing as caring from 2012.
Make a map of your relations. Whom do you think with? Whom do you think for? What do you care? Borrow a dog, if you do not have a dog of your own. Have a walk together. Listen to the dog. What does the dog know that you do not know? What do you know together?

Thread number 5 Design your Thing

Read Pelle Ehn's article about participation in design things from 2008.
Decide what you think about design? Who is designing for whom? Who is using? What is to be designed? Move on and start to play a design game. You are all designers, users, and participants. Design the city as a parliament. What kind of devices do you need? What kind of infrastructure do you need? How can design carry on after you have left the design game?

Thread number 6 Do not avoid contradictions

Read Carl DiSalvo's book about adversarial design from 2012.
Return to your design game of a parliament. The Consensus is not an option. Make sure that controversies can flourish in your democratic design experiment. Arrange a choir of multiple voices. Let the choir sing at the city square. Listen. Do you tolerate disagreement? Does it feel uncomfortable? Do you, by all means, try to reach harmony? Think again. Develop your design game further. Reserve space for polyvocality. Practice. Reflect. Keep on going. Have patience.

Thread number 7 Add a thread of your own choice

7 Final Concluding Thoughts

We would argue that a city is not either or, nor it can be defined or fixed as a problem. The city is in becoming with its citizens. It is a living net of material-discursive relationships [2] and made of different constellations of humans, artefacts, infrastructure and memories, depending on who is playing with the threads. A city is a pattern open to reformulate or change, as you want and a game could be the vehicle for that change [8]. It is about designing living relationships together, to be aware of the unknown and the always there. A city is a living object, a messy condition always with partial understandings of what it could become [12]. The trickster is that we who live in cities do think we know the city, our hoods, we see it as a stable network [11] but it is at another level something undefined, something possible to imagine and construct the opposite to what we know and experience. By stuttering and stumbling, we can sometimes reach further by letting us dwell in the fluidity or the void if you prefer so. A city has as many shapes as there are interpretations.

It is not the rules that dominate and master a game but the relationships evoked when playing [18]. What our rules did was not only shaping a relationship to a city and amidst the players but they additionally designed a place, a Thing [6] to manage players' own imaginations, relations and actions within. Rules that put the adversarial into the light, a city can be a livable place for everyone but not as a fixed place of consensus but rather with tensions to play with [5]. Cities could thus be more of a place for collective articulations [5] and defined by rules at the moment.

Cities should not be defined as in the picture described in the very beginning of this article but more as a caring map of vibrant relations [3]. To create a playfulness by using a site-specific game in a collaborative design process with messy steps is to embrace the imperfect which let us continuously ask questions along the way. Questions important for the exploration and formulation of implicit rules. The imperfections can show what is hidden under the surface and open up for what can be a possibility.

By imperfection, citizens can meet and induce a possible city as a novel everyday collective practice. What is it to participate *with* a place? With the everyday environment? What is it to design a city life?

The work we did initiate is one possible line to start questioning what polyvocality might mean and how we could mutually, in joint playful performances of humans and non-humans, shape and re-shape the accustomed city. We can also relate our process to a figuration of Thing [6] for thinking and practice design processes. According to Pelle Ehn, design is not only about designing objects and systems. Design could be more considered as collaborative assemblages, i.e. the Thing. Participants like the city, citizens, artifacts, infrastructure, culture, values, and economic conditions were the members of our Thing, the explorations and interventions. In our case, the Thing took form because of the members' commitment, which was the prerequisite for initiating the design practice of both citizenship and the future of the city.

We tried on a small intimate scale to challenge beliefs and values of what a livable everyday place might mean. By becoming humble witnesses to an ongoing change there can be potentiality to redraw the pattern of the caring understanding and knowledge that we, the inhabitants, on daily basis, create in urban relationships, both visible and invisible.

In the end, we all dream of cities and places that we can become playful with.

References

1. Ackermann, J., Rauscher, A., Stein, D.: Introduction: Playin' the city. Artistic and Scientific Approaches to playful urban arts. Navigationen, Zeitschrift fur Medien–und Kulturwissenschaften (2016)
2. Barad, K.: Meeting the Universe Halfway: Quantum Physics and the Entanglement of Matter and Meaning. Duke University Press, Durham (2007)
3. de la Bellacasa, M.P.: Nothing comes without its worlds: thinking with care. Sociol. Rev. **60** (2), 197–216 (2012)
4. Braidotti, R.: Nomadic Subjects: Embodiment and Sexual Difference in Contemporary Feminist Theory. Colombia University Press, New York (2011)
5. DiSalvo, C.: Adversarial Design. The MIT Press, Cambridge (2012)
6. Ehn, P.: Participation in design things. In: PDC 2008 Proceedings of the Tenth Anniversary Conference on Participatory Design 2008, pp. 92–101 (2008)
7. Eriksen, M.A., et al.: Collaboratively articulating "urban" participatory design?! In: PDC 2016, Aarhus, Denmark, 15–19 August (2012)
8. Flanagan, M.: Critical Play: Radical Game Design. MIT Press, Cambridge (2009)
9. Haraway, D.: A game of cat's cradle: science studies, feminist theory, cultural studies. Configurations **2**(1), 59–71 (1994)
10. Bernstein, J.H.: Transdisciplinarity: a review of its origins, development, and current issues. J. Res. Pract. **11**(1), 1 (2015). Article R1
11. Latour, B.: Reassembling the Social: An Introduction to Actor-Network-Theory. University Press, Oxford (2005)
12. Law, J., Singleton, V.: Object lessons. Organization **12**(3), 331–355 (2005)
13. Listerbom, C.: Rädslans geografi - om "privata" kvinnor och "offentliga" män. Tidskrift för genusvetenskap, nr 2, pp. 83–98 (2001). ISSN 2001-1377
14. Massey, D.: Space, Place and Gender. Polity Press, Oxford (1994)

15. Montola, M., Stenros, J., Waern, A.: Pervasive Games: Theory and Design. Morgan Kaufmann, Burlington (2009)
16. O'Rourke, K.: Walking and Mapping, Artists as Cartographers. MIT Press, Cambridge (2013)
17. Sadler, S.: The Situationist City. Massachusetts of Technology First. MIT Press, Cambridge (1998)
18. Salen, K., Zimmerman, E. (eds.): The Game Design Reader – A Rules of Play Anthology. MIT Press, Cambridge (2006)
19. Simonsen, J., Robertson, T. (eds.): Routledge International Handbook of Participatory Design. Routledge, New York (2012)
20. Stokes, B., Baumann, K., Bar, F.: Hybrid games for stronger neighbourhoods: connecting residents and urban objects to deepen the sense of place. In: PDC 2016, Aarhus, Denmark, 15–19 August 2016 (2016). http://dx.doi.org/10.1145/2948076.2948103

Designing User Centred Intelligent Classroom Lighting

Diana Georgieva, Kathrine Marie Schledermann,
Stine Maria Louring Nielsen, and Ellen Kathrine Hansen[(⊠)]

Lighting Design, Department of Architecture, Design and Media Technology,
Aalborg University, A.C. Meyers Vænge 15, 2450 Copenhagen, Denmark
diana.z.georgieva@gmail.com,
{kat,stm,ekh}@create.aau.dk

Abstract. Through a case study, this paper presents a new way of designing intelligent classroom lighting to meet the users' needs. A mix of ethnographic methods (field observations and interviews) were used to investigate the everyday learning activities at a middle school in Copenhagen in order to determine how lighting can support the learning environment. Based on the investigations, lighting design criteria and three predefined lighting scenes are proposed as a new design for meeting the needs of students and teachers during three types of activities. The scenes focus on smartboard visibility and on creating a visual focus on the teacher who is the centre of attention during most activities. It is hypothesised that if the scenes are used according to the different types of activities this would enable the teacher to create structure in the lessons and through this improve the behaviour of the students.

Keywords: Lighting for learning · Design research
User centred lighting design · Learning environment · Intelligent lighting
Design methodologies · Design of innovative learning environments

1 Introduction and Background

The aim of this paper is to present how a qualitative approach to investigating the needs of the students and teachers can be beneficial for developing intelligent user-centred classroom lighting. The paper will illustrate how understanding the needs and issues faced by the users in their current environment can be translated into design criteria for classroom lighting to support them in the process of learning and their daily school activities. This is especially important to consider when working with complex environments, such as learning environments of the 21st century, which need to be supported by flexible lighting systems.

The development of intelligent lighting has led to new possibilities for supporting classroom occupants in their daily activities. New LED technologies can provide users with the possibility to change gradually the intensity, distribution, and colour of the light, to separate the room easily into zones, to choose from predefined settings which the teacher or students can activate with one press of a button. Additionally, such systems allow for reprogramming of the lighting as many times as needed after the installation of the luminaires. This makes the job of a lighting designer and the

© ICST Institute for Computer Sciences, Social Informatics and Telecommunications Engineering 2018
A. L. Brooks et al. (Eds.): ArtsIT 2017/DLI 2017, LNICST 229, pp. 314–323, 2018.
https://doi.org/10.1007/978-3-319-76908-0_30

decisions they face much more complex, as their designs can be much more flexible and can have greater impact on the learning environment than lighting installed just a few years ago. Such solutions are becoming increasingly common with the advancement of technologies, thus it is important to understand how they can support the needs of teachers and students.

Research on the effects of light on cognitive performance shows that higher correlated colour temperature (CCT) positively affects reading [1] and concentration [2]. According to other studies, lower CCT positively affects prosocial and aggressive behaviour, and fidgetiness [3], and is also recommended for students with special educational needs [4]. Additionally, Xu and Labroo [5] and Baron et al. [6] found that brightness has an effect on the strength of affective responses. Intelligent lighting provides the opportunity to combine all light parameters, such as CCT, intensity, and distribution, in various ways when creating advanced innovative systems to influence learning and classroom activities, which makes its effects and design much more complex than standard classroom lighting.

These new opportunities of using advanced technologies in the learning environment come at the same time as the introduction of new school reforms and teaching tools, such as interactive boards. For example, a school reform was implemented in Denmark in 2014 [7], and as consequence students and teachers have to spend more time in classrooms. Additionally, it suggests that the classroom activities are more diverse, including physical ones. Due to these demands, there is a need for a physical environment which should be easily modified throughout the day and fitting the constantly changing tasks [8]. Nowadays many more tools are available for students and teachers to use, such as smartboards and other interactive boards, laptops, and tablets. This makes proper visibility very important as glare has to be avoided for projectors and for various types of displays (as discussed by Ramasoot and Fotios [9]).

This growing complexity of technologies and learning environments calls for an innovative way of designing these environments, and therefore an adjusted design process. The aim of this paper is to address how involving the users in the design process through qualitative research methods can be beneficial for developing lighting design solutions which meet the needs of students and teachers of 21st century classrooms. This paper addresses a case study at a Copenhagen school which was about to be renovated with an intelligent lighting system, and was done in the classrooms before they were renovated. In this initial phase of the research project, before the classrooms were renovated or the lighting system designed, the authors were asked to conduct investigations of the users' needs and to define design criteria and a concept based on them. During summer 2017 the classrooms were renovated and intelligent lighting was installed based on the criteria defined in this project. The renovated classrooms are being tested in a later project.

2   Method

In this case study, the needs of the users regarding lighting were explored through analysing *how they used the space and light* and *what issues they faced*, through a mix of ethnographic methods. Qualitative methods were used as they have the advantage of putting the designer, as a researcher, in the actual environment they design for and close to the daily lives of their users [10, p. 24]. This can be beneficial for developing an empathetic relation with the users, which is important for innovation (discussed by Liedtka and Ogilvie [11]), as well as for imagining how their designs would actually be used based on what they see in the current environment.

2.1 Field Observations

For this project it was important to understand the flow of a school day and the classroom activities, as well as how the occupants use the space and the light, in order to recognise the potentials for supporting the students and teachers through intelligent lighting. For this purpose, semi-structured observations were conducted. The observation guides had two main categories: *Light & use of the light* and *Activities & use of the space*. Photographs were also taken in order to track the changes in light and space occupation throughout the day, as well as the types of activities. This was meant to support the field notes taken during observations.

2.2 Interviews

Interviews were conducted to provide an understanding of how the participants subjectively experienced the space and how they used it throughout the year. Two guides, one for individual teacher interviews and one for student focus group interviews [10, pp. 73–77], were formulated. The guides included questions about their typical school day and issues they face when teaching or studying with respects to their environment, including the light. A semi-structured, as opposed to structured guides, enabled flexibility and the possibility to adjust the course of the interviews according to the questions which emerged [12].

3 Data Collection

The data was collected over two weeks in October 2016 (Table 1). The interview and observation data were collected simultaneously by two researchers, based on the availability of the students and teachers throughout the seven days of the field study. The classes for participation were chosen by the school administration. Two rooms were selected - one 5th grade to the east and one to the west. The teachers were

Table 1. Data collected during the field study.

Type of data	Count
Individual interviews	Three teachers, teaching language, mathematics, and music classes
Focus group interviews with 2–3 students	19 students
Field observations	Seven school days
Photos and times lapses	Seven times lapses, 280 photos

recruited based on convenience, according to who wanted to participate and when they were available [10]. All participants were kept anonymous throughout this study.

4 Findings

The data analysed include field notes, interviews, and photographs, which were additionally made into time lapses. The analysis aimed at contributing to the development of user-centred lighting scenes for supporting the everyday needs of students and teachers. In the following section the most relevant findings are presented.

4.1 Light and Use of the Light

At the beginning of the analysis, it quickly became obvious that the main issue caused by inappropriate lighting was glare on the smartboards. This was a pressing issue as the smartboards were used very frequently in both rooms. This problem led to the students and teachers either (1) blocking the daylight and turning off the artificial light in order to be able to see properly, or (2) leaving the lighting as it was to prevent the students from becoming sleepy and losing their focus. This issue was observed by the researchers and shared by one of the teachers who stated that she preferred to leave the lights on for supporting the students' alertness even if it caused glare. Therefore, the teachers were forced to choose between these two options, both of which were preventing them from teaching and learning in the most efficient and desirable way.

Based on the time lapses it was evident that there were only minor differences in the ambient brightness throughout the day and that the rooms were very evenly lit. This was regardless of whether the main source of light was natural or artificial. It was also evident that the CCT remained mostly constant - the exception was in the early mornings when the main source of light was the fluorescent lighting and the rooms were perceived as being more yellow. This even and consistent lighting was in contrast to the rapidly changing classroom activities and the needs of the occupants.

4.2 Activities and Use of the Space

It was observed that different subjects required different use of the rooms. In language classes students would mostly have discussions and read and write on paper, while in mathematics classes they would more often use the smartboard and the whiteboard in combination with laptops. However, observations of the same subjects led by different teachers showed difference in, for example, what percentage of the time a teaching tool, such as the smartboard or books, would be used. Additionally, in the subject Supported Learning the activities were different each time: doing homework, watching a movie, completing a crafts assignment. Nevertheless, the teacher being the centre of attention was consistent between most tasks: when solving a mathematic problem, music activities, or reading. Another consistency between subjects was observed in the furniture arrangement, which was not dependent on the activities, but was instead changed every other month.

From an observer perspective, the biggest surprise was that the students were using the rooms very actively and often unpredictably during lessons. Additionally, change between different activities, such as reading, writing, using smartboard, whiteboard, or paper was rapid most of the time, and a lot of the time multiple tools were used simultaneously. Due to this rapid change, which was also leading to different use of the space, changes in the students' behaviour and in their concentration, it was sometimes very difficult for an observer to distinguish between lessons and breaks.

5   Discussion

5.1   Defining Design Criteria and Lighting Scenes

Based on the findings, design criteria for meeting the users' needs were formulated (Table 2) and three predefined lighting scenes were proposed (Fig. 1). It was concluded based on the analysis that the main focus of the design should be (1) *to improve the visual comfort during classroom activities, especially in respect to the smartboard,* and (2) *to direct the students' attention to where the activities required it to be* - e.g., teacher or smartboard – in order to provide the teachers with a *tool for structuring the classroom activities.* The main findings contributing to this design proposal were that the smartboard was used frequently but glare was often a problem; and that teachers were the focus of students' attention, but that this is not indicated visually due to the evenly distributed lighting.

Table 2. Design and success criteria for the user-centred intelligent lighting scenes.

Design criteria	Success criteria
1. High visibility of the smartboard projection without the need to turn off the artificial lighting	1. The students and teachers do not express glare issues from the artificial light during interviews and it is not observed that they turn off the lighting when showing something important on the smartboard
2. Possibility for creating a visual focus on the teacher in the front part of the room through lighting	2. The teachers express and it is observed that they use the lighting for creating focus in the front part of the room when the students need to direct their attention there, and not during activities when the students work individually or in groups, where they are focused on their desks

In addition to the analysis presented in the previous section, criteria were also developed through (1) describing each activity that was taking place in regular classrooms during observations; (2) setting lighting criteria for each activity; and (3) grouping the activities into types according to the lighting which is needed. Three types of activities emerged from that analysis and a scene was proposed for each of them: *Watching a video, Focus on teacher,* and *General lighting* (Fig. 1).

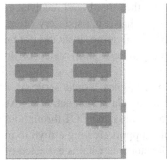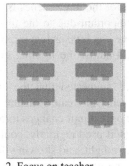

1. Watching a video   2. Focus on teacher   3. General lighting

Fig. 1. Concept for the three predefined lighting scenes. The different shades represent different levels of illumination.

The *first* predefined lighting scene is based on the finding that the smartboard is used a lot, but disability glare is an issue. It was also found that the students and teachers prefer to have bright light throughout the day in order to stay alert. It is proposed that the light in the front part of the room is switched off while the rest of the room is still lit up, although to a lesser extent compared to the other scenes (Fig. 1). This would be most appropriate to use when the students are watching a video for a long period of time; as for instance observed in the class Supported Learning.

The *second* scene is based on the finding that while the teachers are the centre of attention during most activities there is no visual focus on them, since the room is evenly lit. In stage lighting, one of the most commonly used tools for drawing the eye of the audience is to create visual focus through bright light, as 'the human eye is naturally drawn to the brightest part of any composition' [13, p. 194], which is also pointed out by Descottes and Ramos [14, p. 58]. As shown in the illustration (Fig. 1), the design of the second scene suggests that there is a visual focus on the teacher and the front part of the room, which could be achieved through using different light intensity levels in the front and back, possibly supported by different colour temperature, distribution of the light, and/or different types of luminaires. This lighting scene would be appropriate for when the teacher is, for example, introducing an exercise or leading a discussion. However, although it is known that bright light catches the attention initially, more research is needed to determine whether the focus of the students would be sustained for long periods of time through this approach.

The *third* lighting scene proposes general, even lighting in the room (Fig. 1), which would be appropriate during the varied and complex activities which were observed during the field observations, such as when doing a crafts assignment and other types of individual or group work, or a mix of these. These would typically be activities during which the students' attention is not only needed in the direction of the teacher's desk or the boards, but is changing in relation to a combination of activities. It also suggests the highest illuminance of all the scenes as it is probable that the students would need to work more closely on details.

A common recommendation for the three scenes is that the smartboard receives as little light as possible. This is important due to the finding that it is used very often, including for short periods of time - as little as two minutes. Therefore, it should not be assumed that the teachers would adjust the lighting every time a short video or an image is shown.

Additionally, a hypothesis is suggested that the three scenes would serve as a teaching tool by enabling the teacher to create structure in the classroom activities. As during the field study there were only minor changes in brightness and CCT throughout the day, these predefined settings, if used regularly, could support creating a rhythm in the activities through the change in light, and showing the students what is expected of them. Multiple sources discuss the effectiveness of using non-verbal cues for letting students, including ones with ADHD, autism, and other learning disabilities, know what is expected of them at that moment [15–17]. Doerries and Grosser for example state: 'verbal or nonverbal teacher cues signalling upcoming transitions help prepare students for changes in activities or lessons' [17, p. 5]. CASTL similarly point out: 'Cues and visuals work because they quickly and efficiently remind children what behaviours are expected of them' [16, p. 1].

Before the lighting was installed in the classrooms, the concept behind the scenes was introduced to the teachers who pointed out the need for a simple and easy to use system. The teachers only proposed few suggestions, indicating that they need to use the system and get familiar with the functions before they can propose adjustments or changes. Therefore, the design is kept uncomplicated in order to see how the teachers and students will react to it and use it. Although there would be some limitations when changing the settings, the lighting could be made more advanced in future if it is seen or expressed by the occupants that they would prefer more flexibility.

5.2   Limitations of the Methods Used

Observations were conducted to investigate the classroom activities and behaviour, issues regarding the physical environment, as well as how the teachers and students interact with it. Photos and time lapses were important for following the changes in the space and activities more objectively and precisely than through field notes. The personal and mechanical observations were supported with interviews, which contributed to understanding how the students and teachers experience the space, and specific examples of their needs and issues. The interviews were also important for acquiring information about the use and experience of classrooms throughout the year, which is impossible to observe within a short study.

These qualitative methods were useful for avoiding preconceptions of how lessons are conducted and what activities take place in regular classrooms. For example, in the beginning it was assumed that it would be possible to have different lighting distribution based on the activities, as each would have a different furniture arrangement. However, it was found that the arrangement does not depend on the activities taking place. Similarly, an assumption was made that the lighting scenes could be based on the subjects, and each scene would be useful for only some subjects. However, only through conducting field observations it was possible to see that, although there are some differences between how the space is used between subjects, these were too teacher-specific. Therefore, qualitative methods were useful for removing preconceptions and creating knowledge on what activities the environment should be designed for.

Interviews were also relevant for supporting the observations by confirming what is important for the students and teachers during lessons. For example, through field observations a conclusion was reached that there were glare issues with the smartboard, but it was possible that the occupants actually did not experience problems. However, the interviews confirmed this finding and its importance.

A downside to the methods used is that they are time-consuming [10, p. 25] and only limited amount of data were gathered: two classes from the same grade and three teachers participated. It is however possible that other grades and teachers have different experiences and needs. This issue could be overcome by supplementing these methods with other methods: for example questionnaires, which would allow for faster collection of data from more individuals.

5.3 Design Evaluation

As part of the next phase of this project, a renovation of four classrooms, including renovation of the lighting, was carried out in the summer of 2017.

Before the new lighting solution was installed, an additional exploratory research study was carried out by the researchers. Here, ten *other* intelligent lighting solutions in Scandinavian classrooms were studied, including how the teachers experience two of them, both located in Copenhagen and designed within the last five years. The research was done in order to investigate whether these solutions already installed at other schools meet the needs of the users. It was found that solutions similar to the presented proposal, such as focusing on smartboard visibility and on creating a visual focus on the teacher, have not been installed. It was also found that the users are rarely involved in the design process, especially in the beginning when design criteria are defined. The teachers at such schools expressed that visibility of the interactive boards is an issue, causing students to become distracted as they are not able to follow the lessons. Therefore, the design criteria and lighting scenes presented as the outcome of this research show to be unique in the field of classroom lighting, and an evaluation of the lighting installation is important for understanding the *effectiveness of applying qualitative methods in lighting design research.*

The evaluation of the lighting is planned for September and December 2017. It will be carried out through a similar methodology and will investigate whether the lighting supports the criteria and the needs of the users in practice. To analyse how the teachers adjust the lights and window shading according to the students' needs and behaviour, and according to the classroom activities, observations and focus group interviews have been planned. In addition to the methods already used, manual adjustments of the lighting will be tracked automatically during the evaluation, through a datalog. While observations will explain the context of the choice of light, automatic tracking of the light will provide the precise time of the changes and what settings are chosen. During the evaluation it will also be explored through measurements of the general sound levels in the classrooms whether the lighting can be used as a tool by the teachers to influence the level of activity noise during tasks.

5.4 Future Work

Currently, at the case study school the teachers often request from the students to control the artificial light and the curtains. After the implementation of an intelligent system, the teachers would probably have the main responsibility of adjusting the light. However, a risk emerges in this regard since during this study it was observed that the light was adjusted often randomly: e.g., the occupants would close the curtains to watch a video but would not open them again right after its end. Predicting the use of the system and designing it according to these predictions is especially important, since if the lighting is not used in the way intended by the designers, its effects might be undesirable or it might simply be useless.

Furthermore, the knowledge from this project can be used in future research to investigate how lighting can be used as a teaching tool for creating structure, in studies also integrating knowledge from a pedagogical perspective.

6   General Conclusion

This study investigated how the needs of students and teachers regarding lighting can be explored; and how this can be useful in the process of developing innovative intelligent lighting solutions for classrooms. A need for a qualitative approach was recognised and, as an outcome of the study, design criteria and intelligent lighting scenes were developed to be implemented and evaluated at a Copenhagen school.

This paper suggests a different approach to designing classroom lighting, namely involving the users and understanding their needs in order to define the design criteria for intelligent lighting systems. This is achieved not only through focusing on how users experience the lighting and what issues they face in this regard, but also the activities they take part in, the tools they use, and what is important for them in their everyday teaching and learning situations. This way of doing design research was able to lead the designers in a direction that has not been taken before, according to the authors' research of existing solutions. Evaluation of the project after installation will show whether the students and teachers also experience that this lighting meets their needs in practice. It will also show whether the teachers would adopt the lighting as a teaching tool, and whether this would enable them to create structure in the classroom activities, thus improving the learning environment.

Acknowledgments. This study was conducted as part of the project Light and Learning under the Interreg project Lighting Metropolis. The authors would like to thank Albertslund Municipality, and the teachers and students at the case study school for their collaboration on this project; and to express gratitude towards the lighting and architecture firms who shared knowledge and experience throughout the study: Zumtobel, Sweco, and AI Architects.

References

1. Mott, M.S., Robinson, D.H., Walden, A., Burnette, J., Rutherford, A.S.: Illuminating the effects of dynamic lighting on student learning. SAGE Open **2**, 1–9 (2012)
2. Barkmann, C., Wessolowski, N., Schulte-Markwort, M.: Applicability and efficacy of variable light in schools. Physiol. Behav. **105**, 621–627 (2012)
3. Wessolowski, N., Koenig, H., Schulte-Markwort, M., Barkmann, C.: The effect of variable light on the fidgetiness and social behavior of pupils in school. J. Environ. Psychol. **39**, 101–108 (2014)
4. BRANZ Ltd.: Designing Quality Learning Spaces: Lighting. Ministry of Education, New Zealand (2007)
5. Xu, A.J., Labroo, A.A.: Incandescent affect: turning on the hot emotional system with bright light. J. Consum. Psychol. **24**, 207–216 (2014)
6. Baron, R.A., Rea, M.S., Daniels, S.G.: Effects of indoor lighting (illuminance and spectral distribution) on the performance of cognitive tasks and interpersonal behaviors: the potential mediating role of positive affect. Motiv. Emot. **16**, 1–33 (1992)
7. Undervisningsministeriet.: Den nye folkeskole - en kort guide til reformen. https://skolereformgreve2014.files.wordpress.com/2014/06/miniguide-reform.pdf
8. Duelund, B.: En Fleksibel Bordlampe til Forbedring af Lydmiljøet i Folkeskolen (Master Thesis). Aalborg University of Copenhagen (2016)
9. Ramasoot, T., Fotios, S.: Lighting for the classrooms of the future. Electronic classrooms: a new challenge for school lighting guidance. Light Eng. **17**(2), 62–70 (2009)
10. Bjørner, T.: Qualitative Methods for Consumer Research. The Value of the Qualitative Approach in Theory and Practice, 1st edn. Hans Reitzels Forlag, Copenhagen (2015)
11. Liedtka, J., Ogilvie, T.: Designing for Growth: A Design Thinking Tool Kit for Managers. Columbia University Press, New York (2011)
12. Bryman, A.: Social Research Methods, 4th edn. Oxford University Press, New York (2012)
13. Brewster, K., Shafer, M.: Fundamentals of Theatrical Design: A Guide to the Basics of Scenic, Costume, and Lighting Design. Skyhorse Publishing Inc., New York (2013)
14. Descottes, H., Ramos, C.E.: Architectural Lighting: Designing with Light and Space. Princeton Architectural Press, New York (2011)
15. Behavior Management. http://rise.educ.msu.edu/FAQs/FAQ-behavior.htm
16. CASTL: Strategies for Promoting Positive Behaviour. University of Virginia, Charlottesville, VA (2013)
17. Doerries, D., Grosser, D.: Classroom interventions for attention deficit/hyperactivity disorder. T/TAC W&M, 1-800-323-4489 (2015)

On the Design of Digital Game-Based Learning Environments for Education of the General Public on Focused Scientific Topics with an Application to Underwater Acoustics

Michael A. Kalogerakis[1,2(✉)] and Emmanuel K. Skarsoulis[2]

[1] Department of Electrical Engineering, Technological Educational
Institute of Crete, Heraklion, Crete, Greece
mixalis@cs.teicrete.gr
[2] Institute of Applied and Computational Mathematics, Foundation for Research
and Technology-Hellas, Heraklion, Crete, Greece
eskars@iacm.forth.gr

Abstract. Game-based learning environments for educating the general public on focused scientific topics rely upon voluntary engagement of participants usually in presence of competitive attractions, multiple sources of distraction and time constraints. In addition certain educational topics present an inherent complexity that necessitates the implementation of games with sophisticated interfaces and steep learning curves that may discourage players to engage. In this work we analyze the challenges and propose a new model for the design of efficient multistage game-based learning environments based on the general scheme "attract > engage > educate > evaluate". An existing game-based learning environment for introduction to underwater acoustics is presented as a very close design example of the proposed model.

Keywords: Serious games · Ludic game design · Public learning environments
Underwater acoustics

1 Introduction

A fundamental distinction between traditional and serious games is that the latter do not have entertainment, enjoyment or fun as their primary purpose [1]. As such, serious games are used for a variety of professional purposes including training, education and assessment. In our digital era most serious games are software applications running either as standalone programs or integrated in Digital Game-Based Learning Environments (DGBLEs). The design and development of educational software requires the combination of different fields of expertise (scientific core, educational-, graphic-, interaction design, technical programming etc.) represented by different groups or individuals. A recent study distinguishes four main roles in the creation of an educational game (a) educational expert, (b) game designer, (c) instructor and (d) learner [2]. More roles have to be considered if the activity is to lead to a marketable product (market research, product promotion etc.). Although gameplay is commonly considered

© ICST Institute for Computer Sciences, Social Informatics and Telecommunications Engineering 2018
A. L. Brooks et al. (Eds.): ArtsIT 2017/DLI 2017, LNICST 229, pp. 324–336, 2018.
https://doi.org/10.1007/978-3-319-76908-0_31

as a voluntary activity, participation in serious games, which is usually mandatory and pre-designed, may reduce the fun and impulsiveness of the game. Recent studies however suggest that contrary to the opinion of many game designers, being required to play a serious game does not necessarily take the fun out of the game or reduce enjoyment and learning effect [3, 4]. According to the Gameplay/Purpose/Scope (G/P/S) classification model a serious game can be designed for one, several or none of the following purposes: Training, Message-broadcasting and Data exchange [5]. The first category includes serious games used for organized training of specific individuals – or groups – in simulated virtual environments through game playing. In such environments, knowledge and training is accomplished in a binding and organized way and, although "it's a game", participants are aware of their training, feel dedicated to what they are doing, and willing to follow certain rules no matter how strict they might be. On the other hand, the main purpose of message-broadcasting game based learning environments is the introduction and education of the general public (or pre-defined target groups) on specific topics/policies of several disciplines (physics, ecology, economy, art, history etc.) through relaxed and self-controlled participation. In such environments access is open to the general public, there are no strict rules to follow and engagement is entirely voluntary. The third category of this model includes games designed to collect information from their players or encouraging them to exchange data.

In this work we focus exclusively on message-broadcasting public DGBLEs as we attempt to understand and analyze the particular characteristics of such environments and propose effective models for their design. To do so, we initially state a number of essential requirements that have to be satisfied as well as a number of crucial issues to be considered during the design. We then proceed to propose a model based on a set of properties satisfying the above requirements while addressing most of the issues specified. Finally, we conclude by presenting a case study of an existing game-based learning environment called "Ocean Sound Lab" having a design/structure that matches closely most principles of the proposed model.

2   A Proposed Model

An effective message-broadcasting DGBLE installed in a public area must comply with the following two essential requirements:

- Maximize the number of attracted individuals for its specific target group(s)
- Minimize the number of individuals walking away before the completion of its intended course.

A third desirable – although not crucial – requirement is the ability to assess its effectiveness and impact on each individual as a measure of its overall efficacy. This can be achieved by encouraging participants to evaluate themselves through quiz-like applications or games integrated in the learning environment.

A key issue to bear in mind during the design of such a DGBLE is that participation of individuals is voluntary and there is no guarantee that it will last throughout the entire learning session. Other significant issues include the presence of multiple competitive attractions and time scarcity. When wandering in a large hall of a museum or exhibition, most visitors' attention is continuously challenged by a variety of rival visual and audio stimulants all competing for a share of their time. Since there is always a limit to the total time a person is planning – or allowed – to spend in such places, time scarcity is another important issue. In that sense, visitors inevitably are drawn towards the most interesting attractions, opting out the rest. But even when visitors are attracted and engaged to a DGBLE – hence at least their vision is focused – there is always an increased chance of distraction due to other existing stimulants (mostly audio and haptic) that challenge their attention focus. Such stimulants include the proximity of other persons (including friends and family), public noise, loud voices, phones, music etc. Chances of distraction are further increased considering the positive emotional attitude of visitors in such places [6].

All above issues are characterized as universal since they apply to the average person. Wishing to focus on particular target groups of people there are even more person-specific issues to consider including age group, cognition level and physical condition (especially for elder people) special abilities, and communication language. When designing public DGBLEs these issues are equally important to contemplate, especially when the educational topics focus on specific target groups. A summary of all issues discussed above is presented in Table 1.

Table 1. Issues to be considered when designing DGBLEs.

Key Issue
Voluntary engagement - Needs to be refreshed periodically in order to be maintained throughout the entire learning path
Universal issues

- Time scarcity
- Presence of multiple competitive attractions
- Increased probability of distraction -once engaged- due to
    o   Proximity of other persons (friends, family...)
    o   Public environment (noise, loud voices, phones, music etc.)
- Positive emotional attitude

Person-specific issues
- Age group - Cognition level - Physical condition (especially in larger ages) - Special abilities - Communication language

Taking into account the requirements and issues stated above, we initially propose two sets of properties (essential/desirable) serving as design guidelines for implementing effective and pleasurable public DGBLEs.

A. Essential Properties. A successfully designed and implemented public DGBLE must initially demonstrate a considerable level of saliency so that it stands out against other attractions in order to maximize the percentage of by passers diverting towards it. Saliency must be implemented to both software (nice screen graphics, motion, sound etc.) and the physical space area it is placed upon (signs, graphics, flags etc.). However, visitors' attraction through saliency is just the beginning. First time observers must be able to grasp the theme and context of the DGBLE in a very short time. Failing to do so, visitors will most probably walk away especially in the presence of other competitive attractions. Moreover a brief, clear and unambiguous description of context is necessary but not sufficient condition for further engagement particularly if the implemented educational topics are hard or unusual. In such cases visitors have to be guided towards the core of a theme in a series of steps of increasing complexity, starting with simple and enjoyable engagements and proceeding to the more demanding ones. In this way the visitors' overall engagement is preserved throughout the learning path. To further preserve and increase users' engagement, a public DGBLE could implement competition mechanisms among players, e.g. in the form of high scores or time records to be beaten, or even real-time multiple-player competitions if this is technically feasible. On the other hand, since some people are not very keen to rivalry and competition, another way to boost engagement is through more relaxed reward mechanisms where visitors are evaluated for their newly acquired skills or knowledge and not for their competitive abilities. Reward-through-evaluation can be implemented in various forms, like overall performance analysis classification, or post-game knowledge evaluation through quiz-like games.

Finally a successfully designed and implemented public DGBLE must create a positive post-engagement affection so that people continue to reflect upon it later on and discuss it further encouraging others to also try the experience. This type of social advertisement works in tandem with saliency to increase the spreading of knowledge to the general public.

B. Desirable Properties. The properties/guidelines discussed so far are essential for the proper design of an effective DGBLE. We further suggest some additional features/properties that – although not essential – could further boost the effectiveness of the design.

In theory the educational value of a public DGBLE should be similar for all participants, however this is not always the case. In fact the spectrum of people addressed by a public learning environment is very wide, as it includes people from different countries, different ages, and even different educational levels. To maximize the effect on all these people, a public DGBLE must be customizable in different ways. Initially if the learning environment is addressed to people from different countries – as in the case of large museums and exhibitions – then it must have a multilingual user interface supporting at least the most common languages of the expected visitors. Moreover a customizable learning environment may implement different pedagogic approaches for different people groups such as children and adults. The different modes in a customizable DGBLE can be presented as options through the user interface as in the typical example of language selection.

Dynamic adjustability of a DGBLE should not be limited to the example above. In fact, this is another desirable property of a learning environment that contributes to user experience optimization. In fact an intelligent DGBLE can be dynamically adjusted to current user's capabilities by monitoring his actions and fine-tuning the desired level of difficulty accordingly. Moreover, during the course of time the system may collect a number of statistical parameters, analyze them from time to time and use the analysis results to re-adjust several key parameters like speed and difficulty of a game, time to complete a learning course, etc. Finally, another highly desirable – although not essential – design property is system modularity, since it allows large and complex DGBLEs to be configured in alternative ways by adding, substituting or removing separate system components. A summary all properties discussed above is given in Table 2.

Table 2. Essential and desirable properties/guidelines for the design of effective public DGBLEs.

Essential properties
- considerable level of saliency
- brief, clear and unambiguous description of context
- gradually increasing complexity to preserve engagement
- competition mechanisms
- reward-through-evaluation mechanisms
- positive post-engagement experience broadcast

Desirable properties
- customization
o for several target audiences
o interface language
- dynamic adjustability
o to current user capabilities
o to statistical analysis of results
- modularity

Model Description. The core component of a public DGBLE is one or several standalone games, tutorials, presentations, etc., covering all topics and issues that need to be learned (and absorbed). In several situations however, the topics to be taught present an inherent complexity that necessitates the implementation of intricate interfaces with steep learning curves. This might be especially true in topics related to science or mathematics. Consequently even if a person is initially attracted to an educational game, an increased interface complexity might reduce his motivation for further engagement, especially in public areas with other nearby competing attractions and distractions. This becomes even more challenging if we consider that in public DGBLEs the target users are just visitors strolling leisurely around. Hence, users have to be attracted in a voluntary engagement, which in addition must be periodically refreshed in order to be preserved throughout the entire learning path.

An approach to overcome this obstacle is to enrich the learning environment with other attractions and activities that initially "allure" visitors to attend and gradually escalate their engagement towards the subject. Such attractions may include, for example, brief multimedia presentations of certain thought-provoking facts or implications related to the topic. They can also include several stimulating, very simplistic, hands-on interactive digital experiments on the basic principles of the topic. Engagement can be further increased by implementing mechanisms of gratification-through-competition or evaluation such as multiple-player games, high score beating, and self-evaluation procedures. The combination of all the above results in a more "casual" arcade-like digital environment for a person to wander, play, enjoy, compete, and eventually grasp and absorb the basic concepts of the educational topic. In the context of the previous discussion we propose a structural model for the design of digital public game-based learning environments based on the following general scheme:

Attract > Engage > Educate > Evaluate

Our model envisions public DGLEs as integration of a number of discrete application modules under a global shell acting as a home, covering all four stages of the above scheme. Each stage of the proposed model contains one or more standalone application modules that can be invoked either by the user, or run in a demo mode. In the following we present in detail the concept and a general description for each of the four stages of the model, a general outline of which is presented in Table 3.

Stage I. Initial Attraction through Excitement and Curiosity. The main purpose of this stage is to attract the attention of visitors passing-by and make them stop for a while to see what is going on. At this stage visitors will try to assess the situation and decide if they are interested in the subject, or continue with their tour. This is the most critical stage, since all other stages depend on whether or not the visitor remains attracted or walks away. To make a visitor initially attracted, the learning environment must offer an introduction which is (a) brief and accurate so that its context becomes immediately clear and (b) creates excitement and inspires curiosity. Such an introduction may be implemented as one or several brief multimedia presentations running either in standalone or in interactive mode. The content of such presentations must be delivered in a vibrant and playful style, highlighting a combination of well-known aspects of the subject mixed with several strange or unusual ones. Since curiosity-triggering events and surprises can have a positive effect on learning [7] introductory presentations may also contain thought provoking questions, trivia and other stimulating fun facts that entice visitor's attention and curiosity leading them eventually to further engagement.

In public areas such as museums and exhibitions this stage should be backed up with a carefully designed salient physical layout (consoles, booths, posters, flags etc.) to further intensify the attraction effect.

Table 3. Outline of the proposed model

Stage I. Initial Attraction through Excitement and Curiosity.
Purpose: Invite / attract / allure visitors to the topic.   - Interactive multimedia presentations   - Interesting and fun facts on the topic   - Thought-provoking questions and trivia   Works in tandem with a carefully designed salient physical layout
Stage II. Motivation Boost through Relaxed Participation
Purpose: Encourage / motivate visitors to interact with the topic   - Self-explanatory simple and attractive interfaces   - Requiring low mental effort so that people are not discouraged or overwhelmed   - Boost enthusiasm / fortify engagement
Stage III. Core Learning through Game Playing.
Purpose: Engage individuals to core learning of subject through game-playing   - More than one games with overlapping topics   - Progressive difficulty   - Single-player (also multiplayer whenever possible)
Stage IV. Knowledge Confirmation through Self-Evaluation
Purpose: Use rewarding techniques to reinforce attachment to the subject   - Quiz / game like   - Comprehensive answers, further elaborating the subject   - User performance statistics

Stage II. Motivation Boost through Relaxed Participation. As soon as visitors are attracted to the learning environment most of them will start exploring the available content. To further encourage and motivate users, this stage should offer a gallery of elementary simulation games and/or simulation experiments relevant to the fundamental scientific principles of the educational topic. These games/experiments should be kept simple and self-explanatory, having attractive interfaces and requiring low mental effort so that users are not discouraged or overwhelmed. Ideally, this stage must boost the curiosity and enthusiasm of participants and further reinforce their engagement to proceed to the more complex and demanding educational games to follow.

Stage III. Core Learning through Game Playing. This is the fundamental stage of the DGBLE. Visitors proceeding to this stage have already the basic knowledge and enough motivation to engage to more complex and demanding games that require additional mental effort and concentration. If the topics to be covered in this play-and-learn approach are numerous then this stage may contain more than one games each based on a subset of these topics with as much as possible overlapping of topics among games. Ideally games should have a progressive difficulty but not too many levels, since they have to be kept as short as possible, just long enough for the players to ensure that they have mastered the basic laws and principles behind the game. Although all games should be designed primarily as single-player games, a multi-player option could be considered, since the chance of competition with other players – whenever given – enhances the experience and boosts learning.

Stage IV. Knowledge Confirmation through Self-Evaluation. The main purpose of this stage is to rehearse and reinforce the new knowledge using rewarding techniques through game-based self-evaluation. Participants coming through the previous three stages of skilled games and experimentation have already expanded their knowledge on the topics of the DGBLE. Some participants will just walk away at this point, however several others will probably be willing to be challenged further by proving to themselves, to their companions and any watching by-standers how well they master their newly-acquired knowledge. This stage may contain one or more quiz-like evaluation tests with multiple choice answers. To match the overall spirit of the game environment such tests may be also implemented as simple games e.g. with a token-like character having to reach to a target destination by moving forward with right answers and backwards with wrong ones. Evaluation tests/games should feature several user-selected difficulty levels allowing participants to adjust their amount of effort. Tests should terminate giving a total score and a detailed evaluation report containing complete but concise explanations for both right and wrong answers. The report may finish with a short qualification verdict written in high-spirit and maybe containing some well-placed humor. This is especially helpful in case of lower-than-average scores, so that participants are not intimidated but rather encouraged to try again for a better score. Performance statistics taken from this stage from all test scores may be used as a primary indication of the overall value and effectiveness of the learning environment.

Additional GUI Guidelines

To ensure the GUI integrity and uniformity of DGBLEs designed according to this model, the following additional guidelines are proposed:

- Application/game modules may be accessed from within a global "Home Interface" through which participants will be guided along the learning path. Such an interface physically integrates and homogenizes the various components of the DGBLE while it also manages global settings common to all components like for instance interface language, sound preferences, etc.
- Application/game modules should have similar thematic backgrounds and offer identical controls and behaviour for most common actions like getting help, manage settings or getting back to the Home Interface.

- Help and guidance should be provided in a uniform style throughout the environment by means of a theme-related animated pedagogical agent that will be continuously visible and available.
- Content navigation should be clearly suggested but not strictly enforced. Although the stages of the proposed model are logically sequential, some visitors may feel oppressed and discouraged if they are forced to follow a strict roadmap. This is especially true for recurring visitors or users with a partial knowledge of the subject, who want to engage directly on specific game/applications skipping introductory material. The environment should clearly suggest the logical sequence of actions to be taken by novice users but at the same time provide a discrete indication that they can freely navigate around. Chances are that novice visitors will stick to the suggested route, while the more experienced ones will successfully attempt to circumvent it.
- Content redundancy is crucial and should be implemented through dispersion and overlap of the topics to be covered in multiple application modules. In that sense it is desirable to have an arcade of several different games of varying difficulty based on overlapping sets of principles. This variety will permit different visitors to be familiarized with the same set of principles while engaging with different game-learning activities.
- Mechanisms for monitoring user actions and preferences should be implemented throughout the learning environment. Monitoring results may be analyzed in real time predicting users' behaviour and triggering the intelligent help subsystem to provide instructions and guidance [8]. Selected monitoring parameters should be archived for periodical statistical analysis of users' behaviour and system performance. Analysis results may be used as a feedback for adjustments to optimize the efficiency of the system (Fig. 1).

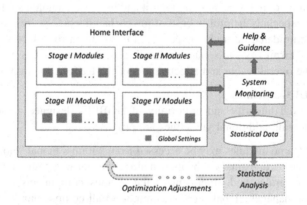

Fig. 1. Intelligent help & guidance and optimization through dynamic system monitoring and statistical analysis

3 Case Study: OCEAN SOUND LAB

Underwater acoustics is the study of sound and sound propagation in water, e.g. in the ocean. OCEAN SOUND LAB (OSL) is a digital game-based learning environment developed by the Institute of Applied and Computational Mathematics of the Foundation for Research and Technology-Hellas (IACM-FORTH). It is designed for installation in public aquaria and museum exhibitions, aiming to offer to the general public a pleasurable introduction to the ocean soundscape and the basic principles of underwater acoustics [9]. It contains a variety of play-and-learn activities, from presentations of underwater sounds and basic physics for the non-expert, to interactive applications and games around ocean acoustic propagation effects. Figure 2 illustrates some representative screenshots of OSL.

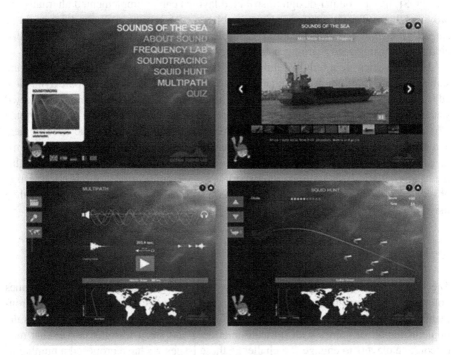

Fig. 2. Screen snapshots of OCEAN SOUND LAB: Main screen (top left), Sounds of the Sea (top right), MultiPath (bottom left) and Squid Hunt (bottom right)

OCEAN SOUND LAB is a game-based learning software environment that fits to the principles mentioned in this work. It exhibits a modular design currently featuring seven modules that span all 4 stages of the proposed model. Initial attraction to the environment (model stage I) is accomplished through two interactive shows/tutorials, called "Sounds of the Sea" and "About Sound". Motivation boost (stage II) is achieved through two other modules called "Frequency Lab" and "Sound Tracing". The core of

OSL (stage III) contains two game-modules called "Squid Hunt" and "MultiPath" and finally knowledge confirmation through self-evaluation (stage IV) is attained through a quiz-like game module of multiple choice type questions of user-selected difficulty levels.

All OSL modules share a global thematic background and offer similar controls and behavior. Help and guidance throughout the environment is provided through an iconic diver "swimming" around the underwater environment (see Fig. 1). The names of the applications and game modules on the main screen are arranged to imply an ordered list that will most probably be followed by first-time visitors. This list is ordered to represent the intended roadmap, and will equally probably be skipped by recurring visitors aiming for specific games.

A standard physical layout for OSL is a single custom-made console with a touch screen running all modules through a main menu that suggests a learning path. Since OSL has a modular design, distributed layouts can be implemented alternatively, provided that sufficient room space is available. In such layouts, OSL modules could be spread at several physical locations (consoles) arranged in a sequential pattern that emulates the suggested learning path.

User activities are monitored throughout the entire learning environment producing statistics about their preferences and action-patterns. OSL does not support dynamical adjustment of its parameters through real-time data analysis, however the collected statistics can be periodically analyzed off-line in an attempt to evaluate its educational efficiency. A systematic analysis of usability tests conducted during the development and testing of Ocean Sound Lab revealed that users/players devote twice as much time in gameplay and quiz solving compared to other activities such as interactive multimedia presentations and simulation/experimentation applications Another interesting observation is that participants are rating the integrated OSL environment higher than the sum of its individual components [10].

4 Discussion

The effective design of public DGBLEs is a challenging task because it presumes voluntary engagement of participants in highly distractive and competitive environments. Moreover the inherent complexity of certain educational topics necessitates the implementation of games with intricate interfaces and steep learning curves that may discourage players to engage. To challenge these issues we have proposed a number of properties serving as guidelines for the design of public DGBLEs. These properties, categorized as either essential or desirable depending on the importance and impact they have on the design, serve as foundations to a comprehensive multistage model for the design of public DGBLEs based on the general scheme "attract > engage > educate > evaluate". The key idea behind this model is to initially attract perspective participants through excitement and curiosity, then gradually increase their motivation through relaxed participation to simple ludic activities on the basic principles of the educational topic. These activities will eventually strengthen participants' engagement which is especially helpful for topics of inherent complexity. When the desired level of motivation is achieved, participants are more prone to enthral to the core game activities of the DGBLE and stay engaged throughout the end. The model completes with a last stage offering ludic self-evaluation to participants wishing to do so. Knowledge confirmation through self-evaluation also provides a way to assess the efficiency of the DGBLE itself by performing statistical analysis of the temporal collected results. In a more flexible and agile scheme the same results could be used to fine-tune the environment in real-time by adjusting certain of its key operational parameters. To complete the model description and ensure its integrity and uniformity a set of additional GUI guidelines are also proposed. This set includes guidelines about the home interface, thematic backgrounds, help and guidance, content navigation and more.

Ocean Sound Lab is an existing DGBLE for introduction to the world of underwater sound and the basic principles of underwater acoustics; an interesting, unusual and rather challenging topic. Since its overall design and organization is largely based to the principles discussed here, we present it as an example of how a DGBLE designed according to the proposed model will look like and behave.

There are more challenges in the design of public DGBLEs that have not been addressed here such as the support of content and GUI adaptation to different target groups, the implementation of adaptive instructional scaffolding techniques for promoting deeper levels of learning and more. Future studies taking into account these and similar issues will definitely produce enhanced models for the design of more effective DGBLEs for public education.

References

1. Michael, D., Chen, S.: Serious Games: Games That Educate, Train and Inform. Thomson Course Technology, Boston (2006)
2. Vidakis, N., Syntychakis, E., Kalafatis, K., Varhalamas, P., Triantafyllidis, G.: Concealing education into games. In: 9th European Conference on Games-Based Learning, pp. 554–563 (2015)
3. Kuindersma, E., van der Pal, J., van den Herik, J., Plaat, A.: Comparing Voluntary and Mandatory Gameplay (2016)
4. Kuindersma, E., van der Pal, J., van den Herik, J., Plaat, A.: Voluntary play in serious games. In: De Gloria, A., Veltkamp, R. (eds.) GALA 2015. LNCS, vol. 9599, pp. 131–140. Springer, Cham (2016). https://doi.org/10.1007/978-3-319-40216-1_14
5. Djaouti, D., Alvarez, J., Jessel, J.P.: Classifying serious games: the G/P/S model. In: Handbook of Research on Improving Learning and Motivation through Educational Games: Multidisciplinary Approaches, pp. 118–136 (2011)
6. Fredrickson, B.L., Branigan, C.: Positive emotions broaden the scope of attention and thought-action repertoires. Cogn. Emot. 19(3), 313–332 (2005)
7. Van Oostendorp, H., Wouters, P.: Narration-based techniques to facilitate game-based learning. In: Wouters, P., van Oostendorp, H. (eds.) Instructional Techniques to Facilitate Learning and Motivation of Serious Games, pp. 103–117. Springer, Cham (2017). https://doi.org/10.1007/978-3-319-39298-1_6
8. Min, W., Wiggins, J.B., Pezzullo, L.G., Vail, A.K., Boyer, K.E., Mott, B.W., Frankosky, M.H., Wiebe, E.N., Lester, J.C.: Predicting dialogue acts for intelligent virtual agents with multimodal student interaction data. In: 9th International Conference on Educational Data Mining, Raleigh, NC, USA (2016)

9. Kalogerakis, M., Skarsoulis, E., Piperakis, G., Haviaris, E.: Ocean Sound Lab: a software environment for introduction to underwater acoustics. In: Proceedings of Meetings on Acoustics ECUA2012, 2 July 2012, vol. 17, no. 1, p. 070008. ASA (2012)
10. Kalogerakis, M., Skarsoulis, E., Piperakis, G.: Evaluating and understanding the usability of an educational software environment for public aquaria and museum exhibitions: In: 1st Virtual International Conference on Advanced Research in Scientific Areas, pp. 2038–2041 (2012)

i-Prolog: A Web-Based Intelligent Tutoring System for Learning Prolog

Afroditi Stathaki[1], Haridimos Kondylakis[2(✉)],
Emmanouil Marakakis[1], and Michael Kalogerakis[3]

[1] Department of Informatics Engineering,
Technological Educational Institute of Crete, 71410 Heraklion, Greece
stathakiafrodith@hotmail.com, mmarak@cs.teicrete.gr
[2] Computational Biomedicine Laboratory,
FORTH-ICS, N. Plastira 100, 70013 Heraklion, Greece
kondylak@ics.forth.gr
[3] Department of Electrical Engineering,
Technological Educational Institute of Crete, 71410 Heraklion, Greece
mixalis@cs.teicrete.gr

Abstract. Intelligent tutoring systems (ITS) incorporate techniques for transferring knowledge and skills to students. These systems use a combination of computer-aided instruction methods and artificial intelligence. In this paper we present a web-based intelligent tutoring system. Although it can be used as a generic learning mechanism, in this paper, as a proof of concept we used it for learning Prolog. We present the architecture of our system and we provide details on each one of its modules. Each lesson includes the corresponding lecture with theory and exercises, a practice module where students can apply the corresponding theory and an assessment module to verify user's understanding. The system can be used with or without a teacher enabling distant learning. Among the novelties of our system is its flexibility to adapt to individual student choices and profile, offering a wide range of alternatives and trying to continuously keep the interest of the final user. The preliminary evaluation performed confirms the usability of our system and the benefits of using it for learning Prolog.

Keywords: Intelligent tutoring systems · Prolog

1 Introduction

Electronic tutors can deliver material through games, videos, movies, and exercises, a more exciting menu for any student and especially for those with learning difficulties. Electronic tutors try to personalize the learning process and to replace human tutors. The course content is personalized based on the evaluation of the student's performance and knowledge and as such the presentation of the material can differ for each student. In addition, computer tutors in many cases inflict less anxiety in students when compared to human tutors: Learners can practice as much as they want and make mistakes without anyone observing them.

© ICST Institute for Computer Sciences, Social Informatics and Telecommunications Engineering 2018
A. L. Brooks et al. (Eds.): ArtsIT 2017/DLI 2017, LNICST 229, pp. 337–346, 2018.
https://doi.org/10.1007/978-3-319-76908-0_32

To this direction, many intelligent tutoring systems (ITS) have been constructed the last decades. According to Graesser [5], «ITSs are computerized learning environments that incorporate computational models from the cognitive sciences, learning sciences, computational linguistics, artificial intelligence, mathematics, and other fields». As such, ITSs have the common goal of enabling learning in a meaningful and effective manner by using a variety of computing technologies.

The primary goal of an ITS system is to mimic a human tutor by adapting its instructions according to individual student's performance, strengths and weaknesses [18]. There are many benefits associated with ITSs since they ease the work of instructors and can replace them in situations where they may not be present, such as with an embedded training system which may be used out in the field. Training is tailored and customized according to the potential of the individual student, enabling a more efficient student learning. Furthermore, the knowledge of the best instructors can be captured and incorporated into an ITS, and distributed to all students.

This paper focuses on the development of a web-based intelligent tutoring system. As a proof of concept we implemented the tool for Prolog, but it is built as generic as possible, able to be used for other lessons as well. Prolog is a logic programming language as its implementation is based on Horn Clause logic, a subset of first-order logic [19]. Prolog has built-in a unification algorithm and the only way to do a repetition is through recursion. As such many students coming from procedural programming find Prolog difficult to understand and use. To this direction, we designed a novel system enabling students to learn and experiment with Prolog. The designed system has many novel features and aims to teach Prolog programming and to be deployed in real-time education and/or in distance learning. The system presents the theory behind Prolog and examples and instructs the learners on how to construct Prolog programs. Then the practice module is used to enable practicing allowing students to use among three types of practicing: *hint-based*, *schema-based* or *open practice*. The whole learning environment is personalized according to individual profiles. It provides examples and appropriate instructions according to the personal learning style, making the whole learning process as personalized as possible. Then, an assessment module evaluates user understanding enabling or not the next lecture. A teacher is optional, and if present she/he can supervise the whole process asynchronously and identify the progress of the individual students.

The rest of this paper is structured as follows: In Sect. 2, we present related work. Then in Sect. 3 we present the architecture of our system and describe the components of our system. In Sect. 4, we present an initial evaluation of our system. Finally, Sect. 5 concludes this paper and presents directions for future work.

2   Related Work

There have been many ITSs developed over the last 20 years to help students learn geography, circuits, medical diagnosis [4], mathematics, physics, genetics, and chemistry.

For computer programming, ACT programming Tutor (APT) [2] offers hints for learning LISP, produced using a set of expert-defined production rules. Ask-Elle [3] is a Haskell tutor that tries to help students by identifying program errors, whereas in ITAP [12] programming hints are employed using past student's data in order to debug Python programs. Those recent works show that hints are essential in tutoring systems. However, they mostly focus on debugging programs and not on combing theory teaching with program debugging.

For Prolog, there have been developed many university ITS for teaching programming, used with positive results [16, 17] and tools helping students to construct logic programs [10].

The Augmented Prolog Programming Environment (APPE) [11], for example, accepts student programs and detects errors from five categories: (1) Incorrect Solutions, (2) Uncovered Solutions, (3) Non termination, (4) Redundant Solutions, (5) Invalid Parameters. When an error is detected, advices are also provided to the students. Another ITS system for debugging Prolog programs by Looi [9], analyzes input programs and uses task-specific knowledge to detect bugs and to correct them. Belikova [1] on the other hand, separate the errors identified into two categories: The programs that cannot run because of errors and the ones that may work but possibly contain other errors. The work uses a set of recursive program schemata which cover several aspects of recursion such as simple recursion, monotonic or non-monotonic recursion etc. All these aforementioned works provide outdated tools and mostly focus on error-detection to guide Prolog learning. In our case however, the whole platform goes beyond simple debugging, provides lectures and example exercises and is personalized according to individual learning style. In addition, our system supports a more pedagogical learning approach and it is available for use on the web.

Another work closer to our vision is by Vlahavas et al. [15]. The system created can be used for distance learning and contains text, images and animated lessons. The system provides examples, bibliographic resources, exercises and many links for each lesson. Initially it provides the basic concepts to the amateur users and then progresses on information on more advanced topics. Finally, at the end, the user is guided in developing small Prolog programs. In our approach, we go beyond guided development of Prolog programs and we allow hint-based, schema-based and open practice. In addition, our system includes an assessment module for capturing user's progress and understanding.

Overall, although most of the developed systems can detect errors and some of them already provide useful resources to the end-users, still the intelligence used is limited. For example, the emotional status of the student could affect his/her learning curve and an ITS should be adaptable and personalized according to individual user profiles. In our approach however, user profiling is the central point of our implementation.

3 Architecture

The architecture of our system is shown in Fig. 1. It consists of six basic components: (1) The interface; (2) the tutoring/pedagogical module; (3) the teacher module; (4) the student/learner module; the (5) APIs for updating the Knowledge base and finally (6) the Knowledge Base. Bellow we provide more details for each one of these modules.

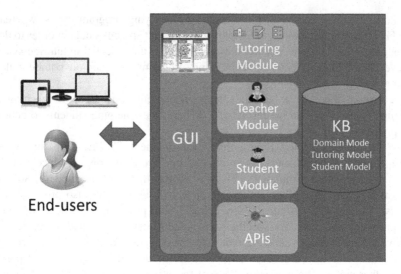

Fig. 1. The architecture of i-Prolog

We have to note that the system is developed both in the Greek and English language. The interface is developed using CSS, AJAX and HTML 5, whereas the back-end of the system is developed using Prolog.

3.1   The Tutoring/Pedagogical Module

This module in essence is the cognitive model that contains the concepts, the rules, and the problem-solving strategies of the domain to be learned. It controls the presentation of the material to be presented to the student and has a feedback mechanism in order to answer end-user's questions. It is responsible for selecting teaching goals, and for determining appropriate teaching strategies according to the selected student model, learner's needs and/or preferences, learning experiences, the domain of discourse and the instructional objectives of the intelligent tutoring system.

In our system, the information is structured as "lessons". For each lesson, we have the teaching goals and the teaching strategies. In addition, each lesson is divided into three parts: (a) the lecture (b) the practice and (c) the assessment part.

The *lecture part* supports several teaching methods, like question-answering, class style lecturing, etc. that can be combined, trying to keep alive the interest of the learner. In any case, the selection of the teaching method is guided by an underlying instructional theory, the theory of Skinner [14]. According to Skinner, a question is a stimulus and the answer is a reaction. If a student reacts, there is positive amplification and then a student can learn. As such, in general, a lecture first presents some theory items to the student, and then, in order to progress to the next theory item, he has to answer one or more small exercises/examples, based on the taught theory. To do that he can revisit the theory. However, she/he can progress to the next theory item, independent of the correctness of his/her answer.

The *practice part* on the other hand, includes different techniques for exercising. The system allows learners to discover which technique is more appropriate for them. The underling theories of this section are the theories of *"discovery learning"* and *"fact-finding learning"* claiming that learners must have a critical thinking and should discover by themselves what is important to learn [13]. As such, the learner can select according to his/her preference among *hint-based practice, schema-based practice* and *open-practice.* In the hint-based practice, many hints guide the learner to complete a certain task. In the schema-based approach example, schemata are suggested for completing the task showing examples and guiding the end-user on constructing accordingly his/her programs. Finally, in the open-practice approach, no help is provided to the learner and he has to identify possible strategies by himself for solving the exercises.

Finally, the *assessment part* incorporates tests and exercises trying to identify the outcome of the selected teaching methods and to construct the profile of the end-user. This part can be used by teachers to evaluate the progress of their students, or by students to evaluate themselves and understand their progress. The assessment of each lesson should be completed within 45 min and if the available time runs out without answering more than 50% of the exercises the lesson is considered uncompleted and the student has to do the assessment again. Users can evaluate the assessment methods and procedures and all comments are saved to the knowledge base as well for future reference and extraction of statistics.

A use case-diagram of the functionality of the tutoring module is shown in Fig. 2.

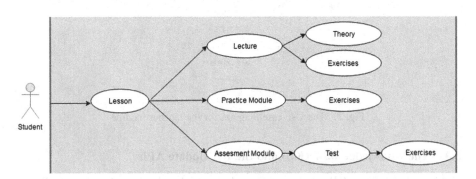

Fig. 2. The Use-case diagram of i-Prolog

3.2   The Student/Learner Module

The student module incorporates the cognitive processes (e.g. information retrieval, calculation and problem solving), the meta-cognitive strategies (e.g. learning from errors) and the psychological attributes (e.g. developmental level, learning style, interests) for each student. As such, the student module represents the learner's emerging knowledge and skills. Information such as learning preferences, past learning experiences may also be relevant for adapting the teaching process. It also records the learner's errors and misconceptions. It continuously monitors and assesses student performance and updates accordingly the student model. This module provides the dynamicity in student-centered tutoring personalizing the teaching process. In order to do so, information for each unique user is used (his/her email) that are registered by the administrator of the system.

3.3   The Teacher Module

The teacher module enables a distant teacher to communicate with the students using messages, providing him with a complete view of a student's progress through the system and with statistical information. The teacher has the ability to detect the mistakes of his/her students, their selections and their comments and to observe the student's assessments. A use-case diagram of the functionalities of the teacher module is shown in Fig. 3.

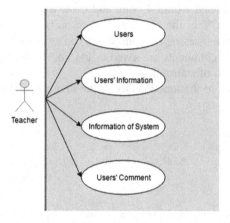

Fig. 3. The Use-case diagram for the teacher module

3.4   The Knowledge Base (KB) and the KB Update APIs

The knowledge Base (KB) contains knowledge related to the subject matter, i.e. Prolog programming. It contains knowledge about Prolog programming and learning in order to make inferences and/or to solve problems. In addition, it contains explanations for problem solutions, providing also alternative explanations for the same topic. Furthermore, it includes a user manual for using the system.

3.5   The User Interface

The user interface provides the means for the students and teachers to interact with the system through a graphical user interface. Some screenshots of the GUI are show in Figs. 4 and 5.

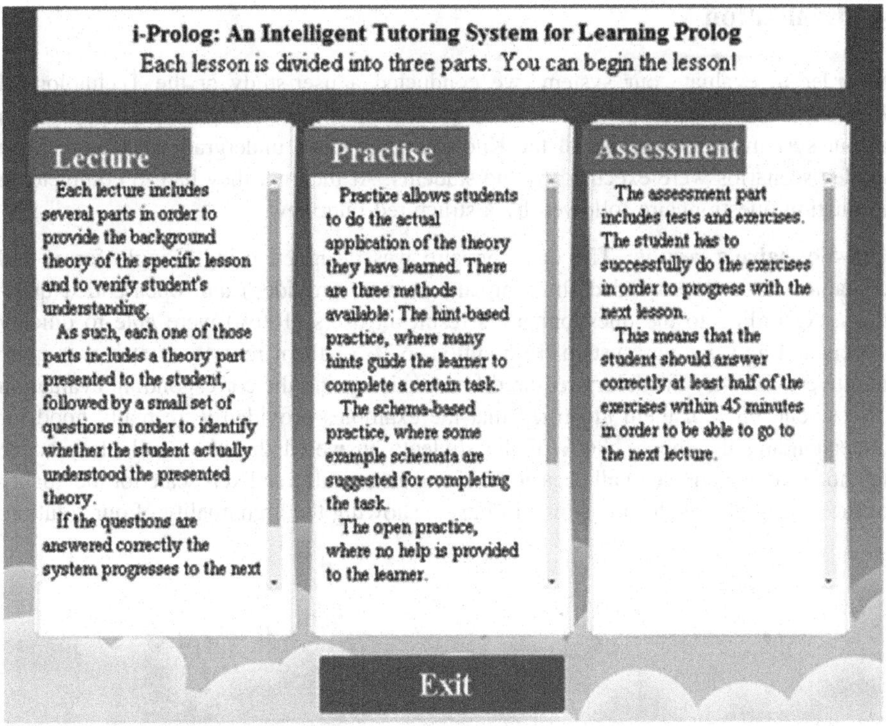

i-Prolog: An Intelligent Tutoring System for Learning Prolog
Each lesson is divided into three parts. You can begin the lesson!
Lecture
Each lecture includes several parts in order to provide the background theory of the specific lesson and to verify student's understanding.
As such, each one of those parts includes a theory part presented to the student, followed by a small set of questions in order to identify whether the student actually understood the presented theory.
If the questions are answered correctly the system progresses to the next
Practise
Practice allows students to do the actual application of the theory they have learned. There are three methods available: The hint-based practice, where many hints guide the learner to complete a certain task.
The schema-based practice, where some example schemata are suggested for completing the task.
The open practice, where no help is provided to the learner.
Assessment
The assessment part includes tests and exercises. The student has to successfully do the exercises in order to progress with the next lesson.
This means that the student should answer correctly at least half of the exercises within 45 minutes in order to be able to go to the next lecture.
Exit

Fig. 4. Selecting lecture, practice or evaluation

SWISH
Create a Program Notebook here
Open source file containing

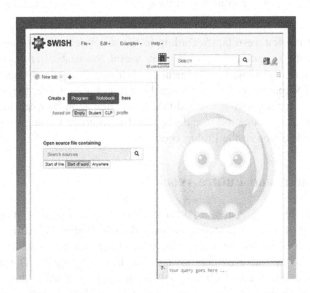

Fig. 5. Practicing using the online Prolog compiler

4   Evaluation

In order to evaluate our system, we conducted a user-study at the Technological Educational Institute (T.E.I) of Crete. More specifically, we made a short introduction of our system to 15 students of the Knowledge Systems undergraduate lesson. Then guided scenarios were executed by the students. At the end, they had to complete an evaluation questionnaire followed by a structured interview.

Questionnaire's results: The questionnaire was designed using Google forms and contained both closed-ended (limiting the answers provided) and open-ended questions. According to the questionnaire's result all users (100%) were able to quickly understand and use our system. In addition, 67% of them reported that it was quite intuitive to identify the theory required for practicing and the corresponding evaluation assessment. 93% of them identified that the examples provided were really good for understanding the theory. 86% of the students answered that the available practice methods were adequate in all occasions. Using an overall five likert scale for the quality of the system the results are shown in Fig. 6, showing the high quality of our solution.

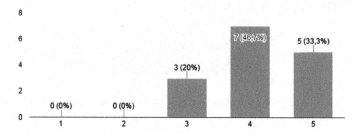

Fig. 6. Overall evaluation of the quality of the system (5 the best)

Structured Interview results: According to the structured interviews conducted, all students liked the system and found it really useful and usable. They considered that the system offers a pleasant environment for learning Prolog and they reported that there are no unexpected errors or strange behavior. Furthermore, the students made some proposals for improving the real-time communication between the teacher and the students in the practice mode and suggested to improve the suggestions provided after the error-detection in the Prolog code.

5   Conclusions and Future Work

i-Prolog is an e-learning system used for student-centered teaching. It focuses on the learner and gives specific attention to provide knowledge by letting the students themselves to discover the learning style that best suits them. As such, the tool helps students to gain a positive attitude towards the learning process. The use of such a system can offer significant benefits for both the teacher and learners due to its ability to be used in many ways and to adapt according to individual student profiles. It can be applied to both traditional education and distance learning. In traditional education, it can be a tool enriching the teaching process, while it can be used remotely to replace completely the physical presence of the teacher. The main objective of this work is to enhance the interest of students and teachers and to become a precursor for new research that will evolve and improve its construction and its use.

We have to admit, that there is a margin of improvement from both the computer and the education side. Until now, there are systems that offer asynchronous communication with the teacher who manages the system. The new challenge is to turn the ITS into a system that will enable communication between not only a student and an educator but among all students as well. The aim of this improvement is to integrate the theories of cooperative and socio-cultural learning that are not yet included in these systems. This of course, will add new ways of practicing, where students could be divided into groups and performing collaboratively the training through constructive communication. As such, the teaching will be transformed to an interactive game, available online, designed to make the learning process more enjoyable and effective. Finally, it is in our immediate plans to exploit the currently implemented tool in order to further educate patients for the management of their disease exploiting our intelligent recommendation [6–8] and see how this tool can be adapted in a versatile new domain.

References

1. Bielikova, M.N.: A schema-based approach to teaching programming in Lisp and Prolog. PEG (2003)
2. Corbett, A., Anderson, J.: Locus of feedback control in computer-based tutoring: impact on learning rate, achievement and attitudes. In: SIGCHI 2001, pp. 245–252 (2001)
3. Gerdes, A., Heeren, B., Jeuring, J., van Binsbergen, L.T.: Ask-Elle: an adaptable programming tutor for haskell giving automated feedback. IJAIED **27**(1), 1–36 (2016)
4. Giannoulis, M., Marakakis, E., Kondylakis, H.: Developing a collaborative knowledge system for Cancer Diseases, IEEE CBMS (2017)
5. Graesser, A.C., Conley, M.W., Olney, A.: Intelligent tutoring systems. In: APA Handbook of Educational Psychology. Department of Psychology & Institute for Intelligent Systems, pp. 1–54 (2010)
6. Kondylakis, H., Kazantzaki, E., Koumakis, L., et al.: Development of interactive empowerment services in support of personalized medicine. eCancer Med. Sci. J. **8**, 400 (2014). https://doi.org/10.3332/ecancer.2014.398
7. Kondylakis, H., Koumakis, L., Kazantzaki, E., et al.: Patient empowerment through personal medical recommendations. Health Biomed. Inf. **216**, 1117 (2015)
8. Kondylakis, H., Koumakis, L., Ruping, S., et al.: PMIR: a personal medical information recommender. In: Proceedings of Medical Informatics Europe (MIE), vol. 205, p. 1193 (2014)
9. Looi, C.K.: Automatic debugging of prolog programs in a prolog intelligent tutoring system. Instruct. Sci. **20**, 215–263 (1991)
10. Marakakis, E., Kondylakis, H., Papadakis, N.: A knowledge-based interactive verifier for logic programs. Innov. Knowl. Intell. Eng. Syst. **18**(3), 143–156 (2014)
11. Moon-Chuen, L.: An augmented prolog programming for tutoring applications Environment Components. In: AIE, pp. 898–906 (1990)

12. Rivers, K., Koedinger, K.R.: Data-driven hint generation in vast solution spaces: a self-improving python programming tutor. IJAIED **16**(1), 37–64 (2015)
13. Robins, A., Rountree, T., Rountree, N.: Learning and teaching programming: a review and discussion. Comput. Sci. Educ. **13**, 137–172 (2003)
14. Skinner, B.F.: About Behaviorism. Vintage, New York (2011)
15. Vlahavas, I.P., Sakellariou, I., Futo, I., Pasztor, Z., Szeredi, J.: CSPCONS: A communicating sequential prolog with constraints. In: Vlahavas, I.P., Spyropoulos, C.D. (eds.) SETN 2002. LNCS (LNAI), vol. 2308, pp. 72–84. Springer, Heidelberg (2002). https://doi.org/10.1007/3-540-46014-4_8
16. Webb, G.I.: Inside the unification tutor: the architecture of an intelligent educational system. In: ASCILITE, pp. 677–684 (1991)
17. Webb, G.I.: The unification tutor - an intelligent educational system in the classroom. In: ASCILITE, pp. 408–420 (1989)
18. Wikipedia Article: intelligent tutoring system. https://en.wikipedia.org/wiki/Intelligent_tutoring_system. Accessed Aug 2017
19. Yang, S.M.: Approaches for learning prolog programming. Innov. Teach. Learn. Inf. Comput. Sci. **6**, 88–107 (2007)

Training the Mind: The GARDINER Platform

Nikolas Vidakis[✉], Maria Skalidaki, Kostas Konstantoulakis,
Lefteris Kalikakis, Michail Kalogiannakis, and Kostas Vassilakis

Department of Informatics Engineering,
Technological Educational Institution of Crete,
Estavromenos, 71004 Heraklion, Crete, Greece
{nv,mkalogiannakis,k.vassilakis}@staff.teicrete.gr,
m.skalidakh@gmail.com,koskonstant@gmail.com,
lepter91@gmail.com

Abstract. Recent research has shown that the systematic involvement of a person with games, which are designated to exercise memory and concentration, contributes to the long-term preservation of the human memory and therefore leads to the prevention of dementia. Our work seeks to capitalize on the positive effects of serious games' use in a variety of ways. In particular, we provide insights into the design and development process of two serious games dedicated to being used by elderly people with dementia. In their context, we also elaborate on the basic elements of a novel web-oriented platform, namely GARDINER (Games plAtform foR minD traIning aNd mEmory peRk), aimed at making available various memory games which may have been crafted by various sources. Finally, some empirical data derived from the use of our platform and games in practice is provided.

Keywords: Serious games · Games for elderly · Game-based training
Memory training · Game data · Dementia · Dementia-related games
Serious games hub

1 Introduction

Today, a large proportion of people worldwide, approximately forty-eight million, live with dementia, a serious, progressive and fatal disease causing the gradual attenuation of elderly people's mental processes [1]. This figure is expected to get dramatically increased in the near future as the global population ages [2]. Dementia comprises several stages which are characterized by common symptoms. The more advanced the stage is, the more the patient loses his initial abilities including, among others, concentration, problem solving skills and memory. At the final stage, critical body functions are dramatically deteriorated resulting to patients' death. Despite the ever-increasing need for efficient and effective means for dementia's prevention and treatment, no traditional medications still exist [3]. However, some very encouraging and promising results have been achieved during the last few years by the serious game research community [4]. In particular, some researchers turned themselves towards serious games, in order to measure their potential in cognitive training of aged gamers and affected by dementia users. More precisely, experimental results have shown

© ICST Institute for Computer Sciences, Social Informatics and Telecommunications Engineering 2018
A. L. Brooks et al. (Eds.): ArtsIT 2017/DLI 2017, LNICST 229, pp. 347–356, 2018.
https://doi.org/10.1007/978-3-319-76908-0_33

significant improvement in players' performance after the systematic play of dementia-oriented games. The type of these games is varied depending on their orientation, which may be diagnostic assessment or rehabilitative care [5]. The former is primarily concerned with the early detection of the disease and focuses on the delay of cognitive decline while the latter on restoring cognitive functions. Serious games used for dementia also vary significantly with respect to the type of impairment at which they are aimed (i.e. physical [6], cognitive [7] and emotional [8]). Different types of impairment may necessitate the use of radically different game-design elements (e.g. avatars, 3d worlds or 2D boards) and raise a number of implementation-specific requirements (e.g. multi-modal interaction) which, in every case, seriously affects the game design and its computational implementation processes.

Generally, the field of serious games for dementia remains highly unexplored. It is indicative that most of the published works make use of conventional games, in the context of mostly commercial platforms like Wii or Nintendo DS, which have been properly adapted for the needs of this purpose. Our work seeks to contribute to the state of the art in many folds. Firstly, we propose a generic web-based architecture capable of hosting and unifying serious games for dementia which might have been crafted by various sources yet being made accessible via a unified interface. As a result, properties and qualities supported by our platform (i.e. monitoring API) will also become properties of the hosted applications. Secondly, we provide insights on the design details of two games which we have specifically developed to help users with dementia. Finally, we provide practical evidence on an experiment we have carried out and we elaborate on the results which have been properly traced and which persisted in their context. The role of the data which is collected is critical since it is given to professional experts of the domain for further analysis, comments and/or suggestions.

2   Related Work

During the last years, the serious games industry appears to have made some very early but significant efforts in the domain of dementia-related games whose aim is to facilitate the prevention, rehabilitation and deceleration of the development of cognitive impairment in elderly people via cognitive training methods. As a result, a wide range of games has been made available with great impact on the consumer audience. Even though dementia related-games have been proved to work in practice, there is only a limited number of works available. One of the few taxonomies which have been proposed for their classification is presented in [5]. Classification schemes are crucial for the success of the serious games for dementia (SG4D) since they establish the grounds for researchers to reason about, compare and evaluate different works yet with compatible characteristics and similar objectives. According to [9] SG4D can be classified with regards to their type, as preventative, rehabilitative, educative and/or assessing and regarding their category as cognitive, physical and social emotional.

Other more technologically driven criteria also exist which mainly concern platform availability, including PCs, smartphones, the Nintendo Wii or even the MS Kinect and the I/O capabilities and instruments supported on top of the hosting environments [4]. Depending on the axes upon which a SG4D falls, the mechanics underpinning the game design, the metrics which need to be measured and the type of experiment that should be carried out, are significantly affected [18]. Therefore, the focus of the application and its objectives must be known before its execution and they need to be seriously considered throughout the design phase. Nonetheless, so far, no design principles have been proposed for SG4D game development. Therefore, their development is grounded merely on designers' personal experience, if any, and ad-hoc or random design choices whose success can be accessed only at runtime by "trial and error" efforts in the context of experiments explicitly set out for this purpose. The state of the art seems to have been focusing on determining whether and to what extent serious games can play a role in preventing or ameliorating the effects of dementia.

An indicative work in the context of SG4D is Lumosity [10], a popular online suite comprising more than fifty brain training games whose aim is to strengthen cognitive abilities of users in a way tailored to the individual needs of each one. In particular, each user can interactively define their personal training schedule and goals via their profile, choosing from selected categories the exact games to be played and their sequence of being played. At all times, a user-specific dashboard is sustained which provides detailed insights on a user's performance, in terms of certain metrics depicted through dedicated visual means, in accordance with the goals set by this user. These metrics include speed, memory, attention, flexibility and problem solving rate. Social and emotional engagement is supported via the ability to contradict personal performance with that of specific community users or with the community's average. Based on the experiment undertaken in 2006 [11] with twenty-three participants of an average age of fifty-four, the group which received Lumocity training for twenty minutes per day for five weeks, displayed improvement in their working memory and in their visual attention performance.

Brain Age [12] has been developed to stimulate users' brain, being available for the Nintendo DS platform. There is a diversity of games provided which includes simple math problems, a variety of puzzles, sudoku puzzles, reading classic literature out loud and so on with the users being able to interact either via the touch screen or the integrated microphone. Despite the fact that the game is not targeted to people with dementia, lots of neurologists suggest its use due to its positive impact on users' cognitive activities [13]. In fact, the outcome of some experiments which have been carried out in the context of the 'Brain Age' game, with the aim of measuring its effects on the elderly and non-gamer users, has shown improvement in users' executive functions and processing speed [14].

Wii Sports, developed by Nintendo, comprises a simulator of group-games including tennis, baseball, bowling, golf and boxing. In the context of a series of experiments, in which patients diagnosed with dementia took part, Wii Sports have shown that within a timespan of nine weeks, participants improved their score and managed to memorize the game rules with great success [15]. According to another research in which two elderly females with mild cognitive impairment were engaged in Wii playing for a narrow period, results have shown an increase in the attention of both participants while they have also indicated that the participants found the game entertaining and fun [16].

MasterQuiz [19] is a reminiscence game which is specially designated for patients suffering from mild dementia. The game has been compiled against the Android API instead of that of the Web since it is specifically targeted on patients who live in Norway where the Wi-Fi coverage is quite limited. The core of the game is a quiz with an image displayed on the left-hand side and a set of alternative text-based answers displayed on the right-hand side. In case of a correct answer users are congratulated, while on the contrary, they are asked to try again, for as many times it is necessary until they find the correct one. As the game progresses, it monitors and updates the number of failed attempts required to the correct answer. Users are allowed to show their preference either for generic or personalized questions via the game settings menu. The personalized questions must have been previously uploaded to a custom web database. The generic questions can be filtered by decade or customizable tags for each of the images such as sports, home, science, arts, just to name a few.

3   The GARDINER Platform

The aim of this study is to provide a valid and novel way to assist clinicians in assessing a person's cognitive status by means of analysis of data collected throughout the gameplay of two well-known serious game prototypes, the 'Face Name' game and the 'Matching Tiles' game (see Fig. 1). Both games focus on two cognitive functions, which severely decline as dementia progresses, the short-term memory and word and object recognition. Regarding the first game, the focus is on assessing the capacity for retrieving information from the short memory, while on the second game the goal is to match card pairs by means of object recognition. Their implementation addresses requirements which have been derived from various existing serious games dedicated for elderly people [20]. The game environment is straightforward and with clear challenges while being primarily designed for elderly players strives to minimize possible negative feelings of tension and confusion. The games present an adapted difficulty, providing a unique experience for each user based on their individual abilities, thereby encouraging them to play the games frequently. It is also important to note that various data are collected throughout the gameplay which are stored under each user's personal profile for further analysis and assessment.

Fig. 1. Game selection

Our platform, the GARDINER (**G**ames pl**A**tform fo**R** mind tra**I**ning a**N**d m**E**mory pe**R**k) is designed and implemented in such a way and with the use of the proper interactions artifacts that support the existence of more serious games for training the mind. When a new game is ready to be uploaded to GARDINER, a shortcut icon for the game is placed at the carousel type game menu (see Fig. 1). The positioning of the game in the carousel menu interaction artifact depends on the placement criteria set up by the platform administrator, these criteria can be one or more of the following: chronological (i.e. creation date), difficulty level, random order etc.

The main idea behind the development of these serious game prototypes is to map challenges in the design of serious games applied to assessment and cognitive stimulation with people suffering from Alzheimer or elderly people. The collection of in-game data and player performance can be used as part of a diagnostic test for cognitive decline. This recorded information can be very useful for health professionals in the diagnosis of any suspected cognitive problems, while it could also help in monitoring the progression of these conditions and provide a potential alert for signs of cognitive deterioration. The great expectation of this study, is to help users train and evaluate their four cognitive spheres which are memory, planning skills, initiative and perseverance [17] while being entertaining, interactive and easy to use in the same time.

The general architecture of GARDINER (see Fig. 2) includes tools and services for (a) enabling players to have authorized access to the platform and the games,

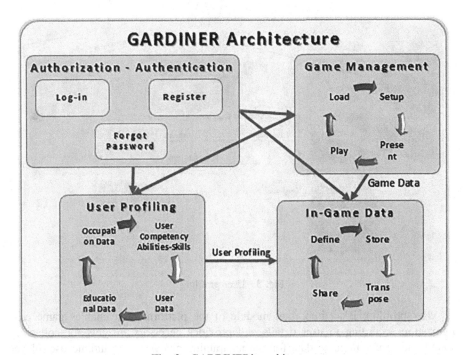

Fig. 2. GARDINER's architecture

(b) allowing trainers and platform administrators to upload, setup, present within the platform and initiate serious games, (c) permit trainers and trainees to define use centered data related to occupation, education, competences and abilities and hence define the user profile which can be used to customize games according to user preferences, abilities and desires and (d) enable the platform to define, store, transpose and share in-game data and therefore provide information to trainers or carers to evaluate training sessions and achieve mind training and recovery conclusions as well as allow game guidelines to be updated from in-game metrics and trainee choices while playing.

The GARDINER platform and the games are implemented with Php, Mysql, JavaScript and HTML. The combination of these technologies was selected for the ease of the development and the flexibility in the access as it is working in a browser without demanding any further installation. The design of GARDINER includes not only textual instructions output modality yet visual and audio modalities as well. Multimodality output is used to make our serious game prototypes, accessible to people with hearing or vision issues. Audio technology can help elderly people interact with technology in general and with the games of the GARDINER platform in specific.

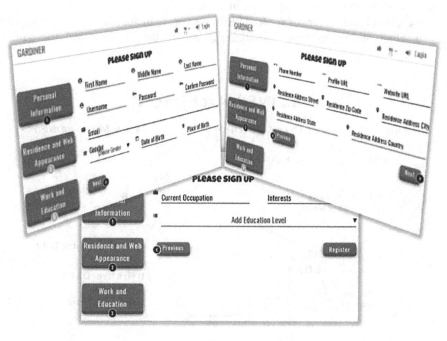

Fig. 3. User profiling

User profiling is an important module of the platform as it enables game customization according to user details and provides necessary insights for collecting sound and useful in-game data for further training analysis. The unique user-player profile is created by the user and apart from some few data that are mandatory such as username and password for accessing the platform all other user information are optional. The registration i.e. user profiling processes, services and interaction screens (see Fig. 3) are designed and implemented in such a way that protect user rights and preserve user anonymity. In more detail GARNIDER's user profiling module includes three data tabs namely the "Personal Information" tab, the "Residence and web Appearance" tab and the Work and Education" tab. At the "Personal Information", the user is asked to enter the username and password as minimum mandatory data and other personal data such as name surname gender etc. optionally. The "Residence and web Appearance" tab urge user to submit residence address, telephone number(s), web URL, profile URL etc. and therefore enhance its user information. As a last step at the user profiling module the user is asked to provide information such as current occupation, education, preferences, abilities and interests. All data collected is anonymous and assigned a unique user-id at GARDINER's Data Base (RDB).

The user profile contains relevant demographic data about the trainees which will be used to enrich the analysis of user's progress over the game training sessions (Fig. 3). Furthermore, the user profile contains relevant data about the user's performance for a set of game activities, such as completion time for each individual game and final score of the completed activity, number of hints that the player used and the overall errors that the user committed during the game training session.

Authorization and authentication are facilitated via the Login process and are realized as illustrated in the upper left module of Fig. 2.

The Game Management module allows trainees, trainers and platform administrators to upload, setup, present and play the serious games supported by GARDINER according their role permissions. The trainee, in our pilot implementation, can choose between the two memory training games namely the "Face Name Game" and the "Matching Tiles".

In the "Face Name game", the player is invited to remember and write down the name of the people depicted in the section. The game starts with the presentation of the faces with their names respectively. The user can control the game pagination, so she/he can take her/his time to observe each face with its name and she/he could have the opportunity to remember the matches while playing the level (Fig. 4).

When the presentation of all face pictures of the specific game level is finished, a "start the game" button is shown up. When the user enters the play mode (see Fig. 5), the faces are shown as before but instead of the name label, now a blank text field takes place where the user fills with his answer. The main difference at this stage of the game is that the navigation button "Previous" is replaced with the operation button "Hint", as shown in Figs. 4 and 5, which helps the user to complete the level and go on. Thus, the user can only navigate forward which means that she/he cannot go back and correct or complete a previously given answer and she/he can ask the system for help, with a point penalty, by pressing the "Hint" button. Each time the user presses the "Hint" button one more letter of the name is given by the system. When each level finishes the "next level" button shows up to take the user to the next level.

The "Matching Tiles" game aims to reveal every tile by matching pairs of identical tiles. The user can continue to guess until matching right each tile. The game promotes point-and-click interactions. When the user turns over a tile there is an audio and visual feedback regarding the attached tile (Fig. 7). All these simple mechanisms have been designed in order to make the game easy to learn and play. The game completes when the user has matched every tile on the board. The game settings allow the user to select

Fig. 4. Memorizing names & faces, training the mind

Fig. 5. Remembering names & faces, testing the mind status

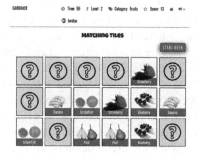

Fig. 6. Matching tiles settings

Fig. 7. Matching tiles

the level and the category of the game she/he is going to play as shown in Fig. 6. He can choose between different categories such as fruits, faces or color and between three levels of difficulty.

When the user completes either of the two games in our pilot implementation or any other game, when more games will be added to the GARDINER platform, all in-game data is recorded into log files for further processing.

4 Conclusions and Future Work

Our work proposes a generic web-based platform capable of hosting and unifying serious games for dementia which might have been crafted by various sources yet being made accessible via a unified interface. We provide insights on the design details of two classical games which we have specifically developed to help users with dementia. Furthermore, we have carried out a preliminary experiment on a small number of volunteers (approximately 15). The volunteers have tested the web-based architecture as well as the two memory games by playing them twice in a time interval of 20 days. Initial results showed a general overall enhancement on numbers which force us to carry out more extensive and elaborate experiments with more users and from a more dispersed age, occupational and educational user group. The role of the collected data is critical since it can be made available to professional experts of the domain of memory training i.e. neurologists for further analysis, comments and/or suggestions. Further research on the field of multimodal input/output has to be carried out in order to provide support to non-visual and gesture-based interaction schemes. Additionally, more serious games need to be crafted and be introduced to the GAR-DINER platform so as to address even more cognitive abilities.

References

1. Kazmi, S., Ugail, H., Lesk, V., Palmer, I.: Interactive digital serious games for the assessment, rehabilitation, and prediction of dementia. Int. J. Comput. Games Technol. **2014**, 1–11 (2014)
2. Dementia statistics|Alzheimer's Disease International. Alz.co.uk (2017). http://www.alz.co.uk/research/statistics. Accessed 03 June 2017
3. Singh-Manoux, A., Kivimäki, M.: The importance of cognitive ageing for understanding dementia. Age **32**(4), 509–512 (2010)
4. McCallum, S., Boletsis, C.: Dementia games: a literature review of dementia-related serious games. In: Ma, M., Oliveira, M.F., Petersen, S., Hauge, J.B. (eds.) SGDA 2013. LNCS, vol. 8101, pp. 15–27. Springer, Heidelberg (2013). https://doi.org/10.1007/978-3-642-40790-1_2
5. McCallum, S., Boletsis, C.: A taxonomy of serious games for dementia. In: Schouten, B., Fedtke, S., Bekker, T., Schijven, M., Gekker, A. (eds.) Games for Health, pp. 219–232. Springer, Heidelberg (2013). https://doi.org/10.1007/978-3-658-02897-8_17
6. Padala, K., Padala, P., Malloy, T., Geske, J., Dubbert, P., Dennis, R., Garner, K., Bopp, M., Burke, W., Sullivan, D.: Wii-fit for improving gait and balance in an assisted living facility: a pilot study. J. Aging Res. **2012**, 1–6 (2012)
7. Rosen, A., Sugiura, L., Kramer, J., Whitfield-Gabrieli, S., Gabrieli, J.: Cognitive training changes hippocampal function in mild cognitive impairment: a pilot study. J. Alzheimers Dis. **26**, 349–357 (2012)
8. Boulay, M., Benveniste, S., Boespflug, S., Jouvelot, P., Rigaud, A.: A pilot usability study of MINWii, a music therapy game for demented patients. Technol. Health Care: Off. J. Eur. Soc. Eng. Med. **19**(4), 233–246 (2011)
9. Sawyer, B.: From cells to cell processors: the integration of health and video games. IEEE Comput. Graph. Appl. **28**(6), 83–85 (2008)
10. Brain Games & Brain Training – Lumosity. Lumosity.com (2017). http://www.lumosity.com. Accessed 04 June 2017
11. Scanlon, M., Drescher, D., Sarkar, K.: Improvement of visual attention and working memory through a web-based cognitive training program, Lumos Labs (2007)
12. B. Day!, "Brain Age: Train Your Brain in Minutes a Day!". Nintendo.com (2017). http://www.nintendo.com/games/detail/Y9QLGBWxkmRRzsQEQtvqGqZ63_CjS_9F. Accessed 04 June 2017

13. Kawashima, R., Okita, K., Yamazaki, R., Tajima, N., Yoshida, H., Taira, M., Iwata, K., Sasaki, T., Maeyama, K., Usui, N., Sugimoto, K.: Reading aloud and arithmetic calculation improve frontal function of people with dementia. J. Gerontol. Ser. A: Biol. Sci. Med. Sci. **60**(3), 380–384 (2005)

14. Nouchi, R., Taki, Y., Takeuchi, H., Hashizume, H., Akitsuki, Y., Shigemune, Y., Sekiguchi, A., Kotozaki, Y., Tsukiura, T., Yomogida, Y., Kawashima, R.: Brain training game improves executive functions and processing speed in the elderly: a randomized controlled trial. PLoS One **7**(1), e29676 (2012)

15. Fenney, A., Lee, T.: Exploring spared capacity in persons with dementia: what Wii^{TM} can learn. Activities Adapt. Aging **34**(4), 303–313 (2010)

16. Weybright, E., Dattilo, J., Rusch, F.: Effects of an interactive video game (Nintendo Wii™) on older women with mild cognitive impairment. Ther. Recreation **44**, 271–287 (2010)

17. Imbeault, F., Bouchard, B., Bouzouane, A.: Serious games in cognitive training for Alzheimer's patients. In: 2011 IEEE 1st International Conference on Serious Games and Applications for Health (SeGAH) (2011)

18. Bouchard, B., Imbeault, F., Bouzouane, A., Menelas, B.-A.J.: Developing serious games specifically adapted to people suffering from Alzheimer. In: Ma, M., Oliveira, M.F., Hauge, J.B., Duin, H., Thoben, K.-D. (eds.) SGDA 2012. LNCS, vol. 7528, pp. 243–254. Springer, Heidelberg (2012). https://doi.org/10.1007/978-3-642-33687-4_21

19. McCallum, S.: Gamification and serious games for personalized health. Stud. Health Technol. Inform. **177**, 85–96 (2012)

20. Tong, T., Chan, J., Chignell, M.: Serious games for dementia. In: Proceedings of the 26th International Conference on World Wide Web Companion (WWW 2017 Companion), pp. 1111–1115 (2017)

Facilitating Learning in Isolated Places Through an Autonomous LMS

Kostas Vassilakis[1]([⊠]), John Makridis[2],
Michail Angelos Lasithiotakis[2], Michail Kalogiannakis[2],
and Nikolas Vidakis[2]

[1] Department of Electrical Engineering,
Technological Educational Institute of Crete,
Stauromenos, 71410 Heraklion, Greece
kostas@teicrete.gr
[2] Department of Informatics Engineering,
Technological Educational Institute of Crete,
Stauromenos, 71410 Heraklion, Greece
j.makridis7@gmail.com, m.a.lasithiotakis@gmail.com,
{mkalogiannakis,nv}@staff.teicrete.gr

Abstract. Current research argues that eLearning and mobile learning are forms of learning that could take place outside the classroom and the traditional learning environments. In addition, recent advancement in technology and increased use of smart devices permit students to carry with them a kind of portable smart device. Inevitably, sooner or later, these devices will become integral educational tools, such as pencils and books, while learning outside the classroom will continue to gain popularity as another form of learning. Ubiquitous learning aims to stimulate the wide use of ICT in Education and the enactment of autonomous digital resources for Outdoor learning. Technology could provide innovative ways of conducting outdoor courses, encompassing knowledge and physical activity. This paper presents the eClass-Pi system that facilitates outside the classroom eLearning and m-learning educational processes. It provides all the functionalities of a typical Learning Management Systems as well as synchronous and asynchronous teaching, portability and energy autonomy.

Keywords: Learning outside the classroom · Mobile learning
Blended Learning · Hybrid courses · Digital and educational tools & practices
Educational strategies

1 Introduction

Recently in the field of education the old-fashioned style of teaching has been abandoned. Teachers have begun to embrace new and more interactive ways of learning by asking for more active student involvement. A key role in this development has been the evolution of technology, reaching a point where education is now easier to provide individualized information anytime, anywhere, and on any device [1, 2]. On their part, teachers observed and explored the potential impact of this emerging technology on students, helping them to learn better in a dynamic environment [3].

© ICST Institute for Computer Sciences, Social Informatics and Telecommunications Engineering 2018
A. L. Brooks et al. (Eds.): ArtsIT 2017/DLI 2017, LNICST 229, pp. 357–365, 2018.
https://doi.org/10.1007/978-3-319-76908-0_34

More specifically, eLearning made a spectacular introduction to the academic world and changed it radically. It is widely known, in many forms and types, such as online learning, cyber learning, virtual learning, mobile learning and is described by a majority of authors as access to learning experiences through the use of technology. Watson and Kalmon [4] simply defining eLearning as *"providing instruction and content that includes a combination of educational modes, delivery methods and technologies, learning theories, pedagogical dimensions, mainly through the Internet"*.

There are many innovations developed in the recent years that support and assist eLearning. For example, teachers can easily share information with students that have access to exercises, can start a discussion or further research and elaborate their assignments online [5]. Other learning innovations include the gamification and ludi-fication of the educational processes where learning is transformed into playing with the use of smart devices, field teaching, 3D printing rewards and feedback, giving students more motivation, collaboration and interest in the learning process [6–8]. Furthermore, recent reviews and studies show that portable mobile devices, used in outdoor informal environments (e.g. backyards, rural areas, nature centers or parks) support outdoor and field based education and stimulate knowledge acquisition outside the classroom [9]. These innovative implementations in eLearning can be hosted, integrated and provided through Learning Management Systems. This study proposes and presents the eClass-Pi system that facilitates educational processes outside the classroom. It provides functionality similar to Learning Management Systems (LMS) as well as Blended Learning.

The paper is divided as follows. Section 2 presents the findings on the literature review conducted. Section 3 introduces the development of the autonomous LMS eClass-Pi and presents a use scenario of learning outside the classroom and Sect. 4 concludes the paper.

2   Background

Outdoor education is often referred as a synonymous to education outside the class-room, adventure education, outdoor learning, outdoor school, expeditionary learning, experiential education, and environmental education [10]. Education outside the classroom is a concept, that is currently enjoying a revival due to the recognition of its benefits [11]. Interactions that support learning outside the classroom are made more accessible by using portable devices which are equipped with essential features of personal computer. According to [12], *"The mobile devices can connect to Internet through wireless communication technologies creating a spectrum of educational opportunities and a new type of student-technology partnership in learning"*.

Mobile technologies and the Information and Communication Technologies (ICT), in general, will not change the teaching principles and the educational process. However, it is the pedagogical practices of teachers which can be facilitated using ICT [13, 14].

Nowadays, there is an increasing demand for Learning Management Systems (LMS). Educational institutions integrate these systems since they provide significant benefits and facilitate the educational process [15]. Choosing the right LMS is a crucial decision for an educational institution since it should consider all the features it needs to offer via system platform. The most powerful and popular LMSs across the world are Moodle [16], Blackboard [17] and Canvas [18]. These systems can provide the necessary features to conduct and manage a course, through a modern user interface. Beyond the ordinary use of Learning Management Systems, they could also be used in a different approach such as offline-portable LMS. This approach serves outdoor activities in isolated or rural places, where internet connection is limited. In our literature review for related work we have found some efforts and preliminary projects that could support a USB based LMS edition to cover teachers' course conducting needs. Such preliminary products are the StratBeans ATUM [19], the ATutor [20] and the NetDimensions Talent Slate [21].

3   An Autonomous LMS: The eClass-Pi

Teachers through portable LMSs can create offline courses and offer them to their students, implementing an eLearning environment for practicing education outside the classroom. The eClass-Pi autonomous LMS system facilitates educational processes outside the classroom. Unlike the previous mentioned portable LMS, our system uses a single-board computer instead of USB based installations. In more detail, it provides functionality similar to a traditional LMS augmented with synchronous and asynchronous learning services (Blended Learning), portability, energy autonomy and database synchronization mechanisms.

3.1   System Analysis

To achieve an outdoor activity, we implement the eClass-Pi system that satisfies requirements such as portability and energy autonomy. Our system uses the Open eClass LMS which is developed by the Greek Universities Network [22] and an implementation of a database synchronization mechanism with the server which hosts the institution's LMS. However, we designed our system in such a way that any other LMS can be supported by the hardware used. Table 1 summarises the main requirements that our system fulfils.

Table 1. eClass-Pi functional & non-functional main requirements

Portability	It is the most basic and necessary feature of systems that support outdoor learning. Portability is mandatory in order to facilitate course teaching in different locations, habitats and surroundings. eClass-Pi meets this strict requirement and supports full portability
Energy Autonomy	Energy autonomy is a principal element of systems that facilitates learning in rural or isolated locations. eClass-Pi along with portability, supports energy autonomy with the use of a power bank with integrated solar panel. The idea is to combine portability and energy autonomy to serve long-term course sessions in detached places

(continued)

Table 1. (*continued*)

Use of existing learning infrastructure	Our implementation hosts the Open-Source eClass LMS. It is an academic effort with a community of experienced researchers, developers and academic staff. It is provided to the majority of universities and institutes around Greece facilitating the educational process. Open eClass has a variety of features (modules) such as file exchange, exercises, assignments, gradebook, attendances, analytics, teleconference and forum which are accessible through an easy-to-use environment
Two different instances of the LMS	Our implementation must support two different installations of a LMS. The first installation is the main LMS environment of the educational institute which is installed on a web server and the second installation is a limited LMS installation on a portable computing system
Course Synchronization	The system must support synchronization features. In more detail, our system must implement a synchronization algorithm in order to achieve bidirectional data flow between the two LMS instances (base and portative)

3.2   System Architecture

Our proposed architecture of eClass-Pi (Fig. 1) consists of two main settings. The two settings represent the "Indoor" and "Outdoor" installation of the LMS respectively. On both LMS installations, we have installed LAMP [23] which is an open source Web development platform that uses Linux (OS), Apache (Web server), MySQL (RDBMS) and PHP (OO-scripting language) which are suitable for building webpages and applications. We have named "base-LMS" the setting that is on the institutions main server and "portative-LMS" the setting that is on the portable device supporting the outdoor learning activities.

base-LMS: That corresponds to the main institutional LMS installation. For testing purposes, we could not use the official institutional LMS. Our needs for LMS hosting is fulfilled through the Okeanos virtual compute and network service offered by the National Network for Research and Technology (GRNET) [24]. Our academic network provides us a virtual machine with one CPU core, 4 GBs of RAM, and 40 GBs of disk storage.

portative-LMS: It is a limited LMS installation on a portable computing system. We used a Raspberry Pi 3 Model B [25], a developer board, provided by the Raspberry Pi Foundation which is a low-cost computer system with a 1.2 GHz 64-bit quad-core ARMv8 CPU, one GB of RAM and flexible storage depends on MicroSD card. It also has a built-in Ethernet port, Wireless LAN module, Bluetooth low-energy (BLE) and four USB ports. To connect users (mobile devices) to the Raspberry Pi server, we customized the source files of the operating system by converting the board's Wi-Fi receiver to a transmitter, creating that way a private ad hoc network.

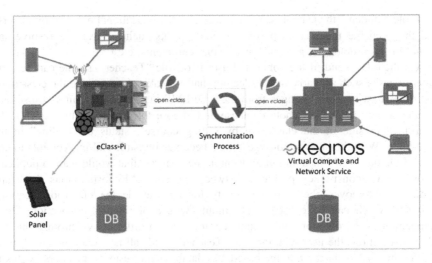

Fig. 1. The eClass-Pi architecture.

The communication between the two LMS-Stations is established through HTTP requests. Since, Raspberry Pi is a complete, portable computer system that can act as a server and it is difficult to assign a static external IP address, our system performs the GET and POST method requests exclusively from the Portable-LMS-Station. To achieve this, our system should be connected to a LAN (802.3) or WLAN (802.11) network. Alternatively, a 3G/4G USB Broadband modem could be used to achieve connectivity.

3.3   The eClass-Pi

The UML activity diagram of our system (Fig. 2) presents all available actions offered to users for outside the classroom (outdoor) courses. eClass-Pi supports two different user roles, namely the "Teacher" and the "Student". In the case that the connected user

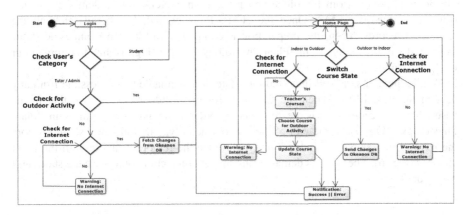

Fig. 2. The eClass-Pi "Indoor" & "Outdoor" activity diagram.

is of role "Student" then she/he can have access to the educational material of a course and the available modules to perform different tasks such as: exercise resolve and digital material upload (e.g. snapshots, textual comments, etc.).

On the other hand, if the connected user is of role "Teacher", she/he can perform different tasks such as: carry out the lecture that will take place outside the classroom, fetch the latest course's changes from the base-LMS installation, monitor course data transfer to and from the remote database and choose the lecture of his desire to be performed outside of the classroom by setting course's status to "Offline" in the base-LMS. With the latter action, the course becomes invisible and inaccessible to any user of the base-LMS installation, preventing new entries that would lead to duplicate records and inconsistency problems between the two LMS installations (base and portative). Moreover, the course is ready for the outside the classroom learning activities which can be carried out without the use of internet connection. Upon completion of the outdoor educational activities and in order to synchronize the two LMS installations the user with the role "Teacher" sends all new data produced, from the portative-LMS database to the base-LMS database and restores the course status to "Online" i.e. visible. Synchronization of the two LMS installations (base and portative) requires the eClass-Pi portable device to be connected to the internet, otherwise, a warning message will be displayed to the user.

3.4   The Use Case of Plant Physiology Laboratory Course Outside the Classroom

To illustrate some of the concepts described so far and to provide insight into the features of eClass-Pi, we will briefly describe a representative use case scenario emphasizing on teaching a laboratory course outside the classroom (Exhibit 1).

Exhibit 1: Let us assume that we have imported teachers, students, and courses from the base-LMS installation to the portative-LMS installation and we are ready to provide, support and exercise a course outdoors. In our indicative scenario the connected user, is tutor "John Doe" which is tutoring the above imported courses and has the rights to create and initiate an outdoor activity. John Doe can manage the "Plant Physiology" course from his office and prepare an exercise for student's evaluation (Fig. 3) on the base-LMS. Once the eClass-Pi is booted, he should fetch all the associated records. Then, the preparation is completed and he can change the status from "Indoor" to "Outdoor" in "Plant Physiology" course (Fig. 4) that he tutors in our use case scenario.

While the course is still in a "Indoor" state, it is available and accessible from any user in the base-LMS. When the course is set to "Outdoor", we notice that in the base-LMS, it becomes invisible to users in order to avoid any conflicts in "Plant Physiology" (Fig. 5). In the end of the outdoor activity, Mr. John Doe should restore the state of the course to "Indoor" to synchronize the remote database with the latest changes (Fig. 6). The process demands an internet connection, otherwise the state can't be restored.

Fig. 3. Exercise creation.

Fig. 4. Change course status.

Fig. 5. Okeanos & eClass-Pi aspects.

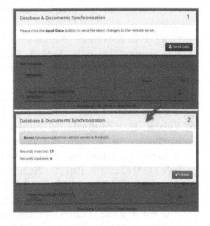

Fig. 6. Send records in Okeanos.

4 Conclusions and Future Work

In this paper, we have attempted to sketch the organizational underpinnings of the eClass-Pi – a pilot effort aiming to build an autonomous and portable LMS for facilitating learning in rural or isolated places. Our primary design target is to set up a fully operational LMS system on a portable computing system such as the Raspberry Pi that is energy autonomous and supports specific course activities and synchronizes to the base-LMS installation of an educational institute which resides on the institute's main server. We have implemented the eClass-Pi that offers a fully energy autonomous and portative-LMS. Using eClass-Pi, we can provide hybrid courses which satisfy synchronous learning in environments that lack energy sources and internet communications and asynchronous learning inside educational institute environment. In specific scientific sectors, the eClass-Pi can offer significant improvements in practical education as it gives students the possibility to bring technology outside the classroom, interact with surrounding artifacts and engage the environment in the learning process in isolated places. Our ongoing work covers a variety of issues of both technological and educational engineering character. Some of the issues to be addressed in the immediate future include synchronization conflicts with databases' records, system features restrictions and limited user's connections based on hardware. Evolving our work, we are going to evaluate how the promotion of democratic dialogic behavior and democracy could be promoted through a system such as eClass-Pi.

References

1. Motiwalla, L.F.: Mobile learning: a framework and evaluation. Comput. Educ. **49**(3), 581–596 (2007)
2. Gikas, J., Grant, M.M.: Mobile computing devices in higher education: student perspectives on learning with cellphones, smartphones & social media. Internet High. Educ. **19**, 18–26 (2013)
3. Dang, T.T., Robertson, M.: Impacts of learning management system on learner autonomy in EFL learning. Int. Educ. Stud. **3**, 3–11 (2010)
4. Watson, J., Kalmon, S.: A Review of State-Level Policy and Practice. Learning Point, Naperville (2005)
5. Dicheva, D., Dichev, C., Angelova, G., Agre, G.: Gamification in education: a systematic mapping study. Educ. Technol. Soc. **18**, 75–88 (2015)
6. Vidakis, N., Christinaki, E., Serafimidis, I., Triantafyllidis, G.: Combining ludology and narratology in an open authorable framework for educational games for children: the scenario of teaching preschoolers with autism diagnosis. In: Stephanidis, C., Antona, M. (eds.) UAHCI 2014, Part II. LNCS, vol. 8514, pp. 626–636. Springer, Cham (2014). https://doi.org/10.1007/978-3-319-07440-5_57
7. Vidakis, N., Syntychakis, E., Kalafatis, K., Christinaki, E., Triantafyllidis, G.: Ludic educational game creation tool: teaching schoolers road safety. In: Antona, M., Stephanidis, C. (eds.) UAHCI 2015, Part III. LNCS, vol. 9177, pp. 565–576. Springer, Cham (2015). https://doi.org/10.1007/978-3-319-20684-4_55
8. Groh, F.: Gamification: state of the art definition and utilization. Res. Trends Media Inf. **14** (02), 39–46 (2012)
9. Zimmerman, H.T., Land, S.M.: Facilitating place-based learning in outdoor informal environments with mobile computers. TechTrends **58**(1), 77–83 (2014)
10. Quay, J., Seaman, J.: John Dewey and Education Outdoors: Making Sense of the 'Educational Situation' through more than a Century of Progressive Reforms. Sense Publishers, Rotterdam (2013)
11. Dillon, J., Rickinson, M., Teamey, K., Morris, M., Choi, M.Y., Sanders, D., Benefield, P.: The value of outdoor learning: evidence from research in the UK and elsewhere. School Sci. Rev. **87**, 320 (2006)
12. Churchill, D., Kennedy, D., Flint, D., Cotton, N.: Using handhelds to support students' outdoor educational activities. Int. J. Contin. Eng. Educ. Life Long Learn. **20**, 54–71 (2010)

13. Kalogiannakis, M., Papadakis, S.: Combining mobile technologies in environmental education: a Greek case study. Int. J. Mob. Learn. Organ. **11**(2), 108–130 (2017)
14. Lai, H.C., Chang, C.Y., Wen-Shiane, L., Fan, Y.L., Wu, Y.T.: Support students' outdoor educational activities with handheld technology. In: International Conference on Information Communication Technology in Education, pp. 10–12 (2008)
15. Adzharuddin, N.A., Ling, L.H.: Learning management system (LMS) among university students: does it work? Int. J. e-Educ. e-Bus. e-Manag. e-Learn. **3**(3), 248–252 (2013)
16. Moodle Learning Management System, Moodle Pty Ltd. https://moodle.com/. Accessed 1 May 2017
17. Blackboard Learning Management System, Blackboard Inc. http://www.blackboard.com/. Accessed 1 May 2017
18. Canvas Learning Management System, Instructure Inc. https://www.canvaslms.com/. Accessed 1 May 2017
19. Stratbeans e-Learning and Learning Management System Solutions, Stratbeans Consulting Pvt. Ltd. http://stratbeans.com/. Accessed 1 May 2017
20. ATutor Learning Content Management System, ATutor. http://www.atutor.ca. Accessed 1 May 2017
21. NetDimensions Enterprise Learning Management System, NetDimensions Ltd. http://www.netdimensions.com/. Accessed 1 May 2017
22. The Greek Universities Network, GUNET. http://www.gunet.gr. Accessed 1 May 2017
23. Official Documentation - Ubuntu Server Guide, Ubuntu. https://help.ubuntu.com/lts/serverguide/lamp-applications.html. Accessed 10 May 2017
24. National Network for Research and Technology, GRNET. https://grnet.gr/. Accessed 1 May 2017
25. Raspberry Pi Foundation. https://www.raspberrypi.org/. Accessed 1 May 2017

Using Gamification for Supporting an Introductory Programming Course. The Case of ClassCraft in a Secondary Education Classroom

Stamatios Papadakis(✉) and Michail Kalogiannakis

Department of Preschool Education, University of Crete, Rethymnon Campus, Rethymno, Crete, Greece
stpapadakis@gmail.com, mkalogian@edc.uoc.gr

Abstract. Old teaching methods mechanisms are no longer beneficial to the students. In traditional instructional methodology, where the lecture classes are perceived to be tedious by students, the gamification technology has a great advantage to solve the problem as it can improve learning motivation of students. Various studies have shown that gamification under appropriate conditions may create an environment conducive to learning and lead to large increases in students' interest in programming. ClassCraft is a game that it can be used in the classroom to help students to have fun, promote teamwork, and become better learners. In this paper, we present a pilot teaching intervention. The results showed that the general students' performance has not been affected positively. On the other hand, their engagement has been affected positively.

Keywords: ClassCraft · Gamification · Introductory programming courses
Secondary education

1 Introduction

A recent report (August 2017), highlights the fact that "regardless of race/ethnicity or gender, 80% of students who have learned Computer Science (CS) claimed that they learned CS in a class at school, about twice the rate of any other means of learning, including on their own, through afterschool clubs, online, or in any other program outside of school" (p. 26) [30]. As Wang states, this data strongly suggests that formal education remains the best way to ensure widespread and equitable access to CS learning [30].

At the same time, various other reports highlighted the fact that in CS classes the dropout rate seems much higher compared to other classes and indeed, many CS classes face a "lack of interest" from the general school population [2, 23, 31, 32]. There are concerns among researchers and education professionals that students in our classrooms are bored, unmotivated and disengaged from school [4, 26]. One of the reasons is that old teaching methods are no longer beneficial to the students. On the other hand, game-based learning can improve learning motivation of students [1, 14, 15, 21]. Compared with traditional lectures, digital game-based approaches can indeed

© ICST Institute for Computer Sciences, Social Informatics and Telecommunications Engineering 2018
A. L. Brooks et al. (Eds.): ArtsIT 2017/DLI 2017, LNICST 229, pp. 366–375, 2018.
https://doi.org/10.1007/978-3-319-76908-0_35

produce better learning effects, which underscore the need to develop appropriate instructional materials [1, 26].

ClassCraft is a role-playing game which aims to transform any classroom into a role-playing platform that fosters stronger student collaboration and encourages better behavior [5, 28]. Gamification systems such as ClassCraft add an adventure game layer on top of the existing course infrastructure. Students create a character, play as part of a team, and gain experience points and rewards based on class-related behaviors [1].

The rest of paper is organized as follows. Section 2 describes the use of computer games in education, and Sect. 3 describes the role-playing video game ClassCraft. Section 4 describes the comparative study of different teaching methods. Finally, Sects. 5 and 6 present the results and conclusion of the teaching intervention.

2 Gamification

Digital games are an important part of most adolescent's leisure lives nowadays and are expected to become the predominant form of popular culture interaction in our society. Studies show that even young children under the age of 8 are frequent users of digital games and applications [10, 21, 24]. Many educators see digital games as powerfully motivating digital environments [23, 27] because of their potential to enhance student engagement and motivation in learning, [13] as well as an effective way to create socially interactive and constructivist learning environments [6]. According to [11], "Video games engage players in powerful forms of learning, forms that we could spread in various guises, into schools, workplaces, and communities where we wish to engage people with "education" (p. 216)".

There are a lot of studies that demonstrate the advantages of digital games in learning, not only for transversal skills like communication, collaboration, fine motor skill, to name but a few but also for specific skills in particular knowledge domains [18, 21]. Through gamification of education, the intention has been to incorporate the aspects of games that produce flow into the school setting, increasing thus student school engagement [4].

Gamification is defined as the application of game elements to non-game contexts [4]. In education overall, the conversation about gamification posits that this approach when used in the classroom could be an effective tool for increasing student learning and engagement, compared to the traditional lecture format [4, 11, 21]. The reason is that through gamification, we can not only create a mindset that encourages students to try new things and not be afraid of failing, but also enable students to engage in enjoyable experiences for the purpose of learning [1]. Another key advantage of gamification is the low cost of development and the possibility of making learning content more appealing or interesting using game elements [1].

Gamification will not on its own ensure the engagement of students in class, but it can provide another means of promoting students' active participation and investment into something beyond the academic expectations of a lesson. Gamification should be used as an adjunct to other well-supported engagement strategies [4].

3 ClassCraft

Inspired by role-playing video games, ClassCraft (https://game.ClassCraft.com/home) was created by a high school science teacher Shawn Young to help engage his students [29]. The first public version of ClassCraft was made available in February 2014 as a beta version. The official global launch of the game was in August 2014 [28].

ClassCraft is a game that students and teacher play together to transform how both members experience class every day. It can be considered to metaphorize the functioning of a classroom as a battlefield combining collaboration and competition [5, 28]. The service requires no installation (other than mobile apps, if one decides to use them). The game operates on a real-time web engine, so events in the game are pushed in real time to other users' devices, much like in a normal online video game [28]. ClassCraft is not related to a specific school subject, and the duration of the game depends on the teacher's expectations (from a few class hours to the entire year). The students play the game during school hours and outside of class [28].

Game rules are quite simple. A student by demonstrating positive behavior in class can earn "Experience Points (XP)" that will allow him/her to level up and learn new powers. If a student "breaks" the class rules, he/she will lose "Health Points (HP)"— his/her life energy in the game—and eventually, he/she will fall in battle. For instance, if a student earns XP points, these powers have real benefits for the student and for his/her team (see Fig. 1). Accordingly, if a student loses HP points the rest of his/her team will take damage, too. In any case, students need to work together to succeed. In ClassCraft, students are placed in teams of four to six members and play as Mages, Warriors, or Healers [28]. Each group has unique properties and powers and is designed for different types of students [12]. Each team has at least one Warrior, one Mage, and one Healer so they can help each other succeed in class tasks [8].

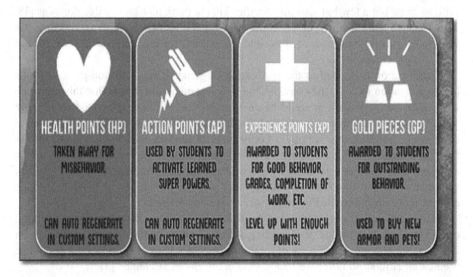

Fig. 1. ClassCraft point system (Reproduced from Dylan Peters EDU. Source: https://goo.gl/btWWf9).

The teacher played the game with his students in the school computer lab. He used the video projector in order for the students to watch the game during the whole teaching hour. At the beginning of the teaching hour, the teacher used the game class announcement tool to send messages to students, to reward or punish them for their performance, e.g., arriving in class late. Also during the teaching hour, the students were rewarded, or punished, for good or bad behavior of for their contribution in class, accordingly.

4 The Study

To determine the effectiveness of gamification compared to traditional approaches, the implementation of an experimental intervention was chosen. Class consisted of students attending the 1st grade of Senior High School (Lyceum), in the region of Crete, Greece. An experiment has been conducted to evaluate the effectiveness of the proposed approach via investigating the following research questions:

H1: The implementation of ClassCraft will have a positive impact on students' attitudes toward the programming course.

H2: The implementation of ClassCraft, will have a positive impact (improvement) in the overall grades of students in the programming course.

4.1 The Research Procedure

According to the working hypothesis of this work, the study followed an independent-subjects design. A random representative sample of subjects is selected and then the subjects are randomly assigned to either an experimental group or a control group. This procedure ensured that there was no systematic relationship between features of the subjects and to the group in which they were designated. One group, the experimental group, receives a treatment designed to produce some effect (the teaching intervention using ClassCraft). The other group, the control group, is left alone or given a fake treatment. Data is gathered; the dependent variables are measured. Results from the two groups are compared and analyzed to see if the experimental treatment made any difference [4, 9].

The sample consisted of 30 students enrolled in a public high school in Heraklion, (M age = 15.72 years, SD age = 1.22 years). At the beginning of the school year 2016–2017 the students were voluntarily enrolled in a lesson entitled "IT Applications". Students were distributed at random in two groups. Both groups of students were taught the same teaching material, in the same school computer lab but at different days and/or hours. All the lessons were taught by the same Computer Science teacher.

The intervention was applied in a special section of the lesson entitled "Programming environments for creating applications" (teaching duration of 16 h). The researcher randomly decided that the students of the first group would be used as a control group. The second group of students was assigned to the experimental group that would be taught the basic programming principles. The teacher implemented ClassCraft in the classroom to examine if this game can create an environment conducive to learning, leading to an increasing student interest in programming. Among the students, 51% were boys and 49% were girls. The two groups had an equal number of students and were similar with respect to age and gender. App Inventor for Android (AIA) for various pedagogical and practical reasons [19, 20, 22, 24, 25, 27] was qualified for the overall experimental design and implementation of the intervention.

In order to take results comparable with other studies the teacher followed the procedure given by [28] in the experimental group: Once students were introduced to the game, the students were asked whether they wanted to play or not. After the students of both genders, voluntarily agreed to play, they were asked to choose their five teammates following the teacher's instructions: Each team should contain different kinds of students, slow achievers and good learners, with or without behavioral difficulties. Prior the intervention, a pre-test evaluation focused on student's knowledge in the basic programming skills and attitudes toward programming showed that the two groups were statistically equivalent. The teacher used the computer lab video projector to show students the various messages during the course (announcements, penalties, rewards, assignments etc.).

As far as the ClassCraft implementation in the experimental group is concerned, the teacher did not use the game just as a simple badge system, but instead he tried to make lesson adjustments directly. For instance, if a student was a warrior and his/her teammate arrived late in class (which meant HP loss) the student could act and save his/her friend. If players lose all their HP, they receive a sentence and their teammates also lose HP [28]. In other cases, a student could use his/her power to bring a homework late, etc. Consequently, the students knew that their behavior in class affected the overall outcome. Concerning the learning content, the teacher regularly introduced personalized questions in the game and rewarded the students with in-game bounties. The students also earned XP points when they helped other students, collaborated during school activities, and got good grades. In general, the teacher used ClassCraft as an alternative way to empower students to take control of their learning process by reinforcing teamwork and collaboration rather than competition among students. Although students' parents had been informed, they did not show much interest for the intervention. Some parents disagreed with the idea of playing a game in the school. For that reason, the teacher did not use the parent mode of the game. Unlike similar studies [28] the teacher did not face any technical problems. Even the game's internationalization didn't pose a problem, although the Greek language was not supported by the game. Figure 2 shows the experimental design of this study.

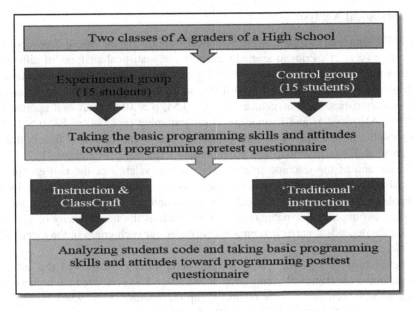

Fig. 2. Experimental design for the learning activities.

4.2 Evaluation

The teacher used a variety of data collection methods. First, the teacher collected and analyzed the correctness and complexity of the code created by students in various projects in both experimental conditions. Then, the teacher used the data from the students' final knowledge evaluation using an online questionnaire. The study of Kleinschmager and Hanenberg was used as a basis for creating the questionnaire [16]. The third tool was an appropriately designed questionnaire which was created by the teacher and composed of measures taken directly or adapted from previous studies. All aspects were measured with the use of four-point Likert scales (Not at all true to Very true). The questionnaire contained questions about students' attitudes towards programming. The questionnaire was developed on the basis of the Computer Attitude Scale (CAS) [17].

The adaptation of both the pre-test and the post-test were made by two experienced teachers who had taught the science course for many years [24, 27]. This is a common approach for developing achievement tests [20, 25]. All questionnaires were pilot tested prior to the main study to establish reliability, validity, and feasibility. They were distributed to 20 students who did not participate in the study to minimize potential problems related to the students' understanding of the questionnaires, the translation from English into Greek, the process of conducting the investigation etc. No problems were encountered during the pilot study. The Cronbach's alpha value of both the pre-test and the post-test questionnaire were .82 and .84 respectively, showing good reliability in internal consistency.

4.3 Statistical Analysis

The whole data was analyzed in the Statistical Package for the Social Sciences SPSS application (ver. 21). Prior to teaching intervention, statistical analyses of differences between the experimental and the control groups were performed. The results after applying suitable statistical tests showed that both groups did not differ significantly in their characteristics, such as gender ($X^2(2) = 0.54$, $p > .05$), behavioral approach (F (1, 28) = .51, $p > .05$) and knowledge in programming ($F(1, 28) = .82$, $p > .05$). In summary, the results show that both groups are equivalent in term of factors that are thought to underlie behavioral and programming knowledge differences [3, 7].

At the end of the teaching intervention, the equivalence of the two groups was checked using the independent samples t test. As it is a parametric test prior to its use, the application of standard statistical analysis techniques assumed that data met the necessary assumptions for parametric analyses such as the homogeneity of variances and that the dependent variable normally distributed for each group of the independent variable.

The analysis of students' projects (code complexity etc.) showed that although students in the experimental group ($M = 66.60$, $SD = 8.84$) recorded the highest score compared with their peers in the control group ($M = 64.87$, $SD = 9.96$), those results were not statistically significant ($t = -.29$, $df = 28$, $p > .05$).

Similarly, the analysis of the results of the online test at the end of the teaching session showed that there was not a clear progression in learning and understanding of basic programming concepts and problem-solving ability in the experimental group. Again, although the experimental group ($M = 74.60$, $SD = 7.21$) had slightly better performance than the control group ($M = 73.47$, $SD = 8.11$), the difference in performance between the two groups was not statistically significant ($t = -.41$, $df = 28$, $p > .05$).

The teacher, therefore, wanted to verify whether the attitudes of students toward programming varied in relation to the group to which they belonged. The results showed that the difference in performance between the two groups was statistically significant ($t = -7.78$, $df = 28$, $p < .001$), indicating that the method brought about a crucial difference between the two groups. Further analysis showed that the experimental group ($M = 92.27$, $SD = 2.09$) had significantly better performance than the control group ($M = 72.87$, $SD = 9.43$).

5 Discussion of Results - Intervention

Regarding the research hypotheses, the results of the present analysis are somewhat ambiguous. The first hypothesis seems to be confirmed by the findings as they showed that the use of ClassCraft in the classroom contributed positively to the growth of students' interest and attitudes for programming. It also seems that students involved with the game gave a more playful and pleasant feel to the learning process compared the 'traditional' approach. Regarding the acquisition of knowledge and skills, the results indicate that students in the experimental group did not significantly outperform their counterparts in the control group in terms of their understanding of the basic programming concepts, skills concepts, and problem-solving ability. From this first part of our study, we can conclude that the second hypothesis was not confirmed statistically in this small sample.

These markings are also consistent with those noted in other studies, which show that the use of ClassCraft in the classroom helps increase motivation, improves classroom behavior, and forms meaningful collaboration [28]. In the same study [28] note that ClassCraft helps to make appropriate and non-appropriate behavior clearer to students through a system of rewards and penalties, depending on the school rules. Overall, students feel they have had a more engaging and enjoyable experience. We can consider that the implementation of ClassCraft in the classroom/computer lab is appealing to students because it brings the language and culture of digital games which are part of their daily life to the school environment, [4]. In general, students in the experimental group, reported positive feelings towards the system and increased motivation to participate in similar courses in the future.

On the other hand, this game in no way affects the curriculum or in class assessments. The main drawback is that it does not provide integration with the course curriculums in a direct and simple way [29]. As [5] note, making effective use of commercial games in the classroom requires careful thought and explicit direction in the extraction of this unintended pedagogical value. However, the role of the teacher and his/her own appropriation of the game are key [28]. Finally, one of the more encouraging elements of this intervention is that both genders appeared to equally be involved in the game and it is compliant with the results of [28].

6 Conclusion

There are a lot of studies that demonstrate the advantages of digital games in learning, not only for transversal skills such as communication, collaboration, fine motor skill, etc., but also for specific skills in particular knowledge domains [18]. Through gamification of education, the intention has been to incorporate the aspects of games that produce flow into the school setting and to increase student school engagement [4].

Though this study has a number of limitations (small sample, short duration etc.) similarly to other studies, it provides implications that gamification can ensure the engagement of students in the class, in means of promoting students' active participation [4].

However, the proper application of an innovative method requires a thorough understanding of its various subsets and careful attention to exclude potential pitfalls, a thorough preparation on the part of the teacher and proper training of students [20, 25]. Prior to the implementation of gamification in the classroom teachers need to determine the needs and interests of them and their students, as well as what they wish to achieve through the implementation of a gamification system [4]. One of such barriers is the lack of methodologies and tools that would allow teachers to embrace their approach in an appropriate manner [18]. Undoubtedly, to generalize the use of games in formal education settings, educators need additional support [5].

Thus, further research into this area is required as it will provide valuable understanding of the potential of gamification as a tool for increasing student engagement.

References

1. Al-Azawi, R., Al-Faliti, F., Al-Blushi, M.: Educational gamification vs. game based learning: comparative study. Int. J. Innov. Manag. Technol. **7**(4), 131 (2016)
2. Bennedsen, J., Caspersen, M.E.: Failure rates in introductory programming. ACM SIGCSE Bull. Inroads **39**(2), 32–36 (2007)
3. Berdousis, I., Kordaki, M.: Gender differences and achievement in computer science: a case study. Procedia-Soc. Behav. Sci. **191**, 1161–1166 (2015)
4. Bond, L.: Mathimagicians quest: applying game design concepts to education to increase school engagement for students with emotional and behavioral disabilities. Doctoral dissertation, University of Washington (2015)
5. Calvo, A., Rotaru, D.C., Freire, M., Fernandez-Manjon, B.: Tools and approaches for simplifying serious games development in educational settings. In: Global Engineering Education Conference (EDUCON), pp. 1188–1197. IEEE (2016)
6. Chan, K.Y.G., Tan, S.L., Hew, K.F.T., Koh, B.G., Lim, L.S., Yong, J.C.: Knowledge for games, games for knowledge: designing a digital roll-and-move board game for a law of torts class. Res. Pract. Technol. Enhanced Learn. **12**(1), 7 (2017)
7. Chan, V., Stafford, K., Klawe, M., Chen, G.: Gender differences in Vancouver secondary students interests related to information technology careers. In: Balka, E., Smith, R. (eds.) Women, Work and Computerization. ITIFIP, vol. 44, pp. 58–69. Springer, Heidelberg (2000). https://doi.org/10.1007/978-0-387-35509-2_8
8. ClassCraft Studios Inc. http://www.ClassCraft.com/overview/
9. Dewey, R.A.: Psychology: an introduction. http://www.intropsych.com/ch01_psychology_and_science/independent_dependent_and_subject_variables.html
10. Gee, J.P.: Learning by design: games as learning machines. Digit. Educ. Rev. **8**, 15–23 (2004)
11. Gee, J.P.: What Video Games Have to Teach us About Learning and Literacy. Palgrave Macmillan, New York (2007)
12. Haris, D.A., Sugito, E.: Analysis of factors affecting user acceptance of the implementation of ClassCraft e-learning: case studies Faculty of Information Technology of Tarumanagara University. In: 2015 International Conference on Advanced Computer Science and Information Systems (ICACSIS), pp. 73–78. IEEE (2015)
13. Hsu, C.-Y., Tsai, M.-J., Chang, Y.-H., Liang, J.-C.: Surveying in-service teachers' beliefs about game-based learning and perceptions of technological pedagogical and content knowledge of games. Educ. Technol. Soc. **20**(1), 134–143 (2017)
14. Kalogiannakis, M., Papadakis, S.: A proposal for teaching ScratchJr programming environment in preservice kindergarten teachers. In: Proceedings of the 12th Conference of the European Science Education Research Association (ESERA), «Research, Practice and Collaboration in Science Education». Dublin City University and the University of Limerick, Dublin, Ireland, 21–25 August 2017 (2017)
15. Kalogiannakis, M., Papadakis, S.: Pre-service kindergarten teachers acceptance of "ScratchJr" as a tool for learning and teaching computational thinking and Science education. In: Proceedings of the 12th Conference of the European Science Education Research Association (ESERA), «Research, Practice and Collaboration in Science Education». Dublin City University and the University of Limerick, Dublin, Ireland, 21–25 August 2017 (2017)

16. Kleinschmager, S., Hanenberg, S.: How to rate programming skills in programming experiments? A preliminary, exploratory, study based on university marks, pretests, and self-estimation. In: Proceedings of ACM SIGPLAN Workshop on Evaluation and Usability of Programming Languages and Tools, pp. 15–24. ACM Press (2011)

17. Loyd, B.H., Gressard, C.: Reliability and factorial validity of computer attitude scale. Educ. Psychol. Measur. **44**(2), 501–505 (1984)

18. Moreno, J., Méndez, N.D.: Teaching sciences in K-12 using 2D educational massive online games. Anais temporários do LACLO **10**(1), 394 (2015)

19. Orfanakis, V., Papadakis, S.: A new programming environment for teaching programming. A first acquaintance with enchanting. In: The 2nd International Virtual Scientific Conference - Scieconf 2014, pp. 268–273. EDIS - University of Zilina, Slovakia (2014)

20. Orfanakis, V., Papadakis, S.: Teaching basic programming concepts to novice programmers in secondary education using Twitter, Python, Ardruino and a coffee machine. In: Hellenic Conference on Innovating STEM Education (HISTEM), Greece (2016)

21. Papadakis, S.: The use of computer games in classroom environment. Int. J. Teach. Case Stud. **9**(1), 1–25 (2018)

22. Papadakis, S., Orfanakis, V.: Comparing novice programing environments for use in secondary education: App Inventor for Android vs. Alice. Int. J. Technol. Enhanced Learn. **10**(1/2), 44–72 (2018)

23. Papadakis, S., Kalogiannakis, M., Orfanakis, V., Zaranis, N.: The appropriateness of Scratch and App Inventor as educational environments for teaching introductory programming in primary and secondary education. Int. J. Web Based Learn. Teach. Technologies (IJWLTT) **12**(4), 58–77 (2017)

24. Papadakis, S., Kalogiannakis, M., Orfanakis, V., Zaranis, N.: Using Scratch and App Inventor for teaching introductory programming in secondary education. A case study. Int. J. Technol. Enhanced Learn. **8**(3/4), 217–233 (2016)

25. Papadakis, S., Orfanakis, V.: The combined use of Lego Mindstorms NXT and App Inventor for teaching novice programmers. In: Alimisis, D., Moro, M., Menegatti, E. (eds.) Edurobotics 2016 2016. AISC, vol. 560, pp. 193–204. Springer, Cham (2017). https://doi.org/10.1007/978-3-319-55553-9_15

26. Papadakis, S.: Creativity and innovation in European education. 10 years eTwinning. Past, present and the future. Int. J. Technol. Enhanced Learn. **8**(3/4), 279–296 (2016)

27. Papadakis, S., Kalogiannakis, M., Orfanakis, V., Zaranis, N.: Novice programming environments. Scratch & App Inventor: a first comparison. In: Fardoun, H.M., Gallud, J. A. (eds.) Proceedings of the 2014 Workshop on Interaction Design in Educational Environments, pp. 1–7. ACM, New York (2014)

28. Sanchez, E., Young, S., Jouneau-Sion, C.: ClassCraft: from gamification to ludicization of classroom management. Educ. Inf. Technol. **22**(2), 497–513 (2017)

29. Sant, C.: Leveling Up: Evaluating Theoretical Underpinnings and Applications of Gamification in the Classroom. Vanderbilt University, Peabody College of Education and Human Development (2014)

30. Wang, J.: Is the US education system ready for CS for all? Commun. ACM **60**(8), 26–28 (2017)

31. Watson, C., Li, F.W.: Failure rates in introductory programming revisited. In: Proceedings of the 2014 Conference on Innovation and Technology in Computer Science Education (ITiCSE 2014), pp. 39–44. ACM, New York (2014)

32. Yardi, S., Bruckman, A.: What is computing?: Bridging the gap between teenagers' perceptions and graduate students' experiences. In: Proceedings of the Third International Workshop on Computing Education Research, pp. 39–50. ACM (2007)

Access Moodle Using Smart Mobile Phones.
A Case Study in a Greek University

Stamatios Papadakis[1(✉)], Michail Kalogiannakis[1], Eirini Sifaki[2],
and Nikolas Vidakis[3]

[1] Department of Preschool Education, University of Crete,
Rethymnon Campus, Rethymno, Crete, Greece
stpapadakis@gmail.com, mkalogian@edc.uoc.gr
[2] Hellenic Open University, Patras, Greece
eirini_sifaki@yahoo.gr
[3] Department of Informatics Engineering, Technological Educational Institution
of Crete, Stavromenos, Heraklion, Crete, Greece
nv@ie.teicrete.gr

Abstract. The use of learning management systems (LMS) has grown considerably in universities around the world. This study investigated how often students used a mobile phone to access various activities on Moodle. The students' point of view is important since they are the main users of the offered teaching technique and can cooperate in implementing and improving an e-course as a very important stakeholder in the e-learning process. A survey on self-reported usage was filled by 122 university students in a course offered by the faculty of Preschool Education at the University of Crete. Follow-up interviews were conducted to solicit students' perceptions on mobile access to Moodle and the underlying reasons. The results show significant differences in students' usage of various Moodle activities via mobile phones. Students' responses also suggest that Moodle is used merely as an electronic document repository and not as an effective learning tool due to the limitations of mobile access on usability and reliability.

Keywords: Moodle · Mobile access · LMS · Smart mobile devices

1 Introduction

Information and communication technology (ICT) is increasingly becoming a bigger and more important part of students' everyday life [17, 18, 23, 25–27]. Consequently, the role of e-learning has transformed completely as recent advances in Information Technology (IT) and the advent of Web 2.0 technologies enabled the creation of learning content that is no longer based on textbooks and learning guides [24–26, 30]. The traditional idea of "classroom" now incorporates the use of both physical and virtual space [33]. A significant trend in universities has been to implement so-called learning management systems (LMS) (Moodle and other web-based learning systems), which are used as a common platform where students and teachers can interact digitally [6, 32, 34].

© ICST Institute for Computer Sciences, Social Informatics and Telecommunications Engineering 2018
A. L. Brooks et al. (Eds.): ArtsIT 2017/DLI 2017, LNICST 229, pp. 376–385, 2018.
https://doi.org/10.1007/978-3-319-76908-0_36

In recent years, instructors have been concerned about mobile devices as the new media for learning content delivery, the collaboration between the members of the educational community, at primary, secondary and tertiary levels of education [14, 20, 23, 25, 26, 28, 29, 35]. In this way, they go along with the new generations of students that were 'born with smartphones' and are very familiar with the latest technologies [3, 23]. It is not uncommon to see university students, as well as those in secondary school, using smartphones to access learning resources on Moodle and other LMSs [15]. However, despite the increase in LMS adoption in universities, concern has been expressed as to whether LMSs are being used as effective learning tools or merely as electronic document repositories [5, 6]. [4] state that the findings of various researchers indicate that while many staff in the universities worldwide use LMSs to some extent, a large majority fail to make use of the potential pedagogical advantages offered by the full functionality of the software. [32] state that LMSs are still inadequate in supporting the level of interaction, personalization, and engagement demanded by the tech-savvy students.

Students' perceptions of an LMS is mainly influenced by how the system correlates with their educational needs and expectations [32]. Research results confirm that the LMSs are used more as electronic document repositories than as active learning tools and students are much more likely to assume a passive role rather than becoming active players [4, 5]. In a research in the University of Minho (UM) Portugal, researchers found that the students seem to appreciate the contribution of an LMS to their learning, viewing it as a complement rather than a substitute for classroom activities [5]. [15] in a similar study found that students did not prefer using their mobile phones to access Moodle, due to the limitations of mobile access on usability and reliability. In terms of Moodle activities, it was found that students preferred carrying out easy and low-stake Moodle tasks on their mobile phones, such as accessing learning materials.

The current research aims at examining how students use Moodle via smart mobile devices to carry out different Moodle activities and the possible reasons behind such usage patterns.

2   Mobile Learning and LMS

An LMS is a tool that performs among other functions: mediation of knowledge appropriation, administration of such mediation, access to educational and communication tools [12]. An LMS not only provides academic institutions with efficient means to train and teach individuals but also enables them to efficiently codify and share their academic knowledge [1]. As a result, the state of the eLearning market globally continues to shift, grow, and evolve. According to [8], global revenues for self-paced eLearning (LMS, authoring tools, packaged content, and services) reached $46.6 billion in 2016. In 2004, the eLearning market was worth more than US$18 billion [16]. The global learning management system (LMS) market is expected to grow at a CAGR of 24% during the 2016 to 2020 period [8]. Currently, there are many brands of web-based learning systems, for example, WebCT, Moodle, OLAT, and Sakai [34]. According to literature, there are three LMS generations (see Fig. 1) [31].

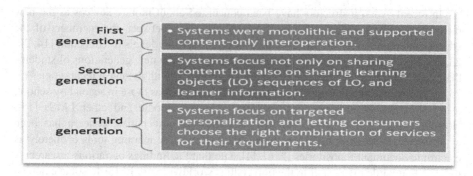

Fig. 1. The three LMS generations

When deciding on the introduction of an LMS and when measuring its effectiveness and usefulness, many factors must be taken into account [3]. Successful implementation of LMSs is not an easy step and depend not only on providing training and support for instructors but also on the level of student active engagement and student and instructor satisfaction with the LMS used [5]. Motivation and positive perceptions and attitudes of tutors and students toward e-learning and digital literacy should be taken into consideration for successful e-learning adoption [2]. The students' point of view is very important since they are the main users of the offered teaching technique and can cooperate in implementing and improving an e-course as a very important stakeholder in the e-learning process [3]. There are three e-learning modes of engagement, which correspond to growing levels of complexity and depth in LMS usage (see Fig. 2) [11].

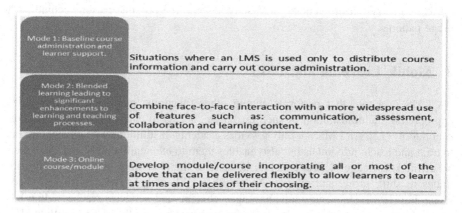

Fig. 2. Three e-learning modes of engagement in LMS usage.

[13] in a cross-institutional study revealed both institutional and cultural barriers for e-learning to transform, rather than sit uncomfortably alongside, institutional practice.

Previous studies had found that most universities were at mode 1 of the Francis and Raftery model [5]. Similarly, as for the level of engagement to which the LMSs are used, studies had found that the vast majority of students seem to experience no higher engagement than Francis and Raftery mode 1 [5, 15].

3 Methodology

3.1 The LMS

The open-source LMS Moodle, (http://moodle.org/) can be found in many segments of education and higher education is no exception. Its popularity, except for the fact it is free, is mainly based on its flexibility, adaptability and the possibility of personalization while, on the other hand, the system contains many standard features which make the learning process easy to implement [3]. The University of Crete (Faculty of Preschool Education) has adopted Moodle (version 2.9) as one of its official LMS. One course of one instructor was selected for this study. The instructor was in the faculty of Preschool Education and the course was entitled "Introduction to the Informatics II". The scope of the course was for preservice kindergarten teachers to learn on how to use ScratchJr for educational purposes. The instructor used Moodle in multiple roles: as a repository of teaching materials, a platform for making course announcements and as discussion forums for student–student and student–instructor interaction. Also, the students could submit assignments, take quizzes, conduct group projects and receive feedback from the instructor. Although there is a mobile app for Moodle, it cannot be used directly by the students' due to University security policy. The students had to used their preferred browsers in their mobile devices to access Moodle.

3.2 The Sample and the Procedure

This study adopts a mixed method with survey and interview data collected and analyzed. The study design was based on the work of [5] to get comparable results. The participants were 3rd-year students. Although the study targeted about 160 respondents, a total of 122 valid submissions were obtained, (76% response rate). After the online survey data were collected, the students were voluntarily asked to participate in the interviews. 25 students took part in the follow-up interviews. All interviews were conducted face-to-face.

A questionnaire asking about the experience of using Moodle was used for collecting quantitative data. It included two parts: demographic information and frequency of course Moodle use. Part 1 asked for basic demographic information as well as their experience with Moodle and self-perceived IT competency level; Part 2 asked about the frequencies of using different categories of Moodle activities with variables in a 5-point Likert scale: ranging from 1 (never) to 5 (several times a day). Some of the questionnaire questions are as follows: "What did you usually do when you access the Moodle of this course via your phone?", "Did you have any difficulties in using the Moodle of this course using your mobile phone? If yes, what were they?", etc.

4   Results

4.1   Questionnaire Responses

Table 1 shows the statistics of student self-reported usage of Moodle via mobile phones. Access to learning materials was the most frequent activity, while interacting with instructors and other students were the least frequent one.

Table 1. Students usage of Moodle via smart mobile phones.

Moodle activities	Mean	SD
Accessing resources	3.8	1.12
Submitting assignments	1.3	0.26
Taking tests	2.1	0.71
Interaction	1.5	0.33
Collaboration	1.1	0.17

Experience of using Moodle may have affected students' usage of Moodle via mobile access. We used Kruskal–Wallis tests as a non-parametric equivalent of the ANOVA control. The tests revealed that students with different Moodle experience reported significantly different usage frequency ($p < .05$). Follow-up pair-wise tests revealed that students with "2 years' or more" experience with Moodle reported higher frequencies than those with "less than 1 year" or "1 year to less than 2 years" experience. Besides, a difference in the frequency of using Moodle via mobile phones across IT competency was also analyzed. As a statistically significant difference of access frequencies in interaction and collaboration activities was found ($p < .05$) a follow-up pair-wise test was used by the researchers. It was found that students who rated themselves as "competent" reported significantly more frequent access than those who rated themselves as "not or somewhat competent" or "less competent." In terms of collaboration, students who rated themselves as "competent" reported significantly more frequent access than those who rated themselves as "not or somewhat competent" or "less competent". There was no significant difference between other pairs of IT competency values. These results are completely different compared to the work of [5]. As all the students of the Department of Preschool Education were females in this study, there was no gender-based statistical analysis.

4.2   Interview Responses

The semi-structured interviews were conducted after a regular university day. A separate isolated room was used to avoid distractions and outside influences. All students interviewed answered that they used mobile phones to access the Moodle of their courses, as mobile phones allowed them to access the LMS at any place and anytime. Mobile access also enabled them to read announcements, comments, and feedback as soon as they were available online. At the same time, they also stated that they preferred content to be more well-organized and clearly presented in comparison with the

LMS access via desktop PCs, due to the technological limitations of smart mobile devices. For example, some said they preferred to see the necessary announcements as soon as they accessed the application to feel more comfortable with the course content or they reported the inability to find information in a quick and efficient way. Students' tendency in using Moodle for resource depository and information retrieval in this study demonstrated consistency with previous studies on students' perception on Moodle [4, 32]. Students statements (Table 2) revealed that they see LMS as a complement rather than a substitute for the formal class.

Table 2. Students representative answers.

Moodle activities	Sample views
Accessing resources	It may be a convenient option to see changes in the material made by the professor. On the other hand, one respondent expressed a worry that the mobile access stressed her out as she felt she should constantly check her phone for new updates, similar to the 'Facebook-syndrome'
Submitting assignments	I do not use it because I find it a cumbersome process
Taking tests	Most importantly, it gives me a sense of freedom, as I am not obliged to constantly sit in front of a PC. It's very easy to access, so sometimes you end up sitting at a cafe and checking whether there is anything new
Interaction	If there was no social media, the system would be important for communication with instructors and other students. I prefer to use other social media platforms, such as students' closed group on Facebook
Collaboration	Although I own a mobile device with a large touch screen, I prefer for this type of activities to work on my PC

In general, students indicated that using mobile phones was not a preferred method to access Moodle. Although there are mobile device monitors with larger screens - which can render higher resolutions at more readable sizes - students still referred to usability issues such as the screen size. Thus, they would only be comfortable to conduct simple and low-stake tasks using mobile access (see Fig. 3).

Fig. 3. Moodle content in a 5.5-in mobile device screen.

5 Discussion

This study set out to investigate how university students perceive the use of learning management systems. As many studies show, the success of web-based learning systems will not be achieved if students fail to use such systems [34]. Both the survey and interview data indicated that students used mobile phones to access Moodle for learning materials much more often than for other uses, which indicates that the use of mobile access to Moodle was still at the lowest level as suggested in [11]. Incomplete system use signifies that the LMS is perceived as a tool with a few isolated functions, not as the 'multi tool' the system it is designed to be [32]. Like other studies [5, 31, 32], the major findings from the results show that students' perception of the LMS is affected by several factors related to social influences, perceived easiness to use and perceived usefulness. Students highlighted that mobile phones present usability and compatibility problems while trying to access websites meant for desktop or laptop computers. Thus, this is one of the main reason why students do not prefer mobile access for accessing the LMSs. If mobile phones are to be used to effectively access LMSs, the LMSs must be optimized for mobile access. This could happen through the provision of a few selected services by the instructors, with the necessary detail for each service. The design challenge is to optimize the LMS in such a way that the mobile site satisfies at least most of the mobile users' needs for the LMS [31]. Therefore, managers and developers of e-learning need to improve the content quality of their e-learning systems to encourage students to use them more extensively [34]. Furthermore, the findings of this study, like other studies, emphasize the importance of the LMS delivering quality content to its users, as well as the fact that it is up-to-date, easily available and relevant [1, 22, 32, 34]. In contrast to other studies such as the ones reported by [32], the students didn't report that the LMS contained a lot of unnecessary information.

In this study, like those reported by [5], the results suggest that simply the creation of Moodle activities that are designed for interaction and collaboration does not necessarily result in more frequent access to those activities via mobile phones. Besides, instructors and teaching assistants need to be more responsive and more active in facilitating student interactive activities. As [32] indicate the teacher's way of using the system is a major source of influence on how students perceive and use an LMS.

The results also revealed that students who had used Moodle for a longer period tended to use mobile access more often to take tests and collaborate on Moodle than those who had used Moodle for less time. In addition, students with high self-perceived IT competency used more mobile access to Moodle for interaction and collaboration activities. These seem to comply with many studies where experience and IT competency are positively associated with technology usage [7, 10, 19, 21].

6 Conclusion and Future Work

Recent technological advances have led universities to an introduction of innovative modes of teaching and learning. Studies have found that students may react differently to the online learning environment, depending on their skill level and attitude [9]. In general, students in this study did not prefer using their mobile phones to access Moodle due to the limitations of mobile access on usability and reliability. However, most of them indeed used mobile phones to access Moodle when it was necessary. In terms of Moodle activities, it was found that students preferred carrying out easy and low-stake Moodle tasks on their mobile phones, such as accessing learning materials. The students expressed the need for a more user-friendly mobile access.

This study, much like other studies of similar nature, had limitations. A possible limitation is that the data collection was limited to a single university department in Greece. Follow-up studies can expand the sample by recruiting participants from different universities and in different regions. Another limitation is that the findings of this study are solely based on self-reported data from participants, which might be subject to the difference in students' own perception. Future studies could rely on objective data sources such as the usage patterns as reflected in the LMS system logs. Additionally, as it is clear from the results, the students' perceptions reflect issues that are both technical and social in nature, a fact which in many ways supports previous research on user acceptance of the technology. So, it will be of interest in future studies to try to identify, the individual, organizational, and technological factors that could be influencing the use of LMS, using the Technology Acceptance Model.

The feature of blended learning on which we would like to focus is the increasing emphasis on 'learner collaboration' [11]. We soon expect the use of LMS in the University of Crete to be being utilized closer to Francis and Raftery's Mode 2 as students make more use of communication and collaboration tools.

References

1. Al-Busaidi, K.A.: Learners' perspective on critical factors to LMS success in blended learning: an empirical investigation. Commun. Assoc. Inform. Syst. (CAIS) **30**(2), 11–34 (2012)
2. Alkoudmani, R.M., Elkalmi, R.M.: Challenges to web-based learning in pharmacy education in arabic language speaking countries. Arch. Pharma Pract. **6**, 41–47 (2015)
3. Aristovnik, A., Keržič, D., Tomaževič, N., Umek, L.: Determining factors of students' perceived usefulness of e-learning in higher education. In: McPherson, M., Nunes, M.B. (eds.) Proceedings of the International Conference e-Learning 2016, Part I, pp. 3–10 (2016)
4. Badge, J., Cann, A., Scott, J.: E-Learning VersusE: seeing the pedagogic wood for the technological trees. Biosci. Educ. **5**(1), 1–11 (2005)
5. Carvalho, A., Areal, N., Silva, J.: Students' perceptions of blackboard and moodle in a Portuguese University. Br. J. Edu. Technol. **42**(5), 824–841 (2011)
6. Chipps, J., Kerr, J., Brysiewicz, P., Walters, F.: A survey of University students' perceptions of learning management systems in a low-resource setting using a technology acceptance model. CIN Comput. Inform. Nurs. **33**(2), 71–77 (2015)
7. Cochrane, T.D.: Critical success factors for transforming pedagogy with mobile web 2.0. Br. J. Edu. Technol. **45**(1), 65–82 (2014)
8. Docebo: Elearning market trends and forecast 2017–2021. https://www.docebo.com/resource/elearning-market-trends-and-forecast-2017-2021/
9. Drennan, J., Kennedy, J., Pisarski, A.: Factors affecting student attitudes toward flexible online learning in management education. J. Educ. Res. **98**(6), 331–338 (2005)

10. Elstad, E., Christophersen, K.A.: Perceptions of digital competency among student teachers: contributing to the development of student teachers' instructional self-efficacy in technology-rich classrooms. Educ. Sci. **7**(1), 27 (2017)
11. Francis, R., Raftery, J.: Blended learning landscapes. Brookes eJournal Learn. Teach. **1**(3), 1–5 (2005)
12. Gomez, F.S., Ordóñez, A.: Application of a reference framework for integration of web resources in DOTLRN-Case study of Physics-topic: waves. In: McPherson, M., Nunes, M.B. (eds.) Proceedings of the International Conference e-learning 2016, Part I, pp. 112–119 (2016)
13. Gunn, C.: Sustainability factors for e-learning initiatives. ALT-J. **18**(2), 89–103 (2010)
14. Heng, W., Zhong, D.: A practice of mobile learning on cloud computing. In: McPherson, M., Nunes, M.B. (eds.) Proceedings of the International Conference e-Learning 2016, Part I, pp. 88–95 (2016)
15. Hu, X., Lei, L.C.U., Li, J., Iseli-Chan, N., Siu, F.L.C., Chu, S.K.W.: Access moodle using mobile phones: student usage and perceptions. In: Churchill, D., Lu, J., Chiu, T.K.F., Fox, B. (eds.) Mobile Learning Design. LNET, pp. 155–171. Springer, Singapore (2016). https://doi.org/10.1007/978-981-10-0027-0_10
16. ITP.net: E-Learning Curve - ITP Technology. http://www.itp.net/482772-e-learning-curve
17. Kalogiannakis, M., Papadakis, S.: An evaluation of Greek educational Android apps for preschoolers. In: proceedings of the 12th Conference of the European Science Education Research Association (ESERA), Research, Practice and Collaboration in Science Education, Dublin City University and the University of Limerick, Dublin, Ireland, 21–25 August 2017 (2017)
18. Kalogiannakis, M., Papadakis, S.: A proposal for teaching ScratchJr programming environment in preservice kindergarten teachers. In: Proceedings of the 12th Conference of the European Science Education Research Association (ESERA), Research, Practice and Collaboration in Science Education, Dublin, Ireland, 21–25 August 2017 (2017)
19. Kalogiannakis, M., Papadakis, S.: Investigating pre-service kindergarten teachers' intention to adopt and use table into teaching practice for natural sciences. Int. J. Childhood Stud. (IJCS) **1**(1) (forthcoming article)
20. Kalogiannakis, M., Papadakis, S.: Pre-service kindergarten teachers acceptance of "ScratchJr" as a tool for learning and teaching computational thinking and Science education. In: proceedings of the 12th Conference of the European Science Education Research Association (ESERA), Research, Practice and Collaboration in Science Education. Dublin City University and the University of Limerick, Dublin, Ireland, 21–25 August 2017 (2017)
21. Li, K., Li, Y., Franklin, T.: Preservice teachers' intention to adopt technology in their future classrooms. J. Educ. Comput. Res. **54**(7), 946–966 (2016)
22. Ozkan, S., Koseler, R.: Multi-dimensional students' evaluation of e-learning systems in the higher education context: an empirical investigation. Comput. Educ. **53**(4), 1285–1296 (2009)
23. Orfanakis V., Papadakis, S.: A new programming environment for teaching programming. A first acquaintance with Enchanting. In: The 2nd international virtual Scientific Conference - Scieconf 2014, pp. 268–273. EDIS - University of Zilina, Slovakia (2014)
24. Papadakis, S., Kalogiannakis, M., Zaranis, N.: Designing and creating an educational app rubric for preschool teachers. Educ. Inform. Technol., 1–19 (2017)
25. Papadakis, S., Kalogiannakis, M., Zaranis, N.: Comparing tablets and PCs in teaching mathematics: an attempt to improve mathematics competence in early childhood education. Preschool Primary Educ. **4**(2), 241–253 (2016)

26. Papadakis, S., Kalogiannakis, M., Zaranis, N.: Developing fundamental programming concepts and computational thinking with ScratchJr in preschool education: a case study. Int. J. Mobile Learn. Organ. **10**(3), 187–202 (2016)
27. Papadakis, S., Kalogiannakis, M.: Mobile educational applications for children. What educators and parents need to know. Int. J. Mobile Learn. Organ. **11**(3), 256–277 (2017)
28. Papadakis, S.: Creativity and innovation in european education. 10 years eTwinning. past, present and the future. Int. J. Technol. Enhanced Learn. **8**(3/4), 279–296 (2016)
29. Papadakis, S.: The use of computer games in classroom environment. Int. J. Teach. Case Stud. **9**(1), 1–25 (2018)
30. Papadakis, S., Orfanakis, V.: The combined use of Lego Mindstorms NXT and app inventor for teaching novice programmers. In: Alimisis, D., Moro, M., Menegatti, E. (eds.) Edurobotics 2016 2016. AISC, vol. 560, pp. 193–204. Springer, Cham (2017). https://doi.org/10.1007/978-3-319-55553-9_15
31. Shokri, A., Dafoulas, G.: A Quantitative analysis of the role of social networks in educational contexts. In: McPherson, M., Nunes, M.B. (eds.) Proceedings of the International Conference e-Learning 2016, Part I, pp. 43–52 (2016)
32. Ssekakubo, G., Suleman, H., Marsden, G.: Designing mobile LMS interfaces: learners' expectations and experiences. Interact. Technol. Smart Educ. **10**(2), 147–167 (2013)
33. Suorsa, J., Eskilsson, N.: Students' perceptions of learning management systems. An explorative case study of upper secondary school students (Bachelor's thesis). Department of Applied Information Technology, University of Gothenburg, Sweden (2014)
34. Wilson, G., Randall, M.: The implementation and evaluation of a new learning space: a pilot study. Res. Learn. Technol. **20**, 14431 (2012)
35. Yeou, M.: An investigation of students' acceptance of moodle in a blended learning setting using technology acceptance model. J. Educ. Technol. Syst. **44**(3), 300–318 (2016)
36. Zaranis, N., Kalogiannakis, M., Papadakis, S.: Using mobile devices for teaching realistic mathematics in kindergarten education. Creative Educ. **4**(1–10), 22 (2013)

Detecting Depression Using Voice Signal Extracted by Chatbots: A Feasibility Study

Alexandros Roniotis[(✉)] and Manolis Tsiknakis

Department of Informatics Engineering,
Technological Educational Institute of Crete, Heraklion, Greece
alexandros.roniotis@gmail.com,
tsiknaki@staff.teicrete.gr

Abstract. This work aims at proposing a novel framework for detecting depression, like commonly met in cancer patients, using prosodic and statistical features extracted by voice signal. This work presents the first results of extracting these features on test and training sets extracted from the AVEC2016 dataset using MATLAB. The results indicate that voice can be used for extracting depression indicators and developing a mobile application for integrating this new knowledge could be the next step.

Keywords: Virtual coach · Cancer · Detecting depression · Machine learning
MFCCs

1 Introduction

Cancer is a major health problem in developed countries and accounts for almost 15% of all deaths [1]. Apart from physical exhaustion, knowledge about the forthcoming death has a serious impact on the psychological condition of the patient, resulting in increased identification of depression [2–4]. Clinical depression can only be diagnosed by a professional psychologist or clinician and treated through antidepressants or psychotherapy [5–7]. Depression in cancer patients seems to accelerate disease progression [8]. However, proper assessment and recognition of mental disorders requires intensive training and experience [9]. Developing an automatic machine learning mechanism for automatically detecting signs of depression could prove handful to clinicians during the early detection and start of psychotherapy [10, 11].

Developing e-health applications for smartphones or tablets is a rapidly growing sector [12]. Automated health monitoring using a software that interacts with the patient, called virtual coach, can help in self-treatment of the patient, reducing monitoring costs in a clinical environment and the timely notification of the supervising clinician [13, 14]. Not only the cost of using a system of this type is low, but also the familiarity of patients with modern devices increases over the years.

By installing a virtual coach in the smart device of a patient, the patient could monitor his or her mental state at anytime, anywhere and without the use of additional equipment or the need to get monitored within any hospital. Moreover, the technical requirements of modern phones allow the processing of complex data, such as voice signals, as they currently have powerful processors, large storage space and memory [15].

© ICST Institute for Computer Sciences, Social Informatics and Telecommunications Engineering 2018
A. L. Brooks et al. (Eds.): ArtsIT 2017/DLI 2017, LNICST 229, pp. 386–392, 2018.
https://doi.org/10.1007/978-3-319-76908-0_37

This work presents some first results on extracting signal features from voice for the purpose of detecting depression in cancer patients (or in general cases). The program has been applied on real voice segments, provided by the AVEC2016 dataset (www.avec16.com). The first results indicate that the features extracted are correlated to depression and we could move to the next future step; to apply the detection algorithms to cancer patients through mobile application and augmented reality chatbots.

2 Background

Clinical depression affects mood, thinking, behavior and physical condition [16]. Especially, voice and articulation of a person are directly affected by mental state [17], therefore voice features can be used as biomarkers of depression [18]. Voice features correlate with the presence and grade of depression and are often used to develop automatic classifiers. These features are classified as normal, mild, moderate, severe or very severe mental disorder according to the Hamilton Rating Scale for Depression (HAM-D), the 9-item Patient Health Questionnaire (PHQ-9) or Beck Depression Index (BDI) [19–21].

Depression affects speech production by differentiating stimulation of muscles and vocal cords [22] and altering respiratory rate [23]. Therefore, the quality of the produced sound is affected and is objectively measurable [24]. Some features that are used for the classification of emotional state are categorized as prosodic or spectral. Prosodic features include the rate of speech, the fundamental voice frequency ($f0$), the intensity and the energy of the voice and glottal features [25, 26]. Some frequent spectral features include the formants (the eigenfrequencies of the vocal organ), the power spectral density (PSD) and Mel Frequency Cepstral coefficients (MFCCs) [24, 27, 28].

3 Objectives

High costs and modest effectiveness of health system is often attributed to lack of patient's engagement at home [29]. The effective engagement is considered the "trillion opportunity" [30] and many companies have invested in developing m-Health applications for smart devices to involve in self-monitoring their health state, following their therapeutic scheme, reporting symptoms, etc. However, the devotion of patients proved moderate to low, mainly because they were not prompted by a third party to keep using the application. Instead, when using the application under the constant presence of a clinician, the results turned very encouraging [31]. Thus, it appears that the existence of a coach during the usage of the application could improve its effectiveness [32].

After the usage increase of the first years, applications for smart devices have lost their initial momentum [33]. Now the new generation of applications is considered that of chatbots, i.e. automated communication programs where the user chats with the device [29]. Chatbots are considered the next challenge for healthcare applications where a virtual coach will discuss with the patients, encourage them to pursue an action, raise questions and guide the discussion according to the answers received and processed [29, 34, 35]. Such an application could extract depressive biomarkers.

4 The Framework

The proposed scientific work is divided into two main sections. At first the extraction of audio data is performed for each subject, parallel to filling a depression questionnaire. Then, data is processed and feature vectors are extracted to compose the training set.

In the second stage, the speech of a subject is recorded and is then processed to generate a feature vector with the same features of the first stage. The vector is then classified into a depression class, according to the training set of the previous stage. Then, depending on the results of the classification, the virtual coach urges the patient to perform more psychotherapeutic activities, adhere to the therapeutic scheme, and notify the supervising clinician when depression scale is classified as severe.

4.1 Training Set

Initially, an application for mobile devices will be developed in order to generate some data. The application will be installed on a mobile device such as a mobile phone or tablet. The first time it runs, the program will show the patient a BDI questionnaire [20]. The answers will be stored for processing at a later stage.

Then, the virtual coach appears, developed with the open source environment BotLibre (www.botlibre.com), which, based on Positive psychology theory [36, 37], will start one interactive chat with the individual. The speech signal is then stored on the device for post-processing.

The answers on the BDI questionnaire are used as the ground truth towards defining the depression scale of the training set. Speech signal from the user is used to extract feature vectors. The features include the Mel-frequency cepstral coefficients (MFCCs) [36], speech duration, the duration of pauses, speech rate and the response-to-question delay and several more described in the next section. These features and the gender of the user form the training set.

4.2 Classification of Depression Scale

During the second stage a user is classified in one of the fore-mentioned depression scales. The user's responses to the chatbot's queries are recorded. The resulting signal will be recorded for producing the feature vector to be classified using the training set.

Another stage is to assess the effectiveness of classification. Towards evaluation the leave-one-out method is used, where each vector of the training set is sorted after removing the same vector. Finally, the resulting Confusion Matrix is used for estimating accuracy [39].

5 Methods

5.1 Extracting the Audio Features

The first step of our study before developing the framework is to evaluate the performance of voice features for detecting signs of depression. Therefore, the audio data provided by

AVEC has been used, accompanied by their respective transcripts. The dataset consists of a series of pre-extracted features using the COVAREP toolbox at 10-ms intervals over the entire recording ($f0$, NAQ, QOQ, H1H2, PSP, MDQ, peakSlope, Rd, Rd conf, MCEP 0–24, HMPDM 1–24, HMPDD 1–12, and Formants F1–F3).

For the purposes of the present work, the resulting time series data were submitted to additional preprocessing steps as follows: First, the participant's voice was isolated using the time stamps in the transcripts. Segments with values of "<synch>", "<laughter>", "[laughter]", "<sigh>" and "scrubbed entry" were ignored as non informative segments. Next, segments containing unvoiced segments (VUV = 0) were removed from the final concatenated time series. Furthermore, to correct for instances of apparently inaccurate annotation analyses were restricted to continuous voiced segments lasting >5 ms. To control for speaker dependency, the $f0$ was normalized to a scale of 0 to 1, and the deltas and delta-deltas were extracted for $f0$ and MFCCs.

The main analyses consisted in computing three sets of features to be used in subsequent classification approaches using Matlab Treebagger (n = 100 trees) classifier. The first set of audio features consisted of a series of statistical descriptors for each pre-extracted descriptor, while the second set consisted of Discrete Cosine Transform (DCT) coefficients for each descriptor. The first 10 values of the DCT were retained, reducing the number of parameters and therefore complexity. The third set of audio features consisted of 8 high level features which were computed for the entire duration of the concatenated time-series. The Pause Ratio was extracted measuring the frequency of pauses during the participant's speech. Pauses were detected automatically using a pause detector, which relied on a low loudness detection function based on the Perceptual Quality measure.

Some other features include the Voiced Segment Ratio (computed as the number of voiced segments divided by the length of the entire speech segment) and the Speaking Ratio (computed as the number of speaking instances that there is participant's speech), divided by the total number of selected recorded segments, as

$$SpeakingRatio = (\#allinstants - \#pauses)/\#allinstants$$

Some more are the Mean Laughter Duration, defined as the duration of laughter segments divided by the total number of laughter instances; the Mean delay in response to chatbot's questions; the Mean duration of pauses; the Maximum duration of pauses; The Fraction of pauses in overall time.

Finally, the former two sets of features were individually combined in feature level with the high level features into single feature vectors. The final set of statistical descriptors with high-level features was of size 494, and the set of DCTs with high-level features was of size 1278.

5.2   Classification

Gender-based classification for depression seems to substantially improve depression detection. In the present work, gender-based classification was implemented by building two different classifiers, one for men and another for women. The classifier for men was trained on feature-sets extracted from data of male participants and the women classifier from data of female participants. The classifier used was Matlab's treebagger using a forest of 100 trees.

6 Experimental Results

Performance of classification was evaluated through training with the training set and subsequent testing with the development and test sets provided by AVEC. In addition, the algorithms were assessed using the leave-one-out procedure on the joined training and development sets. The gender-based approach outperformed gender-independent models with the audio statistical descriptors.

More specifically, the F1-score for gender-independent classification was 0.24 for depression and 0.75 for non-depression. On the other hand, F1-score for depressed is 0.59 and for non-depressed is 0.87.

7 Conclusion

The F1-score of the gender-specific audio feature classification depicts that there is correlation of voice to depression, as expected by literature. However, it is interesting to study if the features could be fused with more features extracted by more modalities, such as video or text transcripts.

Future works include integrating the feature selection and classifications algorithms in a mobile application, where a chatbot will chat with patients. Patient replies will be recorded and post-processed for depression detection.

Acknowledgments. This research is supported by IKY scholarships programme and co-financed by the European Union (European Social Fund - ESF) and Greek national funds through the action "Reinforcement of Postdoctoral Researchers" in the framework of the Operational Programme "Human Resources Development Program, Education and Lifelong Learning" of the National Strategic Reference Framework (NSRF) 2014–2020.

References

1. World Health Organization, World Cancer Report 2014 (2014)
2. Dalton, S., Laursen, T., Mortensen, P., Johansen, C.: Risk for hospitalization with depression after a cancer diagnosis: a nationwide, population-based study of cancer patients in Denmark from 1973 to 2003. J. Clin. Oncol. **27**(9), 1440–1445 (2009)
3. Greek National Research Institute, Mental Health - Contemporary Approaches and Reflections, Athens (2011)
4. Moussas, G., Papadopoulos, A., Christodoulaki, A., Karkanias, A.: Psychological and psychiatric problems in patients with cancer: relationship with the localization of the disease. Psychiatry **23**(1), 46–60 (2012)
5. American Psychiatric Association, Diagnostic and statistical manual of mental disorders, Fourth Edition, Text Revision: DSM-IV-TR. American Psychiatric Publishing Inc., Washington, DC (2000)

6. Karapoulios, D., Getsios, I., Rizou, V., Tsiklitara, A., Kostopoulou, S., Balodimou, Ch., Margari, N.: Anxiety and depression in patients with lung cancer under chemotherapy. Evaluation with the hospital anxiety and depression scale HADS. In: Asclepios Step, pp. 428–440, Athens (2013)
7. Mathers, C., Boerma, T., Ma Fat, D.: The Global Burden of Disease: 2004 Update. WHO, Geneva (2008)
8. American Cancer Society, Depression Increases Cancer Patients' Risk of Dying (2009)
9. Fotiadou, A., Priftis, F., Kiprianos, S.: The role of primary health care in the treatment of people with mental disorder. Brain 41(1) (2004)
10. Cesar, J., Chavoushi, F.: Depression, WHO - Priority Medicines for Europe and the World (2013 Update) (2013)
11. Kampakis, S., Tsironis, Th.: The role of engineering Learning in Clinical Psychiatry - Application on depressed patients data, Thessaloniki (2011)
12. Gay, V., Leijdekkers, P.: A health monitoring system using smart phones and wearable sensors. Int. J. ARM 8, 29–35 (2007)
13. van Wissen, A., Vinkers, C., van Halteren, A.: Developing a Virtual coach for chronic patients: a user study on the impact of similarity, familiarity and realism. In: Meschtscher-jakov, A., De Ruyter, B., Fuchsberger, V., Murer, M., Tscheligi, M. (eds.) PERSUASIVE 2016. LNCS, vol. 9638, pp. 263–275. Springer, Cham (2016). https://doi.org/10.1007/978-3-319-31510-2_23
14. Ellis, T., Latham, N., DeAngelis, T., Thomas, C., Saint-Hilaire, M., Bickmore, T.: Feasibility of a virtual exercise coach to promote walking in community-dwelling persons with parkinson disease. Am. J. Phys. Med. Rehabil. 92(6), 472–485 (2013)
15. Free, C., Phillips, G., Watson, L., Galli, L., Felix, L., Edwards, P., Patel, V., Haines, A.: The effectiveness of mobile-health technologies to improve health care service delivery processes: a systematic review and meta-analysis. PLoS Med. 10, e1001363 (2013)
16. Albrecht, T., Herrick, C.: 100 Questions and Answers About Depression, p. 212. Jones & Bartlett Publishers, Sudbury (2010)
17. Sahu, S., Espy-Wilson, C.: Effect of depression on syllabic rate of speech. J. Acoust. Soc. Am. 138, 1781 (2015)
18. Ozdas, A., Shiavi, R., Silverman, S., Wilkes, D.: Analysis of fundamental frequency for near term suicidal risk assessment. In: 2000 IEEE International Conference in Systems, Man, and Cybernetics (2000)
19. Hamilton, H.: A rating scale for depression. J. Neurol. Neurosurg. Psychiatry 23, 56–62 (1960)
20. Beck, A., Steer, R., Brown, G.: Beck Depression Inventory-II. The Psychological Corporation, (1961–1996)
21. Kroenke, K., Spitzer, R., Williams, J.: The PHQ-9, validity of a brief depression severity measure. J. Gen. Intern. Med. 16, 606–613 (2001)
22. Roy, N., Nissen, S., Sapir, S.: Articulatory changes in muscle tension dysphonia: evidence of vowel space expansion following manual circumlaryngeal therapy. J. Commun. Disord. 42(2), 124–135 (2009)
23. Kreibig, S.: Autonomic nervous system activity in emotion: a review. Biol. Psychol. 84(3), 394–421 (2010)
24. Cummins, N., Scherer, S., Krajewski, J., Schnieder, S., Epps, J., Quatieri, T.: A review of depression and suicide risk assessment using speech analysis. Speech Commun. 71, 10–49 (2015)

25. Pampouchidou, A., Simantiraki, O., Fazlollahi, A., Manousos, D., Pediaditis, M., Roniotis, A., Giannakakis, G., Meriaudeau, F., Simos, P., Marias, K., Yang, F., Tsiknakis, M.: Depression assessment by fusing high and low level features from audio, video, and text. In: 6th International Workshop on Audio/Visual Emotion Challenge, Amsterdam, Netherlands, pp. 27–34 (2016)

26. France, D., Shiavi, R., Silverman, S., Silverman, M., Wilkes, M.: Acoustical properties of speech as indicators of depression and suicidal risk. IEEE Trans. Biomed. Eng. **47**(7), 829–837 (2000)

27. Laosaphan, T., Yingthawornsuk, T.: Classification of depressed speakers based on MFCC in speech samples. In: ICAEEE 2012, Pattaya, Thailand (2012)

28. Sturim, D., Torres-Carrasquillo, P., Quatieri, T., Malyska, N., McCree, A.: Automatic detection of depression in speech using Gaussian mixture modeling with factor analysis. In: Proceedings of Interspeech (2011)

29. Yuan, M.: Chatbots: Building Intelligent Bots. Addison-Wesley, New York (2016)

30. Greene, J., Hibbard, J., Sacks, R., Overton, V., Parrotta, C.: When patient activation levels change, health outcomes and costs change, too. Health Aff. **34**(3), 431–437 (2015)

31. Bloss, C., Wineinnger, N., Peters, M., Boeldt, D., Ariniello, L., Kim, J.Y., Sheard, J., Komatireddy, R., Barrett, P., Topol, E.: A prospective randomized trial examining health care utilization in individuals using multiple smartphone-enabled biosensors. PeerJ **4**, e1554 (2016)

32. Freeney, D.: Usability Versus Persuasion in an Application Interface Design. Institute for Innovation Design & Engineering, Mälardalen University, Eskilstuna, Sweden (2014)

33. The Nielsen Company, So Many Apps, So Much More Time for Entertainment (2016)

34. Zillman, M.P.: Healthcare Bots and Subject Directories (2016)

35. Bots, the next frontier, The Economist (2016)

36. Versluis, A., Verkuil, B., Spinhoven, P., van der Ploeg, M., Brosschot, J.: Changing mental health and positive psychological well-being using ecological momentary interventions: a systematic review and meta-analysis. J. Med. Internet Res. **18**(6), e152 (2016)

37. Proyer, R., Gander, F., Wellenzohn, S., Willibald, R.: Positive psychology interventions in people aged 50–79 years: long-term effects of placebocontrolled online interventions on well-being and depression. Aging Mental Health **18**(8), 997–1005 (2014)

38. Sahidullah, M., Goutam, S.: Design, analysis and experimental evaluation of block based transformation in MFCC computation for speaker recognition. Speech Commun. **54**(4), 543–565 (2012)

39. Dasarathy, B.: Nearest Neighbor (NN) Norms: NN Pattern Classification Techniques (1991)

Implementing an Adaptive Learning System with the Use of Experience API

Koralia Papadokostaki, Spyros Panagiotakis[✉], Kostas Vassilakis, and Athanasios Malamos

Department of Informatics Engineering,
Technological Educational Institute of Crete, Heraklion, Crete, Greece
mtpl30@edu.teicrete.gr,
{spanag,amalamos}@ie.teicrete.gr, kostas@teicrete.gr

Abstract. With the evolution of e-learning and its transformation into mobile learning, SCORM fails to keep up with learner's need to discover knowledge through multiple and diverse sources. ADL's Experience API (xAPI) fills this gap and offers a novel and flexible way to keep track of a learner's activities and progress. In this paper, the xAPI and the concept behind it are shortly discussed, a brief comparison with SCORM is attempted and an innovative implementation of an adaptive LMS-free learning system with the use of xAPI is presented.

Keywords: Experience API · Tin Can API · xAPI · LRS · SCORM
ADL · Activities tracking · ADL's LRS · Adaptive learning

1 Introduction

As mobile devices gain constantly popularity and conquer our everyday lives and habits, online learning has shifted from traditional LMSs (Learning Management Systems) to an everyday and everywhere process [1, 2]. Games, augmented reality applications, virtual worlds, streaming platforms and social networks may nowadays serve as training or teaching sources, while mobile equipment of different types plays the role of the medium. This new mobile learning model offers surplus value to a user's learning environment [2, 3].

Identifying the need to support mobile and non-traditional sources of learning and to host tracking information for each user's learning curve, ADL (Advanced Distributed Learning) [4] has developed a new specification, the Experience API [1, 5], which is also known as xAPI. In a few words, xAPI is a "platform and content agnostic" [5] tool that can dynamically track and store activities from any platform or software system, as those aforementioned.

In this paper we will shortly address the concept of xAPI, explore its basic infrastructure and compare it to its predecessor, SCORM (Sharable Content Object Reference Model) [6]. Finally, we will present our novel implementation which consists of two standalone courses that seamlessly communicate without a Learning Management System making use of xAPI. To the best of our knowledge there is no LMS- independent application that enables adaptive sequencing path according to a user's previous activities and the interaction of two courses through xAPI. Our xAPI

© ICST Institute for Computer Sciences, Social Informatics and Telecommunications Engineering 2018
A. L. Brooks et al. (Eds.): ArtsIT 2017/DLI 2017, LNICST 229, pp. 393–402, 2018.
https://doi.org/10.1007/978-3-319-76908-0_38

enabled application needs not the setup and configuration of an LMS and users only use their email in order to enter a personalized course. This is achieved by employing the JavaScript libraries which implement xAPI to store and track learning activities.

The rest of this paper is structured as below: in Sect. 2 the Experience API (xAPI) specification is introduced, in Sect. 3 xAPI's uses in education are presented, and in Sect. 4 our novel implementation is described. Finally, in Sect. 5, conclusions upon our implementation and plans for future work are discussed.

2   xAPI: Inside the Specification

2.1   ADL's SCORM: The Predecessor of Experience API

The ADL (Advanced Distributed Learning) Initiative is a US government program aiming to augment flexible, lifelong learning through the use of technology [4]. It is widely known for its SCORM specification [6], introduced in 2001, and revised up to the SCORM 2004 4th Edition. SCORM (Sharable Content Object Reference Model) intended to overcome the major problems of interoperability and reusability of learning content. Before SCORM was proposed, the process of tracking the learner's progress was tailor-made for each platform; if the company or foundation changed its LMS, the tracking process had to be redesigned and re-implemented. With the use of the SCORM model, the learning content is packaged into a format which can be transferred through various Learning Management Systems (LMSs) [3, 6, 7] accomplishing thus not only interoperability, but also reusability, traceability and longer lifecycle.

Although SCORM was welcomed with applauses, adopted, supported and compliant with popular LMSs and perhaps the most "widely used e-learning format" [8], rapid rise of technology caused its glory to gradually fade away. To start with, SCORM is tightly connected to the LMS ("LMS-centric" as stated in [3]) and cannot exist autonomously [2]. However, in a constantly changing world, where learning happens also beyond the LMS and through mobile devices (tablets, smartphones, smart television sets even gaming consoles), there is a need for support of informal and ubiquitous education [2], which is neatly described with the motto "Learning is happening everywhere" [1].

That was the vision Learning-Education-Training Systems Interoperability (LETSI) tried to realize in 2008, when it started investigating the requirements of the next generation of SCORM (SCORM 2.0). After lots of whitepapers and suggestions [9], ADL focused on standardized experience tracking capabilities and in 2010 a Broad Agency Announcement (BAA) project evolved: the "Experience API." Rustici Software - the company that undertook the project - renamed it to "Project Tin Can" as this term implied the two-way conversation between the company and the e-learning industry [1, 5] and today the two terms are synonymous.

2.2   Experience API - Understanding the Basics

The new technical specification called Experience API (also known as xAPI or Tin Can API) was launched in 2012, under the version 0.9 and up to today several versions have been launched adding extra functionality and clarifying many issues. The current version at the time of writing is version 1.0.3 and was launched in September, 2016 [10]. The xAPI was and remains an open source, learning technologies interoperability specification that describes tracking of learner activities and experiences between technologies [11]. It is licensed under the Apache License, Version 2.0 and is widely updated and supported by the community [5].

Based on the concept of activity streams that popular social media, such as the Facebook and the Twitter, already use, xAPI can capture learning activities in the form of activity streams originating from various means and contexts [2, 7]. These records are transferred and kept in a server, called Learning Record Store (LRS), which is responsible for receiving, storing, and providing access to them. The xAPI not only specifies the structure of the streams of learning experiences, but also defines the details for their transfer and storage [7, 11]. The core elements of the specification, the (learning) activity streams are called "Statements" (xAPI statements) and describe how the learner interacted with an object, e.g. whether a learner completed a course, accomplished a quiz or watched a video. In their basic format they follow the structure of <Actor, Verb, Object>, but as the object can be of various types this structure can be extended by adding extra optional information, such as the result of a quiz, the timestamp of the activity or the context of an activity [11, 12]. The statements are identified by a unique UUID (Universally Unique Identifier) and are transferred and stored in JSON (JavaScript Object Notation) format.

xAPI supports a predefined Vocabulary, comprising of a large set of Verbs and Activity Types to support various cases. Verbs include *attempted, failed, experienced, shared*, while Activity Types may be *simulation, course, media, meeting, assessment* or *file* among others. Both sets are updated regularly and extended [13].

An LRS is not only a data store for statements, but it can also allow the retrieval of these statements by external applications and serves as a provider of these statements to be aggregated and analyzed. It may provide the source for data aggregation and analytics and can be the repository for extraction of precious information from basic statements [2, 7]. Apart from reporting and analytics, an LRS can be a valuable tool for personalized approaches, as activities stored in the format <*who did what*> can be easily processed. Additionally, it can host activities from various sources and that is its main advantage: whether the statement comes from a serious game, a mobile application or a webpage it can be stored under the same format in the LRS. Finally, an LRS can exchange data with other LRSs, meeting thus different requirements.

2.3   xAPI vs. SCORM

xAPI was advertised as the evolution of SCORM and similarities should be self-evident. Nevertheless, xAPI is a much wider technology than SCORM, can be used in various circumstances and has many advantages compared to SCORM. Firstly, in order to use SCORM, the learning contents should be delivered in SCORM packages, which can be a serious limitation for the content developer. In xAPI, though, learning activities or contents can be totally independent of data formats [14], as simple web content can be a learning activity and libraries or applications implementing the xAPI specification can provide the infrastructure for the delivery of the statements to an

LRS. This makes tracking activities from various sources a reality; statements concerning the same learner may originate from webpages, mobile applications, simulators, virtual games or social networking tools [1, 2]; all these diverse technologies can be used as training systems and data from them should end up in the same storage unit, the same LRS. The xAPI extends learning environments further than SCORM and provides independence from LMSs, fulfilling this way the vision of 'lifelong learning', since learning can happen everywhere. Additionally, as xAPI is based on the delivery of statements relative to the content and not the content itself, they are easier to implement and give the content-developers flexibility concerning the content and the hosting of the content. For example, the content may be offline and xAPI may deliver the statements to the LRS through an occasional connection to the Internet [2, 11]. This is a major advantage for xAPI, as the learner need not be constantly online, but may still contribute to the LRS with the activities that he accomplished in form of statements. Moreover, xAPI may prove to be a priceless mechanism in the hands of data analysts, as it can cooperate well with Business Analytics and reporting tools, contrary to LMSs, the traditional hosts of SCORM content [1, 14]. Finally, xAPI may simultaneously integrate with one or several LRSs, and optionally with an LMS offering this way extra value to the administrator of the data. Figure 1 illustrates the vast diversity of sources for the statements of xAPI and the flexibility in use of the data, that xAPI and its essential component, LRS, provide.

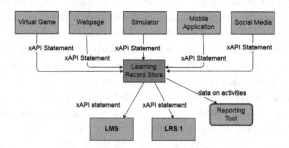

Fig. 1. xAPI supports a distributed architecture, where statement streams can originate from diverse sources and may be delivered to several endpoints.

3   xAPI in Education

xAPI broadens e-learning and its potentials, by adding tracking to various learning activities in a seamless manner. It is suitable for tracking learning activities that happen in a learning system, i.e. an LMS or an online course, but it is also ideal for recording learning activities that are not hosted in traditional learning systems. As Internet becomes the main repository of knowledge nowadays, online resources are potential sources of informal learning. In real life informal learning can happen everywhere and anytime and informal e-learning should follow these trails.

With Internet and mobile devices, YouTube videos, serious games, simulations or posts on social media can provide valuable knowledge to the learner; with the use of xAPI and its implementations, all these learning activities can be captured and may contribute to the definition of each learner's personal profile. Till now, only knowledge that was delivered through formal e-education could be recorded, now tracking informal learning may give us additional information upon the learner, the content and the learning process. Keeping a record of an individual's learning experiences can play an important role in providing him with the proper content in the most efficient manner, which is the goal of Adaptive Learning/training [15]. Building an adaptive learning system may alter the content to meet the learner's needs or might change the way the content is presented according to the learner's profile [7, 15, 16].

From the perspective of Learning Analytics, where educational data is collected and analyzed aiming in the discovery of patterns in learning process or problems in student performance, xAPI is indeed a very promising technology [17]. In the five stages of collecting, reporting, predicting, acting and refining [17], xAPI can pioneer in collecting data from various sources (not necessarily LMSs) and provide aggregate or summarized data to third-party tools for reporting and predicting [17]. Extracting Analytics and therefore knowledge from gathered data can be used by students as self-awareness tools; by teachers for self-evaluation and detection of issues in their classroom or as a motive for improvement, while schools may use tools for their planning, decision-making and as part of Business Intelligence [17, 18].

Furthermore, xAPI can promote collaborative learning through the use of collaborative applications, social media or even serious or virtual games. Using it may augment teamwork and may convert e-learning from personal learning to team-learning [2, 19].

4   Implementing an Adaptive Learning System with xAPI

4.1   Our Implementation

Our vision was to take advantage of the capabilities of xAPI in order to create an adaptive learning system [7, 15] which will adjust its content according to the previous activities a learner has accomplished. For the learning system to be effective and accurate we had to use the online delivery of the statements from the activity provider towards the LRS. Additionally, our learning system should have access to the statements in the LRS, in order to change the content accordingly. In our case, the Activity Provider and the Activity Consumer are actually parts of the same application. The intermediate service, the LRS, stores the statements and acts as a server to our client-server application. However, the decision-making is made in the client as the course runs on the browser.

Our implementation is addressed towards fifth and sixth grade students of Primary Education. It is a brief course on spreadsheets that includes a short introduction on their use and usability and demonstrates basic concepts about sheets, cells and their format. As spreadsheets belong to the same office suite with word processors and presentations software, students may be familiar with some features of this software. Therefore, our application consists of two independent courses which are two separate webpages.

Course 1 is about text formatting and may be included in word processors, spreadsheets and presentations, whereas Course 2 provides learning content for spreadsheets.

When the learner accomplishes Course 1, a statement is sent to the LRS. When he launches Course 2, the course 'asks' the LRS if that statement exists in the LRS (Fig. 2) and if it does, it does not show the content which was included in Course 1. If the statement does not exist - i.e. the learner has not come across text formatting - the content regarding the Course 1 is displayed to the learner. For instance, if Course 1 was offered as part of a word processing lesson but the student was absent at that time or failed that course, he should revise this content and therefore our implementation in Course 2 should provide him with the information included in the Course 1. This way, our implementation offers personalized pathway to the learner according to his previous activities and adapts the content according to the learner's history and needs.

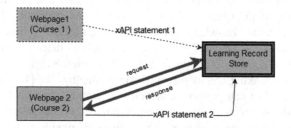

Fig. 2. The architecture of our implementation. A dashed box suggests that the course is not required and dashed lines that the relevant statement may not be sent to the LRS. Thick arrows show the communication between the course and the LRS regarding the existence of xAPI statement1.

4.2   Constructing a Course with the Use of xAPI

For our implementation, an instance of ADL's Open Source Learning Record Store (LRS) [20] was installed in an UBUNTU server. Inventors of xAPI along with the community have developed libraries in several languages, e.g. JavaScript, C, Java, PHP and Python in order to implement the xAPI specification. The library in JavaScript, called Tin Can.js, is constantly supported and updated by developers and seemed the ideal solution for us to implement our course.

The courses are webpages (.html files) with JavaScript code which performs the communication between the courses and the LRS. In order to develop user-friendly courses that would be enriched with attractive interface, multimedia content and interactive quizzes, we used a demo version of Articulate Storyline 2 [21], which is a popular software for creating learning content. Articulate Storyline 2 efficiently supports Tin Can API, but its integrated features provided one-way delivery of statements, i.e. from the course to the LRS and not vice versa, and were not sufficient in our implementation. Therefore, the Tin Can API JavaScript library [22] has been used to provide all the necessary functions making bidirectional communication between our html courses and the LRS possible. Our courses in Articulate Storyline 2 were augmented with JavaScript code calling functions to make delivery of the statements to and from the LRS possible. As stated earlier, Course 1 is an optional part which might have been attempted in the past by a student and may belong to a different class. If it is completed successfully, our implementation sends a statement (via the JavaScript Tin Can function *sendStatement*) to the LRS with the indication that the student has completed Course 1. The Tin Can JavaScript function *sendStatement* is implemented via Restful HTTP *PUT (or POST)* method [11]. Figure 3 shows the statement that is sent via a PUT function towards the LRS.

[18/May/2017 13:30:31] "OPTIONS /xAPI/statements?statementId=e5a7d141-b4d2-4acd-8c37-8880f4b0cc02 HTTP/1.1" 200 0
[18/May/2017 13:30:32] "PUT /xAPI/statements?statementId=e5a7d141-b4d2-4acd-8c37-8880f4b0cc02 HTTP/1.1" 500 30

Fig. 3. An example of the delivery of the statement from Course 1 to the LRS.

The statement is stored in our instance of ADL's LRS (available at: http://83.212. 100.157:8000/) and is shown in JSON format below.

```
{   "verb": {
  "id":
"http://adlnet.gov/expapi/verbs/completed",
        "display": {
            "und": "completed"        }      },
    "version": "1.0.2",
    "timestamp": "2017-05-18T17:30:32.680Z",
    "object": {
        "id": "http://koralia/Test_in_text_Formatting",
        "objectType": "Activity"},
    "actor": {
        "mbox": "mailto:koraliap@test.com",
        "objectType": "Agent"},
    "stored": "2017-05-18T17:30:31.282349+00:00",
    "result": {
        "completion": true,
          "score": {
            "scaled": 1 },
        "success": true      },
    "id": "e5a7d141-b4d2-4acd-8c37-8880f4b0cc02",
    "authority": {
        "mbox": "mailto:mtp130@edu.teicrete.gr",
        "name": "koralia",
        "objectType": "Agent"      }}
```

The short format of the statement is

mailto:koraliap@test.com   (*Actor*)

http://adlnet.gov/expapi/verbs/completed   (*Verb*)

http://koralia/Test_in_text_Formatting   (*Object*)

and follows the structure of <*Actor, Verb, Object*> which was mentioned earlier in this paper.

When the student attempts Course 2, which might be in a posterior point in time, the student need not repeat Course 1. Therefore, our implementation sends – via JavaScript Tin Can *getStatements* function– a request towards the LRS asking whether the statement with the indication that the student has completed Course 1 exists. Again Tin Can JavaScript function *getStatements* is implemented via a Restful HTTP method (illustrated in Fig. 4), the *GET* method [11].

```
[18/May/2017 13:33:29] "OPTIONS /xAPI/statements?verb=http%3A%2F%2Fadlnet.gov%2Fexpapi%2Fverbs%2Fcompleted&activity=http%3A%2F
%2Fkoralia%2FTest_in_text_Formatting HTTP/1.1" 200 0
[18/May/2017 13:33:30] "GET /xAPI/statements?verb=http%3A%2F%2Fadlnet.gov%2Fexpapi%2Fverbs%2Fcompleted&activity=http%3A%2F%2Fk
oralia%2FTest_in_text_Formatting HTTP/1.1" 200 6375
[18/May/2017 13:33:44] "OPTIONS /xAPI/statements?statementId=37f2150b-d2bf-45aa-8e22-af0aa3e3656c HTTP/1.1" 200 0
```

Fig. 4. An example of the request of a statement towards the LRS.

The LRS responds and if the requested statement is found, our implementation skips this part and continues with new content (Fig. 5). If the statement is not found, our implementation shows the content of the first course as well as the new content (Fig. 6). To avoid bottlenecks and delays, the request to the LRS has been sent at the beginning of the second course and the response is stored in a local variable.

Fig. 5. The user has previously completed Course 1 and automatically skips the slides concerning this content. In the menu on the left, the slides concerning the content of Course 1 appear to have been skipped.

The exported courses are in html format and can be hosted in any website together or independently. They are standalone applications that need not an LMS to integrate, but instead need an LRS to communicate with. Along with the course files, the tincan.js file should be uploaded in the web servers, whereas the browser should support JavaScript.

Fig. 6. If the user has not completed Course 1, he watches the slides concerning relevant content.

5 Conclusion

In this paper we have attempted a short description of xAPI, its functionality and architecture. We have compared it to its predecessor SCORM and have manifested its advantages in a constantly changing world where learning becomes ubiquitous and mobile. As activity streams gain popularity and tracking them offers valuable knowledge, xAPI is being constantly extended, updated and widely adopted in the Learning Industry [23]. Following this trend, we have created an adaptive learning system, making use of xAPI, which modifies its content according to the learner's history, without the use of an LMS.

Our implementation consists of two separate short courses illustrating the features and flexibility of xAPI. Although it was developed in a commercial e-learning authoring tool, it demonstrates the xAPI open source specification and implements the seamless communication between web content and LRS with the use of JavaScript libraries. It only requires an email address for the identification of the user and no extra authentication for him. It does not need the setup of an LMS and is totally platform independent. Additionally, the content may be scattered across various servers and platforms and each part need not coexist with the other parts, offering thus boundless potentials to the distribution of learning content.

Our implementation was evaluated by 36 students of fifth grade of a Primary School in Crete, Greece. Although the statements were massively sent to the LRS and the communication between the LRS and the course was two-way, our implementation responded with stability and accuracy; the young students noticed no delay or inconsistency during their engagement with the course. Despite the fact that the architecture of our implementation is distributed, i.e. the course and the LRS are hosted in diverse systems, the response time of our system is satisfactory (about 260 ms, where 200 ms is the roundtrip time between the user and the LRS) and does not affect the responsiveness of our implementation.

It is within our intentions to expand our application with extra functionalities, enrich it with mobile content, video streaming applications and social media integration. This way we will fully exploit the capabilities of xAPI and make a completely personalized and adaptive course without the use of LMS. Finally, we intend to conduct Learning Analytics on statements generated by our application, hoping to form significant conclusions.

References

1. Experience API/ Tin Can API. http://experienceapi.com
2. Murray, K., Berking, P., Haag, J., Hruska, N.: Mobile Learning and ADL' s Experience API Overview of the xAPI, pp. 45–49 (2013)
3. Lim, K.C.: Case Studies of xAPI Applications to E-Learning, pp. 11–12 (2015)
4. ADL. http://www.adlnet.gov/
5. The xAPI Overview. https://www.adlnet.gov/xAPI
6. SCORM Overview. http://www.adlnet.gov/SCORM
7. Moisa, V.: Adaptive learning management system. J. Mob. Embed. Distrib. Syst. 5, 70–77 (2013)
8. Ruano, I., Cano, P., Gámez, J., Gómez, J.: Advanced LMS Integration of SCORM Web Laboratories, p. 4 (2016)
9. The LETSI SCORM 2.0 White Papers. https://scorm.com/tincanoverview/the-letsi-scorm-2-0-white-papers/
10. Experience API, Appendix A: Revision History. https://github.com/adlnet/xAPI-Spec/blob/master/xAPI-About.md#Appendix1A
11. xAPI-Spec. https://github.com/adlnet/xAPI-Spec/
12. Glahn, C.: Using the ADL experience API for mobile learning, sensing, informing, encouraging, orchestrating. In: 2013 Seventh International Conference on Next Generation Mobile Apps, Services and Technologies (NGMAST), pp. 268–273. IEEE (2013)
13. Rustici Software: Tin Can API Registry. https://registry.tincanapi.com/#home
14. Benedek, A.: Learning design versus learning experience design: is the experience API making the difference? In: Edulearn13 Proceedings, pp. 1926–1936 (2013)
15. Paramythis, A., Loidl-Reisinger, S.: Adaptive learning environments and e-learning standards. In: 2nd European Conference on e-learning, vol. 1, pp. 369–379 (2003)
16. Poeppelman, T., Hruska, M., Long, R., Amburn, C.: Interoperable performance assessment for individuals and teams using experience API. In: Proceedings of the 2nd Annual GIFT Users Symposium, pp. 1–8 (2014)
17. Del Blanco, A., Serrano, A., Freire, M., Martinez-Ortiz, I., Fernandez-Manjon, B.: E-learning standards and learning analytics. Can data collection be improved by using standard data models? In: EDUCON, 2013, pp. 1255–1261. IEEE (2013)
18. Long, P., Siemens, G.: Penetrating the fog: analytics in learning and education. In: EDUCAUSE Review, vol. 46 (2011)
19. Nine Practical Uses of the Tin Can API (xAPI). https://www.youtube.com/watch?v=8LFhDdqQ13A
20. ADL's Open Source Learning Record Store (LRS). https://github.com/adlnet/ADL_LRS
21. Articulate Storyline. https://www.articulate.com/downloads/storyline-2/
22. TinCan Javascript Library. http://rusticisoftware.github.io/TinCanJS/
23. Rustici Software: Experience API Adopters. https://experienceapi.com/adopters

Note Recognizer: Web Application that Assists Music Learning by Detecting and Processing Musical Characteristics from Audio Files or Microphone in Real-Time

Markos Fragkopoulos, Athanasios G. Malamos$^{(\boxtimes)}$,
and Spyros Panagiotakis

Media, Networks and Communications Lab, Department of Informatics
Engineering, P.O. Box 71500, Heraklion, Crete, Greece
exog3n@gmail.com, {amalamos,spanag}@ie.teicrete.gr

Abstract. Note recognizer is an online web application. In order to overcome the performance issues of the internet infrastructure (browser, devices, OS platforms) traditional algorithms have been re-designed and novel processes based on the Web Audio API have been implemented. It is the first time that open standard web tools offered in all the commercial browsers are used to build an application that usually required dedicated signal processing libraries. These novel processes and algorithms provide MIDI (Musical Instrument Digital Interface) information out of audio files or microphone. Our application may assist musical education by allowing students to transform their inspiration or a performance into notes.

Keywords: Web audio · Javascript · HTML5 · Pitch detection
Onset detection · MIDI

1 Introduction

Automatic Music Transcription (AMT) is the conversion of an acoustic signal (music) into a formal musical representation, such as a MIDI file or a score format. It is considered to be a significant technology area in music signal processing. In [10] it is defined as the process of converting an audio signal (natural or recorded) into a piano-roll notation (a representation of musical notes across time), while in [11] it is defined as the process of converting a music signal into a common music score. A typical formal music representation format includes pitches, onsets and offsets of the notes, tempo and (ideally) the instruments [4].

Automatic music transcription (AMT) could be analyzed into the following major tasks:

- Pitch detection, which is the process to estimate the pitch or fundamental frequency of a digitized music sample [4, 5]. This process results to the music note or tone that corresponds to the sample. This process may be performed in time, frequency or both domains according to the algorithm we choose

© ICST Institute for Computer Sciences, Social Informatics and Telecommunications Engineering 2018
A. L. Brooks et al. (Eds.): ArtsIT 2017/DLI 2017, LNICST 229, pp. 403–412, 2018.
https://doi.org/10.1007/978-3-319-76908-0_39

- Note onset detection that is the beginning of a musical note [4, 6]. It is affected by the transient of a note switch but it is not expressing this transition which is independent by the note but rather the beginning of the pure note waveform. Both pitch and onset detection are considered open problems.
- Tempo estimation, which refers to the perceived tempo of a music sample [4]. It is an objective estimation that differs even between human experts that hear the same song. It is considered as an open problem as well, thus new algorithms appear every year in the competitions (ex MIREX).

In the AMT tasks we may include also some pre-conditioning actions that may be applied to the audio signal that improve the music characteristics estimation efficiency such as, Loudness Estimation that is related to potential amplification of the signal and instrument related filtering that might improve the pitch estimation.

In the past years, the problem of automatic music transcription has gained considerable research interest due to novel high impact and widespread applications, such as automatic search and retrieval of musical information features, interactive music systems (e.g. computerized performances, score following, and rhythm tracking), as well as musicological analysis [11, 12, 14]. The current research efforts focus in the development of innovative algorithms that extract efficiently musical features of multi-instruments recordings [4]. The problem of single instrument AMT may be considered solved from the algorithmic and fundamental research point of view. On the other hand, production and usability of a service or a product is not only a matter of algorithmic efficiency but furthermore is a matter of viability of production under the customer and market requirements. In the case of music applications, the new area of interest for customers and professionals is considered to be the web [8, 9]. The web improves accessibility and makes easier the application adoption and success. However, a significant disadvantage of the web is that applications are executed in the user (usually portable) device and we have to be sure that even a "weak" device may "decently" execute the application. Thus, web requires applications to be of low computational complexity.

In the market there is a limited number of applications that extract music information from recordings and even less applications that may be able to extract information in real-time (e.g., Ableton Live 9, AudioScore, ScoreCloud, AnthemScore). There are also some key demos over the web like Pitchdetector and Beats Audio API. Especially in the case of web or mobile platforms, there are no efficient applications appeared.

The idea for this application came from the music school student's involvement with music in all its aspects (electronic/instrumental). The main motivation for the creation of this application is the need of any student musician to log those scattered moments of inspiration and creativity and maintain them documented as ideas. Therefore, knowing that inspiration is coming suddenly, any minute, any place, this application has to overcome the barriers of a standalone application (like those appearing in the market) that requires personal computers to execute. Instead the purpose of this work is the development of a fully web-based real-time application that can be executed seamlessly in a mobile phone or tablet or a personal computer, free of any application installations and plug-ins. As might be expected, web increases significantly the usability and usefulness of the application, however, imposes additional constraints to the, anyway, difficult problem of Automatic Music Transcription.

The implementation of this application is presented over the next chapters of the paper. The evaluation that is quoted has been done with some different instrument samples in two specific axes: note-by-note separately and comparative to some other similar commercial software.

2 Implementation

Note recognizer was developed as a proof of concept of an online automatic transcriber. In this application the user can track the recording of music notation over time on piano roll. The minimum requirements of the system limited only on a computer with satisfying performance capabilities, a major browser and a microphone or a music file. The user also can set a few details for more accurate results. To accomplish the purposes of this work, the implementation needs to interlock a series of functionalities. These consist of audio sound routing and processing, onset detection, pitch detection, tempo calculation, characterization of music events, note representation and interoperability mechanism. This application implements a part of the algorithms studied and creates some more. It was decided to present a limited range of functionalities, that the application is first stable, functional and give its mark on future objectives. At the end of this paper we will discuss some of the candidate features for future Note Recognizer features.

2.1 Sound Routing

The application sound routing and retrieval achieved with an implementation using the Web Audio API along with custom algorithms. Instead of using PCM data for retrieving the audio signal in our workflow, AnalyserNode (Web audio API) have been engaged. The AnalyserNode interface represents a node able to provide real-time frequency and time-domain analysis information. It is an AudioNode that passes the audio stream unchanged from the input to the output, but allows you to take the generated data, process it, and create audio processing functions.

2.2 Music Information Retrieval

In music information retrieval there are three basic estimation procedures: onset detection, BPM calculation and pitch detection.

Onset detection and BPM calculation. Onset detection, typically follows a flow of actions in order to increase efficiency [1, 7]. Initially, pre-processing of the raw audio signal to increase the performance of the following steps, generation of the Detection Function, post-processing, applying a peak selection algorithm in the detection function to select adequate peaks (Fig. 1).

Pre-processing indicates the transformation of the original signal to the weakening or strengthening of some aspects of the signal. For the pre-processing step

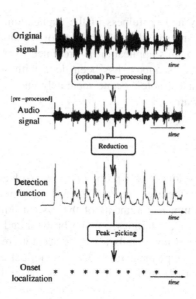

Fig. 1. Flow chart of a typical onset detection algorithm [1]

implementation of Short-Time Fourier Transform (STFT) have been engaged [1]. The Detection Function that is implemented is the High Frequency Content.

$$f(x) = \sum_{m=-\frac{N}{2}}^{\frac{N}{2}-1} x(\text{ns} + \text{m})H(m)e^{\frac{2\pi mk}{N}}$$

where n is the time, s is the window step size, i.e., H (m) is the Hamming windowing function, which reduces spectral smudging and the k frequency. When using the STFT, we do not use a sliding window, instead we hop window by step s to create successive STFT overlapping Windows.

For the implementation a Dynamic Compressor (Web audio API) have been used for pre-processing the sound. The *DynamicsCompressorNode* interface provides a compression effect, which lowers the volume of the loudest parts of the signal in order to avoid clipping and distortion that may occur. In general, a clearer sound without distortion may improve onset detection algorithms accuracy and performance.

The process is as follows: An audio file or microphone is loaded in webaudio component. If it has multiple channels they are summed into a single channel. Then the music signal is cut into overlapping sections. A windowing function is applied; in this case, the algorithm uses a hamming window. Apply the FFT algorithm with some zero padding to the windowed, overlapping signal. Then move the next frame of music and repeat this procedure until the recording has stopped and all parts of the signal have been processed. While the general procedure of the STFT is straightforward, the STFT has two tunable parameters that need to be appropriately adjusted: the percentage of overlap between successive frames and the time length of each window.

The windowing function is used to reduce smudging of adjacent frequency components. This is done by multiplying the time domain signal by the windowing function. Using a windowing function comes at a cost. The windowing function will decimate the amplitude of the signal, throwing away information. To solve this, each STFT window has some percentage of overlap between its current window and its previous windows so that if an onset is located in a weak part of one window, it is caught by the next window; unless otherwise stated, an overlap of 50% is used in all cases.

High Frequency Content and Post-processing. HFC based on the assumption on which: onsets have most high-density energy in areas where the mixing with other parallel components is lower, a condition that usually occurs in high frequency regions. This can be utilized by weighting each STFT window with a factor proportional of its frequency [1].

Post-processing used to facilitate procedures of thresholding and peaks selection by increasing the uniformity and consistency of the events related to the characteristics of the detection function, ideally turning on isolated readily detectable local maxima. Normalization of the signal is described in the theoretical implementation as part of the STFT which is used in pre-processing. In current application normalization have been implemented after the detection function because the quality of the results was better in this position after various tests. Then a moving median filter [2] is applied based on a previous implementation in [17], which is customized to run on the client-side. Afterwards the only remaining task to get the onsets is a dynamic threshold picking method which is built from scratch.

For the BPM calculation some code snippets from Beats Audio API have been implemented including the counting of intervals between nearby onsets, where is measuring time duration between beats [3] and grouping the neighbors by tempo where is produced a statistical histogram of measurements. Then by extracting the most significant (according rules) periodicity a tempo estimation, in beats per minute (BPM), can be achieved [13].

Pitch detection. Pitch specified as property of an acoustic signal which is determined by the frequency of the waves that produce it, so the pitch represents how high or low the sound is. For music, the assessment pitch corresponds the detected frequencies in some musical notes. For more accurate results we need to cut some amount of noise form the signal before the pitch detection algorithm. This is achieved by implementing a parametric EQ with some instrument oriented presets. These presets based on each instrument frequency range and can be selected by the user from a simple select box. According to the pitch detection code snippets from Wilson C. PitchDetect demo [15] have been implemented. So the method that been used for pitch detection is Auto-correlation. This is the cross-correlation of a signal with itself at different time points, in other words is the similarity between observations as a function of time elapsed between them [16].

2.3   Music Information Processing

The main requirements posed by this application during the information processing are the results pump ability from the algorithms in real-time and the handling of them in time oriented way.

Thread and snapshot handling. To achieve extraction results by the algorithms in real time there should be a continuous flow of the incoming signal to these algorithms, and in the same time a continuous recording of the music information by the algorithms in the system. For these purposes the application uses an execution thread (thread) as a key pillar implemented with the *setInterval()* javascript function. This thread basically sends and receives information from subroutines finite times (cycles) per second. From each cycle a single snapshot is produced whose time position is equal to the deviation of the time position of the current cycle from the time position of the first cycle. The flow of the incoming signal to the detection and calculation algorithms controlled by two AnalyserNodes. The allocation of the detection algorithms results made in a central snapshots array, whose positions are directly-linked with cycles and thus with time. We can say that as a digital audio signal is expressed in an array of values, so the music information of this signal is expressed by its snapshots array. The sampling rate of the snapshots array is different from the signal sample rate and equal to the number of cycles per second that thread executed. In the present application the sampling rate of the snapshots array is about 50 Hz.

Auto-correction. Through constant experimentation we estimated the accuracy of the autocorrelation algorithm. Errors usually have to do with noise and reverberation. Improving the algorithm itself was not possible due to lack of advanced theoretical knowledge in signal processing. Hence, we decided to use some reasonable assumptions to achieve rudimentary correction of the results in real-time. In fact, the main tool in this case is the snapshots array through which we can make time based comparisons between snapshots and apply some basic rules. Thus, in each cycle the executing thread calls a function that examines music information snapshots of the present note along with the previous and following two notes.

Characterization and objects. The characterization is based on the onset and the offset of each note with the logical assumption that each onset of a note that detected has also an offset and all intermediate snapshots have the same pitch. This function is based on the information of the offset of each note so it cannot operate in real-time as if one note is played at a particular time the system does not know in advance when it will end. So this algorithm is executed serially in snapshots array with a small delay. The results are recorded in the system, but only on demand of the user are represented and shall replace the previous ones. More specifically, when the algorithm detects that a snapshot is an onset and another is an offset of a certain note then finds the most common pitch between snapshots and defines the pitch of the note. Then is the moment that the note object which consists of snapshots created. By characterizing the items, we can correct pitches and instances for which we have no information. The auto-correlation algorithm recognizes them as gaps or errors, providing they are within the limits of an onset and offset. Each notes' offset, detected by a function which sets a threshold and in a particular sequence comparisons of the wavelength of each snapshot, provides a snapshot as the end of the note.

2.4   Music Information Representation

Time and space relevance. The representation of the diluted music information based on the conversion of time in space. The key factor here is the time and space relevance. It would be very simple if the display of musicological characteristics took place in demand, this because we would have the total length of the signal and we could easily compute the relativity of space and time. Seconds are not the only unit of time to be used in the application, also used musical units beat and bars which duration, such as their length on axis x, determined by the tempo. When the render of the music information should be achieved in real-time we do not know the duration of the audio clip. We also know that the algorithm for calculating the tempo make some initial time to calculate the first result. These two parameters are indispensable for fixing sizes in space. To overcome this problem, the application employs two initial assumptions. The first is that the piano roll (canvas) has a finite size, and the second that the application starts with an agreed average of 120 BPM, until the tempo calculation algorithm return the first result. So the sizes of the measures planned at the start of the application base of calculations based on the original values and then by user request can be redesigned based on new figures calculated based on the actual speed of the music clip.

Music information rendering. Piano roll is divided into notes on the y axis and time/beats in axis x. The display is in the form of rectangular shapes which grow depending on the duration of each note in real-time. The rendering also executed through the main thread, and its implementation contains snapshots instances draw on the canvas

3   Evaluation and Perspectives

The application tested in real use cases with different instruments and sources. The tests were both system and subsystem oriented. Some tests achieved with the musical instrument recorded under ideal studio conditions without any external noise at all, and others with a regular microphone on a PC.

The first evaluation has been done on each note separately, with piano. Due to the time-domain approach of the pitch detection algorithm we see that we have no results until the middle of the second octave (Fig. 2 (a) and (b)). The second evaluation (Table 1) is a comparative evaluation that has been done with two different instruments (Guitar, Trumpet) in two commerce software and Note Recognizer.

We note that the result of the application is sufficiently accurate to the original, especially when the track is played at a slow speed. The results' accuracy depends on the kind of the instrument, with the major differentiation factor to be the amount of

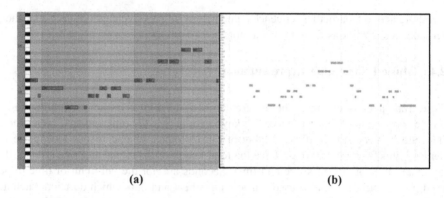

(a)   (b)

Fig. 2. (a) Part of the original notes of the song "Hit the road Jack", (b) Capturing part of the song "Hit the road Jack" played with piano at 110 BPM, with redraw corrected functionality

Table 1. Comparative evaluation with two different instruments (Guitar, Trumpet) in two commerce software and Note Recognizer

Instruments	Ableton live 9	WIDI 4.4 Pro	Note Recognizer (real-time)	Note Recognizer (corrected)	Original notes
Guitar	25/25 (+6 errors)	25/25 (+9 errors)	24/25 (+1 error)	24/25 (+1 error)	25
Trumpet	32/32 (+1 error)	31/32 (+15 errors)	32/32 (+3 errors)	32/32 (0 errors)	32

resonance they produce (Fig. 3 (a) and (b)). When the instrument has resonator the application can have numerous adverse results. Also there has been an evaluation of some subsystems. As for Auto-correction functionality we note that it provides correction of the greater percentage of errors that arise at lower frequencies but also discontinuities near or within the notes. The on demand redrawing of the corrected notes is also functioning efficiently. After comparison of our implementation with some professional applications, we noticed that Note Recognizer is quite satisfactory. The application currently has very high computational requirements, especially because of the thread that executes about 50 times per second drawing and onset detection among other functions.

The upcoming version of Note Recognizer covers the performance issue (currently it implements only two web workers), the pianoroll redrawing, the replacement of AnalyserNodes with AudioWorkerNodes and the offset detection function. There are also some goals regarding the creation of some new subsystems. It would be very efficient, for example, to extend the pianoroll to be interactive, so it is possible for the user to edit the rendered notes, play them back and export them as a MIDI file.

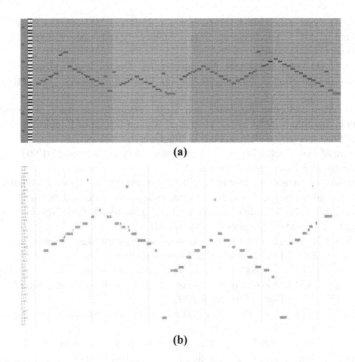

Fig. 3. (**a**) Music information recording on Ableton live by playing piece on bouzouki, (**b**) Music information recording on Note Recognizer by playing piece on bouzouki

4 Conclusion

In this paper we presented Note Recognizer, a web browser application for processing, retrieval and demonstration of music information from music recordings or music files. Note Recognizer may assist a student to express his/her musical inspiration and at the same time to understand more about the nature of music. The current version is stable and runs on most recent browsers, desktop or mobile. As an experience with web audio development, Note Recognizer is already a usable tool that can be found online at: http://medialab.teicrete.gr/2015_ptixiakes/note_recognizer/.

References

1. Bello, J.P., Daudet, L., Abdallah, S., Duxbury, C., Davies, M., Sandler, M.B.: A tutorial on onset detection in music signals. IEEE Trans. Speech Audio Process. **13**(5), 1035–1047 (2005)
2. Rosão, C., Ribeiro, R., Matos, D.M.: Comparing onset detection methods based on spectral. In: Proceedings of the Workshop on Open Source and Design of Communication, pp. 71–78. ACM (2012)
3. Man, T.K.: Tempo Extraction using the Di. Hong Kong University of Science and Technology, Hong Kong (2006)

4. Cai, W.: Analysis of Acoustic Feature Extraction. University of Rochester, New York (2013)
5. Cnx. (n.d.) (2017). http://cnx.org/contents/8b900091-908f-42ad-b93d-806415434b46@2/Pitch-Detection-Algorithms
6. Bello, J.P., Duxbury, C., Davies, M., Sandler, M.: On the use of phase and energy for musical onset detection in the complex domain. IEEE Signal Process. Lett. **11**(6), 553–556 (2004)
7. Hess, A.: Beat Detection for Automated Music Transcription: An exploration of Onset Detection Algorithms. MSc thesis, Thomas J. Watson School of Engineering and Applied Science State University of New York at Binghamton (2011)
8. The future of music technology (2017). http://www.yalescientific.org/2012/03/the-future-of-music-technology/. Accessed 2 June 2017
9. The future of music technology (2017). http://spectrum.ieee.org/tech-talk/consumer-electronics/audiovideo/the-future-of-music-technology. Accessed 2 June 2017
10. Bayesian Music Transcription: A. Taylan Cemgil Radboud, PHD Thesis, University of Nijmegen, Netherlands (November, 2004) (2004)
11. Klapuri, A., Davy, M. (eds.): Signal Processing Methods for Music Transcription. Springer, New York (2006). https://doi.org/10.1007/0-387-32845-9
12. Bello, J.P., Sandler, M.: Phase-based note onset detection for music signals. In: Proceedings of the IEEE International Conference on Acoustics, Speech, and Signal Processing (ICASSP-03), Hong Kong, 6–10 April 2003
13. Beat detection using web audio (2017). http://joesul.li/van/beat-detection-using-web-audio/. Accessed 2 June 2017
14. Goto, M.: A predominant-f0 estimation method for polyphonic musical audio signals. In: 18th International Congress on Acoustics, pp. 1085–1088 (2004)
15. Implementation of Pitch Detection (2017). https://github.com/cwilso/pitchdetect. Accessed 2 June 2017
16. Wikipedia. (n.d.) (2017). https://en.wikipedia.org/wiki/Autocorrelation. Accessed 2 June 2017
17. Implementation of the Moving Median filter (2017). https://github.com/mikolalysenko/moving-median. Accessed 2 June 2017

Blocks as Symbolic Tools for Children's Playful Collaboration

Cristina Sylla[1(✉)], Eva Brooks[2], and Lisa Tümmler[3]

[1] Centre for Child Studies/EngageLab, University of Minho, Campus de Gualtar,
4710-057 Braga, Portugal
sylla@engagelab.org

[2] Xlab: Design, Learning, Innovation, Department of Learning and Philosophy,
Aalborg University, Kroghstræde 3, 9220 Aalborg, Denmark
eb@learning.aau.dk

[3] Institute for Educational Science, Otto-Von-Guericke-University Magdeburg,
Universitätspl. 2, 39106 Magdeburg, Germany
lisatuemmler@me.com

Abstract. This paper reports on two intervention studies conducted in two Danish kindergartens where a Digital Manipulative (DM) was investigated in relation to children's interactions, experiences and playful processes. The DM, in the form of physical blocks was developed following a user-centred design approach. Research indicated how children's interaction with the physical blocks generated a democratic collaboration between their peers, which triggered engagement and sustained children's attention for a long time. Children's play with the blocks unfolded two levels of articulation; one level where they used the blocks to create visual narratives and a second level where they used the blocks as construction material. This double function was analysed as fostering playful learning processes indicating that the design conveyed potentials to function as a pedagogical resource.

Keywords: Children · Digital manipulatives · Co-discovery analysis
Collaboration · Designs for play and learning · Pedagogy

1 Introduction

The central aspect of Constructionism is the understanding of children as builders [1]. This understanding is grounded on an assumption that children actively construct knowledge through interactions with their surrounding environment [2]. According to this understanding, children do not "get" ideas but instead they build ideas [3]. This process can be stimulated when children interact with meaningful artefacts that promote active engagements [3]. In particular, culturally rooted objects that can be used by children to express and materialize their ideas strongly support the building of intellectual structures [1]. Papert speaks of "objects-to-think-with", referring to "objects in which there is an intersection of cultural presence, embedded knowledge, and the possibility for personal identification" [1:11]. In this context, he emphasizes the absence of 'learning-richness' of children's activities, such as building and playing

© ICST Institute for Computer Sciences, Social Informatics and Telecommunications Engineering 2018
A. L. Brooks et al. (Eds.): ArtsIT 2017/DLI 2017, LNICST 229, pp. 413–423, 2018.
https://doi.org/10.1007/978-3-319-76908-0_40

with sandcastles, LEGO bricks, dolls and collectible cards. This kind of learning activities should be taken into consideration as models for the design of new tools for children's play. In particular, while taking advantage of new technologies, which have the potential to "expand the scope of activities with that quality" [4:6].

However, digital technologies do not always afford potentials for children to creatively express themselves [5]. Indeed, whereas tangible interfaces have features that encourage both individual and social play, the size of the groups of children influences the kind of play that evolves through their interaction with the tool [6]. Difficulties in mastering the technology, such as handling a computer mouse, can have a negative impact on the interaction with technology. This affects children's play and level of creativity, thus their collaborative peer interactions. From a practical side a further hindering can be the size of the technological artefacts that makes it too difficult to fit into the kindergarten environment [5]. This shows how design and pedagogical concerns are interwoven and not only connected to individual or collective interests and desires, but also to the material affordances involved in such situations.

Digital manipulatives (DMs)[1] build on the tradition of using objects as learning scaffolds [7, 8] affording a more natural interaction than traditional interfaces [9] while promoting embodied and exploratory learning [10]. Considering the learning benefits of DMs over their digital counterparts, several works have shown that DMs have the potential to foster creativity [8] providing a higher level of engagement and immersion resulting in more active learning [11–15]. One of the characteristics of digital manipulatives is that they support collaboration [16] encouraging verbalizations and discussion among children while solving tasks, thus, naturally promoting the achievement of social skills [17–19]. Yet, in early childhood curriculum, play as a condition for learning is often separated from the use of digital tools, which are merely seen as facilitators of learning outcomes (cf. [20–22]. This highlights that an understanding of children's play could pave a way about how to best fill the gap between pedagogical understandings of play and children's use of and experience with digital tools.

This paper describes two intervention studies carried in two Danish kindergartens where a Digital Manipulative (DM) was used to investigate (1) how the design of the DM fostered playful processes in a collaborative environment, and (2) the children's collaborative interactions and play experiences. The Digital Manipulative that was used is further described below in Sect. 2. The results provided new insights for the further development of the tool. Section 3 details the method, and Sect. 4 the actual interventions. Finally, Sect. 5 presents the discussion and concludes the paper.

2 Description of the Digital Manipulative

The Digital Manipulative used in this study is named TOK, which stands for Touch, Organize, Create [13]. It is composed as an electronic platform with six or eight slots that connects to a computer or a tablet through USB or Bluetooth (see Fig. 1).

---

[1] The term Digital Manipulatives has been coined by Resnick et al. [4] referring to objects with embedded computational properties that are used to manipulate digital content, other authors use the term Tangible Interfaces or TUIs.

Additionally, microphone, and a set of 23 physical blocks with images are used to manipulate digital content on the connected unit. In the current implementation, the system can identify up to 250 different blocks. This number can be extended.

The backside of each block as well as the electronic system have embedded magnets on its surface. This correctly snap the blocks into the system, making it easy for the users to place the blocks. Simultaneously, this assures a stable contact between the blocks and the platform. The size of the blocks, 4.5 × 4.5 × 1 cm, offers a good grip and easy manipulation (see Fig. 1). Placing a block on the platform renders the corresponding digital content on the device's screen, creating a direct mapping between input and output. The sequence of blocks placed on the platform unfolds a narrative. The system presents the content of the picture-blocks on the screen following the order in which they are placed, thus enabling the random placement of the blocks on the slots (see Fig. 1). Similarly, when a block is removed from the TOK platform its corresponding animation immediately disappears from the screen. The blocks represent classical scenarios and 'actants' from narratives for children - basically, heroes and opponents [23, 24], composed by characters, objects and nature elements. Five different scenarios (a castle landscape, a forest, a desert, the woods and a circus) allow locating the stories in different settings.

Fig. 1. Two girls grabbing and placing blocks on the TOK platform to build and exploring the corresponding animated narrative.

Children can change the scene, mix and remix the characters, try out different plots, shift direction and start all over again. As the system only provides visual feedback (except for the ambient sounds), children can imagine and create their own spoken narratives. TOK was developed following a user-centred design approach and empirically validated in a long-term study with various groups of children in a Portuguese preschool [13, 19, 25]. The interventions reported here, provided new insights for the further development of the TOK as a tool for fostering non-formal learning processes in a collaborative environment.

3 Methods

The two intervention studies took place in two public kindergartens (KG1 and KG2) in the southwestern part of Denmark. Twenty-two children – twelve from KG1 and ten from KG2 – all at five years-of-age, took part. Both kindergartens regularly use iPads and different educational digital media.

3.1 Procedure

The intervention in each of the kindergartens was carried out in a separate room where also three researchers attended. In KG2 the teacher also was present in the room. Two TOK systems were connected to a computer via USB, a set of 23 blocks and a microphone respectively) were placed on two separate tables, which were facing each other. The blocks were scattered on each table in front of the computer. The DMs were turned on when the children entered the room. In each kindergarten, two groups of children at the time played with the DM for 30 min. They were in groups of two and three, which were counterbalanced with the same number of boys and girls. At KG1 there were four groups of three children: group 1 with three girls; group 2 two boys and one girl; group 3 three boys; and group 4 two boys and one girl. At KG2 the children were divided in two groups of three and two groups of two children: group 1 with two girls and a boy; group 2 two boys and a girl; group 3 two girls; and group 4 two boys. After that children went back to the class and two new groups came to the room to play with the DM. The same procedure was carried in both kindergartens. The three researchers were available to offer support, when and if the children needed, otherwise they were in the background, observing and taking field notes.

3.2 Data Collection and Methodology

The study followed a qualitative, explorative and inductive methodology. Thus, the children were allowed to collaborate with each other, without interruptions from the three researchers, to learn how to interact with the system [26, 27]. The data was collected through (1) field notes; (2) video observations; and (3) situated interviews. Two video cameras were discreetly placed behind each table respectively and synchronized to record each group from the back and from the front to allow different observation angles. The children were informed about and shown the cameras, but did not pay any further attention to them. Following the children's interaction with the TOK a situated interview [28] was carried out with each teacher after the session.

The researchers applied a co-discovery analysis of the observation of the children's activities [29, 30]. Directly after each session, the researchers discussed and noted impressions of the intervention. This was to keep a fresh record from the observations contributing to a reliable analysis of the data [31]. The video recordings were later analysed.

4 Kindergarten Interventions

In the following sections, the results from the two intervention studies are presented. After an initial introduction of the TOK, the children organised themselves into smaller groups (see Sect. 3.1) and were ready to explore the TOK. In line with the co-discovery approach [29, 30], the functioning of the TOK was not explained, instead the children were encouraged to explore and find it out by themselves. It did not take long time until the children found out that they had to place the blocks on the TOK platform to render digital animations. Initially, the children started to place the blocks on the TOK platform very carefully, but they became increasingly confident trying out different blocks and exploring the interactions between the different elements. They also shared their explorations and, thereby, also learnt the TOK functionalities from each other. The following sub-sections focus on how the children in both kindergartens (KG1 and KG2) played with the Digital Manipulative. The children in both kindergartens were divided into four groups (Group 1, 2, 3, and 4), where two groups at the time played with the TOK – first groups 1 and 2 and thereafter groups 3 and 4. While two groups were playing with the TOK, the other two groups were in another room.

4.1 Handling of the Blocks and Group Dynamics

The handling of the TOK blocks interrelated with the way the group dynamics evolved during the intervention sessions. In KG1, Group 1 (three girls), they all took turns and handled the blocks; in Group 2 (two boys and one girl) the girl just observed while both boys handled the blocks; Group 3 and Group 4 were unstable and the members of each group were merging, going apart, and building new constellations, while some of them observed the others handling the blocks with changing roles.

In KG2, all children in three out of four groups handled the blocks. In the fourth group, Group 4 (two boys and one girl), the boys predominantly handled the blocks.

In both kindergartens, the children maintained the groups except in KG1, Group 3 and Group 4, instead of two groups with three children by each of the two tables as planned, the five boys gathered together around one table and the girl was alone by the other table. The boys were visibly excited, three of them manipulated the blocks while one of them spoke into the microphone, and the other boy observed. From time to time they changed roles. After some time, two boys left the table and joined the girl that was alone. One of these boys stayed by this table for the rest of the activity. By doing so, he could easier access and play with the TOK, not having to 'compete' with the other boys about the space closest to the blocks. The other boy moved between both tables. In both kindergartens, sometimes the children from one group joined the other group. This happened when something aroused their curiosity. Sometimes one group called the other group to show something they liked or that had surprised them. After having shared their experiences, the children continued to play with the DM within their own group.

In summary, the evolving group dynamics in KG1 and KG2 showed that the children after only a short while understood how to use the TOK. They were concentrated and placed the blocks on the platform and, accordingly, observed the interactions. One of the groups (KG1, Group 3), did so in an intense way by enthu-siastically and continuously placing and removing blocks.

4.2 Involvement and Collaboration

The way the children were involved in the interactions with the TOK, influenced their modes of collaboration. In particular, the children's collaboration was shown through their negotiations and construction activities while playing with the TOK. At first the children were predominantly observers, placing and removing blocks to explore the interactions between the different elements. Except for the group of five boys, they were all focused and concentrated, taking time to observe what was happening on the screen. After that, they started to systematically replace some of the blocks.

Sometimes children reconstructed an action rendered on the display by repeatedly removing and placing the same blocks on the platform. This was done when the children wanted to understand the interactions that took place as well as when they liked something and repeatedly wanted to watch the unfolded animation. For instance, a girl from KG2, Group 1 placed and removed several times a block of a witch as well as a block of Zorro. Always, after Zorro defeated the witch, the girl lifted both blocks and placed them again, repeating this action several times while commenting the fight together with her peers. A block showing a cloud and its blowing effect created a great interest among the children, generating an intense interaction in KG1, Group 1 and Group 2. They explored the cloud in combination with a lot of other blocks and discussed about different effects that emerged.

Except for one girl from KG1, Group 2 and another girl from KG1, Group 4, all children wanted to continue to play after the time was over. Signs of involvement were visible through children's body movements. For example, they were clapping hands, showing thumbs up, mimicking the movements of the characters. This was done by moving an imaginary sword in the air, mimicking the sound of the cloud blowing wind, or the sounds of the fights, pointing at the screen, to raise the other's attention and commenting on the action, interjections of joy, surprise or disappointment.

Negotiation and Construction
Playing with the TOK generated many verbal interactions between the children. They commented on the actions, called for each other's attention, e.g. regarding specific interactions between block elements that they liked. Some children took blocks from the table and held the blocks in their hands, or to their chest, signalling that they wanted to keep them for their own manipulation. However, generally the children shared the blocks and let each other freely choose which blocks to place. Often, the children applied an implicit agreement by taking turns in choosing which blocks to choose. But sometimes they had divergent opinions and wanted to place different blocks on the platform, or they wanted to handle the same block or the microphone simultaneously (see Fig. 2b). Such conflicting interests led to discussions and negotiations between the children. In general, they negotiated until all in the group were happy with a solution, sometimes the stronger won possession over one block (see Fig. 2c). This behaviour was observable in all the groups.

Fig. 2. Children calling the attention for a specific action (a), fighting for the microphone (b), and fighting for a block (c).

Besides playing with the Digital Manipulative on the computer, five out of eight groups also used the blocks to make their own free-standing constructions (see Fig. 3). In KG1, Group 1 the girls built towers with blocks, all of the piles with the same height. They then placed the piles on the platform slots and lifted the piles to change the block that was in contact with the platform and, thereby, triggering different interactions (Fig. 3d). In Group 4 the girl built piles and divided them into smaller ones followed by ordering the piles in front of the computer. In KG2, Group 1 a girl built piles and then slowly glided the block on the top until all of it fell down (Fig. 3a). In Group 2 a girl built a square with all blocks facing her (Fig. 3c) and in Group 3 the girl ordered the blocks near the platform creating different patterns (Fig. 3b). From there she and the other girl in the group jointly chose the blocks to place on the platform.

Fig. 3. Children's constructions (a) building piles and gliding the block on the top until it falls down; (b) ordering the blocks creating different patterns; (c) building a square with the blocks (d) building piles and placing them on the platform slots; (e) building a pile with all the blocks; (f) holding several blocks.

In summary, during the intervention the children showed interest and involvement in collaborative actions and interactions with the TOK. Their collaboration included negotiations, sharing of the blocks, as well as unexpected ways to, as part of the play, use the blocks for different kinds of constructions.

4.3   Pedagogical Dimensions of the Digital Manipulative

The teacher from kindergarten 2 identified that the blocks representing different settings triggered the children's fantasy and ideas and as such they formed opportunities for the children to create different kinds of stories. According to the novelty factor, she furthermore suggested to increase the number of blocks to maintain children's interest over time.

Relatively to the ideal number of children playing with one TOK, the teachers had different opinions, the teacher from kindergarten 2 preferred to have two children at a time, whereas the teacher from kindergarten 1 considered that three children was a good number. Both teachers thought that it could be a good idea to connect the Digital Manipulative to a projector, as a bigger screen would be beneficial for activities involving bigger groups of children.

Relatively to the ideal number of slots for the electronic platform, the teacher from kindergarten 2 considered that six slots (for placing six blocks) are enough, since she observed that children most often merely used four slots out of six slots.

The teachers also referred the importance of extending the activities into the home context to share the created stories with parents and family. The teacher from kindergarten 1 expressed that the interface due to its visual design, is a good tool to integrate children from different cultural backgrounds into play activities.

5   Discussion and Conclusions

This explorative and inductive study involved 22 children from two Danish kindergartens and investigated how the design of a Digital Manipulative (DM) could foster playful processes among children in a collaborative environment. Furthermore, what kind of collaborative interactions and play experiences that emerged during the use of the DM.

Regarding the ease of use of the TOK system, the children were able to explore the tool and find out its functions without any help. Along the interaction, they created their own play rules [32] through negotiations with each other over the ways of handling the blocks. This experience of being autonomous contributed to the children's sense of 'being able to', which in turn generated playful interactions and collaborations [5].

The children engaged with the blocks at *two levels of articulation* [33]. At one level they used the blocks to create visual narratives on the computer screen, at a second level they used the blocks as construction material. This double function allowed them to engage in a diversity of activities, which were not merely confined to the computer, but independent from it.

The multimodal (tactile, visual, and audio) feedback encouraged exploration and gesturing, generating concentrated activities. Sometimes the children seemed to engage in problem solving, for example when they reconstructed the visual interactions in order to understand what happened. This indicates that playing with the Digital Manipulative supports a 'debugging philosophy' [1: 114].

The blocks, as input devices, generated a form of *democratic interactions*, this is, they gave children equal power to interact with the device. This democratisation through the sharing of the input devices, encouraged social interaction and collaboration. In this regard, our observational data indicates that the collaboration in the groups with two children from the same gender (two boys or two girls) and the groups with three children (where two of them were girls and one of them a boy), showed a tendency for a more balanced cooperation. However, in the groups with two boys and one girl, the girls tended to take an observer role rather than being active in the interplay. These findings are in accordance with [9].

The Digital Manipulative created a collaborative environment and fostered playful experiences and as such it showed potentials as a pedagogical resource. Regarding the further development of the Digital Manipulative, the intensified interaction among the children when using the block of the cloud, indicates a sensory dimension of the interaction. This influenced the quality of the playful activity in a positive way as it contributed to the collaboration between the children. In other words, the cloud block promoted the children's involvement in the story they were creating and building upon. Furthermore, the physical blocks contributed to the children's awareness, control and accessibility to different kinds of actions [34]. The physical blocks helped the children to coordinate their verbalisations as the child who held a specific block also was in charge of the next coming part of the story that they jointly created. Veraksa and Veraksa [35] and Björklund et al. [36] state that symbolic tools grounded in, for example, fantasy and metaphors, support children's intellectual development. These are all crucial inputs to the further development of TOK, including the need to develop a guideline for the pedagogical use of the Digital Manipulative (DM).

In conclusion, emerging 'design for play' guidelines are based on the above-mentioned two-level articulation wherein children's understanding of DM is emphasized. This through their apprehension of the material, which inspired and fostered joint discussions, sharing and negotiations. Furthermore, the children in this study understood the Digital Manipulative through their collaborative constructions and realisations of ideas, which, in turn, contributed to new and creative knowledge.

Acknowledgments. We would like to sincerely thank teachers and children at Toftlund and Skærbæk Kindergartens, and our host Prof. Eva Irene Brooks, and the Xlab: Design, Learning & Innovation at Aalborg University, Denmark.

The first author was financed by the COST Action IS1410, Digital literacy skills and practices in the early years (DigiLitEY) and the Portuguese Foundation for Science and Technology (FCT) within the Postdoctoral Grant: SFRH/BPD/111891/2015.

References

1. Papert, S.: Mindstorms: Children, Computers and Powerful Ideas. Basic Books, New York (1980)
2. Ackermann, E.: Piaget's Constructivism, Papert's Constructionism: What's the difference? (2001), http://learning.media.mit.edu/content/publications/EA.Piaget%20_%20Papert.pdf
3. Kafai, Y., Resnick, M.: Constructionism in Practice: Designing, Thinking, and Learning in a Digital World. Lawrence Erlbaum Associates, Mahwah (1996)
4. Resnick, M., Martin, F., Berg, R., Borovoy, R., Colella, V., Kramer, K., Silverman, B.: Digital manipulatives: new toys to think with. In: Proceedings of the Conference on Human Factors in Computing Systems, pp. 281–287. ACM Press, New York (1998)

5. Brooks, E.P., Brooks, A.L.: Digital creativity: children's playful mastery of technology. In: Brooks, A.L., Ayiter, E., Yazicigil, O. (eds.) ArtsIT 2014. LNICSSITE, vol. 145, pp. 116–127. Springer, Cham (2015). https://doi.org/10.1007/978-3-319-18836-2_14

6. Petersson, E., Brooks, A.: Virtual and physical toys: open-ended features for non-formal learning. Cyberpsychology Behav. 9(2), 196–199 (2006)

7. Brosterman, N.: Inventing Kindergarten. Harry N. Adams Inc., New York (1997)

8. Montessori, M.: The Montessori Method: Scientific Pedagogy as Applied to Child Education in the "Children's Houses". R. Bentley, Cambridge (1912)

9. Fails, J.A., Druin, A., Guha, M.L., Chipman, G., Simms, S., Churaman, W.: Child's Play: A Comparison of Desktop and Physical Interactive Environments (2005)

10. Marshall, P.: Do tangible interfaces enhance learning? In: Proceedings of the 1st International Conference on Tangible and Embedded Interaction, pp. 163–170. ACM Press, New York (2007)

11. Sylla, C., Coutinho, C., Branco, P.: A digital manipulative for embodied "Stage-Narrative" creation. Entertainment Comput. 5(4), 495–507 (2014)

12. Lauricella, A.R., Barr, R., Calvert, S.L.: Parent-child interaction during traditional and computer storybook reading for children's comprehension: implications for electronic storybook design. Int. J. Child-Comput. Interact. 2(1), 17–25 (2014)

13. Price, S., Rogers, Y.V.: Let's get physical: the learning benefits of interacting in digitally augmented physical spaces. Comput. Educ. 43(1, 2), 137–151 (2004)

14. Chi, M.T.H., Wylie, R.: The ICAP framework: linking cognitive engagement to active learning outcomes. Educ. Psychol. 49(4), 219–243 (2014)

15. Cho, J., Jyoo, J., Shin, J.-Y., Cho, J.-D., Bianchi, A.: Quantifying children's engagement with educational tangible blocks. In: TEI 2017 Proceedings of the 11th International Conference on Tangible, Embedded, and Embodied Interaction, pp. 389–395 (2017)

16. Hornecker, E., Buur, J.: Getting a grip on tangible interaction: a framework on physical space and social interaction. In: Proceedings of the Conference on Human Factors in Computing Systems, pp. 437–446. ACM Press, New York (2016)

17. Sylla, C., Coutinho, C., Branco, P., Müller, W.: Investigating the use of digital manipulatives for storytelling in pre-school. Int. J. Child-Comput. Interact. 6, 39–48 (2015)

18. Zuckerman, O., Arida, S., Resnick, M.: Extending tangible interfaces for education: digital montessori-inspired manipulatives. In: Proceedings of CHI 2005, pp. 859–868 (2005)

19. Olson, I.C., Leong, Z.A., Wilensky, U., Horn, M.S.: It's just a toolbar!: using tangibles to help children manage conflict around a multi-touch tabletop. In: Proceedings of TEI 2011, pp. 29–36. ACM (2011)

20. Ministeriet for Børn, Undervisning og Ligestilling, Lov om Dag-, Fritids- og Klubtilbud m.v. til Børn og Unge, jf. Lovbekendtgørelse nr. 30, 22 Januar (2015), https://www.retsinformation.dk/pdfPrint.aspx?id=168340

21. Digitaliseringsstyrelsen, Et stærkere og mere trygt digitalt samfund - Den fællesoffentlige digitaliseringsstrategi (2016–2020), https://www.fm.dk/publikationer/2016/et-staerkere-og-mere-trygt-digitalt-samfund

22. SUS Implement Consulting Group, Forskning i og praksisnær afdækning af digitale redskabers betydning for børns udvikling, trivsel og læring, https://www.sus.dk/wp-content/uploads/forskning-i-digitale-redskabers-betydning_sammnfattende-rapport_dec2015-1.pdf

23. Greimas, A.J.: Actants, actors, and figures. On meaning: selected writings in semiotic theory. In: Theory and History of Literature, vol. 38, pp. 106–120. University of Minnesota Press, Minneapolis (1973/1987)

24. Propp, V.: Morphology of the Folktale, 2nd edn. University of Texas Press, Austin (1928/1968)

25. Sylla, C., Pereira, I., Coutinho, C., Branco, P.: Digital manipulatives as scaffolds for preschoolers' language development. IEEE Trans. Emerg. Top. Comput. **4**(3), 439–449 (2016)

26. Mazzone, E., Xu, D., Read, J. C.: Design in evaluation: reflections on designing for children's technology. In: Proceedings of 21st British HCI Group Annual Conference on People and Computers: HCI but not as we know it. BCS, vol. 2, pp. 153–156 (2007)

27. Almukadi, W., Boy, G.A.: Enhancing collaboration and facilitating children's learning using TUIs: a human-centered design approach. In: Zaphiris, P., Ioannou, A. (eds.) LCT 2016. LNCS, vol. 9753, pp. 105–114. Springer, Cham (2016). https://doi.org/10.1007/978-3-319-39483-1_10

28. Yliriskiu, S., Buur, J.: Designing with Video. Focusing on the User-Centred Design Process. Springer, London (2007). https://doi.org/10.1007/978-1-84628-961-3

29. Kemp, J.A.M., van Gelderen, T.: Co-discovery exploration: an informal method for the iterative design of consumer products. In: Jordan, W.P., Thomas, B., McClelland, I.L., Weerdmeester, B. (eds.) Usability Evaluation in Industry. CRC Press (1996)

30. Als, B.S., Jensen, J.J., Skov, M.B.: Comparison of think-aloud and constructive interaction in usability testing with children. In: Proceeding IDC 2005, pp. 9–16. ACM Press, New York (2005)

31. Flanagan, J.: The critical incident technique. Psychol. Bull. **51**(4), 327–358 (1954)

32. Kudrowitz, B.M., Wallace, D.R.: The play pyramid: a play classification and ideation tool for toy design. Int. J. Arts Tech. **3**(1), 36–56 (2008)

33. Van Leeuwen, T.: Introducing Social Semiotics. An Introductory Textbook. Routledge, Oxon (2005)

34. Wright, S.: Graphic-narrative play: young children's authoring through drawing and telling. Int. J. Educ. Through Arts **8**(8), 1–27 (2007)

35. Veraksa, A., Veraksa, N.: Symbolic representation in early years learning: the acquisition of complex notions. Eur. Early Child. Educ. Res. J. **24**(5), 668–683 (2016)

36. Björklund, C., Nilsen, M., Pramling Samuelsson, I.: Berättelser som Redskap för att Föra och Följa Resonemang. Nordic Early Child. Educ. Res. J. **12**(5), 1–18 (2016)

Change of Learning Environment Using Game Production – Theory, Methods and Practice

Lars Reng, Lise Busk Kofoed$^{(\boxtimes)}$, and Henrik Schoenau-Fog

Department of Architecture, Design and Mediatechnology,
Aalborg University, Aalborg, Denmark
{lre, lk, hsf}@create.aau.dk

Abstract. Game Based Learning has proven to have many possibilities for supporting better learning outcomes, when using educational or commercial games in the classroom. However, there is also a great potential in using game development as a motivator in other kinds of learning scenarios. This study will focus on cases in which development of games did change the learning environments into production units where students or employees were producing games as part of the learning process. The cases indicate that the motivation as well as the learning curve became very high. The pedagogical theories and methods are based on Problem Based Learning (PBL), but are developed further by combining PBL with a production-oriented/design based approach. We illustrate the potential of using game production as a learning environment with investigation of three game productions. We can conclude that using game production is a powerful pedagogic tool for establishing learning, motivation and engagement.

Keywords: Purposeful game development · Problem based learning
Change of learning environment · Design based learning
Integrating theory & practice

1 Introduction

Development of learning is a very important part of today's agenda for learning institutions and for private companies. This calls for new teaching strategies to establish new teaching and learning possibilities in companies, in higher education as well as in primary schools. For all, the teaching strategies have to be focused on specific knowledge as part of the learning goals for the future, but also to establish motivation and engagement. Furthermore, the skills of collaboration, creativity and innovation have been stressed as some of the most important 21st century skills together with critical thinking which count for both companies and educational institutions [1].

Using games as learning tools have been studied for several years [2, 3, 4], and the learning outcomes are often reported to be rather successful [5, 6, 7]. Designs with narrative role-play based learning goals is an interactive approach to learning that involves the participants in collaborative, creative problem solving in a meaningful context, which can be implemented with non or varying degrees of technology [8].

© ICST Institute for Computer Sciences, Social Informatics and Telecommunications Engineering 2018
A. L. Brooks et al. (Eds.): ArtsIT 2017/DLI 2017, LNICST 229, pp. 424–434, 2018.
https://doi.org/10.1007/978-3-319-76908-0_41

This study will focus on cases where the learning environments are transformed into different kind of game production units where employees or students are producing games with a purpose as part of the learning process. In this paper, we present the pedagogical theories and methods which are based on Problem Based Learning (PBL) as used at Aalborg University, Denmark [9], but are developed further combining PBL with a design based approach. We illustrate the potentials of using such purposive game productions as a learning environment with investigation of three cases of game productions, which involved 54 employees from a process company producing a non-digital problem-solving game, 25 students from Aalborg University, Media Technology Bachelor study producing a purposeful digital game, and 7 teachers plus 55 pupils from a public school also producing purposeful digital games. The cases are described and analyzed and the main results indicate that all participants who worked on the game production was very motivated and engaged and acquired several new technical, social and analytical skills and competences. Furthermore, the results also indicate that the university students as well as the employees also increased their knowledge of production of and skills in project management. The findings illustrate great potentials in changing the learning environment and using production oriented activities, such as game development in all kind of learning scenarios. We conclude that using purposive game production is a powerful pedagogic tool for establishing motivation and engagement, and thereby foundation for learning.

2 Pedagogical Approach

In order to heighten learners' engagement and motivation in getting new knowledge we have experienced that learning through simulated praxis offer a highly efficient approach to working with subjects of high complexity [8]. Producing games make it possible to simplify, categorize and structure the relevant factors in a way that creates clarity and strategic outlook. This function as a map where the scaling helps eliminate the noise and call attention to the essential factors [10]. Furthermore, fabricating their own games is a powerful approach to learning that involves learners in a collective and creative problem solving processes [8, 5]. The pedagogical theories and didactic methods are based on Problem Based Learning and project organized teamwork (PBL) as used at Aalborg University, Denmark [9], but are developed further combining PBL with a production-oriented or design based approach [11]. According to theories of Problem Based Learning and situated learning, design based learning creates contextualized and authentic learning as design tasks which force students to work in an environment which demands are close to real life skills and domain knowledge when practiced in project work [12]. Developing knowledge and skills required in such situations are in addition more transferrable to future situations [13]. Design-based learning using 'enactivism', which is a framework that argues that a close connection between affordance of a learning environment and a learner's capacity of action is implicit in the PBL learning process, and a close connection between affordance of a learning environment, and a learner's capacity of action and perception in knowledge development [14] seems to fit to our pedagogical approach. In the case of a fabrication of a non-digital game the learners were employees working in a company, and it was important for their motivation that they would be able to understand a learning process to see and understand how to change their own and others knowledge, skills and competences. Therefore, we have added a simplistic learning model based on Kolb's experiential learning cycle [15], Schön's theories about the reflective practitioner [16] and Cowan's reflection loops [17] with emphasis on meta-learning processes, shared visions and common mental models [18]. To deal with motivation we have used Kellers' ARCS model for motivational design and performance, which is based on a synthesis of motivational concepts and characteristics within three conceptual categories: attention, confidence and satisfaction [29, 20]. These categories are integrated in the design of the game, where the learners' attention is directed towards the interaction, the problem analyses, the problem-solving activities and implementation strategies, which has relevance through the simulations which occur in the game process. In the cases of the digital games, the development of purposeful games has been examined as a 'powerful learning environment' to stimulate active, autonomous learning via rich contexts and authentic tasks of compositions and construction [21]. Purposeful educational game production, that requires content application, can be applied as a micro world where designers or learners get to explore, represent and test their domain knowledge and skills for integrating them into the game [22], so we find that design based learning in general and computer game development in particular is well connected to PBL and project work. According to self-determination theory there are three basic cognitive needs that are universally applicable: the need for competence, autonomy and relatedness which is related to two main types of motivation: extrinsic and intrinsic motivation. Intrinsic motivation refers to those actions that students engage in as they are inherently interesting and enjoyable, while extrinsic motivation refers to individuals engaging in actions because they lead to separable outcomes (e.g. rewards) [23].

In order to fully integrate the value for students/employees in a learning situation it is important that the learning environment support the teaching to satisfy the learners need for autonomy [25]. To get a sense of relatedness it is important to be encouraged and valued by significant others (teachers, peers etc.) [24]. Construction of the learning process to suit the individual learner is embedded in the process of learning (here making the game), where the teacher/facilitator support the different stages of game-construction to the group of learners in a need-and/or desire-driven instruction so the outcome is tailoring of new knowledge and experience [24]. (See Fig. 1) Summing up, non-digital as well as digital game production can be based on the concept of PBL and

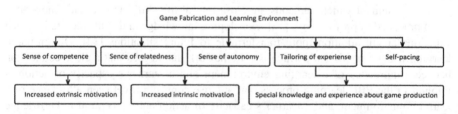

Fig. 1. The pedagogical elements in the fabrication of games and learning in a virtual production environment. (Inspired by Abeysekera and Dawson [24])

project work with a production-oriented/design based strategy, combined with a focus on motivation and engagement.

3 Method

The cases are from three different studies of game productions. The pedagogical approach has been the same with minor additions related to the specific case situation and the aim of the game. We have used action research [26] combined with an exploratory case-study approach [27] in combination with the descriptive, mixed-method case study [28, 29] to investigate the learning/teaching processes in each case.

This study explored the process of learning by design within the context of game development, project management and production. In particular, we addressed the following research questions in all three cases:

1. Did participating in a production of game development enhance motivation towards further learning?
2. How did the different aspects of the process of game production give knowledge and understanding of the different problems connected to each game production?
3. How did the game production strengthen confidence in own competence?

4 The Three Cases

4.1 Case 1: Crossing the Borders – a Game in a Change Process

Case 1 is an example from a larger technological and organizational change in a mid-sized Danish processing company. A characteristic of the organization is that there is a very distinct division between the employees in the production and those performing the administrative and management functions which cause a major problem because a lack of communication between the departments and no understanding or common knowledge of each department's problems. During several workshops using the PBL approach the employees themselves identified problems about delaying of test results, missing information, no sufficient planning and IT-problems [30]. A two hours' pre-workshop was organized where representatives from three departments (which has the problems); production, IT and Laboratory should analyze the problems, and they found a distinct lack of communication and almost no common knowledge about the different departments. Representatives from each department then set up the following questions: Where are the borders to other departments? Which departments do we have to be in close contact with? What important information and knowledge are needed from the different departments so they understand our need and we understand their need? What do each department expect from the other department and what are the departments able to deliver according the common goals? During a co-creating design process those questions were transformed into a non-digital game, where a process during the 3 departments were designed as a problem-solving game e.g. the process of a sample from production has to go through the Lab and IT and feed-back should be given back to production. Very motivated employees from the three departments played the game, and they should interact when they could see a problem. Each problem was projected on a screen. Playing the game was an eye-opener for all participants. They suddenly recognized why it sometimes was problematic e.g. to get some test results very fast from one department. Another department also found that they had to be much more specific when they asked for information if it should be useful for the planning task. And one department realized that they did not know which support they actually could get from the IT-department.

After this game, each department started to formulate projects to solve the problems they had met during the game. They did their project work according to the previous learned PBL method, and quite fast they had solutions to be tested and implemented in their daily work. It was projects about an improved planning system for the production process and the planning department, projects about how to share knowledge and information between three departments etc. One project was about efficiency at the laboratory which had always got complaints. All departments wanted their tests to be prioritized highest. When different departments worked together on a solution they developed a priority system and recommended that an extra laboratory assistant was absolutely necessary. The management agreed with the project proposals, and they were all implemented. Making and playing the game was successful and the employees all felt very motivated and found they had gained not only new knowledge and experience but also a feeling of competence in relation to understand and being able to contribute to the change process, and later the game was played and modified several times by the employees them self [30].

4.2   Case 2: Purposive Game Production – Experiment for University Students

All technical programs at Aalborg University are based on Problem Based Learning. Each semester is divided between courses (15 ECTS) and problem based project work (15 ECTS). The idea behind the purposive game production was mainly motivated by three major issues: Students at the end of their Media Technology bachelor education seem to have a growing concern about the skills and abilities they have learned would fit the needs and requirements of the industry. Another issue was that the students did not feel they had enough time to focus on a single skill/discipline in order to truly understand what was required to fully master it. The third major issue was a general lack of motivation [4]. In order to create a format that would allow the teacher full control of the production, giving the students an experience as close to that of being in a company, and still staying within the requirements and rules of the current study plan, and a very limited time frame; the format chosen is illustrated in Fig. 3. The students would have their semester split in two. First a three-month period where the students would be part of the virtual company for the purposive game production. Second a one month academic project where the students would work in smaller PBL project-groups, and use their product of the game production to develop and investigate an academic problem within the theme of their semester. 20 students were accepted for the experiment. Each of the 20 roles for the production was carefully decided upon based on industry practice, the students' previous experience, and the short timeframe of the production. It was decided to use SCRUM method to manage and control projects [31]. Most SCRUM models function with a project owner role being part of the company, but not part of the development team. The project owner set the requirements for the product. By giving these roles to the teachers, there would be full control over the production, but the daily management tasks should be done by the students. All students were allowed to apply for the positions they felt most passionate about. The number of students who accepted the terms was 20, and the distribution of roles was also almost as desired.

The most important requirements for the game were:

- The game must be a meaningful, purposive game, build with the purpose to enhance teaching of a real, critical, and important topic in public schools (kids age 13–16). The students chose to work with the theme "Global Warming".
- The game had to be 100% factual valid, and true to the latest research in the field.
- The game must give the young people an experience that would facilitate a fact-based discussion about the topic and its possible solutions in the classroom.
- The game had to meet a professional quality that would allow the students to use it when applying for a future job.

Caused by the short timeframe a simplified timetable with only a few of the traditional phases of a game production was given to the students. As the students were in an unfamiliar situation compared to their traditional semester projects, it was decided to keep a fairly high amount of regularly spaced deadlines to ensure that mismanaged activities were detected early. (See Fig. 2).

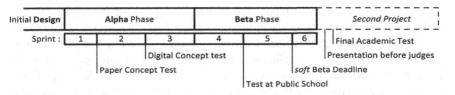

Fig. 2. The purposive game production time table for Media Technology students.

The production facilities were organized in a large group room at Aalborg University's campus where the purposive game production team members organized their own area and divided it into sections based on their roles – e.g. programmers, 3D designers, 2D designers and production management. A group of seven game company CEOs came to judge the quality of the final product. It can be concluded that the group organized project-work does have the flexibility and framework for establishing a learning/teaching environment which could enhance students' motivation for further studies and at the same time gain knowledge and experience within aspects of game production and management of larger productions. This approach can supports students' different interests within the different semesters study-regulations as well as it can give experiences very close to a real production situation. The main findings of surveys, observations and interviews were that students learned more than the learning goals in the study regulation, and that the game-based learning strategy seems rather efficient and demanding for the students [5]. Students experienced a lot of frustration due to the overwhelming challenge of managing a team of 20+ team-members, causing them to truly understand the importance of good project management. They also experienced that sufficient communication, planning and coordination of the game production as a whole as well as the team production is very important, and that they had to be better equipped regarding those aspects. These reflections might be the best starting point for new learning processes – which furthermore was emphasized by the fact, that members of the jury committee offered jobs to some of the students.

In summary, it can be concluded that the new learning environment together with the elements in the pedagogical model have given students increased motivation and self-confidence (see Fig. 1) not only to continue their study the next semester, but they also had shown that they were able to obtain their goals. Furthermore, they improved their special knowledge and experience about game production [5].

4.3   Case 3: Game Production in a Danish Public School – the Teachers' Challenges

The lack of motivation among pupils in secondary schools is a big problem in many Danish public schools. At the same time, there is a political pressure on the public schools that there should be more focus on math and natural science, hoping to motivate more students to get interested in technical areas and to continue their education either in college or in training schools. A general question is then how a game production activity can be developed as a teaching and learning tool in a Public School. A team of teachers from a smaller public school embraced one of the most challenging new game based learning methods, and wanted to implement it on their 9th grade pupils [5]. Their latest evaluation of their 8th grade pupils had shown a low level of motivation and ability to continue their education [32]. None of the teaching staff had any experience with game development. Making a purposeful game production is one of the most demanding teaching activities for a teacher [4]. Therefore a prof. game developer should educate the teachers in game development based on the professional Game Engine 'Unity'. A few weeks before the start of the pupils' project the teachers had agreed on a challenging project. They would like the pupils to create a game that would give the player a realistic experience of being a refugee. With all the current news of European countries daily closing new borders and changing their rules on immigration, they were asking if it would be possible to create a game that could teach the pupils how it would be for a refugee from Syria or Libya to make it all the way to Denmark. The idea was very interesting, but 'Purposive Game Productions' is a challenge even for experienced teachers and pupils [33]. We agreed to assist the teachers building the framework for this challenging production. In this activity, our focus was on the process of making the game as we see the biggest learning potentials in the production of a game - not in playing them - for the teachers as well as for the pupils. We investigated how the team of teachers developed and planned how to organize their teaching and get their pupils started to make the game. The teachers' overall idea of the game was based on the question about how refugees came to Denmark, and the process confirmed that teachers who are using purposive game development as a teaching tool are confronted with big challenges which are connected to all phases of the coordination, planning, implementation and continuation of the teaching and learning (see Fig. 3). The process identified several challenges:

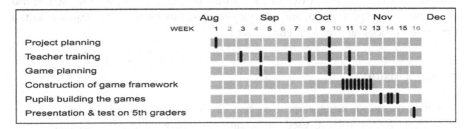

Fig. 3. Timetable of the project

1. The teachers had to be introduced to game development (incl. programming) which was part of working with the game engine; Unity. This was done with a series of six intense workshops of four hours. The goal was that the teachers would remember enough to help the pupils in their game development phases.
2. The teacher's daily time schedule made it very difficult to find a common time for planning. So, it was decided that it should be after school hours.
3. It was difficult to get all teachers to meet at the same time because of other tasks.

Four months was a long process for the teachers, and there seem to be some level of fatigue among almost all teachers.

At the day of presentation, 14 games were demonstrated - each dealing with a different country. The classroom was organized so the name of each country was hanging on a sign above each game. The plan was that you could walk from one country to another and experience the different problems the refugees meet during their escape.

All games except one did function, and all groups had made their own game development and graphics. The young game developers were very enthusiastic about their game and tried "to sell" their product. In general, they were proud of the results, even some groups said they could have done better if they have had more time. They liked to show their game and explain how they have made it. The teachers found that the main part of the pupils was rather motivated during the process, but some of the students had difficulties. About 10% had difficulties keeping focus and concentration, so a full day may be too much, because they are not used to work like that. It was also difficult to keep them in their groups for so long, but teachers reported that some groups were much more active than they used to be, and especially the girls became very motivated and determined. The teachers agreed that most of the students had learned a lot besides programming and game-development: geography, Danish, culture subjects and especially collection of data as well as working in a group being part of a large project with 14 groups. A big surprise for the teachers was that the game activity was so time-and resource consuming. It was difficult to make a proper schedule for planning and implementation [33]. The teachers would like to develop the use of games as a teaching strategy, but they would need to have more knowledge and skills using Unity, and they need more time and experience about using games so they would be able to analyze what the students had learned. The teachers also reflected that their pedagogical strategy should be very clear; the learning objectives and the tool to "measure" the students' learning process as well as the learning outcome. The head of the school had also followed the production, and was very surprised to see the great improvement in the students focus and well-structured work.

5 Conclusion

The main reason for using purposive game development as a teaching method is that learners are forced to be focused, and cannot proceed without fully understanding in depth the material they are trying to model into a game, as well as every detail of the essential information to use. Furthermore, to end with a successful game production, they have to decide how to best model the knowledge into an enjoyable game for the users/players. Combined with the fact that most people find this type of challenge highly motivating, they very often turn from extrinsic motivation into a series of intrinsic motivational goals that drive them way beyond solving the minimum requirements of their project. It can be concluded that learning through game production does have the flexibility and framework for establishing a learning/teaching environment which can enhance learners' motivation and engagement and provide the necessary qualifications aimed for. The pedagogical approach including Problem Based Learning using project work has been very useful when planning and implementing the games. All the involved persons, employee, students, teachers and pupils got valuable experiences and knowledge related to the specific topics in the different games they constructed.

References

1. Bellance, J., Brandt, R. (eds.): 21st Century Skills: Rethinking How Students Learn. Solution Tree Press, Leading Edge (2010)
2. Bowman, S.: The function of role-playing games: how participants create community, solve problems and explore identity. McFarland, Jefferson (2010)
3. Spires, H., Turner, K., Lester, J.: Twenty – First century skills and game based learning. In: EdMedia: World Conference on Educational Media and Technology, June 30, 2008 in Vienna, Austria. Association for the Advancement of Computing in Education (AACE). ISBN 978-1-880094-65-5 (2008)
4. Reng, L., Schoenau-Fog, H.: The game enhanced learning model: mapping game-based learning for educators. In: European Conference on Games Based Learning, p. 559. Academic Conferences International Limited (2016)
5. Schoenau-Fog, H., Reng, L., Kofoed, L.: Fabrication of games and learning: - a purposive game production. In: Munkvold, R., Kolås, L. (eds.) Proceedings of The 9th European Conference on Games-Based Learning: ECGBL 2015, pp. 480–488. Academic Conferences and Publishing International, Reading (2015)

6. Wang, L.C., Chen, M.P.: The effects of game strategy and preference-matching on flow experience and programming performance in game-based learning. Innov. Teach. Int. **47**(1), 39–52 (2010)
7. Yang, Y.-T.C.: Building virtual cities, inspiring intelligent citizens: digital games for developing students' problem solving and learning motivation. Comput. Educ. **59**(2), 365 (2012)
8. Gjedde, L.: Designing for motivational immersive learning through narrative role-play scenarios. In: E-Learn: World Conference on E-Learning in Corporate Government, Healthcare and Higher Education. Association for the Advancement of Computing in Education (AACE), Chesapeake (2015)
9. Kolmos, A., et al.: Facilitation in a PBL-environment. Centre for Engineering Education Research and Development (2008). ISBN 978-87-991994-8-8
10. Thomsen, M.: workz (2016). http://workz.dk/
11. Ke, F.: An implementation of design-based learning through creating educational computer games: a case study on mathematics learning during design and computing, Computers and Education. Elsevier Ltd. (2013)
12. Savin-Baden, M.: Using problem-based learning: new constellations for the 21st century. J. Excellence Coll. Teach. **25**(3, 4), 197–219 (2014)
13. De Vries, E.: Students' construction of external representations in design-based learning situations. Learn. Instructions **16**, 213–222 (2006)
14. Lo, Q.: Understanding Enactivism: a study of affordance and constraints of engaging practicing teachers as digital game designers. Educ. Technol. Res. Dev. **60**, 785–806 (2012)
15. Kolb, D.: Experiential Learning: Experience as the Source of Learning and Development (1984). 2015 By Parson Education Inc.
16. Schön, D.: The Reflective Practitioner. How Professionals Think in Action. Ashgate Publishing Limited, England (2009)
17. Cowan, J.: On Becoming an Innovative University Teacher – Reflection in Action. SHRE and Open University Press, England (2006)
18. Stacey, R.D.: Strategic Management and Organizational Dynamics. The Challenge of Complexity. Pearson Education Limited, Upper Saddle River (2003)
19. Keller, J.M.: An integrative theory of motivation, volition and performance. Technol. Instr. Cogn. Learn. **6**, 79–104 (2008)
20. Keller, J.M.: Motivational Design for Learning and Performance: The ARCS Model Approach. Springer, New York (2010)
21. Robertson, J., Howells, C.: Computer game design: opportunities for successful learning. Comput. Educ. **50**(2), 559–578 (2008)
22. Mitchell, J., Kelleher, H., Saundry, C.: A multimedia mathematics project in a teacher education program. In: Darling, L.F., Erickson, G., Clarke, A. (eds.) Collective improvisation in a teacher education community, pp. 101–118. Springer Science Business Media, Dordrecht (2007). https://doi.org/10.1007/978-1-4020-5668-0_9
23. Ryan, R., Deci, E.: Self-determination theory and the facilitation of intrinsic motivation, social development and well-being. Am. Psychol. **55**(1), 68–78 (2000)
24. Abeysekera, L., Dawson, P.: Motivation and cognitive load in the flipped classroom: definition, rationale and a call for research. High. Educ. Res. Dev. **34**(1), 1–14 (2015)
25. Pintrich, P.: A motivational science perspective on the role of student motivation in learning and teaching context. J. Educ. Psychol. **95**(4), 667–686 (2003)
26. Barry, W.J.: Modern American Education Handbook of Action Research Enquiry and Practice. Sage, London (2012)
27. Stebbins, R.A.: Exploratory Research in the Social Sciences. Sage Publications, Thousand Oaks (2001)

28. Stake, R.: The art of case research. Sage Publications, Thousand Oaks (1995)
29. Yin, V.K.: Case Study Research: Design and Methods. Sage Publications, Thousand Oaks (2008)
30. Busk Kofoed, L., Joergensen, F.: The learning process as a key factor in changes – A theoretical learning approach. In: Proceedings of the 5th International CIN Conference, Sydney (2004)
31. Schwaber, K.: Argile Project management With SCRUM. Microsoft Cooperation (2004)
32. Holm, P.: Headmaster; Højby Skole, Odsherred, Denmark (2016)
33. Reng, L., Kofoed, L.: New teaching strategies for engineering students: new challenges for the teachers. In: Proceedings of International Conference on Engineering Education and Research. Western Sydney University (2016)

Mapping Situations in Implementing Learning Platforms

Andreas Lindenskov Tamborg[(✉)] and Benjamin Brink Allsopp

Department of Learning and Philosophy, Aalborg University,
AC Meyers Vænge 15, Copenhagen, Denmark
{alt,ben}@learning.aau.dk

Abstract. The implementation of digital learning platforms can be a complex process as it involves change for multiple stakeholders such as teachers, school managers and staff from the municipality. This paper draws on video observations from workshops held at two schools in a project intended to support implementation. The aim of this paper is to map the stakeholders' beliefs about the platforms and their implementation, to identify cultural logics underlying these beliefs and to investigate how these affect opportunities for implementing the platforms.

Keywords: Learning platforms · Cultural logics · Arcform

1 Introduction

The research literature suggests that digital learning platforms hold the potential to improve student learning [1–5], but also that the implementation of platforms is a complex process that often awakens concerns and uncertainties among school staff [6, 7]. Research has shown that teachers often associate learning platforms with an increase of standardization at the cost of professional judgment [8], and that school leaders view digital platforms as an expression of increased demands of accountability and cost reduction [9]. Such concerns among the intended users of platforms in themselves represent a threat to exploiting the platforms' potential of improving student learning. On top of this, different stakeholders[1] experience different concerns. This can lead to divergent and potentially conflicting strategies in the implementation process [10]. To achieve successful implementations of digital learning platforms there is a critical need to better understand the views and priorities underlying these strategies and how they affect implementation processes.

In this paper, we investigate this matter in a Danish context. We do so by drawing on video observations of discussions among teachers, school leaders and municipal consultants participating in future workshops [11] at two different Danish schools as a part of a large-scale research project. We describe the process of analyzing this material in a visual mapping notation where we show key stakeholder beliefs. We then identify the strategies and underlying priorities from these maps and discuss how these affect the opportunities for the local implementation of learning platforms. In the following

---

[1] In this paper, we refer to groups of actors (e.g. teachers) as stakeholders.

© ICST Institute for Computer Sciences, Social Informatics and Telecommunications Engineering 2018
A. L. Brooks et al. (Eds.): ArtsIT 2017/DLI 2017, LNICST 229, pp. 435–444, 2018.
https://doi.org/10.1007/978-3-319-76908-0_42

section, we describe the political initiative behind the learning platforms and the project this paper reports from in more detail.

2 Background

The implementation of learning platforms in Danish elementary schools is an ambitious political decision that is associated with many aspirations and visions. The platforms are designed to support teachers in planning lessons, sharing teaching materials and evaluating lessons, as well as to support teachers during class [12]. The platforms should also support the adoption of an objective-oriented curriculum reform requiring teachers to set learning goals for each lesson [12]. The responsibility of choosing, purchasing and implementing a platform that meets local needs was left to the municipalities. All Danish municipalities are required to start implementation by 2017.

The project from which this paper reports is part of a large-scale research initiative aiming at supporting local implementation of the platforms. Approximately 80 teachers from 15 different schools across the country participated in the project. At each school, the project conducted future workshops, which is a participatory method that supports democratic problem solving by involving actors directly in decision-making about matters that affects their everyday (professional) lives [11]. Future workshops typically consist of three phases, namely a critique phase, a fantasy phase and a realization phase. In this project, the critique phase consisted of a brainstorming session that supported the stakeholders in expressing their concerns. The fantasy phase then supported the stakeholders in expressing aspirations and visions for how they themselves, students and parents could benefit from the platforms. In the final realization phase, the focus was to assist the schools in developing concrete initiatives or interventions that aimed at realizing the aspirations and visions articulated in the fantasy phase.

This paper has its roots in the critique and fantasy phases from two schools. We chose these phases as they allow us to gain an insight into the stakeholders' concerns, priorities and strategies relating to the implementation of the platforms.

3 Theoretical Framework and Research Question

In our analysis, we draw on Nielsen's [13] concept of dynamic stabilities or cultural logics originally developed to study teacher collaboration. According to Nielsen, teachers' collaborations are dynamic because they involve numerous ongoing activities that are oriented towards one or more objectives. At the same time, they are stable in that they involve a perceived regularity suggesting consistent priorities underlying these activities [13]. These logics are ways of seeing the world that affect the way people act. In this line of thinking, the stakeholders involved in the implementation of the learning platforms are each bearers of distinct cultural logics, which are expressed in certain concerns, priorities and strategies. Using this concept, we investigate and identify the dynamic stabilities among the stakeholders at the future workshops, thereby answering the following research question: *Which cultural logics can be identified among the stakeholders participating in the workshops and how do these affect the opportunities for the local implementation of the learning platforms?*

4 Data and Methodology

The data used in this paper consists of observations from future workshops held at two schools that participated in the research project. The workshops lasted approximately six hours and were facilitated by one of the authors of this paper (in collaboration with another facilitator). At school 1, three teachers and two school leaders participated and at school 2, six teachers and one consultant participated. The role of the facilitators during the workshops was to structure and organize group conversations according to the three phases of the future workshops. They also observed and took field notes from the dialogues between the participants. The observations were focused on how the actors related to the platform, and which criticisms, aspirations and visions the actors articulated. We also video recorded the workshops.

Cultural logics are however difficult to identify in this data because they occur in complex situations and are expressed in many different ways by different participants. The challenge after the workshops was to identify clear stakeholder beliefs from the many hours of recordings. The researchers needed to interpret hundreds of different utterances and not only agree on what beliefs were being expressed, but also on how representative they were of the stakeholder. This required prolonged discussion among the researchers. To support this we have used Arcform [14] to map the stakeholders' beliefs to thereby open a discussion about the cultural logics of the stakeholders among multiple researchers.

4.1 Mapping with Arcform

Arcform [14] resembles many network notations by using nodes to represent objects (for example stakeholders) and arcs to relate the objects to each other. Arcform differs from most network notations by allowing more flexible arcs that for example can point from or to other arcs. This allows meanings to use other meanings recursively. Nodes and arcs have labels that can be read in sequence as grammatically normal English sentences, however meanings are always represented by a single token. For example Fig. 1 allows us to read the sentence "Teachers try to use learning platforms", but the single arc labeled "try to" represents the meaning of this sentence. We can also read the sentence "teachers use learning platforms" where the single arc labeled "use"

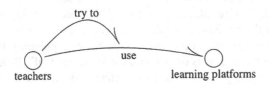

Fig. 1. The Arcform expression "teachers try to use learning platforms" represented by the arc labeled "try to"

represents this meaning. Arcform maps allow us to add any number of additional expressions that reuse existing nodes and arcs when they include the meanings of these tokens.

We used this syntax to create maps of stakeholders, their relations to each other, the platforms and non-human actors which helped us identifying stabilities in the actors' utterances. These were identified from watching the video recordings and negotiating adequate interpretations of these over many iterations until arriving at a stable map. The central epistemological idea in this process is that mapping understandings of the stakeholder beliefs makes this understanding more transparent and therefore more open to scrutiny among the researchers. Examining these maps raised questions, which called for further examination of the utterances and sometimes led to modifications of the map. This could again raise questions until a kind of stability was reached where further changes became increasingly small. The process is illustrated with snapshots of the map as we discuss stakeholder beliefs. It is worth noting that in the maps below we have merged the arcs labeled "try to" and "use" shown in Fig. 1 into a single arc labeled "try to use".

5   Stakeholder Beliefs

In this section, we present the stakeholders' beliefs that we interpreted from their utterances as tokens in a sequence of Arcform maps. Although this has been a nego-tiation where we have both added and removed from the map and returned to the workshop conversations looking for confirmation or challenges to our interpretations, we can only present a simplification of this process. In the following, we present beliefs from school leaders and teachers at school 1 and consultants and teachers at school 2 and we only show beliefs that survive to be included in the stable map.

5.1   School Leaders at School 1

From the conversations at school 1, our interpretation of school leaders' utterances identified the beliefs shown in Fig. 2. We understood that school leaders did not question the value of the learning platforms, but believed that learning platforms help the teachers. This is drawn as the arc labeled "help" pointing from the node labeled "learning platforms" to the node labeled "teachers". However, the school leaders also believed that the teachers do not try to use the learning platforms. This is drawn with the arc labeled "do not". The school leaders spent much time reconciling these two beliefs. This is exemplified in a comment from a school leader: "You need to use it over time. We have many highly competent teachers at our school, but they are not willing to experiment. And I have difficulties accepting that people refuse to see if it works. I really think that the platform can help the teachers and streamline their work".

The belief reflected here and elsewhere is that learning platforms help teachers *if* the teachers try to use them. This is drawn with the arc labeled "if". When listening to the school leaders describing what teachers are willing to do and what will help them, it is not just important to consider the beliefs that they express, but also that they are beliefs

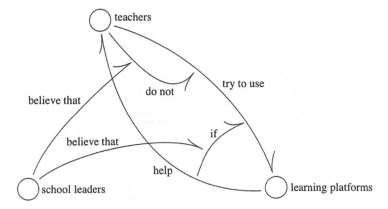

Fig. 2. A version of the Arcform map showing that school leaders believe that teachers do not try to use learning platforms and that learning platforms help teachers if they try to use them.

held by the school leaders. This is drawn as the two arcs labeled "believe that" pointing from the node labeled "school leaders".

5.2   Teachers at School 1

From the teachers' utterances, we identified the beliefs shown in Fig. 2. The teachers were forthright about not trying to use the learning platform, which was already drawn in the map. The teachers provide many explanations for this, but most of these suggested that they believe that learning platforms prioritize learning goals over content opportunities. This is exemplified in one teachers comment: "The whole didactical frame in the learning platform that focuses on learning objectives is way too narrow. One of the key ideas behind the learning platform is that we should focus on learning objectives instead of the content. But for me the content is the most important factor and a key motivational factor for the students. And I don't believe that we always are capable of predicting the content, and writing it in advance in a platform. So from my point of view the platforms should be able to do something different than they do now". The belief reflected here is drawn as the arc labeled "prioritize goals over opportunities" pointing from the node labeled "learning platforms" and pointing back onto the arc itself[2]. On top of these understandings there is also a higher level understanding that the teachers do not try to use the learning platforms *because* they believe that learning platforms prioritize goals over opportunities. This is drawn with the arc labeled "believe that" pointing from the teacher node to the arc labeled "prioritize goals over opportunities", and with the arc labeled "because" pointing from the arc labeled "do not" to the arc labeled "believe that" (Fig. 3).

---

[2] It is a feature of Arcform that statements can be drawn in this way when they do not have a subject or object, or when the subject or object is not needed in other statements in the map.

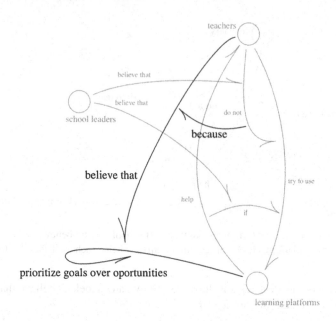

Fig. 3. A version of the Arcform map showing that teachers do not try to use learning platforms because they believe that they prioritize goals over opportunities.

5.3   Consultants at School 2

The map shown in Fig. 4 shows our most stable interpretation of the beliefs underlying the utterances of the consultants at school 2. Conversations between the consultants and the teachers focused around technical skills drawn with the node labeled "technical skills". Our field notes from the workshop describe an observation in which a number of beliefs about technical skills became apparent: *There is a tendency that the discussions are centered on the consultants because they know how the platform works. The teachers do not possess this knowledge and are very interested in learning from the consultants. The consultants are positive and willing to share their knowledge with the teachers. At the end of the meeting, the teachers agree with the one consultant that he will help them use the learning platform.* We understood that the teachers did not have the necessary technical skills (drawn with the arc labeled "do not have") while the consultants do have these skills (drawn with the arc labeled "have"). The consultants have these skills to support teachers when they try to use the learning platform; this is drawn with the arc labeled "to" pointing to the arc labeled "support when".

As a part of a municipal initiative, the consultants had also introduced the principle of evaluation for learning (EVL) at several schools including school 2. EVL is a didactical approach that can be used by teachers to work systematically with formative assessment with the purpose of increasing student learning and has been added as a node in the map. The consultants clearly supported EVL and expressed that the learning platforms also support it (drawn with the two arcs labeled "support").

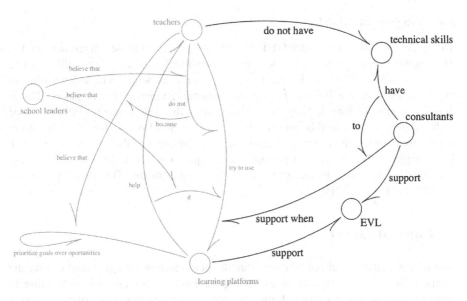

Fig. 4. A version of the Arcform map showing that consultants have technical skills to support when teachers try to use learning platforms and that teachers do not have these technical skills, as well as that both consultants and learning platforms support EVL.

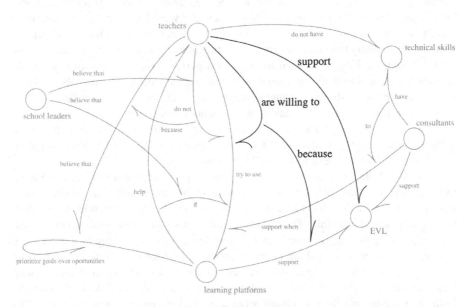

Fig. 5. A version of the Arcform map showing that teachers also support EVL and that they are willing to try to use learning platforms because learning platforms support EVL.

5.4   Teachers at School 2

The teachers at this school added different perspectives from those offered at school 1. The teachers were also quick to add their support to EVL. This is exemplified in one teachers comment: "We need a place were we can work with EVL, and we want to experiment with how and to what extent the platform can provide such a place". This is drawn as a new arc labeled "support" pointing from the node labeled "teachers" to the node labeled "EVL". In this context, the teachers were also assertive that they were willing to try to use the learning platform (drawn with the arc labeled "are willing to"). We interpreted the context that prompted this expression was at least in part because learning platforms support the evaluation for learning principle. This is drawn with the arc labeled "because" (Fig. 5).

6   Cultural Logics

The school leaders at school 1 believe that the platform holds the potential to save the teachers' time. According to them, exploiting these potentials requires investing time to learn how to use the platforms. From this perspective, the teachers' concerns were a consequence of their limited hands-on experience with the platforms. This view shows a cultural logic that prioritizes saving the teachers' time and supporting them in streamlining their work. The teachers from this school were however unhappy that the learning platform required them to plan and define learning objectives for each lesson. They found this problematic because they believed it would require them to anticipate exactly how the students would engage with the academic content. This would deprive them the opportunity to pursue unanticipated student interests emerging while engaging with the content. Therefore, from the teacher's perspective, the platforms' focus on defining learning objectives threatened their pedagogical values. This reveals a cultural logic orientated towards maintaining pedagogical values. It is clear that the points of view of the teachers and the leaders at this school were quite different. They each represent cultural logics, which are oriented towards fundamentally different priorities. If these cultural logics remain tacit it will be difficult for the two parties to agree on how, when and to what extent the platforms can be used.

At school 2, the consultants participating in the workshops were one of the driving forces for implementing EVL, which all schools in the municipality had adopted. They were keen to maintain EVL and therefore had a cultural logic that prioritized maintaining a didactical principle. The teachers at this school were new to the platform, but had successfully used EVL, which also they were keen on continuing to use. Because of this, the teachers were willing to invest the required time to experiment with using the platform to see how it could support them in using EVL. The cultural logic among these teachers was also oriented towards maintaining a particular didactical principle. Both the teachers and the consultants were interested in continuing to use EVL. This alignment of cultural logics between the teachers and the consultants enabled the stakeholders to collaborate towards the same objective.

The examples from the two schools show how different cultural logics cause different opportunities for implementing the learning platforms. Our analysis of the first school identified that these different views caused a collision between the cultural logics. It also meant that the discussion between the stakeholders was about whether the teachers tried to use the platforms or not, and not *how* the platforms could be used in ways that would be beneficial. Such a discussion however requires the stakeholders to align their conceptions of what must be prioritized in the implementation of the learning platform. The discussion at the second school showed that the common didactical footing among the stakeholders enabled a productive collaboration in which the teachers could benefit from the technical knowledge and skills of the consultants.

7 Conclusion

By using data from future workshops in which teachers, school leaders and consultants discussed the implementation of learning platforms we identified key beliefs among stakeholders. We used Arcform [14] as a visual notation technique to make this transparent and open to scrutiny. By using the concept of cultural logics [13], our analyses revealed that the stakeholders at school 1 were oriented towards different priorities and objectives, making an implementation of the platform difficult. At school 2 however, the priorities and objectives of the participating stakeholders where aligned. This enabled the parties to support each other in experimenting with using the platform to obtain common objectives. This suggests that aligned cultural logics are necessary for a successful implementation of learning platforms.

Acknowledgments. This paper is part of the Digital Learning Platforms project financed by Local Government Denmark and The National Agency for It and Learning, The Digital Strategy 2016-2020.

References

1. Edmunds, B., Hartnett, M.: Using a learning management system to personalise learning for primary school students. J. Open Flex. Distance Learn. **18**(1), 11–29 (2014)
2. Lu, J., Law, N.W.Y.: Understanding collaborative learning behavior from moodle log data. Interact. Learn. Environ. **20**(5), 451–466 (2012)
3. Liu, F., Cavanaugh, C.: High enrollment course success factors in virtual school: factors influencing student academic achievement. Int. J. E-Learn. **10**(4), 393–418 (2011)
4. Psycharis, S., Chalatzoglidis, G., Kalogiannakis, M.: Moodle as a learning environment in promoting conceptual understanding for secondary school students. EURASIA J. Math. Sci. Technol. Educ. **9**(1), 11–21 (2013)
5. Misfeldt, M.: Digitalt Understøttede Læringsmål: Udviklingsprojekt med demonstrations-skoleforsøg vedr. it i folkeskolen (Slutrapport). (1 ed.) København: Institut for Læring og Filosofi, Aalborg Universitet (2016)
6. Misfeldt, M., Tamborg, A.L.: Læringsmålstyret undervisning og målforståelser - statiske og dynamiske mål. Cursiv **19**, 113–139 (2016)
7. Underwood, J.D., Stiller, J.: Does knowing lead to doing in the case of learning platforms? Teach. Teach. Theor. Pract. **20**(2), 229–246 (2014)

8. Lochner, B., Conrad, R., Graham, E.: Secondary teachers' concerns in adopting learning management systems: A U.S. perspective. TechTrends Linking Res. Pract. Improv. Learn. **59**(5), 62–70 (2015)

9. Selwyn, N.: "It's all about standardisation"–exploring the digital (re)configuration of school management and administration. Camb. J. Educ. **41**(4), 473–488 (2011)

10. Tamborg, A.L., Allsopp, B.N., Fougt, S.S., Misfeldt, M.: Mapping the logics in practice oriented competence development. In: Proceedings of the Tenth Congress of The European Research in Mathematics Education, Dublin, Ireland (2017). forthcoming

11. Jung, R., Müllert, N.R.: Håndbog i fremtidsværksteder. København: Politisk Revy (1984)

12. K.L. Aftale om konkretisering af det fælles brugerportalsinitiativ for folkeskolen (2014)

13. Nielsen, L.T.: Teamsamarbejdets Dynamiske Stabilitet. En Kulturhistorisk Analyse Af Læreres Læring i Team. Ph.D.-afhandling, Aarhus: Aarhus Universitet (2012)

14. Allsopp, B.B.: Introducing arc form: designing a satisfactory highly non-linear alternative to texts for general-purpose idea development. Ph.D dissertation. Kbh: Aarhus Universitet, Institut for Uddannelse og Pædagogik (2013)

BioSpil: Bringing Interactivity and Gaming into a Cinema-Context

Tobias Tretow-Fish, Dan Andersen, Lisa Klemm Larsen,
and Eva Brooks(✉) ⓘ

Department of Learning and Philosophy, Aalborg University,
Kroghstræde 3, 9220 Aalborg, Denmark
{ttreto16,dandel6,lklal4}@student.aau.dk,
eb@learning.aau.dk

Abstract. This paper presents a study on a current phenomenon conceptualized as BioSpil, which brings interactivity and gaming into a cinema context. The study focused on two questions, namely in what way BioSpil can be called a game, and how it functions as a social game. The study applied an ethnographic approach. The analysis showed that BioSpil had a game-like character, but were, to a certain extent, in conflict with two of Calliois' categories that can define a game, namely being free and separate in time and space. The aspect of a game as being free, is not only dependent on accessibility in terms of devices, but also on cultural and contextual factors. This influenced the conditions of what constitute accepted and expected behaviors of visitors in a cinema-context. Furthermore, the analysis identified that BioSpil offered three kinds of social spaces; an active, a passive, and an external space.

Keywords: BioSpil · Interactivity · Games · Commercials · Mobile phones
Cinema · Game design theory · Explorative study · Thematic analysis

1 Introduction

In this study, we have explored the concept of *BioSpil* from *Dansk Reklame Film* A/S (Danish Advertising Film) [1] *'Bio'* referring to the Danish word *'Biograf'*, which means 'cinema' and *'Spil'*, the Danish word for 'game'. BioSpil is a platform where different kinds of games are available for movie-goers to log on and play approximately five minutes before the regular commercials in Nordic Film Cinemas in Denmark[1]. The games are commercials presented in a game format with game-design elements and game principles [2]. The basic idea behind BioSpil is to bring interactivity and gaming into a cinema-context. However, this does not only comprise potential entertainment values for the movie audience, but also offer advertisers opportunities to interact with the audience in a new way. By allowing the BioSpil participants to continue some of the games at home on Facebook, the developers have an intention to build a bridge between the offline BioSpil in cinemas and online on Facebook. An example of this is

---

[1] The project BioSpil is developed in collaboration between MEC Access and MediaCom Beyond Advertising. The concept and the technological platform is developed by the TechAdd company AddThunder.

© ICST Institute for Computer Sciences, Social Informatics and Telecommunications Engineering 2018
A. L. Brooks et al. (Eds.): ArtsIT 2017/DLI 2017, LNICST 229, pp. 445–457, 2018.
https://doi.org/10.1007/978-3-319-76908-0_43

the DolceWord game[2] from Danish Advertising Film, which can be continued after the cinema-visit and, thereby, increase the possibilities for the participants to win prizes at Nescafé Dolce Gusto's Facebook-page[3] (Egmont, 2013) (Fig. 1).

Fig. 1. Left image shows the interface of the DolceWord BioSpil. A coffee word appears on the canvas, and the user should as fast as possible swipe the word on their mobile phone on a 4 × 4 words letter plate. The winner participates in a weekly competition about a Nescafé (NDG) coffee machine. At NDG's Facebook site it was possible to enter the competition also after the cinema visit and continue to play against other people. The image to the right shows the DolceWord game and how it is exposed on the movie screen (http://groupmdanmark.dk/cases/mediacom-udviklingen-af-biospil/)

Phillips and Noble [3] identified attributes that formed movie-goers attitudes toward advertisements in cinemas. The respondents found their movie experience diminished due to the advertising, as well as to the sense that they, at the same time, had to pay more and more to go to the movies. Also, the respondents indicated that due to the commercials, they choose to arrive late to the cinema to miss out the commercials.

Statistical analyses from Danes' Cultural Habits [4] show that young people more often visit the cinema compared to older people. 24% of young people between 15 and 19 years of age and 26% of people between 16–29 years of age have visited the cinemas in 2012. Generally, more females than men visit the cinema. Recent statistics from Danish Cinemas[4] indicates a positive development when it comes to an increase of cinema visitors, which is explained by the digitalization of Danish cinemas as well as the 3D technology. Furthermore, it is expected that cinemas will earn more money on advertisements compared to what was the case in 2014[5].

The Entertainment Software Association (ESA) [5] presents in their report from 2016 that 27% of people below 18 years of age are game players and 29% of people

---

[2] For more details, see link: https://www.youtube.com/watch?v=c70r6EgwT50.

[3] See link: https://www.facebook.com/NESCAFEDolceGustoDanmark/.

[4] Danske Biografer, 2014. Brancheforening for Landets Biografer: http://danske-biografer.dk/danskerne-ser-stadig-film-i-biografen/.

[5] This prediction comes from Global Entertainment & Media Outlook, PwC: https://www.pwc.com/gx/en/industries/entertainment-media.html.

between 18–35 years of age play games. The gender division shows that 59% of males and 41% of females represent the game players. Furthermore, the statistics from ESA informs that 48% of the game players play social games, where 36% use their smartphone as a game device and 31% a wireless device. The most frequent type of games that the most frequent gamers play on their wireless of mobile devices is puzzle, board game, card game or game shows.

Whereas related research indicates that movie-goers are not so positive to cinema advertisements, the Global Entertainment and Media Outlook predict an up-going trend regarding both cinema visitors and advertisements. Considering the above-presented statistics, which show that both in the case of being a movie-goer and a game-player, young people are the most frequent representatives, this could indicate that *BioSpil* as a form for combining game play with advertisement could be of interest for the most frequent movie-goers. Based on this and the fact that BioSpil as a phenomenon has not been widely examined, we have conducted an explorative study investigating (1) in what way BioSpil can be called a game, and (2) how it functions as a social game.

2   Background

While cinema advertising is not a new phenomenon, the first advertising film appeared in 1897 for Admiral cigarettes [6], presenting it in an interactive game-format is novel. To date and to our knowledge, advertising as gameplay has not been a field of scientific study. The only reference to this phenomenon that we have found is a Russian paper from 2016: 'Linguistic Characteristics of Modern Danish Advertisements', which contains an analysis of Danish advertising texts from different kinds of media (print editions, television, radio, the Internet) created between 2005 and 2016. The analysis was linguistic and focused the language of advertising in terms of grammar, syntax and other qualities of sentences. In this study, BioSpil is referred to as an object of advertising where it is possible to win prizes in a movie-context [7].

Sega Games started a new advertising trend when they in the 1980s inserted Marlboro billboards in its racing games [8, 9]. This refers to in-game advertising, where products or brands are included within a digital game, for example, different brands are placed in games in the form of billboards and posters [10, 11]. Similar to advertisements in movies, slots are offered by game producers to advertisers to include their product in a game [11]. Another way to advertise, is by means of so called advergames and constitute a form of gamification of advertising [10]. Advergames are similar to BioSpil, as they are designed to advertise a specific brand or product. The games are downloadable or playable on the advertiser's website and are supposed to convey an entertaining message for the advertised product or brand [10]. Advergames are most often casual games that offer short time playing and can be played on smartphones or tablets [12].

3   Methodology

The study is grounded in an ethnographic approach, where the empirical work has been explorative and carried out in the field and characterized by the people we have met during the field studies [12]. Based on that the topic we investigated previously has not been so widely explored, we have worked inductively in the sense that the gathered data guided as well as directed us through an interchangeable field of study. The data was collected on the basis of negotiations and discussions between the members of the research team, where each data set led to the next data set aiming towards a form of theory-building [11].

The study was carried out in Aarhus, the second biggest city in Denmark and consisted of observations in cafes and in a cinema (Sects. 3.1 and 3.2), an expert interview, and an additional questionnaire survey (Sect. 3.3). A more detailed description of each of these studies is presented in the below text.

3.1 Observing in Cafes

In order to better understand visitors' interaction with BioSpil in a cinema context, we conducted an initial study in two different cafe-contexts with the overall intention to explore human's interaction with mobile phones – the device with which BioSpil is played. In particular, our interest was to explore what happens when people use mobile phones in public spaces. In this regard, we were interested in the mobile phone as a tool for users to accomplish their goals, rather than specifically as an entertainment system.

Cafes constitute gathering areas for different kinds of people to meet socially or to individually have a break and something to drink and eat. Often, also, cafes offer opportunities for people to charge their mobile devices. We conducted two observations in cafe-contexts; one in a regular cafe and one in a board game cafe. In both cases, the observations were unstructured, as we would not be limited in relation to new discoveries as the observations progressed. In order to get an authentic and accurate data collection, where our presence would not affect the observed behavior and appearance of the cafe visitors, we chose to take on a nomadic observer role and apply a covert/disguised observation technique [13]. The benefit of this approach was to try to achieve a more nuanced understanding toward a field that still is under-researched, in particular regarding theories related to cinema advertisement in the form of games. Covert observations are in some instances criticized as they do not include any informed consent, which can violate the informants position [14]. However, Lugosi [15], in his ethnographic study of commercial hospitality, states that covert observations sometimes is necessary, but that this concealment needs to be negotiated throughout the fieldwork. This is in line with Calvey [13], who also argues that in such covert research, engagement with the ethics of research should not become a ritualistic tick box process, but should run throughout the lifetime of a project. Based on this, we considered that the data collection, which took place in public domains, would not violate the informants' privacy or identity. Ethically, we have based this on the Research Ethics Framework by ESRC [16].

Accordingly, we have applied a form of situated and reflective ethics [13], where we were aware of that observations in public spaces are influenced by people acting differently depending on their social context. People, their environment and their social context are factors that always mutually influence each other and, thereby, it is not possible to directly replicate this study as the results can only be valid for those specific people and contexts [17].

The observation in the regular cafe included seventy-five guests (forty-eight females and twenty-seven males) with a varied but not noted age range. Here, we were interested in how the informants used the mobile phone in the cafe space and in what way the interaction with the mobile phone unfolded potential social interaction. As the mobile phone can be used anywhere and everywhere, private and public lives of the user merge [18].

The board game cafe observations included twenty-seven board gamers (seventeen females and ten males) all of them approximately in their twenties. This age-group is in line with the above-mentioned statistics regarding the ages of most frequent game-players as well as movie-goers (see Sect. 1). Similarly, as in the observation in the regular cafe, our interest was directed towards how the cafe visitors used the mobile phone in the cafe space, in particular in what way it functioned in a gaming context.

3.2 Observing in a Cinema

In the cinema observation study, we applied a similar method approach as in the cafe contexts, namely unstructured observation (see Sect. 3.1 for further description). The overall intention was to explore how movie-goers interact when playing BioSpil (BioSpil is further elaborated in Sect. 1). Furthermore, through the informants' BioSpil gameplay, our interest was to investigate whether and in what way BioSpil represented a game. Different from the cafe observations, we considered the mobile phone as an entertainment system with social potentials. The observation included 14 BioSpil and was carried out at the Nordic Film Cinema in a city located in southwest of Denmark. Sixty-two moviegoers equally distributed between females and males were included in the study, and had a varied but not noted range of age.

We applied similar nomadic observer role as in the cafes and we applied a covert/disguised observation technique [13] (for further description, see Sect. 3.1). We chose to place ourselves at the back of the cinema to have an overview of the whole space and to not fall outside the norm of being a moviegoer, in order to (1) record authentic data on the moviegoers' actions and interactions with BioSpil, individually and interpersonally, and (2) leave the cinema when BioSpil was over, so we did not disturb the daily operations or the moviegoers' experience, or at least as little as possible.

3.3 Expert Interviews and Questionnaire Surveys

Due to that the concept of BioSpil is not so widely researched, we targeted additional data from experts to broaden the understanding of the concept as such and how the games, from their perspectives, function when played in the cinemas. Therefore, we conducted four semi-structured interviews [19] with experts: one with the developer of BioSpil, two with employees from the operating staff in a Nordic Film Cinema, which has a daily contact with the users of BioSpil and the system running BioSpil, and, finally, one interview with the owner of a board games cafe in Aalborg.

To qualify the collected data, we used triangulation including different sources of data and different respondents [20]. In this regard, we added questionnaire surveys to a selection of BioSpil users. Twenty-five users replied and they were mostly men in their late twenties. Users of the board games cafe in Aalborg supplied eleven answers (on Facebook), where nine were men and two were women, all of them also in their late twenties. The questions in the questionnaires were primarily aimed at people's experiences of playing BioSpil.

3.4 Thematic Analysis

We followed a thematic analysis to identify, analyze and describe patterns in the collected data. These patterns were, then, gathered into themes. This method can be seen as a minimization and organization of data, opening up for interpretation of the data [21]. Usually codes are used in the early stages of thematic analysis, to ground the themes strongly in the data. For our analysis, we instead chose to apply a detailed focus using flexible themes formed from Patton's idea of sensitizing concepts [22]. Grounded in the study's explorative and inductive approach, guiding theories emerged alongside the analysis. In line with this, the formulated research questions regarding in what way BioSpil can be classified as a game and how it functions as a social game, were systematically narrowed down along the way. The emerging themes were found iteratively, first as a tool in initiating assumptions and continuously developed, as data was gathered, assembled and analyzed into fewer and overarching themes.

We consider the collection of data as small bits of reality, through which we investigated events, meanings and experiences, such as the effects of discourses that operate in social contexts [21].

4   Analysis

BioSpil represents a concept where a certain commercial is presented in a game format with game-design elements and game principles. The BioSpil games can be played in a cinema before the movie starts. The gameplay can also continue afterwards by being available on the product's website or Facebook-site. In this way, the BioSpil concept brings interactivity and gaming into a cinema-context, which opens up for potential entertainment values for the audience as well as opportunities for advertisers to interact with the audience in new ways.

In order to find out in what way BioSpil can be called a game, and how it functions as a social game, we performed a thematic analysis. We have reviewed observations and interviews to identify these themes and ended up with a collection of eleven initial themes presented in Table 1.

After having identified initial themes, we made a comparative analysis of them, where we reduced the eleven themes to two [21].

The two themes were:

- Devices and accessibility
- The game as a social space

To process these themes, we applied a framework from Roger Calliois' theory [23] on games and play to understand BioSpil as a game in relation to the theme 'Devices and availability'. For the other theme 'The game as a social space', we used Richard

Table 1. Initial themes.

Informants	Method	Initial themes
Users of BioSpil in the Nordic Film Cinema	Unstructured observations	1.How the informants interact with the device 2.How the informants interact with each other
Developer of BioSpil	Semi-structured interview	3.The social aspect of BioSpil 4.The BioSpil development process 5.The meaning of the device
Operating staff in the Nordic Film Cinema	Semi-structured interview	6.The cinema vs. BioSpil 7.BioSpil: commercial or game? 8.The operation of BioSpil
Owner of the board game cafe	Semi-structured interview	9.The interaction between the informants 10.The role of the phone 11.The visitors

Rouse's theory [2] on game design, which helped us to understand what motivated the informants to use BioSpil.

4.1 Devices and Accessibility

The analysis showed that the devices (e.g. smartphone, iOS or Android operating systems, the BioSpil and Facebook apps) and the accessibility to the BioSpil were crucial ingredients for their participation in the gameplay. Calliois' theory [23] defines a game by introducing six elements, namely: free, separate, uncertain, unproductive, governed by rules and make belief. In addition, he also includes four types of experiences in relation to game-players and games and these are: competition, chance, vertigo and simulation. Since this study is not about game-play experiences, we only look closer into the six game defining elements, which are:

- Games are *free* when players can participate spontaneously and leave them when they want to.
- Games are *separate* when they are limited in time and space. If games are interrupted, the continuation is defined by players.
- Games are *uncertain* when there is no predefined outcome. Players initiatives define the outcome of the game.
- Games are *unproductive* when no goods are produced and when they end as they begin.
- Games are *governed by rules* when they suspend ordinary laws and behaviours that must be followed by players.
- Games involve *make-believe* that confirm for players the existence of imagined realities that may be set against "real life" [23].

Through observations of the BioSpil players in the cinema, we found that two of the above-mentioned elements was more outstanding than the others, namely *Free* and *Separate*. They are further described in the below Sects. (4.1.1 and 4.1.2)

4.1.1   Free

The participants in the study experienced the BioSpil game as accessible in terms of being free to play. The necessary devices (e.g. smartphone, iOS or Android operating systems, the BioSpil and Facebook apps), however, limited the accessibility. If a game should be considered as free to play, it must not be a forced participation. Simultaneously every player must have the opportunity to participate spontaneously and to withdraw from the game [23]. In this sense, BioSpil is free as it is accessible in the cinema context and afterwards on social media. The participants in the study could choose both to participate and to leave the game at any moment when it was playable. They retrieved the BioSpil app in the dedicated timeslot before the regular commercials and the movie started. The participants were guided through visual and verbal instructions how they should download the app and get going with the game. This resulted in that the participants experienced the introduction to the BioSpil and to join and start playing the games as an easy and accessible way, also for beginners. Spontaneous participation in the game is therefore also possible and likewise is the option of spontaneous withdrawing from the game since no repercussions exists from closing the app or to stop interacting with the phone. However, there is a limitation of the accessibility and spontaneous participation in the gameplay since the participants needed to possess all the necessary devices to interact with the BioSpil app and the games.

4.1.2   Separate

The second of Calliois' elements that BioSpil had a notable conflict with, was whether or not BioSpil as a game was separated in a spacious sense. According to Calliois [23], a game must have an established place and time for where and when it can be played. The games in this study, therefore, constituted a closed and protected universe, which Calliois describes as a pure space.

The physical spatial element of BioSpil is defined by three factors: (1) the cinema room; (2) the cinema screen; and (3) the phone. These physical elements of BioSpil can be related to Calliois' definition of a game's spacious separation. Since the games have a start and end, it is possible for the players to enter or leaves these spatial spaces (the cinema space, the cinema screen and the phone). However, the results from this study showed that BioSpil also has experience-based spatial elements regarding visibility and audibility. The technical segment behind the game (hardware and software) creates an apparent conflict in relation to these experience-based spatial elements. During the gameplay in the cinema that was observed, the games crashed or a technical error occurred. In these situations, the participants lost the ability and opportunity to correct the game and continue playing. Thereby, they lost the interaction as such as they could not resume the game. In other words, the participants in the study lost the defined space of the game and the motivation to continue playing.

In the following section, we have applied Rouse's theory [2] of game design to the BioSpil concept, including a closer look at the aspects that motivated the participants in the study to play BioSpil.

4.2 The Game as a Social Space

The analysis showed that the BioSpil participants experienced the aspects of socializing and bragging rights as the main components to why they participated in the BioSpil gameplay. Rouse (2015) describes that players in particular request four types of game-experiences, either isolated or mixed up [2]:

- *Challenge*: Players are motivated by facing challenges and succeeding in overcoming them.
- *Socialize*: Players will engage themselves and are motivated by games set in a social context.
- *Bragging rights*: Players also engages in winning the game to gain respect from their peers and the rights to brag about it.
- *Fantasize*: Players are motivated to play games so they can be released in another world, a fantasy world, and explore it.

The below sub-sections describe the two types of game-experiences that the participants in this study put forward, namely socializing and bragging rights.

4.2.1 Socializing

The analysis of interviews and observations showed that the participants primarily found the game to be a social game. The importance of this aspect was further confirmed by the BioSpil's developer, who stated that BioSpil focuses on social aspects of gameplay experiences as these essentially are motivating the participation in BioSpil. The gameplay activity in the cinema, along with the games' subsequent invitation to share the participants experience on Facebook, was put forward as building stones that helped to create a social dimension of the game. In addition, some games, such as horse races, helped the participants to create a sense of "being in a team" as they in this game worked together to get their horses to win the race. This social aspect of the gameplay experience is in line with Rouse [2], who emphasizes that a lot of games provide a social context and most people enjoy the socializing aspect of these games. Despite the fact that single-player games exist and thrives, there are more multiplayer games and social games because people want game experiences that are social [2].

4.2.2 Bragging Rights

The participants in the study experienced that BioSpil encouraged them to share their results from the gameplay activity in the cinema on Facebook. The "bragging rockets" feature in the games and the sharing of the experiences on Facebook created an opportunity for the participants' "bragging rights". These bragging rights are also established after the end of a game, where the winning participant got their names on the cinema screen. Beside the social aspect of the BioSpil gameplay, the participants also engaged in the gameplay to win. Having a high score or beating an opponent in a game gave the opportunity to brag and support the participant's self-esteem. Rouse [2] states that the emotions that a game can bring to the player, are stronger than what is experienced in other kinds of media, where the experiences are less profound and the personal involvement is less extensive [2].

The discussion section will further elaborate on the game and gameplay aspects of accessibility, socializing and bragging rights.

5 Discussion

The discussion is centered around whether game design theory supports BioSpil as a game and in what way this is compliant to the outcomes from the thematic analysis of the empirical study. The findings from the observations in the board game cafe, the expert interviews and the supplementing questionnaire data, are part of the discussion. Following this section, the paper concludes with a question about BioSpil having a future potential of being a disruptive innovation.

5.1 Accessibility and Contextual Factors

Calliois [23] defines games based on certain categories, e.g. they have to be free, governed by rules, and separate in time and space. In this study, the category of being free was emphasized as it should be accessible. The results showed that BioSpil was not fully accessible as it is dependent on the users having a number of devices. The devices contribute to defining the gameplay environment, the desired behavior and culture of the users. The differences in the contextual culture are clearly visible in the difference between board games in cafes and BioSpil in cinemas. At the board game cafes, the phones are undesirable. Considering the preferred behavior in board game cafes, the same mirroring of desired behavior and culture as in the cinema was observed, where the phone is not a welcomed device [24]. BioSpil's location, i.e. before the advertisements and the start of the movie, now serves as an exceptional break as it challenges the cinema behavior and culture [24]. In this sense, the cinema culture and users' behavior limit BioSpil's accessibility. If the cinema as an institution prevents users against using their phones, the users are, as well, prevented to join BioSpil games.

5.2 The Game as a Social Space and Its Mediators

External mediators, which for BioSpil is the game itself, are significant for a gameplay activity. The mediators contribute to defining the space in relation to a game. For example, in BioSpil, as well as at the board games cafes, non-players also were included in socializing, and as such they became mediators maintaining players' interest in the game activity. They did so by, for example, giving advices to the player regarding a next step in the game, or notifying the player when he succeeded in the game. In this way, the mediators had a more important role, and to a greater extent, than initially assumed.

From the investigations into the social space of BioSpil and at the board game cafe, three dimensions of interactions were identified, which describe emerging social spaces applicable within this study:

- An *active space*, which concerns those who play and shoots bragging rockets or talk about the game. In addition, this space also includes the mediators, who actively support specific players.
- A *passive space*, which concerns those who are watching the gameplay and cheers, sit at other tables or stand as observers.
- An *external space*, which concerns the interactions that reaches out from the executive space. For example, sharing results via Facebook or chatting on forums with people from the cafe.

6   Concluding Remarks

This paper presents the current phenomenon of BioSpil, which brings interactivity and gaming into a cinema context. In particular, the study focused on two questions, namely in what way BioSpil can be called a game, and how it functions as a social game. The study applied an ethnographic approach, including observations, expert interviews, and an additional questionnaire. Further studies are needed to confirm the outcomes of this study.

According to Calliois' categories [23] of what can define a game, BioSpil had a game-like character, but were, in particular and to a certain extent, in conflict with two of Calliois' categories, namely being free and separate in time and space. The aspect of a game as being free, is not only dependent on accessibility in terms of devices, but also on cultural and contextual factors. This, in turn, influences the conditions of what constitute accepted and expected behaviors of visitors (potential players) in a cinema-context. In line with Rouse [2], BioSpil constituted three kinds of social spaces; an active, a passive, and an external space.

The analyses of the empirical data indicate that BioSpil in its current form embraces an innovation with a future opportunity to become disruptive [25]. According to Christensen [25], disruptive innovations starts in the form of simple applications related to a limited market and moves up market to displace established competitors. BioSpil as a concept and the technology behind it, can be applied to several other social contexts, where it can impact the way consumers use this kind of technology. BioSpil offers consumers something they did not have before in terms of social and digital gaming-based experiences in the cinema, which can be extended to other contexts. In addition, the concept creates a new market for the advertising industry, by offering a new platform where large proportions of consumers do not necessarily consider the platform as advertisement, but rather as entertainment. At the same time, it can be concluded that the practical and technical application still is a hurdle that retains the concept. Consequently, for now BioSpil can only be regarded as a sustaining innovation on its way to open the door towards disruptive innovation [25].

References

1. Egmont (2013). http://www.egmont.com/dk/presse/Nyheder-og-pressemeddelelser/Verdens-forste-interaktive-biografspil/
2. Rouse, R.: Game Design: Theory and Practice. Wordware Publishing Inc., Plano (2005)
3. Phillips, J., Noble, M.S.: Simply captivating: understanding consumers' attitudes toward the cinema as an advertising medium. J. Advert. **36**(1), 81–94 (2007)
4. Bak, L., Madsen, A-S., BHenrichsen, B., Troldborg, S.: Danskernes Kulturvaner. Kulturministeriet, Epinion A/S og Pluss Leadership A/S, Viborg (2012)
5. Essential Facts about the Computer and Video Game Industry, Entertainment Software Association (ESA) (2015)
6. Austin, B.: Cinema screen advertising: an old technology with new promise for consumer marketing. J. Consum. Market. **3**(1), 45–56 (1986)
7. Vinogradova, V.: Linguistic characteristics of modern danish advertisements (2016). https://dspace.spbu.ru/handle/11701/3576?locale=en
8. Chambers, J.: The sponsored avatar: examining the present reality and future possibilities of advertising in digital games (2006). http://ir.lib.sfu.ca/retrieve/1630/8878e0c3d9c0a0bc676 70b8d9a0f.doc
9. Chang, Y., Yan, J., Zhang, J., Luo, J.: Online in-game advertising effect: examining the influence of a match between games and advertising. J. Interact. Advert. **11**(1), 63–73 (2013)
10. Terlutter, R., Capella, L.-M.: The gamification of advertising: analysis and research directions of in-game advertising, advergames, and advertising in social network games. J. Advert. **42**(2–3), 95–112 (2013)
11. Yang, M., Roskos-Ewoldsen, R.D., Dinu, L., Arpan, M.L.: The effectiveness of 'In-Game' advertising. J. Advert. **35**(4), 143–152 (2006)
12. Redondo, I.: The effectiveness of casual advergames on adolescents' brand attitudes. Eur. J. Market. **46**(11/12), 1671–1688 (2012)
13. Calvey, D.: The art and politics of covert research: doing 'Situated Ethics' in the field. Sociology **42**(5), 905–918 (2008)
14. Baker, L.M.: Observation: a complex research method. Libr. Trends **55**(1), 171–189 (2006)
15. Lugosi, P.: Between overt and covert research: concealment and disclosure in an ethnographic study of commercial hospitality. Qual. Inq. **12**(3), 541–561 (2006)
16. Research Ethics Framework, ESRC (2005). http://www.esrcsocietytoday.ac.uk/ESRCInfoCentre/opportunities/research_ethics_framework/index.aspx?ComponentId=11292&SourcePageId=19165
17. Thyer, B.A., Dulmus, C.N., Sowers, K.M.: Human Behavior in the Social Environment. Wiley, Hoboken (2012)
18. Fortunati, L.: The mobile phone as technological artefact. In: Glotz, P., Bertschi, S., Locke, C. (eds.) Thumb Culture: The Meaning of Mobile Phones for Society, pp. 149–160. Transaction Publishers, New Brunswick, London (2005)
19. Kvale, S., Brinkmann, S.: Interview - Det kvalitative forskningsinterview som håndværk. Hans Reitzels Forlag, Copenhagen (2015)
20. Brinkmann, S.: Kvalitativ udforskning af hverdagslivet. Hans Reitzel, Copenhagen (2013)
21. Braun, V., Clarke, V.: Using thematic analysis in psychology. Qual. Res. Psychol. **3**, 77–101 (2006)
22. Patton, M.Q.: Qualitative Research & Evaluation Methods, 3rd edn. Sage Publications, Thousand Oaks (2002)

23. Caillois, R.: Man, play and games. The Free Press of Glencoe, Inc., Egmont (1961). http://www.egmont.com/dk/presse/Nyheder-og-pressemeddelelser/Verdens-forste-interaktive-biografspil/
24. Telia (2015). https://www.youtube.com/watch?v=aoRxI3mFvjI
25. Christiansen, C.: The ongoing process of building a theory of disruption. J. Prod. Innov. Manage. **23**(1), 39–55 (2006)

Computer Coding at School
and Game Creation

Isabel Barbosa[1], João Magalhães[1], Vasilis Manassakis[2(✉)],
Giorgos Panselinas[2], Castália Almeida[3], Ermelinda Alves[3],
Loredana Mataresse[4], Pasqualle Mossa[5], Amílcar Baptista[6],
Sara Brandão[6], and Katarzyna Azevedo[7]

[1] Code for All, Lda – Academia de Código, Santarém, Portugal
{isabel.barbosa, joao.magalhaes}@academiadecodigo.org
[2] Regional Directorate of Primary and Secondary Education of Crete,
Heraklion, Greece
manassakisv@gmail.com, panselin@gmail.com
[3] Agrupamento de Escolas de Aveiro, Aveiro, Portugal
castalia_almeida@hotmail.com, duxinha@yahoo.com
[4] Instituto d' Instruzione Superiore Secondaria Marco Polo, Bari, Italy
lorimatal3@yahoo.it
[5] Scuola Media Statale Dante Alighieri, Lucera, Italy
pasqualemossa@libero.it
[6] INOVA+, Lisbon, Portugal
{amilcar.baptista, sara.brandao}@inovamais.pt
[7] INnCREASE SP.Z O.O, Rzeszów, Poland
inncrease@inncrease.eu

Abstract. Education and schools are facing serious problems to motivate and prepare the new generations. A multidisciplinary educational approach, where students are taught to program, can contribute to a better school. Game creation is a multidisciplinary strategy supported on computer programing that can contribute to set school into the right direction and turn students into effectively active participants on their education. Development and sustainability in a global society are only possible with informed consumers and a good digital task force. Introducing computer programming in European school is a trend and a challenge that is being embraced by several initiatives. This paper emerges from one of those initiatives and describes the strategy adopted to integrate technology in students' curriculum in schools from Portugal, Greece and Italy, through coding and multidisciplinary projects design and development.

Keywords: Coding skills · Game creation · Digital task force
Computer programming

1 Introduction

Technology is evolving at such a pace that digital literacy is a growing issue to be addressed by all sectors of the society [1, 2]. Development and sustainability in this global society is only possible with informed consumers and a good digital task force

© ICST Institute for Computer Sciences, Social Informatics and Telecommunications Engineering 2018
A. L. Brooks et al. (Eds.): ArtsIT 2017/DLI 2017, LNICST 229, pp. 458–468, 2018.
https://doi.org/10.1007/978-3-319-76908-0_44

[3]. This means to prepare young students for a digital society, for the upcoming digital jobs, to gain the skills and confidence they need to use digital technology, not only to support their learning but also in their future workplace and so on [3]. In this social economic environment, coding represents one of the key competences that must be acquired by all young students in the scope of 21st Century Skills [4, 5]. Coding is the art of telling a computer how to perform complex tasks. Once students know how to code, they can create virtual worlds within the computer where the only limits are their own imagination.

It's important to bridge the gap between students' skills developed at schools and young people skills needed in the working society. At school, the dominant pedagogy remains "chalk and talk" [6]. Schools "kill" students' creativity and they must change to meet students' needs, because schooling time is short and must be recognized as an important phase of students' lives by all the educational stakeholders and mainly by themselves [7]. It's almost common sense that it's time to adopt more active pedagogies. Technology projects are one way to bring students and their enthusiasm back to school [8]. It's important to create a fertile environment for learning, adopting pedagogies and methods, design and technology projects, that embrace interdisciplinary approaches, usually associated to liberal arts such as studio based learning [6].

Technology can be the instigator for the revolution to happen in education, just as it is doing with several workforces around the world that are being transformed by devices ant the cloud. But, we can't forget that technology at school is just a tool, to truly benefit of digital transformation, schools must recognize that students today learn different than the generations before them [9]. Furthermore, technology doesn't need to replace the curriculum, it can enhance it, leading to deeper student engagement and boosting important skills like creativity and collaboration that students will need in tomorrow's workforce [9]. Peachey's insight on this tells it all:

> Technology can empower the students of today to create the world of tomorrow. The students we equip with digital skills today will work in careers we haven't even thought of yet, and build new technology that we can't even begin to imagine. Educators, parents, and technology companies have a responsibility to provide them with the best education and tools possible to make this future a reality. Technology is the key to helping our students succeed, think creatively, and ultimately create a better world. [9, np]

Additionally, the concept of Science, Technology, Engineering, the Arts and Mathematics (STEAM) education, is emerging as a model of how boundaries between traditional academic subjects can be removed so that science, technology, engineering, arts and mathematics can be structured into an integrated curriculum [6].

It's important to reinforce that schooling time is short and it is important to make the most of it, preparing students for life. For this to be possible, school must evolve, endorsing pedagogy changes and learning approaches.

In this scenario, problem-based and project based learning approaches can be examples of strategies that encourage students to become more actively engaged in their own learning [3]. They must be given the opportunity to learn by doing, developing projects, using technology, learning to code and even being able to create their own programs and computer games.

Game creation as an educational strategy supported on computer programing or coding and in a multidisciplinary pedagogical approach can contribute to change the way schools are preparing young people for life [10]. Learning to code isn't easy. A few years ago, learning to code included lots of books, some basic online tutorials and a whole lot of experimentation. Last years, many changes have happened, there exist interactive courses, tons of online tutorials and games to practice coding [11]. A game itself probably isn't going to teach someone to program or code. Games make practice fun and it's easy to spend hours reinforcing coding skills without even realizing it. The potential benefits of using games for learning are clear and they can be more successful than teaching traditional approaches [12]. Furthermore, these games can help students to learn curriculum topics but also improve motivation, intellectual openness, work ethic, conscientiousness, and positive self-evaluation [12].

Thus, coding is an emerging globally priority, much remains to be done in Europe, especially concerning the need to promote real initiatives that can support coding activities in schools. Even though the trend to introduce computing and programming at school as a core curriculum subject has been identified, this task hasn't been easy [5]. Some countries have already done so, and many others are intending to. Portugal, Greece and Italy are among the later or trying to consolidate a few lose initiatives.

Besides the will to introduce computing at school, it is important to help teachers developing the competences to teach coding to students, as well as their own coding competences. Junior Code Academy (JCA) is an European project that also aimed to help teachers at this task. The scenario from Portuguese school's partner was the ignition to establish a set of lessons to help teachers teach students from 10 to 15 years old to code. Another Important contribute to help teachers introducing programming in school, pointed out a set of resources, from which Scratch and Massachusetts Institute of Technology (MIT) App Inventor were elected as learning tools to use at JCA [13]. Scratch and MIT App Inventor are both Creative Commons licenses [13].

JCA project mission is to expand the minds of young students (10–15 years old) and provide them with the right set of tools and skills to meet the needs of tomorrow, implementing a learning strategy under the scope of the demands of 21st century key competences, such as logical reasoning and problem solving.

An overview of the methodology used developing JCA project is described next, as well as the preliminary results gathered and analyzed till now, since this is an ongoing research yet.

2 Methodology

The ongoing project lies down on a design research methodology. Globally, the project intended to design and test a strategy for introducing coding at school, for students between 10 to 15 years old, in the European countries involved. To achieve this main goal, the project consortium conducted a survey to collect data about the state of art on coding at school, in Portugal, Greece and Italy. Then a pilot guide was created and tested in the Portuguese school partner. From this pilot, a functional set of 10 lessons per school year were defined and materials and resources compiled, for the international implementation at the project partner schools'.

This paper describes the ongoing research and presents the main data collected, so far.

Research methodology was developed into these phases: (A) survey on state of art on coding implementation at each school partner, (B) pilot test at Portuguese school partner and (C) international implementation at the Italian and Greek school partners'.

In this scope, several instruments were constructed, validated by experts and deployed to all the participants intervenient in the study. These instruments included a survey and monitoring tools that were applied to students and teachers during the pilot and international implementation phases. Preliminary results as well as data collected was analyzed and are presented in next sections.

3 Ongoing Research

The preliminary results presented now are organized accordingly to the design research steps previously mentioned: (A) state of art on coding implementation at each school partner; (B) pilot testing, and (C) international implementation.

3.1 State of Art on Coding Implementation at Each School Partner

The survey conducted represents the efforts to identify and analyze the state of art on coding implementation at each partner school in what concerns: (a) Policies in the field, and (b) Contextual needs based on data about available infrastructures, connectivity and equipment.

It was answered mostly by schools' partner project coordinators or headmasters and it was reported that:

(i) *Agrupamento de Escolas de Aveiro* (AEA) - 2449 students, 104 classes, 233 teachers and 62 staff members, and comprises all grades from kindergarten to 12th grade. AEA is a schools' cluster with 7 schools' buildings in a 30 km area;

(ii) *5th Gymnasium* (Junior High School*) of Heraklion* (GH) - 420 students, 18 classes, 41 teachers and no staff members, and comprises the following grades: 7th grade, 8th grade and 9th grade;

(iii) *Scuola Media Statale Dante Alighieri* (DA) - 700 students, 30 classes, about 70 teachers and 8/10 staff members and it comprises the following grades: 6th grade, 7th grade and 8th grade;

(iv) *Istituto D'Istruzione Superiore Secondaria Marco Polo* (MP) - 1500 students, 65 classes, about 110 teachers and 20 staff members and it comprises the following grades: 8th grade, 9th grade, 10th grade, 11th grade and 12th grade.

Information and Communication Technologies (ICT) was reported to already be part of the curriculum at Italian and Greek schools', but not at Portuguese ones. It was indicated that in Portugal there were plans to integrate ICT as part of the curriculum soon, because, and we quote, "the government has projects to implement ICT in the next years".

About computer programming or coding it was reported that it was not part of the curriculum in Portugal and Italy (see Fig. 1) and it was reported to be unknown if there were any plans to integrate it in the Portuguese and Italian schools soon.

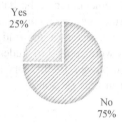

Fig. 1. Computer programming/coding is already part of the curriculum.

The respondent from DA reported computer programming or coding not to be part of the curriculum in Italy, neither to be part of any plans to be integrated in Italian schools soon.

About the contextual needs, it was reported by each school partner that:

(i) AEA - students had access to computers with internet in specific classrooms and library, and that the equipment available in the school were computers and internet. Finally, it was reported that it was unknown if any other equipment would be needed to be acquired for the JCA project.

(ii) GH - students had access to computers with internet in specific classrooms and computer labs, and that the equipment available in the school were computers, internet, printer, scanner and digital camera. Finally, it was reported that it was unknown if any other equipment would be needed to be acquired for the JCA project.

(iii) DA - students had access to computers with internet in specific classrooms, computer labs and library, and that the equipment available in the school were computers, laptops, tablets, internet and printer. Finally, it was reported that it wouldn't be needed to acquire equipment for the JCA project.

(iv) MP - students had access to computers with internet in computer labs and laptops that students could request, and that the equipment available in the school were computers, laptops, tablets, internet, printer, scanner and digital camera. Finally, it was reported that it might be needed to acquire any other equipment for the JCA project, but it was not identified which.

Globally, the school partners reported that they were at an early stage of adopting strategies to implement computer programming or coding in their schools and JCA project was considered an important step in that process.

3.2   Pilot Phase

The pilot phase consisted on the preparation of a set of lesson plans and its implementation at AEA, in Portugal. Five classes, one per school grade, two teachers and about 130 students, 10 to 15 years old were involved. The pilot was started in the third week of September 2016 and was developed till the end of the first scholar term, December 2016.

The results presented here emerged from the analysis of the monitoring data collected with the tools created for that purpose for both, students and teachers. A total of 1072 responses were collected from students of all the 5 classes along at least 10 lessons (see Fig. 2). And, a total of 53 responses were collect from teachers along at least 10 lessons (see Fig. 4) per class.

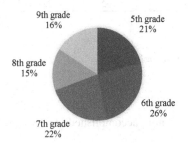

Grade	No. responses	%
5th grade	228	21,3%
6th grade	275	25,7%
7th grade	241	22,5%
8th grade	158	14,7%
9th grade	170	15,9%

Fig. 2. Students responses by school grade

Students inquiry and scales used were the following:

  (i)   Lesson liking (Scale: 1 = not at all to 5 = very much);
  (ii) Lessons activities difficulty (Scale: 1 = not at all to 5 = very much);
  (iii) Time to finish the activities in each lesson (Scale: 1 = no time to finish to 5 = time to finish all activities); and,
  (iv) Global lesson evaluation (Scale: 1 = lesson didn't go well at all to 5 = Lesson did go very well).

Students perceptions indicated that the majority, 67,6% liked the lessons very much, and only 3%, reported that they didn't like the lessons. A great number of students, 38,7% considered that they didn't have difficulties doing the activities. Most of the students, 73% considered that they had enough time to finish the tasks proposed for each lesson. And, globally students' evaluation considered that lessons went well or very well by 88,3% of the students (see Fig. 3).

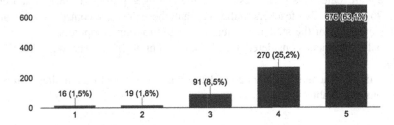

Fig. 3. Students global lessons evaluation (Scale: 1 = the lesson didn't go well at all to 5 = the lesson did go very well)

There were 2 teachers assigned to these classes, but not both were present in lesson at the same time, one was responsible to teach classes from 5th to 7th grade and the other was responsible to teach classes from 8th and 9th grade.

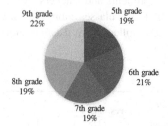

Grade	No. responses	%
5th grade	10	18,9%
6th grade	11	20,8%
7th grade	10	18,9%
8th grade	10	18,9%
9th grade	12	22,6%

Fig. 4. Teachers responses by school grade

Teachers inquiry and scales used were the following:

(i)   Lesson plan accomplishment (Scale: 1 = not accomplished to 5 = fully accomplished);
(ii) Activities purposed adjusted to students' capacities (Scale: 1 = not adjusted to 5 = well adjusted);
(iii) Difficulties revealed by most students (Scale: 1 = lots of difficulties to 5 = no difficulties at all);
(iv) Interest revealed by most students doing the activities purposed (Scale: 1 = no interest to 5 = lots of interest);
(v)   Enthusiasm revealed by most students doing the activities purposed (Scale: 1 = no enthusiasm to 5 = lots of enthusiasm);
(vi) Contribute of the lessons towards a higher motivation of the students to learn how to program computers (Scale: 1 = nothing to 5 = a lot); and
(vii) Global lessons evaluation (Scale: 1 = the lesson didn't go well at all to 5 = the lesson did go very well).

Teachers reported that most of the lesson plans were fully accomplished, 81,1%, and that they had the perception that the activities purposed were well adjusted to the students' capacities, 77,4%. They also pointed out that most of the students didn't reveal difficulties, 60,4%, or difficulties at all, 39,6%. Teachers considered that almost all students revealed lots of interest doing the activities purposed, 98,1%, and enthusiasm, 96,2%. Finally, teachers indicated that these lessons contributed towards a higher motivation of the students to learn how to program computers.

Globally, teachers considered that lessons went well or very well, 96,2% (see Fig. 5).

Most of the teachers' answers considered that there weren't anomalies to report in the lessons (see Table 1).

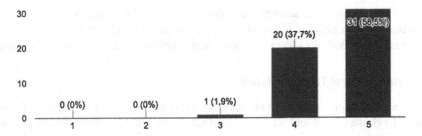

Fig. 5. Teachers global lessons evaluation (Scale: 1 = the lesson didn't go well at all to 5 = the lesson did go very well)

Table 1. Anomalies reported that affected the lessons

Anomalies	No. responses	%
Nothing to report	43	81,1%
No electricity	0	–
No Internet access	0	–
Several computers were or went out of order	0	–
Students arrived late to the lesson	0	–
There were behavioral/discipline issues to report	1	1,9%
Other	10	18,9%

As "other" anomalies teachers reported the following:

- JCA questionnaire complexity (5th, 6th and 7th grade) – reported 3 times, one by school year.
- Students' behavior, they speak too loud (8th grade) – reported 1 time.
- App Inventor is not working or working badly (9th grade) – reported 1 time.
- Noisy students (8th grade) – reported 1 time.
- Slow Internet access, so apps testing time was longer than expected (9th grade) – reported 1 time.
- Noisy students and to many for one class (8th grade) – reported 1 time.
- 45 min were not enough to help and support properly all the students, using a new app. Students revealed low autonomy skills. (8th grade) – reported 1 time.
- To many students in the class to support (8th grade) – reported 1 time.

The pilot monitoring highlighted several issues, such as that students liked coding classes and wanted to learn more. Students were keen on project based learning strategy. These findings were shared with international school project partners and three main suggestions were made:

- lessons should be longer than 45 min;
- classes should have a maximum of 20 students; and,
- lessons would gain if there were at least 2 teachers in the classroom.

These suggestions were adopted accordingly with the possibilities of each school partner, and, besides other variations, all adopted 60 min duration lessons.

Next, preliminary data form Italy and Greek implementations are briefly presented.

3.3   International Implementation

In Greece, the implementation took place at GH, in Crete, Greece. It started in the first week of February 2017 and was developed till the end of May. A 12-lesson plan was implemented.

A total of 292 responses were collected from students. In summary, 38,7% of the students reported that they liked the lessons very much and some students, about 11%, considered that they didn't like the lessons.

When asked about the difficulty of the activities, students reported that they felt that those were not difficult at all, 45,9% and only a few, 7,9%, stated they were very difficult. Many students, 49%, considered that they had enough time to finish all the activities purposed during the lessons and 9,6% considered they didn't. Several students, 35,6% evaluated the lessons globally went very well and 10,6% considered the lessons didn't go well.

A total of 47 responses were collected from teachers, during the same reported period.

Globally, teachers considered that most of the lesson plans have been fully accomplished, 72,3%, and that the purposed activities were adjusted to students' capacities, 76,6%. Teachers also considered that students didn't reveal difficulties doing the activities, 68,1%, and the majority, reported that students did, both, participate with interest and enthusiasm doing the activities purposed, 76,6%. Most teachers also pointed out that the lessons contributed to motivate the students to learn how to program computers, 80,9%. Teachers considered that only a minority of students, 2,1%, revealed difficulties, but that none of them revealed lack of interest or enthusiasm.

Overall teachers considered the lessons went well or very well, 72,3%.

Finally, teachers involved considered that there weren't almost any anomalies to report. However, there were 4,3% reported referrals on behavioral/discipline issues and 6,4% referrals on other anomalies. As "other" anomalies teachers reported the following:

- There was not enough time to complete the lesson – reported twice.
- There was a problem with the Internet.

In Italy, the implementation is still taking place at both schools in Bari, Italy, MP and DA, by the time this paper was written. In Italy, the implementation started later and was not finish yet, nevertheless we could present just a few preliminary results.

A total of 310 responses were collected from students till the 25th of May (103 from MP and 207 from DA). In summary, students liked the lessons very much, 70% and reported that those were not at all difficult, 42% and only a few, 1%, stated they were very difficult. Most students, 62%, considered that they had enough time to finish all the activities purposed during the lessons and 1% considered they didn't. Most of the students, 74%, stated the lessons went very well.

A total of 23 responses were collected from teachers, during the same reported period (7 from MP and 12 from DA). Globally, teachers considered that most of the lesson plans, 96%, have been fully accomplished, and that the activities were adjusted to students' capacities, 95%. Teachers also considered that students didn't reveal difficulties doing the activities, 61%, and the majority, 83%, did both, participate with interest and enthusiasm doing the activities purposed. Teachers, 82%, also considered that the lessons contributed to motivate the students to learn how to program computers. Overall the lessons were going well and very well, 100%.

Data collected so far, allowed us to understand that students were very interested in learning how to code, but that there were some factors, like lesson duration, number of lessons in the plan, number of students per class and number of teachers in the classroom that must be further analyzed.

Final thoughts are presented next as the first conclusions of this ongoing project and research.

4   Main Findings and First Conclusions

The main ideas that emerge from a preliminary data analysis pointed out that 10 lessons to introduce programming at school is the minimum lesson number required. So, we recommend a minimum of 12 lessons, if the school year is organized in terms of about 12 weeks, or between 12 to 15 lessons if the school year is organized in semesters. Classes should ideally have 20 students' maximum. If classes are bigger they should be broken apart in smaller groups for the coding lessons (e.g. 12 students). And, there should be ideally 2 teachers in the classroom, to better support the students work, since project based learning strategy must be the learning methodology to explore.

Even though the research presented here is still an ongoing project, we are aware that more than the impact, that Erasmus + project - Junior Code Academy (JCA): Enhancing coding skills in European schools, might have in the consortium of partners created to develop it and in the students and teachers involved, it is expected that the ongoing research can provide significant data that will allow to better achieve the project goals, namely to help European teachers and schools' leaders to promote the introduction of coding at schools. This paper intends to be a contribution on that way.

Further research and data analysis must be made to enrich the preliminary findings identified. We expect to raise the awareness for the need to prevent some flaws that might influence the introduction of coding at European schools, so they can be minimized. By achieving this, we believe our findings may contribute towards the access and the enhancing of coding skills for all students.

A new school, with interested and enthusiastic students is easier to achieve when they can learn meaningful subjects while participating in project based learning activities and gaming... or even developing their own games, learning to master the basics of game creation. Introducing computer programming or coding at school is a must for European schools and students.

Acknowledgments. With the support of the European Commission, EU Erasmus + Program, under the action type Strategic Partnerships for School Education: "Junior Code Academy – Enhancing Coding Skills in European Schools" (2015-1-PT01-KA201-013121), coordinated by Code for All, Lda.
This article is responsibility of the authors and not from European Commission.

References

1. Binkley, M., Erstad, O., Herman, J., Raizen, S., Ripley, M., Rumble, M.: ACTS Draft White Papers. University of Melbourne. Cisco. Intel. Microsoft: ATCS (2010)
2. McCormack, A.: The e-Skills Manifesto - A Call to Arms. EuropeanSchoolnet (2010)
3. Ertmer, P.A., Ottenbreit-Leftwitch, A.T.: Teacher technology change: How knowledge, confidence, beliefs, and culture intersect. J. Res. Technol. Educ. **42**(3), 255–284 (2010). http://www.iste.org/jrte
4. Balanskat, A., Engelhart, K.: Computing our future: Computer programming and coding - Priorities, school curricula and initiatives across Europe. European Schoolnet (2014). http://www.eun.org/c/document_library/get_file?uuid=521cb928-6ec4-4a86-b522-9d8fd5cf60ce&groupId=43887
5. Balanskat, A., Engelhart, K.: Computing our future: Computer programming and coding - Priorities, school curricula and initiatives across Europe – Update 2015. European Schoolnet (2015). http://www.eun.org/c/document_library/get_file?uuid=3596b121-941c-4296-a760-0f4e4795d6fa&groupId=43887
6. Connor, A.M., Karmokar, S., Whittington, C., Walker, C.: Full STEAM ahead: a manifesto for integrating arts pedagogics into STEM education. In: Proceedings of the 2014 IEEE International Conference on Teaching, Assessment and Learning in Engineering (2015)
7. Robinson, K.: The Element: How Finding Your Passion Changes Everything. Penguin, New York (2009)
8. Barbosa, I., Pombo, L., Moreira, F., Loureiro, M.J., Loureiro, M.J., Guimaraes, D., Magalhães, J.: Junior code academy: an innovative project in Portugal. In: Proceedings of the ICEM 2015 "Any Time, Any Place Learning", Medellin - Colombia, 29 September–2 October 2015 (2015)
9. Peachey, N.: "Nik Peachey's insight: Very utopian view of edtech. From news.microsoft.com - The technology revolution transforming education, 14 June 2017. https://news.microsoft.com/europe/2017/06/13/the-technology-revolution-transforming-education/#sm.000n79v2u10j4eax10b7ze6ox8fhd%23KP8p58HRu3PHOFKq.97
10. Kapp, K.M.: The Gamification of Learning and Instruction: Game-Based Methods and Strategies for Training and Education. Wiley, New York (2012)
11. Chapman, C.: 15 free games that will help you learn how to code. Business Insider: Tech Insider, 5 April 2017. http://www.businessinsider.com/15-free-games-that-will-help-you-learn-how-to-code-2017-4/#-14
12. Sharples, M., de Roock, R., Ferguson, R., Gaved, M., Herodotou, C., Koh, E., Kukulska-Hulme, A., Looi, C.-K, McAndrew, P., Rienties, B., Weller, M., Wong, L.H.: Innovating Pedagogy 2016: Open University. Innovation Report 5. Milton Keynes: The Open University (2016)
13. García-Peñalvo, F.J., Rees, A.M., Hughes, J., Jormanainen, I., Toivonen, T., Vermeersch, J.: A survey of resources for introducing coding into schools. In: Fourth International Conference on Technological Ecosystems for Enhancing Multiculturality – TEEM 2016 (2016)

Creativity in Co-design for Physical Education: Comparing Contributions of Children and Professionals

Danića Mast[1,2(✉)], Sylvia Schipper[1,3], Fenne van Doorn[2,4],
Alice Schut[5], Mathieu Gielen[4], and Sanne de Vries[1]

[1] Research Group Healthy Lifestyle in a Supporting Environment,
Faculty for Health, Nutrition and Sports,
The Hague University of Applied Sciences, Johanna Westerdijkplein 75,
2521 EN The Hague, The Netherlands
{d.mast, s.j.schipper, s.i.devries}@hhs.nl
[2] Faculty for IT and Design, Communication and Multimedia Design,
User Experience Design, The Hague University of Applied Sciences,
Johanna Westerdijkplein 75, 2521 EN The Hague, The Netherlands
f.a.p.vandoorn@hhs.nl
[3] Faculty Technology, Innovation and Society, Industrial Design Engineering,
The Hague University of Applied Sciences, Johanna Westerdijkplein 75,
2521 EN The Hague, The Netherlands
[4] Faculty of Industrial Design Engineering, Delft University of Technology,
Landbergstraat 15, 2628 CE Delft, The Netherlands
m.a.gielen@tudelft.nl
[5] Department of Science Education and Communication,
Faculty of Applied Sciences, Delft University of Technology, Lorentzweg 1,
2628 CJ Delft, The Netherlands
a.schut@tudelft.nl

Abstract. This study is carried out within the context of a research and inno-vation project *Co-design with Kids* that aims to support teaching of broad so-called '21st century' skills. In this project, design toolboxes for use within primary education are developed and studied, with real life clients and assign-ments. In the case described in this paper, the assignment was to create new concepts for physical education (PE). To be able to assess the value of design outcomes created in a co-design trajectory by children, we compared their design outcomes to those created in a similar design process by professionals. Six teams of children (n = 21, 11–12 years old) and three teams of professionals (n = 10, with a background in design, sports or physical education) developed concepts in separate co-creation sessions. We present a first assessment of the differences and similarities in creativity of the design outcomes of the two groups. This assessment of textual summaries shows no remarkable differences between design outcomes of children and those of professionals in terms of elaboration, originality and relevance. This indicates that children could be involved as design partners. Further research is needed to gain insight into the specific value of involving children as design partners.

© ICST Institute for Computer Sciences, Social Informatics and Telecommunications Engineering 2018
A. L. Brooks et al. (Eds.): ArtsIT 2017/DLI 2017, LNICST 229, pp. 469–478, 2018.
https://doi.org/10.1007/978-3-319-76908-0_45

Keywords: Co-design · Physical education · Children · Professionals Co-creation

1 Introduction

In this study, we involved teams of professionals with a background in design, sport or physical education and teams of children as designers to invent new concepts for exercises in physical education. This paper describes the differences and similarities between the design outcomes of these two groups.

1.1 Involving Children in Physical Education Development

Children generally like to move and be physically active, but for physical education (PE) to be more effective, PE exercises should match their perceptual world [13, 20]. There are many efforts to make PE more motivating, better targeted and more effective. However, children are often participants in studies on PE, but they are rarely involved in the development of its content. Involving children in the development of PE can make children more motivated to participate, leading to increased effectiveness of physical education.

1.2 Context of the Research

The study is carried out within the context of a research and innovation project *Co-design with Kids* that aims to support teaching of broad so-called '21st century' skills. These skills are hard to train by themselves; they need a coherent setting and content to train them. As many of the 21st century skills are also addressed within design processes and professional design education has a large array of tools and techniques to train design skills, a project is carried out to develop and study design toolboxes for use within primary education.

This project is carried out with real clients (companies and public organizations), to ensure a realistic and motivating setting for the children. In the case described in this paper, the client asked for ideas for a 'Gym of the Future'. As part of this research project, the question is addressed what the creative quality of the design outcomes from children is, and thus the value of such projects for the clients.

1.3 Research Questions/Goal

To be able to assess the value of design outcomes created in a co-design trajectory by children, we will compare their design outcomes to the design outcomes of a similar design process by professionals. With this approach, we aim to gain insights that can contribute to answering the following questions:

- What are the differences and similarities of (physical education game-) design outcomes created in co-design sessions by professionals vs. Children in terms of creativity?
- What is the value of children as design partners and what is the quality of their design outcomes?

2   Related Research

2.1   Co-creation: Involving Children in Design Assignments

In co-design (also known as participatory design), stakeholders are involved in a design process [3, 5, 8], often during several stages. Previous research shows many benefits from involving children in the co-design of technology [7, 8]. Innovations often originate in the user domain (instead of the manufacturer) [16] and children can come up with great, creative, outside the box solutions for problems [4], being experts on their own user experiences.

Though co-design with children (CDC) is widely acknowledged and applied, especially in the Interaction Design community, views on its value vary widely. Van Doorn [6] argues for a co-research approach in which the value of children's contributions lies in mapping the context of their current lives as an inspiration ground for design. Van Mechelen et al. [15] argue that CDC outcomes can be analyzed to uncover children's underlying values. Iversen et al. [9] see CDC as a form of child emancipation and emphasize that "the objective of design is not only technological products, but for participants to develop new insights, design abilities, and a critical and reflective stance toward technology through their engagement in design work", thus assigning the merit of CDC to children's development rather than to a direct design outcome.

Criticism on co-design with children focuses primarily on the proper inclusion of children in all stages of the design process [17]. Van Mechelen et al. [14] have analyzed forms of group dynamics that challenge the co-design process with children. A critical reflection of design solutions stemming from children's participation is harder to come by.

Given that the current academic debate points at such different merits of CDC as emancipation, uncovering underlying values, or mapping a context, the basic question rises why the design outcome itself is no longer a central theme. It may be time to once again evaluate if design solutions of CDC have a better or different quality from those of professionals.

2.2   Comparing Design Outcomes of Different Types of Designers

Little research has been done into the comparison of designs by children vs. adults or professionals. Related research does compare the outcomes of design trajectories using different types of design tools and with different age groups.

In a study by Thang et al. [21] outcomes of brainstorming vs. prototyping by children have been compared and assessed by an expert jury on creativity, novelty, non-obviousness, workability, relevance and thoroughness of ideas. The ideas were judged on transcripts of the explanation of the outcomes. Brainstorming outcomes were considered more creative, novel and surprising and prototyping outcomes were more relevant and workable.

A comparison of design outcomes by young children vs. teenagers by Chimbo et al. [5] showed that young children focused on decoration and graphical content, while teenagers emphasized on textual content and usability. This shows that when designing technology for different age groups it would be important to involve different groups of children and not consider all children (of different ages) as one homogenous group.

Druin [7] argues for inter-generational design teams, suggesting that the contributions from children and adults are different and complementary.

2.3 Assessing Creativity

To be able to assess the value of design outcomes we will assess and compare their level of creativity to be able to give a first indication of similarities and differences.

Creativity is the creation, innovation, expression, production and discovery [19] of ideas. It is about bringing something into being. This can be done through generating something novel or through transforming the existent [10].

Assessing creativity is considered complex and difficult [12]. Nonetheless multiple research approaches generally identify similar componential factors: originality/novelty, usefulness/appropriateness/relevance and fluency/quantity, elaboration/variation [16, 18, 22].

The Consensual Assessment Technique (CAT) [2] is an approach where multiple expert judges assess the actual creativity of things that have been produced as a whole. Instead of assessing predefined criteria. However, correlations have been found with other judgements such as 'novel use of materials' and 'complexity' [1] corresponding with aspects defined by other researchers.

3   Method/Execution

3.1   Co-design with Kids

In the first part of this study, 21 children (11–12 years old), were divided in 6 teams of 3 or 4 children. Each team chose one out of four assignments based upon problems they experience in PE lessons: 'Making explanation more fun', 2 teams; 'Making Balancing more fun', 2 teams; 'Game that allows cheating', 1 team; 'Fair teams', 1 team. In six weekly one-hour sessions they developed a concept using various design tools for divergent thinking (sensitizing, mind maps, brainstorming, prototyping), convergent thinking (dots-method [11], C-box, user-testing) and reflection (process wall). The sessions took place in the classroom and in the school gymnasium. During these sessions children were guided by their own classroom teacher. The assignment was introduced by a external PE teacher, to whom the children also presented interim results on which they received feedback. The final concepts were presented in the school gymnasium and were recorded on film.

3.2   Co-design with Professionals

In the second part of this study, 10 professionals, of which 3 had a background in design and 7 in sports/physical education were invited to a 4-h design session on one evening. The design session took place in a class room. The professionals were divided in three groups, with an as much as possible even distribution of people with different backgrounds. Each group had one member with a design background that could guide the design process. They had the freedom to choose their own method for their creative process, as they would in a real design context. Each group received one assignment (based on the assignments that were chosen most by the children): 'Fair teams'; 'Making explanations more fun'; 'Making Balancing more fun'. The final presentations were recorded on film.

3.3   Creativity Assessment Criteria

Based on Torrance Test of Creative Thinking [22], a toolkit for idea competitions by Piller and Walcher [16] and work by Reinartz and Saffer [18] we identified three criteria to assess the creativity of the concepts of children and professionals:

- *Elaboration:* The degree in which concepts are complete and detailed. To which extent the ideas are thought through [16].
- *Originality:* The extent in which results are novel and not a derivative of existing concepts [18].
- *Relevance:* The degree in which a solution is useful for a given problem [16].

3.4   Summary and Assessment of Design Concepts

Each design outcome from both children and professionals was summarized in text by a researcher based on the videos of the final presentations and checked by a second, independent researcher who compared the summaries to the presentation videos ensuring a truthful explanation of all concepts and to make sure that the summarizer didn't fill in any blanks. This ensured a similar representation of children's and professional's ideas.

The summaries were assessed based on the previously drafted criteria (elaboration, originality, relevance) by a third independent designer/researcher who described noticeable substantive differences and similarities between concepts. This designer/researcher has a background in design education and is experienced in objectively assessing design outcomes. In this study, due to practical constraints, this researcher was aware which group (children or professionals) had created each concept.

4   Results

4.1   Elaboration

Differences
Children seemed more specific in identifying physical devices and physical actions. They describe them and the rules of the game in a clear and specific manner. Furthermore, they describe the giving of instruction to players and the type of penalties within a game more often. Additions (such as projections or augmented reality) are to situations or surroundings that are familiar to the children. Their ideas are mostly based on existing situations and play forms. They combine different, existing gym and sports equipment and materials (such as using a stick while standing on a Pedalo balancing board), tasks (such as different angles of computer questions) and actions (such as ball

throwing). They don't mention adjusting difficulty to the skill levels of individuals or offering help, in contrast to professionals.

The concepts of professionals are all rather complex, with various phases in game play. They add complexity to exercises by adding different phases or levels (such as the help of a virtual Messi in a higher level). Because they are less specific in describing the rules and actions, they just give an impression of the game play, these concepts seemed more abstract.

Another noticeable difference between concepts of children and professionals is that professionals gave their concepts a title, adding more context and explanation to their concepts.

Similarities

Professionals added complexity through phases which often makes the game play too complex and incomprehensible. In the 'three-stage rocket' concept ('Making balancing more fun' assignment) there is an accumulation of many activities (Mastermind, traditional exercises) that have no good coherence and are not well thought out in why and in which way they succeed each other.

The concepts of children are more simple, but when they do add complexity (which happened in a concept where goals that function as 'free zones' were introduced), their concepts also seem somewhat incoherent.

Conclusion

Both groups seem to elaborate in their concepts by either adding objects (children) or phases (professionals), but often this made the concepts more complex instead of adding value.

For this criterion, it is not possible to conclude if children executed the assignment better or worse compared to professionals in terms of elaborateness, at most in a different way, more explicitly and at a lower level of abstraction than the professionals.

4.2 Originality

Differences

The design outcomes of children are variations on existing concepts, to which they add more freedom and surprising elements. That does seem to make the concepts more motivating to play, but only slightly more original than existing concepts.

Professionals invent new elements, such as a Teacher in a control room (in the 'Escape Room' concept) or AR-characters and a sorting hat (in the 'Sorting Hat' concept). These are novel elements to PE, but often already existing concepts outside PE. Through combining with and adding these new aspects from other areas to more known PE practices, the originality of their design outcomes increases.

Similarities

The children's and professionals' solutions are novel and not similar to existing concepts. Allocating freedom (such as a play situation/environment that adjusts to a child's preferences) makes instruction more fun in concepts created by both groups.

Conclusion

Overall, professionals perform slightly better than children on originality. The difference between both groups is caused by the slightly higher novelty and richer context of the concepts described by professionals.

4.3   Relevance

Differences

The differences for this criterion are not so much found between the groups but much more between the assignments. Both children and professionals created relevant ideas for the 'Making explanation more fun' and 'Making balancing more fun' assignments. Neither managed to create a solution for 'Fair teams' that will last longer than just one game play. This might be because this assignment has a more psychological aspect than just a physical setting with straightforward rules for game play; we suspect the rules designed by both children and professionals can be manipulated once someone is familiar with the game. For example, in the 'without talking' concept, where teams are made based on questionnaire answers, players can discuss beforehand what preferences they fill in in the questionnaire.

The adults are better with 'The escape room' concept (where different rooms have different physical tasks that have to be accomplished before moving to the next room), making the implicit explanation more surprising and rewarding (such as Messi as a virtual guide when a higher level is reached) and therefore seems more 'fun', than the intertwined explanation of the children's ideas.

In "Making balancing more fun" implicit balancing is enhanced in different forms. In both concepts created by children, teams battle each other making the movement more complex (striking back a ball with a stick while crossing the floor on a Pedalo board), while the competition makes it fun. One of the professionals' concepts consisted of a virtual reality environment that makes the balancing exercise more complex and also more motivating and exciting.

Similarities

Both children and adults use implicit instruction for different elements to create interesting exercises. Both have difficulties designing a solution for a more psychological problem.

Conclusion

Children and professionals create relevant concepts that solve the given problem. They give different accents, but this has no effect on the value of the outcome relevancy.

5   Conclusion

This first assessment of differences and similarities of the design outcomes of children and professionals show that the design outcomes of both groups are more or less equivalent on the whole in terms of creativity, although there are some differences in details.

For Physical Education, our results show that input from children aged 11–12 years can be of equal value as input from professionals in the early ideation stage. In developing PE curricula, children could be valuable co-design partners and could be involved more.

Since our first findings demonstrate no remarkable differences between the design outcomes of children and professionals, this justifies follow-up research that looks in more detail at the aspects influencing the creative quality of design outcomes of children versus professionals.

Amidst the academic debate on the various reasons for CDC and the shift away from valuing the design outcomes as such, this study suggests that the quality of the design solutions is still a relevant focus.

6 Discussion and Further Work

This study has some strengths and limitations that should be taken into account when interpreting the results.

Spatial Context. The different contexts (gymnasium & classroom for the children; workshop room for the professionals) in which both groups carried out their assignment could have resulted in differences in focus. For example, the use of gym equipment by children because of their presence in the gym.

Personal Context. Some differences in the design outcomes can be explained by personal context, (such as the age difference between groups). The use of a title (and consequently increased context and explanation) for the concepts by professionals is something professionals would be more accustomed to. That children name penalties and instructions more often is likely because these are aspects that they come into contact with in their school context daily.

Background Professionals. Only three professionals had a professional design background (most had a PE background). Even though each team of professionals had one designer as a member, in a normal design setting a design team would consist of more designers. In future research, it would be interesting to see what the differences would be between groups of professionals with just a PE background or groups of professionals with just a design background and groups of children.

Trajectory. Both groups followed different design trajectories that might have been of influence on the design outcomes. Professionals spent less time on their assignment (4 h) than children (6 h, divided over 6 weeks). The difference in weeks over which the design process was spread gave children more time to let their ideas settle. Nonetheless, we didn't see this in the results. In further research, more similar trajectories would be preferable to be better able to identify the cause of similarities and differences.

Tools & Instruction. The professionals had complete freedom in their approach while the children had a specified toolkit to work with and instructors to guide them. This could have had effect on the outcomes and therefore the judgment of the concepts.

Further research is needed to explore what variables are of influence on the design outcomes for both children and professionals.

Concept Summaries. All concepts were summarized textually. A good addition would be to graphically summarize the concepts, all in the same manner. This allows objective evaluation solely based on design features although there will always be an element of interpretation in the translation of concepts into a 'neutral' format that cannot be attributed to either of the groups.

Anonymous & Objective Assessment. The assessing researcher knew which concepts were designed by which group. To be able to objectively assess the outcomes, in the next stage of this project an objective jury, consisting of multiple members, will assess anonymized concepts.

More Teams. We examined the design outcomes of one class of children. For further research, we should review the design outcomes of more classes from other schools to investigate the difference between different age groups, school types, and the contents of the toolkit that the children have worked with.

Creativity. The value of design outcomes doesn't solely rely on the level of creativity. Although it gives an indication and a way of comparing amongst results, in future research we should look into additional methods of assessing the value of design outcomes by children as design partners.

Acknowledgements. This project is funded by NWO-NRO under the 'Human Capital: 21st century skills' program. We would like to thank the professionals, the children and teacher of the participating school.

References

1. Amabile, T.M.: The social psychology of creativity: a componential conceptualization. J. Pers. Soc. Psychol. **45**(2), 357 (1983)
2. Baer, J., McKool, S.S.: Assessing creativity using the consensual assessment technique. In: Handbook of Research on Assessment Technologies, Methods, and Applications in Higher Education, pp. 65–77. IGI Global (2009)
3. Benton, L., Johnson, H., Ashwin, E., Brosnan, M., Growemeyer, B.: Developing IDEAS: supporting children with autism within a participatory design team. In: Proceedings of CHI 2012, pp. 1759–1764 (2012)
4. De Bono, E.: Children solve problems (1972)
5. Chimbo, B., Gelderblom, J.H.: Comparing young children and teenagers as partners in co-design of an educational technology solution. In: Proceedings of the ISI e-Skills for Knowledge Production and Innovation Conference, pp. 17–21, November 2014
6. Van Doorn, F., Gielen, M., Stappers, P.J.: Children as co-researchers: more than just a role-play. In: Proceedings of IDC 2014, pp. 237–240 (2014). https://doi.org/10.1145/2593968.2610461
7. Druin, A.: The Design of Children's Technology. Morgan Kaufmann Publishers, San Francisco (1999)

8. Druin, A.: The role of children in the design of new technology. Behav. Inf. Technol. **21**(1), 1–25 (2002)
9. Iversen, O., Smith, R., Dindler, C.: Child as protagonist: expanding the role of children in participatory design. In: Proceedings of IDC 2017, pp. 27–37 (2017)
10. Kaufman, J.C., Sternberg, R.J.: The Cambridge Handbook of Creativity. Cambridge University Press, Cambridge (2010)
11. Klapwijk, R.: De kunst van het kiezen: to stip or not to stip, 26 October 2011. https://www.wetenschapsknooppuntzh.nl/blog/de-kunst-van-het-kiezen-to-stip-or-not-to-stip/. Accessed 07 July 2017
12. Klapwijk, R.M.: Formative assessment of creativity. In: de Vries, M. (ed.) Handbook of Technology Education. SIHE, pp. 1–20. Springer, Cham (2017). https://doi.org/10.1007/978-3-319-38889-2_55-1
13. KVLO Topic Beleven in bewegen (BO) number 1, 31 January 2014. https://www.kennisbanksportenbewegen.nl/?file=6298&m=1459423514&action=file.download
14. van Mechelen, M., Gielen, M., vanden Abeele, V., Laenen, A., Zaman, B.: Exploring challenging group dynamics in participatory design with children. In: 13th International Conference on Interaction Design & Children, pp. 269–272 (2014). https://doi.org/10.1145/2593968.2610469
15. van Mechelen, M., Derboven, J., Laenen, A., Willems, B., Geerts, D., vanden Abeele, V.: The GLID method: moving from design features to underlying values in co-design. Int. J. Hum Comput Stud. **97**, 116–128 (2017). http://dx.doi.org/10.1016/j.ijhcs.2016.09.005
16. Piller, F.T., Walcher, D.: Toolkits for idea competitions: a novel method to integrate users in new product development. R&d Manage. **36**(3), 307–318 (2006). http://onlinelibrary.wiley.com/doi/10.1111/j.1467-9310.2006.00432.x/epdf
17. Read, J.C., Fitton, D., Sim, G., Horton, M.: How ideas make it through to designs: process and practice. In: Proceedings of the 9th Nordic Conference on Human–Computer Interaction (Nordi - CHI 2016), New York, Article 16, 10 p. ACM (2016). https://doi.org/10.1145/2971485.2971560
18. Reinartz, W., Saffert, P.: Creativity in advertising: when it works and when it doesn't. Harv. Bus. Rev. **91**(6), 106–111 (2013)
19. Schasfoort, B.: Beeldonderwijs en didactiek. Wolters-Noordhoff (2007)
20. Slot-Heijs, J., Lucassen, J., Collard, D.: Effecten van bewegingsonderwijs op sport- en beweeggedrag op latere leeftijd. Mulier Instituut (2017)
21. Thang, B., Sluis-Thiescheffer, W., Bekker, T., Eggen, B., Vermeeren, A., de Ridder, H.: Comparing the creativity of children's design solutions based on expert assessment. In: Proceedings of the 7th International Conference on Interaction Design and Children, pp. 266–273. ACM, June 2008
22. Torrance, P.: Verbal Tests. Forms A and B-Figural Tests, Forms A and B. The Torrance Tests of Creative Thinking-Norms-Technical Manual Research Edition, p. 6. Personnel Press, Princeton

The Impact of Dynamic Lighting in Classrooms. A Review on Methods

Ellen Kathrine Hansen[(✉)] , Stine Maria Louring Nielsen,
Diana Georgieva, and Kathrine Marie Schledermann

Lighting Design, Department of Architecture, Design and Media Technology,
Aalborg University, A.C. Meyers Vænge 15, 2450 Copenhagen, SV, Denmark
{ekh,stm,kat}@create.aau.dk,
diana.z.georgieva@gmail.com

Abstract. In order to understand how research can support lighting designs to improve nurturing environments for learning, a literature review was carried out. The review examined lighting research methods and parameters used for evaluating the effect of dynamic lighting in classrooms. The test parameter gaining most attention in the studies is academic performance; whereas qualitative test parameters, such as behaviour and mood, are addressed in less than a third of the selected studies. The analysis of these methods leads to a conclusion that learning environments to a broader extent should be studied and designed holistically through a mixed method approach. It is suggested that the potentials of dynamic lighting in learning environments are explored through design driven innovation and the use of mixed methods, in order to be able to put more emphasis on the students' and teachers' needs for dynamic lighting scenarios.

Keywords: Design research · Learning environment · Lighting in classrooms
Mixed methods · User-centric lighting design · Design driven innovation
Dynamic lighting

1 Introduction

Lighting technology has undergone a revolution, revealing new potentials of integrating lighting as a central parameter for improving the learning environment and nurturing the passion for learning in schools. Potentials of meeting new needs for differentiated learning situations and human needs for dynamic lighting are in focus, but not yet validated and specified as design parameters in the design of dynamic lighting. In order to approach a design perspective which can support learning environments more holistically, it is relevant to investigate *how the effects of dynamic lighting in classrooms can be evaluated* and to discuss *how this knowledge can be integrated in the process of designing dynamic lighting for classrooms.*

This review provides an overview and a critical perspective on research and methods used to measure the effects of dynamic classroom lighting. To address the real-life effects of lighting, this review focuses on field studies in classrooms, gathered from the library of Aalborg University, ProQuest search engine, ResearchGate, and Google Scholar.

© ICST Institute for Computer Sciences, Social Informatics and Telecommunications Engineering 2018
A. L. Brooks et al. (Eds.): ArtsIT 2017/DLI 2017, LNICST 229, pp. 479–489, 2018.
https://doi.org/10.1007/978-3-319-76908-0_46

In this paper, the *learning environment* is defined as the combination of the physical environment (the classrooms); the learning activities which take place in this environment during school hours, and the behaviour of the students which affects or might affect these activities.

The term *dynamic lighting* refers to intelligent, automatic systems with one or more parameters changing over time - such as light intensity, correlated colour temperature (CCT), or distribution. It also includes lighting, which consists of scenes with predefined light parameters. The term *daylight* is used for light of natural origin, including sunlight and skylight, while incandescent, fluorescent, LED, HPSV, and others, are referred to as *artificial* or *electrical* lighting.

The definition of a *mixed methods* approach refers to Creswell [1]: the use of both qualitative and quantitative methods in a study; the data from both of which are analysed; and are merged, connected, or embedded. This is as opposed to a quasi-mixed approach, which includes both methodologies without them being integrated.

2   Reviews

2.1   Academic Performance as Test Parameter

One of the most common ways to measure the effects of light on students is to test their progression in test scores or concentration over time. Many researchers choose to do so by analysing the scores from specifically chosen or prepared *standardised tests*, rather than exploring the school grades. Over forty years ago, this method was employed by Mayron et al. [2] in investigating the effects of cool white and full-spectrum fluorescent light on the reading performance of first-grade children. Their results were inconclusive as it was not possible to isolate the variables and an assumption was made that the observed difference in the performance of students was due to differences in teaching.

Through the use of standardised tests, the influence of two predefined light settings on reading performance - accuracy, speed, and expression - were tested by Mott et al. [3]. The analysis showed that the reading improved more under the *focus* setting (6000 K, 1000 lx) in comparison to the *normal* (3500 K, 500 lx), during the study. Another experiment on dynamic light tested the effects of three settings, with different CCT and intensity levels, on student performance through field and laboratory experiments [4]. First, a preliminary study investigated effects of light on arousal as a potential mediator of performance. It showed that warmer colour temperature (3500 K) had a relaxing effect on the seventeen adult subjects. Afterwards, a laboratory experiment was conducted which, in contrast, showed no change in the performance of students when solving an arithmetical problem. However, the field study that took place afterwards confirmed the results from the pre-test, revealing a possible strong influence on performance for the setting with the highest CCT (6500 K). A similar contradiction between a field and a controlled experiment was present in a study on dynamic light by Sleegers et al. [5]. Mott et al. [3] also reported that their field study showed no effect of lighting on motivation, in contrast to a laboratory experiment conducted by Knez [6]. This could indicate that field experiments, which test in conditions much closer to everyday life, could be more precise in predicting the effect of lighting on the learning potentials of students in real-life situations.

The method of comparing the school grades of children was also utilised in a study on the effects of increased horizontal and ambient illumination on multiple factors, including academic achievement [7]. The experimental classrooms were equipped with fluorescent luminaires emitting direct and indirect light, plus extra fixtures to increase the light levels on the walls. The findings showed an interesting discovery in that, while there was a small difference between the progression in achievement for the experiment and control groups over the time of the study, a pronounced effect was evident during the dark season.

Between 2012 and 2014, four field studies have examined the effects of light on *concentration*. All of them used the d2 Test of Attention and experimented with LED, fluorescent lights, or both. Barkmann et al. [8] conducted an experiment where seven fluorescent lighting settings were presented to the teachers and it was up to them to decide when, how, and how often to use them. The results showed that under the *Concentrate* lighting scenario (5800 K, 1060 lx) the students made fewer errors of omission compared to the *Standard* setting (4000 K, 300 lx). The effect of dynamic LED light, as opposed to fluorescent light, was investigated by Sleegers et al. [5] in one laboratory and two field experiments. The light differed in CCT and intensity and was controlled by the teacher, similarly to Barkmann's experiment. The results of the field studies showed that the children performed better on the d2 test in the experimental *Focus* setting (6500 K, 1000 lx) compared to the *Standard* (3000–4000 K, 300 lx). However, the controlled study showed no effect. The findings of another field study on dynamic lighting from the same year showed no improvement in the students' concentration under 6000 K, 1000 lx compared to 3500 K, 500 lx [3].

Regarding the effects of light on student performance, there are still questions that remain unanswered. There is an indication that field experiments, which test in conditions much closer to everyday life, could be more precise in predicting the effect of lighting on the learning potentials of students in real-life situations. This indicates a need for developing methods for holistic field research, in contrast to merely using quantitative methods and studying quantitative parameters, such as test scores and grades. Hereto, Keis et al. [9] point out that the long-term exposure to blue-enriched light in the morning needs to be further investigated. Choi and Suk [4] suggest that future research should address how light affects students of different ages, and Sleegers et al. [5] point out that future studies could examine the effects of light on children with cognitive and behavioural learning disabilities. In addition, there is a lack of studies comparing the effects of fluorescent, LED light, and other light sources.

2.2 Behavior and Mood as Test Parameters

In this section, field research on the impact of dynamic light on behaviour, mood, and use of light in classrooms is presented. The inattentive and the off-task *behaviours* of students were observed under full-spectrum fluorescent light with shielded electromagnetic radiation by Wohlfarth [10]. This was measured by documenting the direction in which the students were looking and various other behaviours, using structured observations. The results of the study were contradictory as some of the behaviours increased in occurrence while others decreased under the experimental lighting. Another study which investigated concentration as a dependent variable was conducted by Kuller and Lindsten [11]. First they assessed the classroom behaviour of students through a scale consisting of 18 items, including concentration, and they later compared it to the levels of cortisol (a stress hormone which is affected by light). What they reported was a possible negative relationship between the cortisol levels and concentration. However, no further research has examined this in relation to classroom environments. In 2016, another investigation was conducted using a qualitative approach. The effects of colour temperature (3000 K and 4100 K, fluorescent light) on students' on-task behaviour was explored by Pulay et al., by documenting their physical location during class, using structured observations [12]. The analysis showed an increase in their concentration under the cooler light setting. Another field study by Keis et al., investigated the effects of blue-enriched LED light on the cognitive performance (processing speed, concentration, and memory) of high-school students in morning classes [9]. The control group was under warm fluorescent lighting (3000 K, 3500 K), while the experimental group was under blue-enriched LED light (5500 K). They found a positive impact of the experimental light on the concentration of the participants.

Wessolowski et al. tested the effects of the Philips SchoolVision system, which is based on fluorescent lighting, and compared its *Relax* setting (3500 K, 325 lx) to its *Standard* setting (4000 K, 300 lx) in order to evaluate the effects on fidgetiness, aggressive, and pro-social behaviour [13]. The impact was explored through detecting the pixel changes in a digital recording through structured observations and by self-rating assessments. Under *Relax*, a decline in restlessness and aggressive behaviour was observed. A tendency towards an increased pro-social behaviour was also reported.

The effects of light on *mood* were studied in a static-group comparison by Wohlfarth [10], where the students were exposed to either (1) a combination of interior colours, (2) full-spectrum light, (3) colours and light, or control lighting. A significant correlation was found between *light and colours* and *mood*, which was examined through a mood variation test. In the schools with the *light* and *colour/light* conditions, the students had a greater feeling of Surgency and Mastery/Self-Esteem. However, the children in the control and in the *colour/light* school both scored higher on Aggression in comparison to the other two. Another study by Raynham et al. examined the impact of indirect light on the mood of students on the ground and first floors of a school, measured through a self-rating scale [7]. The results showed a difference between the experimental and control classrooms on the ground floor, revealing a steady improvement of the mood after December under the indirect light setting as opposed to a heavy decline followed by a slight improvement in the control.

The analysis of the selected field research on the impact of dynamic light on behaviour and mood indicates that concentration is increased under cooler blue-enriched light, whereas exposure to warmer light reduces restlessness and aggressive behaviour and affects positively pro-social behaviour. This indicates that there is a need for flexible learning environments meeting various needs through different lighting scenarios. The methods used for studying the effects of light on *behaviour and mood* are qualitative, whereas the data are typically quantified. These data would be valuable for setting up and testing design criteria, as well as for performing correlational analysis. The use of advanced technologies for generating quantitative data on behaviour (as in Wessolowski et al. [13]) could also mean that researchers would be able to work with large sample sizes of students and achieve results that are more generalizable. However, it should be considered that providing designers with qualitative data on the most human aspect of the classroom environment - the human behaviour and mood - could lead them to developing a more empathetic relation with the people they design for, and could add "meaning and individuality to the statistics" [14, p. 114]. Thus, this review identifies a need to rethink the methodologies applied when investigating and measuring the potentials and effects of innovative technologies (such as lighting) that can spark and nurture passions for learning in the real-life learning environments of children.

3   Result

The selected studies, which include academic performance as a test parameter, made up more than 75% of the reviewed literature (half of which studies solely the effects on performance). In comparison, around one third investigates the effects of light on behaviour, mood, and/or use of light (Fig. 1, Left). Half of the studies applied exclusively quantitative methods, while only less than 10% applied qualitative ones; 22% used mixed methods, and 18% - quasi-mixed (Fig. 1, Right).

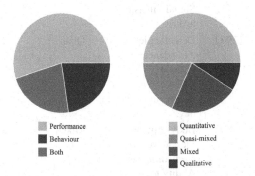

Fig. 1. Methods and parameters included in selected studies

The effects of light on *academic performance* are almost exclusively studied quantitatively - fifteen out of the seventeen reviewed studies. This approach allows the acquisition of data for very large, comparable sample sizes of students (Table 1).

However, Mott et al. [3] suggest that other ways of measuring student performance, such as behavioural observations (applied in: [10, 12]) might show better results. Analysing the concentration of students through documenting their spatial location in the classroom [12], despite the quantification of data, provides an image and allows the designer to get a glimpse of what is happening in the real-life environment. While Wohlfarth [10] did not obtain conclusive findings after measuring on-task behaviour

Table 1. List of included studies on the learning environment and investigated effects.

Author(s)	Year	Investigated the effects of light on	Methods used	Tools
Mayron, Ott, Nations, Mayron	1974	Performance Hyperactive behaviour Sick days	Mixed	Academic tests Performance objectives Observation timelapse
Ne'eman et al.	1976	Preference for sunlight Use of light	Mixed	Interviews Questionnaires
Wohlfarth	1986	Mental development Performance Attitudes toward school Misbehaviours Absences due to illness Refractive eye problems Blood pressure Dental caries Off-task behaviours Sound intensity levels	Quasi-mixed	Structured observations Achievement tests The School Subjects Attitude Scales (SSAS) Discip. actions taken Sound level Measurements Pre-adolescent Mood Variation tests (PAMS) Blood pressure
Hathaway	1992	Dental caries Attendance rates Rates of achievement Health and general dev.	Quan	Test of Basic Skills
Kuller, Lindsten	1992	Body growth Sick leave Cortisol levels Ability to concentrate Sociability	Mixed	Structured observations Cortisol
Heschong Mahone Group	1999	Academic performance Mood	Quasi-mixed	Iowa Test of Basic Skills (ITBS) Grades from schools Interviews
Yarbrough	2001	Student achievement	Quan	Iowa Test, Basic Skills
Axarli, Meresi	2008	Use of light Visual comfort	Mixed	

(continued)

Table 1. (*continued*)

Author(s)	Year	Investigated the effects of light on	Methods used	Tools
Tanner	2009	Student achievement	Quasi-mixed	Iowa Test, Basic Skills
Raynham, Govén, Laike	2011	Mood Sleepiness Quality of sleep Academic performance Sick-leave Cortisol, Melatonin	Quan	Scores School Tests Self-rating scale
Barkmann, Wessolowski, Schulte-Markwort	2012	Attention Reading speed Reading comprehension Achievement Motivation Classroom atmosphere	Quan	d2 Test of Attention ELFE 1–6 LGVT 6–12 Questionnaire for Emotional and Social Exp. (FEESS)
Mott, Robinson, Walden, Burnette, Rutherford	2012	Concentration Motivation Oral reading fluency	Quan	d2 Test of Attention AIMSweb An instrument adapted from Pintrich (1990)
Sleegers et al.	2013	Concentration	Quan	d2 Test of Attention
Keis, Helbig, Streb, Hille	2014	Concentration Cognitive processing Memory retention Attitude to the lighting	Quan	d2 Test of Attention Test (ZVT) Visual and Verbal Memory Test
Wessolowski, Koenig, Schulte-Markwort, Barkmann	2014	Fidgetiness Prosocial behaviour Aggressive behaviour	Quasi-mixed	Change of pixels CRS; Conners, (1973) Observation System Aggressiveness Self-assessment tools
Buckley	2014	Use of light Visual comfort	Qual	Interviews Observations
Barrett, Zhang, Davies, Barrett	2015	Academic performance	Quan	Progression in test scores from the schools
Choi and Suk	2016	Arousal Accuracy, Speed Sense time passed	Quan	Electrocardiogram Solving arithmetical pr.

(*continued*)

Table 1. (*continued*)

Author(s)	Year	Investigated the effects of light on	Methods used	Tools
Ahadi et al.	2016	Performance Feeling of drowsiness	Mixed	Academic scores Daylight quality
Drosou et al.	2016	Use of the light	Quan	Documenting HDRI
Pulay et al.	2016	On-task behaviours	Qual	Mapping stud. location

through qualitative methods, the contradictory results raise questions such as what the right way is to measure the effects of light on performance and whether qualitative methods could help explain the results in more detail.

Behaviour has an impact on classroom activities, academic performance of students [15], and the use of physical space, including light, making it one of the most influential factors. Additionally, interpersonal and hyperactive behaviour also have an impact on the well-being and mood of teachers, who in turn affect the students and the classroom environment [16]. This means that exploring and mastering the relationship between behaviour and light can lead to opportunities for creating lighting designs with great impact on classroom environments. Nevertheless, it should be considered that through observing behaviour it is not possible to understand what the students are learning and how much. Thus, despite its importance, behaviour cannot be the only factor used for measuring the effects of light on students and learning.

Research indicates that warm CCT and low light intensity are conducive to reducing aggression and restlessness, boosting pro-social behaviour and feeling of relaxation, and supporting students with special educational needs [4, 13, 17], which might actually be the opposite of what is good for performance [4, 5, 8, 9, 18]. However, other research shows a positive correlation between pro-social classroom behaviour and academic performance [19]. This shows how little we still know about the effects of light on different aspects, and indicates to the authors that a more holistic and user-centric approach is necessary.

When people are involved, it is crucial to consider that only they can reveal what really generates value for them. An example of this can be found in a study by Keis et al. [9] who found a positive effect of blue-enriched light on the concentration of students. Despite this effect, questionnaires regarding the satisfaction with light showed that the students preferred the appearance of the standard lighting, and only 50% wanted to keep the new one.

Good communication between users and designers can potentially lead to innovative design solutions [20]. Qualitative data can be used as a tool for improving the conversation between users, researchers, and designers, by providing different tools for communication, such as images, videos, and stories [21]. Having these tools is important when users, researchers and designers of different ages, backgrounds, and roles in the study and design process, need to communicate experiences, knowledge, and ideas (an issue increasingly addressed in healthcare research and design: [22–24]).

The UK Design Council report emphasizes the need for involving the students and school staff in the design process, stating that the "genuine involvement of users empowers individuals, produces greater satisfaction [with the renovated spaces] and should improve the design" [25, p. 7]. According to another British report "the learning environment should 'belong' to the community, involving teachers, students and community members in the design process" [26, p. 17]. Mixing qualitative and quantitative methods might be the most suitable approach for analysing the complex experiences and needs of the users, the relations between the various human and environmental factors, as well as the long-standing issues of energy efficiency and optimization of resources (addressed in: [27, 28]). In recent years, qualitative and quantitative methods are increasingly being mixed in order to address these complex issues [14, 29]. According to Wisdom and Creswell, a mixed methods study "reflects participants' point of view" and gives "a voice to study participants, and ensures that study findings are grounded in participants' experiences" [30, p. 3]. When applying mixed methods in investigating multiple factors, combining knowledge and practices from different fields is essential. Such a transdisciplinary approach is valuable for understanding how light can become a multidimensional design element, meeting criteria validated through methodologies from different scientific fields [31].

4 Conclusion

This literature review examined lighting research methods used for evaluating the effects of dynamic light in classrooms. The overall aim for this study was to understand how research can support innovative lighting designs for meeting the needs of users, and thus supporting environments for learning.

The reviewed literature uncovers potentials of dynamic lighting for improving the learning environment. Especially the effects of changing CCT and light intensity during the dark seasons, long-term exposure to blue-enriched light in the morning to increase concentration, and warm light to reduce aggression and promote a prosocial behaviour have potentials that need to be investigated.

The test parameter gaining most attention in the reviewed field studies is academic performance, which is investigated in the majority of the studies and mostly through quantitative methods. Behaviour and mood are addressed in one third of the selected papers and predominantly studied through qualitative methods, analysed through a quantification of collected data. Additionally, field tests could be more precise in predicting the effect of lighting on the learning environment, which points out needs for developing methods for holistic field research.

This review leads to a recommendation that more test parameters and the relations between them should be studied through a holistic approach. This could include elements of the physical environment - light, air, temperature, noise, colours - as well as human parameters, such as behaviour, performance, health, mental well-being, and perception.

It is suggested that the relation between dynamic light and these test parameters is explored through the use of mixed methods to draw from the strengths and minimize the weaknesses of qualitative and quantitative methods - and to be able to put more emphasis on the users' perspective. Studying multiple variables through different methods requires the collaboration of specialists from various disciplines of technology, design, and social sciences, such as lighting design, architecture, pedagogy, and anthropology, in a transdisciplinary approach.

References

1. Creswell, J.W.: Research Design: Qualitative, Quantitative, and Mixed Methods Approaches, 4th edn. SAGE Publications Inc., USA (2014)
2. Mayron, L.W., Ott, J., Nations, R., Mayron, E.L.: Light, radiation, and academic behavior. Acad. Ther. **X**(1), 33–47 (1974)
3. Mott, M.S., Robinson, D.H., Walden, A., Burnette, J., Rutherford, A.S.: Illuminating the effects of dynamic lighting on student learning. SAGE Open **2012**, 1–9 (2012)
4. Choi, K., Suk, H.J.: Dynamic lighting system for the learning environment: performance of elementary students. Opt. Soc. Am. (OSA), **24**(10) (2016)
5. Sleegers, P.J.C., Moolenaar, N.M., Galetzka, M., Pruyn, A., Sarroukh, B.E., van der Zande, B.: Lighting affects students' concentration positively: findings from three dutch studies. Lighting Res. Technol. **45**, 159–175 (2013)
6. Knez, I.: Effects of indoor lighting on mood and cognition. J. Environ. Psychol. **15**, 39–51 (1995)
7. Raynham, P.J., Govén, T., Laike, T.: Influence of ambient light on the performance, mood, endocrine systems and other factors of School children. In: Proceedings of the 27th Session of the CIE Sun City, South Africa (2011)
8. Barkmann, C., Wessolowski, N., Schulte-Markwort, M.: Applicability and efficacy of variable light in Schools. Physiol. Behav. **105**, 621–627 (2012)
9. Keis, O., Helbig, H., Streb, J., Hille, K.: Influence of blue-enriched classroom lighting on students' cognitive performance. Trends Neurosci. Educ. **3**, 8–92 (2014)
10. Wohlfarth, H.: Colour and Light Effects on Students' Achievement, Behavior and Physiology. Alberta Department of Education, Edmonton (1986)
11. Kuller, R., Lindsten, C.: Health and behavior of children in classrooms with and without windows. J. Environ. Psychol. **12**, 305–317 (1992)
12. Pulay, A., Read, M., Tural, E., Lee, S.: Examining student behavior under two correlated color temperature levels of lighting in an elementary school classroom. Educ. Plann. **23**(3), 57–69 (2016)
13. Wessolowski, N., Koenig, H., Schulte-Markwort, M., Barkmann, C.: The effect of variable light on the fidgetiness and social behavior of pupils in school. J. Environ. Psychol. **39**, 101–108 (2014)
14. Kington, A., Sammons, P., Day, C., Regan, E.: Stories and statistics: describing a mixed methods study of effective classroom practice. J. Mixed Methods Res. **5**(2), 103–125 (2014)
15. Straus C., Tiffany D.M.: Strategies to Improve Low-Performing Schools Under the Every Student Act (2016). https://www.americanprogress.org/issues/education/reports
16. Nierenberg, C.: Depression in Teachers Impacts Classroom Learning (2015). http://www.livescience.com/49771-depression-teachers-impacts-classroom-learning.html
17. BRANZ Ltd.: Designing Quality Learning Spaces: Lighting. New Zealand: Ministry of Education (2007). ISBN 0-478-13619-6; WEB ISBN 0-478-13624-2
18. Hathaway, W.E.: A Study Into the Effects of Types of Light on Children - A Case of Daylight Robbery. IRC Internal Report, Canada (1992)

19. Wentzel, K.R.: Does being good make the grade? social behavior and academic competence in middle School. J. Educ. Psychol. **85**(2), 357–364 (1993)
20. Sidawi, B.: The impact of social interaction and communications on innovation in the architectural design studio. Buildings **2012**(2), 203–217 (2012)
21. Fraser, H.M.A.: Design Works: How to Tackle Your Toughest Innovation Challenges Through Business Design. University of Toronto Press, Toronto (2012)
22. Hamilton, D.K.: Collaborators must work together to share results. Res. Des. J. **9**(1), 107–109 (2015). Health Environments
23. Kasali, A.: Architects in interdisciplinary contexts: representational practices in healthcare design. Des. Stud. **41**, 205–223 (2015)
24. Lehoux, P., Hivon, M.: The worlds and modalities of engagement of design participants: a qualitative case study of three medical innovations. Des. Stud. **32**, 313–332 (2011)
25. Higgins, S., Hall, E., Wall, K., Woolner, P., McCaughey, C.: The Impact of School Environments: A Literature Review. UK Design Council report (2005)
26. Building Futures: 21st Century Schools. Learning Environments of the Future. Building Futures, UK (2004)
27. Drosou, N., Brembilla, E., Mardaljevic, J., Haines, V.: Reality bites: measuring actual daylighting performance in classrooms. In: Proceedings of PLEA 16, Los Angeles, 11–13 July 2016 (2016)
28. Plympton, P., Conway, S., Epstein, K.: Daylighting in Schools: improving student performance and health at a price schools can afford. Paper presented at American Solar Energy Society Conference, NREL/CP-550-28049 (2000)
29. Strudsholm, T., Meadows, L.M., Vollman, A.R., Thurston, W.E., Henderson, R.: Using mixed methods to facilitate complex, multiphased health research. Int. J. Qual. Methods **15**(1), 1–11 (2016)
30. Wisdom, J., Creswell, J.W.: Mixed Methods: Integrating Quantitative And Qualitative Data Collection And Analysis While Studying Patient-Centered Medical Home Models. Agency for Healthcare Research and Quality, Rockville, MD, AHRQ Publication No. 13-0028-EF, p. 3 (2013)
31. Hansen, E.K., Mullins, M.: Lighting design: toward a synthesis of science, media technology and architecture. eCAADe, **2**(1), 613–620 (2014)

Design Fiction as Norm-Critical Practice

Linda Paxling$^{(\boxtimes)}$ ⓘ

Blekinge Institute of Technology, Karlshamn, Sweden
linda.paxling@bth.se

Abstract. The transdisciplinary fields of design and feminist technoscience share a common interest in focusing on the world in a state of always becoming, always changing. Within feminist technoscience, norm-critical perspectives are implemented to shed light on unequal sociotechnical infrastructures. Within design research, generative methods of critical design and design fiction encourage processes of fictional prototyping and storytelling that infuse discussions on what kind of world we want to live in. The purpose of this paper is to illustrate how design fiction can be used as a method to address norm-criticality in media technology education. Based on a week-long design fiction workshop with undergraduate students, three student projects are analyzed in detail. The analysis suggests design fiction can be used as a norm-critical practice to invoke discussions on values and beliefs within media design processes as well as established narratives of futuring.

Keywords: Design fiction · Norm-criticality · Media technology
Education

1 Introduction and Aim

Design fiction is a hybrid practice that functions in the borderlands between actual and possible worlds. It is an approach for visualizing and materializing alternative scenarios using design and storytelling and is being used as a platform for questioning status quo, invoking discussion on social and ethical consequences of emerging technologies and increasing political and civic engagement [1]. Vermeulen & Van Looy [2] show in their study on stereotypes in game culture how discriminating norms can affect playing frequency as well as motivation among female players. Racial, gender and cultural stereotypes have been quite persistent in the film industry, where marginalized groups are depicted in a negative manner or often not at all [3]. While portrayals are gradually changing for the better it is important to shed light on these issues so as to encourage positive change in the future media landscape.

Similar to intersectional feminism, norm-critical practices in media education can provide fruitful critiques on how and for whom digital games and films are produced and distributed. The practices highlight question such as; which stories are we telling? How and which characters are portrayed? How does this effect differences within and between cultures? How do dominant technologies, information systems and software affect our perceptions of the future?

The purpose of this paper is to illustrate how design fiction can be used as a method to address norm-critical perspectives in media technology education. Norm-critical

© ICST Institute for Computer Sciences, Social Informatics and Telecommunications Engineering 2018
A. L. Brooks et al. (Eds.): ArtsIT 2017/DLI 2017, LNICST 229, pp. 490–499, 2018.
https://doi.org/10.1007/978-3-319-76908-0_47

perspectives stem from research fields such as feminist research and education [4], and while the terminology has not yet gained ground within design research, the emphasis on questioning norms and values in design, technology and information systems is well established in the areas of human-computer interaction and critical and speculative design [5].

Norms signify the 'normal' and address behaviors acceptable in a social setting. Lifestyle choices, clothes, greetings, table manners, public and personal behaviour – we are inscribed with many social norms in our daily lives - norms that are implicit and functional. The intention of a norm-critical perspective is not to create a society without norms and social rules of behaviour, but rather to place attention to certain dominant norms excluding and discriminating people and ultimately creating unequal cultures. Heterosexuality, ableism and whiteness are for instance critiqued as norms that can exclude and discriminate people, who do not follow the socially accepted behaviors within these discourses [6, 7]. Other norms of interest embedded and embodied in media design processes concern the relation between media designer and the presumptive users, technologies of choice, digital infrastructures and how stories of futures are framed.

2   Feminist Technoscience

Feminist technoscience is a transdisciplinary research field, which stem from decades of feminist critique within science and technology [8]. It is, similar to posthumanism, an epistemological knowledge production that challenges the anthropomorphical assumption of humans being at the center of the world [9]. The research field further critiques a positivist approach as being too limited and negligible towards knowledge production because of how it ontologically tends to separate researcher, objects and users. The theoretical framework of feminist technoscience suggests that we should view the world in a constant becoming where researcher, objects and users are much more inter-dependent and the relations between actors temporally and spatially change [4].

The fields of science and technology are entangled with sociotechnical networks and the relations (human and non-human) occurring between them need to be made ethically and politically accountable. Reshaping humanist concepts such as body, identity and gender through technoscientific practices can create more equal worldings [10]. Haran & King writes how the "'now' is not necessarily a shared experience, as we are materially embodied on different continents. We are subject to different local political economies, however transnational we might imagine our shared projects to be" [11:2] Science fiction, speculative fabulation, design fiction, critical design or even story-telling are all different genres, discourses and methods that can deconstruct and reframe our different temporal and spatial experiences of social norms and values [12].

3   Norm-Criticality

Criticality is rooted in a design tradition of questioning the ideas, exposing structures and creating a space for discussion of power, inequality, capitalism, industry and technology that underpins conceptions of design [7, 13]. Jonsson & Lundmark provide a framework for making the invisible values in design visible through norm-critical design analysis. They suggest "norm-critical design can be understood as a sub-field of critical design where the specific focus is on the relationship between design and social norms" [7:5]. They introduce four perspectives - cultural representations, technology, interactivity and context of use - in their framework of norm-critical design analysis for interactive systems. The different perspectives illustrate identity markers such as gender, race, ethnicity and social groupings, interactions, or lack thereof, between people and artefacts and technologies can strengthen certain values and diminish others, for instance photo manipulation. The perspective of context reflects the diffractive approach of understanding how norms are manifested in everyday life and how this can differ temporally, spatially and geographically [4]. These perspectives focus on interactive systems and constitute an analytical framework relevant for similar mediations i.e. games, film and sound design.

4   Critical Practice in Design

I contextualize design fiction within design research by making use of Malpass' umbrella term critical practice in design [14]. Malpass' differentiates the practice with the subcategories associative design, speculative design and critical design. Associative design focuses primarily on confronting dominant traditions in product design and while this approach can certainly be useful in design fiction scenarios, speculative and critical design are closer at hand when situating design fiction. Speculative design creates a discursive space between science and technology and material culture. The designers work closely with materials and concepts which are often related to scientific practices and "the process of doing science itself figures as the design process" [14:339]. Speculative design places the attention on how our present development in science and technology is directed towards certain futures and advocates a dialogue on whether these are the futures we desire. In for instance Auger-Loizeau's speculative design project 'Afterlife' the debate concerns the ethics of human death. The design concept consisted of intervening with the usual decomposition process by connecting the body with a fuel cell that can produce electricity from organic matter. The electricity is then enclosed within a regular dry cell battery that can be used by friends and family of the deceased [15].

Dunne and Raby define the concept critical design as using "speculative design proposals to challenge narrow assumptions, preconceptions and givens about the role products play in everyday life. It is more of an attitude than anything else, a position rather than a method. [...] Its opposite is affirmative design: design that reinforces the status quo" [16]. Practitioners in critical design offer alternatives to existing design objects and practices thereby providing a commentary on social, cultural and ethical matters. In Dunne & Raby's project *Robots* [17] normative values of how humans perceive existing and future relations with robots are highlighted. The robot bodies further challenge the popular cultural notions of robots in science fiction film and literature and suggest alternatives to what kind of material and form can be used.

Ambiguity in research is a risky thing and design artefacts can certainly become meaningless and confusing and lack the intended outcome of the design researcher, especially with artefacts having an intended audience. Gaver et al. explain how an ambiguity of information, context and relationships moves us toward a 'relational ambiguity', where we need to interpret incomplete information, implement references seemingly incompatible and consider subjective individual experiences and attitudes onto new situations [18]. However, working with research through design and design fiction in an educational context ambiguity can become a useful design method for asking questions of how and why we use certain techniques, concepts, tools and methods and how these choices affect our futuring. Just as critical and speculative design are intentionally non-rational, so too are design fictions. The intent is to compel the audiences to simultaneously relate and question the design artefact thereby (re-) considering one's beliefs, values and behaviors [14]. According to Auger, the practices of design fictions, critical and speculative design share certain premises, where they "all remove the constraints from the commercial sector that define normative design processes; use models and prototypes at the heart of the enquiry; and use fiction to present alternative products, systems or worlds" [15:11].

5   Design Fiction

Design fiction is often used as an approach, or a technique, for creating exploratory and discursive spaces between the actual and the possible [19–21]. Sterling describes "the deliberate use of diegetic prototypes to suspend disbelief about change" [22]. Lindley and Coulton unpack Sterling's definition through the following criteria

1. something that creates a story world,
2. has something being prototyped within that story world
3. does so in order to create a discursive space" [23:210]

However, what this 'something' can be is far from easily defined. There have been many attempts to pin down a definition of this 'something', be it artefact, prototype, poetry, system or world, but it persists an intricate, fickle path [23, 24]. Gonzatto et al. proclaim that design fictions are not innocent creative plays [25]. The fictions are always created by someone, who has a specific intent of (re-)acting with present structures and Gonzatto et al. suggest that design fictions can have "both naïve and critical interpretations" [25:43]. Design fictions become naïve when they are exclusive, deterministic and disregard stakeholders without power. Yet, when the projects are inclusive, open-ended and a multitude of perspectives and values are considered, they become critical.

6   The Design Fiction Workshop

The workshop was part of a method course for third-year students at an undergraduate program in media technology. The students represent four different orientations within media technology – digital games, digital visual production, digital audio production and digital infrastructure. The aim of the week-long design fiction workshop was to introduce design fiction as a concept and method for undergraduate students to explore their roles as media designers and critically reflect on the normative narratives of design by engaging with different design manifests. The students could either choose a manifest from a list of design manifests on the Social Design Notes website [26] or they could locate one on their own. I provided the students with a few directives on what the manifests should entail. It should hold a statement with aim and method, focus on design practices and preferably include some ethical considerations. What these ethical considerations entailed were later discussed when the students started experimenting with the manifests. This ultimately led to the selected design manifests differing greatly in genre, style, aim and age.

On the first day of the workshop the students were given a lecture on design fiction, allocated reading of Bleecker's essay "Design Fiction: a short essay on design, science, fact and fiction" [28], and a brainstorming workshop on the relation of design fiction and media technology. The students were then introduced to the assignment, which was conducted in smaller groups of 2 to 5 persons throughout the week. A few students chose to work with the assignment individually. The assignment was as follows:

1. Select a design manifest.
2. Create an artefact that challenges, problematizes or plays with the chosen manifest.
3. The mandatory documentation at the end of the week included a link to the chosen manifest, a minimum of one illustration of the artefact, a description of the artefact and an explanation on the difference occurring between the chosen manifest and the created artefact.

The student projects were about 30 in total and quite diverse in style and outline. One student group, for instance, created a narrative of a fictive advertising agency that was forced to create these absurd and confrontational images for a company. Another group sketched a house on water were their discussion points concerned the future of architecture and housing solutions from an environmental perspective. One student created a game concept where the player was rewarded doing actions that he or she normally would have been punished for. Malpass explains how designers work closely with materials and concepts often related to scientific practices and "the process of doing science itself figures as the design process" [14:339]. This mindset resembles the work done by several undergraduate students in how they worked with future scenarios on how the relation between humans and technology will manifest in a possible future. The three student projects described in more detail below were chosen based on the students' distinct discussions and prototypes in relation to the chosen design manifest.

6.1   Project MaybePhone

The selected design manifest The Ten Principles of Good Design [29] by Rams makes use of concepts such as innovative, unobtrusive, long-lasting and aesthetic to define what good design is. The students wanted to challenge the conformity of Ram's design principles by creating a design artefact that challenged the perception of how a communication tool should behave. They chose to illustrate a design artefact called MaybePhone with the intention of making the relationship between the user and communication tool less functional. The idea behind MaybePhone is it may or may not work like you expect it to. It can bounce away from you, become invisible or suddenly play loud music. The students worked with questions such as what will personal communication tools look like in the future and how will the changing boundaries between body and tool change our communication?

6.2 Project Through Coloured Lenses

The selected design manifest The Karimanifesto [30] by Karim Rashid focuses on the work ethics of a designer. The project Through coloured lenses is an experiment with colours and lenses to explore how colours can work with and against each other. The students began their exploration by working with different digital colour schematics and then proceeded to create a prototype consisting of a set of glasses with different colour filters. The students also outlined a concept where the glasses can be used as voluntary self-censorship to erase certain objects, events or people.

6.3 Project HumTec

The selected design manifest is 1000 Words: A Manifesto for Sustainability in Design [31] by Chocinov relates design to ethics, sustainability and the anthropocene worldview. The project HumTec consists of a story world concept and illustrations of an artificial intelligence which in part follows the guidelines of the manifest. The critique of the manifest is visible, when the student discusses the prototype in relation to sustainability and technological access. The story concept is as follows; through human development and an increased consumption nature has turned into roads, housing and merchandise. Fertile soil has been covered with asphalt and forests are destroyed to make room for factories and buildings. Eco-friendly cities have sprung out of this development and HumTec is one of the companies working with the plant biospheres. HumTec's prototype is an artificial intelligence based on studies of the hummingbird. The students describe how the prototype will eventually work with pollinating and planting seeds based on the long-term strategy of rebuilding nature.

7 Discussion

In this paper design fiction is positioned through various branches of critical practices in design and further entangled with norm-critical perspectives. The situatedness and interests of the students as well as how the chosen manifests differed in style and aims was reflected in the diversity of the design fiction prototypes.

7.1 Analysis of MaybePhone

This project challenged the chosen manifest outlining what 'good' design is by distorting the functionality of a smart phone. The students made the phone unpredictable and difficult to use with the purpose of challenging the normative values and purposes of design and when discussing the future of communication and the fluid boundaries between humans and technology. MaybePhone is similar to associative design as it subverts an everyday object, the smartphone, and plays with its functionality and the relationship between humans and technology. The project also contains speculative and critical design perspectives, where they contextualize their artefact with discourses of communication and values of 'good' design.

The project holds critical interpretations of the chosen manifest when the students worked with creating a set of opposing principles. The students' discussions revolved around future communication and how the MaybePhone implore new kinds of relations between the user and the phone when it doesn't work over distance. The norm-critical perspectives of the project are narrated in the ambiguity of the design attributes and helps designers question and re-evaluate what we are expecting of future communication tools. We are designing technology that should suit the user's behaviours but can the user also benefit from changing its behaviours for the sake of technology?

7.2   Analysis of Through Coloured Lenses

The students behind the project chose a manifest on how a designer should work, which led to a design artefact and a work process that conversed on censorship and the practices of a designer. The prototype itself holds both naïve and critical interpretations when it was initially created as a playful activity for experimenting with colour and material and then proceeded to become more critical as a practice of self-censorship. The students mentioned lenses can be used for avoiding certain objects, events or people, creating hidden messages or for subtitling films.

The Karimanifesto focuses on expected norms of designers, which turned the students in the direction of focusing more on how they perceive their own work ethics in relation to Rashid's principles. In this case the norm-critical perspectives is visible in relation to the students work process and the outcomes of their design artefact. Rashid doesn't value reflection or the past as meaningful and the students are very critical of this perspective. They consider their backgrounds as valuable for creating the design artefact and their learning outcomes has taught them things on how to design differently in the future. This project illustrates how one's own boundaries demarks the outlines of a design fiction project, which creates further responsibilities for the designer, or in this case, the students. The ethical aspects of their prototype should be further explored in terms of what is rendered invisible when using the lenses, who is excluded from using them or how can the lenses be beneficial in media outlets?

7.3   Analysis of HumTec

The student created an artefact and a story world that discusses the work practices of an engineer and implicitly a designer. The student differentiates its prototype with the manifest through two examples. One is the manifest suggesting it is important people understand how artefacts works, while the student discusses the challenges of creating technological artefacts that are understandable for everyone. The second example concerns material choice and longevity. The student prefers to create a product that is sustainable and has longevity rather than creating products that can't be recycled as the manifest suggests. However, this seems to be a misunderstanding from the student as the author of the manifest compares designers' tendency to work with inorganic materials rather than organic and how these materials are far from sustainable or recyclable.

The design fiction prototype creates a future-making narrative when it suggests a plausible future of less nature and more urban environments. Furthermore it creates critical focal points on the changing relations and inter-dependency of human and non-human actors (the humming bird). The student illustrates norm-criticality when creating fictive solutions to a changing future environment and also when discussing what is preferable when creating technological artefacts for specific users.

8   Conclusion

The multi-dimensional structuring of design fictions pose interesting challenges when attempting to shed light on norms and belief systems in media technology. The selected student projects bring forward norm-critical discussions on the intended role of a media designer and future relations between humans, animals and (communication) technologies. How we narrate our future-making practices in the present holds real-world consequences for our socio-material futures. Within an educational context design fiction works well as a critical, ambiguous and deconstructive form of meta-design and it also has the potential of encouraging students to act as change agents for creating alternative future-making socio-material practices.

Combining the processes of making (games, websites, graphic and sound design) with design fiction works well to disrupt the established narratives of the digital media in and out of the academy. Based on the student prototypes presented in this paper I consider design fiction a promising method for creating discursive spaces in learning situations so as to stimulate vital discussions on social, cultural, technological and ethical implications of the past, present and future.

Future work with design fiction, together with norm-critical and feminist technoscience perspectives, can include invisible infrastructuring in technological systems, cultural representation, diversity, interactivity, context, manipulation, the list goes on and on. Acknowledging these different socio-political discourses as well as the individual and collective situatedness of knowledges students and media designers embody, we can work to deconstruct and reframe the media landscape to be more inclusive and diverse.

References

1. Hanna, J.R., Ashby, S.R.: From design fiction to future models of community building and civic engagement. In: Proceedings of the 9th Nordic Conference on Human-Computer Interaction - NordiCHI 2016 (2016)
2. Vermeulen, L., Van Looy, J.: "I Play So I Am?" A gender study into stereotype perception and genre choice of digital game players. J. Broadcast. Electron. Media **60**(2), 286–304 (2016)
3. Towbin, M.A., Haddock, S.A., Zimmerman, T.S., Lund, L.K., Tanner, L.R.: Images of gender, race, age, and sexual orientation in disney feature-length animated films. J. Fem. Fam. Ther. **15**(4), 19–44 (2004)
4. Ehrnberger, K.: Tillblivelser - En trasslig berättelse om design som normkritisk praktik. Doctoral dissertation, KTH (2017)

5. Dunne, A., Raby, F.: Speculative Everything: Design, Fiction, and Social Dreaming. The MIT Press, Cambridge (2013)
6. Swedish Secretariat for Gender Research. http://www.genus.se/en
7. Jonsson, F., Lundmark, S.: Norm-critical Design Analysis: A Framework. SIRR 2014:1 (2014)
8. Trojer, L.: Sharing Fragile Future, Feminist Technoscience in Contexts of Implication. Lean Publishing (2017). http://leanpub.com/sharingfragilefuturefeministtechnoscienceincontext sofimplication
9. Åsberg, C., Lykke, N.: Feminist technoscience studies. Eur. J. Women's Stud. **17**(4), 299–305 (2010)
10. Weber, J.: From science and technology to feminist technoscience. In: Davis, K., Evans, M., Lorber, J. (eds.) Handbook of Gender and Women's Studies, pp. 397–414. SAGE Publications Ltd., London (2006)
11. Haran, J., King, K.: Science fiction feminisms, feminist science fictions and feminist sustainability. Ada J. Gend. New Media Technol. **2** (2013)
12. Haraway, D.: SF: science fiction, speculative fabulation, string figures, so far. Ada J. Gend. New Media Technol. **3** (2013)
13. Lundmark, S., Normark, M.: Reflections on norm-critical design efforts in online youth counselling. In: Proceedings of the 7th Nordic Conference on Human-Computer Interaction: Making Sense Through Design (NordiCHI 2012), pp. 438–447. ACM, New York (2012)
14. Malpass, M.: Between Wit and reason: defining associative, speculative, and critical design in practice. Des. Cult. **5**(3), 333–356 (2013)
15. Auger, J.: Speculative design: crafting the speculation. Digit. Creat. **24**(1), 11–35 (2013)
16. Dunne, A., Raby, F.: Designing Critical Design FAQ. http://www.z33.be/debat/files/dunnerabyfaq.pdf
17. Dunne, A., Raby, F.: Technological dreams series: No. 1. Robots (2007). http://www.dunneandraby.co.uk/content/projects/10/0
18. Gaver, W.W., Beaver, J., Benford, S.: Ambiguity as a resource for design. In: Proceedings of the SIGCHI Conference on Human Factors in Computing Systems (CHI 2003), pp. 233–240. ACM, New York (2003)
19. Morrison, A.: Design prospects: investigating design fiction via a rogue urban drone. In: Proceedings of DRS 2014 Conference, Umeå, Sweden (2014)
20. Franke, B.: Design fiction is not necessarily about the future'. In: Sixth Swiss Design Network Conference, Negotiating Futures – Design Fiction, pp. 80–90 (2010)
21. Sterling, B.: Design fictions. Interactions **16**(3), 21–24 (2009)
22. Sterling, B.: Bruce Sterling Explains the Intriguing New Concept of Design Fiction, Slate (2012). http://www.slate.com/blogs/future_tense/2012/03/02/bruce_sterling_on_design_fictions_html
23. Lindley, J., Coulton, P.: Back to the future: 10 years of design fiction. In: Proceedings of the 2015 British HCI Conference (British HCI 2015), pp. 210–211. ACM, New York (2015)
24. Markussen, T., Knutz, E.: The poetics of design fiction. In: Proceedings of the 6th International Conference on Designing Pleasurable Products and Interfaces (DPPI 2013), pp. 231–240. ACM, New York (2013)
25. Gonzatto, R.F., van Amstel, F.M.C., Merkle, L.E., Hartmann, T.: The ideology of the future in design fictions. Digit. Creat. **24**(1), 36–45 (2013)
26. Social Design Notes. http://backspace.com/notes/2009/07/design-manifestos.php
27. Coulton, P., Lindley, J., Sturdee, M., Stead, M.: Design fiction as world building. In: Proceedings of the 3rd Biennial Research Through Design Conference, 22–24 March 2017, Edinburgh, UK, pp. 163–179 (2017). Article 11

28. Bleecker, J.: Design Fiction: A Short Essay on Design, Science, Fact and Fiction. Near Future Laboratory, Los Angeles (2009)
29. Rams, D.: The Ten Principles of Good Design. https://www.vitsoe.com/eu/about/good-design
30. Rashid, K.: Karimanifesto. https://tianickels.wordpress.com/2013/04/18/todays-dose-of-designspiration-karim-rashids-karimanifesto/
31. Chochinov, A.: 1000 Words: A Manifesto for Sustainability in Design. http://www.core77.com/posts/40586

New Forms of Creative Artistic Expression Through Technology: An Alternative Perspective to Education

Andrei-Ducu Predescu and Georgios Triantafyllidis[✉]

Department of Architecture, Design and Media Technology, AAU Copenhagen,
A.C. Meyers Vænge 15, 2450 København SV, Denmark
{adp,gt}@create.aau.dk

Abstract. The paper tries to address the relationship between creativity and technology, having as a basis the idea that implementing cross disciplinarily approaches has a great potential in generating innovation. The recurring theme of the paper revolves around identifying the catalysts of disruptive ideas hence supporting the need of creative thinkers in our society as opposed to hyper specialization of knowledge. We look at the current educational system, analyze different technologies and their impact as well as the influence of technology upon art. Finally, through the NEO-David light art installation case study, we hope to find evidence in supporting the importance of creativity and cross-disciplinary thinking.

Keywords: Creativity · Education · Cross-disciplinary thinking
Art and technology · Light installation · Creative expression · Lighting design
Kinetic light · Voxel display system

1 Introduction

Since the dawn of human kind, several driving forces have been spearheading the development of our civilisation. This paper focuses on two of these high momentum entities, creativity and technology. Even though in the last couple of centuries these have been perceived as distinct explorative fields, studies based on divergent thinking begin to direct our attention towards a holistic paradigm, which addresses these fields through a cross-disciplinary methodology.

1.1 A Brief History of Creativity, Art and Technology

If we are to consider one of the most basic technological developments, such as the harnessing of fire, and its implementation, in the different aspects of the life of early sapiens, we can quickly identify creativity as a development tool. The use of fire as a means of protection, a source of heat and light, or using it as a weapon against others, showcases the ability to iterate upon a technology based on creative input.

An extreme form of creativity, showcasing the highest level of abstraction, has manifested its self throughout history in the form of art. The definition of art has always

© ICST Institute for Computer Sciences, Social Informatics and Telecommunications Engineering 2018
A. L. Brooks et al. (Eds.): ArtsIT 2017/DLI 2017, LNICST 229, pp. 500–509, 2018.
https://doi.org/10.1007/978-3-319-76908-0_48

been a controversial subject, during the 20th and in the first decades of the 21st centuries, when the means of expression have evolved, morphed and transitioned, hand in hand with emerging technologies and social development. But one constant has remained during the ages, art appeals to our humanity and it is tied to psychological, sociological and political issues relevant to its time.

The technological and cultural development of proto-societies, such as the production of colouring pigments, the use of burned clay, later ceramics, the desire of "cultural colonisation" of the inhabited space, is a clear example of an emerging symbiotic relationship between art and technology, and their co-evolution as a hallmark of humanity, transcending ages.

It is a common idea that the scientific field and art share many of their core principles, both involving overlapping methodologies, such as the development of ideas, hypothesis and theories which are later tested in an environment, engaging both mind and body, such as the studio or the laboratory [1]. Artists and scientists alike, tackle diverse subjects ranging from materials, people, history, quantum physics etc. to transform the acquired knowledge into something else.

In classical Greek, the word "art" is translated as "techne", from which the words technique and technology would arise, thus presenting us with another ancestral connection between these two fields. [2].

1.2   The Shortcomings of the Educational System

Until the middle of the 18th century this connection between creativity and technology was much more evident, then it is today, having an educational methodology relying on a truly holistic approach, the seven years apprenticeship, which combined thinking and making in an unbroken learning experience [3].

Due to the economic changes brought in by the industrial age, and the geopolitical circumstances of the period, a new model was developed, one that would be able to cater to the needs of the era. With the rise of the public education systems, a range of ideas were put in place, mainly having a focus on standardisation, and specialisation of knowledge while at the same time creating a socio-intellectual division between economical classes. This approach has been successfully propagated throughout our civilisation, resulting into a society which fails to see the interconnectivity of knowledge, often marginalising creative efforts in favour of more gainful aspects of productivity.

Now society faces yet another paradigm shift. We are at the moment when we have past the first timid steps into the digital age. The computer has forever changed the social landscape, by slowly eliminating arduous tasks and allowing us to assume creative positions. Unfortunately, the current educational system seems to have forgotten to adapt to these new circumstances. By trying to create professionals whom we consider specialist in a certain area it is often forgotten that the development of innovation relies on an individual's ability for abstraction. If the industrial age needed a workforce which could operate as the brain controlling a machine, the information age needs a workforce which can transcend this role, and regain its humanity through great thinkers, focusing at working with a technology rather than being a part of it. The economy of the 21st century will not be driven by human "drones", but by individuals whom are able to connect apparently invisible dots.

1.3   Re In-powering the People

The empowering of individuals through technology has already began to have disruptive consequences, throughout the professional fields. In the case of art and technology we start to identify a reunification of the disciplines. In many cases the boundaries between the technologist and the artist having been blurred to an almost indistinguishable level.

It is through this mashup that innovation can emerge. The so-called thinking outside the box or divergent thinking is what allows individuals to make unusual cross-disciplinary connections. To pursue such endeavours, knowledge has to be mixed and span different fields, hence the argument for an approach combining the extremes, art and technology. The bridge connecting these fields is the proving ground of our future.

2   The Relationship Between Creativity, Technology and Innovation

The relation between creativity and technology has been a subject of debate between scholars for decades if not centuries. Taking into consideration this complex relationship, the paper tries to analyse different aspects of how creativity drives innovation in technological development.

It seems to be quite ironic that innovation has always made its self-present, when individuals have taken established concepts and applied them to new domains. A curious fact is that of the establishment of the Theory of Natural Selection [4]. Darwin's magnum opus, was not the direct result of his knowledge in biology, but his power of abstraction, his investigation of an economic paper by Thomas Malthus, demonstrating that populations grew faster than the resources to sustain them, Darwin realised that only the best adapted to their environment would be able to survive. This curiosity presents us with evidence the catalyst for innovation can often lye outside of the inquired subject, while at the same time proving the need of creative thinking in extrapolating information.

The rapid spread of technology is an irrefutable fact, as computing power rises, devices get cheaper, and access to information is made available to the masses, our perspective is shifted towards other aspects of human development.

The availability of high-end technology to the general population, results in routine tasks being a thing of the past rather than the future. This expansion of possibilities, leaves us more time for experimentation and allows us to fail in a safe environment. If throughout recent history creativity has been regarded as a "luxury", it is the unburdening brought by technology, that expands our creative power. It is in many ways a transition from a creative "oligarchy" to a creative "democracy", in the sense of making more space for individuals to be at the discussion table.

Such a process of democratisation has a direct impact on the way we work and deal with problem solving. Meaning that due to technology we now have access to specialised knowledge, in a matter of seconds, however it is up to us to put together this figurative puzzle.

One of the most turbulent technologies, when having a focus on art, has been the invention of the photographic process. From its very early beginning in the 19th century it has had a very controversial position within the art world. This technology allowed individuals to bypass years of training in mastering the craft of image reproduction, yet allowing the artist to focus on the aesthetic message he or she intended to communicate.

The controversy around how photography qualifies as art has been an ongoing discussion since the development of the first images. If in the beginning artists were trying to imitate traditional landscape oil paintings, this quickly matured towards embracing the qualities of the medium, working with, rather than against it. As an example, conceptual photography turns an idea into a photograph. Even though what is depicted in the photographs are real objects, the subject is strictly abstract, trying to establish an emotional relationship with the viewer [5].

The general availability of technology has given amateurs the opportunity to experiment as well as allowing them the chance to express themselves creatively, thus further encouraging a liberalisation of the arts, sparking an initial wave of techno-artistic democratisation.

Furthermore, iteration on the photographic technology lead to another crucial cultural development. The Kinetoscope is an early motion picture device; it introduced the basic principles on which cinematography would be built. As soon as moving images were available, their commercial value was immediately identified. First as a technological curiosity and soon after it reached a certain maturity it became an artistic medium. Transposing theatrical live performance to this medium was imminent. As such, an art form dating back to antiquity, got the opportunity to morph and evolve into a similar yet much more accessible means of entertainment. Cross-disciplinary thinking, is the catalyst for, what a century later would become, one of the most lucrative entertainment industries.

In the field of computer science, an important piece of it has been absorbed by the video game industry. In the early sixties, developments were setting the stage for this "brave new world" and in 1962 one of the first video games, Spacewars [6], was developed by Harvard and MIT employees Martin Graetz, Steven Russel and Wayne Wiitanen [7]. This initial proof of concept showcased the possibility of a new form of creative expression, one which could combine narrative elements, visual design and user interactivity. By the 1980 this became a booming industry, which resulted in the birth of countless employment positions focused on creative aspects. In 2015 the revenue generated by the video game industry summed up to 91.5 billion US$ [8].

It seems that a pattern could be identified, when looking at the link between creativity and technology. It can be explained as follows, firstly a technology is developed, due to previous conditions. As soon as the technology in question reaches a certain maturity its application is questioned, at this point creatives begin a process of infusing human centred qualities. If this initial process proves to have economic potential, it is then when the technology goes in a second stage of development it reaches its to full maturity. At this second stage of development creative input is one of the major driving forces, it is also responsible for the development of spin-off technologies. the process then is repeated until the technology becomes obsolete (Fig. 1).

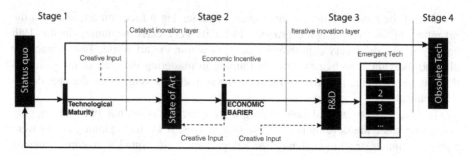

Fig. 1. Showcasing the process of innovation and its necessary inputs

In the world of fine art, particularly installation based art, modern technology has had several timid attempts at a holistic implementation. It somehow seems that arts enter more easily in the world of technology then the other way around. However, general availability and low cost is slowly making this a reality. One of the very first modern technologies used in the art world has been the light emitting diode. Since its wide commercial availability at the beginning of the 1970s it has been a catalyst for the development of light-art installations. Artists such as Jenny Holzer [9] have used them to create public works, in many cases occupying the position of advertising billboards, which have managed to draw the attention of the public to art, outside the exhibition gallery, hence making art available to a wider audience. The creative possibilities brought to the creative field by technology has inspired an entire generation of artists. A great leap forward has been the introduction of programming in the context of installation art, allowing individuals to further express their creative ambitions. In 2003 Cerith Wyn Evans marries his interest in ciphered communication and literature in the work entitled "Diary: How to improve the world (you will only make it worse)" [10]. He uses a plasma screen to reveal letter by letter, the English translation of the Morse code that is being conveyed through the flickering lights of an opulent chandelier. Such a work even if not truly technically impressive is showcasing a tendency to shift the trajectory of art towards a holistic approach to technology, in the hopes that the artistic scope can reach the apotheosis of the work in question.

One of the most interesting works combining advanced technological concepts with artistic sensibility, makes its self-known in 2006. Mariko Mori's Tom Na H-iu [11] is a monolith like, free-standing sculpture. It has been designed having in mind the symbolism of light as a representation of the soul, and translates that through a very unusual connection. The mysterious internal light of the installation is driven by the data-output generated by the Kamiokade neutrino detector. Which means that the neutrinos, governing the aesthetic effect of the installation come from a dying star. Such connections across the scientific field and fine art serve to further demonstrate the value and power of cross-disciplinary thinking and the empowering effect of technology within socio-cultural activities.

In 2009 on a remote forested hilltop, artist Doug Aitken produced a work which can only be described as a "sonic earthwork" [12]. The work implied the drilling of a 30 cm in diameter shaft with depth of 1.6 km on top of which a pavilion was standing. By lowering a series of microphones and accelerometers at different intervals, the artist was attempting to translate the movement of the earth to sound, hence establishing a new relationship to our planet.

No matter what the chosen means are, whether using light, sound, moving images electronics or all of them together, artists have repeatedly challenged the boundaries of their media and have expanded their possibilities in artistic expression exponentially throughout the last two decades. This has been a direct result of the general availability of powerful yet easy to use technology and most importantly the human factor, generally relying on cross-disciplinary thinking and knowledge.

3   Conceptual Framework of the NEO-David Installation

To further understand the creative process and how it is involved in the development of a project we will look at a specific case study. Our case follows the creative approach in producing a feasible, yet strong concept rooted in the fields of art, technology and lighting design. The Neo-David installation was the result of a theoretical investigation and physical experimentation in the possibility of form and movement representation using the medium of light.

In 1501 the Renaissance Italian sculptor, painter, architect, and poet Michelangelo di Lodovico Buonarroti Simoni begins work on what would become one of the most celebrated masterpieces in classical sculpture, widely known as David. The piece is a celebration of the human figure and stands as a testament to the understanding of form in it's most realistic representation. However, "David" deals only with form, but fails to address the issue of movement, in the sense of a changing form, therefor David will forever be frozen in time. Movement is a critical aspect of an individual's identity, it is a form of expression, which cannot and should not be ignored. Movement expresses freedom and through abstraction it can embody a physical manifestation of uncensored democracy. Hence the installation should communicate movement to holistically celebrate an individual.

Lastly the installation had to establish an emotional relationship with the individual with which it was interacting, as such, the idea of mirroring was introduced. As a conceptual statement, there is no higher praise to one's self then the literal staring in a mirror. This allows the creation of an alter ego, a manifestation of the individual which could be translated to the installation using light. Thus the alter ego, receives a new identity, a pure manifestation of energy.

Conceptually all these parameters involve a high degree of abstraction but irrefutably cater to the desired intention, while allowing the potential apotheosis of an individual's sculptural representation.

4 Design Challenges

As the concept idea was established, it has drawn inspiration from the art world, psychology and philosophy, having a wide cross-disciplinary span over humanistic "sciences", it is now time to expand our research over how NEO-David was seeking to become a reality, and what will its physical manifestation be.

Traditional sculpting technics rely on the addition or subtraction of material with the goal of unveiling a form. This is a critical principle, which we will need to understand, as it means that we will need to do the same with the material of our choice. In our situation, the "material" will be light. Unfortunately, light has several disadvantages such as it's lack of plasticity in creating a form, and the fact that we cannot see light, just its effects on different surfaces.

In this context, the sculpture must be composed by two elements: An interaction area and the display area. The first element is defined by a physically delimited area. It is the interaction zone of the sculpture where the individual's form and movement is analyzed with the help of depth imaging. The second element is the display area. Here a three-dimensional model is displayed through the individual manipulation of the constituting voxels.

4.1 Anthropomorphic Form Generation

To generate a form that could later be used as an output, we need to employ some advanced technological means, by which we refer to scanning methods, particularly the generation of cloud points or depth maps. To keep things simple, we will not discuss the technical details of such operations, but we will limit ourselves to a short conceptual description. The generation of a real-time three-dimensional model can be achieved through several means, one of which could be the use of electronical components which now are readily available.

The Microsoft Kinect [13] was first introduced in November 2010 and ever since has been used a wide variety of applications, and has generated a great interest in technological oriented artistic circles. Using IR imaging it has the capacity to generate a real-time point cloud which can be translated to a partial 3D model of an environment. It is to be emphasised partial as the Kinect has the limitation of "not seeing through objects". A visual comparison of the resulting real-time 3D output of the Kinect could be that of a bas-relief. In order to overcome this issue and create a fully tree-dimensional model we will need to make investigations in the field of trigonometry, particularly triangulation methods. Through the employment of such technics we can develop a computational model which is able to generate the data set required for driving the display area of the project.

4.2 Display Area and Output Method

After the issues in generating form have been solved we need to look at how it can be translated to a system able to communicate form and movement. Yet again we are obligated to analyse form in an abstract manner to understand how we can physically reproduce it.

Mathematically a form is the equivalent of a volume, which can be described as a quantity of three-dimensional space rapped by a closed surface, and it can be numerically quantified using cubic meters [14]. However, what we are particularly interested in, is what the constituent components of a volume are. Further inquiry requires us to borrow notions from Euclidian geometry, in which three-dimensional space is a geometric setting, in which three values, also known as parameters, are required to determine the position of an element. Such notions allow us to understand physical space as a three-parameter model in which all known matter exists. This mathematical notion leads us to a relatively abstract conclusion which is, that a volume can be represented through a collection of such parameters, that visualized as a group can perform the task of mimicking a volume, this collection of parameters can be identified in mathematics as a three-dimensional matrix or grid.

Previous research in the domain on volumetric displays has been done at ETH Zurich, through the development of the NOVA system [15]. The investigation was very successful from a technological perspective, however the lack of 3D content available was limited and its development hindered by a slow adoption rate of users. This issue however does not concern NEO-David as it is limited to the content previously discussed (Fig. 2).

Fig. 2. Showcasing the NOVA system displayed in the Zurich main train station

4.3   Design Research Outcome and Potential Applications

The system designed for the implementation of the NEO-David installation, has proven to be dealing with highly complex issues and as such the process has been one requiring new ways of using technologies and creative means. As a result, the research done in these directions has proved very useful in the development of further research across different fields as well as applications.

One of these directions refers to the development of real-time modelling techniques, based of scanning technologies, further development and research in this direction could potentially lead to improvements in fields of computer science, medicine and spatial navigation via augmented reality.

Secondly, based on findings in projects such as the NEO-David display system and previous research in the NOVA system, strongly suggest the need for further research on the aesthetic and utilitarian aspect of volume lighting solutions. Applications can include dynamic lighting systems, media facades and implementation of voxel screens within the modern architectural language.

The last point is with regards to the cross disciplinary research methodology and development process as a perspective towards how educational institutions can develop a teaching model in response to the socio-economical changes of the 21st century.

5 Conclusion

The paper at hand has dealt into many aspect of creativity and its irrefutable connection with technology, as result of this investigation we can draw a series of informed conclusions regarding several aspects.

Concerning the NEO-David installation, we can state that without a cross-disciplinary approach, having an emphasis on creative thinking, its development would have been highly unlikely. From the highly abstract concept, relating to a theoretical model, to the development and physical implementation of a prototype, none of these could have been possible without employing a process of borrowing, and expanding as well as the mutation of knowledge coming from an array of scientific and artistic fields.

As the NEO-David installation has been developed in the context of a Master's Thesis in the Lighting Design Master's program at AAU Copenhagen, we can also draw conclusions on the programs cross-disciplinary approach. By combining three fields of study, architecture, lighting engineering and media technology, the program succeeds in bringing together students from all the above-mentioned domains. This cultural and knowledge based melting pot becomes a catalyst for the development of bold projects and encourages individuals to think and work outside of their own comfort zone through the uses of collaborative methodologies. This educational model, although not perfect, proves to be cultivating innovative professionals, ready to tackle the controversies of the 21st century.

As we have seen in the previous discussion, technology has been a clear means through which individuals have been pushing de boundaries of conceptual thinking. This process has given birth to new ways of interaction between the public, art and technology, bringing new valences to the creative intent and broadening experiences from both a conceptual perspective as well as a sensorial one.

It seems that art and technology have a bright future ahead, and that the relationship between the two is a symbiotic one, stimulating each other and pushing each other's boundary having as a main catalyst creativity, both fuelled by cross-disciplinary thinking and the desired to improve our lives.

References

1. The Art Institute of Chicago. http://www.artic.edu
2. Definisions of Technology. http://web.engr.oregonstate.edu

3. Sennete, R.: The Craftsman, pp. 53–81. Yale University Press, New Haven (2008)
4. Darwin, C.: The Autobiography of Charles Darwin, London (1887)
5. Clarke, G.: The Photograph: A Visual and Cultural History, pp. 32–44. Oxford University Press, Oxford (1997)
6. Ceruzzi, J.: A History of Modern Computing. MIT Press, Cambridge (2003)
7. Spacewar. https://en.wikipedia.org/wiki/Spacewar!
8. Game Market World Revenue in 2015. https://www.statista.com
9. Moszynska, A.: Sculpture Now, pp. 64–65. Thames & Hudson, London (2013)
10. Arts Council Collection. http://www.artscouncilcollection.org.uk/
11. Benesse Art Site Naoshima. http://benesse-artsite.jp/en/
12. Moszynska. A.: Sculpture Now, pp. 155–156. Thames & Hudson, London (2013)
13. Microsoft. https://developer.microsoft.com
14. Math Open Reference. http://www.mathopenref.com/
15. Schubiger-Banz, S., Eberle, M.: The NOVA display system. In: Adams, R., Gibson, S., Arisona, S.M. (eds.) Transdisciplinary Digital Art. Sound, Vision and the New Screen. CCIS, vol. 7, pp. 476–487. Springer, Heidelberg (2008). https://doi.org/10.1007/978-3-540-79486-8_37

Learning History Through Location-Based Games: The Fortification Gates of the Venetian Walls of the City of Heraklion

Kostas Vassilakis[1]([✉]), Orestis Charalampakos[2],
Georgios Glykokokalos[2], Persefoni Kontokalou[2],
Michail Kalogiannakis[2], and Nikolas Vidakis[2]

[1] Department of Electrical Engineering,
Technological Education Institution of Crete,
Stauromenos, 71410 Heraklion, Greece
kostas@teicrete.gr
[2] Department of Informatics Engineering,
Technological Education Institution of Crete,
Stauromenos, 71410 Heraklion, Greece
Orestischaral@gmail.com, glykokokalos@gmail.com,
Kont_per@hotmail.com,
mkalogiannakis@staff.teicrete.gr, nv@ie.teicrete.gr

Abstract. Games in education have always been a tool for increasing motivation and interest of learners. We present Location-Based Games (LBG) as a tool to involve and motivate students in the learning process. LBGs require the player to move around in order to complete a task and proceed in the storyline and use localization technology such as Global Positioning System (GPS). LBGs are built on physical worlds, while virtual world augmentations enable the interaction of physical and other related (cultural, historical etc.) data with the player. Augmented reality (AR) is used to provide this extra layer with 3D objects, avatars and animations for player's interaction. In our paper we present a history learning LBG with the use of augmented reality in the form of 3D objects. We explore the concept, of having both virtual and physical worlds available within the same visual display environment.

Keywords: Game-based learning (GBL) · Location based educational games
Mobile learning · Augmented reality (AR) · Digital storytelling
Education outside the class · Global Positioning System (GPS)

1 Introduction

Gaming has always been a fun way to learn new things and acquire skills. Many learning theories align with the gaming process [1]. In games students are highly motivated by involvement with the subject of study and stimulation comes with learning by doing. Gamification applies game elements to real life tasks. In this way, it helps in the behavioral change, improves motivation and enhances engagement [1, 2]. The constructivism theory is embedded in Game- Based learning approach [3].

© ICST Institute for Computer Sciences, Social Informatics and Telecommunications Engineering 2018
A. L. Brooks et al. (Eds.): ArtsIT 2017/DLI 2017, LNICST 229, pp. 510–519, 2018.
https://doi.org/10.1007/978-3-319-76908-0_49

Ubiquitous computing [4] which describes the technology and the use of a computer that is not static could be the early foundations of Mobile Computing and Location Based Games. In the middle of the 90 s mixed reality was in attention. In [5] Miligram argues: "The next generation telecommunication environment is envisaged to be one, which will provide an ideal virtual space with [sufficient] reality essential for communication".

The purpose of our game -The Heraklion Fortification Gates- is to provide the means for teaching the history of the Venetian walls of the city of Heraklion (Crete). Every time the players reach one of the nine gates/bastions of the walls, they get notifications to answer questions which are related to the history of that gate. Players visit the Fortification's gates all around the city and get information about them. The game ends when the players have passed all the Gates.

The rest of the paper is structured as follows. Section 2 presents the Background based on findings of the literature review conducted. Section 3 introduces the development of the Heraklion fortification gates game and Sect. 4 concludes the paper.

2 Background

With the growth of digital games there was a new academic interest in how gaming could contribute through new perspective in education.

Gamification in Education attempts to harness the power of videogames for motivation and put it into practice at classrooms [6]. Teachers achieve this, by translating the kind of engagement that students experience with games, into an educational context which includes influencing students' behavior and goals of facilitating learning [7]. The localization technology evolvement opens a new way in gaming and furthermore on Game-Based Learning. The arenas are now entire cities for many games [8]. Role-playing games, hunts and searching for treasures are just some of the types of Location Based games [9].

2.1 Location Based Games and Augmented Reality

Location Based Games require the player to move around in order to complete a task and proceed further [10]. The basic idea with these games is that the players combine knowledge and physical activities that take place in the real world, especially in sights that are rich in educational value, like historic city centers.

Location Based Games are used for academic and pedagogic reasons. LBGs are ludic games which combine learning with pleasure [8]. The characteristics of such games enforce the ability to involve students into meaningful learning activities indoors and outdoors [11].

Augmented Reality (AR) is a technology that allows people to integrate virtual objects and live data directly on the user's surrounding environment [12]. Since 2000, many articles mention LBGs as the new trend. In the following years, more and more location based and AR applications were developed, especially for mobile equipment. "Pirates!" [13] is one of them, a multi-player game implemented on handheld devices connected in a Wireless Local Area Network (WLAN). The players in "Pirates!" used the physical environment as the game arena [13]. But there was no accuracy in determining the player's location and this assume limits on designing the game. The development in mobile computing and telecommunication with the global positioning system (GPS) was the next big step towards Location Based services and games. In 2003, the game "Can You See Me Now (CYSMN)" [14] was implemented with GPS technology. Players could move around within the city-arena with a fixed speed, they could see the city map and the position of the other players and they could also communicate with each other using walkie-talkies [14].

To serve the goal of education a game must provide the players-students with new information, or relate their background knowledge with the real world. In this case LBGs can connect digital media and metadata with the locations, cultural objects, monuments etc. for the learning gain [15]. This is consolidated by the fact that people are learning easily when they're combining words, patterns and other media within a structured learning environment, in comparison to the use of mere words according to the Cognitive Theory of Multimedia [16].

Augmented Reality elements and digital mapping can be implemented for the creation of educational material by using information on a geo-location with visual references to digital resources [17]. Virtual content could be anything, 3D scenes or objects, a textual display of the data. Augmented Reality enriches the sensorial perception of a person because she/he can see and hear more than others, and perhaps even touch, smell and taste things that others cannot [12]. The main task of AR in our game is the continuous calculation and replacement of the visual angle, so that the virtual image can be accurately projected on an object. Therefore, AR calculates the distance and orientation from the observation device to the predefined pattern in real world and accurately projects the setup model on that predefined pattern, by using computer vision technology.

The first educational location-based game with augmented reality elements was "Environmental Detectives" [18]. It was created by Massachusetts Institute of Technology (MIT) Teacher Educational Program (TEP) and it was targeted to high school and university students. By using hand-held devices, students investigate outdoors to determine the source of a toxin spill on their campus. Some ways of investigation are by taking interviews with virtual people, conducting environmental measurement simulations and analyzing the data.

Another application is a mobile city game called "Frequency 1550" [19]. It was developed by the Waag Society and helped students to acquire historical knowledge of medieval Amsterdam. An experimental design used 458 students from 20 classes of 5 different schools and its results showed that students who played the game and were engaged in the project gained more knowledge about medieval Amsterdam than those who did not play the game and attended regular projects.

2.2 Learning History of Venetian Walls in the Digital Era

The Gates of Heraklion consist a remarkable element of the Venetian Walls of the city. The Venetian Walls are a series of fortifications and defensive walls that surround the center of Heraklion. They are one of the best-preserved fortifications of Europe. Their goal was to protect the coastal city from invaders, fact that is proven by the Siege of Candia that lasted for 21 years (1648–1669) and it is the second longest recorded siege in history.

They were first built by the Byzantines although they started being shaped to the way they look nowadays, after the conquest of the city by the Arabs (Saracenes) in 824. A full reconstruction of the walls took place after the island of Crete fell into Venetian control in 13th century.

Municipality of Heraklion in its application "A Tour of Venetian Candia" for its visitors, the Candia of 1640 is enlivened through a dynamic implementation of a virtual tour [20], allows the user (inhabitant, visitor, educational community) to travel digitally through time and space and draw multileveled and diverse information in Greek and English. As the user moves, the application within the old city limits, through specific routes, the Venetian Candia unfolds in front of his/her eyes. An "experiential" in physical space and real-time tour of the historic town center, through new technologies and photorealistic three-dimensional representations [20].

Another application is "E-Guide to the Modern City" [20], which is a contemporary electronic city tour guide for smart mobile devices where the user can tour the city sights in an attractive aesthetic environment, with many photographs, text and audio tours depending on the interests and time. For guests who do not have enough time for extensive tours, the "top ten" offers the most important sights of the city, while the "automatic audio guide" gives information about the monuments located in their way [20].

The work presented in this paper defers from the above application as it follows the game based learning approach which improves motivation and enhances engagement of the player. Our LBG offers knowledge through a game by searching places and answering questions.

3   The Heraklion Fortification Gates LBG

3.1   Description of the Game

The "Heraklion Fortification Gates LBG" is a game that gives players the opportunity to explore Heraklion in a playful way.

At first, the game locates the player's position and then gives him or her instructions on how to get to a specific location. During the search of the location, cards with information about the place the player has to go are displayed on the screen. When the player reaches the required area, she/he should scan with her/his smart device this area for a pattern, in order to have the 3D augmented reality object appear on her/his screen. When she/he finds it, a question about the place with four possible answers will appear. After answering the question, the player is prompted to take a selfie and moves on to the next place. At the end of game, the player can see the solutions and find out which of them she/he answered correctly and which wrong and all the selfies she/he took in each stop (see Figs. 3 and 4).

The "Heraklion fortification gates" is a game for smart devices. The few things that players need are a smart device with a camera (smart phone, tablet) and zest for knowledge. Once the game is downloaded into the device, the user can initiate the learning experience by login into the game. After login, the camera of the device is activated and starts reflecting the real surrounding environment as background on the device's screen.

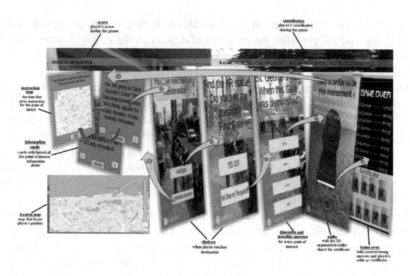

Fig. 1. Game graphical presentation & pattern

3.2   Implementation

The use of localization technology makes it possible to locate the player's position and display the game elements depending on the location. Our LBG, as all Location Based Games do, builds upon the physical world, and with the addition of a virtual world (AR) it enables the interaction of physical and other related (cultural, historical etc.) data with the player.

For the virtual word in our game we have used Vuforia5 [21] which is an AR Software Development Kit (SDK) for smartphones or other similar mobile device that allows the execution of AR applications into a real-time video obtained from these devices. This software uses the capabilities of the computer vision technology to recognize and make the individual tracking of the objects captured by the video camera in real time.

As basic technology for our game development, we have used the Unity Game Engine [22] which allows the developer to create 2D or 3D games. It combines a design platform with C# or JavaScript code. The outcome can be exported in different platforms.

Furthermore, we have used innovative pedagogical approaches for the learning aspect of our game. We mixed the art of traditional storytelling and the use of multimedia technology and thus compiled digital storytelling. By digital storytelling students can be engaged in deep, meaningful learning and enhance their motivation. Digital storytelling provides students with opportunities to organize information in a more familiar way and echoes their use of technology outside of the classroom [4].

The interaction space of the game is divided into three main areas, which act independently or in combination to each other, depending on the game pattern section and the game storytelling stage. These areas are: (a) the top of the device screen which is a bar with informative data, such as scoring and GPS coordinates (see Figs. 1 and 3) with no interaction capabilities, (b) the middle area of the device screen, which presents instructions prompting the player to move to the next point of interest and information about these points, and quiz questions and (c) the lower screen area which shows an open layer map which locates the player's position when acting independently and answers to multiple choice questions when acting in combination with the rest of the game screen.

Fig. 2. Learning history & locating the point of interest

During the game, the player is notified about the score and coordinates by information which appears on the upper right corner of the screen. As soon as the player is located within the radius of the point of interest, a menu is activated that enables him or her to either proceed to the game flow or continue reading the information cards with the historical data of the point of interest. With the option "PROCEED", the player is encouraged to find the AR element which is a projection of a 3D augmented reality object (see Fig. 2). If the player succeeds on identifying the augmented reality object, a 3D object will be displayed on the screen, and the question will appear in a 3D form. The player then can interact with the 3D AR object by selecting the "YES I DO" option and display possible answers to the quiz question.

In case that the player scans the surrounding place with her/his smart device and cannot locate the 3D augmented reality object, she/he can select the option "NO! Show me the question" and bypass the 3D and AR options of the game. A question in 2D form will appear and simultaneously one mark will be subtracted from her/his game score as a penalty for not locating the AR object.

The scoring scheme of the game is as follows: +1 if the answer is correct, 0 if it is wrong, −1 if the player does not locate the AR object (see Fig. 3).

In every question the player completes, either in a 2D or a 3D question, she/he is asked to take a photograph with the monument and/or the 3D AR object that belong to the point of interest. When the rewarding selfie has been taken the player proceeds to the next point of interest i.e. the next fortification gate of the Heraklion Venetian walls. The map appears again and the steps described above are repeated. By visiting all points of interest, answering all the questions and taking all the rewarding selfies, the game reaches the end. The player is informed with the score, correct and wrong

Fig. 3. Quiz with or without AR & player rewarding

answers and receives the certificate which is a compilation of all taken photographs from each point as reward (see right screen shot of Fig. 3).

3.3 Player's Position and Game Patterns

Determining players' position and defining the game patterns are important architectural elements, in order to create engaging games. In our game architecture (see Figs. 3 and 4) we thoroughly define those elements and support player positioning and game pattern. In the following paragraphs, we elaborate further these architectural elements.

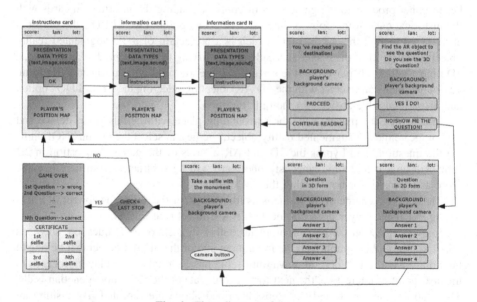

Fig. 4. Flow diagram of the game

Determining player position: The main problem on Location Based Games is to determine the player's position as more accurate as you can. There are many approaches for doing so, such as: GPS, cell tower triangulation, Wi-Fi, single cell tower and IP. In more detail, Cell- Id is based on geolocating a smartphone [10]. Using the connected cell-tower the mobile telephone provider can locate through the id of the tower. IP geolocating is an interesting approach of determining the position of a mobile device. Although the IP is unique for its device, it changes really fast and furthermore, similar IPs may be used in different places. Other methods use Radio-frequency Identification (RFID) tags to identify smart devices with RFID readers installed, or QR-codes etc. A combination of methods is the best and most accurate way of locating the device, eliminating the environment factor [13].

In our implementation, we use GPS to determine the player's position. GPS is the most popular technology for this scope due to its high accuracy [10]. It consists of a GPS sensor which is discoverable by the GPS satellites. Because of that, it is available everywhere, without the need of a tower cell or any other signals. It is expected to face problems regarding the signal within close spaces, like buildings etc. Another disadvantage is the high energy consumption although many devices nowadays have enough reserve.

Game Pattern: Every Location-Based game is built on a pattern, so that the player can use it to move around. "Search and Find" pattern refers to the games that have instructions and guide the players to a specific location. Instead of asking the player to move in specific coordinates, this pattern may let the player find a specific object, such as a monument, a school or a store.

Our game is using this pattern, as it leads the player through the city of Heraklion, so they can find the spots of interest (gates and bastions) and answer the questions. While moving around, the player is presented with useful information about the destination gate in the form of text, mini videos and photos. Figure 4 presents our game flowchart which is according to the game pattern approach. More specifically, the player is provided with instructions as to how she/he will reach the next point of interest. While moving around toward the next location the game provides educational information about the location in the form of text, mini-videos and sound. The player can navigate between information and instruction as she/he pleases until the next point of interest, as shown in the upper row of the flow diagram of Fig. 4. According to our game pattern once the player has reached a point of interest she/he is immediately notified by the game and can decide to look for the AR artifact or not. The decision about the AR artifact affects the interaction elements of the next steps of the game, as presented in rows two and three of Fig. 4. Once the player has played the quiz, she/he is permitted to take a selfie with the AR element at the point of interest, as a reward for achieving an intermediate goal. The above flow of events is repeated until the player visits all points of interest and according to our game pattern, she/he will receive a game certificate, which is an assemblage of all points of interest selfies with the AR elements.

4 Conclusion

Location Based Games in education could be the way for producing learning outcomes by increasing the motivation and interest of students about subjects that demand sightseeing. Current handheld devices (smartphones, tablets, etc.) with embedded geolocation technologies and video cameras are ideal medium for such games. Usually, LBG require from the player to move around in order to complete a task and proceed through a storyline. School outdoor activities would be more fun and more pedagogic with the use of LBG adapted in a learning context.

In this paper, we've introduced "The Heraklion Fortification Gates", a LBG that offers to students the opportunity to learn about the history of the Venetians gates of the city of Heraklion. When the student reaches the place of interest she/he gets information about the gate and has to answer to related questions. The game arena is the physical space of the city, while the visual display environment consists of both physical and virtual worlds and augmented reality is used in the form of 3D objects. The structure of the game, the subject matter and the questions involve real historical information resulting adequate educational value and in essence, the game becomes a vehicle that transfers "unseen" information to the player [23].

The new version of the game would have a background scenario for leading the player from place to place. Also a story, perhaps a crime-solving story, that lead the game-flow could make the LBG more ludic and increase further the interest of the players.

References

1. Marczewski, A.: Gamasutra-The Art & Business of Making Games (2013)
2. Flatla, D., Gutwin, C., Nacke, L., Bateman, S., Mandryk, R.: Calibration games: making calibration tasks enjoyable by adding motivating game elements (2011)
3. De Grove, F., Bourgonjon, J., Van Looy, J.: Digital games in the classroom? A contextual approach to teachers' adoptionintention of digital games in formal education. Comput. Hum. Behav. **28**, 2023–2033 (2012)
4. Weiser, M.: The computer for the 21st century. Sci. Am. **265**, 94–104 (1991)
5. Milgram, P., Kishino, F.: Taxonomy of mixed reality visual displays. IEICE Trans. Inf. Syst. **25**(12), 1321–1329 (1994)
6. Lee, J.J., Hammer, J.: Gamification in education: what, how, why bother? Acad. Exch. Quart. **15**, 146 (2011)
7. Vidakis, N., Christinaki, E., Serafimidis, I., Triantafyllidis, G.: Combining ludology and narratology in an open authorable framework for educational games for children: the scenario of teaching preschoolers with autism diagnosis. In: Stephanidis, C., Antona, M. (eds.) UAHCI 2014. LNCS, vol. 8514, pp. 626–636. Springer, Cham (2014). https://doi.org/10.1007/978-3-319-07440-5_57
8. Vidakis, N., Syntychakis, E., Kalafatis, K., Christinaki, E., Triantafyllidis, G.: Ludic educational game creation tool: teaching schoolers road safety. In: Antona, M., Stephanidis, C. (eds.) UAHCI 2015. LNCS, vol. 9177, pp. 565–576. Springer, Cham (2015). https://doi.org/10.1007/978-3-319-20684-4_55
9. Duncan, G.R.: Gamers turn cities into a battleground. New Sci. **186**, 26–27 (2005)

10. Lehmann, L.: Location-based mobile games (2012)
11. Wijers, M., Jonker, V., Drijvers, P.: MobileMath: exploring mathematics outside the classroom. Math. Educ. **42**, 789–799 (2010)
12. Daponte, P., De Vito, L., Picariello, F., Ricci, M.: State of the art and future developments of the augmented reality for measurement applications. ScienceDirect **57**, 53–70 (2014)
13. Björk, S., Falk, J., Hansson, R., Ljungstrand, P.: Pirates! using the physical world as a game board (2001)
14. Benford, S., Anastasi, R., Flintham, M., Drozd, A.: Coping with uncertainty in a location-based game. IEEE Pervasive Comput. **2**, 34–41 (2003)
15. Brown, E., Börner, D., Sharples, M., Glahn, C., De Jong, T.: Location-based and contextual mobile learning. A STELLAR Small-Scale Study (2010)
16. Mayer, R.: Cognitive theory and the design of multimedia instruction: an example of the two-way street between cognition and instruction. New Dir. Teach. Learn. **2002**, 55–71 (2002)
17. Joo-Nagata, J., Abad, F., Giner, J., Garcia-Peñalvo, F.: Augmented reality and pedestrian navigation through its implementation in m-learning and e-learning: evaluation of an educational program in Chile. Comput. Educ. **111**, 1–17 (2017)
18. MIT: MIT Handheld Augmented Reality Simulations. http://web.mit.edu/mitstep/ar/index.html. Accessed June 2017
19. Huizenga, J., Admiraal, W., Akkerman, S., Ten Dam, G.: Mobile game-based learning in secondary education: engagement, motivation and learning in a mobile city game. Authors J. Compilation **25**, 332–344 (2009)
20. Municipality of Heraklion: Municipality of Heraklion: Mobile Applications (2015). https://www.heraklion.gr/ourplace/her-mobile-apps/heraklion-mobile-apps.html. Accessed 2 June 2017
21. Vuforia Developer Portal: PTC Inc. (2011). https://developer.vuforia.com/. Accessed 2 May 2017
22. UNITY: UNITY. https://unity3d.com/. Accessed 10 Apr 2017
23. Sintoris, C., Yiannoutsou, N., Demetriou, S., Avouris, N.: Discovering the invisible city: location-based games for learning in smart cities. Inter. Des. Archit. J. **16**, 47–64 (2013)

A Collaborative Video Sketching Model in the Making

Peter Gundersen, Rikke Ørngreen$^{(\boxtimes)}$, Birgitte Henningsen,
and Heidi Hautopp

Research Center for VidEO, ILD-lab, Aalborg University, Aalborg, Denmark
{pgu, rior, bhe, hh}@learning.aau.dk

Abstract. The literature on design research emphasizes working in iterative cycles that investigate and explore many ideas and alternative designs. However, these cycles are seldom applied or documented in educational research papers. In this paper, we illustrate the development process of a video sketching model, where we explore the relation between the educational research design team, their sketching and video sketching activities. The results show how sketching can be done in different modes and how it supports thinking, communication, reflection and distributed cognition in design teams when developing educational theories.

Keywords: Sketching · Reflection · Design · Distributed cognition
Education

1 Introduction

Design methods have increasingly found their way into educational research, especially with the emergence of design-based research [1, 2], which has seen a steady rise in popularity over the last few decades [3]. Although there are many articles that provide an overview of the approach [3], as well as articles discussing its merits as a scientific methodology [4, 5], articles focusing on the early stages of design-based research remain scarce [6]. A recent analysis of the 47 most cited articles from 2002 to 2012 shows that early iterative methods, such as sketching and prototyping, are hardly mentioned in the literature. When they are, they seem to be understood as longer, often annual, cycles of analysis rather than short alternative design trials, as for instance using rough disposable sketching techniques [7, 8]. It is not clear whether these processes take place and are simply not reported on or they are not implemented at all.

In this paper, we therefore seek to open the black box regarding sketching processes. Our point of departure is a network of information technology (IT) and learning design researchers at Aalborg University who for the last year have implemented different sketching techniques in various settings for knowledge sharing and learning. The preliminary culmination of this work is the development of the video sketching framework shown in Fig. 1. This model is inspired by the work of several researchers in the field, most notable Olofsson and Sjölén [18]. Herein, we explore how the video sketching model came about and ask: What are the steps that lead from any number of ideas to a single model finding its place as an academic contribution? In what ways do

© ICST Institute for Computer Sciences, Social Informatics and Telecommunications Engineering 2018
A. L. Brooks et al. (Eds.): ArtsIT 2017/DLI 2017, LNICST 229, pp. 520–529, 2018.
https://doi.org/10.1007/978-3-319-76908-0_50

video sketching techniques contribute to the development of educational theory? We start by presenting our theoretical framework, elaborating on how sketching can be perceived and what purposes it fulfils. We then analyse different steps in our process as an educational research (ER) design team in an investigation and discussion of the research questions raised above.

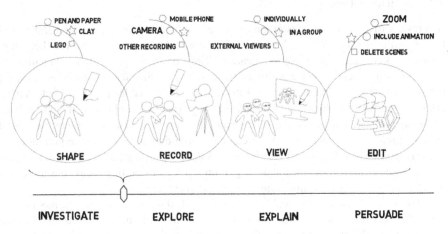

Fig. 1. Video sketching framework. To learn more about this framework, see [9]

2 Theoretical Framework

2.1 Moving Beyond Words

Here, we present our point of departure by considering the question of why researchers in education, or any discipline, should concern themselves with alternative thinking tools besides their minds and words. Western culture, not least within academia, has consistently privileged the spoken and written word as the highest form of intellectual practice, relegating visual representations to second-rate status as illustrations of ideas [10]. In 'Unflattening', Sousanis [11] makes a compelling argument for words not being the only vehicle for communicating thought. While referring to the written word, he states that linear sequences of rows have their strengths but that they are not the only option. When conveying meaning, the relationship between components, such as words and pictures, matters in terms of size, shape, placement, etc. For Sousanis, cartoons are a means to capture and convey thoughts with more complexity than do written words. Drawing becomes a way to tap into our imaginative system and extend our thinking, engaging both conception and perception simultaneously. As we elaborate below: 'Drawing is not to transcribe ideas from our heads but to generate them in search of greater understanding'[11, p. 79].

Further, the visuals and the process of making and discussing these in collaboration, supports knowledge creation beyond the individual. Hutchins framed the distributed cognition concept in the 1990s, and he elaborated on it from a human–computer interface (HCI) perspective with Hollan and Kirsch in 2000 [12]. A vital perspective, in view of our research, is that distributed cognition rests not only in the materials but also in the interplay between the participants and the material. Thus, cognition may be distributed among group members, across time and space, and be part of physical, digital and mental representations.

2.2   Sketching Theory

In a review of sketching in design processes in the literature from the mid-1960 s until the beginning of this decade, Vistisen [13] identified two perspectives on sketching: visual thinking and visual communication. The dominant perspective, sketching as visual thinking, focuses on the ability of sketching to mediate the sense-making process between the designer and the design problem. Sketching enables the designer to have a conversation with the drawing, also referred to by Goldschmidt [14] as 'the backtalk of self-generated sketches'. On the other hand, Buxton [15] places sketches as shared points of reference against which we can compare other ideas or re-interpretations of the existing designs. In support of this view, Hutchins [16] regards sketches as artefacts that may act as a form of distributed cognition – a way of putting ideas 'out there' for debate, critique, and most importantly new interpretations [13].

Oxman [17] contributes with an important distinction between the medium of sketching and the series of actions carried out by the designer which result in transformations of the representations. With this differentiation, it is possible to look at vastly different sketching media (not only pen and paper) and the different purposes tied to the actions of a designer working with these processes separately.

Olofsson and Sjölén [18] argue for four different purposes of sketching: investigative, exploratory, explanatory and persuasive. Investigative sketches work on the problem identification level. The purpose of explorative sketches focuses on possible solutions to identified problems. In explanatory sketches, the aim is to communicate a clear message to others outside the design group in a neutral, straightforward manner to get feedback from users, clients and external experts. Persuasive sketches have the function of trying to 'sell' a proposed design concept to influential stakeholders and are therefore often artistically impressive. Consequently, there is a big difference between the numerous, rough, pencil drawn and disposable explorative sketches and the highly detailed 3D-rendered persuasive sketches.

Apart from categorising sketching according to purpose, it can be categorised according to medium and subject. Traditional media counts pencil, pastel, airbrush, etc., but new research in the field proposes an expansion of this category to include temporal media, for example, in Vistisen's [19] approach to sketching with animation, where he, in the model of expressive capacity, sums up different media use (Fig. 2).

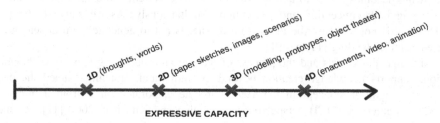

Fig. 2. Scale of expressive capacities in sketching (Fig. 11 in [19], p. 32)

In our video sketching framework, we add yet another layer. All sketching processes with their different purposes and expressive capacities can be recorded through different setups. Our argument is that this creates an interesting hybrid of visual thinking and visual communication. The thinking processes of a design group while sketching suddenly become (more) transparent and editable when recorded, and a visual communicative sketch gains temporality, creating opportunities for the designers to re-enter the design situation with different purposes as new ideas emerge while watching the session (see Fig. 1).

The question is, what kind of sketch is a video sketch? On one side, recorded investigative pen and paper and digital sketch sessions gain an additional sketch layer through which the designers are able to re-view and retain otherwise elusive thought processes. On the other side, a recording of an explanatory sketch in the making can change its purpose completely as new understandings arise in the editing phase.

3 Our Process

We now turn our attention to the process of developing the video sketch framework and unravelling the applied sketching techniques. We start with an early paper sketch, where the ER design team is investigating the problem space. Next, we look at early solution proposals, closing with an implementation of video sketching techniques.

3.1 Early Sketchwork

The early sketch in Fig. 3 investigates a pivotal aspect of our understanding of how sketching and video interact. At the sketch's upper edge, the team investigate the functionalities of the involved media. Initially, it seems simple to conclude that the camera provides a means of retaining the sketching process. Recording sketching sessions enables re-viewing and re-analysing thought processes materialised through either ink on paper or recorded words. However, in the lower right corner, an

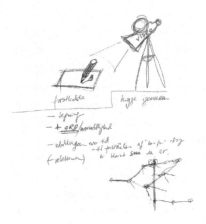

Fig. 3. Early sketch

interesting figure emerges. Here the ER design team collaboratively discuss and imagine the multiple decisions made over the course of a sketching session. What if we had taken a different route? What ideas were discarded without sufficient investigation? Is it possible for a group of designers to restart a discussion from a given point in the video?

3.2   From Sketch to Model

In the early sketches (above), we primarily focused on the investigative sketching mode, i.e. we strived to identify the problem. In the following sketches, we primarily sketched in an explorative mode, exploring possible solutions to the problem we had identified. In this explorative phase, we produced multiple sketches and multiple sketching materials' using pen and paper and a blackboard, which gave more space for drawing and a better overview. The following sketches are examples from this process.

In the sketch in Fig. 4, we explore various approaches to how we can identify, understand and visualise different phases in video sketching and how these phases can loop into each other. For example, one loop could be: A person records him or herself and views the recording (symbolised by the eye). After viewing, the person decides to redo the act/recording and view again, or perhaps the person decides to move on and edit the recording. After editing, the person decides to go back to recording with new insights from the process just completed. At the bottom of the sketch, a wavy line both visualises time going from A to B and visualises how the process from A to B can take place in different types of sketching modes (investigative, explorative, etc.) symbolised by the crosses on the wavy line. In this sketch, we also debated and strived to clarify the understanding of sketching modes in relation to video sketching. Are the phases supposed to be understood as purposes (focusing on the outcome) or as approaches (focusing on maintaining a specific mind-set throughout the process)?

Fig. 4. From early sketch to draft model

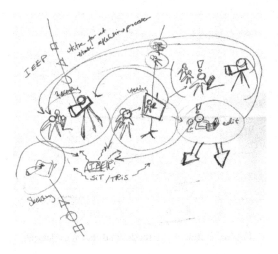

Fig. 5. From draft model to model

The sketch in Fig. 5 is a clarification of the sketch in Fig. 4. One can argue this sketch enters the purpose of explanatory sketch and we move from visual thinking into the area of visual communication. We explicitly sketch the phases: shaping, recording, viewing and editing and the possible loops between the phases (shown by the curved arrows). At the same time, we continue exploring the possible visualisations of the various parameters (shown by the 'arm'/line with a circle, triangle and square).

In the sketch in Fig. 5, we did not explore the relation between the sketching phases (shape, record, view, edit) and the sketching modes (investigative, explorative, etc.). We had briefly touched on this relation with the waved line and crosses earlier (see Fig. 4), and we returned to this issue in the sketch below, in Fig. 6, where a 'slider' emerged under the phases, shown as four intertwined circles. We strived through the slider to visually express that each sketching phase (shaping, recording, viewing, editing) can be combined with various sketching modes (investigate, explore, explain, persuade). For example, an editing phase can be done in either an investigative, explorative, explanatory or persuasive mode. Similarly, in a recording phase, it is also possible to be in either an investigative, explanatory or persuasive mode.

After working our way through the different sketches with pen and paper, we closed in on the final model presented in the introduction (Fig. 1). In the sketching and production of this final model in the software VideoScribe (http://www.sparkol.com/), we focused on explaining the model. We strived to clarify and communicate the content/the model in the video editing phase. Even though the primary purpose of this phase was explanatory/persuasive, the switch in material from pen on paper to video software initiated a new round of exploration. At first, we made a very rough version, using existing template icons. We then moved on to our own digital drawings. To ensure clear communication of the different elements of our video sketching model, the ER design team viewed and discussed the draft versions in VideoScribe. We also experimented with the graphics and temporal details in the video, making it more

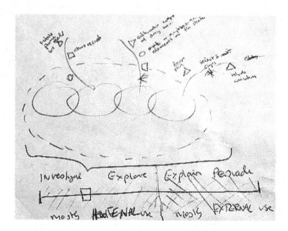

Fig. 6. Refining the model and its interrelations

convincing. Thus, we argue that the video also has the purpose of persuading the viewers through seductive and corporate-type graphics.

3.3 The Meta Layers and Process Over Time

When exploring the process, we revisited not only our sketches but also the photos taken on the days of collaboration. Here, it became clear how the situational factors (sitting around a table, drawing on the same paper from different angles) and time (the layering of papers on top of each other) constitute important relational factors that co-construct our meaning [12]. We also experienced this as supporting our historical recall and reasoning when revisiting and choosing the significant examples later on, as the timely progression shown in Fig. 7 illustrates.

Fig. 7. Progression over time in the work with the model

3.4   From Model to Video Sketch and to Model-in-Use

The empirical research behind the model, i.e. the case studies related to its development, was presented at the Association for Visual Pedagogies Conference in 2017 [9]. The ER design team made an explanatory video which was presented virtually and discussed. In the video, we used an informal panel discussion (see Fig. 8). We first sketched (pen and paper) ideas for the content and form, and the video was then recorded in one shot with two cameras. Later, in the edit mode, the VideoScribe movie was superimposed to the screen, camera angle was chosen, etc. This presentation video supported a process of thinking about how to utilize video sketching in the explanatory form. After submitting the video to the conference, we reviewed it and found that our recorded and edited panel-like discussion, while sketching on top of our model (Fig. 1), gave insight into three different ways of utilising the model-in-use in future scenarios.

Fig. 8. Screendump from the conference video

4   Discussing the Learning Potentials in Video Sketching

In the introduction to this paper, we asked two questions: whether we could identify steps in the process of formulating academic contributions, and in what way video sketching techniques contribute to the development of educational theory. In the previous paragraphs, we have zoomed in on our sketching processes and the steps involved, and we have showed how it influenced our development of the video sketching framework. To further understand the reflective processes that occur when working with the development of the video sketching model, we draw upon the work of Schön [20]. Schön focuses on reflective practices among practitioners and notes that it is vital to combine the ability to operate in uncertain and unique contexts in the field of design. According to Schön, a design situation is unique because there is not just a single way to solve the problems that may occur. This places a demand on the designer to reflect in terms of reflection in action and reflection over action [20]. In the ER design team, we switched fluently between reflection modes, using different expression formats, e.g. drawings, dialogues, and videos.

We argue that the use of video sketching potentially supports and enlarges reflective processes through the possibilities of: (1) re-viewing and re-entering thought processes via the recorded video sessions, thereby triggering memories [21] about the intention of the sketch which can open a new round of collaborative exploration and re-analysis; (2) providing a collaborative log of drawings and video sketches which is easily accessible, supports coherence through fragmented processes and scattered meetings and supports knowledge sharing and distributed learning over time; and (3) making the research process transparent to fellow researchers or project stakeholders.

In relation to the first point, we acknowledge the potential weakness of not having sufficient time in a given research project to make numerous iterative recordings and holding re-viewing and reflecting sessions, although we stress that doing so among research peers strengthens not only the theory under discussion but also the professional development of the participants. Regarding point two, the notion of having a collective log of materials relates to portfolio thinking – and having a common portfolio may not be for all researchers. Some find working with academic matters a more solitary matter and do not feel comfortable sharing knowledge with peers, especially in the early stages of a given project. Future investigation into the research on (e)Portfolio, could provide knowledge that can be explored with regard to video sketching as well, for example in relation to the (e)Portfolio concepts of ownership, the meaning of volunteering and mandatory participation for the result, etc. [22, 23]. On a positive note, we found the materialisation of early ideas and, not least, the discussions along the way to be pivotal in our understanding of the framework we were generating, and we have retained several ideas for future research topics that would have been discarded.

Thinking and communicating with sketches and video sketches has in our case been a pivotal part of educational research and has impacted theoretical development.

5   Conclusion

In this paper we have outlined our sketching processes in order to make our development of the video sketching model transparent. Our purpose is to contribute a detailed description of these processes, which is typically omitted in papers in the field of design-based research. Based on design literature, we argue that these processes are pivotal in order to grasp learning potentials, and we find our process underlines how sketches in many forms, with many purposes and with various expressive capacities, play a significant role in academia, especially when it is desirable to prioritise short iterations on ideas and alternative designs, such as when developing educational theory.

References

1. Brown, A.: Design experiments: theoretical and methodological challenges in creating complex interventions in classroom settings. J. Learn. Sci. **2**, 141–178 (1992)
2. Collins, A.: Toward a design science of education. In: Scanlon, E., O'Shea, T. (eds.) New Directions in Educational Technology, pp. 15–22. Springer, Heidelberg (1992). https://doi.org/10.1007/978-3-642-77750-9_2
3. Anderson, T., Shattuck, J.: Design-based research: a decade of progress in education research? Educ. Res. **41**, 16–25 (2012)
4. Barab, S., Squire, K.: Design-based research: putting a stake in the ground. J. Learn. Sci. **13**, 1–14 (2004)
5. Dede, C.: Why design-based research is both important and difficult. Educ. Technol. **45**, 5–8 (2005)
6. Wyche, S.P., Grinter, R.E.: Using sketching to support design research in new ways: a case study investigating design and charismatic pentecostalism in São Paulo, Brazil. In: Proceedings of the 2012 iConference, pp. 63–71. ACM (2012)
7. Gundersen, P.: Understandings of the concept of iteration in design-based research. In: Cumulus REDO Conference Proceedings, 30 May–2 June (2017)
8. Ørngreen, R.: Reflections on design-based research. In: Abdelnour Nocera, J., Barricelli, B. R., Lopes, A., Campos, P., Clemmensen, T. (eds.) HWID 2015. IAICT, vol. 468, pp. 20–38. Springer, Cham (2015). https://doi.org/10.1007/978-3-319-27048-7_2
9. Henningsen, B., Gundersen, P., Hautopp, H., Ørngreen, R.: Collaborative video sketching. In: Otrel-Cass, K. (ed.) Undervisning og Læring, Proceedings of the 2nd Association for Visual Pedagogy Conference, pp. 43–51, Dafolo (2017)
10. Mirzoeff, N.: The Visual Culture Reader, 2nd edn. Psychology Press, Routledge (2002)
11. Sousanis, N.: Unflattening. Harvard University Press, Boston (2015)
12. Hollan, J., Hutchins, E., Kirsh., D.: Distributed cognition: toward a new foundation for human-computer interaction research. ACM Trans. Comput. Hum. Interact. **7**, 174–196 (2000)
13. Vistisen, P.: The roles of sketching in design: mapping the tension between functions in design sketching. In: Nordic Design Research Conference (2015)
14. Goldschmidt, G.: The backtalk of self-generated sketches. Des. Issues **19**, 72–88 (2003)
15. Buxton, B.: Sketching user experiences - getting the design right and the right design. Focal Press Morgan Kaufman, San Francisco (2007)
16. Hutchins, E.: Cognition in the Wild. MIT Press, Boston (1995)
17. Oxman, R.M.: The reflective eye: visual reasoning in design. In: Koutamanis, A., Timmerman, H., Vermeulen, I. (eds.) Visual Data Bases in Architecture, Averbury, U.K. (1995)
18. Olofsson, E., Sjölén, K.: Design Sketching. KEEOS Design Books AB, Sundsvall (2007)
19. Vistisen, P.: Sketching with Animation - Using Animation to Portray Fictional Realities Aimed at Becoming Factual. Aalborg University Press, Aalborg (2016)
20. Schön, D.: Designing as reflective conversation with the materials of a design situation. Knowl. Based Syst. **5**, 3–14 (1992)
21. Kumar, J., Yammiyavar, P., Nielsen, J.: Mind tape technique: a usability evaluation method for tracing cognitive processes in cross cultural settings. eMinds, **1**, 83–99 (2007)
22. Barrett, H., Carney, J.: Conflicting paradigms and competing purposes in electronic portfolio development, unpublished paper retrieved via helen barrets blog, pp. 1–14. http://electronicportfolios.com/portfolios/LEAJournal-BarrettCarney.pdf
23. Smith, K., Tillema, H.: Clarifying different types of portfolio use. Assess. Eval. High. Educ. **28**(6), 625–648 (2003)

Author Index

Printed in the United States
By Bookmasters